Brief Contents

Interpersonal Communication
Relating to Others

● Steven A. Beebe
Southwest Texas State University

● Susan J. Beebe
Southwest Texas State University

● Mark V. Redmond
Iowa State University

Allyn and Bacon

BOSTON   LONDON   TORONTO   SYDNEY   TOKYO   SINGAPORE

Editor-in Chief: Karen Hanson
Senior Editor: Karon Bowers
Developmental Editor: Carol Alper
Editorial Assistant: Sarah Kelly
Marketing Manager: Jacqueline Aaron
Production Coordinator: Mary Beth Finch
Editorial-Production Service: Thomas E. Dorsaneo/Publishing Consultants
Text Design and Composition: Schneck-DePippo Graphics
Photo Research: Helane Manditch-Prottas
Cover Administrator: Linda Knowles
Composition Buyer: Linda Cox
Manufacturing Buyer: Megan Cochran

Copyright © 2002, 1999, 1996 by Allyn & Bacon
A Pearson Education Company
75 Arlington Street
Boston, MA 02116

Internet: www.ablongman.com

Library of Congress Cataloging-in-Publication Data

Beebe, Steven A.
      Interpersonal communication : relating to others / Steven A. B eebe, Susan J. Beebe,
  Mark V. Redmond.—3rd ed.
          p.   cm.
      Includes bibliographical references and index.
      ISBN 0-205-33537-3
      1. Interpersonal communication. I. Beebe, Susan J. II. Redmond, Mark V., 1949–. III. Title
  BF637.C45 B43 2001
  153.6—dc21   00-066388

Printed in the United States of America.

10 9 8 7 6 5 4 3 2   05 04 03 02 01

Dedicated to our families

Mark and Matthew Beebe

Peggy, Nicholas, and Eric Redmond, and Beth Maroney

List of Features

Contents

Contents

Chapter 3

Interpersonal Communication and
Perception 72

Chapter 4

Interpersonal Communication and Cultural
Diversity: Adapting to Others 96

Part II Interpersonal
Skills 132

Chapter 5

Listening and Respondi

Chapter 10

Chapter 11

Preface

If we could distill the central focus of this book into a bumper sticker, it would be this: Become other oriented. We believe the most important principle in understanding and enhancing interpersonal communication is to focus on others, rather than only on yourself. By being other-oriented, we don't mean that you are not self-reflexively aware of who you are or that you abandon any sensitivity to your own thoughts and behavior. We do suggest, however, that being other-oriented involves the mindful process of considering the thoughts, needs, and values of others, rather than an egocentric focus on self. The opposite of being other-oriented is being self-absorbed. We didn't invent this principle of being other-oriented; it is the foundation of every major faith movement, religion, and human value system in the world. It was also the foundation of the first two editions of *Interpersonal Communication: Relating to Others,* and it continues as the central theme of the third edition.

This book was written to be the primary text for college-level courses in interpersonal communication. Although there are many different approaches to teaching interpersonal communication, we have endeavored to include the essential principles and skills to help students learn how to understand and improve their relationships with others. Our balance of principles and skills is designed to help students enhance their own repertoire of communication skills, as well as giving them insights into the hows and whys of human relationships. As with our first two editions, we continue to emphasize the importance of relationship development and present skills to help maintain quality interpersonal relationships.

Our Approach To Interpersonal Communication

An Emphasis on Others

Although becoming other-oriented can often be a challenge, we believe it is worth the effort; mastering this ability will result in life-long relationship rewards. Considering the thoughts and feelings of others is an essential prerequisite for understanding and improving interpersonal communication. Throughout the book, our other-oriented approach gently but consistently reminds students about the importance of the challenging process of seeing the world as others see it. At the heart of understanding and developing relationships with others is the process of considering how others are affected by our communication. Becoming other-oriented is not a single skill, but rather a composite of principles and skills. Foremost among them are self-awareness and self-knowledge; throughout the book we suggest that true empathy and sensitivity are possible only when we feel secure about our own identify. In addition, becoming other-oriented includes all of the classic skills and principles typically taught in interpersonal communication courses, such as listening, feedback, conflict management skills, verbal and nonverbal skills, and places additional emphasis on the importance of the perceptions, thoughts, attitudes, beliefs, values, and the emotions of others. To emphasize the importance of our other-oriented approach, each chapter includes a feature called "Considering Others," which provides observations and research conclusions designed to help students connect to others.

An Emphasis on Diversity

Imbedded in our other-oriented approach is the theme that others are different from us. To help students understand and sensitively consider those differences when interpersonally communicating with others, we place considerable emphasis on presenting principles and research conclusions about communication diversity. In recent years, the body of research on gender- and culture-based differences in communication behavior has grown significantly. We do more, however, than just point out that we are different from one another. Using a competency-based approach, we present practical, research-based strategies for increasing communication competence when interacting with people who are different from ourselves. Using research observations about both culture and gender, we stress that the competent interpersonal communicator is knowledgeable, motivated, and skilled in communicating with people from diverse backgrounds. Our "Understanding Diversity" boxes featured in every chapter highlight both interpersonal principles and skills that help students relate to others who are different from themselves.

An Emphasis on Relationships

From the opening chapter until we conclude the book, we discuss how relationships work and how to improve them. Students are consistently curious about how to improve their relationships with others. We link communication skills with principles that help explain and predict how relationships begin, develop, and sometimes decline. As suggested by our subtitle, *Relating to Others,* we highlight the importance of cultivating relationships by developing an increased awareness of and sensitivity to others. Our emphasis on relationships is reflected in the broad range of relationship types we consider in our discussions, including relationships with friends, lovers, family, and co-workers, and even relationships formed and developed over the Internet. Communication researchers have contributed significant insights to relationship development and maintenance. We rely on the latest communication research to give students the benefit of state-of-the-art thinking about how relationships can be improved.

An Emphasis on How Technology Influences Interpersonal Relationships

The advent of the Internet and other technological tools have affected how we relate to others, not just on-line but off-line as well. We build upon our previous discussion of the role of technology by including new "e-Connections" boxes in every chapter that will help students see how relational cues are both similar to and different from their live-and-in-person connections to others. A new feature to this edition is the inclusion of several Web sites that can extend students' knowledge of interpersonal relationships that are included in our "e-Connections" boxes. In addition, an expanded discussion in Chapter 1 and a new section in Chapter 11 reviews contemporary re-

- **Teaching Tool for the Interactive Companion** This tool by Sue Stewart of St. Edward's University contains activities, teaching suggestions, and test questions to help the instructor integrate the media assets in the Interactive Companion into his or her own teaching style and classroom environment. *Available Spring 2002!*

- **PowerPoint Presentation** This package by Nan Peck of Northern Virginia Community College consists of a collection of lecture outlines and graphic images keyed to every chapter in the text and is available on the Web at *www.ablongman.com/ppt.*

- **Allyn & Bacon Digital Media Archive for Communication, Version 2.0 (CD-ROM) (Windows and Macintosh)** This resource, available on CD-ROM, offers more than 200 still images, video excerpts, Web links, and assorted lecture resources that can be incorporated into multimedia presentations in the classroom.

- **CourseCompass** Powered by Blackboard, CourseCompass is the most flexible online course management system on the market today. Log on at *www.coursecompass.com* and find out how you can get the most out of this dynamic teaching resource. *Available for Spring 2002!*

Student Supplements:

- **SkillBuilder Workbook** This guide by Mark Redmond helps students reinforce and enhance their understanding of the principles and skills of interpersonal communication. Filled with exercises, activities, and study aids, it provides students with a wealth of opportunities to review and apply concepts introduced in the text.

- **Interactive Companion Website** This Website, by Sue Stewart of St. Edward's University offers video and audio clips, activities, and practice tests, all keyed to the text objectives. The site can be accessed when you activate the PIN code available with a new text at *www.abinteractive.com/login. Available Spring 2002!*

- **Companion Website with Online Practice Tests** Accessed at *www.ablongman.com/beebe*, this site provides Web links and Internet activities to enrich the course. The site also contains online learning objectives, practice tests, and interactive discussions.

- **Speech Communication on the Net** This booklet by Terrence Doyle, Northern Virginia Community College, includes the basics of using the Internet, conducting Web searches, and critically evaluating and documenting Internet sources. It also contains Internet activities and URLs specific to the discipline of speech communication.

- **Allyn & Bacon Communication Studies Website** By Terrence Doyle, Northern Virginia Community College, and Tim Borchers, Morehead State University, this site includes modules on interpersonal and small communication and public speaking and includes Web links, enrichment materials, and interactive activities to enhance students' understanding of key concepts. Access it at *www.ablongman.com/commstudies*

- **E-Book** The e-book is a digitized version of your textbook, enhanced with versatile study tools and a powerful search engine. The e-book duplicates the print textbook, following the exact page format and numbering of the print book. Students can search, highlight, make notes, and print text directly from their e-books. *Available Spring 2002!*

---

search conclusions about how relationships can develop, be maintained, and be terminated when connected via computer-mediated communication. Although our primary emphasis remains on face-to-face interactions, we believe we should not ignore the significant role technology plays in affecting our relationships with others.

Features of the Third Edition

The features that made our first two editions successful have been retained in the third edition. Our other-oriented approach, emphasis on diversity, focus on relationships, and expanded coverage of technology, coupled with our balanced discussion of principles and skills, are the key reasons both students and instructors praise the book.

We've retained the over-arching structure of the second edition of the book. In Part I we present foundation principles by introducing the study of interpersonal communication in Chapter 1. It includes new material about the role of technology in communication, as well as new material about myths of interpersonal communication. Our revised Chapter 2, "Communication and Self," now includes a discussion of self disclosure which was previously discussed in Chapter 9. Chapter 3 offers a streamlined discussion of the power of perception to influence our interpersonal communication with others. New research conclusions and a continued emphasis on diversity are presented in Chapter 4 as one of our foundation principles of interpersonal communication.

Part II includes our coverage of essential interpersonal skills. Chapter 5 presents what many users believe is an exceptionally strong, clear coverage of listening and responding. We've bolstered our discussion with new research about listening styles and other new research conclusions. Communicating verbally is the focus of Chapter 6, and we've added new material about avoiding biased language. Chapter 7 includes our crisp, clear, get-to-the-point discussion of using and interpreting nonverbal messages; new material throughout the chapters, including a new discussion of deceitful communication, has been added. "Conflict Management Skills," Chapter 8, concludes our discussion of communication skills. This edition offers new, practical research conclusions about managing emotions during conflict as well as many other research-based principles and strategies for managing conflict in interpersonal relationships.

Part III, "Interpersonal Communication Relationships," continues our applications of interpersonal skills to the context of relationship development, maintenance, and termination. Chapter 9 presents essential principles which help explain how relationships work. Chapter 10 offers both descriptive and prescriptive information for developing interpersonal relationships. Our last chapter has been retitled; it's now called "Interpersonal Relationships at Home, at Work, and on the Internet." We continue our applications of interpersonal communication in families and at the workplace, and have added exciting new research observations about how interpersonal communication research applies to on-line connections.

Here's a summary of some of the key revisions we've made to the third edition:

- Updated research conclusions about interpersonal communication in every chapter. We've continued to emphasize research observations from communication scholars.

- A further expanded discussion of the role of the Internet in the process of building and maintaining interpersonal relationships with others. We've written a new section called "Interpersonal Communication on the Internet," included in Chapter 11.
- New, revised "e-Connections" boxes in every chapter which highlight research conclusions and illustrations of how electronic means of communication affects our relationships. We've also included new Web addresses which provide a wealth of additional information about interpersonal communication; our companion Web site www.ablongman.com/beebe contains links for all of the Web sites included in the book.
- New cartoons, stories, examples, and illustrations have been added in every chapter to apply the principles and skills we discuss.
- We've revised our discussion of self disclosure and included this new material in Chapter 2.
- We added several new self-assessment tests throughout the book.
- New material in Chapter 4 helps students better adapt their behavior when communicating with others who are different from themselves.
- A new section on listening styles in Chapter 5 helps students adapt to people-oriented, action-oriented, content-oriented, and time-oriented listeners.
- A new section, called "Improving Critical Listening and Responding Skills," helps improve both critical thinking and critical listening skills.
- New material in Chapter 6 helps students use language to develop dialogue and supportive communication skills.
- An expanded discussion of how to avoid biased, insensitive language is included in Chapter 6.
- New material on detecting deceitful nonverbal communication has been included in Chapter 7.
- Chapter 8 includes new information to help students better manage pseudo-, simple-, and ego-conflict, as well as expanded coverage of conflict management skills
- Relational theory has been reorganized in Chapter 9 and now includes a discussion of relationships from the social exchange and dialectal perspectives.
- New to Chapter 10 is a discussion of relational escalation and maintenance as it applies to diverse friendships and romantic relationships.
- A discussion of communication between spouses, parent and children, and siblings has been added to Chapter 11.

Our Partnership with Instructors

n Chapter 1 we claim that it's a myth that information equals communication. Information is a necessary but not sufficient condition for communication to occur. So it is with a textbook. A textbook is only an inanimate repository of information; in the hands of a gifted instructor, however, the information comes to life in the minds and hearts of students. In our third edition we continue to offer a wide array of tools and resources to help instructors teach and students learn the

information we have distilled in these pages. Our goal is to provide a wealth of teaching tools that can make the material applicable and memorable.

Within the text we've included chapter opening learning objectives and content outlines. We've incorporated "Recap" boxes that help remind students of key content, "e-Connection" boxes that point out applications of technology to students, "Understanding Diversity" boxes that highlight applications of learning interpersonal communication in a diverse world, "Building Your Skills" boxes that help students see the connection between knowing and doing, and "Considering Others" boxes that remind students about our central other-oriented theme. We conclude each chapter with a cogent summary of the key ideas, as well as discussion questions that focus on comprehension, critical thinking, and ethical issues. In addition, each chapter ends with suggestions for students who are writing an interpersonal journal, as well as activities and exercises for collaborative learning. Numerous self-assessment instruments are liberally sprinkled throughout the text.

In addition to the built-in learning tools, we offer a briefcase full of instructor and student resources.

Instructor's Supplements

- *Instructor's Resource Manual* This comprehensive guide by Nan Peck of Northern Virginia Community College provides a wealth of teaching tips, lecture outlines, sample syllabi, Internet exercises, class assignments, student activities, and more.
- *Test Bank* This test bank by Thomas E. Jewell of Marymount College contains questions including multiple choice, true false, matching, fill-in-the-blank, short answer, and essay.
- *Computerized Test Bank* An integrated suite of testing tools for Windows and Macintosh. Using the best-selling ESATEST III software, this computerized test bank allows instructors to edit, create, and print tests using any combination of questions from the printed test bank.
- *The Blockbuster Approach: Teaching Interpersonal Communication with Video, 2nd Edition* This guide by Thomas E. Jewell, Marymount College, provides lists and descriptions of commercial video that can be used in the classroom to illustrate interpersonal concepts and complex interpersonal relationships. Sample activities are available.
- *Allyn & Bacon Interpersonal Communication Video* This 30 minute video includes three scenarios that illustrate concepts in interpersonal communication including communication fundamentals, perception, the self, listening, conflict, intimacy, and relationships. Comes with an accompanying video user's guide.
- *Video: Interpersonal Communication* Covers concepts such as perception, ethics, self-disclosure, sexual harassment, and dysfunctional relationships in the 50 minute video and accompanying video user's guide.
- *Interpersonal Movie Library* This collection is available to adopters and contains feature films dealing with a range of interpersonal topics (some restrictions apply).
- *Allyn & Bacon Communication Video Library* Contains a collection of communication videos produced by Film for the Humanities and Sciences (restrictions apply).

Acknowledgements

This book is a team project. The three of us represent only one component of the team. Without the contributions of hard-working, creative scholars who have studied interpersonal communication and published their results, a book of this breadth would not be possible. We also thank our students who are a constant source of insights, challenges, questions, and curiosity about interpersonal communication and keep our perspective fresh and alive.

We are most appreciative of the continuing high-quality editorial support that kept our multi-author team on track and on schedule. Editor Karon Bowers consistently provides support, encouragement, ideas, and inspiration for this book; she is the best editor with whom we have worked in our two decades of authoring texts. Development editor Carol Alper again provided outstanding assistance, advice, and ideas to keep us on schedule; we continue to be thankful for her gifts of working with words, ideas, and people.

We also appreciate the many outstanding interpersonal communication teachers and scholars who read the manuscript and offered suggestions that have made this a better book. We thank the following people for sharing their time, talent, and teaching tips with us:

Reviewers for the third edition:

Norman Clark
Appalachian State University

Cameron Smith Basquiat
Community College of Southern Nevada

Carolyn P. DeLeCour
Palo Alto College

Claire Sullivan
University of Maine

Patricia M. Harris-Jenkinson
Sacramento City College

Sheryl L. Williams
University of Wisconsin—Whitewater

Elizabeth R. Lamoureux
Buena Vista University

Richard L. Wiseman
California State University—Fullerton

Timothy P. Mottet
Southwest Texas State University

Reviewers for the first and second editions:

Rebecca Anderson
Johnson County Community College

Terrence Doyle
Northern Virginia Community College

Leonard Barchak
McNeese University

Sherry J. Holmen
Albuquerque T–VI Community College

Judyth Betz-Gonzales
Delta College

David D. Hudson
Golden West College

Marion Boyer
Kalamazoo Community College

Diana K. Ivy
Texas A&M University—Corpus Christi

Carol Z. Dolphin
University of Wisconsin —Waukesha

Thomas E. Jewell
Marymount College

Nan Peck
Northern Virginia Community College

Dickie Spurgeon
Southern Illinois University

Terry Perkins
Eastern Illinois University

Glen H. Stamp
Ball State University

Susan Richardson
Prince George Community College

Dick Stine
Johnson County Community College

Michael Schliessman
South Dakota State University

James J. Tolhuizen
Indiana University—Northwest

Cheri Simonds
Illinois State University

Sally Vogl-Bauer
University of Wisconsin—Whitewater

Anntarie Lanita Sims
Trenton State College

We are continually grateful for the support and ideas of our friends and colleagues. Steve and Sue thank Thompson Biggers, a valued friend and colleague, who helped conceptualize the project and provided many suggestions. Phil Salem, a friend and colleague at Southwest Texas State University, influenced our work through his talent and enthusiasm for teaching. Lee Williams, Maureen Keeley, Cathy Fleuriet, also at SWT, offered ongoing support and encouragement. Our friend and colleague, John Masterson, Provost at Texas Lutheran University, shared his knowledge of interpersonal communication, and models effective interpersonal skills as a trusted and cherished friend. Special thanks go to Michael Argyle at Oxford University, Oxford, England who sponsored Steve as a Visiting Scholar at Oxford's Wolfson College and generously shared his research findings. Thanks, too, to Peter Collett of Oxford University for his assistance, support, and friendship. Thayne McCollough, also a colleague whom Steve met in Oxford, provided valuable support for this project.

Over the years Mark has had the opportunity to interact with a number of colleagues who have helped shape his views and understanding of interpersonal communication. Particularly, Mark thanks Kay Mueller, Denise Vrchota, Terry Pickett, David Waggoner, Judith Bunyi, and Steve Ralston for help in the earlier editions. Denise has continued to provide her unique insights for improving the text that can be found woven into the third edition. Beth Lamoureux at Buena Vista University continues to be a extraordinary supporter of our text, as well as a supportive friend. Mark's office neighbor and colleague, Eric Abbott, has provided invaluable advice, counsel, and support during the development of this third edition.

We have had outstanding staff support from many people. Sue Hall, senior administrative assistant in the Department of Speech Communication at SWT, continues to provide valuable, support, assistance, and friendship. Stephanie Cook's word processing skills were most appreciated. Bob Hannah in his role as technical support specialist also provided important help. Kathy Box, a staff member in the Greenlee School of Journalism and Communication at Iowa State University, went above the call of duty in helping Mark meet deadlines.

Finally, our family and friends made a special contribution to this book by teaching us so much about human relationships. Mark thanks his parents, Jack and Alice Redmond; his brother, Jack; and his sisters, Ruthann, Mary Lynn, and Tina, who helped shape a family environment that planted the seeds for studying and appreciating interpersonal communication. Those seeds have been nurtured into a full-grown fascination with how communication shapes our lives and personal development by his wife, Peggy, his daughter Beth, and his sons, Nicholas and Eric. On a practical level Mark owes a lot of his understanding of chat rooms and instant messaging to them.

Steve and Sue want especially to thank their parents, Russell and Muriel Beebe and Herb and Jane Dye, their first and finest teachers of interpersonal communication; combining more than 115 years of marriage, both sets of parents model the quintessential skill of being other-oriented. We also thank our sons, Mark and Matthew Beebe, who offer their continuing love and support.

Steven A. Beebe
Susan J. Beebe
San Marcos, Texas

Mark V. Redmond
Ames, Iowa

Interpersonal
Communication

Interpersonal Communication Foundations

The first four chapters present fundamental concepts that frame our study of interpersonal communication. In Chapter 1 you will learn answers to these questions: What is interpersonal communication? What is the connection between interpersonal communication and interpersonal relationships? Why is it important to study relationships? What can I do to improve my relationships with others? Chapter 2 offers concepts and skills to help you understand more about who you are and how your self concept and sense of self-worth influence your relationships, as well as how you reveal yourself to others. In Chapter 3 you will learn that perception plays a key role in effective interpersonal communication. By recognizing the factors that influence your perceptions and actively analyzing the meaning of perceptual information, you can become more adept at sharing your sense of the world with others. Chapter 4 explores principles to help you better understand people who are different from you and explain how developing an other-oriented perspective helps bridge cultural differences.

1

Introduction to Interpersonal Communication

After you study this chapter

you should be able to . . .

1. Compare and contrast definitions of communication, human communication, and interpersonal communication.

2. Explain why it is useful to study interpersonal communication.

3. Compare and contrast communication as action, interaction, and transaction.

4. Describe the key components of the communication process.

5. Discuss five principles of interpersonal communication.

6. Describe four interpersonal communication myths.

7. Identify strategies that can improve your communication effectiveness.

- Defining Interpersonal Communication

- The Importance of Interpersonal Communication to Our Lives

- An Evolving Model for Human and Interpersonal Communication

- Mediated Interpersonal Communication: A New Frontier

- Principles of Interpersonal Communication

- Interpersonal Communication Myths

- How to Improve Your Own Interpersonal Communication Effectiveness

Communication is to a relationship what breathing is to maintaining life.

VIRGINIA SATIR

Interpersonal communication is like breathing; it is a requirement for life. And, like breathing, it is inescapable. Unless you live in isolation, you communicate interpersonally every day. Listening to your roommate, talking to a teacher, meeting for lunch with a friend, or talking to your parents or your spouse are all examples of interpersonal communication.

It is impossible *not* to communicate with others. Even before we are born, we respond to movement and sound. With our first cry we announce to others that we are here. Once we make contact with others, we communicate, and we continue to do so until our last breath. Even though many of our messages are not verbalized, we nonetheless intentionally, and sometimes unintentionally, send messages to others. Without interpersonal communication, a special form of human communication that occurs as we manage our relationships, people suffer and even die. Recluses, hermits, and people isolated in solitary confinement dream and hallucinate about talking with others face-to-face.

Human communication is at the core of our existence. Think of the number of times you communicated with someone today, as you worked, ate, studied, shopped, or went about your other daily activities. Most people spend between 80 and 90 percent of their waking hours communicating with others.[1] It is through these interactions with others that we develop interpersonal relationships.

Because these relationships are so important to our lives, later chapters will focus on the communication skills and principles that explain and predict how we develop, sustain, and sometimes end relationships. We'll explore such questions as the following: Why do we like some people and not others? How can we interpret other people's unspoken messages with greater accuracy? Why do some relationships blossom and others deteriorate? How can we better manage disagreements with others? How can we better understand our relationships with our family, friends, and coworkers?

This chapter charts the course ahead, addressing key questions about what interpersonal communication is and why it is important. We will begin by seeing how our understanding of the interpersonal communication process has evolved. And we will conclude by examining how we initiate and sustain relationships through interpersonal communication.

Defining Interpersonal Communication

To understand interpersonal communication, we must begin by understanding how it relates to two broader categories: communication in general and human communication. Scholars have attempted to arrive at a general definition of communication for decades, yet experts cannot agree on a single one. One research team counted more than 126 published definitions;[2] however, in the broadest sense, **communication** is the process of acting on information.[3] Someone does or says something, and others think or do something in response to the action or the words as they understand them.

Communication is not unique to humans. It is possible, for example, for you to act on information from your dog. He barks; you feed him. This definition also suggests that your dog can act on information from you. You head for the cupboard to feed him; he wags his tail and jumps up in the air, anticipating his dinner. Researchers do study communication between species as well as communication systems within single animal species, but these fields of study are beyond the scope of this book. The focus of our study is on a form of human communication: people communicating with other people.

To refine this definition, we can say that **human communication** is the process of making sense out of the world and sharing that sense with others.[4] We learn about the world by listening, observing, tasting, touching, and smelling; then we share our conclusions with others. Human communication encompasses many media: speeches, songs, radio and television broadcasts, e-mail, letters, books, articles, poems, advertisements.

Interpersonal communication is a distinctive form of human communication that occurs when you interact with another person and mutually influence each other, usually for the purpose of managing relationships. Three essential elements of this definition determine the unique nature of interpersonal communication apart from other forms of human communication.

Interpersonal Communication Is a Distinctive Form of Communication

For years many scholars defined interpersonal communication simply as communication that occurs when two people interact face-to-face. This limited definition suggests that if two people are interacting, then they are interpersonally communicating. Today, interpersonal communication is defined not just by the number of people who communicate, but also by the quality of the communication. Interpersonal communication occurs not when you simply interact with someone, but when you treat the other as a unique human being.

Think of all human communication as ranging on a continuum from impersonal to interpersonal communication. **Impersonal communication** occurs when you treat people as objects, or when you respond to their roles rather than to who they are as unique people. Philosopher Martin Buber influenced our thinking about human communication when he presented the concept of true dialogue as the essence of true, authentic communication.[5] He described communication as

---

communication. Process of acting on information.

human communication. Process of making sense out of the world and attempting to share that sense with others.

interpersonal communication. Process of interacting simultaneously with another person and mutually influencing each other, usually for the purpose of managing relationships.

impersonal communication. Communication that occurs when we treat people as objects, or when we respond to their roles rather than who they are as unique persons.

In face-to-face encounters, we simultaneously exchange both verbal and nonverbal messages that result in shared meanings. Through this kind of inter-relation, we build relationships with others. (Bob Daemmrich/Stock Boston)

consisting of two different qualities of relationships. He discussed an "I–It" relationship as an impersonal one; the other person is viewed as an "It" rather than as an authentic, genuine person. When you buy a pair of socks at a clothing store, you have a two-person, face-to-face, relatively brief interaction with someone. You communicate. Yet that interchange could hardly be described as intimate or personal. When you ask a server in a restaurant for a glass of water, you are interacting with the role, not necessarily with the individual. You know nothing personal about him (or her), and he knows nothing personal about you (unless he eavesdrops by your table).

Interpersonal communication occurs when you interact with another person as a unique, authentic individual rather than as object or "It." Buber calls this kind of relationship an "I–Thou" relationship. There is true dialogue. An "I–Thou" relationship is not self-centered. The communicators have developed an attitude toward each other that is honest, open, spontaneous, nonjudgmental, and based on equality rather than superiority.[6] The exchanges with the sock-seller or server have the potential to become true interpersonal communication dialogue if you begin to interact with these people as unique individuals. If, for example, during your conversation with the server, you discover you were born in the same town and develop other personal links, the impersonal, role-oriented communication becomes more personal, and the quality of the communication moves toward the intimate end of the continuum.

We're not suggesting that the goal of every communication exchange is to develop a personal, intimate dialogue. As with buying socks or asking for a glass of water at a restaurant, it may not be appropriate to develop personal relationships with others just because you are talking with them.

Although interpersonal communication is more intimate and reveals more about the people involved than does impersonal communication, not all interpersonal communication involves sharing closely guarded personal information. As we

Table 1.1

The Continuum Between Interpersonal Communication and Impersonal Communication

Interpersonal Communication	Impersonal Communication
● People are treated as unique individuals.	● People are treated as objects.
● People communicate in an "I–Thou" relationship. You are special.	● People communicate in an "I–It" relationship. You have a role to perform.
● There is true dialogue and honest sharing of self with others.	● There is mechanical, stilted interaction; no honest sharing of feelings.
● Interpersonal communication often involves communicating with someone you care about, such as a good friend or cherished family member.	● Impersonal communication involves communicating with people such as sales clerks and waitpersons—you have no history with them and you expect no future with them.

discuss later in the book, there are degrees of intimacy when interacting with others. Table 1.1 compares and contrasts interpersonal communication with impersonal communication.

Interpersonal Communication Involves Mutual Influence Between Individuals

Mutual influence means that *all* partners are affected by the interactions, not just one person. Interpersonal communication may or may not involve words. The interaction may be fleeting or enduring. While you are talking and your mother is listening, you are also simultaneously observing your mother's nonverbal expressions. Just because she is not speaking does not mean she is not communicating. She not only hears *what* you have to say, but also observes *how* you say it.

The degree of mutual influence varies a great deal from interaction to interaction. You probably would not be affected a great deal by a brief smile that you receive from a traveling companion on a bus, but would be greatly affected by your lover telling you he or she is leaving you. Every interpersonal communication interaction influences us. Sometimes it changes our lives dramatically, sometimes in small ways. Long-lasting interpersonal relationships are sustained not by one person giving and another taking, but by a spirit of mutual equality. Both you and your partner listen and respond with respect for each other. There is no attempt to manipulate others. True dialogue, says researcher Daniel Yankelovitch, involves a collaborative climate. It's not about winning and losing an argument. It's about being understood and accepted.[7]

Buber defines the quality of being fully "present" when communicating with another person as an "I–thou" relationship.[8] To be present is to give your full attention to the other person. The quality of interpersonal communication is enhanced when both you and your partner are simultaneously present and focused on each other.

Interpersonal Communication Is the Fundamental Means We Use to Manage Our Relationships

An interpersonal **relationship** is the ongoing connection you make with others through interpersonal communication. Relationships go through a series of developmental stages. The initial stages of relationships often involve sharing less intimate or personal information. Later stages evolve to include more intimate conversations and behaviors.

You initiate and form relationships by communicating with others whom you find attractive in some way. You seek to increase your interactions with people with whom you wish to develop relationships, and you continually interpersonally communicate to maintain the relationship. You also use interpersonal communication to end relationships that you have decided are no longer viable.

You can usually identify the stage of a relationship by simply observing the interpersonal communication. People interact differently as they move toward or away from intimacy. Your interactions with a new acquaintance differ from those with a close friend. When interacting with a stranger, you stand farther away, use different words, are more likely to feel awkward, and are less certain about how to interpret body language than when you interact with a good friend. We more fully describe the nature and development of interpersonal relationships with others in Chapters 9, 10, and 11.

In this book we define interpersonal communication as a unique form of human communication. There are other forms of communication, as well. **Mass communication** occurs when someone communicates the same message to many people at once, but the creator of the message is usually not physically present, and listeners have virtually no opportunity to respond immediately to the speaker. Messages communicated via radio and TV are examples of mass communication. **Public communication** occurs when a speaker addresses a large audience in person. **Small-group communication** occurs when a group of from three to fifteen people meet to interact with a common purpose and mutually influence one another. The purpose of the gathering could be to solve a problem, make a decision, learn, or just have fun. While communicating with others in a small group, it is also possible to communicate with others interpersonally—to communicate to manage a relationship with one or more individuals in the group. Finally, **intrapersonal communication** is communication with yourself. Thinking is perhaps the best example of intrapersonal communication. In our discussion of self and communication in Chapter 2, we discuss the relationships between your thoughts and your interpersonal communication with others.

The Importance of Interpersonal Communication to Our Lives

Why learn about interpersonal communication? Because it touches every aspect of your life. It is not only pleasant or desirable to develop quality interpersonal relationships with others, it is vital for your well-being. Learning how to understand and improve interpersonal communication can improve relationships

relationship. An ongoing connection made with another person through interpersonal communication.

mass communication. Type of communication that occurs when one person issues the same message to many people at once; the creator of the message is usually not present and there is virtually no opportunity for listeners to respond to the speaker.

public communication. Type of communication that occurs when a speaker addresses a large audience in person.

small-group communication. Type of communication that occurs when a group of from three to fifteen people meet to interact with a common purpose and mutually influence one another.

intrapersonal communication. Communication with yourself; thinking.

with family, loved ones, friends, and colleagues and can enhance the quality of physical and emotional health.

1. *Being skilled in interpersonal communication can improve relationships with family.* Relating to family members can be a challenge. The divorce statistics in the United States document the difficulties that can occur when people live in relationship with each other: About half of all marriages end in divorce. We don't claim that you will avoid all family conflicts or that your family relationships will always be harmonious if you learn principles and skills of interpersonal communication. You can, however, develop more options for how to respond when family communication challenges come your way. You will be more likely to develop creative, constructive solutions to family conflict if you understand what's happening and can promote true dialogue with your spouse, parent, brother, or sister. Furthermore, family relationships play a major role in determining how you interact with others. Family communication author Virginia Satir calls family communication "the largest single factor determining the kinds of relationships [people make] with others."[9]

2. *Being skilled in interpersonal communication can improve relationships with friends and lovers.* You don't choose your biological families, but you do choose your friends. Friends are people you choose to be with because you like them, and usually they like you. For unmarried people, developing friendships and falling in love are the top-rated sources of satisfaction and happiness in life.[10] Conversely, losing a relationship is among life's most stressful events. Most people between the ages of 19 and 24 report that they have had from five to six romantic relationships and have been "in love" once or twice.[11] Studying interpersonal communication may not unravel all the mysteries of romantic love and friendship, but it can offer insight into behaviors.

Effective interpersonal skills are essential for people to develop meaningful, caring relationships. (Lori Adamski Peek/Tony Stone Images)

3. *Being skilled in interpersonal communication can improve relationships with colleagues.* In many ways, colleagues at work are like family members. Although you choose your friends and lovers, you don't always have the same flexibility in choosing those with whom or for whom you work. Understanding how relationships develop on the job can help you avoid conflict and stress and increase your sense of satisfaction. In addition, your success or failure in a job often hinges on how well you get along with supervisors and peers.

Several surveys document the importance of quality interpersonal relationships in contributing to success at work.[12] The abilities to listen to others, manage conflict, and develop quality interpersonal relationships with others are usually at the top of the list of the skills employers seek in today's job applicants.

4. ***Being skilled in interpersonal communication can improve physical and emotional health.*** Research has shown that the lack or loss of a close relationship can lead to ill health and even death. Physicians have long observed that patients who are widowed or divorced experience more medical problems such as heart disease, cancer, pneumonia, and diabetes than do married people.[13] Grief-stricken spouses are more likely than others to die prematurely, especially around the time of the departed spouse's birthday or near their wedding anniversary.[14] Being childless can also shorten one's life. One study found that middle-aged, childless wives were almost two-and-one-half times more likely to die in a given year than those who had at least one child.[15] Terminally ill patients with a limited number of friends or no social support die sooner than those with stronger ties.[16] Without companions and close friends, opportunities for intimacy and stress-managing interpersonal communication are diminished. Studying how to enhance the quality of your communication with others can make life more enjoyable and enhance your overall well-being.

recap   **Comparing Key Definitions**

Term	Definition
Communication	The process of acting on information
Human communication	The process of making sense out of the world and sharing that sense with others
Interpersonal communication	The process of interacting with another and mutually influencing each other, usually for the purpose of managing relationships

An Evolving Model for Human and Interpersonal Communication

Interpersonal communication involves more than simply transferring or exchanging messages; it is a complex process of creating meaning in the context of an interpersonal relationship. To understand this process more fully, it is useful to see how our perspective on the human communication process has evolved over the past half century. We will begin with the simplest and oldest model of the human communication process and then discuss more contemporary models.

Human Communication as Action: Message Transfer

"Did you get my message?" This simple sentence summarizes the communication as-action approach to human communication. Communication takes place when a message is sent and received. Period. It is a way of transferring meaning from sender to

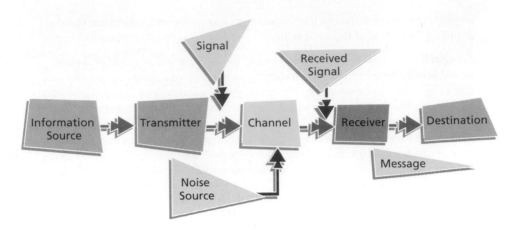

Figure 1.1

A Model for Communication as Action

From: *The Mathematical Theory of Communication* by Claude E. Shannon and Warren Weaver. Copyright 1949 by the Board of Trustees of the University of Illinois. Used by permission of the University of Illinois Press.

receiver. In 1942, communication scholar Harold Lasswell summarized the process as follows:

Who (sender)

Says what (message)

In what channel

To whom (receiver)

With what effect[17]

Figure 1.1 shows a basic model formulated in 1949, seven years after Lasswell's summary, that depicts communication as a linear input/output process. Today, although they view the process differently, researchers still define most of the key components in this model in basically the same way.

Information Source and Transmitter

The **information source** for communication can be a thought or an emotion. The transmitter (nowadays called the **source**), the conveyor of that thought or emotion, puts it into a code that can be understood by a receiver. Translating ideas, feelings, and thoughts into a code is called **encoding.** Vocalizing a word, gesturing, or establishing eye contact are signals that we use to encode our thoughts into a message that can be decoded by someone. **Decoding,** the opposite process of encoding, occurs when the words or unspoken signals are interpreted by the receiver.

Receiver

The **receiver** is the person who decodes and attempts to make sense out of what the source encoded. Think of a radio station with a source broadcasting to a receiver that picks up the station's signal. In human communication, however, there is something in between the source and the receiver: People filter messages through past experiences, attitudes, beliefs, values, prejudices, and biases.

Signal, Received Signal, and Message

Today, all these components—signal, received signal, and message—are simply called the **message.** Messages are the written, spoken, and unspoken elements of communication to which people assign meaning. You can send a message intentionally (talking to a professor before class) or unintentionally (falling asleep dur-

information source. Thought or emotion that triggers communication.

source. Originator of a thought or emotion, who puts it into a code that can be understood by a receiver.

encode. To translate ideas, feelings, and thoughts into a code.

decode. To interpret ideas, feelings, and thoughts that have been translated into a code.

receiver. Person who decodes a message and attempts to make sense out of what the source has encoded.

message. Written, spoken, and unspoken elements of communication, to which people assign meaning.

e-connections
Impersonal America

A few weeks back, I bought an upgrade card for my computer. Being inexpert at such things, I soon found myself out of my depth and placed a call to the company's technical-support line. After going through the menu of options offered by the machine that answered the phone, I was connected to a recorded voice that said I would be on hold for five or ten minutes before someone could help me.

I was actually on hold for about an hour, but my ordeal finally ended.

When the machine hung up on me.

Undaunted, I called the company back—did I mention that this was long-distance?—and spent another hour listening to the same three elevator tunes repeated endlessly. Fed up, I hung up, only to repeat the sequence over the next few days without getting even a smidgen of technical support from the technical-support line.

Which brings us to the question: Where have all the human beings gone?

You know, the people who used to answer your questions, explain your options . . . service with a smile and all that? What happened to them?

It's not just the computer company that makes me wonder. It's the utility company, the bank, the subscription department, the telephone operator and, yes, the automated phone system at my very own office.

It wasn't always like this. Remember when you took your questions to a human who gave you a human response? Now, you listen to a menu and input information. We live in Impersonal America, an acquaintance said the other day as he swiped his money card to buy gas at the pump. Not so long ago, he mused, filling the tank meant dealing with another human being. Maybe shooting the breeze for a moment or two. Now, we just pump and run. Granted, the new way is quicker and easier.

Less painful sometimes, too. Once, years ago, I needed to get an extension on a utility bill. I'm sitting there on hold, trying to frame a hard-luck tale for the clerk, when suddenly a machine picks up the phone. It instructs me to key in some information and quickly approves my request. Never even asks for my tale of woe. It seemed a good deal to me at the time. Only now do I find myself questioning whether the trade-off was worth it. Only now that humanity has been exchanged for cost-effectiveness and service swapped for speed.

And that's a term which seems especially apropos because I don't think this happened just because we were looking for greater efficiency. No, I think we also wanted greater uniformity. We wanted—and have made—our encounters sterile and personality-free. Know how bad it is? A cashier, an older woman who works in a cafeteria in Washington, got in hot water a while back for her habit of calling customers "honey" and "sweetie."

We wanted it to be like that. Wanted correctness over personality. Wanted one-size-fits-all customer service free from the messiness—bad moods, biases, idiosyncrasies, small talk—that characterizes human interaction. But I find that I miss the mess. Indeed, when I went through back channels and finally got a live human to answer my computer question, I was more pumped than an OPEC oil well. The guy even got snippy with me, and it was like hearing a favorite song for the first time in years.

It made me wonder: Are we really better off now than we were when human beings—snippy and otherwise—answered the phones and provided the service? OK, so maybe real live people aren't cost-effective. But I can tell you this: I wound up taking that upgrade card back to the store. Asked the clerk to recommend one from a company that could actually put a living breathing human being on the line in a reasonable amount of time. The card he showed me costs about $100 more. And you know something? It's worth it.

Leonard Pitts, *Miami Herald*. Distributed by Knight-Ridder/Tribune Information Services.

---

ing class); verbally ("Hi. How are you?"), nonverbally (a smile and a handshake), or in written form (this book).

🔵 Channel

A message is communicated from sender to receiver via some pathway called a **channel.** Channels correspond to your senses. When you call your mother on the telephone, the channel is an auditory one. When you talk with your mother face-to-face, the channels are many. You see her: the visual channel. You hear her: the

channel. Pathway through which messages are sent.

auditory channel. You may smell her perfume: the olfactory channel. You may hug her: the tactile channel.

Noise

Noise is interference. It keeps a message from being understood and achieving its intended effect. Without noise, all messages would be communicated with sublime accuracy. But noise is always present. It can be literal (the obnoxious roar of a gas-powered lawn mower), or it can be psychological (instead of concentrating on your teacher's lecture, you may start thinking about the chores you need to finish before the end of the day). Whichever kind it is, noise gets in the way of the message and may even distort it. Communicating accurate messages involves minimizing both external and psychological noise.

The action approach is simple and straightforward, but it has a key flaw: Human communication rarely, if ever, is as simple and efficient as "what we put in is what we get out." Others cannot automatically know what you mean just because you think you know what you mean. Although by Lasswell's time, communication scholars had already begun identifying an array of key elements in the communication process, the action approach overlooked their complexity.

Human Communication as Interaction: Message Exchange

The next big leap in understanding human communication came in the late 1940s and early 1950s. The communication-as-interaction perspective used the same elements as the action models but added two new ones: feedback and context.

Think of a Ping-Pong game. Like a Ping-Pong ball, messages bounce back and forth. We talk; someone listens and responds; we listen and respond to this response. This perspective can be summarized using a physical principle: For every action there is a reaction.

Feedback is the response to the message. Without feedback, communication is rarely effective. When you order your black olive pizza and the server says in response, "That's a black olive pizza, right?" he has provided feedback to ensure that he encoded the message correctly.

Feedback is really a response message. Like other messages, it can be intentional (your mother gives you a hug when you announce your engagement to be married) or unintentional (you yawn as you listen to your uncle tell his story about bears again); verbal ("That's a black olive pizza, right?") or nonverbal (blushing after being asked to dance).

A second component recognized by the interaction perspective is **context**, the physical and psychological communication environment. All communication takes place in some context. As the cliche goes, "Everyone has to be somewhere." A conversation with your good friend on the beach would likely differ from one the two of you may have in a funeral home. Context encompasses not only the physical environment but also the number of people present and their relationship with the communicators, the communication goal, and the culture in which the communicators are steeped.

This perspective, as shown in Figure 1.2, is more realistic, but it still has limitations. Although it emphasizes feedback and context, it does not quite capture the complexity of the interpersonal communication process if the communication takes place simultaneously. The interaction model of communication still views communication as a linear, step-by-step process. But in interpersonal situations, both the source and the receiver send and receive messages at the same time.

noise. Information, either literal or psychological, that interferes with accurate reception of the communication of the message.

feedback. Response to a message.

context. Physical and psychological communication environment.

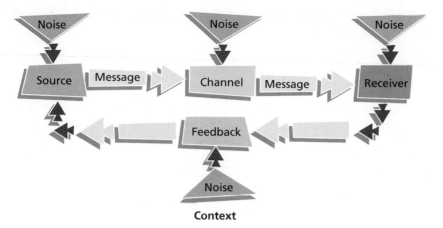

Figure 1.2
**A Model for
Communication as
Interaction**
Interaction models of
communication include
feedback as a response to
a message sent by the
communication source.

Components of the Human Communication Process

Term	Definition
Source	Person who has an idea or emotion
Receiver	Person or group toward whom the source directs messages, intentionally or unintentionally
Message	Written, spoken, and unspoken elements of communication to which people assign meaning
Channel	Pathway through which messages pass between source and receiver
Noise	Anything, either literal or psychological, that interferes with the clear reception and interpretation of a message
Encode	Translation of ideas, feelings, and thoughts into a code
Decode	Interpretation of ideas, feelings, and thoughts that have been translated into a code
Context	Physical and psychological communication environment
Feedback	Verbal and nonverbal responses to messages

Human Communication as Transaction: Message Creation

The communication-as-transaction perspective, which evolved in the 1960s, acknowledges that when you talk to another, you are constantly reacting to what your partner is saying. Most scholars today view it as the most realistic model for interpersonal communication. Like action and interaction, transaction uses various components to describe communication. However, in this model, all the components are simultaneous. As Figure 1.3 indicates, you send and receive messages concurrently. Even as you talk, you are also interpreting your partner's nonverbal and verbal responses.

Transactional communication also occurs within a context defined more broadly than by action or interaction. Transactional communication suggests that your communication is influenced by a force that may not be immediately evident to you or your communication partner. The past experiences and culture of the people involved in the communication, the setting of the communication, and the thoughts and emotions of the communicators are all influencing how messages are being interpreted.

Figure 1.3
A Model for Communication as Mutual Transaction The source and receiver of a message experience communication simultaneously.

Whereas communication as action or interaction views communication as linear—there are specific causes and effects that can explain how messages are interpreted—communication as transaction is much more complicated. An understanding of the relationships you establish changes from moment to moment as the conversation unfolds and your thoughts influence how you are responding to the message. A transactional approach to communication suggests that no single cause explains why you interpret messages the way you do. In fact, it is inappropriate to point to a single factor to explain how you are making sense of the messages of others; communication is messier than that. The meaning of messages in interpersonal relationships evolves from the past, is influenced by the present, and is affected by visions of the future.

As we communicate messages, we monitor the degree to which the other person understands each message. We mutually define the symbols we use. If one partner misunderstands a message, both can work to clarify the meaning. For example, if I ask you to hand me the book off my desk and you hand me a pad of paper, we have failed to create a shared meaning. I might then say, "No, not the pad of paper, the red book next to the phone"; you then would hand me the book. Your action would require me to explain and be more specific. We would not simply transfer or exchange meaning; we would create it during a communication transaction.

 **An Evolving Model for Interpersonal Communication**

Human Communication as Action 	Human communication is linear, with meaning sent or transferred from source to receiver.
Human Communication as Interaction	Human communication occurs as the receiver of the message responds to the source through feedback. This interactive model views communication as a linear action–reaction sequence of events.
Human Communication as Transaction 	Human communication is mutually interactive. Meaning is created based on a concurrent sharing of ideas and feelings. This transactive model most accurately describes human communication.

One researcher says that interpersonal communication is "the coordinated management of meaning" through **episodes,** during which the message of one person influences the message of another.[18] Technically, only the sender and receiver of those messages can determine where one episode ends and another begins.

Mediated Interpersonal Communication: A New Frontier

Today's technology allows us to expand our definition of interpersonal communication. Instead of having to rely on face-to-face contact for our interpersonal exchanges, we can now use various types of media to carry our interpersonal messages: Telephones, faxes, e-mail, and electronic chat rooms are among the sometimes bewildering assortment of devices through which we can interact, exercise mutual influence, and develop interpersonal relationships. When we use one of these media to carry the message, we are using **mediated interpersonal communication.** But as Leonard Pitts suggests in e-Connections: Impersonal America, mediated interpersonal communication may sometimes be less satisfying than a face-to-face encounter. Even in this electronic age, interacting with machines instead of humans may be uncomfortable for some people.

At present, the most effective interpersonal communication, especially for expressing feelings, occurs when there are no media filters to interfere with the clarity of the message or to delay feedback from the receiver of the message. For this reason, our key focus in this book is on unmediated interaction between people.

But we will also begin to explore the new frontier in interpersonal communication. Can you communicate interpersonally with someone on the Internet? Can relationships be developed with another without meeting others face-to-face? There is evidence that people can and do develop meaningful relationships with others without meeting them in person. If you are attending a college or university away from family, friends, or loved ones, you may have found that sending e-mail messages can help keep you in touch with others who are important to you. College freshmen and their parents report that e-mail connections reduce homesickness and the sadness parents often feel as their son or daughter leaves home. The past few years have seen an increase in the number of people who meet in a chatroom on the Internet and eventually develop a real-time relationship. In special e-Connections features throughout the text, we will highlight the ways that today's technology is affecting our relationships.

Do you think there's anything to those reports about the Internet making people more isolated and lose social graces?

Of course not, you idiot.

episode. Sequence of interaction between individuals, during which the message of one person influences the message of another.

mediated interpersonal relationship. Communication with others established or maintained by using media (such as e-mail, telephone, or a fax) rather than a face-to-face encounter.

e-connections
An Electronic Relationship

Today's technology makes it possible for people to develop relationships with others without meeting face-to-face. He was in Australia. She was in New York. They had never met. Their only contact was through an electronic bulletin board on the Internet. At first it was just a few e-mail messages a week. But as their relation- ship developed, they were soon communicating at least twenty times a day. As is the case with most face-to-face encounters, their early messages were about mundane topics such as the weather and daily activities. Eventually, their electronic correspondence became more personal. Then, nine months after they first logged on, Robert popped the question to his cyberspace sweetheart Charlene. "We are having some difficulty in getting people to understand that we know all about one another," newlywed Robert told the *Buffalo News.* "But e-mail is the resurgence of correspondence—which has essentially died out. It was the way many people used to get to know one another." The difference, of course, is that partners can measure the intervals between these "letters" in nanoseconds instead of days or weeks. Although such exchanges are not simultaneous, they certainly can have the kind of spontaneity that people usually associate with interpersonal communication.

As e-Connections: An Electronic Relationship illustrates, e-mail allows intimate relationships to develop between people who are separated by thousands of miles.

People have even developed new ways to communicate the feelings, emotions, and other responses that make it possible to communicate nonverbally. You are probably familiar with emoticons (keyboard symbols typed sideways, like :-O. (Note several other emoticons identified in the following e-Connections box.) You can also communicate emotions via e-mail by "screaming," TYPING IN ALL CAPITAL LETTERS TO SHOUT THE MESSAGE. In still other situations, you might respond to someone by verbally describing nonverbal behaviors: "I am frowning right now as I read what you are sending me."

Of course, just as not all face-to-face communication is interpersonal communication, not all mediated communication results in unique relationships with others. One of the key differences in these mediated communication situations is the reduced level of nonverbal cues. Even if you use emoticons, when you can't see the other person's facial expression, amount of eye contact, or whether he or she seems interested in what you are saying, accurately communicating your meaning, especially your feelings and emotions, can be challenging.

A growing body of research, however, suggests that when you interact with people using computer-mediated communication, you can compensate for the lack of nonverbal cues. If you've been interacting with someone over a period of several weeks or months, you begin to pick up cues about his or her emotions and feelings just from the words he or she uses and from what you have learned about that person and his or her behavior.

Communication researcher Joseph Walther and his colleagues have developed a **social information-processing theory** that explains how you can develop quality relationships with others via e-mail and other electronic means.[19] According to this theory, a key difference between face-to-face and computer-mediated communication is the rate at which information reaches you. During live, in-person communication, you process a lot of information quickly; you process the words you hear as well as the myriad of nonverbal cues you see (facial expression and body posture) and hear (tone of voice and use of pauses). During e-mail interactions, there is less information to process, so it takes a bit longer for the relationship to develop—but

social information-processing theory. Explains how people use information they receive from others via e-mail and other electronic ways to develop relationships with others.

e-connections
Emoticons

A kiss is just a : *, a sigh is just a : - (

Electronic-mail writers have adopted a lighthearted system of shorthand known as "emoticons." These clever combinations of keyboard characters punctuate a message with just the right spirit. To read them, simply look at the line with your head tilted slightly to the left.

For example, in the most basic emoticon, the smiley face, a colon, hyphen, and a right parenthesis become the eye, nose, and mouth of glee : -).

Here's a sample of some frequently used emoticons that will help you get across the nuances of your message:

: - I)	smiley with a mustache
: D	big smile
; -	wink
: - @	scream
: X	keeping mouth shut
: - &	tongue-tied
: - J	tongue in cheek or joking
: p	sticking out tongue or giving a raspberry
: *	kiss
: * ^ :	returning kiss
( )	hug
(((()))))	lots of hugs
: -)8	sharply dressed person
: - >	hey hey
I -)	hee hee

I - D	ho ho
: /	not funny
: - }	smirk
: - o	shocked (or singing the national anthem)
: I	bored
> : - <	angry
< : -)	dumb question or dumb person
(: - $	sick person or person is sick
: - (	sad
: -	really sad
:' (	crying
; - ?	licking your lips

From: Charles Bowen, *HomePC*, (January 1995), 109.

Want to see more emoticons? Click on the following Web addresses to enrich your emoticon vocabulary:

http://www.chatlist.com/faces.html
http://www.pressanykey.com/emoticons.html
http://www.pars.com.cz/clients/smiles/index

it does develop as you learn more about your e-mail partner's likes, dislikes, and feelings. Also, if you expect to communicate with your electronic communication partner again, there is evidence that you will pay more attention to the relationship cues that develop. In one study, Joseph Walther and Judee Burgoon found that the development of relationships between people who met face-to-face differed little from those between people who had computer-mediated interactions.[20] In fact, they found the computer-mediated group actually developed *more* socially rich relationships than the face-to-face groups. Because of technology, some electronic interpersonal exchanges may not be simultaneous. Nonetheless, there is mutual understanding, and the communication can be truly personal rather than impersonal. We suggest that these electronic communication exchanges, even though not as rich in nonverbal and relational information, can mirror characteristics of face-to-face interpersonal communication in the sense that you are developing or maintaining a unique relationship with someone. In addition, electronically mediated relationships can involve mutual influence. And e-mailing someone that you'd like to marry—or divorce—that person, or just get together for a cup of coffee, illustrates how e-messages can alter both lives and relationships. Clearly, not all e-mail correspondence is interpersonal communication; today's technology, however,

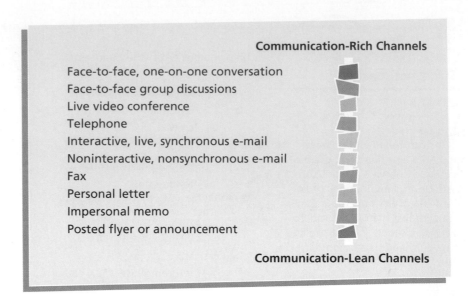

Figure 1.4

**A Continuum of
Communication-Rich and
Communication-Lean
Channels of Communication**
Adapted from L. K. Trevino,
R. L. Draft, and R. H. Lengel,
"Understanding Managers'
Media Choices: A Symbolic
Interactionist Perspective." In
*Organizations and Communi-
cation Technology,* edited by
J. Fulk and C. Steinfield
(Newbury Park, CA: Sage, 1990),
71–94.

sometimes makes it possible to emulate in cyberspace the characteristics of inter-personal transactions.

One research team suggests that the richness of a communication channel can be measured by four criteria: (1) the amount of feedback that the communicators can receive; (2) the number of cues that the channel can convey and that can be interpreted by a receiver; (3) the variety of language that communicators use; and (4) the potential for expressing emotions and feelings.[21] Using these four criteria, researchers have developed a continuum (communication-rich to communication-lean) of communication channels. The model presented in Figure 1.4 illustrates this continuum.

In summary, we believe this new frontier of electronic communication makes it possible for people to develop interpersonal relationships with others who are miles away. We agree with Joseph Walther and Lisa Tidwell that

> The "Information Superhighway" is clearly not just a road for moving data from one place to another, but a roadside where people pass each other, occasionally meet, and decide to travel together. You can't see very much of other drivers at first, unless you do travel together for some time. There are highway bandits, to be sure, who are not as they appear to be—one must drive defensively—and there are conflicts and disagreements on-line as there are off-road, too.[22]

Principles of
Interpersonal Communication

As we introduce the study of interpersonal communication in this chapter, it is useful to present fundamental principles that help explain the nature of inter-personal communication. Underlying our current understanding of interpersonal communication are five principles: Interpersonal communication connects us to

understanding
dive*r*ʂi*ty*

The World Is Here

*O*ne of our most visionary politicians said that he envisioned a
time when the United States could
become the brain of the world, by
which he meant the repository of
all the latest advanced information
systems. I thought of that remark
when an enterprising poet friend
of mine called to say that he had
just sold a poem to a computer
magazine and that the editors were
delighted to get it because they
didn't carry fiction or poetry. Is that
the kind of world we desire? A
humdrum homogenous world of all
brains but no heart, no fiction, no
poetry; a world of robots with
human attendants bereft of imagi-
nation, or culture. Or does North
America deserve a more exciting

*destiny? To become a place where
the cultures of the world crisscross.
This is possible because the United
States is unique in the world: The
world is here.*[23]

These words from Ishmael Reed's
essay, "The World Is Here," remind
us that America is not a one-dimen-
sional culture. You need not travel
to far-off places to develop interpersonal relationships with people
from other cultures, races, or ethnic
backgrounds. America has long
been known as a melting pot—a
place where people from a variety
of cultures and traditions have come
together to seek their fortunes.
Others think America is more like a
tossed salad than a melting pot—in
a salad each ingredient retains its
essential character rather than
melting together to form a united
whole. Focusing on communication
and diversity means much more than
focusing on cultural differences.
Culture consists of the learned values, behaviors, and expectations
shared by a group of people. You

need skill and sensitivity to develop
quality interpersonal relationships
with others whose religion, race,
ethnicity, age, gender, or sexual
orientation differ from your own.
Throughout the text, we include
boxes like this one to help you develop your sensitivity to important
issues related to cultural diversity.
As you embark on your study of
interpersonal communication,
consider these questions either in-
dividually or with a group of your
classmates:

1. What are the implications of this
   melting-pot or tossed salad culture for your study of interpersonal communication?

2. Is there too much emphasis on
   being politically correct on college campuses today? Support
   your answer.

3. What specific interpersonal skills
   will help you communicate effectively with others from different
   cultural and ethnic traditions?

others, is irreversible, is complicated, is governed by rules, and involves both content and relationship dimensions.

Interpersonal Communication Connects Us to Others

Unless you are a living in a cave or have become a cloistered monk, you interact with
others every day. Even if you work at home in front of a glowing computer screen,
you encounter other people in the course of living your life. The opportunities for
interpersonal communication are ubiquitous—they are everywhere. It is through inescapable interpersonal communication with others that we affect and are affected
by other human beings.

We agree with author H. D. Duncan, who said, "We do not relate and then talk,
but relate in talk." Fundamental to an understanding of interpersonal communication is the assumption that the quality of interpersonal relationships stems from the
quality of communication with others. It's been said that people can't *not* communicate. Even though this perspective is debated among communication scholars because people often don't intend to express ideas or feelings, without question interpersonal communication is inescapable in the 21st century. Try to think of a time
when you are *not* communicating. Hard to do, isn't it? How about when you're

asleep? If you fall asleep while reading this book, others who see you may draw conclusions about you; perhaps they will think you attended a great party last night, when in reality you stayed up late studying for a biology exam. In your interpersonal conversations with others, people may similarly draw an unintended conclusion about your interest in them if you inadvertently yawn while a friend of yours is telling you about the record-size fish he caught on his recent trip to the Ozarks. You didn't intend to offend him; you were just exhausted. Our point is that even when you may not be conscious of what you're doing, you are connecting to others through the ever-present process of communication.

The inescapable nature of interpersonal communication doesn't mean others will *accurately* decode your message; it does mean that others are drawing inferences about you and your behavior—they may be right or they may be wrong. Even as you silently stand in a crowded elevator, your lack of eye contact with others communicates your unwillingness to interact with fellow passengers. Your unspoken messages, even when you are asleep, provide cues that others interpret. Remember: People often judge you by your behavior, not your intent. Your interpersonal communication is how you develop connections to others. Even in well-established interpersonal relationships, you may be evoking an unintended response to your behavior.

Interpersonal Communication Is Irreversible

"Disregard that last statement made by the witness," instructs the judge. Yet the clever lawyer knows that once her client has told the jury that her husband gave her a black

Figure 1.5

Interpersonal Communication Is Irreversible
This helical model shows that interpersonal communication never loops back on itself. It begins at the bottom and expands infinitely as the communication partners contribute their thoughts and experiences to the exchange.
Copyright © F. E. X. Dance in *Human Communication Theory* (Holt, Rinehart and Winston, 1967), 294. Reprinted with permission.

eye during an argument, the client cannot really "take it back." This principle applies to all forms of communication. We may try to modify the meaning of a spoken message by saying something like "Oh, I really didn't mean it." But in most cases, the damage has been done. Once created, communication has the physical property of matter; it can't be uncreated. As the helical model in Figure 1.5 suggests, once interpersonal communication begins, it never loops back on itself. Instead, it continues to be shaped by the events, experiences, and thoughts of the communication partners. A Russian proverb nicely summarizes the point: "Once a word goes out of your mouth, you can never swallow it again."

Interpersonal Communication Is Complicated

No form of communication is simple. If any were, we would know how to reduce the number of misunderstandings and conflicts in our world. Because of the number of variables involved in interpersonal exchanges, even simple requests are extremely complex. Communication theorists have noted that whenever you communicate with another person, there are really at least six "people" involved: (1) who you think you are; (2) who you think the other person is; (3) who you think the other person thinks you are; (4) who the other person thinks he or she is; (5) who the other person thinks you are; and (6) who the other person thinks you think he or she is.[24] Whew! And when you add more people to the interaction, it becomes even more involved.

Moreover, when humans communicate, they interpret information from others as symbols. A **symbol** is merely a representation of something else, and it can have various meanings and interpretations. Language is a system of symbols. In English, symbols do not resemble the words they represent. The word (symbol) for *cow* does not look at all like a cow; someone, somewhere decided that *cow* should mean a beast that chews a cud and gives milk. The reliance on symbols to communicate poses a communication challenge; you are often misinterpreted. Sometimes you don't know the code. Only if you are up-to-date on contemporary slang will you know that "homeskillet" means a good friend, "circle of death" means a lousy pizza, and "papaflauge" means you are hiding something from your father.

"I'm afraid you misunderstood . . . I said I'd like a mango."

Messages are not always interpreted as we intend them. Osmo Wiio, a Scandinavian communication scholar, points out the messiness of communicating with others when he suggests the following maxims:

> If communication can fail, it will.
>
> If a message can be understood in different ways, it will be understood in just that way which does the most harm.
>
> There is always somebody who knows better than you what you meant by your message.
>
> The more communication there is, the more difficult it is for communication to succeed.[25]

Although we are not as pessimistic as Professor Wiio, we do suggest that the task of understanding each other is challenging.

Interpersonal Communication Is Governed by Rules

When you play *Monopoly,* you know that there are explicit rules about how to get out of jail, buy Boardwalk, or pass "Go" and get two hundred dollars. The rules are written down. When you play a game with others, there may even be some unwritten rules, such as when you play *Monopoly* with Grandpa, always let him buy Boardwalk. He gets grumpy as a bear before breakfast if he doesn't get to buy it. Similar rules govern how you communicate with others. Most of these rules are embedded in your culture or discussed verbally rather than in a written rulebook.

According to communication researcher Susan Shimanoff, a **rule** is a "followable prescription that indicates what behavior is obligated, preferred, or prohibited in certain contexts."[26] The rules that help define appropriate and inappropriate communication in any given situation may be *explicit* or *implicit.* For your interpersonal communication class, explicit rules are probably spelled out in your syllabus. But your instructor has other rules that are more implicit. They are not written or

symbol. Word, sound, or visual device that represents a thought, concept, or object.

rule. A followable prescription that indicates what behavior is obligated, preferred, or prohibited in certain communication situations or contexts.

For many of us, friendships are vital to our personal well-being. By improving our interpersonal communication skills, we can learn how to improve our friendships. (Ian Shaw/Tony Stone Images)

verbalized, because you learned them long ago: Only one person speaks at a time, you raise your hand to be called, you do not pass notes.

Interpersonal communication rules are developed by the people involved in the interaction and by the culture in which the individuals are communicating. Many times we learn communication rules from experience, by observing and interacting with others.

Interpersonal relationships are also shaped by both explicit and implicit rules. You may explicitly ask your friend not to phone you after 9 P.M. But you also have implicit expectations of others. In an early stage of a relationship, for example, you do not expect to learn private family secrets. At a later stage, you might be offended if an intimate friend does not reveal such secrets. Understanding rules helps you understand what is expected in a relationship.

Rules are developed both by those involved in the interaction and by the culture in which individuals are interacting. British researcher Michael Argyle and his colleagues asked people to identify general rules for relationship development and maintenance and then rate their importance. Here are the most important rules:[27]

Partners should respect the other's privacy.

Partners should not reveal each other's secrets.

Partners should look the other person in the eye during conversation.

Partners should not criticize the other person publicly.

Although we may modify rules to achieve the goals of our relationships, these general rules remain fairly constant. In interpersonal relationships the rules of a relationship are mutually defined and agreed on. Most of us don't like to be told what to do or how to behave all the time. The expectations and rules are continually renegotiated as the relationship unfolds. Few of us learn relationship rules by copying them from a book. Most of us learn these rules from experience, through observing and interacting with family members and friends. Individuals who grow up in environments in which these rules are not observed may not know how to behave in close relationships.

Interpersonal Communication Involves Both Content and Relationship Dimensions

What you say (your words) and how you say it (your tone of voice, amount of eye contact, facial expression, and posture) can reveal much about the true meaning of your message. If one of your roommates loudly and abruptly bellows, "HEY, DORK! CLEAN THIS ROOM!" and another roommate uses the same verbal message but more gently and playfully suggests, "Hey, dork. Clean this room," both are communicating a message seeking the same outcome. But the two messages have different relationship cues. The first, shouted message suggests that your roommate may be frustrated that the room still has echoes of last night's pizza party, whereas roommate number two's teasing request suggests he or she may be fondly amused by your untidiness.

The **content** of a communication message consists of the new information, ideas, or suggested actions that the speaker wishes to share. The **relationship dimension** of a communication message is usually more implied; it offers cues about the emotions, attitudes, and amount of power and control the speaker feels toward the other.[28]

Another way of distinguishing between the content and relationship dimensions of communication is to consider that the content of a message refers to *what* is said. Relationship cues refer to *how* it is communicated. This distinction explains why reading a transcript of what someone says can reveal a quite different meaning from actually hearing the person say the message.

Interpersonal Communication Myths

Several common misconceptions about interpersonal communication can undermine the quality of your interpersonal relationships with others. As we embark on our study of interpersonal communication, it's just as important to unlearn some commonly held misconceptions as it is to learn research conclusions and time-tested principles of interpersonal communication. Don't believe the following myths.

Myth: "More Words Will Make the Meaning Clearer"

More is not necessarily better. Just as there is a time to talk, there is a time to be silent. Piling on more words when your interpersonal communication partner is already baffled by what you are talking about can make matters worse. If someone is confused, hurt, or angry, continuing to add verbiage may hurt, not help. Maybe

content. New information, ideas, or suggested actions that a speaker wishes to share.

relationship dimension. The implied aspect of a communication message, which conveys information about emotions, attitudes, power, and control.

you just need to stop and listen rather than talk. Or ask a question and then just silently wait for an answer. Or perhaps, rather than words, your friend needs a nonverbal message of reassurance, a hug, a smile, or a nod of your head in agreement. And just as a picture can be worth a thousand words, so demonstrating to someone what you mean can be more powerful than continuing to pile on the words. To keep going and going like the Energizer Bunny may only make matters worse. When you communicate feelings and attitudes, your nonverbal, unspoken expressions are where the action is.

Are we suggesting that more communication is always bad? No. Just don't fall into the trap of believing that more words will solve all problems, enhance the quality of interpersonal relationships, and make the meaning clearer. There is a time to stop talking and listen.

Myth: "Meanings Are in Words"

In and of itself, spoken or written, a word has no meaning. It's just a sound, marks on paper, or characters on a computer screen. Meaning resides in people, not words. Others provide the meaning to connect the dots between the word you've spoken and the meaning you intend to create. But sometimes people connect the dots in a way you had not intended. Words are symbols we use to communicate with others. Because a symbol is something that represents something else, a symbol, by its very nature, can have different meanings for different people. Even the best wordsmith or professional speechwriter can use words that result in missed meaning and uncertainty. Differences in culture, background, education, and experience often explain why words create different meanings for different people. When you greet your aunt by enthusiastically demanding, "What's up?" she may find such a greeting a bit too informal and think you're being rude. But to your best buddy, offering a slurred "What's up?" is just a normal way of saying "hello." You intended no disrespect to your aunt, but she took your colloquial welcome the wrong way. Our point: Just because you've spoken it, don't assume others will always catch what you threw to them. Meanings are in people, not in words.

Myth: "Information Equals Communication"

"How many times do I have to tell you not to use the copy machine?" "Can't you read? It's in the syllabus." "It's in the policy and procedure manual." "Are you deaf? I've told you that I love you several times." Each of these exasperated communicators seems to have thought erroneously that information is the same thing as communication. It's not. Information is not communication. This simple, yet powerful principle helps combat the myth that if you say it or write it, then communication has taken place.

Earlier in the chapter we defined communication at the most basic level as acting on information. If you say it, but no one hears it—does that mean there has been communication? Like the proverbial tree that falls silently in the forest because no one is there to hear it, the message you thought you sent is not really communication just because you've put your thoughts into a code. Encoding does not always ensure decoding. And as we already discussed, even if someone has decoded the message, it could be different from the one you intended. Information is not communication.

Instead of focusing entirely on the message we want to convey, we can sometimes communicate even more effectively when we take the time to be other-oriented—to listen to what others are saying. (Bob Daemmrich/Stock Boston)

Myth: "Interpersonal Relationship Problems Are Always Communication Problems"

"You don't understand me!" shouts Paul to his exasperated partner Pat, "We just can't communicate anymore!" Paul seems to think the problem he and Pat are having is a communication problem. But Paul and Pat may understand each other perfectly; they may simply disagree. Although it's certainly true that conflict and discord in interpersonal relationships can occur because of misunderstandings, not *all* conflict and bumpy relationships stem from misunderstandings. There could be several explanations for why a relationship is experiencing turbulence. Perhaps the communication partners are very clear when communicating, but are so self-centered or self-absorbed that the quality of the relationship suffers. Or perhaps the communication partners just don't like each other; or, if they do like and understand each other, they just disagree. The message has been understood but rejected. Although missed meaning may be a contributing factor in interpersonal conflict, it's a myth to assume that all relational discord stems from misunderstanding.

Even though one purpose of this course is to help you enhance the quality of your relationships by becoming a better communicator, we don't claim that *all* interpersonal conflict stems from misunderstanding one another. Nor are we claiming that learning principles and skills of interpersonal communication will solve all your interpersonal relationship problems. One of us three authors was approached by a potential client who said, "I understand you are a communication consultant. I need help with my communication skills. *Do something to me* to make me a better communicator." But communication skill development does not work like Harry Potter's magic wand; there's not something that can be "done to" someone to enhance communication ability. And even if there were a wizard's wand to make all your communication perfectly understood by others, and theirs by you, your interpersonal relationships would undoubtedly still experience stress and conflict.

How to Improve Your Own Interpersonal Communication Effectiveness

Now that we have previewed the study of interpersonal communication, you may be saying to yourself, "Well, that's all well and good, but is it possible to improve my own interpersonal communication? Aren't some people just born to have better interpersonal skills than others?" Just as some people have more musical talent or greater skill at throwing a football, evidence suggests that some people may have an inborn, biological talent for communicating with others.[29] You probably know people who have never had a course in communication, but who develop sensitive, caring interpersonal relationships with others.

A growing body of research called the **communibiological approach** to communication suggests that some people inherit certain traits or characteristics that affect the way they communicate with others. There may be a genetic basis for why people communicate as they do. For example, you or people you know may have been born to have more stage fright or anxiety when communicating with others.[30] And some people may not be as comfortable interacting in interpersonal situations as others are. Some researchers and teachers believe, however, that the communibiological approach gives too much weight to biology and not enough to how we can learn to compensate for what nature did not give us.[31]

So what are the implications of the communibiological approach to communication? Does this mean you can't improve your interpersonal communication? *Absolutely not!* The underlying premise of our study of interpersonal communication is that you can learn ways to enhance the quality of your interpersonal relationships with others. We suggest the following six-part strategy for becoming a more effective communicator.

Become Knowledgeable

By reading this chapter you have already begun improving your communication skills. Effective communicators are knowledgeable. They know how communication works. They understand the components, principles, and rules of the communication process. As you read further in this book, you will learn theories, principles, concepts, and rules that will help you explain and predict how humans communicate.

Understanding these things is a necessary prerequisite for enhancing your interpersonal effectiveness, but this kind of knowledge alone does not make you an effective communicator. You would not let someone fix your car's carburetor if he or she had only read a book. Knowledge must be coupled with skill. And we acquire skill through practice.

Become Skilled

Effective communicators know how to translate knowledge into action. You can memorize the characteristics of a good listener but still not listen well. To develop

communibiological approach. Theoretical perspective that suggests people's communication behavior can be predicted based on personal traits and characteristics that result from their genetic or biological background.

skill requires practice and helpful feedback from others who can confirm the appropriateness of your actions.

Learning a social skill is not much different from learning how to drive a car or operate a computer.[32] To learn any skill, you must break it down into subskills that you can learn and practice. "Hear it, see it, do it, correct it" is the formula that seems to work best for learning any new behaviors. In this book we examine the elements of complex skills (such as listening), offer activities that let you practice the skills, and provide opportunities for you to receive feedback and correct your application of the skills.

Become Motivated

Practicing skills requires work. You need to be motivated to use your information and skill. You must want to improve, and you must have a genuine desire to connect with others if you wish to become a competent communicator. You may know people who understand how to drive a car and have the skill to drive, yet hesitate to get behind the wheel. Or maybe you know someone who took a course in public speaking but is reluctant to stand in front of a crowd. Similarly, someone may pass a test about interpersonal communication principles with flying colors, but unless that person is motivated to use those newfound skills, his or her interactions with others may not improve.

Become Flexible

In this book we do not identify tidy lists of sure-fire strategies that you can use to win friends and influence people. The same set of skills is not effective in every situation, so competent communicators do not assume that "one size fits all." Rather, they assess each unique situation and adapt their behavior to achieve the desired outcome. They examine the context, the situation, and the needs, goals, and messages of others to establish and maintain relationships.

Become Ethical

Ethics are the beliefs, values, and moral principles by which we determine what is right or wrong. Ethics and ethical behavior have long been a critical component of human behavior. Effective interpersonal communicators are ethical. To be an ethical communicator means to be sensitive to the needs of others, to give people choices rather than forcing them to act a certain way. Unethical communicators believe that they know what other people need, even without asking them for their preferences. As we discuss in Chapter 6, being manipulative and forcing opinions on others usually results in a climate of defensiveness. Effective communicators seek to establish trust and reduce interpersonal barriers, rather than erect them. Ethical communicators keep confidences; they keep private information that others wish to be kept private. They also do not intentionally decrease others' feelings of self-worth. Another key element in being an ethical communicator is honesty. If you intentionally lie or distort the truth, then you are not communicating ethically or effectively. At the end of each chapter, we offer a section called "Focus on Ethics," in which we pose ethical questions to help you explore the ethics of interpersonal relationships.

ethics. The beliefs, values, and moral principles by which people determine what is right or wrong.

Ethical communicators are sensitive to the needs of others.
(Frank Siteman/Stock Boston)

Become Other-Oriented

Most of us are egocentric—self-focused; our first inclination is to protect ourselves. Scholars of evolution might argue that our tendency to look out for number one ensures the continuation of the human species.

Yet when we focus *exclusively* on ourselves, it is difficult to communicate effectively. If we fail to adapt our message to our listener, we may not be successful in achieving our intended communication goal. Adapting messages to others does not mean that we tell them only what they want to hear; that would be unethical. Nor does being considerate of others mean we abandon all concern for our own interests. Other-oriented communication suggests that we consider the needs, motives, desires, and goals of our communication partners, while still maintaining our own integrity. The choices we make in forming the message, and selecting the time and place to deliver it, should consider the other person's thoughts and feelings.

How do you become other-oriented? Being other-oriented is really a collection of skills rather than a single skill. We devote considerable discussion throughout the book to developing this collection of essential communication skills.[33]

Focusing on others begins with an accurate understanding of your self-concept and self-esteem; we discuss these foundation principles in the next chapter. As you will learn in Chapter 3, developing an accurate perception of both yourself and others is an important element of effectively relating to others.

Becoming other-oriented also involves adapting to those who may be considerably different from you. Your communication partner may have a different cultural background, be of the opposite sex, or be older or younger than you. In Chapter 4 we explore some of these differences, especially cultural differences, that can sometimes challenge effective and appropriate communication with others; we also suggest specific strategies to help you adapt to others who differ from yourself.

Being other-oriented is more than just having a set of skills or behaviors. It also includes developing positive, healthy attitudes about others. In 1951 Carl Rogers

Role Play: Other-Oriented or Self-Focused

With a communication partner, role-play the following interpersonal situations in two ways. First, role-play the scene with communicators who are not other-oriented—they are self-focused. Then role-play the same scene with communicators who are other-

oriented—they consider the thoughts and feelings of the other person.

Suggested situations:

- Return a broken VCR to a department store salesperson.
- Correct a grocery store cashier who has scanned an item at the wrong price.
- Meet with a teacher who gave your son or daughter a failing grade.
- Ask your professor for a one-day extension on a paper that is due tomorrow.

- Ask someone for a donation to a worthy cause.
- Ask a professor for permission to get into a class that has reached its maximum enrollment
- Accept an unappealing compact disc as a gift from a friend.
- Remind your son or daughter that he or she needs to practice the piano.

---

wrote a pioneering book called *Client-Centered Therapy,* which transformed the field of psychotherapy. In it Rogers explains how genuine positive regard for another person and an open and supportive communication climate lay the foundation for trusting relationships. Rogers emphasizes the importance of listening in connection to another human being, which we explore in depth in Chapter 5.

People gain insight into others' feelings by being sensitive to nonverbal messages as well as the explicit verbal statements they make. We discuss verbal communication skills in Chapter 6 and nonverbal communication skills in Chapter 7. The skills and principles of managing conflict presented in Chapter 8 provide tools and ideas for understanding others when you disagree.

Chapters 9 and 10 build on the principles of interpersonal relationships introduced in this chapter to help you understand how relationships evolve, are maintained, and sometimes end. The final chapter applies our discussion of other-oriented interpersonal communication to various contexts such as families, friends, and colleagues. Our goal is to help you both to understand better how you relate to others and to develop enhanced interpersonal skill.

How Can You Improve Your Communication Effectiveness?

Become Knowledgeable	Learn principles, concepts, and ideas.
Become Skilled	Translate knowledge into action.
Become Motivated	Resolve to use your knowledge and skill.
Become Flexible	Select the right behavior; one size does not fit all.
Become Ethical	Offer choices, establish trust, and reduce barriers to interpersonal communication.
Become Other-Oriented	Focus on others rather than only on your needs.

Summary

At the most basic level, communication is the process of acting on information. Human communication is the process of making sense out of the world and sharing that sense with others. Interpersonal communication is the process of developing a unique relationship with another person by interacting and sharing mutual influence. Early models viewed human communication as a simple message-transfer process. Later models evolved to view communication as interaction and then as transaction. Contemporary approaches to interpersonal communication emphasize the simultaneous nature of influencing others. They identify seven key components in the interpersonal communication process: source, receiver, message, channel, noise, context, and feedback. Electronic media may encourage further evolution of our models for interpersonal communication.

The goal of this book is to help you improve your interpersonal skills and relationships. Interpersonal relationships range from impersonal to intimate, are complementary or symmetrical, are governed by rules, and involve both content and relationship dimensions. The most effective interpersonal communicators are not swayed by common myths about communication. Rather, they are knowledgeable, skilled, motivated, flexible, ethical, and other-oriented. Learning to connect with others is the key to establishing satisfying relationships.

For Discussion and Review

Focus on Comprehension

1. Discuss key differences among the models of communication as action, interaction, and transaction.

2. Define communication, human communication, and interpersonal communication. Discuss the differences among them.

3. Identify the characteristics of interpersonal relationships.

4. Explain how to improve your interpersonal communication.

Focus on Critical Thinking

5. Analyze a recent interpersonal exchange that did not go well. Write down some of the dialogue. Did the other person understand you? Did your communication have the intended effect? Was your message ethical?

6. Make a relationship scale on a piece of paper, and label it "impersonal" at one end and "intimate" at the other. Place your family members and closest friends on the scale; then compare and discuss your entries with your classmates.

7. What rules govern your relationship with your mother? Your father? Your communication teacher? Your roommate? Your spouse?

Focus on Ethics

8. Think about your primary goal for this course. Is it to develop strategies to achieve your own personal goals? Is it to develop sensitivity to the needs of

others? What is behind your desire to achieve your goal? Is your purpose ethical?

9. Your parents want you to visit them for the holidays. You would rather spend the time with a friend. You don't want to hurt your parents' feelings, so you tell them that you have an important project that you are working on; you won't be able to come home for the holidays. Your message is understood. It achieves the intended effect; you don't go home. Explain why you think your message is ethical or unethical.

For Your Journal

1. Try to identify at least three personal goals for improving your interpersonal relationships. Write several specific objectives that you hope to accomplish by the end of this course.

2. Briefly describe a recent communication exchange that was not effective. Perhaps you or your communication partner did not understand the message, or the message may not have achieved its intended goal, or it may have been unethical. Analyze the communication exchange, applying the components of communication discussed in this chapter. For example, what was the communication context? What were sources of internal and external noise? Did you have problems encoding and decoding? Were there problems with the communication channel?

3. Keep a one-day log of your electronically mediated interactions, such as phone calls, e-mail messages, fax messages. Describe each one, noting whether there was a greater emphasis on the content or emotional elements of the messages you exchanged during the interaction.

Learning with Others

1. Working with a group of your classmates, develop a five-minute lesson to teach one of the following concepts to your class:
   a. How interpersonal relationships range from impersonal to intimate
   b. Human communication as action
   c. Human communication as interaction
   d. Human communication as transaction
   e. How interpersonal relationships are governed by rules
   f. How to improve communication effectiveness

2. Working with a group of your classmates, develop your own model of interpersonal communication. Include all of the components that are necessary to describe how communication between people works. Your model could be a drawing or an actual object (such as a Slinky toy) that symbolizes the communication process. Share your model with the class, describing the decisions your group made in developing it. Illustrate your model with a conversation between two people, pointing out how elements of the conversation relate to the model.

2

Interpersonal Communication and Self

After you study this chapter

you should be able to ...

1. Define, compare, and contrast the meanings of self-concept and self-esteem.

2. Identify factors that shape the development of your self-concept.

3. List and describe strategies for improving your self-esteem.

4. Describe how your self-concept affects your relationships with others.

5. Describe the process of appropriate self-disclosure, including two models of self-disclosure.

- Self-Concept: Who Are You?

- Self-Esteem: Your Self-Worth

- Improving Your Self-Esteem

- How Self-Concept and Self-Esteem Affect Interpersonal Communication and Relationships

- Self-Disclosure: Connecting Self to Others Through Talk

- Characteristics of Self-Disclosure

There's only one corner of the universe you can be certain of improving, and that's your own self.

ALDOUS HUXLEY

Philosophers suggest that there are three basic questions to which people all seek answers: (1) "Who am I?" (2) "Why am I here?" and (3) "Who are all these others?" In this chapter we focus on these essential questions about the self. We view them as progressive. Grappling with the question of who you are and seeking to define a purpose for your life are essential to understanding others and becoming other-oriented in your interpersonal communication and relationships.

Fundamentally, all your communication starts or ends with you. When you are the communicator, you intentionally or unintentionally code your thoughts and emotions to be interpreted by another. When you receive a message, you interpret the information through your own frame of reference. Your self-image and self-worth, as well as your needs, values, beliefs, and attitudes, serve as filters for your communication with others. As you establish and develop relationships, you may become more aware of these filters, and perhaps want to alter them. A close relationship often provides the impetus for change.

To understand the role that self concept plays in interpersonal communication, we will explore the first two basic questions—"Who am I?" and "Why am I here?"— trying to discover the meaning of self. We will examine the multifaceted dimensions of our self-concept, learn how it develops, and compare self-concept to self-esteem. Then we will move to the third basic question, "Who are all these others?" What you choose to tell and not tell others about you reveals important clues about who

you are, what you value, and how you relate to another person. We will explore the process of self-disclosure—purposefully revealing information about yourself—later in this chapter.

Self-Concept: Who Are You?

You can begin your journey of self-discovery by doing the exercise in Building Your Skills: Who Are You? on this page.

How did you answer the question "Who are you?" Perhaps with activities in which you participate, or groups and organizations to which you belong. You may have listed some of the roles you assume, such as student, child, or parent. All these things are indeed a part of yourself, the sum total of who you are. Psychologist Karen Horney defines **self** as "that central inner force, common to all human beings and yet unique in each, which is the deep source of growth."[1]

Your answers are also part of your **self-concept.** Your self-concept is your subjective description of who you *think* you are—it is filtered through your own perceptions. For example, you may have great musical talent, but you may not believe in it enough to think of yourself as a musician. You can view self-concept as the labels you consistently use to describe yourself to others.

Who you are is also reflected in the attitudes, beliefs, and values that you hold. These are learned constructs that shape your behavior and self-image. An **attitude** is a learned predisposition to respond to a person, object, or idea in a favorable or

self. Sum total of who a person is; a person's central inner force.

self-concept. A person's subjective description of who he or she is.

attitude. Learned predisposition to respond to a person, object, or idea in a favorable or unfavorable way.

building your skills

Who Are You?

Consider this question: Who are you? More specifically, ask yourself this question ten times. Write your responses in the spaces provided here or on a separate piece of paper. It may be challenging to identify ten aspects of yourself. The Spanish writer Cervantes said, "To know thyself . . . is the most difficult lesson in the world." Your answers will help you begin to explore your self-concept and self-esteem in this chapter.

I am _____   I am _____

I am _____   I am _____

I am _____   I am _____

I am _____   I am _____

I am _____   I am _____

unfavorable way. Attitudes reflect what you like and what you don't like. If you like school, butter pecan ice cream, and your brother, you hold positive attitudes toward these things. You were not born with a fondness for butter pecan ice cream; you learned to like it just as some people learn to enjoy the taste of snails, raw fish, or pureed turnips.

Beliefs are the way in which you structure your understanding of reality—what is true and what is false. Most of your

Figure 2.1

Values, Beliefs, and Attitudes in Relation to Self

beliefs are based on previous experience. You trust that the sun will rise in the morning and that you will get burned if you put your hand on a hot stove.

How are attitudes and beliefs related? They often function quite independently of each other. You may have a favorable attitude toward something and still believe negative things about it. You may believe, for example, that your school football team will not win the national championship this year, although you may be a big fan. Or you may believe that God exists, yet not always like what God does. Beliefs have to do with what is true or not true, whereas attitudes reflect likes and dislikes.

Values are enduring concepts of good and bad, right and wrong. Your values are more resistant to change than either your attitudes or your beliefs. They are also more difficult for most people to identify. Values are so central to who you are that it is difficult to isolate them. For example, when you go to the supermarket, you may spend a few minutes deciding whether to buy regular or cream-style corn, but you probably do not spend much time deciding whether you will steal the corn or pay for it. Our values are instilled in us by our earliest interpersonal relationships; for almost all of us, our parents shape our values. The model in Figure 2.1 illustrates that values are central to our behavior and concept of self, and that what we believe to be true or false stems from our values. Attitudes are at the outer edge of the circle because they are the most likely to change. You may like your coworker today but not tomorrow, even though you *believe* the person will come to work every day and you still *value* the concept of friendship.

beliefs. Way in which you structure your understanding of reality—what is true and what is false.

values. Enduring concept of good and bad, right and wrong.

recap

Who You Are Is Reflected in Your Attitudes, Beliefs, and Values

	Definition	Dimensions	Example
Attitude	Learned predisposition to respond favorably or unfavorably to something	Likes–Dislikes	You like ice cream, incense, and cats.
Belief	The way in which you structure reality	True–False	You believe your parents love you.
Value	Enduring concepts of what is right and wrong	Good–Bad	You value honesty and truth.

One or Many Selves?

Shakespeare's famous line "To thine own self be true" suggests that you have a single self to which you can be true. But do you have just one self? Or is there a more "real you" buried somewhere within? "I'm just not myself this morning," sighs Sandy, as she drags herself out the front door to head for her office. If she is not herself, then *who is she*? Most scholars conclude that we have a core set of behaviors, attitudes, beliefs, and values that constitutes our self—the sum total of who we are. But our *concept* of self can and does change, depending on circumstances and influences.

In addition, our self-concepts are often different from the way others see us. We almost always behave differently in public from the way we do in private. Sociologist Erving Goffman suggests that, like actors and actresses, we have "on-stage" behaviors when others are watching and "backstage" behaviors when they are not.

Perhaps the most enduring and widely accepted framework for describing who we are was developed by the philosopher William James. He identified three components of the self: the material self, the social self, and the spiritual self. We will continue our exploration by examining these components.

The Material Self

Perhaps you've heard the statement "You are what you eat." The **material self** goes a step further by suggesting that "You are what you have." The material self is a total of all the tangible things you own: your body, your possessions, your home. As you examine your list of responses to the question "Who are you?" note whether any of your statements refers to one of your physical attributes or something you own.

One element of the material self gets considerable attention in this culture: the body. Do you like the way you look? Most of us, if we're honest, would like to change something about our appearance. When there is a discrepancy between our desired material self and our self-concept, we may respond to eliminate the discrepancy. We may try to lose weight, change nose shape, or acquire more hair. The multibillion-

material self. Your concept of self as reflected in a total of all the tangible things you own.

---

building your skills

Dimensions of Your Self

Take another look at your responses to the question "Who are you?" Divide your list according to James's description of self-concept as material, social, or spiritual self. If, for example, nothing on your original list relates to your spiritual self, make an entry here so that you have a response for each of the three "selves."

Material Self	Social Self	Spiritual Self
References to physical elements that reflect who you are	References to interactions with others that reflect who you are	References to your reflections about values, morals, and beliefs
Example:	**Example:**	**Example:**
I collect antiques.	I am a member of the Chess Club.	I believe the *Book of Mormon* is an inspired book.
_____	_____	_____
_____	_____	_____
_____	_____	_____
_____	_____	_____

dollar diet industry is just one of many that profit from our collective desire to change our appearance.

We also attempt to keep up with the proverbial Joneses by wanting more expensive clothes, cars, and homes. By extension, what we own becomes who we are. The bigger, better, and more luxurious our possessions, we may subconsciously conclude, the better *we* are.

The Social Self

Look at your "Who are you?" list once more. How many of your responses relate to your **social self,** the part of you that interacts with others? William James believed that you have many social selves—that, depending on the friend, family member, colleague, or acquaintance with whom you are interacting, you change the way you are. A person has, said James, as many social selves as there are people who recognize him or her.

 Peter Blake sought to explore his self-dimensions by painting his self-portrait. What qualities does this self-portrait reveal about the artist? (Tate Gallery, London/Art Resources)

For example, when you talk to your best friend, you are willing to "let down your hair" and reveal more thoughts and feelings than you would in a conversation with your communication professor, or even your parents. We discuss this process of self-disclosure later in the chapter. Each relationship that you have with another person is unique because you bring to it a unique social self.

The Spiritual Self

Your **spiritual self** consists of all your internal thoughts and introspections about your values and moral standards. It does not depend on what you own or with whom you talk; it is the essence of who you *think* you are, and of your *feelings* about yourself, apart from external evaluations. It is an amalgam of your religious beliefs and your sense of who you are in relationship to other forces in the universe. Your spiritual self is the part of you that answers the question "Why am I here?"

social self. Your concept of self as reflected in your personal, social interactions with others.

spiritual self. Your concept of self based on your thoughts and introspections about your values, moral standards, and beliefs.

---

recap

William James's Dimensions of Self

	Definition	Examples
Material Self	All the physical elements that reflect who you are	Body, clothes, car, home
Social Self	The self as reflected through your interactions with others; actually, a variety of selves that respond to changes in situations and roles	Your informal self interacting with your best friend; your formal self interacting with your professors
Spiritual Self	Introspections about values, morals, and beliefs	Belief or disbelief in God; regard for life in all its forms

How Your Self-Concept Develops

James's three elements define the dimensions of the self, but they do not tell us where "Who are you?" responses come from. In truth, we can only speculate about their origins. But some psychologists and sociologists have advanced theories that suggest you learn who you are through five basic means: (1) interactions with other individuals, (2) association with groups, (3) roles you assume, (4) your own labels, and (5) your personality. Like James's framework, this one does not cover every base in the study of self, but its constructs can provide some clues about how your own self-concepts develop.

Interaction with Individuals

In 1902, Charles Horton Cooley first advanced the notion that we form our self-concepts by seeing ourselves in a kind of figurative **looking glass:** We learn who we are by interacting with others, much as we look into a mirror and see our reflection. Like Cooley, George Herbert Mead also believed that our sense of who we are is a consequence of our relationship with others. And Harry Stack Sullivan theorized that from birth to death our self changes primarily because of how people respond to us. One sage noted, "We are not only our brother's keeper; we are our brother's maker."

The process begins at birth. Our names, one of the primary ways we identify ourselves, are given to us by someone else. During the early years of our lives, our parents are the key individuals who reflect who we are. If our parents encouraged us to play the piano, we probably play now. As we become less dependent on our parents, our friends become highly influential in shaping our attitudes, beliefs, and values. And friends continue to provide feedback on how well we perform certain tasks. This, in turn, helps us shape our sense of identity as adults—we must acknowledge our talents in math, language, or art in our own minds before we say that we are mathematicians, linguists, or artists.

Fortunately, not *every* comment affects our sense of who we think we are. We are likely to incorporate the comments of others into our self-concept under three conditions.

First, we are more likely to believe another's statement if he or she repeats something we have heard several times. If one person casually tells you that you have a good ear for singing, you are not likely to launch a search for an agent and a recording contract. But if several individuals tell you on many different occasions that you have a talent for singing, you may decide to do something about it.

Second, we are more likely to value another's statements if we perceive him or her to be credible. If we believe the individual is competent, trustworthy, and qualified to make a judgment about us, then we are more likely to believe it. You would be more likely to think you were a talented singer if

BALLARD STREET copyright © Van Amarongen. Reprinted with permission of Creators Syndicate.

"Thinking can be my hobby if I want it to be!"

looking-glass self. Concept that suggests you learn who you are based on your interactions with others, which are reflected back to you.

understanding
di ve r s i ty

Being Other-Oriented in Other Cultures

How we view others is an extension of how we view ourselves. Most religions of the world emphasize a common spiritual theme known in Christianity as the Golden Rule: Do unto others as you would have others do unto you. This "rule" is the basis for most ethical codes throughout the world. This fundamental principle of other-orientation is expressed in similar ways among the world's people.

Hinduism	This is the sum of duty: Do nothing to others that would cause pain if done to you.
Buddhism	One should seek for others the happiness one desires for one's self.
Taoism	Regard your neighbor's gain as your own gain, and your neighbor's loss as your loss.
Confucianism	Is there one principle that ought to be acted on throughout one's whole life? Surely it is the principle of loving-kindness: do not unto others what you would not have them do unto you.
Zoroastrianism	The nature alone is good that refrains from doing unto another whatsoever is not good for itself.
Judaism	What is hateful to you, do not do to others. That is the entire law: all the rest is but commentary.
Islam	No one of you is a believer until he desires for his brother that which he desires for himself.
Christianity	Do unto others what you would have others do unto you.

Adapted from Wayne Ham, *Man's Living Religions* (Independence, MO: Herald Publishing House, 1966), 39–40.

---

you heard it from opera star Luciano Pavarotti rather than your Aunt Sally. Again, while we are very young, our parents are the dominant voices of credibility and authority. If they tell us repeatedly that we are spoiled and sloppy, then we will probably come to view ourselves that way. If they tell us we are loving, gifted, and charming, we are likely to believe it.

Third, we are likely to incorporate another's comments into our own concept of self if the comments are consistent with other comments and our own experience. If your boss tells you that you work too slowly, but for years people have been urging you to slow down, then your previous experience will probably encourage you to challenge your boss's evaluation.

Association with Groups

I'm a Democrat. I'm a Girl Scout. I'm a rabbi. I'm a coach. I'm a member of the Marching Mules Band. Each of these self-descriptive statements has something in common. Each one answers the "Who are you?" question by providing identification with a group or organization. Reflect once more on your responses to the "Who are you?" question. How many associate you with a group? Religious groups, political groups, ethnic groups, social groups, study groups, and occupational and professional groups play important roles in determining your self-concept. Some of these groups you are born into; others you choose on your own. Either way, these group associations are significant parts of your identity.

As we have already noted, peer pressure is a powerful force in shaping attitudes and behavior, and adolescents are particularly susceptible to it. But adolescents are not alone in allowing the attitudes, beliefs, and values of others to shape their expectations and behavior. Most adults, to varying degrees, ask themselves, "What will the neighbors think? What will my family think?" when they are making choices.

In American culture it is often accepted, or even encouraged, for boys to exhibit rough and tumble, aggressive behavior when they interact with one another. (Tony Freeman/PhotoEdit)

Associating with groups is especially important for people who are not part of the dominant culture. Gays and lesbians, for example, find the support provided by associating with other gays and lesbians to be beneficial to their well-being. The groups you associate with not only provide information about your identity, but also provide needed social support.

Roles You Assume

Look again at your answers to the "Who are you?" question. Perhaps you see words or phrases that signify a role you often assume. Father, aunt, sister, uncle, manager, salesperson, teacher, and student are labels that imply certain expectations for behavior, and they are important in shaping self-concept. Couples who live together before they marry often report that marriage alters their relationship. Before, they may have shared domestic duties such as doing dishes and laundry. But when they assume the labels of "husband" and "wife," they slip into traditional roles. Husbands don't do laundry. Wives don't mow the grass. These stereotypical role expectations that they learned long ago may require extensive discussion and negotiation. Couples who report the highest satisfaction with marriage have similar role expectations for themselves and their spouses.[2]

One reason we assume traditional roles automatically is that our gender group asserts a powerful influence from birth on. As soon as parents know the sex of their child, many begin placing their children in the group by following cultural rules. They paint the nursery pink for a girl, blue for a boy. Boys get a catcher's mitt, a train set, or a football for their birthdays; girls get dolls, frilly dresses, and tea sets. These cultural conventions and expectations play a major role in shaping our self-concept and our behavior. People often describe male babies as strong, solid, and independent; little girls are cute, cuddly, and sweet.[3] Recent research suggests that up until the age of 3, children themselves are not acutely aware of sex roles. Between the ages of 3 and 5, however, masculine and feminine roles begin to emerge,[4] and they are usually solidified between the ages of 5 and 7.

Stereotypical Labels for Males and Females

Terms for Males	Terms for Females
Aggressive	Appreciative
Arrogant	Considerate
Assertive	Cooperative
Conceited	Dependent
Dominant	Feminine
Forceful	Fickle
Frank	Friendly
Handsome	Frivolous
Hard-headed	Helpful
Outspoken	Submissive
Strong	Timid

From Judy C. Pearson, Lynn H. Turner, and William Todd-Mancillas, *Gender & Communication* (Dubuque, IA: William C. Brown, 1995).

Although it is changing, American culture is still male-dominated. What we consider appropriate and inappropriate behavior is often different for males and for females. For example, in group and team meetings, task-oriented, male-dominated roles are valued more than feminine, relationship-building roles.[5] We applaud fathers who work sixty hours a week as "diligent and hard-working," but criticize mothers who do the same as "neglectful and selfish." The list "Stereotypical Labels for Males and Females" illustrates more of these contrasts.

Although our culture defines certain roles as masculine or feminine, we still exercise individual choices about our gender roles. One researcher developed an inventory designed to assess whether we play traditional masculine, feminine, or androgynous roles.[6] Because an **androgynous role** is both masculine and feminine, this role encompasses a greater repertoire of actions and behaviors.

Self-Labels

Although our self concept is deeply affected by others, we are not blank slates for them to write on. The labels we use to describe our own attitudes, beliefs, values, and actions also play a role in shaping our self-concept.

From where do we acquire our labels? We interpret what we experience; we are self-reflexive. **Self-reflexiveness** is the human ability to think about what we are doing while we are doing it. We talk to ourselves about ourselves. We are both participants and observers in all that we do. This dual role encourages us to use labels to describe who we are.

When you were younger, perhaps you dreamed of becoming an all-star basketball player or a movie star. Your coach may have told you that you were a great player or a terrific actor, but as you matured, you probably began observing yourself more critically. You scored no points; you did not get the starring role in the local production of *Annie*. So you self-reflexively decided that you were not, deep down, a basketball player or an actor, even though others may have labeled you as

androgynous role. Gender role that includes both masculine and feminine qualities.

self-reflexiveness. Human ability to think about what you are doing while you are doing it.

"talented." But sometimes, through this self-observation, people discover strengths that encourage them to assume new labels. One woman we know never thought of herself as "heroic" until she went through seventy-two hours of labor before giving birth and then nursed her baby right after delivery.

◗ Your Personality

The concept of personality is central to **psychology,** the study of how your thinking influences how you behave. According to psychologist Lester Lefton, your **personality** consists of a set of enduring internal predispositions and behavioral characteristics that describe how you react to your environment.[7] Understanding the forces that shape your personality is central to increasing your awareness of your self-concept and how you relate to others. Your personality influences whether you are outgoing or shy, humorous or serious, mellow or nervous, and a host of other descriptions that could be used to describe general traits or characteristics about you. There remains a considerable debate as to how much of your personality is influenced by genetics—traits you inherit from your ancestors—and how much is learned behavior. Does nature or nurturing play the predominant role in your personality? As we noted in Chapter 1, the **communibiological approach** to communication suggests that a major factor affecting how people communicate with others is genetic makeup.[8] Others argue that although it's true that communication behavior is influenced by genes, we should not forget that humans can learn to adjust and adapt.[9]

One personality characteristic that communication researchers have spent considerable time studying is whether you are comfortable or uncomfortable interacting with other people. Some people just don't like to talk with others.[10] In interpersonal communication situations, we may say someone is shy. **Shyness** is the behavioral tendency not to talk with others. One study found that about 40 percent of adults reported they were shy.[11] In public-speaking situations we say a person has stage fright; a better term to describe this feeling is *communication apprehension.* **Communication apprehension,** according to communication experts James McCroskey and Virginia Richmond, is "the fear or anxiety associated with either real or anticipated communication with another person or persons."[12] One study found that up to 80 percent of the population experiences some degree of nervousness or apprehension when they speak in public.[13] Another study found that about 20 percent of people are considerably anxious when they give a speech.[14] What makes some people apprehensive about communicating with others? Again, we get back to the nature–nurture issue. Heredity plays an important role in whether you are going to feel nervous or anxious when communicating with someone else. But so does whether you were reinforced for talking with others as a child, as well as other experiences that are part of your culture and learning.

Your overall **willingness to communicate** with others is a general way of summarizing the shyness or apprehension that you feel when talking with others in a variety of situations, including interpersonal conversations. If you are unwilling to communicate with others, you will be less comfortable in a career that forces you to interact with others. To assess your willingness to communicate, take the self-test developed by McCroskey and Richmond in the Building Your Skills box on page 45. The test will give you an overall score as well as a score in specific communication situations such as meetings, interpersonal conversations, communicating with strangers, and communicating with friends.

Understanding the factors that influence your self-concept—such as your interactions with individuals and groups, the roles you assume, your self-labels, and

psychology. Study of how thinking influences behavior.

personality. Set of enduring internal predispositions and behavioral characteristics that describe how people react to their environment.

communibiological approach. Perspective that suggests that genetics and biological influences play a major role in influencing communication behavior.

shyness. Tendency not to talk or interact with other people.

communication apprehension. Fear or anxiety associated with either real or anticipated communication with other people.

willingness to communicate. General characteristic that describes an individual's tendencies to be shy or apprehensive about communicating with others.

building your skills

Assessing Your Willingness to Communicate

Willingness-to-Communicate Scale
Directions: In the following 20 situations, a person might choose to communicate or not to communicate. Presume you have **completely free choice.** Determine the percentage of times you would **choose to initiate communication** in each type of situation. Indicate in the space at the left what percentage of the time you would choose to communicate. Choose any numbers between 0 and 100.

_100_ 1. Talk with a service station attendant.
_100_ 2. Talk with a physician.
_50_ 3. Present a talk to a group of strangers.
_100_ 4. Talk with an acquaintance while standing in line.
_100_ 5. Talk with a salesperson in a store.
_100_ 6. Talk in a large meeting of friends.
_100_ 7. Talk with a police officer.
_50_ 8. Talk in a small group of strangers.
_100_ 9. Talk with a friend while standing in line.
_100_ 10. Talk with a waiter/waitress in a restaurant.
_100_ 11. Talk in a large meeting of acquaintances.
_100_ 12. Talk with a stranger while standing in line.
_100_ 13. Talk with a secretary.
_100_ 14. Present a talk to a group of friends.
_100_ 15. Talk in a small group of acquaintances.
_100_ 16. Talk with a garbage collector.
_50_ 17. Talk in a large meeting of strangers.
_100_ 18. Talk with a spouse (or girl/boy friend).
_100_ 19. Talk in a small group of friends.
_100_ 20. Present a talk to a group of acquaintances.

Source: James C. McCloskey and Virginia P. Richmond, _Fundamentals of Human Communication: An Interpersonal Perspective_ (Prospect Heights, IL: Waveland Press, 1996), p. 53.

Computing Scores on the Willingness-to-Communicate Scale

Scoring: The WTC permits computation of one total score and seven subscores. The range for all scores is 0–100. Follow the procedures outlined below.

1. Group discussion—add scores for items 8, 15, and 19; divide sum by 3.
   Scores 89 = high WTC, scores below 57 = low WTC in this context.

2. Meetings—add scores for items 6, 11, and 17; divide sum by 3.
   Scores 80 = high WTC, scores below 39 = low WTC in this context.

3. Interpersonal—add scores for items 4, 9, and 12; divide sum by 3.
   Scores 94 = high WTC, scores below 64 = low WTC in this context.

4. Public speaking—add scores for items 3, 14, and 20; divide sum by 3.
   Scores 78 = high WTC, scores below 33 = low WTC in this context.

5. Stranger—add scores for items 3, 8, 12, and 17; divide sum by 4.
   Scores 63 = high WTC, scores below 18 = low WTC with these receivers.

6. Acquaintance—add scores for items 4, 11, 15, and 20; divide sum by 4.
   Scores 92 = high WTC, scores below 57 = low WTC with these receivers.

7. Friends—add scores for items 6, 9, 14, and 19; divide sum by 4.
   Scores 99 = high WTC, scores below 71 = low WTC with these receivers.

To compute the total score for the WTC, add the totals for stranger, friend, and acquaintance; then divide by 3. Scores above 82 = high WTC, below 52 = low WTC.

e-connections

What's Your Personality Type?

Is it possible to learn what personality type you are by taking a simple test? The Myers-Briggs Personality Test is one of the most common ways to describe your personality. Based on Jung's theory of personality, the test assumes that each of us has a preference for how we like to process what we experience. According to the test, there are four dimensions to your personality. The first dimension, Extroversion–Introversion (E or I), describes whether you tend to focus your energy in the outside world or the inner world. The second dimension, Sensing–Intuition (S or N), describes whether you prefer to rely on more objective data or subjective impressions when interpreting what you experience. The third dimension is Thinking–Feeling (T or F); this dimension describes your preference for emphasizing cognitive or emotional information. The final dimension is Judging–Perceiving

(J or P); this dimension describes the way you evaluate what you experience. There are 16 possible combinations of personality types. For example, an INFP is someone who is more introverted, intuitive, emotional, and perceptive. Psychologists debate, however, how accurately this test can measure your personality.[15] Although some research suggests it is a quick and valid way to identify how you interact with others, other studies suggest it may not be accurate, especially because it was designed for students in grades 4 through 12. To take a very brief inventory based on the Myers-Briggs test, go to the following Web site and determine for yourself whether your score accurately describes you.

http://www.halconline.com/psych/

Do you want to explore other personality tests? Check out the following Web site which is packed with more tests and links to other tests:

http://www.mbtypeguide.com/Type/index.html

your personality, including your overall comfort level in communicating with others—can help you understand who you are and why you interact (or don't interact) with others. But it's not only who you are that influences your communication, it's your overall sense of self-esteem or self-worth that affects how you express yourself and respond to others.

Self-Esteem: Your Self-Worth

Your self-esteem is closely related to your self-concept. Through your self-concept, you *describe* who you are. Through your self-esteem, you *evaluate* who you are. The term **self-worth** is often used interchangeably with *self-esteem*. People derive their sense of self-worth from comparing themselves to others, a process called *social comparison*. **Social comparison** helps people measure how well they think they are doing compared to others. I'm good at playing soccer (because I beat others); I can't cook (because others cook better than I do); I'm not good at meeting people (most people I know seem to be more comfortable interacting with others); I'm not handy (but my brothers and sisters can fix a leaky faucet). Each of these statements implies a judgment about how well or badly you can perform certain tasks, with implied references to how well others perform the same tasks. A belief that you cannot fix a leaky faucet or cook like a chef may not in itself lower your self-esteem. But if there are *several* things you can't do well, or *many* important tasks that you cannot seem to master, these shortcomings may begin to color your overall sense of worth.

self-esteem (self-worth). Your evaluation of your worth or value as reflected in your perception of such things as your skills, abilities, talents, and appearance.

social comparison. Process of comparing yourself to others to measure your worth and value in relationship to others who are similar to you.

In the 1960s psychologist Eric Berne developed the concept of a **life position** to describe people's overall sense of their own worth and that of others.[16] He identified four life positions: (1) "I'm OK, you're OK," or positive regard for self and others; (2) "I'm OK, you're not OK," or positive regard for self and low regard for others; (3) "I'm not OK, you're OK," or low self-regard and positive regard for others; and (4) "I'm not OK, you're not OK," or low regard for both self and others. Your life position is a driving force in your relationships with others. People in the "I'm OK, you're OK" position have the best chance for healthy relationships because they have discovered their own talents and also recognize that others have been given talents different from their own.

Improving Your Self-Esteem

We have already discussed how low self-esteem can affect our own communication and interactions. In recent years teachers, psychologists, ministers, rabbis, social workers, and even politicians have suggested that many societal problems also stem from collective feelings of low self-esteem. Feelings of low self-worth may contribute to choosing the wrong partners; to becoming dependent on drugs, alcohol, or other substances; and to experiencing problems with eating and other vital activities. So people owe it to society, as well as themselves, to maintain or develop a healthy sense of self-esteem.

Although no simple list of tricks can easily transform low self-esteem into feelings of being valued and appreciated, you can improve the ways you think about yourself and interact with others. We'll explore seven proven techniques that have helped others.

Self-Talk

Cycling champion Lance Armstrong is also a cancer survivor. When he got sick, he told a friend, "Cancer picked the wrong guy. When it looked around for a body to hang out in, it made a big mistake when it chose mine. Big mistake."[17] The positive self-talk reflected in his words undoubtedly helped Armstrong to overcome the challenge of cancer and go on to win the Tour de France twice.

life position. Your feeling of being either "OK" or "Not OK" as reflected in your sense of worth and self-esteem.

Although positive self-talk will never be able to make all of us become champion cyclists like Lance Armstrong, it can help us focus on our own goals and improve our performance levels. (Lance Armstrong/ Liaison Agency Inc.)

Intrapersonal communication is communication within yourself—self-talk. Realistic, positive self-talk can have a reassuring effect on your level of self-worth and on your interactions with others. Conversely, repeating negative messages about your lack of skill and ability can keep you from trying and achieving. Sports psychologist Karlene Sugarman claims, "Positive self-talk will help your performance, negative self-talk will make matters worse. Positive self-talk helps you to develop secure attitudes toward your performance and validates your capabilities.[18]

Of course, blind faith without hard work won't succeed. Self-talk is not a substitute for effort; it can, however, keep you on track and help you ultimately to achieve your goal.

Visualization

Visualization takes the notion of self-talk one step further. Besides just telling yourself that you can achieve your goal, you can actually try to "see" yourself conversing effectively with others, performing well on a project, or exhibiting some other desirable behavior. Recent research suggests that an apprehensive public speaker can manage his or her fears not only by developing skill in public speaking, but also by visualizing positive results when speaking to an audience.[19] If you are one of the many people who fear speaking in public, try visualizing yourself walking to the lectern, taking out your well-prepared notes, and delivering an interesting, well-received speech. This visualization of positive results enhances confidence and speaking skill. The same technique can be used to boost your sense of self-worth about other tasks or skills. If, for example, you tend to get nervous when meeting people at a party, imagine yourself in a room full of people, glibly introducing yourself to others with ease. Visualizing yourself performing well can yield positive results in changing long-standing feelings of inadequacy. Of course, your visualization should be realistic and coupled with a plan to achieve your goal.

intrapersonal communication. Communication within yourself that includes your self-talk.

visualization. Technique of imagining that you are performing a particular task in a certain way. Positive visualization can enhance your self-esteem.

Avoiding Comparisons

Even before we were born, we were compared with others. The latest medical technology lets us see sonograms of fetuses still in the womb, so parents may begin comparing children with other babies before birth. For the rest of our lives we are compared with others, and rather than celebrating our uniqueness, comparisons usually point up who is bigger, brighter, and more beautiful. Many of us have had the experience of being chosen last to play on a sports team, passed over for promotion, or standing unchosen against the wall at a dance.

In North American culture we may be tempted to judge our self-worth by our material possessions and personal appearance. If we know someone who has a newer car (or simply a car, if we rely on public transportation), a smaller waistline, or a higher grade point average, we may feel diminished. Comparisons such as "He has more money than I have," or "She looks better than I look," are likely to deflate our self-worth. Sisters and centenarians Sadie and Bessie Delaney inspired many by their refusal to let what they didn't have deter their sense of personal accomplishment. In their bestseller, *Having Our Say*, these two family matriarchs write of the value of emphasizing what we have, rather than comparing our lack of resources with the abundance of others who have more.

Rather than finding others who seemingly are better off, focus on the unique attributes that make you who you are. Avoid judging your own value in comparison to that of others. A healthy, positive self-concept is fueled not by judgments of others, but by a genuine sense of worth that you recognize in yourself.

Michael continually measures himself against others.

BALLARD STREET copyright © Van Amarongen. Reprinted with permission of Creators Syndicate.

Reframing

Reframing is the process of redefining events and experiences from a different point of view. Just as reframing a work of art can give the picture a whole new look, reframing events that cause you to devalue your self-worth can change your perspective. Research suggests that in times of family stress, individuals who can engage in self-talk and describe the event from someone else's perspective manage stress more successfully. For example, if you get a report from your supervisor that says you should improve one area of your performance, instead of listening to the self-talk that says you're bad at your job, reframe the event within a larger context: Tell yourself that one negative comment does not mean you are hopeless as a worker.

Of course, not all negative experiences should be lightly tossed off and left unexamined, because you can learn and profit from your mistakes. But it is important to remember that your worth as a human being does not depend on a single letter grade, a single response from a prospective employer, or a single play in a football game. Looking at the big picture—what effect this small event will have on your whole life, on society, on history—places negative experiences, which all people have, in a realistic context. The reading on the next page is a good reminder to maintain this longer perspective.

reframing. Process of redefining events and experiences from a different point of view.

People Who Were Told "You'll Never Amount to Much"

Einstein was 4 years old before he could speak and 7 before he could read. Isaac Newton did poorly in grade school, and Beethoven's music teacher once said of him, "As a composer he is hopeless." When Thomas Edison was a boy, his teachers told him he was too stupid to learn anything. F. W. Woolworth got a job in a dry goods store when he was 21, but his employers would not let him wait on a customer because he "didn't have enough sense." A newspaper editor fired Walt Disney because he had "no good ideas." Caruso's music teacher told him, "You can't sing. You have no voice at all." The director of the Imperial Opera in Vienna told Madame Schuman-Heink that she would never be a singer and advised her to buy a sewing machine. Author Leo Tolstoy flunked out of college; scientist Wernher von Braun flunked ninth-grade algebra. Admiral Richard E. Byrd had been retired from the Navy as "unfit for service" until he flew over both poles. Louis Pasteur was rated as "mediocre" in chemistry when he attended the Royal College. Abraham Lincoln entered the Black Hawk War as a captain and came out as a private. Author Louisa May Alcott was told by an editor that she could never write anything that had popular appeal. Famed choir director Fred Waring was once rejected for high school chorus. Winston Churchill failed the sixth grade.

Adapted from Milton E. Larson, "Humbling Cases for Career Counselors," *Phi Delta Kappan 54*(6), (February 1973): 374.

Developing Honest Relationships

Having at least one other person who can help you objectively and honestly reflect on your virtues and vices can be extremely beneficial in fostering a healthy, positive self-image. As we noted earlier, other people play a major role in shaping your self-concept and self-esteem. The more credible the source of information, the more likely you are to believe it. Having a trusted friend, colleague, clergyperson, or counselor who can listen without judging you and give you the straight scoop about yourself can help you avoid "pity parties." Prolonged periods of self-pity left unchecked and unconfirmed can lead to feelings of inferiority. Later in the chapter we discuss how honest relationships are developed through the process of self-disclosure. As the author of the essay "All the Good Things" (on pages 52–53) learned, honest, positive support can provide encouragement for a lifetime.

Letting Go of the Past

Your self-concept is not a fixed construct. It was not implanted at birth to remain constant for the rest of your life. Things change. You change. Others change. Individuals with low self-esteem may be locking on to events and experiences that happened years ago and tenaciously refusing to let go of them. Someone once wrote, "The lightning bug is brilliant, but it hasn't much of a mind; it blunders through existence with its headlight on behind." Looking back at what we can't change only reinforces a sense of helplessness. Constantly replaying negative experiences in our mental VCR only serves to make our sense of worth more difficult to change. Becoming aware of the changes that have occurred and can occur in your life can help you develop a more realistic assessment of your value. If you were overweight as a child, you may have a difficult time accepting that your worth does not hinge on pounds you carried years ago. Being open and receptive to change in self-worth is important to developing a healthy self-concept. Longfellow's advice to let go of the past remains wise advice today: "Look not mournfully into the past. It comes not back again. Wisely improve the Present. It is thine. Go forth to meet the shadowy future, without fear...." As the following chronology of Abraham Lincoln's life suggests, letting go of the past—coupled with reframing, persistent effort, and talent—served Abraham Lincoln well.

Abraham Lincoln Didn't Quit

The sense of obligation to continue is present in all of us. A duty to strive is the duty of us all. I felt a call to that duty.

Abraham Lincoln

1816	His family was forced out of their home. He had to work to support them.
1818	His mother died.
1831	Failed in business.
1832	Ran for state legislature—*lost.*
1832	Also lost his job—wanted to go to law school but couldn't get in.
1833	Borrowed some money from a friend to begin a business and by the end of the year he was bankrupt. He spent the next 17 years of his life paying off this debt.
1834	Ran for state legislature again—*won.*
1835	Was engaged to be married, sweetheart died, and his heart was broken.
1836	Had a total nervous breakdown and was in bed for six months.
1838	Sought to become speaker of the state legislature—*defeated.*
1840	Sought to become elector—*defeated.*
1843	Ran for Congress—*lost.*
1846	Ran for Congress again—*this time he won*—went to Washington and did a good job.
1848	Ran for re-election to Congress—*lost.*
1849	Sought the job of land officer in his home state—*rejected.*
1854	Ran for Senate of the United States—*lost.*
1856	Sought the Vice-Presidential nomination at his party's national convention—got less than 100 votes.
1858	Ran for U.S. Senate again—*again he lost.*
1860	*Elected President of the United States.*

The path was worn and slippery. My foot slipped from under me, knocking the other out of the way, but I recovered and said to myself, "It's a slip and not a fall."

Abraham Lincoln *(after losing a Senate race)*

From J. Canfield and M. V. Hansen, Eds., *Chicken Soup for the Soul* (Health Communications), 1995.

considering others

All the Good Things

He was in the first third-grade class I taught at Saint Mary's School in Morris, Minnesota. All thirty-four of my students were dear to me, but Mark Eklund was one in a million. Very neat in appearance, he had that happy-to-be-alive attitude that made even his occasional mischievousness delightful.

Mark also talked incessantly. I had to remind him again and again that talking without permission was not acceptable. What impressed me so much, though, was his sincere response every time I had to correct him for misbehaving—"Thank you for correcting me, Sister!" I didn't know what to make of it at first, but before long I became accustomed to hearing it many times a day.

One morning my patience was growing thin when Mark talked once too often, and then I made a novice-teacher's mistake. I looked at Mark and said, "If you say one more word, I am going to tape your mouth shut!"

It wasn't ten seconds later when Chuck blurted out, "Mark is talking again." I hadn't asked any of the students to help me watch Mark, but since I had stated the punishment in front of the class, I had to act on it.

I remember the scene as if it had occurred this morning. I walked to my desk, very deliberately opened the drawer and took out a roll of masking tape. Without saying a word, I proceeded to Mark's desk, tore off two pieces of tape and made a big X with them over his mouth. I then returned to the front of the room.

As I glanced at Mark to see how he was doing, he winked at me. That did it! I started laughing. The entire class cheered as I walked back to Mark's desk, removed the tape, and shrugged my shoulders. His first words were, "Thank you for correcting me, Sister."

At the end of the year I was asked to teach junior-high math. The years flew by, and before I knew it Mark was in my classroom again. He was more handsome than ever and just as polite. Since he had to listen carefully to my instruction in the "new math," he did not talk as much in ninth grade as he had in third.

One Friday, things just didn't feel right. We had worked hard on a new concept all week, and I sensed that the students were growing frustrated with themselves—and edgy with one another. I had to stop this crankiness before it got out of hand. So I asked them to list the names of the other students in the room on two sheets of paper, leaving a space between each name. Then I told them to think of the nicest thing they could say about each of their classmates and write it down.

It took the remainder of the class period to finish the assignment, but as the students left the room, each one handed me the papers. Charlie smiled. Mark said, "Thank you for teaching me, Sister. Have a good weekend."

That Saturday, I wrote down the name of each student on a separate sheet of paper, and I listed what everyone else had said about that individual. On Monday I gave each student his or her list. Some of them ran two pages. Before long, the entire class was smiling. "Really?" I heard whispered. "I never knew that meant anything to anyone!" "I didn't know others liked me so much!"

No one ever mentioned those papers in class again. I never knew

Seeking Support

Some of your self-image problems may be so ingrained that you need professional help. A trained counselor, clergy member, or therapist can help you sort through them. Therapists traditionally take a psychoanalytic approach, inviting you to search for experiences in your past that may help you first to understand your feelings and then to change them. Other counselors use different techniques. If you are not sure to whom to turn for a referral, you can start with your school counseling

if they discussed them after class or with their parents, but it didn't matter. The exercise had accomplished its purpose. The students were happy with themselves and one another again.

That group of students moved on. Several years later, after I returned from a vacation, my parents met me at the airport. As we were driving home, Mother asked the usual questions about the trip—the weather, my experiences in general. There was a slight lull in the conversation. Mother gave Dad a sideways glance and simply said, "Dad?" My father cleared his throat as he usually did before saying something important. "The Eklunds called last night," he began.

"Really?" I said. "I haven't heard from them for several years. I wonder how Mark is."

Dad responded quietly. "Mark was killed in Vietnam," he said. "The funeral is tomorrow, and his parents would like it if you could attend." To this day I can still point to the exact spot on I 494 where Dad told me about Mark.

I had never seen a serviceman in a military coffin before. Mark looked so handsome, so mature. All I could think at that moment was, *Mark, I would give all the masking tape in the world if only you could talk to me.*

The church was packed with Mark's friends. Chuck's sister sang "The Battle Hymn of the Republic." Why did it have to rain on the day of the funeral? It was difficult enough at the graveside. The pastor said the usual prayers, and the bugler played taps. One by one those who loved Mark took a last walk by the coffin and sprinkled it with holy water.

I was the last one to bless the coffin. As I stood there, one of the soldiers who had acted as a pallbearer came up to me. "Were you Mark's math teacher?" he asked. I nodded as I continued to stare at the coffin. "Mark talked about you a lot," he said.

After the funeral, most of Mark's former classmates headed to Chuck's farmhouse for lunch. Mark's mother and father were there, obviously waiting for me. "We want to show you something," his father said, taking a wallet out of his pocket. "They found this on Mark when he was killed. We thought you might recognize it."

Opening the billfold, he carefully removed two worn pieces of notebook paper that had obviously been taped, folded and refolded many times. I knew without looking that the papers were the ones on which I had listed all the good things each of Mark's classmates had said about him. "Thank you so much for doing that," Mark's mother said. "As you can see, Mark treasured it."

Mark's classmates started to gather around us. Charlie smiled rather sheepishly and said, "I still have my list. It's in the top drawer of my desk at home." Chuck's wife said, "Chuck asked me to put his in our wedding album." "I have mine too," Marilyn said. "It's in my diary." Then Vicki, another classmate, reached into her pocketbook, took out her wallet and showed her worn and frazzled list to the group. "I carry this with me at all times," Vicki said without batting an eyelash. "I think we all saved our lists."

That was when I finally sat down and cried. I cried for Mark and for all his friends who would never see him again.

Source: Helen P. Mrosla © Proteus, Shippensburg University.

---

services. Or, if you are near a medical-school teaching hospital, you can contact the counseling or psychotherapy office there for a referral.

Because you have spent your whole lifetime developing your self-esteem, it is not easy to make big changes. But as you have seen, talking through problems can make a difference. As communication researchers Frank E. X. Dance and Carl Larson see it, "Speech communication empowers each of us to share in the development of our own self-concept and the fulfillment of that self-concept."[20]

recap   **Strategies for Improving Your Self-Esteem**

Self-Talk	If you're having a bad hair day, tell yourself that you have beautiful eyes and lots of friends who like you anyway.
Visualize	If you feel nervous before a meeting, visualize everyone in the room congratulating you on your great ideas.
Avoid Comparison	Focus on what you can do to enhance your own talents and abilities.
Reframe	If you experience one failure, keep the larger picture in mind, rather than focusing on that isolated incident.
Develop Honest Relationships	Cultivate friends in whom you can confide and who will give you honest feedback for improving your skills and abilities.
Let Go of the Past	Talk yourself out of your "old tapes"; focus on ways to enhance your abilities in the future.
Seek Support	Talk with professional counselors who can help you identify your gifts and talents.

How Self-Concept and Self-Esteem Affect Interpersonal Communication and Relationships

Your self-concept and self-esteem filter every interaction with others. They determine how you approach, respond to, and interpret messages. Specifically, your self-concept and self-esteem affect your ability to be sensitive to others, your self-fulfilling prophecies, your interpretation of messages, and your typical communication style.

Self and Others

We have suggested the importance of becoming other-oriented—being sensitive to the thoughts and feelings of others—as a requisite for developing quality interpersonal relationships with others.

Becoming other-oriented involves recognizing that your "self" is different from others. As the Peanuts cartoon reminds us, the world does not revolve around our solitary selves. Others influence our actions and our self-image. Mead suggests that we develop an "I," which is based on our own perspective of ourselves, and a "Me," which is an image of ourselves based on the collective responses we receive and interpret from others. Being aware of how your concept of self ("I") differs from the perceptions others have of you ("Me") is an important first step in developing an other-orientation.

When you begin the **decentering** process—taking into account what others may be thinking and feeling—you often interpret your assumptions about others using your own self as a frame of reference, especially if you do not know the other per-

decentering. Cognitive process in which you take into account another person's thoughts, feelings, values, background, and perspective.

PEANUTS

son well.[21] For example, if you are nervous and frightened when you have to take a test, you might assume that your friend will react the same way. You may need to remind yourself that the other person is separate from you and may have a different set of responses.

When you use a **specific-other perspective,** you rely on information that you have observed or that you can imagine about a particular person to predict his or her reactions. For example, if you know firsthand that your sister hates to have someone eat off her plate during dinner, you may use that experience to conclude that she would dislike sharing a bag of popcorn at the movies.

Sometimes a **generalized-other perspective** will be more useful. When you think about and respond to others, you can apply knowledge and personal theories that you have about people in general or about specific subgroups to the person with whom you are interacting. For example, you might think that your economics professor, who holds a Ph.D., would prefer to be addressed as *Doctor* rather than as *Mister* because almost all your other professors with doctorates prefer to be called *Doctor.*

Your ability to predict how others will respond to you is based on your ability to understand how your sense of the world is similar to, and different from, their own. First you must know yourself well. Then you can know and understand others. One of the best ways to improve your ability to be other-oriented is to notice how others respond when you act on the predictions and assumptions you have made about them. You may discover that you have not moved out of your own frame of reference enough to make an accurate prediction about another person.

Self-Fulfilling Prophecy

What people believe about themselves often comes true because they expect it to come true. This is a **self-fulfilling prophecy.** If you think you will fail the math quiz because you have labeled yourself inept at math, then you must overcome not only your math deficiency, but also your low expectations of yourself. The theme of George Bernard Shaw's *Pygmalion* is "If you treat a girl like a flower girl, that's all she will ever be. If you treat her like a princess, she may be one." Your attitudes, beliefs, and general expectations about your performance have a powerful and profound effect on your behavior.

The medical profession is learning the power that attitudes and expectations have over healing. Physician Howard Brody's research suggests that in many instances,

specific-other perspective.
Process of relying on information that a person observes or imagines about another person that is used to predict a person's behavior.

generalized-other perspective.
Process of relying on observed or imagined information about many people or people in general that is used to predict a person's behavior.

self-fulfilling prophecy.
Notion that predictions about your future actions are likely to come true because you believe that they will come true.

As Eliza Doolittle says to Colonel Pickering in George Bernard Shaw's *Pygmalion*, "I know I can be a lady to you because you always treat me as a lady." (Shooting Star)

just giving patients a placebo—a pill with no medicine in it—or telling patients that they have been operated on when they haven't had an operation can yield positive medical results. In his book *The Placebo Response,* a woman with debilitating Parkinson's disease made a miraculous recovery; her only treatment was the doctors' telling her that they had completed a medical procedure.[22] They hadn't. Yet before the "treatment" she could barely walk; now she can easily pace around the room. There is a clear link, suggests Dr. Brody, between mental state and physical health. Patients who believe they will improve are more likely to improve.

Self and Interpretation of Messages

Although it may have been several years since you've read A. A. Milne's classic children's stories about Winnie-the-Pooh, do you remember Eeyore, the donkey friend of Winnie-the-Pooh and his friends? Eeyore lives in the gloomiest part of the Hundred Acre Wood and has a self-image to match. In one story all the animals congregate on a stormy night to check on Eeyore:

> . . . they all came to the part of the forest known as Eeyore's gloomy place. On this stormy night it was terribly gloomy indeed—or it would have been were it not for Christopher Robin. He was there with a big umbrella.
>
> "I've invited Eeyore to come and stay with me until the storm is over," said Christopher Robin.
>
> "If it ever is," said Eeyore, "which doesn't seem likely. Not that anybody asked me, you understand. But then, they hardly ever do."[23]

Perhaps you know or have known an Eeyore—someone whose low self-esteem colors how he or she interprets messages and interacts with others. According to research, such people are more likely to have the following traits:[24]

- Be more sensitive to criticism and negative feedback from others.
- Be more critical of others.
- Believe they are not popular or respected by others.
- Expect to be rejected by others.
- Prefer not to be observed when performing.
- Feel threatened by people who they feel are superior.
- Expect to lose when competing with others.
- Be overly responsive to praise and compliments.
- Evaluate their overall behavior as inferior to that of others.

The Pooh stories offer an antidote to Eeyore's gloom in the character of the optimistic Tigger, who assumes that everyone shares his exuberance for life:

> ... when Owl reached Piglet's house, Tigger was there. He was bouncing on his tail, as Tiggers do, and shouting to Piglet. "Come on," he cried. "You can do it! It's fun!"[25]

If, like Tigger, your sense of self-worth is high, research suggests you will

- Have higher expectations for solving problems.
- Think more highly of others.
- Be more likely to accept praise and accolades from others without feeling embarrassed.
- Be more comfortable having others observe you when you perform.
- Be more likely to admit you have both strengths and weaknesses.
- Prefer to interact with others who view themselves as highly competent.
- Expect other people to accept you for who you are.
- Be more likely to seek opportunities to improve skills that need improving.
- Evaluate your overall behavior more positively than would people with lower self-esteem.[26]

Reflecting the assumption that self-concept influences behavior is the principle of **selective exposure,** which suggests that people tend to place themselves in situations consistent with who they think they are. Whom do you usually find at a Baptist church on Sunday morning? Baptists. Who are the attendees at a Democratic convention? Democrats. If you view yourself as a good student who wants an A in the class, where are you likely to be during class time? People behave in ways that reinforce their perception of self, both in interpretation of messages and in behavior.

Self and Interpersonal Needs

According to social psychologist Will Schutz, our concept of who we are, coupled with our need to interact with others, profoundly influences how we communicate with others. Schutz identifies three primary social needs that affect the degree of communication we have with others: the need for inclusion, the need for control, and the need for affection.[27] The **need for inclusion** suggests that each of us has a need to be included in the activities of others. We all need human contact and fellowship. We need to be invited to join others, and perhaps we need to invite others

selective exposure. Principle that suggests people tend to place themselves in situations that are consistent with their self-concept and self-esteem.

need for inclusion. Interpersonal need to be included and to include others in social activities.

to join us. Of course, the level and intensity of this need differs from person to person, but even loners desire some social contact. Our need to include others and be included in activities may stem, in part, from our concept of ourselves as either a "party person" or a loner.

The second need, the **need for control,** suggests that we also need some degree of influence over the relationships we establish with others. We may also have a need to be controlled because we desire some level of stability and comfort in our interactions with others. If we view ourselves as people who are comfortable being in charge, we are more likely to give orders to others rather than take orders from them.

And finally, we each have a **need for affection.** We need to give and receive love, support, warmth, and intimacy, although the amounts we need vary enormously from person to person. If we have a high need for affection, we will more likely place ourselves in situations where that need can be met. The greater our inclusion, control, and affection needs are, the more likely it is that we will actively seek others as friends and initiate communication with them.

Self and Communication Style

Our self-concept and self-esteem ultimately affect how we treat other people. One dimension of the self that is particularly relevant to our interactions with others is communication style. Each of us has a **communication style,** sometimes called social style, that is identifiable by the habitual ways we behave toward others. The style we adopt helps others interpret our messages and predict how we will behave. As they get to know us, other people begin to expect us to communicate in a certain way, based on previous associations with us.

How do we develop our communication style? Many communication researchers, sociologists, and psychologists believe that we have certain underlying traits or personality characteristics that influence how we interact with others. Some scholars believe these traits stem from genetics—we are born with certain personality characteristics. We are who we are because that's the way we are made.[28] Others emphasize the **social learning approach**—we communicate with others as we do because of our interactions with others such as our parents and friends. The truth is that we cannot yet explain exactly how we come to communicate as we do.

Even though we don't know the precise role of nature or nurture in determining how we communicate, most inventories of personality or communication style focus on two primary dimensions that underlie how we interact with others—assertiveness and responsiveness.[29] **Assertiveness** is the tendency to make requests, ask for information, and generally pursue our own rights and best interests. An assertive style is sometimes called a "masculine" style. By masculine, we don't mean that only males can be assertive, but that in many cultures being assertive is synonymous with being "masculine." You are assertive when you seek information if you are confused, or direct others to help you get what you need.

Responsiveness is the tendency to be sensitive to the needs of others. Being other-oriented and sympathetic to the pain of others, and placing the feelings of others above your own feelings are examples of being responsive. Researchers sometimes label responsiveness a "feminine" quality. Again, this does not mean only women are or should be responsive, only that many cultures stereotype being responsive as a traditional behavior of females.

What is your communication style? To assess your style of communication on the assertiveness and responsiveness dimensions, take the "Sociocommunicative

need for control. Interpersonal need for some degree of domination in our relationships as well as the need to be controlled.

need for affection. Interpersonal need to give and receive love, personal support, warmth, and intimacy.

communication style. Identifiable or habitual way in which you communicate to other people.

social learning approach. Perspective that explains your style of communicating with others is based on learning from and modeling other people.

assertiveness. Tendency to make requests, ask for information, and generally pursue your own rights and best interests.

responsiveness. Tendency to be sensitive to the needs of others, including being sympathetic to the pain of others and placing the feelings of others above your own feelings.

Orientation" test by James McCroskey and Virginia Richmond below. You may discover that you test higher on one dimension than on the others. It's also possible to be high on both or low on both. Assertiveness and responsiveness are two different dimensions; you need not have just one or the other.

Sociocommunicative Orientation*

Directions: The following questionnaire lists 20 personality characteristics. Please indicate the degree to which you believe each of these characteristics applies to *you,* as you normally communicate with others, by marking whether you (5) strongly agree that it applies, (4) agree that it applies, (3) are undecided, (2) disagree that it applies, or (1) strongly disagree that it applies. There are no right or wrong answers. Work quickly; record your first impression.

_____ 4 _____ 1. helpful 5
_____ 5 _____ 2. defends own beliefs 3
_____ 4 _____ 3. independent 4
_____ 4 _____ 4. responsive to others 5
_____ 5 _____ 5. forceful 2
_____ 5 _____ 6. has strong personality 2
_____ 4 _____ 7. sympathetic 5
_____ 4 _____ 8. compassionate 5
_____ 5 _____ 9. assertive 2
_____ 4 _____ 10. sensitive to the needs of others 5
_____ 5 _____ 11. dominant 2
_____ 4 _____ 12. sincere 5
_____ 4 _____ 13. gentle 5
_____ 5 _____ 14. willing to take a stand 2
_____ 4 _____ 15. warm 5
_____ 4 _____ 16. tender 5
_____ 5 _____ 17. friendly 5
_____ 5 _____ 18. acts as a leader 3
_____ 5 _____ 19. aggressive 3
_____ 5 _____ 20. competitive 4

Assert - 50
Resp. 43

Assertiveness – 49 . 26
Responsiveness - 41 . 50

---

*Items 2, 3, 5, 6, 9, 11, 14, 18, 19, and 20 measure assertiveness. Add the scores on these items to get your assertiveness score. Items 1, 4, 7, 8, 10, 12, 13, 15, 16, and 17 measure responsiveness. Add the scores on these items to get your responsiveness score. Scores range from 50 to 10. The higher your score, the higher your orientation as assertive and responsive.

Source: James C. McCroskey and Virginia P. Richmond, *Fundamentals of Human Communication: An Interpersonal Perspective* (Prospect Heights, IL: Waveland Press, 1996), p. 91.

What many people want to know is, "What's the best communication style? Should I be assertive or responsive?" The truth is, there is no one best style for every situation. It depends. Sometimes the appropriate thing to do is to assert yourself—to ask or even demand that you receive what you need and have a right to receive. In other situations, it may be more appropriate to be less confrontational. Maintaining the quality of the relationship by simply listening and being thoughtfully responsive to others may be best. The appropriateness of your communication style involves issues we will discuss in future chapters, such as how you adapt to culture and gender differences, your needs, the needs and rights of others, and the goal of your communication.

How Self-Concept and Self-Esteem Affect Interpersonal Communication and Relationships

	Definition	Examples
Message Interpretation and Interaction	Feelings of high or low self-esteem affect how you understand and react to messages.	If you have high self-esteem, you are more likely to accept praise without embarrassment.
Self-Fulfilling Prophecy	What you believe about yourself will come true because you expect it to come true.	You expect to have a rotten time at a party so you behave in ways that guarantee you won't enjoy the party.
Communication Style	Your self-concept and self-esteem contribute to habitual ways of responding to others.	Your image of yourself influences your responsive or assertive behavior toward others.

Self-Disclosure: Connecting Self to Others Through Talk

One important way people develop and revise their self-concept is through other people's reactions to their self-disclosure. **Self-disclosure** occurs when you purposefully provide information to others about yourself that they would not learn if you did not tell them. People can learn your approximate age, height, and weight by just observing you. But they can't learn your *exact* age, height, or weight unless you tell them. Self-disclosure ranges from revealing innocuous information about who you are, to admitting your deepest fears and most private fantasies. Disclosing personal information not only provides a basis for another person to understand you better, it conveys your level of trust and acceptance of the other person. To help explore relationships among self-concept, self-esteem, and self-disclosure, we will describe how self-disclosure occurs, note how people become aware of who they are through self-disclosure, and identify general characteristics of self-disclosure.

Interpersonal relationships cannot achieve intimacy without self-disclosure. Without true self-disclosure, you form only superficial relationships. You can con-

self-disclosure. Purposefully providing information to others that they would not learn if you did not tell them.

The amount of information we reveal to others through our self-disclosures depends on the type of relationship we have with that person. We are more willing to open up to a close friend than a mere acquaintance. (Cleo/PhotoEdit)

firm another person's self-concept, and have your self-concept confirmed, only if both you and your partner have revealed yourselves to each other.

Understanding the Depth and Breadth of Self-Disclosure: The Social Penetration Model of Self-Disclosure

What makes your best friend your best friend? Undoubtedly, one characteristic is that you have shared your most personal information with him or her. With people you know well and who know you, you share more personal information over a broader range of topics than you do with people you know only superficially. Researchers Irwin Altman and Dalmas Taylor developed a model called **social penetration** that illustrates how much and what kinds of information people reveal in various stages of a relationship.[30] Their model starts with a circle that represents all the potential information about yourself that you could disclose to someone (see Figure 2.2, circle A). This circle is divided into many pieces like a pie, with each piece of pie representing a particular aspect of yourself. For instance, some pieces in your pie might relate to athletic activities, religious beliefs, family, school, recreational activities, political interests, and fears. These pieces of pie represent the breadth of topics or information available about you.

In addition, the concentric circles in the pie represent the depth of information you could disclose. By depth, we mean how personal or intimate the information is; telling your friend about your fear of elevators is more intimate that telling someone that your favorite ice cream is homemade vanilla. The smallest circle represents the most personal information. Each of your relationships represents a degree of social penetration, or the extent to which the other person has penetrated your concentric circles (depth) and shared pieces of your pie (breadth). For example, the shading on circle B shows a relationship that involves a high degree of

social penetration model. Model of self-disclosure and relational development that reflects both depth and breadth of shared information.

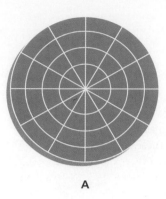

A

Your "self" with all its various dimensions. The pies represent the breadth of your "self," and the rings represent depth.

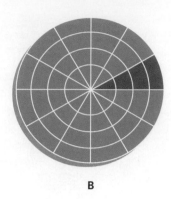

B

A limited relationship in which one dimension of your "self" has been disclosed to another person.

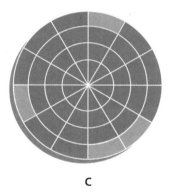

C

A relationship with greater breadth than B but with no intimacy.

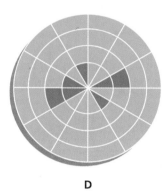

D

A highly intimate, close relationship in which there has been extensive breadth and depth of disclosure.

Figure 2.2
Social Penetration Models

penetration, but of only one aspect of yourself. Perhaps you have a good friend with whom you study and go to the library, but you don't spend much time socializing with your friend; it's all work and no play with this friend. You might have disclosed a depth of information to your friend about your study skills and weaknesses, but little about your family, hobbies, political views, or other aspects of who you are.

Your relationships with your instructors probably look a little like circle B, with its limited breadth. In circle C, more pieces of the pie are shaded, but the information is all fairly safe, superficial information about yourself, such as where you went to school, your hometown, or your major. These would be the kind of disclosures associated with a new friendship. Circle D represents almost complete social penetration, the kind achieved in an intimate, well-developed relationship, in which a large amount of self-disclosure has occurred.

Understanding How We Learn About Ourselves from Others: The Johari Window Model of Self-Disclosure

To disclose information to others, you must first be aware of who you are. **Self-awareness** is your understanding of who you are. In addition to just thinking about who you are, asking others for information about yourself and then listening to what they tell you can enhance your self-awareness. There are a variety of personality tests such as the Myers-Briggs personality inventory (see the e-Connections box on page 46) that may give you additional insight into your interests, style, and ways of relating to others. Most colleges and universities have a career services office where you can take vocational aptitude tests to help you identify careers that fit who you are.

The **Johari Window model** nicely summarizes how your awareness of who you are is influenced by your own level of disclosure, as well as by how much others share information *about* yourself *with* you. (The name "Johari Window" sounds somewhat mystical and exotic, but it is labeled after the first names of the creators of the model, Joe and Harry—Joseph Luft and Harry Ingham.[31]) As Figure 2.3 shows, the model looks like a window. Like the circles in the social penetration model, the window represents your self. This self includes everything about you, including things even you don't yet see or realize. One axis is divided into what you have come to know about yourself and what you don't yet know about who you are. The other axis represents what a particular person knows about you and doesn't know about you. The intersection of these categories creates a four-panel window.

At first glance, all four quadrants in the window seem to be the same size. But that may not be the case (in fact, it probably isn't). Quadrant 1 is called the open area. It contains information that others know about you and that you are also aware of. The more information that you reveal about yourself, that larger quadrant 1 will be. Put another way, the more you open up to others, the larger the open area will

self-awareness. Person's conscious understanding of who he or she is.

Johari Window model. Model of self-disclosure that reflects the movement of information about yourself from Blind and Unknown quadrants to Hidden and Open ones.

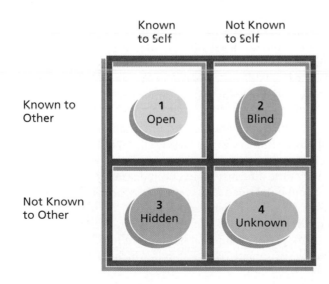

Figure 2.3
Johari Window

be. The open area might include such information as your age, your occupation, and other things you mention about yourself.

Quadrant 2 is called the blind area. This part of the window contains information that other people know about you, but that you do not know. Do you remember when, in grade school, someone may have put a sign on your back that said, "Hit me"? Everyone was aware of it but you. The blind area of the Johari Window works in much the same way. For example, you may see yourself as generous, but others may see you as a tightwad. As you learn how others see you, the blind area of the Johari Window gets smaller. Generally, the more you accurately know about yourself and about how others see you, the better your chances to establish open and honest relationships with others.

Quadrant 3 is the hidden area. This area contains information that you know about yourself, but that others do not know about you. You can probably think of many facts, thoughts, feelings, and fantasies that you would not want anyone else to know. They may be feelings you have about another person or something you've done privately in the past that you'd be embarrassed to share with others. The point here is not to suggest you should share all information in the hidden area with others. It is useful to know, however, that part of who you are is known by some people, but remains hidden from others.

Quadrant 4 in the Johari Window depicts the unknown area. This area contains information that is unknown to both you and others. These are things you do not know about yourself *yet*. Perhaps you do not know how you will react under certain stressful situations. Maybe you are not sure what stand you will take on a certain issue next year or even next week. Other people may also not be aware of how you would respond or behave under certain conditions. Your personal potential, your untapped physical and mental resources, are unknown. You can assume that this area exists, because eventually some, not necessarily all, of these things become known to you, to others, or to both you and others. Because you can never know yourself completely, the unknown quadrant will always exist; you can only guess at its current size, because the information it contains is unavailable to you.

Sometimes our friends observe things about us that we don't realize about ourselves. This kind of unintentional self-disclosure is represented by the blind area. This quadrant is usually small when someone doesn't know us very well, and it grows larger as the person observes more and more information that is in our unknown quadrant. However, as the relationship becomes more intimate, the other person is more likely to reveal his or her perceptions of us, so the unknown and the blind quadrants shrink as information becomes known and accessible to us. As you can see, then, intimate relationships play an important role in the growth of what we know about who we are.

As we did with the social penetration model, we can draw Johari Windows to represent each of our relationships (see Figure 2.4). Window A depicts a new or very restricted relationship for someone who is probably young or at least not very self-aware. Very little information has been disclosed or observed by the other, so the open and blind quadrants are small. Window B shows a new or restricted relationship for someone who knows him- or herself very well. Again, the open and blind quadrants are small, but the unknown quadrant is also small. Window C represents a relationship that has evolved into a good friendship, and window D shows a very intimate relationship in which both individuals are open and disclosing.

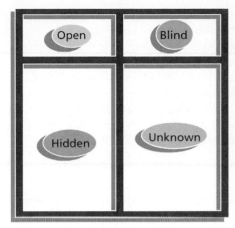

(A) A new relationship, possibly for a young person

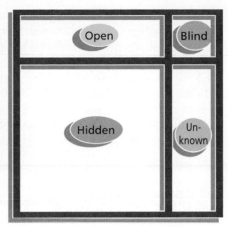

(B) A new relationship for someone who is very self-aware

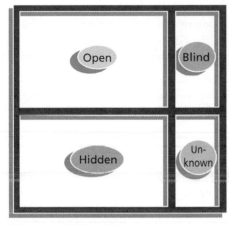

(C) A good friendship

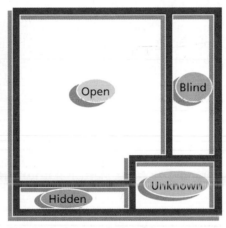

(D) An intimate relationship

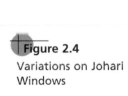

Figure 2.4
Variations on Johari Windows

We've discussed what self-disclosure is and described two models that explain how self-disclosure works and affects your understanding of who you think you are. Next we will describe characteristics of self-disclosure and discuss how disclosure, both appropriate and inappropriate, can affect our interpersonal relationships with others.

Characteristics of Self-Disclosure

Mike was eating alone, sitting at the counter at his neighborhood diner enjoying his favorite meatloaf sandwich. Just as he was reaching for the catsup bottle, a young woman on the dinner stool next to him struck up a conversation with him. Within ten minutes, Mike not only learned where this woman was from, but also whom she dated, how much money she made last year, and how embarrassed she was when her parents found her in a compromising position with her boyfriend on the front porch (which she described in vivid detail, complete with sound effects). Have you had the experience of meeting someone who told you more than you wanted to know about him- or herself? Although self-disclosure is a means to establishing relationships with others, as we presented in both the social penetration and Johari Window models, revealing too much too soon or making the disclosure only a one-way stream of revelatory information violates self-disclosure norms for most North Americans. The following discussion describes characteristics of appropriate self-disclosure.

Self-Disclosure Usually Moves in Small Increments

What made Mike so uncomfortable during his meeting with his dining neighbor was how much information he learned about his companion in such a short period of time. Most people usually reveal information about themselves a little bit at a time, rather than delivering a condensed version of their books-on-tape autobiography. Most North Americans would share Mike's discomfort at learning too much too soon. Monitor your own self-disclosure. Are you revealing information at a greater depth sooner than you should? If you do, others may find your disclosure disquieting. Appropriate self-disclosure should be well timed to suit the occasion and the expectations of the individuals involved.

Self-Disclosure Moves from Less Personal to More Personal Information

As the social penetration model illustrates, we can describe the depth of our self-disclosure by the intimacy level of the information we share. If we move too quickly to more intimate information before we've developed a history with someone, we violate social norms or expectations our partner may have. John Powell, author of the book *why am I afraid to tell you who I am?* notes that the information we reveal about ourselves often progresses through several predictable levels.[32]

> Level 5: *Cliché communication.* We first establish verbal contact with others by saying something that lets the other person know we acknowledge his or her presence. Standard phrases such as "Hello" or "Hi; how are you?" or the more contemporary "What's up?" signal the desire to initiate a relationship, even if it is a brief, superficial one.

> Level 4: *Facts and biographical information.* After using cliché phrases and responses to establish contact, we typically next reveal nonthreatening information about ourselves, such as our names, hometowns, or majors.

> Level 3: *Attitudes and personal ideas.* After noting our name and other basic information, it often follows that we begin talking about more personal information such as our attitudes about work or school, or other relatively safe topics. At this level, the information is not too threatening or revealing, but we do begin to talk about our likes and dislikes of what we might assume are noncontroversial topics.

Level 2: *Personal feelings.* At this level, we discuss topics and issues that are exceedingly more personal. After we've developed rapport with someone, we then share more intimate fears, secrets, and attitudes about other people. Increasingly, we take risks when we share this information. It also involves trust to share these personal feelings.

Level 1: *Peak communication.* Powell calls this the ultimate level of self-disclosure that is seldom reached; his other name for level 1 is "gut level" communication. Only with our most intimate friends do we reveal such personal information. And it's possible, says Powell, that we may not reach this level of intimacy with our life partners, parents, or children. Peak communication is rare because of the risk and trust involved in being so open and revealing.

Self-Disclosure Is Reciprocal

In the mainstream U.S. culture, when people share information about themselves, they expect the other person to share similar information about her- or himself. If you introduce yourself by name to someone, you expect that person to respond by telling you his or her name. This cultural rule allows people to use disclosure as a strategy for gaining information and reducing uncertainty. The reciprocal nature of self-disclosure is called the **dyadic effect.** You disclose to me, and I'll disclose to you.

Self-Disclosure Involves Risk

Although self-disclosure is a building block for establishing intimacy with others, it can be risky. Once you disclose something to someone, that person can now share the information with others; that person has additional power if the information is something you'd rather not have others know.

There is also the risk of rejection when you tell someone something that is personal. As Powell comments, "If I tell you who I am, and you do not like who I am, that is all that I have."[33] Once you reveal what you believe is your true nature or personal feeling and you are rejected or rebuffed, you can't explain your rejection away by saying, "Oh, they don't know the real me." If you've revealed what you honestly believe is "the real you" and you experience disapproval from your partner, that can hurt worse than if your partner did not know "the real you."

Self-Disclosure Involves Trust

As we have already noted, to know something personal about someone is to have power over that person. If information has been shared with you, you have the power to reveal that information to others. To reveal personal information about someone that was shared with you in confidence is unethical. If you've made this promise, you should keep it. Using personal information against others to manipulate and control is a misuse of the trust that was placed in you.[34] According to British social psychologists Michael Argyle, Monica Henderson, and Adrian Furnham, keeping confidences of others is among the most valued expectation your friends have of you. Don't tell what you're not supposed to tell others. When you say, "Oh, I won't tell anyone. Your secret's safe with me," mean it.

dyadic effect. Reciprocal nature of self-disclosure: "You disclose to me, and I'll disclose to you."

recap

Characteristics of Appropriate Self-Disclosure

Self-disclosure usually moves in small increments.	Don't be in a hurry to tell someone too much too quickly about yourself.
Self-disclosure moves from less personal to more personal information.	Revealing personal feelings and intimate information without establishing a foundation of sharing less personal information is likely to make your partner feel uncomfortable.
Self-disclosure is reciprocal.	Appropriate self-disclosure involves dyadic interaction; it should not be a one-way monologue.
Self-disclosure involves risk.	"But if I tell you who I am, you may not like who I am, and that is all that I have." You run the risk of being rejected by others when you disclose to them.
Self-disclosure involves trust.	Disclosing to others means you trust them not to reveal your secrets to others or use the personal information against you. When others self-disclose, you have an ethical responsibility to keep confidential what you've learned.

Summary

We all seek answers to three questions: "Who am I?" "Why am I here?" "Who are all these others?" William James answered the first question by dividing the self into three parts. The material self includes our bodies and those tangible possessions that give us identity. The social self is the part that engages in interaction with others. The spiritual self consists of thoughts and assumptions about values, moral standards, and beliefs about forces that influence our lives. Other theorists conclude that our self-concept develops through interaction with other people. The groups we belong to also give us identity. Our roles as sister, brother, student, and parent are important in how we view who we are; the roles we assume provide labels for who we are. We also self-reflexively make our own observations about ourselves apart from others, and about groups or roles we assume. Our gender plays a key part in affecting our view of who we are in relationship to others.

Given the importance of developing a positive sense of self-esteem, we identified strategies that can enhance your self-worth. Those strategies include engaging in self-talk, using positive visualization, avoiding comparisons with others, reframing, developing honest relationships, letting go of the past, and seeking support when needed.

Our sense of self relates to self-disclosure. Self-disclosure occurs when we purposefully provide information to others that they would not learn if we did not tell them. The social penetration model of self-disclosure describes how the depth and breadth of our disclosure can affect our relationships. The Johari Window model of self-disclosure provides an explanation of the relationship between our self-awareness and self-disclosure. The four quadrants in the Johari Window (Open, Hidden, Unknown, and Blind), reflect how much information we and others know about ourselves. As we develop relationships, the sizes of these windows change relative to one another. Finally, there are five characteristics of appropriate self-disclosure: self-disclosure (1) moves in small increments, (2) moves from less to more personal information, (3) is reciprocal, (4) involves risk, and (5) involves trust.

For Discussion and Review

Focus on Comprehension

1. List and describe the three selves identified by William James. *material, Social, Spiritual*

2. Define, compare, and contrast the terms *self-concept* and *self-esteem*. *— self-worth*

3. Identify and describe four factors that explain how a person's self-concept *persons description of who he/she is* develops. *interacting w Others   roles you assume   Group associations   self labels*

4. Describe and discuss two models of self-disclosure.

5. Identify the characteristics of appropriate self-disclosure. *trust, reciprocal* *Small Steps, move from less personal to more personal   is reciprocal, involves risks, involves trust*

Focus on Critical Thinking

6. Joel, who is 30 years old, married, and has two children, suffers from feelings of low self-esteem. Although he has many friends and a wife who loves him, he feels that others perform much better than he does at work. What strategies would help Joel enhance his self-esteem? *Self talk, visualization*

7. Make a list of all the groups, clubs, and organizations to which you belong. Rank-order them from most important to least important. What does your rank-ordering tell you about these groups in reference to your self-concept?

8. Provide an original example of how visualization might help you enhance your self-esteem. Describe the positive scene. *Graduating w honors*

9. Provide an example from your own experiences that illustrates the Johari Window model of self-disclosure. *my neighbor, don't tell her much she'll take it and run.*

Focus on Ethics

10. Discuss the ethical implications of using untrue flattery to enhance a friend's self-esteem.

11. Many self-help books on the market claim to enrich your social life by providing sure-fire techniques for enhancing self-esteem. Do you think these claims are ethical? Why or why not?

12. Aelish has long planned to attend a top-notch Ivy League college. Her grades, however, are only in the C and B range. Her SAT scores are average. Should she try to reframe this factual information or deal with her problem in another way?

13. Carmelita would like to become better friends with Hector. She decides to disclose some personal information to Hector, hoping that this self-disclosure will increase feelings of intimacy between them. Is it ethical to self-disclose to others as a strategy to enhance intimacy in a relationship?

For Your Journal

1. Record goals for your self-talk and note your self-talk messages day by day. You might want to organize your journal around specific topics such as academic achievement, personal appearance, or social skills. Under academic achievement

you could write, "I will monitor my self-talk messages to keep myself on track while I study for two hours each day." Your personal-appearance self-talk goal may be to tell yourself something positive about your appearance, instead of thinking only about what you don't like.

2. In your journal, write the ten responses you wrote for Building Your Skills: Who Are You? at the beginning of this chapter. At the end of the course, again write ten responses to the "Who are you?" question, without looking at your earlier responses. What are the differences in your responses? How do you explain them?

3. If someone were to walk into one of your favorite rooms in your home, dorm, or apartment, what conclusions might he or she draw about your social style? Are you neat and well organized? Or does your room have the characteristics of an expressive personality? Write a brief description of who you are from a social-style perspective, based on the clues in your room.

Learning with Others

1. Rank the following list of values from 1 to 12. In a group with other students, compare your answers. Discuss how your personal ranking of these values influences your interaction with others.

_____ Honesty	_____ Justice
_____ Salvation	_____ Wealth
_____ Comfort	_____ Beauty
_____ Good health	_____ Equality
_____ Human rights	_____ Freedom
_____ Peace	_____ Mercy

2. You are going to make a shield of your life (like a coat of arms). Draw a large outline of a shield that fills up an entire sheet of paper. Divide your shield into four equal sections. In the upper right-hand section of your shield, draw or symbolize something at which you have skill or talent. In the upper left-hand section, draw or symbolize something you are trying to improve or a new skill you are learning. In the lower right-hand section, draw or symbolize your most prized material possession. Finally, in the lower left-hand section, write three words that you hope someone would use to describe you.

   Share your shield with other students. Tell your classmates why you drew what you did. Discuss how your shield reflects your attitudes, beliefs, and values.

3. Go through your personal music library of tapes or CDs and identify a selection that best symbolizes you. Your selection may be based on either the lyrics or the music. Bring your selection to class and play it for your classmates. (Your instructor will bring a tape or CD player.) Tell why this music symbolizes you. Discuss with classmates how your choice of music provides a glimpse of your culture and a vehicle for self-expression.

4. Johari Window Exercise[35]

The purpose of this exercise is to help you understand the Johari Window as presented in this chapter. In essence, we are asking you to construct a Johari Window for a group in which you participate. Of course, you should realize that the impression you have of the others and the impression they have of you may be based on only a very brief opportunity to meet with one another. Your instructor will give you additional suggestions for completing this activity.

a. Form groups of three to five people.

b. Check five or six adjectives from the folowing list that best describe your personality as you see it.

c. Select three or four adjectives that describe the personality of each person in your group and write them on separate sheets of paper. Distribute these lists to the appropriate group members.

d. Fill in square number A ("known to self and known to others") with adjectives from the list that both you and at least one other member of your group have selected to describe your personality.

e. Fill in square number B ("not known to self but known to others") with those adjectives others in your group used to describe you, but you did not use to describe yourself.

f. Fill in square number C ("known to self but not to others") with adjectives you have used to describe yourself, but no one else used to describe you.

able	dependable	intelligent	patient	sensible
accepting	dignified	introverted	powerful	sentimental
adaptable	energetic	kind	proud	shy
bold	extroverted	knowledgeable	quiet	silly
brave	friendly	logical	reflective	spontaneous
calm	giving	loving	relaxed	sympathetic
caring	happy	mature	religious	tense
cheerful	helpful	modest	responsive	trustworthy
clever	idealistic	nervous	searching	warm
complex	independent	observant	self-assertive	wise
confident	ingenious	organized	self-conscious	witty

	Known to self	Not known to self
Known to others	A	B
Not known to others	C	Unknown

chapter

3

Interpersonal Communication and Perception

After you study this chapter

you should be able to ...

1. Define perception and interpersonal perception.

2. Identify and explain the three stages of interpersonal perception.

3. Describe the relationship between interpersonal communication and interpersonal perception.

4. Explain how we form impressions of others, describe others, and interpret others' behavior.

5. Identify the six factors that distort the accuracy of our interpersonal perceptions.

6. Offer five suggestions for improving interpersonal perceptions.

● Understanding Interpersonal Perception

● Perception and Interpersonal Communication

● Perceiving Others

● Identifying Barriers to Accurate Perceptions

● Improving Your Perception Skills

ook at the picture in Figure 3.1. What is happening and what has happened? What is the relationship among the individuals in the painting? You probably have deduced that the boy was running away from home, the policeman found him, and then he took the boy into the local coffee shop for ice cream or some other treat. Perhaps you think that the counterman is wistfully recalling his own days of running away as a child. What are your feelings about the policeman? Do you see him as a friendly and caring person who has a good understanding of kids?

As human beings, we interpret and attribute meaning to what we observe or experience, particularly if what we are observing is other people. We tend to make inferences about their motives, personalities, and other traits based on their physical qualities and behaviors. The types of conclusions we draw from observing the picture in Figure 3.1 exemplify the process we call *interpersonal perception*. Through interpersonal perception we piece together various bits of information about other people and draw conclusions that may or may not be accurate. Because our feelings and responses to other people are based on our perceptions, those who are skilled at making observations and interpretations have a head start in developing effective interpersonal relationships.

Most of the time, we are unaware of our own perception process. For example, you may not have realized that you were drawing conclusions about the painting until you read the questions above. But we may become aware of the process when differences in perception cause a conflict or disagreement. In truth, no two individuals ever perceive the same thing in exactly the same way. Fortunately, communication tools such as conversation allow us to create shared meanings despite the differences in our perceptions.

Your perceptions are influenced by who you are, including the accumulation of your experiences. If you have had several bad experiences with the police, for example, you may not view the policeman in Figure 3.1 as a friendly person. Or if you know something about the life and work of Norman Rockwell, the illustrator who painted the picture, you may view all his works as representations of an idyllic American culture and society that existed only in his mind. As we noted in Chapter 2, everything people perceive is filtered through their self-concept.[1] It is important to

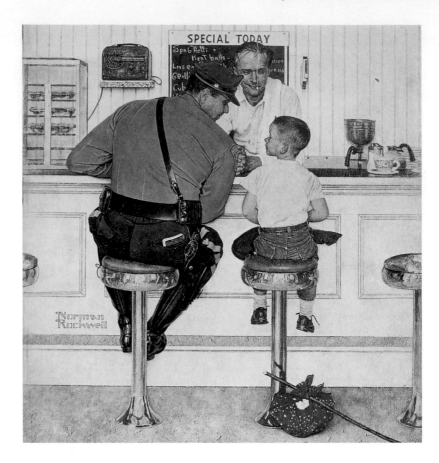

Figure 3.1

Saturday Evening Post cover, September 20, 1958. Old Corner House Collection, Stockbridge, Massachusetts. (Printed by permission of the Rockwell Family Trust. Copyright © The Runaway, the Norman Rockwell Family Trust.)

recognize and examine factors that might distort the accuracy of your interpretations. You can also reduce inaccuracies by applying an other-oriented approach as you interact with people. By focusing on how others perceive the world, you can reduce the amount of distortion that our own self-concepts impose on your perceptions.

Before we turn to the role that perception plays in interpersonal communication, let's first take a closer look at the interpersonal perception process itself.

building your skills

Perceptual Differences

Think of two instances in which you and a friend had a very similar perception of something—perhaps of the food in a restaurant, a scene in a movie, or of some behavior you observed in another person. How did you know that you and your friend had similar perceptions? What factors in your backgrounds influenced the way you each perceived the experience?

Now think of two instances in which you and a friend had different perceptions of the same thing. How did you discover that you and your friend had different perceptions? To what factors in each of your backgrounds do you attribute these different perceptions? What effects did the differences in perception have on your interactions?

Understanding Interpersonal Perception

What is perception? **Perception** is the process of experiencing your world and then making sense out of what you experience. You experience your world through your five senses. For example, a sound travels through the air, vibrates on your eardrum, activates the nerves, and sends a signal to the brain. A similar sequence of events takes place when you see, smell, feel, or taste something. The process of perception also includes organizing and interpreting information provided by the senses. You come out of a building and see wet pavement and puddles of water, hear thunder, smell a distinct odor caused by ions, and observe drops of water falling in front of you. You integrate all those bits of information and conclude that it is raining, and has been for a while.

Your perceptions of people, however, include analysis and interpretation that goes beyond simple interpretation of sensory information. **Interpersonal perception** is the process by which you decide what people are like and give meaning to their actions. It includes making judgments about personality and drawing inferences from what you observed.[2] When you meet someone new, you *select* certain information to attend to: You note whether the person is male or female, has an accent, smiles, uses a friendly tone of voice, as well as particular personal information (she is from Boone, Iowa). You then *organize* the information under some category that is recognizable to you, such as "a friendly Midwesterner." Then you *interpret* the organized perceptions: This person is trustworthy, honest, hardworking, and likable.

In our discussion we focus on this kind of interpersonal perception, which relates to understanding our observations of other people. We begin by examining the three stages of the interpersonal perception process that we have already described: selecting, organizing, and interpreting what we observe.

Stage 1: Selecting

Sit for a minute after you read this passage and tune in to all the sensory input you are receiving: Consider the feel of your socks against your feet, the pressure of the floor on your heels, the pressure of the piece of furniture against your body as you sit, the buzzing sounds from various sources around you—this "white noise" might come from a refrigerator, personal computer, fluorescent lights, water in pipes, voices, passing traffic, or your own heartbeat or churning stomach. What do you smell? What do you see? Without moving your eyes, turn your awareness to the images you see in the corner of your vision. What colors do you see? What shapes? What taste is in your mouth? How do the pages of this book feel against your fingertips? Now stop reading and consider all these sensations. Try to focus on all of them at the same time. You can't.

The number of sensations people can attend to at any given time is limited. Therefore, you are selective about which sensations make it through to the level of awareness. Perhaps you close your eyes or sit in the dark as you listen to music. This allows you to select more auditory sensations because you are eliminating visual ones.

During the selection stage, you attempt to simplify the stimuli that flood in through your senses, using various techniques. You use perceptual filters to screen

perception. Experiencing your world and making sense out of what you experience.

interpersonal perception. Selecting, organizing, and interpreting our observations of other people.

out constant sensations that you have learned are unimportant, such as the sensations of your clothes against your skin and the surrounding white noise and smells. However, you do attend to the sensation of the elastic bands of your underclothes if they pull too tight, because a threshold of arousal is crossed, forcing the brain to attend to that stimulus. Each of your senses has such a threshold.

Directing your attention to specific stimuli and consequently ignoring others is called **selective perception.** Your eye and your brain do not work like a camera, which records everything in the picture. When you develop film, you capture what was in the viewfinder. Your brain doesn't necessarily process *everything* you see through your "viewfinder." Similarly, your ear is not a microphone that consciously picks up every sound. Although the sounds are there, your brain selects sounds that are significant or important to you in some way.

In your interactions with others, you may choose to focus on specific cues such as gestures or foot movement. What specific qualities or features do you tend to focus on when you first meet others? Do you pay particular attention to handshakes, smiles, eye contact, body posture, gestures, or tone of voice? Sometimes people exercise selective perception when they are listening for a specific piece of information.

In a court of law, eyewitness testimony often determines whether someone is innocent or guilty of a crime. Recent research suggests, however, that a witness's powers of observation are not flawless. In fact, scientists have discovered several perceptual errors in eyewitness testimony. Many innocent people have been convicted because of what a witness thought he or she saw or heard.[3] As this evidence documents, the eye is not a camera; the ear is not a microphone.

Stage 2: Organizing

Look at the four items in Figure 3.2. What does each of them mean to you? If you are like most people, you will perceive item A as a rabbit, item B as a telephone number, item C as the word *interpersonal,* and item D as a circle. Strictly speaking, none of those perceptions is correct. We'll discuss why after we explore the second stage of perception: organizing.

After we select certain stimuli, we organize them into convenient, understandable, and efficient patterns that let us make sense of what we have observed. Organizing makes it easier for us to process complex information because it lets us impose the familiar onto the unfamiliar, and because we can easily store and recall simple patterns. For example, when you looked at item A in Figure 3.2, you saw the pattern of dots that you label a rabbit because a rabbit is a concept you know and to which you attach various meanings. The set of dots would not have meaning for you in and of itself, nor would it be meaningful for you to attend to each particular dot or to the dots' relationships to one another. It would be possible to create a mathematical model of the dots indicating their placement on an X–Y grid, but such a model would be extremely complex and difficult to observe and remember. It's much easier to organize the dots in a way that refers to something stored in your memory: a rabbit. For similar reasons, people organize patterns of stars in the sky into the various constellations with shapes like the bear, the crab, and the Big and Little Dippers. People also search for and apply patterns to their perceptions of other people. You might have a friend who jogs and works out at a gym. You put these together and label the friend "athletic." That label represents a pattern of qualities you use in relating to your friend that will be discussed later in the chapter.

selective perception. Directing your attention to specific stimuli and consequently ignoring other stimuli.

The way people organize information depends partly on the way they punctuate it. **Punctuation** is the process of making sense out of stimuli by grouping, dividing, organizing, separating, and categorizing information when communicating with others.[4] Just as punctuation marks on this page tell you when a sentence ends, punctuation in the perception process makes it possible for you to see patterns in information. To many Americans, Item B in Figure 3.2 looks like a telephone number because it has three numbers followed by four numbers. You might also remember that 555 is the prefix you use for calling information. However, the digits could just as easily represent two totally independent numbers: five hundred, fifty-five followed by the number four thousand, four hundred thirty-three. How we interpret the numbers depends on how we punctuate or separate them. When we record information, we use commas, periods, dashes, and colons to signal meanings and interpretations. In our minds we sometimes impose punctuation marks where we believe they should be. For example, we put a dash between 555 and 4433, even though no dash appeared there.

When it comes to punctuating relational events and behaviors, people each develop their own separate set of standards. You will sometimes experience difficulties and disagreements because of differences in how you and your partner choose to punctuate a conversational exchange or shared sequence of events.[5] For example, suppose you and a friend have been talking about her recent school problems. After a few moments of silence, you assume that your conversation on that topic has ended, so you start talking about your recent job interview. Later on, you find out that you offended your friend because she had not punctuated the conversation the same way. She believed that her problems should still have been the focus of the conversation. One classic example of relational problems resulting from differences in punctuation involves a husband who withdraws and a wife who nags.[6] The husband punctuates their interactions in such a way that he sees his withdrawing as a reaction to her nagging. The wife, in contrast, sees herself as nagging her husband because he keeps withdrawing. The husband and wife punctuate their perceptions differently because they each perceive different starting points for their interactions. Resolving such conflicts involves having the parties describe how they have punctuated the event, and agreeing on a common punctuation.

In addition to punctuating, you also **superimpose,** or place a familiar structure on information you select. Looking again at Figure 3.2, you can see that people's inclination to superimpose structure and consistency on what they observe also leads them to create a familiar word from the meaningless assemblage of letters in item C, and to label the figure in item D a circle, even though circles are continuous lines without gaps on the right side. This process of filling in missing information is called **closure.** We apply the same principles in our interactions with people. When we have an incomplete picture of another human being, we impose a pattern or structure, classify the person on the basis of the information we do have, and fill in gaps. For example, when meeting someone for the first time who looks and acts like someone you already know, you may make assumptions about your new acquaintance based upon the characteristics of the person you already know well. You superimpose attributes of the person whom you already know upon the stranger. Many of us are uncomfortable with uncertainty; providing closure and superimposing our assumptions upon a new acquaintance help us make better sense out of what is new and unfamiliar.

A.

B. 5 5 5   4 4 3 3

c. N T R P R S N L

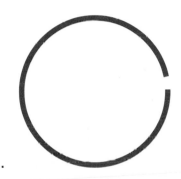

D.

Figure 3.2
What Do You See?

punctuation. Making sense out of stimuli by grouping, dividing, organizing, separating, and categorizing information.

superimpose. To place a familiar structure on information you select.

closure. Filling in missing information.

Stage 3: Interpreting

Once people have selected and organized stimuli, they are ready to interpret the stimuli. We attach meaning to all that we observe. We learn through socialization (what we learn from others) and our own recurring experiences to attribute meaning to particular stimuli. In some cases the meanings are fairly standard, as they are for language, for example. But others are much more personal. As the excerpt from "The Greek Interpreter" shows, the fictional detective Sherlock Holmes was noted for his ability to apply exacting interpretations to what he observed. In general, the heroes in mysteries usually excel in their ability to observe, organize, and interpret the stimuli around them. Sherlock and Mycroft Holmes possess an ability to attend to specific cues that you and I may miss. They also are able to organize the cues to create a unique meaning and interpretation. Seeing that the man in dark mourning clothes is carrying a baby's toy and picture book takes on special meaning when the two clues are combined.

Although not all of us have Sherlock Holmes's perceptual talents, we all attribute meaning to what we observe. If you shake someone's hand and it feels like a

Sherlock Holmes and His Brother Mycroft Make Some Observations
· ·

In this excerpt Sherlock Holmes is visiting his brother Mycroft. Both are looking out a window when Mycroft asks Sherlock what he makes of a very small, dark fellow with his hat pushed back and several packages under his arm standing on the street corner. Dr. Watson records their conversation:

"An old soldier, I perceive," said Sherlock.

"And very recently discharged," remarked his brother.

"Served in India, I see."

"And a non-commissioned officer."

"Royal Artillery, I fancy," said Sherlock.

"And a widower."

"But with a child."

"Children, my dear boy, children."

"Come," said I, laughing, "this is a little too much."

"Surely," answered Holmes, "it is not hard to say that a man with that bearing, expression of authority, and sun-baked skin, is a soldier, is more than a private, and is not long from India."

"That he has not left the service long is shown by his still wearing his ammunition boots, as they are called," observed Mycroft.

"He had not the cavalry stride, yet he wore his hat on one side, as is shown by the lighter skin on that side of his brow. His weight is against his being a sapper [army engineer]. He is in the artillery."

"Then, of course, his complete mourning shows that he has lost someone very dear. The fact that he is doing his own shopping looks as though it were his wife. He has been buying things for children, you perceive. There is a rattle, which shows that one of them is very young. The wife probably died in childbed. The fact that he has a picture-book under his arm shows that there is another child to be thought of."

From Sir Arthur Conan Doyle, "The Greek Interpreter."

building your skills

Perceptual Interpretations

Find a place where you can sit and watch people for a while. Write down as many observations as you can about the people that pass by or that are seated nearby. Try to make some interpretations based on your observations, just as Sherlock Holmes might have. What do you notice about their clothing, their shoes, the manner in which they walk? What are they carrying with them? Do they seem to be in a hurry? Can you tell which are students, teachers, or members of other professions? If you are watching other students, can you tell what their majors are?

If you get the chance, you might approach some of these people and see how accurate your observations are. People are generally open to hearing positive perceptions about themselves. You may want to hold back on sharing negative perceptions.

wet, dead fish, what is your reaction and interpretation? If you notice someone you don't know winking at you from across a room, what do you think? If a toddler is crying in a room full of people and a woman comes over and picks the child up, what do you assume about the woman? If you see a student glance over at another student's exam paper and then record an answer, what do you think the student has done? All these examples show people imposing meaning on what they observe to complete the perceptual process.

recap

The Interpersonal Perception Process

Term	Explanation	Examples
Selecting	The first stage in the perceptual process, in which we select sensations for our awareness	Sitting in your apartment where you hear lots of traffic sounds and car horns, but attending to a particular rhythmic car honking that seems to be right outside your door.
Organizing	The second stage in the perceptual process, in which we assemble stimuli into convenient and efficient patterns	Putting together the car honking with your anticipation of a friend's arrival to pick you up in her car to drive to a movie that starts in five minutes.
Interpreting	The final stage in perception, in which we assign meaning to what we have observed	Deciding the car honking must be your friend signaling you to come out to the car quickly because she's running late.

Perception and Interpersonal Communication

Interpersonal perception is a two-way street. Our perceptions of others affect the ways in which we communicate with them, and their perceptions of us affect the way they communicate with us.

We continually modify the topics, the language, and the manner in which we communicate according to the perceptions we have of others. For example, if you observe a woman in a track suit running in a park, you may conclude that she is a physical fitness fanatic. Then, if you strike up a conversation with her, you may bring up topics such as physical fitness, sports, and diet. But if she informs you that she knows nothing about those things and has just started jogging to offset the time she spends watching videos and eating potato chips, then you would probably shift your focus according to a revised perception. You might start talking about movies and the relative merits of rippled versus plain potato chips. Similarly, if you were talking to a child, you would probably use simple language rather than complex technical terminology. If you were talking to a person who is hearing impaired, you might slow down your speech and raise your speaking volume.

The way that others talk and behave also tells us a great deal about how they perceive us. Maybe you can remember the first time someone younger than you called you Mister, Ms., Mrs., or Miss (if it hasn't happened yet, it will). It probably surprised you to realize that someone perceived you as "old," or as someone with authority. We also analyze others' reactions to us for clues about their perceptions of who we are. For example, suppose your new college friends go out to play basketball, your favorite sport, but do not invite you. When you later ask them why, they say they always thought of you as the unathletic, studious type. Sometimes others' perceptions of us are surprising. If we never ask, we may never discover that they are inaccurate. The degree to which others have a conception of us that differs from our own is often a measure of the quality of the relationship. The stronger the interpersonal relationship, the closer our self-perceptions are to the perceptions others have of us.[7]

How much we notice about another person's communication behavior relates to our level of interest and need. Perception can be either a passive or an active process. **Passive perception** occurs simply because our senses are in operation. We see, hear, smell, taste, and feel things around us without any conscious attempt to do so.

Active perception is the process of seeking out specific information by intentionally observing and questioning; we make a conscious effort to figure out what we are experiencing. We actively perceive information when we are uncertain about what we are seeing or hearing. We've all heard noises that startle us and make us wonder, "What was that?" We then try to recall the sound and identify it, or we might investigate—seek out additional information.

passive perception. Perception that occurs because your senses are in operation.

active perception. Perception that occurs because you seek out specific information through intentional observation and questioning.

e-connections
The Power of Perception

How you make sense out of the world and share that sense with others describes the essential elements of the communication process. The way you make sense out of the world is through perception—the process of selecting, interpreting, and organizing what you experience. To further explore the role of perception in the way people make sense out of the world, click on to the home page of The Perception Lab from the School of Psychology at St. Andrews University in Scotland:

    http://psych.st-and.ac.uk:8080/research/perception lab

Or try this interactive site to explore your powers of perception:

    http://psych.hanover.edu/krantz/sentut.html

If you can gain information and reduce your uncertainty about others, then you can predict their reactions and behaviors, adapt your behaviors and strategies, and therefore maximize the likelihood of fulfilling your social needs.[8] Although this might sound calculating, it really isn't. If you enjoy outdoor activities such as camping and hiking, one of your goals in establishing social relationships is probably to find others who share your interest. So observing, questioning, and processing information to determine a potential friend's interests can help you assess whether the relationship will meet your goals. In Chapter 5 we discuss ways to improve your ability to gain information through more effective listening.

Perceiving Others

 s we collect information about others, we organize and interpret that information in various ways. Interpersonal perception involves three processes: forming impressions of others; applying implicit personality theories and mental constructs, which we use to organize information about people; and finally, developing attribution theories, which help us explain why people behave the way they do.

How We Form Impressions of Others

Impressions are collections of perceptions about others that we maintain and use to interpret their behaviors. Impressions tend to be very general: "She seemed nice," "He was very friendly," or "What a nerd!" According to **impression formation theory,** we form these impressions through perceptions of physical qualities and behavior, information people disclose about themselves, and information that third parties tell us. We select, organize, and interpret all these perceptions to create a general impression. We tend to form these impressions readily and part with them reluctantly. When we first meet someone, we form a first impression without having much information, and we often hold on to this impression throughout the relationship.

In one famous study conducted by Solomon Asch, individuals were asked to evaluate two people based on two lists of adjectives.[9] The list for the first person had the following adjectives: *intelligent, industrious, impulsive, critical, stubborn,* and *envious.* The list for the other person had the same adjectives, but in reverse order. Although the content was identical, respondents gave the first person a more positive evaluation than the second. One explanation for this is that the first words in each list created a first impression that respondents used to interpret the remaining adjectives. In a similar manner, the first impressions we form about someone often affect our interpretation of subsequent perceptions of them.

This effect of attending to the first pieces of information that we observe is called the **primacy effect.** We also tend to put a lot of stock in the last thing we observed, which is called the **recency effect.**[10] For example, if you have thought for years that your friend is honest, but today you discover that she lied to you about something important, that lie will have a greater impact on your impression of her than the honest behavior she has displayed for years. The primacy and recency effects explain why you are more likely to remember information at the beginning or end of a paragraph than you are to remember information in the middle.

impression. A collection of perceptions about others that you maintain and use to interpret their behaviors.

impression formation theory. Theory that explains how you develop perceptions about people and how you maintain and use those perceptions to interpret their behaviors.

primacy effect. Placing heavy emphasis on the first pieces of information that you observe about another, to form an impression.

recency effect. Placing heavy emphasis on the most recent information that you observe about another, to form or modify an impression.

When we're not sure about the meaning intended by another's message, it is wise to actively check out the meaning by asking what he or she meant by the words. (Bob Daemmrich/Stock Boston)

We also attempt to manage the impressions others form of us. We make guesses about how other people will interpret our own physical displays and behaviors; as a result, we attempt to manipulate those displays and behaviors to our advantage. Think about the first day of classes this semester. Did you think about what clothes you were going to wear to classes? Did you worry about how your hair looked, or your breath smelled? Most of us choose clothes that we think will create a positive statement and reflect who we are. In this way we attempt to manage the impressions others form of us. Our ability to manage such impressions effectively depends on our ability to socially decenter (as discussed in the next chapter) by looking at ourselves from other people's perspectives. The more accurate you are at determining how others will react to people's looks and behaviors, the more potential you have for adapting your own looks and behaviors.

How We Describe Others

Do you like to "people watch"? If you have some time on your hands while waiting for a friend, you may just start looking at people and make guesses about what these strangers may do for a living, or whether they are friendly or grumpy, peaceful or petulant, kind or mean. We make assumptions about their personality. Even with people we know well, we don't know everything about them. Most of us have developed an **implicit personality theory,** a pattern of associated qualities that we attribute to people, which allows us to understand them—whether we've met them 10 minutes ago or 10 years ago. We make guesses about who they are, based on what information we already have about them. Implicit personality theory provides a way of organizing the vast array of information we have about people's personalities.[11] Implicit personality theories are essentially stereotypes that we apply to people in general. We accomplish perceptual closure through the use of implicit personality theory; that is, we are able to fill in the blanks about a person's personality without actually having to observe additional qualities. Once you have determined that someone is a "warm" person, you automatically associate other related terms. Your implicit personality theory may be similar to that held by others in your culture, but each person forms his or her own individual theory. There is more consistency between the personality frameworks you would use to judge two strangers

implicit personality theory. Your own set of beliefs and hypotheses about what people are like.

e-connections

The Accuracy of Our Electronic Perceptions of Others

More and more people first "meet" in cyberspace before interacting face-to-face. Precisely how does communicating with someone via e-mail affect how accurately we make impressions of their personality or predict how our electronic partner feels about other issues? Researcher Rodney Fuller asked people to identify a person they hadn't met in person but with whom they had an e-mail exchange. He then asked them several questions to assess how sensitive they were to their Internet partner's feelings about several issues; the subjects answered the same questions about themselves. He also asked people to complete the same questions about people they had met live and in person. The results: People who interacted with others face-to-face were more likely to accurately assess how their colleagues would answer the questions. The e-mail–only group, in general, perceived their electronic partners to be more logical and analytical than they actually were. Patricia Walker, in her excellent book *The Psychology of the Internet,* concludes that we relate to others in type differently from the way we do in person. "Online," concludes Walker, "we appear to be less inclined to perform those little civilities common to social interactions. Predictably, people react to our cooler, more task-oriented impression and respond in kind." Our perception of others is based on the information we discern from our interactions with them. When communicating by e-mail, we have a more limited array of information to share. Electronic perceptions of others may be more "cool" than when meeting others face-to-face.

Source: Rodney Fuller, "Human-Computer-Human Interaction: How Computers Affect Interpersonal Communication," in D. L. Day, and D. K. Kovacs (Eds.) *Computers, Communication and Mental Models* (London: Taylor & Francis, 1996); and Patricia Walker, *The Psychology of the Internet* (Cambridge, England: Cambridge University Press, 1999), p. 17.

than there is between the personality framework you use and the one another person uses to describe the same stranger.

Implicit personality theories allow us to manage a lot of information effectively, but they also can lead us to incorrect conclusions about other people. How accurately does "happy" actually describe a "warm" person? There are probably unhappy warm people. In assuming a connection between these two concepts, you might have reached an erroneous conclusion about the other person. When you assume the warm person is happy, you might not perceive the person's need for support and nurturing. As a result, your responses will be inappropriate and lead to ineffective interpersonal communication.

One feature common to most of our implicit personality theories is the tendency to put people into one of two categories: those we like and those we don't like. Categorizing people as those we "like" often creates a **halo effect** in which we attribute a variety of positive qualities to them without even personally confirming the existence of these qualities. If you like me, you will put a halo around your impression of me, and then apply those qualities from your implicit personality theory that apply to people you like; such as, being considerate of other people, warm, caring, and fun to be with, and having a great sense of humor. However, if you don't like me, you might think of me more as a devil, attributing a variety of negative qualities from your implicit personality theory. This is called the **horn effect.**

Although implicit personality theory describes how we organize and interpret our perceptions of people's personalities in general, we develop categories for people, called *constructs,* that help us explain our perceptions of a specific person. According to psychologist George Kelly, a **construct** is a bipolar (something placed into two categories) quality we use to categorize people.[12] We may pronounce

halo effect. Attributing a variety of positive qualities to those you like.

horn effect. Attributing a variety of negative qualities to those you dislike.

construct. A bipolar quality that you associate with people as you conceptualize them.

To help us understand the people we know, we develop a set of constructs for each person. A highly perceptive person may see a whole array of constructs for this woman: whimsical, warm, dependable, friendly, generous, and kind. A person with a less developed set of constructs may see only the whimsical side of her. (Brigid Allig/Tony Stone Images)

someone as good or bad, athletic or nonathletic, warm or cold, funny or droll, selfish or generous, and so on.

Think about a close friend of yours. What qualities or constructs would you use to describe that person? What qualities differentiate that person from others? What qualities does that person share with others? **Cognitive complexity** is the ability to develop a long list of such personal constructs to describe people. Cognitive complexity varies in terms of differentiation, elaboration, and integration. Differentiation is the development of more and more constructs from which to draw in describing and differentiating among people. Elaboration is how abstract or refined each of your sets of constructs becomes. Integration is how well you organize your constructs. Each of these constructs becomes further developed as you move from childhood to adulthood.

Cognitive complexity affects and is affected by your perceptions. People who develop less complex sets of constructs see the world in simpler terms; they do not differentiate among people as well as a highly cognitively complex person would. A person with a highly developed set of constructs is aware of the motives and causes of people's actions and is able to pick up on their emotional states. Our sensitivity and perceptiveness provide us with the information we need to develop the construct systems we use to describe those people with whom we interact. Most importantly, a highly developed construct system enables us to take on another person's perspective, to empathize, and to orient toward the other person.

How We Interpret the Behavior of Others

"I know why Alice didn't come to our meeting. She just doesn't like me," says Cathy. "She also just wants people to think she's too busy to be bothered with our little group." Cathy seems not only to have made a negative impression of Alice, but Cathy also seems to harbor a hunch as to why Alice didn't come to the meeting. Cathy is attributing meaning to Alice's behavior. Even though Alice could have just

cognitive complexity. Level of ability to develop a sophisticated set of personal constructs

forgotten about the meeting, Cathy thinks Alice's absence is caused by feelings of superiority and contempt. Cathy's assumptions about Alice can be explained by attribution theory.

Attribution theory explains how we proscribe specific motives and causes to the behaviors of others. It helps us interpret what people do. For example, suppose the student sitting next to you in class gets up in the middle of the lecture and walks out. Why did the student leave? Did the student become angry at something the instructor said? No, the lecturer was simply describing types of cloud formations. Was the student sick? You remember noticing that the student looked a little flushed and occasionally winced. Maybe the student has an upset stomach. Or maybe the student is just a bit of a rebel, and often does strange things like leaving in the middle of a class.

Social psychologist Fritz Heider says that we are "naive psychologists,"[13] because we all seek to explain the motives people have for their actions. We are naive because we do not create these explanations in a systematic or scientific manner, but rather by applying common sense to our observations. Developing the most credible explanation for the behavior of others is the goal of the attribution process.

Causal attribution theory identifies three potential causes for any person's action: circumstance, a stimulus, or the person herself or himself.[14] Attributing to *circumstance* means that you believe a person acts in a certain way because the situation leaves no choice. This way of thinking places responsibility for the action outside of the person. You would be attributing to circumstance if you believed the student quickly left the classroom because of an upset stomach. Concluding that the student left because the instructor said something inappropriate would be attributing the student's action to the *stimulus* (the instructor). But if you knew the instructor hadn't said anything out of line, and that the student was perfectly healthy, you would place the responsibility for the action on the student. Attributing to the *person* means that you believe there is some quality about the person that caused the observed behavior. Attributions to the person are the ones we are most concerned with in this text because they are factors in impressions of others.

A number of factors affect the accuracy of our attributions: our ability to make effective and complete observations; the degree to which we are able to observe directly the cause and the effect; the completeness of our information; and our ability to rule out other causes. It is also helpful to know how unique the person's response is to the particular stimulus, to compare the person's response to how other people typically respond, and to know whether the person usually responds each time in the same way to the stimulus. Even with the most complete information, however, we can never completely understand another person's action because we cannot

attribution theory. Theory that explains how you generate explanations for people's behaviors.

causal attribution theory. Theory of attribution that is based on determining whether a person's actions are caused by circumstance, a stimulus, or the person.

become the other person. Fortunately, we can improve our level of understanding by using decentering and by becoming more sensitive to the assumptions or theories we use to make attributions.

recap   How We Organize and Interpret Interpersonal Perceptions

Theory	Description	Examples
Impression Formation Theory	We form global perspectives of others based on general physical qualities, behaviors, and disclosed information.	Categorizing people as nice, friendly, shy, or handsome.
Implicit Personality Theory	We develop a set of relationships among personality characteristics.	"If she is intelligent, then she must be caring, too."
Attribution Theory	We develop reasons to explain the behaviors of others. We attribute others' actions to the circumstance, a stimulus, or to the person.	"I guess she didn't return my call because she doesn't like me." "He's just letting off steam because he had a bad week of exams."

Identifying Barriers to Accurate Perception

Think about the most recent interaction you have had with a stranger. Do you remember the person's age, sex, race, or body size? Did the person have any distinguishing features, such as a beard, tattoos, or a loud voice? The qualities you recall will most likely serve as the basis for attributions you make about that person's behavior. But these attributions, based on your first impressions, might be wrong. Each person sees the world from his or her own unique perspective. That perspective is clouded by a number of distortions and barriers that contribute to inaccurate interpersonal perception. We'll examine these barriers next.

Ignoring Information

People sometimes don't focus on important information, because we give too much weight to information that is obvious and superficial.[15] Why do we ignore important information that may be staring us in the face? It's because of what we learned about attribution theory. We tend to explain the motives for a person's actions on the basis of the most obvious information rather than in-depth information we might have. When meeting someone new, we perceive his or her physical qualities first: color of skin, body size and shape, age, sex, and other obvious physical characteristics. We overattribute to these qualities, because they are so vivid and available, and ignore other details. We have all been victims of these kinds of attributions, some of us more than others. Often we are unaware that others are making biased attributions, because they do not express them openly. But sometimes we can tell by the way others react to us and treat us.

One female student described a job interview in which the male interviewer talked at her for fifteen minutes and then abruptly dismissed her without asking a single question. A male friend of hers with less distinguished academic qualifications and work experience spent forty minutes fielding questions from this same interviewer. Did the interviewer have a sex bias? Probably. Looking only at the female student's gender, he attributed qualities to her that he decided would make her unsuitable for the job. Instead of looking at the more specific information her résumé provided, he simply disregarded it. As discussed earlier, this tendency reflects our desire to simplify stimuli, but it can be dangerous and unfair.

Overgeneralizing

People treat small amounts of information as if they were highly representative.[16] This tendency also leads people to draw inaccurate, prejudicial conclusions.[17] For example, we authors may talk to two students and then generalize the impression we have of those two students to the entire student population. In a similar way, most people tend to assume that the small sampling of another person's behavior is a valid representation of who that person is. As you saw in Figure 3.2, you might create a rabbit even when you have only a few dots on which to base your perception.

Oversimplifying

People prefer simple explanations to complex ones. When Imelda picks you up late to go to a movie, she says, "Sorry, I lost track of the time." The next day, Mary also picks you up late to go to a movie. She says, "Sorry. You wouldn't believe how busy I've been. I ran out of hot water when I was showering and my hair dryer must be busted. It kept shutting off. Then I stopped to get something to eat and it took forever to get my order. And then it turned out they had it all messed up and had to redo it." Whose explanation can you accept more easily, Imelda's or Mary's?

Usually people prefer simple explanations; they tend to be more believable and easier to use in making sense of another's actions. But in reality our behaviors are affected by a multitude of factors, as Mary's explanation indicates. Unfortunately, it takes a lot of effort to understand what makes another person do what he or she does—more effort than we are typically willing to give.

Stereotyping

Preconceived notions about what they expect to find may keep people from seeing what's before their eyes and ears. We see what we want to see, hear what we want to hear. We stereotype others. To **stereotype** someone is to place someone in a rigid category and then interpret all the person's behavior from the framework of that category. The word *stereotype* was originally a printing term, referring to a metal plate that was cast from type set by a printer. The plate would print the same page of type over and over again. When we stereotype people, we place them into inflexible, all-compassing categories. We "print" the same judgments on anyone placed into a given category. We may even choose to ignore contradictory information that we receive directly from the other person. Instead of adjusting our conception of that person, we adjust our perception. The halo and horn effects discussed earlier are reflections of this tendency. For example, if an instructor gets an excellent

stereotype. Set of qualities that you attribute to a person because of the person's membership in some category.

Stereotypes can help us make sense out of the wide range of stimuli we encounter every day. But we also need to be sure that we don't overuse stereotypes and fail to see people as individuals. (Bill Bachmann/The Image Works)

paper from a student who she has concluded is not particularly bright or motivated, she may tend to find errors and shortcomings that are not really there, or she may even accuse the student of plagiarism.

Categorizing individuals is not an inherently bad thing to do, but it is harmful to hang on to an inflexible image of another person in the face of contradictory information. For example, not all mothers are responsible or loving. But because American culture reveres motherhood, we may not easily process our perceptions of a mother who is abusive or negligent.

Imposing Consistency

People overestimate the consistency and constancy of others' behaviors. When we organize our perceptions, we also tend to ignore fluctuation in people's behaviors, and instead see them as consistent. We believe that if someone acted a certain way one day, he or she will continue to act that way in the future. Perhaps you have embarrassed yourself in front of a new acquaintance by acting foolish and silly. At another encounter with this new acquaintance, you realize that the person is continuing to see your behavior as foolish, even though you don't intend it to be seen that way. The other person is imposing consistency on the perception of your inconsistent behavior.

In fact, everyone's behavior varies from day to day. Some days we are in a bad mood, and our behavior on those days does not represent what we are generally like. As intimacy develops in relationships, we interact with our partners in a variety of activities that provide a more complete picture of their true nature.

Focusing on the Negative

People give more weight to negative information than to positive information.[18] Job interviewers often ask you to describe your strengths and weaknesses. If you describe

building your skills

Preconceived Explanations

Think about your own preconceptions about cause–effect relationships. For each of the following, think about what your first explanation of the cause would be:

- A person not calling back after a first date
- A waitress giving you lousy service
- Your car not being repaired after you paid a high service fee
- A teacher being late for class
- A child who beats up on other kids

- A student who copies test answers from the student next to him
- A mother who refuses to let her teenage son drive the car on Friday nights

Now go back and generate as many alternative explanations for each behavior as you can. How can you be sure which explanation is correct?

---

five great strengths and one weakness, it is likely that the interviewer will attend more to the one weakness you mention than to the strengths. We seem to recognize this bias and compensate for it when we first meet someone by sharing only positive information about ourselves.

In another of the Solomon Asch experiments on impression formation, participants heard one of the following two lists of terms describing a person: (1) intelligent, skillful, industrious, warm, determined, practical, cautious; or (2) intelligent, skillful, industrious, cold, determined, practical, cautious.[19] The only difference in these two lists is the use of "warm" in the first list, and "cold" in the second. Despite the presence of six other terms, those with the "cold" list had a much more negative impression of the person than those with the "warm" list. One piece of negative information can have a disproportionate effect on our impressions and negate the effect of several positive pieces of information.

recap   Barriers to Accurate Perception

Ignoring information	We don't focus on important information because we give too much weight to obvious and superficial information.
Overgeneralizating	We treat small amounts of information as if they were highly representative.
Oversimplify	We prefer simple explanations to complex ones.
Stereotyping	We rely on our pre-existing rigid expectations about others to influence our perceptions.
Imposing consistency	We overestimate the consistency and constancy of others' behavior.
Focusing on the negative	We give more weight to negative information than to positive information.

Improving Your Perception Skills

With so many barriers to perceiving and interpreting other people's behavior accurately, what can you do to improve your perceptual skills? Increasing your awareness of the factors that lead to inaccuracy will help initially, and you will find further suggestions in this section. Ultimately, your improvement will depend on your willingness to grow as you expand your experiences, to communicate about your perceptions with others, and to seek out and consider others' perceptions of you. Realize that you have had a lifetime to develop these barriers and that it will take time, commitment, and effort to overcome their effects.

And just by reading this chapter you've gained greater understanding of how the perception process affects your relationships with others. Emulate Sherlock Holmes: Use your knowledge of the perceptual process to sharpen your own perceptions and conclusions. Here are additional strategies to help you become a more accurate perceiver.

Link Details with the Big Picture

Any skilled detective knows how to take a small piece of information or evidence and use it to reach a broader conclusion. Skilled perceivers keep the big picture in mind as they look for clues about a person. In this chapter we have encouraged you to become more sensitive to details when observing others. But be cautious of taking one scrap of evidence and spinning out inaccurate conclusions about a person. Just because someone may dress differently from you, or have a pronounced accent, don't rush to judgment about the person's competence based on such few snatches of information. Look and listen for other cues about your new acquaintance that can help you develop a more accurate understanding of who that person is. As we noted in this chapter, what we see first (primacy) or last (recency) may have the most powerful effect on our overall conclusion. Try not to use the early information to cast a quick or rigid judgment that may be inaccurate. Look at all the details you've gathered.

Become Aware of Others' Perceptions of You

The best athletes don't avoid hearing criticisms and observations from their coaches. Instead, they seek out as much feedback as they can about what they are doing right and wrong. Olympic training often involves the use of videotaped replays and computer analysis so that athletes can see themselves as others see them and use that perspective to improve their performance. It is difficult to be objective about our own behavior, so feedback from others can help us with our self-perceptions. The strongest relationships are those in which the partners are willing both to share and to be receptive of the perceptions of the other.

Increase Your Awareness

Your senses are constantly bombarding you with information, much of which you ignore. You can increase the amount of information you process from your senses by consciously attending to the input. When you interact with others, try to identify one new thing each time to focus on and observe. Watch gestures, eyes, the wrinkles around eyes, foot movements; listen to tone of voice. Each observation will provide information that potentially can improve the quality of your interactions. You may create additional problems, however, if you focus so narrowly on one element that you miss others or overestimate the meaning of irrelevant information. Try to notice as much detail as possible, but keep the entire picture in view.

Become Other-Oriented

Effective interpersonal perception depends on the ability to understand where others are coming from, to get inside their heads, to see things from their perspectives.

Becoming other-oriented involves a two-step process: social decentering (consciously *thinking* about another's thoughts and feelings) and empathizing (*responding emotionally* to another's feelings).[20] What does your boss think and feel when you arrive late for work? What would your spouse think and feel if you brought a dog home as a surprise gift? Throughout this book we offer suggestions for becoming other-oriented, for reminding yourself that the world does not revolve around you. Being other-oriented enables you to increase your understanding of others and improve your ability to predict and adapt to what others do and say.

To improve your ability to socially decenter, and to empathize, strive for two key goals: (1) Gather as much information as possible about the circumstances that are affecting the other person; and (2) gather as much information as possible about the other person. In the next chapter we expand on these ideas as we discuss in more detail how to adapt to others by decentering and empathizing. As we've emphasized before, being other-oriented is not a single skill, but a family of related communication skills (such as socially decentering, empathizing, listening, responding, interpreting verbal and nonverbal messages, appropriately adapting to others, and managing conflict).

Check Your Perceptions

You can check out the accuracy of your perceptions and attributions indirectly and directly. **Indirect perception checking** involves seeking additional information through passive perception either to confirm or to refute your interpretations. If you suspect someone is angry at you but is not admitting it, for example, you could look for more cues in his or her tone of voice, eye contact, and body movements to confirm your suspicion. You could also listen more intently to the person's words and language.

Direct perception checking involves asking straight out whether your interpretations of a perception are correct. This often is not easy to do, for several reasons: You don't like to admit uncertainty or suspicions to others; you might not trust that they will respond honestly; if your interpretations are wrong, you might suffer embarrassment or anger. But asking someone to confirm a perception shows that you are committed to understanding his or her behavior. If your friend's voice sounds weary and her posture is sagging, you may assume that she is depressed or upset. If you ask, "I get the feeling from your tone of voice and the way you're acting that

indirect perception checking. Seeking additional information to confirm or refute interpretations you are making through passive perception such as observing and listening.

direct perception checking. Asking for confirmation from the observed person of an interpretation or a perception about him or her.

It is a good idea to check the accuracy of your perceptions of another person's message by asking outright whether or not they are accurate. (Bill Horsman/Stock Boston)

you are kind of down and depressed; what's wrong?" your friend can then either provide another interpretation: "I'm just tired; I had a busy week"; or expand on your interpretation: "Yeah, things haven't been going very well...." Your observation might also trigger a revelation: "Really? I didn't realize I was acting that way. I guess I am a little down."

Ten Questions That Can Help You Become Other-Oriented

How to Take the Perspective of Another Person

1. What factors or circumstances are affecting the person?

2. How can I determine whether there are factors I don't know about or don't fully understand?

3. What do I know about this person that explains his or her behaviors and feelings?

4. What is going through the other person's mind at this time?

5. What are the other person's feelings at this time?

6. What other explanations could there be for the person's actions?

7. What would I think if I were in the same situation?

8. How would I feel if I were in the same situation?

9. What would other people think if they were in that situation?

10. What would other people feel if they were in that situation?

understanding **diversity**

Moving Beyond a First Impression

Because of the stereotypes that abound, many of us tend to form inaccurate impressions about people of other races. But as this brief story from an article about interracial friendships shows, we can use conversation skills to check out our perceptions directly and move beyond inaccurate first impressions.

Janet, twenty-five, and Eleanor, thirty-three, politely tiptoed around their differences at first, pretending they were both "just people." But when they became roommates on the verge of closeness, they confronted each other, "Why do you play only black music?" "How is your family going to react to me?" "Is it true that whites . . . ?" "Is it true that blacks . . . ?" They found that when they detached themselves from the stereotypes, they became friends despite their differences; in fact, they saluted their differences as part of their interest in each other.

From Bebe Moore Campbell, *MS.*

building your skills

Identifying Your Bias

Write down a list of some recent interpretations you've made about others' behaviors. Identify the specific behavior or quality that you have observed and the resulting interpretation. For example, Joe is a really big man (quality); therefore, he must be a football player (interpretation).

Identify which interpretations might have been affected by any of the biases we've talked about (for example, giving weight to information that is obvious and superficial).

See if you can find out the validity of those interpretations by collecting additional information. Ask Joe if he plays football, or look on the football roster for his name.

Summary

Interpersonal perception is a fundamental element of interpersonal communication. Our communication and interpersonal relationships are affected by the way we perceive those with whom we interact. Interpersonal perception involves more than just the arousal of the senses; it also involves selecting, organizing, and interpreting what we observe in order to decide what people are like and give meaning to their actions.

Our perceptions of others affect how we communicate, and how others perceive us affects how they communicate with us. Interpersonal perception can be a passive or active process. It is passive when only our senses are in operation; it is active when we feel a need for information and intentionally seek it. We are motivated to seek information in situations that have high amounts of uncertainty. Perception of information helps reduce uncertainty and provides us with more control of the situation.

Interpersonal perception affects and is affected by the development of impressions, our own implicit personality theories, and attributions. Our general impressions of individuals are often affected by primacy and recency effects; we pay particular attention to the first things we notice and the most recent things we notice about others. In our interactions with others, we all seem to operate as "naive psychologists," developing and applying our own implicit personality theories. These implicit personality theories represent the general way we believe people behave. We develop specific personal constructs that represent the qualities we associate with specific people we know. Finally, we try to explain the actions and behaviors of others through the process of attribution. According to attribution theorists, we seek to find out the intent and cause of a person's action; we see a person's action as a response to a given circumstance, a particular stimulus, or the person's own personality. To make rational and accurate attributions, we must overcome perceptual barriers. We can identify 10 specific tendencies that distort the accuracy of our attributions, such as focusing on obvious or negative information.

The following suggestions can help you to improve your interpersonal perception: (1) link details with the picture; (2) increase your awareness skills; (3) increase your awareness of others' perceptions of you; (4) become other-oriented; and (5) check your perceptions.

For Discussion and Review

Focus on Comprehension

1. In what ways does interpersonal perception affect interpersonal communication and relationships?
2. Identify and describe the three stages of the interpersonal perception process.
3. Explain the relationships among impression formation theory, implicit personality theory, and attribution theory.
4. Identify and explain five barriers to accurate perception.
5. How can you improve your perceptual skills?

Focus on Critical Thinking

6. Think about some of your recent interpersonal conflicts. How would you describe your perception of the problem in each conflict? How do you think the others would describe their perceptions of it? What role did perception play in contributing to or resolving the conflict?
7. What do you think contributes to the development of tendencies that cause people to perceive others inaccurately? How might the effects of those factors be minimized or eliminated?

Focus on Ethics

8. Do you have a right in an intimate relationship to expect your partner to share his or her perceptions of you, whether those perceptions are positive or negative? Explain your reasoning.
9. If you are aware of how you are distorting your own perceptions and attributions, should you try to change them? Is it a moral obligation? Explain your reasoning.

For Your Journal

1. As you interact with a friend, try to assess your awareness level of the cues that are being communicated. Ask your friend to confirm your interpretation of the cues you have observed. How effective and accurate were you at picking up information?

2. Use the list of barriers to accurate perception to do a self-analysis. Which barriers influence your perceptions the most? What problems do those distortions create in your interactions with others?

3. Choose two of the suggestions for improving your perceptions. Develop a plan for what you will do in your next interaction to apply that suggestion. Try the suggestion; then write an evaluation of how well you applied the suggestion, how well the suggestion worked, and how you might modify your plan to apply the suggestion in the future.

Learning with Others

1. Choose an advertisement, magazine illustration, photograph, or painting that shows a group of people, and bring it to class. In groups of four or five, pass around the pictures. For each picture, write down a few words to describe your perceptions about what you see in the picture. What are the people doing? What is their relationship to one another? What is each one like? How is each one feeling? Why are they doing what they are doing? After you have finished, share with one another what you wrote down. Try to determine why there were differences. What factors influenced your perceptions?

2. Pair up with someone in class whom you do not know and have not interacted with before. Without saying anything to each other, write down the words from the following list that you think apply to the other person. Now converse for five minutes. In a separate section of your paper, write down any additional words that you believe apply to the person. You can go back and put a line through any of the words in the first list that you now think are inaccurate. Share with your partner what words you put down before and during the conversation, and what words you changed. Have your partner share his or her perceptions of you. Discuss, as best you can, the reasons you chose each word.

intelligent	athletic	artistic	studious
nice	funny	conceited	friendly
introvert	extrovert	hard worker	shy
talented	popular	inquisitive	moody
emotional	happy	brave	responsible
leader	follower	uncertain	confused

4

Interpersonal Communication and Cultural Diversity: Adapting to Others

After you study this chapter

you should be able to ...

1. Define *culture*.

2. Identify cultural elements, values, and contexts.

3. Discuss differences and similarities in verbal and nonverbal communication in different cultures.

4. Discuss barriers that inhibit effective intercultural communication.

5. Identify strategies for developing knowledge, motivation, and skills that can improve intercultural competence.

● The Nature of Culture

● Barriers to Effective Intercultural Communication

● Improving Intercultural Competence

Culture is communication, and communication is culture.

EDWARD T. HALL

Perhaps you've heard the saying "Everyone's a little strange except you and me, and I'm not so sure about you." There is a kernel of truth in that sentiment. The simple fact is there is no one else exactly like you, which means that others can seem strange or different from you.

One of life's unprofound principles with profound implications for interpersonal communication is this: People each have different backgrounds and experiences. And, as you learned in the last chapter, people each perceive the world differently. To some degree, each person is estranged from others. There are differences between you and your best friend, even if you grew up together and lived in the same neighborhood.

The greater the difference in background, experience, and the manner in which you perceive others, the more challenging it can be to develop quality relationships with others. A central goal of your study of interpersonal communication is to learn how to better relate to others. Some of the differences that contribute to diversity and thus interfere with developing relationships include differences in age, learning style, gender, religion, ethnicity, sexual orientation, social class, race, and culture.

In the first three chapters, we acknowledged the influence of diversity on interpersonal relationships. In this chapter we examine in more detail the impact that people's differences have on their lives and suggest some communication strategies for bridging those differences in interpersonal relationships. Specifically, we focus on the nature of cultural difference, identify barriers that result from those differences, and suggest strategies that can help you better understand, appreciate, and adapt to people who are different from you. Our premise for this discussion of diversity is that in order to live comfortably in the twenty-first century, people must learn ways to appreciate and understand cultural differences instead of ignoring them, suffering because of them, or wishing that they would disappear.

Some people believe that diversity, especially cultural diversity, is overemphasized. One student overheard before class exclaimed, "I've had it with all this cultural diversity stuff. It seems like every textbook in every class is obsessed with it. My history textbook talks about all these obscure people I've never heard of before. In English lit all we're reading is stuff by people from different cultures. I'm tired of all this politically correct nonsense. I mean, we're all Americans. We're not all going off and live in China. Why don't they just teach us what we need to know and cut all this diversity garbage?"

Perhaps you've encountered this kind of "diversity backlash" among some of your classmates, or you may hold this attitude yourself. It may seem unsettling that textbooks are changing and that educators are concerned with cultural diversity. But these changes are not motivated by an irrational desire to be politically correct. They are taking place because the United States is changing. As suggested by the statistics in Understanding Diversity: A Diversity Almanac on page 99, the United States is becoming increasingly culturally diverse. With this growing diversity comes a growing awareness that learning about cultural differences can affect

A goal in our study of interpersonal communication is to learn how we can put aside differences in age, gender, race, or ability that might cause a barrier to effective communication. (Esbin-Anderson/The Image Works)

every aspect of people's lives in positive ways. You may not plan to travel the world, but the world is traveling to you. Your boss, teacher, religious leader, best friend, or marriage partner may have grown up with different cultural traditions than your own. Textbooks and courses are reflecting the change, not initiating it.

Researchers Guo-Ming Chen and William Starosta argue that the "political and economic effectiveness of the United States in the global arena will depend on individual and collective abilities to communicate competently with people from other cultures."[1] To support this claim, they note that

- Thirty-three percent of corporate profits in the United States stem from international trade.

- Half of the total profits from the twenty-three largest U.S. banks are derived from overseas.

- Foreign trade helps to generate four out of every five new jobs in the United States.

- The United States has more than $300 billion invested abroad.

- Foreign individuals and corporations have invested over $1.5 trillion in the United States in the last twenty-five years.[2]

- The United States does more international trade than any other country in the world.

As noted by one statistician, if the world were a village of 1,000 people, in the village would be 590 Asians, 123 Africans, 96 Europeans, 84 Latin Americans,

understanding
dive**r**sity

A Diversity Almanac

1. Two-thirds of the immigrants on this planet come to the United States.[3]
2. In the United States there are "minority majorities" (where minorities outnumber traditional European Americans) in Miami, Laredo, Gary, Detroit, Washington, DC, Oakland, Atlanta, San Antonio, Los Angeles, Chicago, Baltimore, Houston, New York, Memphis, San Francisco, Fresno, and San Jose.[4]
3. It is estimated that more than 40 million U.S. residents have a non-English first language, including 18 million people for whom Spanish is their first language.[5]
4. Almost one-third of U.S. residents under age 35 are members of minority groups, compared with one-fifth of those age 35 or older. According to U.S. Bureau of the Census population projections, by the year 2025 nearly half of all young adults in this country will come from minority groups.[6]
5. If the current trend continues, by the year 2050 the population of U.S. white ethnics will decrease to 53 percent, down from a current 80 percent. Asians will increase to 16 percent, up from 1.6 percent; Latinos will more than triple their numbers to over 25 percent, up from just over 6.5 percent; and African Americans will increase their proportion slightly from the current 12 percent.[7]
6. It is estimated that during the first ten years of the 21st century Vermont's Asian population will grow by 80 percent, Arizona's will increase by 52 percent, and the state of Delaware's by 56 percent.[8]
7. During the 1990s the U.S. foreign-born population increased four times faster than that of the native-born population.[9]
8. At the end of the 20th century, one in ten U.S. residents were born outside the country.[10]
9. One out of every eight U.S. residents speaks a language other than English at home, and one-third of children in urban U.S. public schools speak a first language other than English.[11]
10. To capture the United States's increasing complexity of racial diversity, the 2000 U.S. Census forms allowed respondents to mark one or more of fourteen categories of race. Because respondents could check more than one box, there were sixty-three racial possibilities. The six primary race categories are American Indian or Alaska Native, Asian, Black or African American, native Hawaiian or Other Pacific Islander, and White. The new multirace categories include American Indian or Alaska Native and White; Asian and White; Black or African American and White; and American Indian or Alaska Native and Black or African American.[12]

55 Former Soviet Union members and 53 North Americans.[13] Clearly, a global economy increases the likelihood that you will communicate with people from many of these different cultures. And you need not travel the world to communicate with people from other cultures. As noted in the Diversity Almanac, two-thirds of all immigrants on this planet come to the United States.[14]

Even though you may not have traveled to the four corners of the world, today's economical and swift transportation system increases the likelihood that you will travel abroad. As Peace Corps volunteer Charles Larson discovered when he traveled abroad, becoming immersed in a new culture has positive benefits. His Peace Corps opportunity was a transforming experience.

> I saw ways of life I would never have seen had I remained within the comfortable domain of my provincial Midwestern upbringing. For the first time, I learned to think of someone besides myself, to consider that there is no single way of observing a problem or answering a troubling question. I discovered that without the mutual tolerance and respect of other people's cultures, there is no possibility for harmony in our world.[15]

His experience helped him become more other-oriented, a quality we will continue to emphasize in this chapter.

Given the importance of culture and cultural differences, we will first turn our attention to defining the nature of culture; then we will identify barriers to effective intercultural communication; and finally, we will identify strategies that can improve your intercultural competence.

The Nature of Culture

Exactly what is culture? **Culture** is a learned system of knowledge, behaviors, attitudes, beliefs, values, and norms that is shared by a group of people.[16] In the broadest sense, culture includes how people think, what they do, and how they use things to sustain their lives. Researcher Geert Hofstede describes culture as the "mental software" that touches every aspect of how we make sense out of the world and share that sense with others.[17] Cultural diversity results from the unique nature of each culture. The elements, values, and context of each culture distinguish it from all others.

Sometimes when we speak of culture, we may be referring to a co-culture. A **co-culture** is a distinct cultural group within a larger culture. For example, about 80 percent of the population of the United States are classified as white, European American, or Caucasian. Members of minority groups such as African Americans, Latinos, and Asians develop a co-culture or what is called a *microculture*. Many communication researchers consider gender one of the most important co-cultures that significantly affect our communication with others. Gays and lesbians constitute another important co-culture in our society. The Amish, Mennonite, Mormon, and Jewish religious groups are examples of important religious co-cultures. Understanding Diversity: Our Range of Differences on page 102 describes both cultural and co-cultural variables that affect our interpersonal relationships with others.

Cultural Elements

culture. Learned system of knowledge, behavior, attitudes, beliefs, values, and norms that is shared by a group of people.

co-culture. Culture that exists within a larger cultural context (such as the gay and lesbian culture).

cultural element. Category of things and ideas that identify the most profound aspects of cultural influence (such as schools, governments, music, theater, language).

enculturation. Process of communicating a group's culture from generation to generation.

Categories of things and ideas that identify the most profound aspects of cultural influence are known as **cultural elements.** According to one research team, cultural elements include the following:

- *Material culture:* things and ideas
- *Social institutions:* schools, governments, religious organizations
- *Individuals and the universe:* system of beliefs
- *Aesthetics:* music, theater, art, dance
- *Language:* verbal and nonverbal communication system[18]

As we grow, we learn to value these cultural elements. You were not born with a certain taste in music, clothes, and automobiles. Through **enculturation,** the process of communicating a group's culture from generation to generation, you learned what you liked by choosing from among the elements available within your culture. Your friends, colleagues, the media, and most importantly, your family, communicate information about these elements and advocate choices for you to make.

The enculturation these women received growing up in Koreatown in Los Angeles was quite different from what they would have received had they lived in another neighborhood. (A. Ramey/Woodfin Camp & Associates)

Cultures are not static; they change as new information and new influences penetrate their stores of knowledge. We no longer believe that bathing is unhealthy, or that we can safely use makeup containing lead. These changes resulted from scientific discoveries. But other changes take place through **acculturation;** we acquire other approaches, beliefs, and values by coming into contact with other cultures. Today, acupuncture, yoga, t'ai chi, and karate studios are commonplace in most cities across America. Taco shells are available in every supermarket, salsa sales now

acculturation. Process through which an individual acquires new approaches, beliefs, and values by coming into contact with other cultures.

building your skills

Assessing Your Communication with Strangers

Your comfort level in communicating with strangers is related to your ability to communicate with people from other cultures. Respond to each statement by indicating the degree to which it is true of your communication with strangers: Always False (answer 1), Usually False (answer 2), Sometimes True and Sometimes False (answer 3), Usually True (answer 4), or Always True (answer 5).

_3_ 1. I accept strangers as they are.

_4_ 2. I express my feelings when I communicate with strangers.

_4_ 3. I avoid negative stereotyping when I communicate with strangers.

_5_ 4. I find similarities between myself and strangers when we communicate.

_5_ 5. I accommodate my behavior to strangers when we communicate.

_21_

To find your score, add the numbers you wrote next to each statement. Scores range from 5 to 25. The higher your score, the greater your potential for developing a strong relationship with someone from a different background.

Source: William B. Gudykunst, *Bridging Differences: Effective Intergroup Communication* (Newbury Park, CA: Sage, 1998), 143.

surpass ketchup sales, and Dunkin' Donuts sells bagels. In less obvious ways, "new" perspectives from other cultures have also influenced our thoughts, actions, and relationships.

Cultural Values

Identifying what a given group of people values or appreciates can provide insight into the behavior of an individual raised within that group. Although there are great differences among the world's **cultural values,** Geert Hofstede identified four variables for measuring values that are significant in almost every culture[19] (see Table 4.1 on page 104). According to Hofstede, each culture places varying degrees of value on masculine and feminine perspectives, avoidance of uncertainty, distribution of power, and individualism. Hofstede's research conclusions have been widely summarized to describe differences among these four key cultural values. Although his research has been criticized as being dated (his information is now more than thirty years old) and based primarily on males who worked at IBM (the primary source for much of his information), his research remains one of the most comprehensive, data-based studies of understanding cultural values.[20] He surveyed more

cultural values. What a given group of people values or appreciates.

---

understanding
diver**s**ity

Our Range of Differences

Cultural diversity includes more than differences in ethnic background or gender. To become other-oriented is to consider a range of differences that affect how we communicate and respond to others. Note the following differences that affect our interactions with others.

Age Different generations, because they share different cultural and historical events, often view life differently. If your grandparents experienced the Great Depression of the 1930s, they may have different attitudes about savings accounts from you or even your parents. Today's explicit song lyrics may shock older Americans who grew up with such racy lyrics as "makin' whoopee." The generation gap is real.

Religion Eating habits and attitudes toward abortion and use of alcohol are just a few of the factors in a person's religious beliefs and traditions that can affect relationships. Although most people in the United States are Christians, there is great diversity in the beliefs and practices of different denominations. Here is a breakdown of the top ten denominations by percentage of total U.S. population:

Percentage of population

1.	Roman Catholic	26.2%
2.	Baptist	19.4%
3.	Protestant (nondenomination)	9.8%
4.	Methodist	8.0%
5.	Lutheran	5.2%
6.	Christian	4.8%
7.	Presbyterian	2.8%
8.	Pentecostal	1.8%
9.	Episcopalian/Anglican	1.7%
10.	Mormon/Latter Day Saint	1.4%

The top five other religions in the United States are:

Percentage of population

1.	Judaism	1.8%
2.	Islam	.5%
3.	Buddhism	.4%
4.	Hinduism	.2%
5.	Bahaism	.01%

Disability Although you may not think of the disabled as part of the cultural diversity equation, there is evidence that we unconsciously alter our communication style when we converse with disabled people. For example, we make less eye contact with people who are in wheelchairs; we also afford them more personal space when conversing. We often speak more loudly and more slowly to those who are blind. Many disabled people find these behaviors insulting.

Social Class The U.S. Constitution declares that all people are created equal, but there is dramatic evidence that class differences exist

than 100,000 employees in more than 50 countries; his research effort has yet to be duplicated or surpassed.

Masculine versus Feminine Perspectives

Some cultures emphasize traditional male values, whereas others place greater value on female perspectives. These values are not really about biological sex differences but about overarching approaches to interacting with others.

People from **masculine cultures** tend to value more traditional roles for both men and women. Masculine cultures also value achievement, assertiveness, heroism, and material wealth. Research reveals that men tend to approach communication from a content orientation, meaning that they view communication as functioning primarily for information exchange. Men talk when they have something to say. This is also consistent with the tendency for men to base their relationships, especially their male friendships, on sharing activities rather than talking.

Men and women from **feminine cultures** tend to value such things as caring for the less fortunate, being sensitive toward others, and enhancing the overall quality of life.[21] Women, as research suggests, tend to approach communication for the purpose of relating or connecting to others, of extending themselves to other people to

masculine culture. Cultural values that emphasize achievement, assertiveness, heroism, and material wealth.

feminine culture. Cultural values that emphasize relationships, caring for the less fortunate, and overall quality of life.

and affect communication patterns. Social psychologist Michael Argyle reports that the cues we use to make class distinctions are (1) way of life, (2) family, (3) job, (4) money, and (5) education. Class differences influence whom we talk with, whether we are likely to invite our neighbors over for coffee, and whom we choose as our friends and lovers. Most of us must make a conscious effort if we want to expand beyond our class boundaries.

Gender In this book we emphasize how gender affects the way we listen, use words, and send and interpret nonverbal messages. Sex differences are biological differences between males and females: only men can impregnate, only women can menstruate, gestate, and lactate. But gender differences focus on learned behavior that is culturally associated with being a man or a woman. Gender role definitions are flexible: a man can adopt behavior that is associated with a female role definition in a given culture and vice versa.

Sexual orientation During the past two decades gays and lesbians have become more assertive in expressing their rights within American society. Issues such as whether gays belong in the military, in the clergy, and in the teaching professions have stirred the passions of many. Being gay has become a source of pride for some, but it is still a social stigma for others. The incidence of suicide among gay teenagers is significantly higher than among non-gay teens. Although gay people are gaining legal rights and protections, they are still subject to discriminatory laws and social intolerance. The gay and lesbian community functions as a co-culture or a culture within the larger U.S. culture.

Race According to the dictionary, race is based on the genetically transmitted physical characteristics of a group of people classified together on the basis of a common history, nationality, or geographical location. Skin color and other

physical characteristics affect our responses and influence the way people of different races interact. Racial prejudice still has a devastating effect on interpersonal communication patterns and relationships.

Ethnicity Ethnicity is a social classification based on a variety of factors such as nationality, religion, language, or ancestral heritage. Nationality and geographical location are especially important in defining an ethnic group. Those of Irish ancestry are usually referred to as an ethnic group rather than as a race. The same could be said of Britons, Norwegians, and Spaniards. Ethnicity, like race, fosters common bonds that affect communication patterns. On the positive side, ethnic groups bring vitality and variety to American society. On the negative side, members of these groups may experience persecution or rejection from members of other groups in our society.

Table 4.1

Examples of Countries that Illustrate Four Cultural Values

Cultural Value	Examples of Countries that Scored Higher on this Cultural Value	Examples of Countries that Scored Lower on this Cultural Value
Masculinity: People from countries with higher masculinity scores prefer high achievement, men being in more assertive roles, and more clearly differentiated sex roles than people from countries with lower scores on this cultural dimension.	Japan, Australia, Venezuela, Italy, Switzerland, Mexico, Ireland, Jamaica, Great Britain	Sweden, Norway, Netherlands, Denmark, Yugoslavia, Costa Rica, Finland, Chile, Portugal, Thailand
Uncertainty Avoidance: People from countries with higher uncertainty avoidance scores generally prefer to avoid uncertainty; they like to know what will happen next. People from countries with lower scores are more comfortable with uncertainty.	Greece, Portugal, Guatemala, Uruguay, Belgium, Japan, Yugoslavia, Peru, France	Singapore, Jamaica, Denmark, Sweden, Hong Kong, Ireland, Great Britain, Malaysia, India, Philippines, United States
Power Distribution: People from countries with higher power distribution scores generally prefer greater power differences between people; they are generally more accepting of someone having authority and power than are people from countries with lower scores on this cultural dimension.	Malaysia, Guatemala, Panama, Philippines, Mexico, Venezuela, Arab countries, Ecuador, Indonesia, India	Austria, Israel, Denmark, New Zealand, Ireland, Sweden, Norway, Finland, Switzerland, Great Britain
Individualism: People from countries with higher individualism scores generally prefer individual accomplishment rather than collective or collaborative achievement.	United States, Australia, Great Britain, Canada, Netherlands, New Zealand, Italy, Belgium, Denmark, Sweden, France	Guatemala, Ecuador, Panama, Venezuela, Columbia, Indonesia, Pakistan, Costa Rica, Peru, Taiwan, South Korea

Source: Adapted from Geert Hofstede, *Cultures and Organizations: Software of the Mind* (London: McGraw-Hill, 1991).

know them and be known by them.[22] What women talk about is less important than the fact that they're talking, because talking implies relationship.

A short way of summarizing this difference: *Men often communicate to report; women often communicate to establish rapport.*[23] So the point of difference isn't in the way the sexes actually communicate, but in the motivations for or reasons they communicate. The *how* may not be that different; the *why* may be very different.[24]

Of course, rarely is a culture on the extreme end of the continuum; many are somewhere in between. For centuries, most countries in Europe, Asia, and the Americas have had masculine cultures. Men and their conquests dominate history books; men have been more prominent in leadership and decision making than women. But today many of these cultures are moving slowly toward the middle—legal and social rules are encouraging more gender balance and greater equality between masculine and feminine roles.

Tolerance of Uncertainty versus Avoidance of Uncertainty

Sven works for a phone company in the United States as a customer service representative. He grew up in Finland, where there is sometimes a higher tolerance for bureaucratic uncertainty than there is in the United States. Jake is from Long Island, New York; he expects (sometimes demands) that his problems be resolved quickly. Sven's higher tolerance for uncertainty and Jake's desire for straight, prompt answers to questions created an oil-and-water confrontation. Jake phoned Sven to complain about the slow response to his request to have a new phone line installed for his fax machine. Sven tried to be reassuring, but Jake got the distinct impression that Sven was not sympathetic and thought that a week's wait for a new line was perfectly reasonable. Jake expected his new line within twenty-four hours. Both had difficulty tuning in to the cultural difference in their expectations about how quickly a bureaucracy should respond to an individual request.

Some cultures tolerate more ambiguity and uncertainty than others. Those in which people need certainty to feel secure are more likely to have and enforce rigid rules for behavior and develop more elaborate codes of conduct. People from cultures with a greater tolerance for uncertainty have more relaxed, informal expectations for others. "Go with the flow" and "It will sort itself out" are phrases that describe their attitudes. Sven and Jake's experience is explained by a study showing that people from Portugal, Greece, Peru, Belgium, and Japan have high certainty needs, but people from Scandinavian countries tend to tolerate uncertainty.[25]

Concentrated versus Decentralized Distribution of Power

Some cultures value an equal or decentralized distribution of power, whereas others accept a concentration of hierarchical power in a centralized government and other organizations. In cultures in which people prefer a more centralized approach to power, hierarchical bureaucracies are common, and people expect some individuals to have more power than others. Russia, France, and China are all high on the concentrated power scale. Those that often strive for greater equality and distribution of power and control include many (but not all) citizens of Australia, Denmark, New Zealand, and Israel. People from these latter countries tend to minimize differences in power between people.

Individual versus Group Achievement

Cealy: We've got this group project to do. Let's divvy up the work and then meet back here next week to see what each of us has done.

Ayako: Wait a minute, Cealy. It might seem to be more efficient to divide up the work into little separate pieces, but in the end we'll have a better report if we all work on every section.

Cealy: Are you kidding? We'll be here all night! Josh, you take the history of the problem. Bert, you look at problem causes and effects. Ayako, why don't you do a literature search on the Internet and start looking up articles.

Ayako: All right. But I still think it would be better to go to the library together. I think we'd have better luck if we worked on each aspect of the problem as a team.

Cealy and Ayako clearly have different strategies for working together. Cealy approaches the project from an individualistic perspective; Ayako prefers a collective or group strategy to achieve the goal. Traditionally, North Americans champion individual accomplishments and achievements. People from Asian backgrounds often value collective or group achievement more highly. One researcher summed up the American goal system this way:

> Chief among the virtues claimed . . . is self-realization. Each person is viewed as having a unique set of talents and potentials. The translation of these potentials into actuality is concurred the highest purpose to which one can devote one's life.[26]

In a collectivistic culture, conversely, people strive to attain goals for all members of the family, group, or community. In Kenyan tribes, for example,

> [N]obody is an isolated individual. Rather, his [or her] uniqueness is secondary fact.
>
> . . . In this new system group activities are dominant, responsibility is shared, and accountability is collective. . . . Because of the emphasis on collectivity, harmony and cooperation among the group tends to be emphasized more than individual function and responsibility.[27]

Individualistic cultures tend to be more loosely knit socially; individuals feel responsible for taking care of themselves and their immediate families.[28] In collectivistic cultures, individuals expect more support from others, also more loyalty to and from the community. Because collectivistic cultures place more value on "we" than "I," teamwork approaches usually succeed better in their workplaces. U.S. businesses have tried to adopt some of Japan's successful team strategies for achieving high productivity.

recap　Cultural Values

Masculine and Feminine	• Masculine cultures value achievement, assertiveness, heroism, material wealth, and more traditional sex roles.
	• Feminine cultures value relationships, caring for the less fortunate, overall quality of life, and less traditional distinctions between sex roles.
Uncertainty and Certainty	• Cultures that value certainty do not like ambiguity, and value feeling secure.
	• Cultures that value uncertainty are comfortable with ambiguity and less information.
Decentralized and Centralized Power	• Centralized cultures value having power in the hands of a small number of people.
	• Decentralized power cultures favor equality and an even distribution of power in government and organizations.
Individualistic and Collectivistic	• Individualistic cultures value accomplishments of individual achievement.
	• Collectivistic cultures value group and team collaboration.

Cultural Contexts

cultural context. Information not explicitly communicated through language, such as environmental or nonverbal cues.

Individuals from different cultures use **cultural contextual** cues in varying degrees to enhance messages and meaning. This led anthropologist Edward T. Hall to categorize cultures as either high- or low-context.[29] As shown in Figure 4.1, in

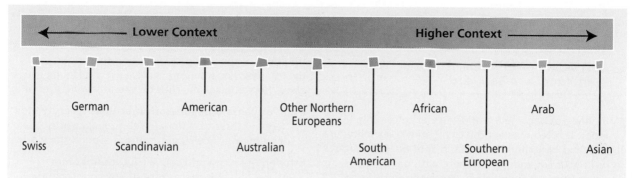

Low-Context Cultures
(Information must be provided explicitly, usually in words.)
- Are less aware of nonverbal cues, environment, and situation
- Lack well-developed networks
- Need detailed background information
- Tend to segment and compartmentalize information
- Control information on a "need to know" basis
- Prefer explicit and careful directions from someone who "knows"
- Consider knowledge a commodity

High-Context Cultures
(Much information drawn from surroundings. Very little must be explicitly transferred.)
- Consider nonverbal cues important
- Let information flow freely
- Rely on physical context for information
- Take environment, situation, gestures, and mood into account
- Maintain extensive information networks

Source: From Donald W. Klopf, *Intercultural Encounters: The Fundamentals of Intercultural Communication.* (Englewood, CO: Morton Publishing 1998, p. 33, and *Meeting News,* June 1993)

high-context cultures, nonverbal cues are extremely important in interpreting messages. **Low-context cultures** rely more explicitly on language, and use fewer contextual cues to send and interpret information. Individuals from high-context cultures may perceive people from low-context cultures as less attractive, knowledgeable, and trustworthy, because they violate unspoken rules of dress, conduct, and communication. Individuals from low-context cultures often are not skilled in interpreting unspoken, contextual messages.[30]

Figure 4.1

High/Low Contexts: Where Different Cultures Fall on the Context Scale

 recap

The Nature of Culture

Cultural Elements	Things and ideas that represent profound aspects of cultural influence, such as art, music, schools, and belief systems.
Cultural Values	What a culture reveres and holds important.
Cultural Contexts	Information not explicitly communicated through language, such as environmental or nonverbal cues. High-context cultures (such as Japanese, Chinese, Korean) derive much information from these cues. Low-context cultures (such as North American, Western European) rely more heavily on words.

high-context culture. Culture that derives much information from nonverbal and environmental cues.

low-context culture. Culture that derives much information from the words of a message and less information from nonverbal and environmental cues.

Barriers to Effective Intercultural Communication

Sari, who had recently moved from New York to New Orleans, couldn't understand it. The dinner party was supposed to start at 7 P.M., but when she drove up, hers was the only car in front of the house. She felt frustrated and began mumbling to herself that she couldn't believe guests could be so discourteous. Finally, after about 20 minutes, another guest arrived. Then another. Not until 7:45 was everyone present who had been invited. What Sari didn't understand was that most of the guests came from a cultural background where a half-hour delay in the starting time for social events was normal. Sari expected punctuality, but most of the other guests assumed that the dinner party would just start when everyone was ready.

Intercultural communication occurs when individuals or groups from different cultures communicate. The transactional process of listening and responding to people from different cultural backgrounds can be challenging. The greater the difference in culture between two people, the greater the potential for misunderstanding and mistrust.

Misunderstanding and miscommunication occur between people from different cultures because of different coding rules and cultural norms, which play a major role in shaping patterns of interaction. The greater the difference between the cultures, the more likely it is that they will use different verbal and nonverbal codes. When you encounter a culture that has little in common with your own, you may experience **culture shock,** or a sense of confusion, anxiety, stress, and loss. If you

intercultural communication. Communication between or among people who have different cultural traditions.

culture shock. Feeling of stress and anxiety a person experiences when encountering a culture different from his or her own.

are visiting or actually living in the new culture, your uncertainty and stress may take time to subside as you learn the values and codes that characterize the culture. But if you are simply trying to communicate with someone from a background very different from your own—even on your home turf—you may find the suggestions in this section helpful in closing the communication gap.[31]

The first step to bridging differences between cultures is to find out what hampers effective communication. What keeps people from connecting with others from other cultures? Sometimes it is different meanings created by different languages or by different interpretations of nonverbal messages. Sometimes it is the inability to stop focusing on oneself and begin focusing on the other. We'll examine some of these barriers first, then discuss strategies and skills for overcoming them.

Ethnocentrism

Marilyn had always been intrigued by Russia. Her dream was to travel the country by train, spending time in small villages as well as exploring the cultural riches of Moscow, Pyatigorsk, and St. Petersburg. Her first day in Russia was a disappointment, however. When she arrived in Moscow, she joined a tour touting the cultural traditions of Russia. When the tour bus stopped at Sparrow Hills, affording the visitors a breathtaking hilltop view of the Moscow skyline, she was perplexed and mildly shocked to see women dressed in elegant wedding gowns mounted on horseback and galloping through the parking lot. Men in suits were cheering them on as a crowd of tipsy revelers set off fireworks and danced wildly to a brass band. "What kind of people are these?" sniffed Marilyn.

"Oh," said the tour guide, "it is our custom to come here to celebrate immediately following the wedding ceremony."

"But in public with such raucousness?" queried Marilyn.

 Colorful celebrations like this ritual purification ceremony in Bali can reinforce healthy ethnic pride. When this pride is taken to the extreme through ethnocentric feelings, barriers between groups may result. (Michael Burgess/Stock Boston)

"It is our tradition," said the guide.

"What a backward culture. They're nothing but a bunch of peasants!" pronounced Marilyn, who was used to more refined nuptial celebrations at a country club or an exclusive hotel.

For the rest of the tour Marilyn judged every Russian behavior as inferior to that of Westerners. That first experience colored her perceptions, and her ethnocentric view served as a barrier to effective interpersonal communication with the Russian people she met.

Ethnocentrism stems from a conviction that our own cultural traditions and assumptions are superior to those of others. In short, it is the opposite of an other-orientation that embraces and appreciates the elements that give another culture meaning. This kind of cultural snobbism is one of the fastest ways to create a barrier that inhibits rather than enhances communication.

The concept of ethnocentrism is not new. Almost 100 years ago W. G. Sumner defined it as "The technical name of this view of things in which one's own group is the center of everything and all others are scaled and rated with reference to it."[32] Many scholars have found that virtually all cultural groups are ethnocentric to some degree.[33] Some even argue that it's not always bad to see one's own cultural group as superior; ethnocentric tendency enhances group pride and patriotism and encourages cultural traditions.[34] A problem occurs, however, when a group views our preferences for doing things as *always* the best way. Extreme ethnocentrism creates a barrier between the group and others.

Different Communication Codes

You are on your first trip to Los Angeles. As you step off the bus and look around for Hollywood Boulevard, you realize you have gotten off at the wrong stop. You see what looks like an old-fashioned corner grocery store with "Bodega" painted on a red sign. So you walk in and ask the man behind the counter, "How do I get to Hollywood Boulevard, please?"

"*No hablo Ingles,*" says the man, smiling and shrugging his shoulders. But he points to a transit map pasted onto the wall behind the counter.

Today, even when you travel within the United States, you are likely to encounter people who do not speak your language. Obviously, this kind of intercultural difference poses a formidable communication challenge. And even when you do speak the same tongue as another, he or she may come from a place where the words and gestures have different meanings. Your ability to communicate will depend on whether you can understand each other's verbal and nonverbal codes.

In the preceding example, although the man behind the counter did not understand your exact words, he noted the cut of your clothing, your backpack, and your anxiety, and he deduced that you were asking directions. And you could understand what his gesture toward the transit map meant. Unfortunately, not every communication between the users of two different languages is this successful.

Even when language is translated, there can be missed or mangled meaning. Note the following examples of mistranslated advertisements:

● A General Motors auto ad with "Body by Fisher" became "Corpse by Fisher" in Flemish.

ethnocentrism. Belief that your cultural traditions and assumptions are superior to others.

building your skills

Assessing Your Ethnocentrism

The following measure of ethnocentrism was developed by communication researchers James Neuliep and James McCroskey. Answer the following questions honestly.

This instrument is composed of 24 statements concerning your feelings about your culture and other cultures. In the space provided to the left of each item indicate the degree to which the statement applies to you by marking whether you (5) strongly agree, (4) agree, (3) are neutral, (2) disagree, or (1) strongly disagree with the statement. There are no right or wrong answers. Work quickly and record your first response.

___2___ 1. Most other cultures are backward compared with my culture.

___3___ 2. People in other cultures have a better lifestyle than we do in my culture.

_4_2___ 3. Most people would be happier if they didn't live like people do in my culture.

___1___ 4. My culture should be the role model for other cultures.

_1_5___ 5. Lifestyles in other cultures are just as valid as those in my culture.

___2___ 6. Other cultures should try to be more like my culture.

___2___ 7. I'm not interested in the values and customs of other cultures.

___3___ 8. It is not wise for other cultures to look up to my culture.

_2_4___ 9. People in my culture could learn a lot from people in other cultures.

___2___ 10. Most people from other cultures just don't know what's good for them.

_2_4___ 11. People from my culture act strange and unusual when they go into other cultures.

___1___ 12. I have little respect for the values and customs of other cultures.

___3___ 13. Most people would be happier if they lived like people in my culture.

___2___ 14. People in my culture have just about the best lifestyles of anywhere.

_4_2___ 15. My culture is backward compared with most other cultures.

___3___ 16. My culture is a poor role model for other cultures.

___1___ 17. Lifestyles in other cultures are not as valid as those in my culture.

___3___ 18. My culture should try to be more like other cultures.

_2_4___ 19. I'm very interested in the values and customs of other cultures.

_2_4___ 20. Most people in my culture just don't know what is good for them.

___2___ 21. People in other cultures could learn a lot from people in my culture.

___3___ 22. Other cultures are smart to look up to my culture.

_2_4___ 23. I respect the values and customs of other cultures.

___3___ 24. People from other cultures act strange and unusual when they come into my culture.

To determine your ethnocentrism **reverse** your score for items 2, 3, 5, 8, 9, 11, 15, 16, 18, 19, 20, and 23. For these items, 5 = 1, 4 = 2, 3 = 3, 2 = 4, and 1 = 5. That is, if your original score was a 5, change it to a 1. If your original score was a 4, change it to a 2, and so forth. Once you have reversed your score for these 12 items, add up all 24 scores. This is your generalized ethnocentrism score. Scores greater than 80 indicate high ethnocentrism. Scores of 50 and below indicate low ethnocentrism.   54

Source: J. W. Neuliep and J. C. McCroskey, "The Development of a U.S. and Generalized Ethnocentrism Scale," *Communication Research Reports,* 14 (1997), 393.

- A Colgate-Palmolive toothpaste named "Cue" was advertised in France before anyone realized that *Cue* also happened to be the name of a widely circulated pornographic book about oral sex.
- Pepsi-Cola's "Come Alive With Pepsi" campaign, when it was translated for the Taiwanese market, conveyed the unsettling news that "Pepsi brings your ancestors back from the grave."
- Parker Pen could not advertise its famous "Jotter" ballpoint pen in some languages because the translation sounded like "jockstrap" pen.
- One American airline operating in Brazil advertised that it had plush "rendezvous lounges" on its jets, unaware that in Portuguese (the language of Brazil) "rendezvous" implies a special room for making love.[35]

Stereotyping and Prejudice

All Europeans dress fashionably.

All Asians are good at math.

All Americans like to drive big cars.

These statements are stereotypes. They are all inaccurate. As we discussed in Chapter 3, to **stereotype** someone is to push him or her into an inflexible, all-encompassing category. Our tendency to simplify sensory stimuli can lead us to adopt stereotypes as we interpret and label the behavior of others. This becomes a barrier to effective intercultural communication when we fail to consider the uniqueness of individuals, groups, or events. Two anthropologists suggest that every person is, in some respects, (1) like all other people, (2) like some other people, and (3) like no other people.[36] The challenge when meeting others is to sort out how they are alike and how they are unique.

Can stereotypes play any useful role in interpersonal communication? It may sometimes be appropriate to draw on stereotypes, or generalizations drawn from limited instances. If, for example, you are alone and lost in a large city at two o'clock in the morning and another car repeatedly taps your rear bumper, it would be prudent to try to drive away as quickly as possible, rather than to hop out of your car to make a new acquaintance. You would be wise to prejudge that the other driver might have some malicious intent. In most situations, however, **prejudice**—prejudging someone on the basis of stereotypes or before you know all the facts—inhibits effective communication, especially if your labels are inaccurate or assume superiority on your part.

Certain prejudices are widespread. Although there are more females than males in the world, one study found that even when a male and a female hold the same type of job, the male's job is considered more prestigious than the female's.[37] Today, gender and racial discrimination in hiring and promotion is illegal in the United States. But some personal opinions have not kept pace with the law. In 1997 a University of Texas professor created a firestorm of controversy with his remarks that certain minorities "come from cultures in which failure is not looked upon in disgrace" and thus cannot compete at selective colleges and universities.[38] Outraged university officials feared that the professor's inflammatory stereotyping would hamper their efforts to attract and retain minority students. The professor's comments resulted in a renewed focus on affirmative action programs and college admissions policies.

stereotype. To place a person or group of persons into an inflexible, all-encompassing category.

prejudice. Prejudging someone before you know all of the facts or background of that person.

Assuming Similarity

Just as it is inaccurate to assume that all people who belong to another social group or class are worlds apart from you, it is usually erroneous to assume that others act and think just as you do. Even if they appear to be like you, all people are not alike. Although this statement is not profound, it has profound implications. Like Sari, who *assumed* that others would value punctuality as she did, people often make the mistake of assuming that others value the same things they do, maintaining a self-focused perspective instead of an other-oriented one. As you saw in Chapter 3, focusing on superficial factors such as appearance, clothing, and even a person's occupation, can lead to false impressions. Instead, you must take the time to explore the person's background and cultural values before you can determine what you really have in common.

Improving Intercultural Competence

Eleanor Roosevelt once said, "We have to face the fact that either all of us are going to die together or we are going to live together, and if we are to live together we have to talk."[39] In essence, she was saying that to overcome differences people need effective communication skills. It is not enough just to point to the barriers to effective intercultural communication and say, "Don't do that." Although identifying the causes of misunderstanding is a good first step to becoming interculturally competent, most people need help with specific strategies to help them overcome these barriers. In this book and in this chapter, we want to focus attention on the interpersonal communication strategies that can lead to intercultural communication competence.

The remaining portion of this chapter presents three sets of strategies to help you bridge differences between yourself and people who come from a different cultural background. These three strategy sets—appropriate knowledge, motivation, and skill—are based on our understanding of how to be a competent communicator.

Our suggestion to enhance your understanding or **knowledge** of others is based on the assumption that knowing more about others is important in quality relationships. One of the barriers to effective intercultural communication is having different communication codes. Improving your knowledge of how others communicate can reduce the impact of this barrier. We offer strategies to help you learn more about other cultures by actively pursuing information about others.

A second set of strategies focuses on becoming motivated to improve our intercultural communication knowledge and skills. **Motivation** is an internal state of readiness to respond to something. A competent communicator wants to learn and improve; an incompetent communicator is not motivated to develop new skills. Technically, no one can motivate you to do something; motivation comes from within. But developing strategies to appreciate others who are different from you may help you appreciate different cultural approaches to communication and relationships. We suggest you endeavor to be tolerant of uncertainty and to avoid knee-jerk negative evaluations of others.

knowledge. One of the elements necessary to become a competent communicator; information that enhances understanding of others.

motivation. Internal state of readiness to respond to something. An element of interpersonal competence.

Ethnocentric Thinking

All good people agree,
And all good people say,
All nice people like Us, are We,
And everyone else is They.

In a few short lines, Rudyard Kipling captured the essence of what sociologists and anthropol-ogists call ethnocentric thinking. Members of all societies tend to believe that "All nice people like Us, are We...." They find comfort in the familiar and often denigrate or distrust others. Of course, with training and experience in other climes, they may learn to transcend their provincialism, placing themselves in others' shoes. Or, as Kipling put it,

... if you cross over the sea,
Instead of over the way,
You may end by (think of it!)
looking on We
As only a sort of They.

In a real sense, a main lesson of the sociology of intergroup relations is to begin to "cross over the sea," to learn to understand why other people think and act as they do and to be able to empathize with their perspectives.

Source: Adapted from Faun B. Evans, Barbara Gleason, and Mark Wiley, *Cultural Tapestry: Readings for a Pluralistic Society* (New York: HarperCollins, 1992).

The final set of strategies, developing **skill** in adapting to others, focuses on specific behaviors that can help overcome the barriers and cultural differences we have discussed. Here, to address the barrier of ethnocentrism, we will identify the advantages of becoming a more flexible communicator. We will also describe the essential competence of becoming other-oriented—focusing on the needs, goals, and values of others, instead of only on yourself. As we discussed in Chapter 1, becoming other-oriented is critical to the process of relating to others.

Developing Knowledge: Strategies to Understand Others Who Differ from Us

Knowledge is power. To increase your knowledge of others who are different from you, we suggest that you actively seek information about others, ask questions and listen for the answers, and establish common ground. Let's discuss these strategies in more detail.

Seek Information About the Culture

Prejudice stems from ignorance. Learning about another person's values, beliefs, and behaviors can help you understand his or her messages and their meaning. Every person has a **world view** based on cultural beliefs about the universe and key issues such as death, God, and the meaning of life.[40] According to communication scholar Carley Dodd, "A culture's world view involves finding out how the culture perceives the role of various forces in explaining why events occur as they do in a social setting."[41] These beliefs shape our thoughts, language, and behavior. Only through intercultural communication can we hope to understand how each individual views the world. As you speak to a person from another culture, think of yourself as a detective watching for implied, often unspoken messages that provide information about the values, norms, roles, and rules of that person's culture.

You can also prepare yourself by studying the culture. If you are going to another country, courses in the history, anthropology, art, or geography of that place can give you a head start on communicating with understanding. Learn not only from books

skill. Behavior that improves the effectiveness or quality of communicating with others.

world view. Perception shared by a culture or group of people about key beliefs and issues, such as death, God, and the meaning of life, which influences interaction with others.

and magazines, but also from individuals whenever possible. Even in a high-context culture, no one will fault you for asking directly for help if you show a sincere desire to learn. If you are trying to communicate with someone closer to home who is from a different background, you can study magazines, music, food, and other readily available sources of information about his or her culture. Or exchange visits to one another's homes or hangouts to observe and learn more about the person.

Given the inextricable link between language and culture, the more you learn about another language, the more you will understand the traditions and customs of the culture. Politicians have long known the value of using even a few words of their constituents' language. President Kennedy impressed and excited a crowd in Berlin by proclaiming, "Ich bin ein Berliner," ("I am a Berliner"). Even though his diction was less than perfect, he conveyed the message that he identified with his listeners. Speaking even a few words can signify your interest in learning about the language and culture of others.

As we noted at the beginning of this chapter, when we speak of culture, we are also referring to co-cultures. A co-culture is a cultural group within a larger culture. Learning how men and women, each a separate co-culture, communicate differently can help us improve our communication with the opposite gender. Men, for example, are more likely to develop friendships through participating in common activities with other men (playing on a baseball team, working together).[42] Women are more likely to develop friendships through talking together rather than working together.

Reading books about differences between the way men and women communicate is one strategy to help both sexes improve understanding and develop insight into different approaches to communication. Deborah Tannen's book *You Just Don't Understand* and John Gray's bestseller *Men Are from Mars, Women Are from Venus* are popular books that can help create a dialogue between men and women about communication differences and thus promote greater knowledge about how to improve communication.

As you read about other cultures or co-cultures, it is important not to develop rigid categories or stereotypes for the way others may talk or behave. Proclaiming "Oh, you're just saying that because you're a man" or "You women always say things like that" can increase rather than decrease communication barriers. Throughout this book we discuss research-based gender differences in the way men and women communicate to enhance your understanding and improve communication with members of the opposite sex. But we don't recommend that you treat men and women as completely separate species from different planets or automatically assume you will immediately misunderstand the opposite sex.

Ask Questions and Listen Effectively

When you encounter a person from another background, asking questions, then pausing to listen, is a simple technique for gathering information and also for confirming the accuracy of your expectations and assumptions. Some cultures, such as the Japanese, have rigid expectations regarding gift giving. It is better to ask what these expectations are than to assume that your good old down-home manners will see you through.

When you ask questions, be prepared to share information about yourself, too. Otherwise, your partner may feel as if you are interrogating him or her as a way to gain power and dominance rather than from a sincere desire to learn about cultural rules and norms.

Communication helps to reduce the uncertainty that is present in any relationship.[43] When you meet people for the first time, you are highly uncertain about who they are and what they like and dislike. When you communicate with someone from another culture, the uncertainty level is particularly high. As you begin to interact, you exchange information that helps you develop greater understanding. If you continue to ask questions, eventually you will feel less uncertain about how the person is likely to behave.

Just asking questions and sharing information about yourself is not sufficient to bridge differences in culture and background. It is equally important to listen to what others share. In the next chapter we provide specific strategies for improving your listening skills.

Develop a "Third Culture"

Several researchers suggest that one of the best ways to enhance understanding when communicating with someone from a different cultural background is to develop a **third culture.** This is created when the communication partners join aspects of separate cultures to create a third, "new" culture that is more comprehensive and inclusive than either of the two separate cultures.[44] The goal of developing a third-culture mentality is to reduce our tendency to approach cultural differences from an "us" versus "them" point of view. Rather than trying to eliminate communication barriers stemming from two different sets of experiences, adopting a third-culture framework seeks to create a new understanding of both participants for each other.[45]

Consider the example of Marsha, a businesswoman from Lincoln, Nebraska, and Tomiko, a businesswoman from Tokyo, Japan. In the context of their business relationship, it would be difficult for them to develop a comprehensive understanding of each other's cultural traditions. However, if they openly acknowledged the most significant of these differences and sought to create a third culture by identifying explicit rules and norms for their interaction, they might be able to develop a more comfortable relationship with each other.

third culture. Establishing common ground by joining separate cultures to create a third, "new," more comprehensive and inclusive culture.

The relationship between this Himalayan Sherpa and Western trekker can be made more comfortable for both of them if they develop a "third culture," different from both of their cultures, with its own rules and expectations. (David Robbins/Tony Stone Images)

As described by communication researcher Benjamin Broome, the third culture "is characterized by unique values and norms that may not have existed prior to the dyadic [two-person] relationship."[46] Broome labels the essence of this new relationship **relational empathy,** which permits varying degrees of understanding, rather than requiring complete comprehension of another's culture or emotions.

One of the barriers to effective intercultural communication is having different communication codes. In seeking a third culture, you are seeking a way to develop a common code or framework to enhance understanding. Developing such a code that both individuals can understand may include each party's learning the language of the other. It can also include discussing meanings of nonverbal communication so that misunderstandings can be reduced. Further, it involves using the perception check skill we discussed in the previous chapter.

The cultural context includes all the elements of the culture (learned behaviors and rules or "mental software") that affect the interaction. Do you come from a culture that takes a tea break each afternoon at 4 P.M.? Does your culture value hard work and achievement, or relaxation and enjoyment? Creating a third culture acknowledges the different cultural contexts and interactions participants have experienced and seeks to develop a new context for future interaction.

Develop Knowledge to Enhance Understanding

Seek Information About the Culture	Learn about a culture's world view.
Ask Questions and Listen	Reduce uncertainty by asking for clarification and listening to the answer.
Develop a Third Culture	Create common ground.

Developing Motivation: Strategies to Accept Others Who Differ from Us

Competent communicators want to learn and improve. They are motivated to enhance their ability to relate to others and to accept others as they are. A key to accepting others is to develop a positive attitude of tolerance and acceptance of those who are different from you. We suggest three strategies to help improve your acceptance and appreciation of others who differ from you: Tolerate ambiguity, develop mindfulness, and avoid negative judgments of others.

Tolerate Ambiguity

Communicating with someone from another culture produces uncertainty. It may take time and several exchanges to clarify a message. Be patient and try to expand your capacity to tolerate ambiguity if you are speaking to someone with a markedly different world view.

When Ken and Rita visited Miami, they asked their hotel concierge to direct them to a church of their faith, and they wound up at one with a predominantly Haitian congregation. They were not prepared for the exuberant chanting and verbal interchanges with the minister during the sermon. They weren't certain whether

realtional empathy. Essence of a relationship that permits varying degrees of understanding, rather than requiring complete comprehension of another's culture or emotions.

Can You Tolerate Ambiguity?

Respond to each statement with a number from 1 to 5: (1) Always False, (2) Usually False, (3) Sometimes False and Sometimes True, (4) Usually True, or (5) Always True.

___4___ 1. I am comfortable in new situations.

___4___ 2. I deal with unforeseen problems successfully.

___5___ 3. I experience little discomfort in ambiguous situations.

___4___ 4. I am relaxed in unfamiliar situations.

___3___ 5. I am not frustrated when things do not go the way I expected.

To find your score, add the numbers you wrote next to each statement. Scores range from 5 to 25. The higher your score, the greater your tolerance for ambiguity.

Source: William B. Gudykunst, *Bridging Differences: Effective Intergroup Communication* (Newbury Park, CA: Sage, 1998), 121.

they should join in or simply sit quietly and observe. Ken whispered to Rita, "I'm not sure what to do. Let's just watch and see what is expected of us." In the end, they chose to sit and clap along with the chanting rather than to become actively involved in the worship. Rita felt uncomfortable and conspicuous, though, and had to fight off the urge to bolt. But after the service, several members of the congregation came up to greet Ken and Rita, invited them to lunch, and expressed great happiness in their visit. "You know," said Rita later in the day, "I'm so grateful that we sat through our discomfort. We might never have met those terrific people. Now I understand why their worship is so noisy—they're just brimming over with joy."

Develop Mindfulness

"Our life is what our thoughts make it," said Marcus Aurelius in *Meditations*. To be **mindful** is to be consciously aware of cultural differences, to acknowledge that there is a connection between thoughts and deeds when you interact with a person from a background different from your own. William Gudykunst suggests that being mindful is one of the best ways to approach any new cultural encounter.[47] Remember that there are and will be cultural differences, and try to keep them in your consciousness. Also try to consider the other individual's frame of reference or world view and to use his or her cultural priorities and assumptions when you are communicating.[48] Adapt your behavior to minimize cultural noise and distortion.

You can become more mindful through self-talk, something we discussed in Chapter 2. Self-talk consists of rational messages you tell yourself to help you manage your emotions or discomfort with a certain situation. Imagine that you are working on a group project with several of your classmates. One classmate, Suji, was born in Iran. When interacting with you, he consistently gets about a foot away, whereas you are more comfortable with three or four feet between you. When Suji encroaches on your space, you could "be mindful" of the difference by mentally noting, "Suji sure likes to get close to people when he talks to them. This may represent a practice in his culture." This self-talk message makes you consciously aware that there may be a difference in your interaction styles. If you still feel uncomfortable, instead of blurting out, "Hey, man, why so close?" you could

mindfulness. Awareness of cultural differences and the connection between thoughts and deeds when interacting with someone from a background different from your own.

Measuring Mindfulness

Respond to each statement with a number from 1 to 5:
(1) Always False, (2) Usually False, (3) Sometimes False and Sometimes True, (4) Usually True, or (5) Always True.

___5___ 1. I pay attention to the situation and context when I communicate.

___4___ 2. I can describe others with whom I communicate in great detail.

___5___ 3. I seek out new information about the people with whom I communicate.

___4___ 4. I try to find rational reasons why others may behave in a way I perceive negatively.

___5___ 5. I recognize that the person with whom I am communicating has a different point of view than I do.

To find your score, add the numbers you wrote next to each statement. Scores range from 5 to 25. The higher your score, the more mindful you are when you communicate.

23

Source: William B. Gudykunst, *Bridging Differences: Effective Intergroup Communication* (Newbury Park, CA: Sage, 1998), 120.

express your own preferences with an "I" message: "Suji, I'd prefer a bit more space between us when we talk."

Avoid Negative Judgments about Another Culture

American tourist on her first visit to France:

Can you believe it. How repulsive! These people actually eat horse meat and think it's a delicacy.

Black teenager watching his white classmates dance:

Man, they don't know anything about good music! And those dances are so dumb. I don't call this a party.

Japanese businessperson visiting Argentina:

These people are never on time. No wonder they can never catch up to us.

German student, after watching a documentary about life in Japan:

No wonder they work so hard. They have dinky little houses. I'd work long hours too if I had to live like that.

The kind of ethnocentrism that underlies judgments like these is a communication barrier. It is also an underlying cause of suspicion and mistrust and, in extreme cases, a spark that ignites violence. Instead of making judgments about another culture, try simply to acknowledge differences and to view them as an interesting challenge rather than as an obstacle to be eradicated.

 Develop Motivation to Accept Others

Tolerate Ambiguity	Take your time and expect some uncertainty.
Develop Mindfulness	Be conscious of cultural differences rather than ignoring the differences.
Avoid Negative Judgments	Resist thinking that your culture has all the answers.

Developing Skill: Strategies to Adapt to Others Who Differ from Us

To be skilled is to be capable of putting into action what you know and want to achieve. The underlying skill in being interculturally competent is the ability to be flexible and adapt to others. We discuss these crucial skills here as an introduction to the communication skills that we present in the next four chapters.

Develop Flexibility

When you interact with someone from another background, your responding skills are crucial. You can only learn so much from books; you must be willing to learn as you communicate. Every individual is unique, so cultural generalizations that you learn from research may not always apply. It is not accurate to assume, for example, that *all* French people are preoccupied with food and fashion. Many members of minority groups in the United States find it draining to correct these generalizations in their encounters with others. Pay close attention to the other person's nonverbal cues when you begin conversing; then adjust your communication style and language if necessary to put the person at ease. And avoid asking questions or making statements based on generalizations.

Become Other-Oriented

Throughout the book we have emphasized the importance of becoming other-oriented—focusing on others rather than yourself—as an important way to enhance your interpersonal competence. We have also discussed the problems ethnocentrism can create when you attempt to communicate with others, especially with those whose culture differs from yours. We now offer three specific ways to increase your other-orientedness: social decentering, empathy, and adaptation.

Although our focus in this discussion is on how to increase other-orientation in intercultural interactions, the principles apply to *all* interpersonal interactions. The

---

building your skills

Predicting How Others Feel

Look at these descriptions and rank-order them from 1 (highest) to 6 (lowest) in terms of how readily you think you could predict each person's reactions to finding out his or her mother or other close relative has just died:

_1_ A. A close friend of yours of the same sex, age, race, and culture

_6_ B. A 60-year-old male Chinese farmer

_2_ C. A college student who is twenty years older than you but of the same race, sex, and culture

_5_ D. A 10-year-old California girl who is the child of Asian and Latino parents

_3_ E. A college student of a different race from you but the same age, culture, and sex

_4_ F. A college student of the opposite sex from you but the same age, race, and culture

What qualities do you feel provide you the best information on which to base your judgments? Why? What would you need to know about each person to feel comfortable in making a prediction? How can you get that information?

major difference between intercultural interactions and those that occur within your own culture is primarily the obviousness of the differences between you and the other person.

1. *Social Decentering.* **Social decentering,** the first strategy, is a *cognitive process* in which you take into account the other person's thoughts, feelings, values, background, and perspectives. This process involves viewing the world from the other person's point of view. The greater the difference between yourself and the other person, the more difficult it is to accomplish social decentering. In doing the Building Your Skills: Predicting How Others Feel exercise, you may find it easier to judge your close friend than any of the other relationships described.

   The rest of your rankings depend on the various experiences you have had. Your interactions with members of the opposite sex, with someone from another race, or with someone of a different age are probably the next most frequent, and next highest ranked. Interactions with people from other cultures are probably the most difficult because your experiences with such interactions are often limited. It is easier to socially decenter about someone who is similar in culture and background to you.

   There are three ways to socially decenter or take another's perspective: (1) Develop an understanding of another, based on how you have responded when something similar has happened to you; (2) base your understanding of others on the knowledge you have about a specific person; or (3) make generalizations about someone, based on your understanding of how you think most people would feel or behave.[49]

   First, when you draw on your direct experience, you use your knowledge of what happened to you in the past to help you guess how someone else may feel. To the degree that the other person is similar to you, your reactions and theirs will match. For example, suppose you are talking to a student who has just failed a midterm exam in an important course. You have also had this experience. Your reaction was to discount it because you had confidence you could still pull a passing grade. You might use this self-understanding to predict your classmate's reactions. To the degree that you are similar to the classmate, your prediction will be accurate. But suppose your classmate comes from a culture with high expectations for success. Your classmate might feel upset over having dishonored his family by his poor performance. In this situation, understanding your own reaction needs to be tempered by your awareness of how similar or dissimilar the other person is to you. Recognition of differences should lead you to recognize the need to socially decenter in another way.

   The second way we socially decenter—or take the perspective of another—is based on specific knowledge we have of the person with whom we are interacting. Drawing on your memory of how your classmate reacted to a previous failed midterm gives you a basis to more accurately predict his reaction. Even if you have not observed your classmate's reaction to the same situation, you project how you think he would feel based on similar instances. As relationships become more intimate, you gain more information to allow you to socially decenter more readily. Your accuracy in predicting and understanding your partners usually increases as relationships become more intimate. In intercultural interactions, the more opportunity you have to interact with the same person and learn more about the person and his or her culture, the more your ability to socially decenter will increase.

social decentering. Cognitive process in which we take into account another person's thoughts, feelings, values, background, and perspectives.

Grief for the loss of a loved one is a universal emotion that cuts across all cultures. (David Barnett/Stock Boston)

The third way to socially decenter is to apply your understanding of people in general, or of categories of people from whom you have gained some knowledge. Each of us develops implicit personality theories, constructs, and attributions of how people act, as discussed in Chapter 3. You might have a general theory to explain the behavior of men and another for women. You might have general theories about Mexicans, Japanese, Canadians, Slovenians, Texans, or Iowans. As you meet someone who falls into one of your categories, you draw on that conceptualization to socially decenter. The more you can learn about a given culture, the stronger your general theories can be, and the more effectively you can use this method of socially decentering. The key, however, is to avoid developing inaccurate, inflexible stereotypes of others and basing your perceptions of others only on those generalizations.

2. *Empathy.* Besides *thinking* about how another may feel (socially decentering), you can have an *emotional* reaction to what others do or tell you. People feel empathy for another. **Empathy,** a second skill for becoming other-oriented, is an *emotional reaction* that is similar to the one being experienced by another person, as compared to social decentering, which is a *cognitive reaction.* Empathy is feeling what another person feels. Our emotional reaction can be either similar to or different from the emotions the other person is experiencing. You may experience mild pity for your classmate who has failed the midterm, in contrast to his stronger feeling of anguish and dishonor. Or you may share his same feelings of anguish and dishonor.

Some emotional reactions are almost universal and cut across cultural boundaries. You may experience empathy when seeing photos or videos depicting emotional scenes occurring in other countries. Seeing a mother crying while holding her sick or dying child in a refugee camp might move you to cry and feel a deep sense of sadness or loss. You empathize with the woman. You might also experi-

empathy. Process of developing an emotional reaction that is similar to the reaction being experienced by another person. Feeling what another person is feeling.

ence empathy for your brother, who has just received the devastating news that his best friend has been killed in an automobile accident. As tears come to your eyes, you grieve with him. Empathy can enhance interpersonal interactions in a number of ways: It can provide a bond between you and the other person; it is confirming; it is comforting and supportive; it can increase your understanding of others; and it can strengthen the relationship. People can empathize most easily with those who are similar, and in situations with which they have had a similar emotional experience.

Developing empathy is different from sympathizing with others. When you offer **sympathy,** you tell someone you are sorry he or she feels what he or she is feeling. Here are examples of statements of sympathy: "I'm sorry your Uncle Joe died" and "I'm sorry to hear you failed your test." When you sympathize with others, you acknowledge their feelings. But when you empathize, you experience an emotional reaction that is similar to the other person's, you, too, feel grief or sadness. We discuss strategies for developing empathic listening skills in the next chapter.

Appropriately Adapt Your Communication to Others

The logical extension of being flexible and becoming other-oriented is to adapt your communication to enhance the quality and effectiveness of your interpersonal communication. To **adapt** means to adjust your behavior to others to accommodate differences and expectations. Appropriate adaptation occurs in the context of the relationship you have with the other person and what is happening in the communication environment. Adapting to others has its roots in **communication accommodation theory,** which suggests that all people adapt their behavior to others to some extent. Those who appropriately and sensitively adapt to others are more likely to experience more positive communication.[50] Adapting to others doesn't mean you only tell others what they want to hear and do what others want you to do. Such spineless, placating behavior is not wise, effective, or ethical. Nor are we suggesting that you adapt your behavior only so that you can get your way; the goal is effective communication, not manipulation. We are suggesting, however, that you be aware of what your communication partner is doing and saying, especially if there are cultural differences, so that your message is understood and you don't unwittingly offend others. Although it may seem common sense, being sensitive to others and adapting behaviors to others are not as common as you might think.

Sometimes people adapt their behavior based on what they think someone will like. At other times they adapt their communication after realizing they have done something wrong. When you modify your behavior in anticipation of an event, you **adapt predictively.** For example, you might decide to buy a friend flowers to soften the news about breaking a date because you know how much your friend likes flowers. When you modify your behavior after an event, you **adapt reactively.** For example, you might buy your friend flowers to apologize for a fight.

There are a number of reasons people adapt communication with another person. People often adapt messages in an attempt to make them more understandable. For instance, in talking to an individual with limited understanding of English, you would probably choose simple words and phrases (people also tend to raise their voices in these situations, under the false assumption that the other person isn't "hearing" what is said). People also adapt messages in order to accomplish goals more effectively. In intercultural interactions, people frequently

sympathy. Acknowledgment that someone may be feeling bad; compassion toward someone.

adaptation. Adjusting behavior in accord with what someone else does. We can adapt based on the individual, the relationship, and the situation.

communication accommodation theory. Theory that suggests that all people adapt their behavior to others to some extent.

adapt predictively. To modify or change behavior in anticipation of an event.

adapt reactively. To modify or change behavior after an event.

Table 4.2

Communication Adaptation Behaviors

Type	Examples
Topical: Choosing a topic or issue to discuss because you know it will interest the other person.	Talking about a mutual friend, talking about a party you both went to, asking if he or she saw a particular play that was in town.
Explanatory/Elaboration: Providing additional information or detail because you recognize that the other person does not know it.	Explaining your mother's eating habits to a new friend, explaining to a neighbor how to keep squirrels away from bean plants.
Withholding Explanation or Information: Not providing an explanation because your partner already knows the information, because it might hurt or anger your partner, because of fear of how the other person might misuse it, or because you wish to avoid violating a confidentiality.	Not elaborating on the parts of an auto engine when you describe a car problem because you know the listener is knowledgeable about cars, not telling a friend you saw his or her lover with another person because the friend would be hurt, not telling someone about your interest in a mutual friend because you are afraid that person would blab about it to the mutual friend.
Examples/Comparisons/Analogies: Choosing examples that you know your partner will find relevant.	Explaining roller blading by comparing it to ice skating, something your partner knows how to do.
Personal Referencing: Referring to your partner's specific attitudes, interests, personality, traits, or ethnic background.	"I've got something to tell you I think you'll find funny." "Could you help me balance my checkbook; you're so good at math." "That's a behavior I'd expect from you, given the way your parents raised you."
Vernacular/Language: Choosing or avoiding certain words because of their potential effect on the receiver. Using words that have a unique meaning for you and your partner. Using words that you think are appropriate to the other person's level of understanding.	A wife asking her husband if he was catching flies during a movie, meaning he was asleep with his mouth wide open. A father telling his child that a criminal is someone who does bad things. Two computer jocks talking about "bytes," "RAM," and "chips."
Disclosure: Consciously deciding to share information about yourself that the other does not know about you.	Telling your lover about your sexual fantasies. Telling your instructor about family problems.
Immediate Follow-Up Questioning: Seeking additional information from the other person about information he or she shares during the interaction.	"So, what was it like growing up in small-town Iowa?" "Tell me more about your vacation in Florida." "Where are you going on your date?"
Delayed Follow-Up Questioning: Seeking additional information from the other person about previous information he or she shared.	"How's your mother doing after her operation yesterday?" "How was your date Saturday night?"
Adapting To Immediate Reaction/Feedback: Modifying your words or behavior because of your partner's reaction.	If your friend starts to cry when you talk about her mother's death, you might quickly change the topic.

Source: © Mark V. Redmond, 1994. Used by permission.

adapt communication behavior in response to the feedback or reactions they are receiving. Table 4.2 lists a variety of ways to adapt verbal messages to others.

Conversants also adapt nonverbal cues. Many times they raise or lower voice volume in response to the volume of a partner, or lean forward toward people in response to their leaning toward the speaker. We'll talk more about such nonverbal cues in Chapter 7.

Adaptation across intercultural contexts is usually more difficult than within your own culture. Imagine shaking hands with a stranger, and having the stranger hold on to your hand as you continue to talk. In the United States, hand-holding between strangers violates our nonverbal norms. But in some cultures maintaining physical contact while talking is expected. Pulling your hand away from this person would be rude. As illustrated in Understanding Diversity: Mind Your Manners—and Theirs (pages 126–127), what may be mannerly in one culture is not always acceptable in another. Adapting to these cultural differences means developing that "third" culture that we talked about earlier in the chapter.

Taking an other-oriented approach to communication means considering the thoughts, feelings, background, perspectives, attitudes, and values of your interpersonal partners and adjusting your interaction with them accordingly. Other-orientation leads to more effective interpersonal communication, regardless of whether you are dealing with someone in your family or from another country.

By careful analysis of the factors that affect communication partners, you can develop understanding and empathy. That understanding and empathy can then help you make the most effective strategic communication choices as you adapt your messages and responses.

In an effective interpersonal relationship, your partner is also orienting him- or herself to you. A competent communicator has knowledge of others, is motivated to enhance the quality of communication, and possesses the skill of being other-oriented.

If you learn the skills and principles we have presented here, will it really make a difference in your ability to relate to others? Recent evidence suggests the answer is yes. A study by communication researcher Lori Carell found that students who had been exposed to lessons in empathy linked to a study of interpersonal and intercultural communication improved their ability to empathize with others.[51] There is evidence that if you master these principles and skills, you will be rewarded with greater insight and ability to relate to others who are different from you.

recap   **Develop Skill to Adapt to Others**

Develop flexibility.	Learn to "go with the flow."
Become other-oriented.	Put yourself in the other person's mental and emotional mindset; adapt to others; listen and respond appropriately.
Adapt your communication to others.	Adjust your behavior to others to accommodate differences and expectation.

Mind Your Manners—and Theirs

If it be appropriate to kiss the Pope's slipper, by all means do so.

Lord Chesterfield, founder of modern etiquette, in 1750

The saying "When in Rome do what the Romans do" suggests that international travelers should adopt an other-oriented approach to the host country's manners and customs. After interviewing hundreds of international businesspeople, Roger Axtell offers the following tips on etiquette when visiting with people from other countries or traveling to international destinations. Realize, of course, that these observations are not true of all individuals. As in the United States, in many of these countries there are dozens of different cultural groups with their own sets of values and customs.

Austrians

- Are punctual
- Use a firm handshake (both men and women)
- Consider keeping their hands in their lap when dining to be impolite
- Are uncomfortable with first names until a friendship is established

English, Scots, Welsh

- Tend to use understatement in business matters
- Value punctuality
- Are accustomed to cooler room temperatures than Americans
- Call a Scot a Scotsman (or Scotswoman), not a Scotchman or Scottish

French

- Rarely use first names, even among colleagues

- Frequently shake hands but their grip is less firm than most
- Usually eat their main meal of the day at midday
- Make decisions after much deliberation

Irish

- Are not overly conscientious about time and punctuality
- Do not typically give business gifts
- May regard refusing a drink or failing to buy your round as bad manners

Italians

- Use strong and frequent hand and body gestures
- May grasp your elbow as they shake hands
- Do not consider punctuality a virtue, at least for social events
- Do not talk business at a social event

Summary

A culture is a system of knowledge that is shared by a larger group of people. It includes cultural elements, values, goals, and contexts. Cultural elements are categories of things and ideas that identify key aspects of cultural influence. Cultural values reflect how individuals regard masculine and feminine behaviors and individual and collective achievements. They also reflect whether individuals can tolerate ambiguity or need a high degree of certainty, and whether they believe in concentrated or decentralized power structures. The goals of a culture depend on the way it values individual versus group achievement. In high-context cultures, the meaning of messages depends heavily on nonverbal information; low-context cultures rely more heavily on words than upon context for deriving meaning.

Intercultural communication occurs when individuals or groups from different cultures communicate. Several barriers inhibit effective intercultural communication.

Russians
- Want to know what Americans really think
- When greeting, shake hands and announce their name
- Among friends, some give "bear hugs" and kiss cheeks

Egyptians
- Like all practicing Muslims, rest on Friday
- Regard friendship and trust as a prerequisite for business
- Usually hold social engagements late in the day

Zambians
- Often shake hands with the left supporting the right
- When dining, may ask for food; it Is impolite not to
- Consider it improper to refuse food

Australians
- Speak frankly and directly; they dislike pretensions

- Will not shy away from disagreement
- Appreciate punctuality
- Have good sense of humor, even in tense situations

Indians
- When greeting a woman, they put palms together and bow slightly
- Do not eat beef and regard the cow as a sacred animal
- Show great respect to elders

Japanese
- Exchange business cards before bowing or shaking hands
- Consider it impolite to have long or frequent eye-to-eye contact
- Rarely use first names
- Avoid the word "no" to preserve harmony

Thais (Thailand)
- Regard displays of either temper or affection in public as unacceptable

- Have a taboo against using your foot to point, or showing your sole
- Don't like pats on the head

Brazilians
- Like long handshakes
- Like to touch arms, elbows, and backs
- When conversing, view interruption as enthusiasm
- Attach a sexual meaning to the OK hand signal

Mexicans
- Are not rigidly punctual
- Take their main meal at about 1 or 4 P.M.
- Refrain from using first names until they are invited to do so
- Consider hands in pockets to be impolite

Source: Adapted from Roger E. Axtell, *Do's and Taboos of Hosting International Visitors* (New York: Wiley, 1989).

Ethnocentrism is the belief that one's own cultural traditions and assumptions are superior to those of others. Differences in language and the way people interpret nonverbal messages also interfere with effective intercultural communication. People stereotype by placing a group or a person into an inflexible, all-encompassing category. A related barrier is prejudice—people often prejudge someone before they know all the facts. Stereotyping and prejudice can keep people from viewing others as unique individuals and therefore hamper effective, honest communication. Finally, assuming that one is similar to others can also be a barrier to intercultural communication. All humans have some similarities, but their cultures have taught them to process the world differently.

Although it is reasonably easy to identify cultural differences, it is more challenging to bridge those differences. To enhance understanding between cultures, we suggest the following: Develop knowledge by seeking information about the culture, ask questions and listen, and develop a "third culture." Increase your motivation to appreciate others who are different from you by tolerating ambiguity, developing mindfulness, and avoiding negative judgments about another culture. Finally, enhance your skill by becoming flexible. Be other-oriented by socially decentering, and becoming more empathic. And adapt your verbal and nonverbal communication to others.

For Discussion and Review

Focus on Comprehension

1. What is culture?

2. What are four contrasting cultural values?

3. What are the differences between high-context and low-context cultures?

4. How do individualistic and collectivistic cultures differ?

5. What is ethnocentrism?

Focus on Critical Thinking

6. Jonna, an American, has just been accepted as a foreign exchange student in Germany. What potential cultural barriers may she face? How should she manage these potential barriers?

7. What's the problem in assuming that other people are like us? How does this create a barrier to effective intercultural communication?

8. If you were to design a lesson plan for elementary age students about how to deal with racial and ethnic stereotypes, what would you include?

9. What are appropriate ways to deal with someone who consistently utters racial slurs and evidences prejudice toward racial or ethnic groups?

Focus on Ethics

10. Marla is the director of the campus multicultural studies program. She wants to require all students in a four-year degree program to take at least four courses that focus on multicultural issues. Is it appropriate to force students to take such a concentration of courses?

11. When Wayne, a Polish American, went to visit Dave, who was from an old Southern Baptist family, Dave's dad made a bigoted statement about African Americans. This upset Wayne, and he wondered whether Dave's father was prejudiced against Catholics, too. Should Wayne have spoken up and told Dave's dad that he did not like the remark?

12. Is it ethical or appropriate for someone from one culture to attempt to change the cultural values of someone from a different culture? For example, culture A practices polygamy: one husband can be married to several wives. Culture B practices monogamy: one husband can be married to only one wife. Should a person from culture B attempt to make someone from culture A change his or her ways?

For Your Journal

1. Describe your perceptions of your cultural values, based on the discussion of cultural values beginning on page 102 in this chapter. On a scale of 1 to 10, rate yourself in terms of masculine versus feminine perspective, individual versus group achievement, tolerance of uncertainty versus need for certainty, and centralized versus decentralized power. Provide an example of your reaction to an interpersonal communication encounter to illustrate each of these values.

2. Write a journal entry discussing how you have experienced one of the barriers to effective intercultural communication described in this chapter. Have you been ethnocentric in your thoughts or behavior or a victim of ethnocentrism? Describe a situation in which communication was difficult because you and your communication partner spoke different languages. Have you been a victim of stereotyping or prejudice? Have you assumed someone was similar to yourself and later found that there were more differences than you had suspected?

3. This chapter presented nine specific strategies or skills to help bridge differences in background and culture. Rank-order these skills and strategies in terms of what *you* need to improve in your interactions with people from different backgrounds. Give a rank of 1 to the skill or strategy that you most need to develop, a rank of 2 to the next area you feel you need to work on, and so on. Rank yourself on all nine strategies.

   Seek information about the culture   _____

   Ask questions and listen effectively   _____

   Develop a third culture   _____

   Tolerate ambiguity   _____

   Develop mindfulness   _____

   Avoid negative judgments about another culture _____

   Be flexible   _____

   Become other-oriented   _____

   Adapt your communication to others   _____

   Based on the areas in which you need greatest improvement, write a journal entry about how you will develop skill in these areas. How will you put into practice what you have learned in this chapter?

Learning with Others

1. Your instructor will guide you in playing Diversity Bingo to help you get better acquainted with the international and intercultural experiences of your classmates.

Diversity Bingo

Your assignment is to locate people who have either done or know about the things listed in the following boxes, and then to obtain their autographs. You must first introduce yourself and share two personal things not listed in any of the boxes. After the introduction, the person may autograph the appropriate boxes for you. The person who collects the most autographs wins. You may not go back to the same person twice.

Was born outside the United States	Has attended a Native American powwow	Knows the significance of Angel Island	Is a morning person	Is a vegetarian	Has worked outside the United States
Has been to Australia	Can communicate in American Sign Language	Has attended a Cinco de Mayo celebration	Likes 20th-century classical music	Knows the significance of the Stonewall Riots	Knows which tribal government the U.S. Constitution was modeled after
Has traveled outside the United States	Celebrates Hanukkah	Has had his or her last name mispronounced	Is a late-night person	Knows who Rosa Parks is	Knows the opening date of the deer hunting or fishing season
Can name at least two traditionally black U.S. colleges	Has been a student for more than five years	Has a lesbian, gay, or bisexual friend	Has a Native American ancestor	Worked while going to high school	Has been to Europe
Is bilingual or multilingual	Knows what Kwanzaa is	Knows the meaning of Juneteenth	Knows the meaning of Jeri Curl	Has danced to Tex-Mex music	Can name the books of the Old or New Testament
Is an avid country music fan	Has been to a longhouse	Knows his or her Chinese birth sign	Has danced to Zydeco music	Knows why many Irish people immigrated to the United States in the 1880s	Is an avid Dilbert fan

Source: Adapted from 3M, Austin, Texas, Diversity Seminar, 1994.

2. Bring to class a fable, folktale, or children's story from a culture other than your own. As a group, analyze the cultural values implied by the story or characters in the story.

3. Working with a group of your classmates, develop an ideal culture based on the combined values and elements of people in your group. Develop a name for your culture. Suggest foods, recreational activities, and other leisure pursuits. Compare the culture your group develops with those that other groups in your class develop. How would the communication skills and principles discussed in this chapter help you bridge differences among those cultures?

4. As a group, go on an intercultural scavenger hunt. Your instructor will give you a time limit. Scavenge your campus or classroom area to identify influences of as many different cultures as you can find. For example, you could go to the cafeteria and make note of ethnic foods that you find. Identify clothing, music, or architecture that is influenced by certain cultures.

5. In small groups, identify examples from your own experiences for each barrier to effective intercultural communication discussed in the text. Use one of the examples to develop a skit to perform for the rest of the class. See if the class can identify which intercultural barrier your group is depicting. Also suggest how the skills and principles discussed in the chapter might have improved the communication in the situation you role-play.

Diversity Bingo, Answers

	There was a devastating potato famine in Ireland in the 1880s.	Chinese birth signs: Rat, Ox, Tiger, Rabbit, Dragon, Snake, Horse, Sheep, Monkey, Rooster.	A longhouse is a Native American meeting place.	
	Tex-Mex music is a country swing style that originated in southern Texas.	Jeri Curl is hair treatment used by African Americans.	Juneteenth celebrates the freeing of slaves in Texas in 1865.	Kwanzaa is an African American holiday.	
				Howard, Hampton, Tuskegee, and Spelman are among notable African-American colleges.
	Rosa Parks is a Black woman who refused to sit down in the back of a bus in Montgomery, Ala.		Hanukkah is a Jewish holiday celebrating rededication of the Temple in 165 b.c.	
	A 1969 police raid on a NY bar started the gay rights movement.	Cinco de Mayo celebrates the Mexican victory over the French in 1862.	American Sign is used by the hearing impaired to communicate.	
		Angel Island is where Chinese immigrants disembarked to enter the United States.	A powwow is a Native American celebration.	

Interpersonal Communication Skills

People judge you by your behavior, not by your intentions. The following four chapters focus on research-based communication skills that can help you monitor and shape your behavior to improve the quality of your relationships. Chapter 5 offers tips and strategies for listening to others and confirming your understanding of what you hear. Chapter 6 explores how the words people use and misuse affect relationships with others. Becoming other-oriented involves both listening to the words and reading the behavior cues of others. Chapter 7 focuses on the scope and importance of unspoken messages. We will explore the implications of the adage "Actions speak louder than words." Chapter 8 presents principles and skills to help you manage conflict and disagreements with others.

Listening and Responding

1. Describe five elements of the listening process.

2. Identify characteristics of four listening styles.

3. Understand why we listen, and list several important barriers to effective listening.

4. Identify ways to improve your other-orientation and listening skills.

5. Identify responding skills and understand strategies for improving them.

Picture your best friend in your mind. What are some of the qualities you most admire in your friend? Many people would respond that one of the most valued qualities in a friend is his or her just being there—supporting, comforting, and listening. As theologian Henri Nouwen so eloquently put it,

> Listening is much more than allowing another to talk while waiting for a chance to respond. Listening is paying full attention to others and welcoming them into our very beings. . . . Listening is a form of spiritual hospitality by which you invite strangers to become friends, to get to know their inner selves more fully, and even dare to be silent with you.[1]

Simply stated, friends listen. They listen even if we sometimes say foolish things. Again, Nouwen describes it well: "True listeners no longer have an inner need to make their presence known. They are free to receive, to welcome, to accept."[2] As we consider the essential skills of interpersonal communication, the skill of listening to others would have to be at or near the top of the list in terms of importance. Skilled communicators do more than impassively listen—they appropriately respond to what we say. They confirm that they understand and care for us by providing both verbal and nonverbal feedback. In this chapter we explore the interpersonal communication skills of listening and responding.

You spend more time listening than participating in any other communication activity. In fact, you spend more time listening to others than almost anything else you do. Typical Americans spend more than 80 percent of an average day communicating with other people, and, as the pie chart in Figure 5.1 shows, they spend 45 percent of that communication time listening to others.[3] Ironically, most people's formal communication training focuses on writing, the activity to which they devote the least amount of communication time. Chances are that until now you have had no formal training in listening. In this chapter, we focus on this often neglected, yet quintessential, skill for developing quality interpersonal relationships. Listening is the process by which people learn the most about others. In addition, we explore ways to respond appropriately to others.

Figure 5.1
What You Do with Your Communication Time

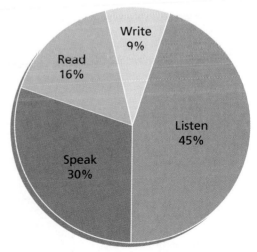

Write 9%

Read 16%

Listen 45%

Speak 30%

Listening Defined

"**D**id you hear what I said?" demanded a father who had been lecturing his teenage son on the importance of hanging up his clothes. In fact, his son did *hear* him, but he may not have been *listening*. **Listening** is the process of creating meaning from verbal and nonverbal messages. When we listen, we hear words and try to make sense out of what we hear. **Hearing** is the physiological process of decoding sounds. You hear when sound vibrations reach your eardrum and buzz the middle ear bones: the hammer, anvil, and stirrup. Eventually, these sound vibrations are translated into electrical impulses that reach the brain. In order to listen to something, you must first select that sound from competing sounds. Listening involves four activities—selecting, attending, understanding, and remembering. A fifth activity—responding—confirms that listening has occurred.

Selecting

To **select** a sound is to choose one sound as you sort through the various sounds competing for your attention. As you listen to someone in an interpersonal context, you focus on the words and nonverbal messages of your partner. Even now, as you are reading this book, there are undoubtedly countless noises within earshot. Stop reading for a moment and sort through the various sounds around you. Do you hear music? Is there noise from outside? How about the murmur of voices, the tick of a clock, the hum of a computer, the whoosh of an air conditioner or furnace? To listen, you must select which of these sounds will receive your attention.

listening. Creating meaning from verbal and nonverbal messages.

hearing. Physiological process of decoding sounds.

selecting. Sorting through various sounds competing for your attention.

Healthy family relations result when parents and children are able to develop people-oriented listening styles. (Michael Newman/PhotoEdit)

Attending

After selecting a sound, you then **attend** to or focus on it. Attention can be fleeting. You may attend to the sound for a moment and then move on or return to other thoughts or other sounds. Typically, you attend to those sounds and messages that meet your needs or are consistent with what you think you should be focusing on. If you are hungry, you may select and then attend to a commercial for a sizzling burger or a crispy-crust pizza. Information that is novel or intense, or that somehow relates to you, also may capture your attention. And conflict, humor, new ideas, and real or concrete things command your attention more easily than abstract theories that do not relate to your interests or needs.

In addition, when someone invites you to participate or respond, you listen much more attentively than you do when someone just talks at you. One of your authors attended a daylong series of lectures at Oxford University, on life in England during the Middle Ages. As a paleoanthropologist droned on about femur measurements and Harris lines, your author struggled to stay awake. But when the lecturer produced several recently unearthed skeletons and invited the audience to participate in drawing conclusions about their lives and environment, your author was all ears.

Understanding

Whereas hearing is a physiological phenomenon, **understanding** is the process of assigning meaning to the sounds you select and to which you attend. There are several theories about how you assign meaning to words you hear, but there is no universally accepted notion of how this process works. We know that people understand best if they can relate what they are hearing to something they already know. A well-advertised series of commercial foreign language tapes bases its guarantees of success on this principle, claiming that speakers of English can quickly learn to speak Spanish like a native by using mnemonic devices—for example, using the word *S-O-C-K-S* to remember the Spanish phrase *"Eso si, que es?"*

A second basic principle about how people understand others is this: The greater the similarity between individuals, the greater the likelihood for more accurate understanding. Individuals from different cultures who have substantially different religions, family lifestyles, values, and attitudes often have difficulty understanding each other, particularly in the early phases of a relationship.

You understand best that which you also experience. Perhaps you have heard the Montessori school philosophy: I hear, I forget; I see, I remember; I experience,

attending. Focusing on a particular sound or message.

understanding. Assigning meaning to messages.

I understand. Hearing alone does not provide us with understanding. People hear over 1 billion words each year, but understand only a fraction of that number. They may not be attending to the words coming their way, or may simply not know what some words mean. In Chapter 3 we discussed the processes involved in perception and observed that different people can reach dramatically different conclusions about the same events and messages, based on their previous experiences. A key to establishing relationships with others is trying to understand those differences in experience in order to arrive at a common meaning for the messages exchanged.

Remembering

To **remember** is to recall information. Some researchers theorize that you store every detail you have ever heard or witnessed; your mind operates like a video camera. But you cannot retrieve or remember all the tapes. Sometimes you were present, yet have no recollection of what occurred.

Human brains have both short-term and long-term memory storage systems. Short-term memory is where you store almost all the information you hear. You look up a phone number in the telephone book, mumble the number to yourself, then dial the number, only to discover that the line is busy. Three minutes later you have to look up the number again because it did not get stored in your long-term memory. Short-term storage is very limited. Just as airports have just a few short-term parking spaces, but lots of spaces for long-term parking, brains can accommodate a few things of fleeting significance, but acres of important information. Most of us forget hundreds of snips and bits of insignificant information that pass through our brains each day.

The information stored in long-term memory includes events, conversations, and other data that are significant. People tend to remember dramatic and vital information, as well as seemingly inconsequential details connected with such information. Most people over the age of 45 today know exactly where they were on November 22, 1963, the day President Kennedy was assassinated. Many over the age of 65 can also recall where they were on December 7, 1941, Pearl Harbor Day. Do you remember what you were doing on April 19, 1995, when you heard the news that the Alfred P. Murrah Federal Building in Oklahoma City had been bombed? Or, do you recall the day in April 1999, when students were indiscriminately shot at Columbine High School in Colorado? Information makes it to long-term memory because of its significance to us.

Responding

Interpersonal communication is transactive; it involves both talking and responding. You **respond** to people to let them know you understand their messages. Responses can be nonverbal; direct eye contact and head nods let your partner know you're tuned in. Or you can respond verbally by asking questions to confirm the content of the message: "Are you saying you don't want us to spend as much time together as we once did?" or by making statements that reflect the feelings of the speaker: "So you are frustrated that you have to wait for someone to drive you where you want to go." We discuss responding skills in more detail later in the chapter.

remembering. Recalling information that has been communicated.

responding. Confirming your understanding of a message.

recap

What Is Listening?

Selecting	Sorting through various sounds that compete for your attention
Attending	Focusing on a particular sound or message
Understanding	Assigning meaning to messages
Remembering	Recalling information that has been communicated
Responding	Confirming your understanding of a message

Listening Styles

What's your listening style? Do you focus more on the content of the message than on the feelings being expressed by the speaker? Or do you prefer brief sound bites of information? Your **listening style** is your preferred way of making sense out of the spoken messages you hear. Listening researchers Kitty Watson, Larry Barker, and James Weaver found that listeners tend to fall into one of four listening styles: people-oriented, action-oriented, content-oriented, or time-oriented.[4]

People-Oriented Listeners

As you might suspect from the label, **people-oriented listeners** tend to be comfortable with and skilled at listening to people's feelings and emotions. They are likely to empathize and search for common areas of interest. People-oriented listeners embody many of the attributes of being other-oriented that we've discussed throughout the book—they seek strong interpersonal connections when listening to others. Preliminary evidence suggests that people-oriented listeners may be less apprehensive when interacting with others in small-group and interpersonal interactions.[5]

Action-Oriented Listeners

An **action-oriented listener** prefers information that is well organized, brief, and error-free. An action-oriented listener doesn't like the speaker to tell lengthy stories and digress. The action-oriented listener may think "Get to the point" or "What am I supposed to do with this information" when hearing a message filled with too many anecdotes or rambling, disorganized bits of information. Whereas a people-oriented listener would be more likely to focus on the feelings of the person telling the story, the action-oriented listener wants to know the point or the punch line. There is new evidence to suggest that action-oriented listeners are more likely to be more skeptical when listening to information. Researchers call this skepticism **second-guessing**—questioning the ideas and assumptions underlying a message. Rather than taking the information they hear at face value, action-oriented listeners are more likely to reinterpret or evaluate the literal message to determine whether

listening style. Preferred way of making sense out of spoken messages to which we listen.

people-oriented listener. Listener who is comfortable with and skilled at listening to people's feelings and emotions.

action-oriented listener. Listener who prefers information that is well-organized, brief, and error free.

second-guessing. Questioning the ideas and assumptions underlying a message; assessing whether the message is true or false.

it is true or false—they make another guess (hence the term *second-guessing*) as to whether the information they are listening to is accurate.[6]

Content-Oriented Listeners

If you are a **content-oriented listener,** you are more comfortable listening to complex, detailed information than are people with other listening styles. A content-oriented listener hones in on the facts, details, and evidence in a message. In fact, if a message does not have ample supporting evidence and specific details, the content-oriented listener is more likely to reject the message. Like the action-oriented listener, content-oriented listeners are likely to make second guesses about the messages they hear. Content-oriented listeners are also less apprehensive when communicating with others in group and interpersonal situations.[7] Content-oriented listeners would make good judges or lawyers; they focus on issues and arguments and listen to see whether a conclusion that a speaker reaches is accurate or credible.

Time-Oriented Listeners

You're a **time-oriented listener** if you like your messages delivered succinctly. Time-oriented listeners are keenly aware of how much time they have to listen. Their lives are filled with many things on their "to do" list; their "in basket" often overflows, so they want messages delivered quickly and briefly. Whereas a people-oriented listener might enjoy spending time over a cup of coffee catching up on the day's activities, a time-oriented listener is more like a drive-by listener—a time-oriented listener may think, "Give me what I need so I can keep on moving to my next task or hear my next message," "Don't ramble, don't digress, just get to the point quickly."

content-oriented listener.
Listener who is more comfortable listening to complex, detailed information than are those with other listening styles.

time-oriented listener.
Listener who likes messages delivered succinctly.

Information overload can prevent us from being able to communicate effectively with people around us. (Bob Daemmrich/Stock Boston)

building your skills

Assessing Your Listening Skills

The purpose of this questionnaire is to assess your listening skill. Respond to each statement with a number as follows: 1 for always false, 2 for usually false, 3 for sometimes false, 4 for usually true, and 5 for always true.

_____ 1. I have a difficult time separating important and unimportant ideas when I listen to others.

_____ 2. I check new information against what I already know when I listen to others.

_____ 3. I have an idea what others will say when I listen to them.

_____ 4. I am sensitive to others' feelings when I listen to them.

_____ 5. I think about what I am going to say next when I listen to others.

_____ 6. I focus on the process of communication that is occurring between me and others when I listen to them.

_____ 7. I cannot wait for others to finish talking so I can take my turn.

_____ 8. I try to understand the meanings that are being created when I communicate with others.

_____ 9. I focus on determining whether others understand what I said when they are talking.

_____ 10. I ask others to elaborate when I am not sure what they mean.

To find your score, first reverse your responses for the odd-numbered items (if you wrote 1, make it 5; if you wrote 2, make it 4; if you wrote 3, leave it as 3; if you wrote 4, make it 2; if you wrote 5, make it 1). Next, add the numbers next to each statement. Scores range from 10 to 50. The higher your score, the better your listening skill.

Source: William Gudykunst, _Bridging Differences,_ 2nd ed. (Thousand Oaks, CA: Sage, 1998), p. 165. Reprinted by permission of Sage Publications, Inc.

Knowing your listening style can help you better understand how to adapt to various listening situations. If, for example, you know that you are a time-oriented or action-oriented listener and your friend or companion is a people-oriented listener, you and your friend will need to adjust both your speaking and listening styles. When speaking to an action-oriented listener, give the listener a brief preview of what you will be talking about. You could say, "Phil, there are three things I'd like to share with you." Stick to that structure. When speaking to a people-oriented listener, realize that he or she will feel rushed or hurried if you skip information about feelings or relationships. A people-oriented listener prefers to spend more time talking about emotions than do those with other listening styles. A time-oriented listener would like information summarized like a crisply written business memo punctuated with bullets and lists of essential information.

What is the best listening style? It depends on the listening situation and the communication context and objectives. In a high-pressure, fast-paced job such as stock trading, you don't have time to listen to stories about clients' families or the latest TV show; you need information delivered quickly and efficiently. A father listening to a daughter talk about what a rotten day at school she had, would find a people-oriented listening style the most effective way of listening to his daughter pour her heart out about life's challenges and frustrations. Being aware of your own preferred listening style and the needs of your communication partner can help you adopt a listening style that best suits the situation.

Listening Barriers

Even though people spend so much of their communication time listening, most don't listen as well as they should. Twenty-four hours after you hear a speech, a class lecture, or a sermon, you have forgotten more than half of what was said. And it gets worse. In another twenty-four hours you have forgotten half of what you remembered, so you really remember only a quarter of the lecture.

Interpersonal listening skills are not much better. If anything, they may be worse. When you listen to a speech or lecture, you have a clearly defined listening role; one person talks and you are expected to listen. But in interpersonal situations, you may have to alternate quickly between speaking and listening. This takes considerable skill and concentration. Often you are thinking of what you want to say next, rather than listening.

One study found that even in the most intimate relationships, our listening skills are not highly developed. Couples who had been married for at least five years were placed in separate rooms, and researchers asked the wives, "During the last six months have you and your spouse talked about who would be responsible for some of the household chores such as taking out the garbage and other domestic responsibilities?" "Yes," recalled at least 71 percent of the wives. Interestingly, when the same question was put to their husbands, only 19 percent recalled a discussion of domestic duties. Intrigued, the researchers next asked a more personal question of the wives: "In the last six months have you and your spouse discussed the possibilities of increasing the size of your family? Have you talked about having children?" An overwhelming majority, 91 percent, of the wives responded affirmatively. Curiously, only 15 percent of the husbands recalled having a conversation about having more children. Although one anecdotal study does not prove conclusively that all intimate relationships suffer from listening lapses, it does illustrate the problem. And as Understanding Diversity: Who Listens Better, Men or Women? reiterates, often the problem is gender related.

Another surprising study found that we sometimes pay more attention to strangers than to intimate friends or partners. Married couples in the study tended to interrupt each other more often and were generally less polite to each other than were strangers involved in a decision-making task.[8] Apparently, we take listening shortcuts when communicating with others in close relationships.

understanding
diversity

Who Listens Better: Men or Women?

Research provides no definitive answer to the question, who listens better, men or women? There is evidence that men and women listen somewhat differently and have different expectations about the role of listening and talking. Deborah Tannen suggests that one of the most common complaints wives have about their husbands, is "He doesn't listen to me anymore" along with "He doesn't talk to me anymore." Another scholar noted that complaints about lack of communication were usually at the top of women's lists of reasons for divorce but mentioned much less often by men. Since both men and women are participating in the same conversation, why are women more often dissatisfied with the listening and talking process than men? Tannen's explanation: Women

expect different things from conversations from what men expect.

One researcher suggests that men and women may have different attention styles. When men listen, they may be looking for a new structure or organizational pattern, or to separate bits of information they hear. They continually shape, form, observe, inquire, and direct energy toward a chosen goal. Men's attention style is reported to be more emotionally controlled than women's attention style. Women are described as more subjective, empathic, and emotionally involved as they listen. They are more likely to search for relationships among parts of a pattern and to rely on more intuitive perceptions of feelings. They are also more easily distracted by competing details. Females may hear more of the message because they reject less of it. These differences in attention styles and the way men and women process information, suggest the researcher can potentially affect listening, even though we have no direct evidence linking attention style to listening skill.

Another researcher suggests that when men listen, they listen to

solve a problem; men are more instrumental and task oriented. Women listen to seek new information to enhance understanding. There is additional evidence that men may be more goal oriented when they listen. What are the implications of these research studies? They may mean that men and women focus on different parts of messages and have different listening objectives. These differences can affect relationship development. Males may need to recognize that while they are attending to a message and looking for new structure to solve a problem or achieve a goal, they may hear less of the message and therefore listen less effectively. And even though many females may hear more of the message, they may need to make connections between the parts of the information they hear to look for major ideas, rather than just focus on the details. In any case, gender-based differences in attention style and information processing may account for some of the relational problems that husbands and wives, lovers, siblings, and male-female pairs experience.[9]

Most interpersonal listening problems can be traced to a single source—ourselves. While listening to others, we also "talk" to ourselves. Our internal thoughts are like a play-by-play sportscast. We mentally comment on the words and sights that we select and to which we attend. If we keep those comments focused on the message, they may be useful. But we often attend to our own internal dialogues instead of others' messages. Then our listening effectiveness plummets.

Inattentive listening is a bit like channel surfing when we watch TV—pushing the remote control button to switch from channel to channel, avoiding commercials and focusing for brief periods on attention-grabbing program "bites." When we listen to others, we may fleetingly tune in to the conversation for a moment, decide that the content is uninteresting, and then focus on a personal thought. These thoughts are barriers to communication, and they come in a variety of forms.

Are we more attentive listeners to TV? Apparently not. One research team phoned TV viewers as soon as the evening news program was over. On average, most people remembered only about 17 percent of what they heard. And even when they were reminded of some of the news coverage, most averaged no better than

25 percent recall.[10] Even though more highly educated viewers did a little better, the overall conclusion is not good: We often don't "catch" what we hear, even a few moments after hearing it.

Being Self-Absorbed

You're in your local grocery store during "rush hour." It appears that most of your community has also decided to forage for food at the same time. As you are trying to get in and out of the store quickly, it seems that many of the harried shoppers are oblivious to those around them. They stop in the aisle, blocking the path for others (including you). They elbow their way into crowded checkout stands. And the "express lane" that limits customers to ten items or fewer, is backed up because more than one shopper is math challenged—has difficulty counting to ten. You find yourself becoming tense—not just because you are hungry and need sustenance, but because it seems the grocery store is filled with people who are self-absorbed; they are focused on getting their needs met, but not the needs of others.

Self-absorbed listeners are focused on their needs rather than yours; the message is about *them,* not *you.* During conversations with a self-absorbed communicator, you have difficulty sustaining the conversation about anything except your self-absorbed partner's ideas, experiences, and stories. This problem is also called **conversational narcissism.** To be narcissistic is to be in love with oneself, like the mythical Greek character Narcissus, who became enamored with his reflection in a pool of water.[11]

conversational narcissism.
Overly focusing on personal agendas and being self-absorbed rather than focusing on the needs and ideas of others.

The self-absorbed listener is actively involved in doing several things other than listening. The self-absorbed person is much more likely to interrupt others in mid-sentence. He or she is seeking ways to focus the attention on him- or herself.

The self-absorbed listener is also not focusing on his or her partner's message, but thinking about what he or she is going to say next. This focus on an internal message can keep a listener from selecting and attending to the other person's message. If you are supposed to be listening to Aunt Mae tell about her recent trip to the Buckner County Fair, but you are eager to hit her up for a loan, your personal agenda will serve as a barrier to your listening ability. Or you may simply decide that Aunt Mae's monologue is boring and unimportant and give yourself permission to tune out as she drones on. Like humorist James Thurber's famous daydreamer, Walter Mitty, you may eventually find yourself unable to respond cogently, lost in your own world.[12]

How do you short-circuit this listening problem? First, diagnose it. Note consciously when you find yourself drifting off, thinking about your agenda rather than concentrating on the speaker. Second, throttle up your powers of concentration when you find your internal messages are distracting you from listening well. If you notice that you are "telling" yourself that Aunt Mae's anecdote is boring, you can also mentally remind yourself to listen with greater energy and focus.

Emotional Noise

Words are powerful symbols that affect people's attitudes, behavior, and even blood pressure. Words arouse people emotionally. **Emotional noise** occurs when emotional arousal interferes with communication effectiveness. If you grew up in a home in which R-rated language was never used, then four-letter words may be distracting to you. Words that insult your religious or ethnic heritage can also be fighting words. Most people respond to certain trigger words like a bull to a waving cape; they want to charge in to correct the speaker or perhaps even do battle with him or her.

emotional noise. Form of communication interference caused by emotional arousal.

---

building your skills

Identifying Your Emotional "Hot Buttons"

The following listening situations and phrases may cause you to be emotional. Check those that are "hot buttons" for you as a listener, and add others that strongly affect you, positively or negatively.

_____ "You never/always . . ,"

_____ Know-it-all attitudes

_____ Individuals who smoke cigarettes or cigars while talking to you

_____ "Shut up!"

_____ Being ignored

_____ Bad grammar

_____ "You never listen."

_____ Obscene language

_____ Whining

_____ "What you should do is . . ."

_____ Being interrupted

Others:

_____

_____

_____

Knowing what your emotional hot buttons are can help prevent your overreacting when they are pushed.

Source: Adapted from Diane Bone, *The Business of Listening* (Crisp Publications, Los Altos, CA, 1995), 52.

Sometimes it is not specific words, but rather concepts or ideas that cause an emotional eruption. Some talk-radio hosts try to boost their ratings by purposely using demagogic language that elicits passionate responses. Although listening to such conflict can be interesting and entertaining, when your own emotions become aroused, you may lose your ability to converse effectively. Strong emotions can interfere with focusing on the message of another.

The emotional state of the speaker may also affect your ability to understand and evaluate what you hear. If you are listening to someone who is emotionally distraught, you will be more likely to focus on his or her emotions than on the content of the message.[13] Communication author R. G. Owens advises that when you are communicating with someone who is emotionally excited, you should remain calm and focused, and try simply to communicate your interest in the other person.[14]

Your listening challenge is to avoid emotional sidetracks and keep your attention focused on the message. When your internal dialogue is kicked into high gear by objectionable words or concepts, or by an emotional speaker, make an effort to quiet it down and steer back to the subject at hand.

Criticizing the Speaker

The late Mother Teresa once said, "If you judge people, you have no time to love them." Being critical of the speaker may distract a listener from focusing on the message. As you learned in Chapter 3, most people are especially distracted by appearances, forming impressions of others based solely on nonverbal information. Superficial factors such as clothing, body size and shape, age, and ethnicity all affect our interpretation of a message. In his essay "Black Men and Public Space," journalist Brent Staples provides this account of an incident that made communication impossible because of the way a woman reacted to his appearance:

> On assignment for a local paper and killing time before an interview, I entered a jewelry store on the city's affluent Near North Side. The proprietor excused herself and returned with an enormous red Doberman pinscher straining at the end of a leash. She stood, the dog extended toward me, silent to my questions, her eyes bulging nearly out of her head.[15]

Again, it is important to monitor your internal dialogue to make sure you are focusing on the message rather than criticizing the messenger. Good listeners say to themselves, "While it may be distracting, I am simply not going to let the appearance of this speaker keep my attention from the message."

Speech Rate versus Thought Rate

Your ability to think faster than people speak is another listening pitfall. The average person speaks at a rate of 125 words a minute. Some folks talk a bit faster, others more slowly. In contrast, you have the ability to process up to 600 or 800 words a minute. The difference between your mental ability to handle words and the speed at which they arrive at your cortical centers can cause trouble, giving you time to daydream and to tune the speaker in and out, and giving you the illusion that you are concentrating more attentively than you actually are.[16]

You can turn your listening speed into an advantage if you use the extra time instead to summarize what a speaker is saying. By periodically sprinkling in mental summaries during a conversation, you can dramatically increase your listening ability and make the speech-rate/thought-rate difference work to your advantage.

Information Overload

We live in an information-rich age. We are all constantly bombarded with sight and sound images, and experts suggest that the volume of information competing for our attention is likely to become even greater in the future. Fax machines, car phones, audio Internet messages, and other technological devices can interrupt conversations and distract us from listening to others.

Be on the alert for these information interruptions when you are talking with others. Don't assume that because you are ready to talk, the other person is ready to listen. If your message is particularly sensitive or important, you may want to ask your listening partner, "Is this a good time to talk?" Even if he or she says yes, look for eye contact and a responsive facial expression to make sure the positive response is genuine.

External Noise

As you will recall, all the communication models in Chapter 1 include the element of noise—distractions that take your focus away from the message. Many households seem to be addicted to noise. Often there is a TV on (sometimes more than one), a computer game beeping, and music emanating from another room. These and other sounds compete for your attention when you are listening to others.

Besides literal noise, there are other potential distractors. A headline in your evening paper about the latest details in a lurid sex scandal may "shout" for your attention just when your son wants to talk with you about his latest science fiction story. A desire to listen to your new compact disk of "Pacific Overtures" may drown out your spouse's overtures to a heart-to-heart about your family's budget problems. The lure of music, TV, books, or your computer can all distract you from your listening task.

Distractions make it difficult to sustain attention to a message. You have a choice to make. You can attempt to listen through the labyrinth of competing distractions, or you can modify the environment to reduce them. Turning off the stereo, setting down the paper, and establishing eye contact with the speaker can help to minimize the noise barrier.

recap **Overcoming Barriers to Listening**

Listening Barriers	To Overcome the Barrier
Being Self-Absorbed	Consciously become aware of the self-focus and shift attention.
Emotional Noise	Use self-talk to manage emotions.
Criticizing the Speaker	Focus on the message, not the messenger.
Information Rate	Use the difference between speech rate and thought rate to mentally summarize the message.
Information Overload	Realize when you or your partner are tired or distracted and not ready to listen.
External Noise	Take charge of the listening environment by eliminating the distraction.

Improving Listening, Comprehension, and Responding Skills

Many of the listening problems that we have identified stem from focusing on oneself rather than on the messages of others. You can improve your listening skills by following three steps you probably first encountered in elementary school: (1) stop, (2) look, and (3) listen, and then (4) ask questions and (5) reflect content by paraphrasing. Although these steps may seem simplistic, they can provide the necessary structure to help you refocus your mental energies and improve your listening power. These three steps to improved listening are supported by a considerable body of listening research. Let's consider each step separately.

Stop

Stop what? What should you *not* do in order to be a better listener? As noted earlier, while you are "listening" you may also be "talking" to yourself—providing yourself with a commentary about the messages you hear. Given that people often produce such mental commentary, it's important to focus consciously on the message, rather than to be distracted by one's own mental tangents. Many of the barriers to improved listening skills relate to the focus people place on themselves and their own messages rather than on others. Your internal, self-generated messages may distract you from giving your undivided attention to what others are saying.

In order to select and attend to the messages of others, people need to become aware of and stop their own internal dialogues about issues and ideas that are self-focused rather than other-oriented. It boils down to this: When you listen, you are either on task or off task. When you are on task, you are concentrating on the message; when you're off task, your mind may be a thousand miles away. What's important is to be aware of what you are doing. A four-stage model of how people learn any skill, often attributed to psychologist Abraham Maslow, suggests that as they practice and develop the skill of decentering, they operate at one of four levels of competence:

- Unconscious incompetence
- Conscious incompetence
- Conscious competence
- Unconscious competence

The first level—*unconscious incompetence*—means you are unaware of your own incompetence. You don't know what you don't know. In this case, before you read this chapter, you may simply not have been aware that you are distracted by your internal dialogue when you interact with others.

The second level is *conscious incompetence.* Here you become aware or conscious that you are not competent; you know what you don't know. You may now be aware that you are an easily distracted listener, but you do not know how to solve the problem.

considering others

Doctors Must Address More Than Physical Complaints

What's wrong with this picture: An eighty-year-old woman visits her doctor, the same one she has been seeing for a long time. He asks about her health, and she starts talking about not being happy in her new apartment after forty-one years living in the same house.

The apartment is in a different part of town and she misses her former neighbors, who used to pick up items for her at the grocery store.

Buying furniture has posed a problem, especially because her failing eyesight makes it difficult to drive places. She also worries about making her retirement money stretch as far as she needs. She says she is so lonely.

The doctor says "Mmm-hmm" and "That's too bad" at the appropriate times during her story. Then he steers the conversation toward the woman's heart condition and whether she has been experiencing any pain or other symptoms.

Stop right there, says Dr. Howard Waitzkin, an internal-medicine physician and sociologist at the University of California at Irvine. He says the doctor is focused on the physical symptom (a weak heart) and not listening to what is really disrupting this woman's life (the loss of community).

"Social problems almost always come up when doctors and patients are talking," Waitzkin says, "but they tend to be marginalized in the conversation."

This added work [of taking more time to listen] may seem a burden for busy doctors, but Waitzkin insists such careful listening has long-term benefits: It helps address patients' underlying concerns in one visit rather than let a stressful situation linger at the potential expense of the patient's health.

Source: Bob Condor, *Chicago Tribune,* January 5, 1995. © copyrighted Chicago Tribune Company. All rights reserved. Used with permission.

The third level is *conscious competence:* you are aware that you know something, but applying it has not yet become an integrated habit. You might have to work at decentering when you first begin using it.

The final level of skill attainment is *unconscious competence.* At this level your skills become second nature to you. After the age of 6, most people are unconsciously competent at tying their shoes; it is automatic. In the same way, you may become so skilled in the decentering process that you do it as the rule rather than as an exception. At this level you will also probably have the capacity to empathize, or "feel with" others as you listen. Understanding Diversity: Doctors Must Address More Than Physical Complaints points out that some doctors, despite their high level of professional training, do not always have highly developed listening skills. If they took time to *stop* and listen, says the writer, they would be far more effective at treating their patients. As a wise person once said, "Take a tip from nature—your ears aren't made to shut, but your mouth is."

Look

Nonverbal messages are powerful. As the primary ways we communicate feelings, emotions, and attitudes, they play a major role in the total communication process, particularly in the development of relationships. Facial expressions and vocal cues, as well as eye contact, posture, and use of gestures and movement, can dramatically color the meaning of a message. When the nonverbal message contradicts the verbal message, people almost always believe the nonverbal message. In listening to others, it is vital that you focus not only on the words, but also on the nonverbal messages. Listen with your eyes as well as your ears.

Another reason to look at another person is to establish eye contact, which signals that you are focusing your interest and attention on him or her. If your eyes are darting over your partner's head, looking for someone else, or if you are constantly peeking at your watch, your partner will rightfully get the message that you're not really listening. Researcher J. Harrigan found that people telegraph desire to change roles from listener to speaker by increasing eye contact, using gestures such as a raised finger, and shifting posture.[17] So it is important to maintain eye contact and monitor your partner's nonverbal signals when you are speaking as well as listening.

It is important, however, not to be distracted by nonverbal cues that may prevent you from interpreting the message correctly. A research team asked one group of college students to listen to a counselor, and another group both to view and to listen.[18] The students then rated the counselor's effectiveness. Students who both saw and heard the counselor perceived him as *less* effective, because his distracting nonverbal behaviors affected their evaluations. In Chapter 7, we provide more information about how to enhance your skill in interpreting the nonverbal messages of others.

Listen

After making a concerted effort to stop distracting internal dialogue and to look for nonverbal cues, you will then be in a better position to understand the verbal messages of others. To listen is to do more than focus on facts and message details; it is to search for the essence of the speaker's thoughts. We recommend the following strategies to help you improve your listening skill.

1. *Determine your listening goal.* You listen to other people for several reasons—to learn, to enjoy yourself, to evaluate, or to provide empathic support. With so many potential listening goals and options, it is useful to decide consciously what your listening objective is.

   If you are listening to someone give you directions to the city park, then your mental summaries should focus on the details of when to turn left and how many streets past the courthouse you go before you turn right. The details are crucial to achieving your objective. If, in contrast, your neighbor is telling you about her father's triple bypass operation, then your goal is to empathize. It is probably not important that you be able to recall when her father checked into the hospital or other details. Your job is to listen patiently and to provide emotional support. Clarifying your listening objective in your own mind can help you use appropriate skills to maximize your listening effectiveness.

2. *Transform listening barriers into listening goals.* If you can transform into listening goals the listening barriers you read about earlier, you will be well on your way to improving your listening skill. Make it a goal not to focus on your personal agenda. Make it a goal to use self-talk to manage emotional noise. Set a goal not to criticize the speaker. Remind yourself before each conversation to do mental summaries that capitalize on the differences between your information processing rate and the speaker's verbal delivery rate. And make it your business to choose a communication environment that is free of distraction from other incoming information or noise.

3. *When your listening goal is to remember a message, mentally summarize the details of the message.* This suggestion may seem to contradict the suggestion to avoid

focusing only on facts; but if your goal is to be able to recall information, it is important to grasp the details your partner provides. As we noted earlier, you can process words much more quickly than a person speaks. So periodically summarize the names, dates, and locations in the message. Organize the speaker's factual information into appropriate categories or try to place events in chronological order. Without a full understanding of the details, you will likely miss the speaker's major point.

4. *Mentally weave these summaries into a focused major point or series of major ideas.* Facts usually make the most sense when you can use them to help support an idea or major point. So, as you summarize, try to link the facts you have organized in your mind with key ideas and principles. Use facts to enhance your critical thinking as you analyze, synthesize, evaluate, and finally summarize the key points or ideas your listening partner is making.[19]

5. *Practice listening to challenging material.* To improve or even maintain any skill, you need to practice it. Listening experts suggest that listening skills deteriorate if people do not practice what they know. Listening to difficult, challenging material can sharpen listening skills, so good listeners practice by listening to documentaries, debates, and other challenging material rather than mindless sitcoms and other material that entertains but does not engage them mentally.

Ask Questions

Sometimes when others share a momentous occurrence, the story may tumble out in a rambling, disorganized way. You can help sort through the story if you ask questions to identify the sequence of events. "What happened first?" and "Then what happened?" can help both you and your partner clarify what happened.

If your partner is using words or phrases that you don't understand, ask for definitions. "He's just so lackadaisical!" moans Mariko. "What do you mean by lackadaisical? Could you give me an example?" asks Reggie. Sometimes asking for an example helps the speaker sort through the events as well.

Of course, if you are trying to understand another's feelings, you can ask how he or she is feeling, or how the event or situation made him or her feel. Often, however, nonverbal cues are more revealing than a verbal disclosure about feelings and emotions.

Reflect Content by Paraphrasing

The only way to know whether you understand a message is to check your understanding of the facts and ideas by paraphrasing your understanding. Verbally reflecting what you understood the speaker to say can dramatically minimize misunderstanding. Respond with a statement such as:

"Are you saying . . ."

"You seem to be describing . . ."

"So the point you are making seems to be . . ."

"Here is what I understand you to mean . . ."

"So here is what seemed to happen . . ."

Then summarize the events, details, or key points you think the speaker is trying to convey. This is not a word-for-word repetition of what the speaker has said, nor do you need to summarize the content of *each* phrase or minor detail. Rather, it is a **paraphrase** to check the accuracy of your understanding. Here is an example:

Juan: This week I have so much extra work to do. I'm sorry if I haven't been able to help keep this place clean. I know it's my turn to do the dishes tonight, but I have to get back to work. Could you do the dishes tonight?

Brigid: So you want me to do the dishes tonight and for the rest of the week. Right?

Juan: Well, I'd like you to help with the dishes tonight. But I think I can handle it for the rest of the week.

Brigid: OK. So I'll do them tonight and you take over tomorrow.

Juan: Yes.

paraphrasing. Checking the accuracy of your understanding by offering a verbal summary of the key ideas of your partner's message.

Research conducted in clinical counseling settings found that when a listener paraphrases the content and feelings of a speaker, the speaker is more likely to trust and value the listener.[20] Paraphrasing to check understanding is also a vital skill to use when you are trying to reconcile a difference of opinion. Chapter 8 shows you how to use it in that context.

Practice Paraphrasing: Identifying Details and Major Ideas

Read each of the following statements. After you have read each statement, cover it with your hand or a piece of paper. First, list as many of the details as you can recall from the message. Second, summarize your understanding of the major idea or key point of the message. As a variation to this activity, rather than reading the statement, have someone read the statement to you and then identify the details and major idea.

Statement 1: "I'm very confused. I reserved our conference room for 1 P.M. today for an important meeting. We all know that conference space is tight. I reserved the room last week with the administrative assistant. Now I learn that you are planning to use the conference room at noon for a two-hour meeting. It's now 11 A.M. We need to solve this problem soon. I have no other option for holding my meeting. And if I don't hold my meeting today, the boss is going to be upset."

Statement 2: "Hello, Marcia? I'm calling on my mobile phone. Where are you? I thought you were supposed to meet me at the circle drive 45 minutes ago. You know I can't be late for my seminar this evening. What do you mean, you're waiting at the circle drive? I don't see you.

No, I'm at Switzler Hall circle drive. You're where? No, that's not the circle drive I meant. I thought you'd know where I meant. Don't you ever listen? If you hurry, I can just make it to the seminar.

Statement 3: "Oh, Mary, I just don't know what to do. My daughter announced that when she turns 18 next week she's going to shave her head, get a large tattoo, and put a ring in her nose and eyebrow. She said it's something she's always wanted to do and now she can do it without my permission. She's always been such a sweet, compliant girl, but she seems to have turned wacky. I've tried talking with her. And her father isn't much help. He thinks it may look 'cool.' I just don't want her to look like a freak when she has her senior picture taken next month."

recap   How to Improve Your Listening Skills

Listening Skills	Definition	Action
Stop	Tune out distracting competing messages.	Become conscious of being distracted; use self-talk to remain focused.
Look	Become aware of the speaker's nonverbal cues; monitor your own nonverbal cues to communicate your interest in the speaker.	Establish eye contact; avoid fidgeting or performing other tasks when someone is speaking to you. Listen with your eyes.
Listen	Create meaning from your partner's verbal and nonverbal messages.	Mentally summarize details; link these details with main ideas.
Ask questions	Clarify words, events, and feelings by questioning the speaker.	Ask for definitions and examples; clarify sequences of events.
Reflect content by paraphrasing when appropriate	Briefly state the essence of what the speaker has said to ensure the accuracy of your understanding.	Summarize the key events, details, or points of what the speaker has said.

Improving Empathic Listening and Responding Skills

Above all, good listening is an other-oriented activity. As we discussed in Chapter 4, at the heart of being other-oriented is cultivating **empathy**—feeling what someone else is feeling. The word *empathy* comes from a Greek word for "passion" and is related to the German word, *Einfuhling*, which means "to feel with." Empathy involves emotions. Empathy and the companion skill of socially decentering—the cognitive process of taking into account another person's thoughts, feelings, and background—are often primary listening goals. Sometimes the purpose of listening to a friend, relative, or colleague is not just to remember what is said, but to demonstrate that you care and are compassionate toward your partner.

Good listening, especially listening to empathize with another, is active, not passive. To listen passively is to avoid displaying any behavior that lets the speaker know you are listening.[21] Passive listeners sit with a blank stare or a frozen facial expression. Their thoughts and feelings could be anywhere, for all the speaker knows. **Active listeners,** in contrast, respond mentally, verbally, and nonverbally to a speaker's message. Responding serves several specific functions. First, it can be a measure of how accurately you understood the message. If you burst out laughing as your friend tells you about losing his house in a flood, he'll know you misunderstood what he was saying. Second, your responses indicate whether you agree or disagree with the comments others make. If you tell your friend that you do not approve of her comments on abortion, she'll know your position on the information she shared. Finally, your responses tell speakers how they are affecting you. When you get tears in your eyes as you listen to your friend describe how lonely he has felt since his father died, he will know that you are affected by the pain he is feeling. Like radar that guides high-tech weapons, your feedback provides information to help others decide whether or not to correct the course of their messages.

empathy. Feeling what others are feeling, rather than just acknowledging that they are feeling a certain way.

active listening. Interactive process of responding mentally, verbally, and nonverbally to a speaker's message.

As you can see, responding is something done for others that also offers great benefits for the responder. It is the key to exchanging mutually understood, emotionally satisfying messages. Responding is especially critical if you are listening to provide support. Of course, listening to empathize is only one of the possible listening goals you may have. We are not suggesting that ferreting out someone's emotions is the goal of every listening encounter. That would be tedious for both you and your listening partners. But when you do want to listen empathically and respond, you must shift the focus to your partner and try to understand the message from his or her perspective.[22]

Empathy is not a single skill but a collection of skills that help you predict how others will respond. Daniel Goleman's book *Emotional Intelligence* is an outstanding resource that discusses the role and importance of our emotions in developing empathy with others.[23] Goleman has found evidence that people who are emotionally intelligent—sensitive to others, empathic, and other-oriented—have better interpersonal relationships. Goleman summarizes the centrality of emotions in developing empathy by quoting Antoine De Saint-Exupery: "It is with the heart that one sees rightly; what is essential is invisible to the eye."[24]

The quiz in Considering Others: Test Your Empathy Ability can help you determine how effectively you empathize with others. We then discuss strategies you can use to enhance your empathy skills.

When your friends have "one of those days," perhaps they seek you out to talk about it. They may not have any real problems to solve—perhaps it was just a day filled with miscommunication and squabbles with their partners or co-workers. But they want to tell you the details. Do you listen empathically, without giving advice? Often that is what your friends are seeking—a listener who focuses attention on them and understands what they are saying. People are willing to listen empathically for the same reasons they like to give friends gifts. It makes people feel good to show that they value others. Psychologist and counselor Carl Rogers summarized the value of empathy when he said, "A high degree of empathy in a relationship is possibly the most potent factor in bringing about change and learning."

e-connections
What's Your EQ?

According to best-selling author psychologist Daniel Goleman, your emotional intelligence is your ability to interact with others by listening, being empathic, and generally being sensitive to others rather than being oblivious to others or self-focused. In essence, your emotional intelligence is the extent to which you are other-oriented, the central premise of this book. What's your EQ (emotional intelligence quotient)? To take a short, ten-question test, click on the following Web address and assess your EQ:

http://www.utne.com/azEq.tmp1

Here's another EQ test to try:

http://homearts.com/depts/relat/olegab5.htm

considering
others

Test Your Empathy Ability

Empathy is an emotional capability that often grows out of a conscious decentering process. It is the ability to move away from yourself enough to "feel for" another person. But it does not mean abandoning your own self. On the contrary, empathic people often have a strong self-concept and high self-esteem, which enable them to be generous with others. Take this short test to assess your empathy. Respond to each statement by indicating the degree to which the statement is true regarding the way you typically communicate with others. When you think of how you communicate, is the statement always false (answer 1), usually false (answer 2), sometimes false and

sometimes true (answer 3), usually true (answer 4), or always true (answer 5)?

_____ 1. I try to understand others' experiences from their perspectives.

_____ 2. I follow the Golden Rule ("Do unto others as you would have them do unto you") when communicating with others.

_____ 3. I can "tune in" to emotions others are experiencing when we communicate.

_____ 4. When trying to understand how others feel, I imagine how I would feel in their situation.

_____ 5. I am able to tell what others are feeling without being told.

_____ 6. Others experience the same feelings I do in any given situation.

_____ 7. When others are having problems, I can imagine how they feel.

_____ 8. I find it hard to understand the emotions others experience.

_____ 9. I try to see others as they want me to.

_____ 10. I never seem to know what others are thinking when we communicate.

To find your score, first reverse the responses for the even-numbered items (if you wrote 1, make it 5; if you wrote 2, make it 4; if you wrote 3, leave it as 3; if you wrote 4, make it 2; if you wrote 5, make it 1). Next, add the numbers next to each statement. Scores range from 10 to 50. The higher your score, the more you are able to empathize.

Source: William Gudykunst, _Bridging Differences_, 3rd ed. (Thousand Oaks, CA: Sage, 1998), p. 234.

Understand Your Partner's Feelings: Imagine How You Would Feel

When your goal is to empathize or "feel with" your partner, you might begin by imagining how you would feel under the same circumstances. If your spouse comes home dejected from being hassled at work, try to recall how you felt when that happened to you. If a friend calls to tell you his mother is ill, try to imagine how you would feel if the situation were reversed. Of course, your reaction to these events might be different from your spouse's or your friend's. You may need to decenter and remember how your partner felt in other similar situations, to understand how he or she is feeling now.

Paraphrase Emotions

The bottom line in empathic responding is to make certain that you accurately understand how the other person is feeling. You can paraphrase, beginning with such phrases as

"So you are feeling . . ."

"You must feel . . ."

You can better understand a partner's feelings—empathize with him or her—if you listen and try to recall how you might have felt in similar situations. (Gerard Loucel/Tony Stone Images)

"So now you feel . . ."

"Emotionally, you must be feeling . . ."

In the following example of empathic responding, the listener asks questions, summarizes content, and summarizes feelings.

David: I think I'm in over my head. My boss gave me a job to do and I just don't know how to do it. I'm afraid I've bitten off more than I can chew.

Mike: (Thinks how he would feel if he were given an important task at work but did not know how to complete the task, then asks for more information.) What job did she ask you to do?

David: I'm supposed to do an inventory of all the items in the warehouse on the VAX computer system and have it finished by the end of the week. I don't have the foggiest notion of how to start. I've never even used that system.

Mike: (summarizing feelings.) So you feel panicked because you may not have enough time to learn the system *and* do the inventory.

David: Well, I'm not only panicked, I'm afraid I may be fired.

Mike: (summarizing feelings.) So your fear that you might lose your job is getting in the way of just focusing on the task and seeing what you can get done. It's making you feel like you made a mistake in taking this job.

David: That's exactly how I feel.

Note that toward the end of the dialogue Mike has to make a couple of tries to summarize David's feelings accurately. Also note that Mike does a good job of listening and responding without giving advice. Just by being an active listener, you can help your partner clarify a problem.

Sympathy versus Empathy

Most card shops have a sympathy card section. Such cards let people know you realize they are feeling bad about the death of someone close to them. To **sympathize** is to say you are sorry—that you want to offer your support and acknowledge that someone is feeling bad. Empathy goes one step further than sympathy. Empathy means that you try to perceive the world from another's perspective; you attempt to feel what someone else feels.

Respond to the sample situations below both with sympathy and with empathy.

1. A good friend of yours just phoned to tell you that her dog, a well-loved fourteen-year old pet, has just died.

   Respond with sympathy: _____

   _____

   Respond with empathy: _____

   _____

   _____

2. Your older brother comes to visit you and tells you that he and his wife are getting a divorce after twenty years of marriage.

   Respond with sympathy: _____

   _____

   _____

   Respond with empathy: _____

   _____

   _____

3. A friend tells you that she just got fired from her job.

   Respond with sympathy: _____

   _____

   _____

   Respond with empathy: _____

   _____

   _____

Source: Adapted from William Gudykunst, *Bridging Differences*, 3rd ed. (Thousand Oaks, CA: Sage, 1998). Reprinted by permission of Sage Publications, Inc.

We have discussed responding and the active listening process from a tidy step-by-step textbook approach. In practice, you may have to back up and clarify content, ask more questions, and rethink how you would feel before you attempt to summarize how someone else feels. Conversely, you may be able to summarize feelings *without* asking questions or summarizing content if the message is clear and it relates to a situation with which you are very familiar. Overusing this skill can slow down a conversation and make the other person uncomfortable or irritated. But if you use it judiciously, paraphrasing can help both you and your partner keep focused on the issues and ideas at hand.

Reflecting content or feeling through paraphrasing can be especially useful in the following situations:

● Before you take an important action

● Before you argue or criticize

● When your partner has strong feelings or wants to talk over a problem

● When your partner is speaking "in code" or using unclear abbreviations

sympathy. Acknowledging that someone may be feeling bad.

- When your partner wants to understand your feelings and thoughts
- When you are talking to yourself
- When you encounter new ideas[25]

Sometimes, however, you truly don't understand how another person really feels. At times like this, be cautious of telling others, "I know just how you feel." It may be more important simply to let others know that you care about them than to grill them in search of "their feelings."

If you do decide to use paraphrasing skills, keep the following guidelines in mind:

- Use your own words.
- Don't go beyond the information communicated by the speaker.
- Be concise.
- Be specific.
- Be accurate.

Do *not* use paraphrasing skills if you aren't able to be open and accepting, if you do not trust the other person to find his or her own solution, if you are using these skills as a way of hiding yourself from another, or if you feel pressured, hassled, or tired.[26] And as we have already discussed, overuse of paraphrasing can be distracting and unnatural.

building your skills

Listening and Paraphrasing Content and Emotion

Working in groups of three, ask person A to briefly identify a problem or conflict that he or she is having (or has had) with another person (coworker, supervisor, spouse, or family member). Person B should use questioning, content paraphrasing, and emotion paraphrasing skills to explore the problem. Person C should observe the discussion and evaluate person B's listening and paraphrasing skills, using the Observer Checklist. Make a check mark next to all of the skills that person B uses effectively.

Observer Checklist

Nonverbal Skills

_____ Direct eye contact

_____ Open, relaxed body posture

_____ Uncrossed arms

_____ Uncrossed legs

_____ Appropriate hand gestures

_____ Reinforcing nods

_____ Responsive facial expression

_____ Appropriate tone of voice

_____ Appropriate volume

Verbal Skills

_____ Effective and appropriate questions

_____ Accurate paraphrase of content

_____ Accurate paraphrase of emotion

_____ Timely paraphrase

_____ Didn't interrupt the speaker

Don't be discouraged if your initial attempts to use these skills seem awkward and uncomfortable. Any new skill takes time to learn and use well. The instructions and samples you have seen here should serve as guides, rather than as hard-and-fast prescriptions to follow during each conversation.

How to Respond with Empathy

Responding with Empathy	Action
Understand Your Partner's Feelings	Ask yourself how you would feel if you had experienced a similar situation or recall how you *did* feel under similar circumstances. Or recall how your *partner* felt under similar circumstances.
Paraphrase Emotions	When appropriate, try to summarize what you think your partner may be feeling.

When I ask you to listen to me and you start giving advice,
you have not done what I asked.
When I ask you to listen to me and you begin to tell me why I shouldn't feel that way
you are trampling on my feelings.
When I ask you to listen to me and you feel you have to do something
to solve my problems, you have failed me, strange as that may seem.
Listen! All I asked, was that you listen. Not talk or do—just hear me.
Advice is cheap: 50 cents will get you both Dear Abby and Billy Graham
in the same newspaper.
And I can do for myself; I'm not helpless. Maybe discouraged and faltering,
but not helpless.
When you do something for me that I can and need to do for myself,
you contribute to my fear and weakness.
But when you accept as a simple fact that I do feel what I feel,
no matter how irrational, then I quit trying to convince you
and can get about the business of understanding what's behind this irrational feeling.
And when that's clear, the answers are obvious and I don't need advice.
Irrational feelings make sense when we understand what's behind them.
Perhaps that's why prayer works, sometimes, for some people
because God is mute, and doesn't give advice or try to fix things,
God just listens and lets you work it out for yourself.
So, please listen and just hear me, and, if you want to talk,
wait a minute for your turn: and I'll listen to you.

Anonymous

Improving Critical Listening and Responding Skills

After putting it off for several months, you've decided to buy a mobile phone. As you begin to talk to your friends, you're surprised to find a bewildering number of factors to consider: Do you want digital? Cellular? Voice mail? How many weekend minutes, evening minutes, or daily minutes of calling time do you need? You decide to head to a store to see if a salesperson can help you sort through the maze of options. The salesperson is friendly enough, but you become even more overwhelmed with the number of options, bells, and whistles to consider. As you try to make this decision, your listening goal is not to empathize with those who extol the virtues of mobile phones. Nor do you need to take a multiple-choice test over the information they share. To sort through the information, you need to listen critically.

Critical listening involves listening to evaluate the quality, appropriateness, value, or importance of the information you hear. *The goal of a critical listener is to use information to make a choice.* Whether you're selecting a new phone, deciding whom to vote for, choosing a potential date, or evaluating a new business plan, you will be faced with many opportunities to use your critical listening skills in interpersonal situations.

A critical listener is not necessarily one who offers negative comments. A critical listener seeks to identify both good information and information that is flawed or less helpful. We call this process *information triage. Triage* is a French term that usually describes the process used by emergency medical personnel to determine which of several patients is the most severely ill or injured and needs immediate medical attention. **Information triage** is a process of evaluating and sorting out issues. An effective critical listener performs information triage; he or she is able to distinguish useful and accurate information and conclusions from information that is less useful, as well as conclusions that are inaccurate or invalid.

How do you develop the skill of information triage? Initially, listening critically involves the same strategies as listening to comprehend that we discussed earlier. Before you evaluate information, it's vital that you first *understand* the information. Second, examine the logic or reasoning used in the message. And finally, be mindful of whether you are basing your evaluations on facts—something that is observed or verifiable, or inference—a conclusion based on partial information. Although courses in logic, argumentation, and public speaking often present skills to help you evaluate information, it's also important to listen critically during interpersonal conversations.

Look for Faulty Logic: Wrong Reasoning

Effective critical listeners can spot whether or not a speaker is logically reaching a valid, well-supported conclusion. **Logic** is the application of appropriate evidence to reach a valid, well-reasoned conclusion. People who are thinking illogically often use reasoning fallacies to reach a flawed conclusion. The point they are making or the conclusion they are reaching does not make logical sense. A **fallacy** occurs when someone attempts to persuade without adequate evidence or uses arguments that are

critical listening. Listening in which the goal is to evaluate and assess the quality, appropriateness, value, or importance of information.

information triage. Ability to sort good information from less useful or valid information.

logic. Use of appropriate evidence to reach a valid, well-reasoned conclusion.

fallacy. False reasoning that occurs when someone attempts to persuade without adequate evidence or with arguments that are irrelevant or inappropriate.

irrelevant, inaccurate, or inappropriate. The study of logic and reasoning is usually included in courses in debate, argumentation, persuasion, public speaking, and philosophy. But because people often listen critically in interpersonal situations, we include a brief overview of classic reasoning fallacies.[27] You can enhance both your critical listening and responding skills if you can avoid or spot the following fallacies.

Causal Fallacy

A **causal fallacy** occurs when someone makes a faulty cause-and-effect connection between two things or events. A popular children's book titled *Wilbur, the Dog Who Chased the Sun Up* is about a dog, Wilbur, who thought that his barking every morning caused the sunrise. It made sense to him: He barked; the sun came up. But simply because one thing follows another does not mean that the first event caused the second event. Be wary of someone who claims such a cause-and-effect relationship without evidence or proof. For example, the salesperson who claims, "People who buy mobile phones make more money" cannot guarantee that buying a phone will cause you to have increased income. Another logical explanation could be that mobile phone purchasers already have well-paying jobs—that's why they need a mobile phone.

Bandwagon Fallacy

Some people will try to get your vote or money by claiming that "everybody thinks this is a good idea, so you should too." Such a person is guilty of the **bandwagon fallacy.** Because someone says that "everyone" is "jumping on the bandwagon" or agrees with an idea or supports a point of view does not necessarily make it accurate or correct. Examples of bandwagon fallacies are "Everyone knows you will be more popular if you purchase a convertible" and "Everyone believes we need to increase the sales tax to support education for our children."

Either/Or Fallacy

The **either/or fallacy** practically defines itself. It occurs when someone argues that there are only two alternatives to a problem or issue. It's a fallacy because life is rarely that simple; there are virtually always more than only two options to consider. "It's either increase taxes or fire several teachers," bellows a member of the school board. Although those may be two choices, there are undoubtedly more options than just those. Be skeptical when you hear someone boil an issue down to only two options. Another example of an either/or fallacy is "Either we put trigger locks on all guns, or we limit the sale of handguns."

Hasty Generalization

A generalization is simply a conclusion someone has reached. A **hasty generalization** is a conclusion without adequate evidence to support it. For example, Ben claimed you shouldn't eat shrimp, because his nephew ate shrimp and became ill. Ben was guilty of using a hasty generalization fallacy. One case does not prove the point. Even if two or three out of the millions of people who eat shrimp every day became ill after dining on shrimp scampi, those instances are not adequate evidence to claim that no one should enjoy a shrimp cocktail. In another instance, your coworker tells you, "You don't need to worry about kids joining street gangs. My two sons went through high school and were never tempted to join a gang. Gangs are no real threat in our community." This, too, is an example of making a hasty generalization.

causal fallacy. Making a faulty cause-and-effect connection between two things or events.

bandwagon fallacy. Reasoning that suggests that because everyone else believes something or is doing something, then it must be valid, accurate, or effective.

either/or fallacy. Oversimplifying an issue as having only one or two outcomes or choices (either this *or* that).

hasty generalization. Reaching a conclusion without adequate evidence to support the conclusion.

Attacking the Person

At your office holiday party you overhear someone say, "We know Karl's idea of expanding the parking garage is stupid, because Karl grew up in the country. He just isn't sophisticated." The person making this claim is guilty of a reasoning fallacy called attacking the person. **Attacking the person** occurs when you critique someone's idea because of an irrelevant personal characteristic, rather than evaluating the idea itself. "She grew up in China. She could not possibly have an insightful thing to say about the need for a new airport." This is another example of inappropriately attacking the person rather than the idea the individual is proposing. Don't dismiss what someone says only because you have been turned against the person who presented it. Focus on the merit of the message or idea rather than the irrelevant qualifications of the messenger.

Red Herring

When someone tries to divert attention from the real issue or idea being discussed, by using irrelevant facts or information rather than directly responding to the issue at hand, the person is using the **red herring** fallacy. This fallacy gets its name from an old trick of dragging a red herring fish across a trail to divert the dogs who were sent to track someone down. When asked a difficult or potentially embarrassing question, politicians often respond with a completely different issue or irrelevant piece of information. Here's how one politician used a red herring to divert attention from something she'd rather not talk about: "So the question is, did I illegally raise campaign money? Well, the issue is really 'Did my opponent sponsor legislation to support underage drinking?' Too many teenagers are abusing alcohol, and this abuse must stop!" Did you see how the issue of teenage drinking was used to divert attention from charges of the use of illegal campaign funds? Watch out for speakers who try to divert your attention from issues they'd rather not talk about.

Non Sequitur

"Non sequitur" is a Latin term for "it does not follow." A **non sequitur fallacy** occurs when one idea or conclusion does not logically follow the previous idea or conclusion. Non sequitur arguments don't make sense. "We need to hire more workers because we have fluoridated water in our community." After hearing a non sequitur argument, you may scratch your head and mentally or audibly say, "Huh?" "Because we have a new campus radio station, we should pick up the trash around city hall." Or going door-to-door, the mayoral candidate says, "I will make a wonderful mayor because I have five children and sixteen grandchildren." These, too, are non sequitur conclusions. There is no logical connection between radio stations and picking up trash. And it's a stretch to argue that you'd make a better mayor because you have children and grandchildren.

Being able to spot the use of faulty logic is an important ability when trying to evaluate the soundness of a speaker's conclusion. Being knowledgeable about reasoning fallacies can also help you better respond to flawed arguments developed by others.

Avoid Jumping to Conclusions: Fact–Inference Confusion

Imagine this scene. You are a detective investigating a death. You are given the following information: (1) Leo and Moshia are found lying together on the floor, (2) Leo and Moshia are both dead, (3) Leo and Moshia are surrounded by water

attacking the person. Critiquing irrelevant personal characteristics of the person who is proposing an idea, rather than critiquing the idea itself.

red herring. Using irrelevant facts or information to distract someone from the issue that needs to be discussed.

non sequitur. Idea or conclusion that does not logically follow the previous idea or conclusion. Latin for "it does not follow."

and broken glass, (4) on the sofa near Leo and Moshia, a cat is seen with its back arched, apparently ready to defend itself.

Given these sketchy details, do you, the detective assigned to the case, have any theories about the cause of Leo and Moshia's demise? Perhaps they slipped on the water, crashed into a table, broke a vase, and died (that would explain the water and broken glass). Or maybe their attacker recently left the scene, and the cat is still distressed by the commotion. Clearly, you could make several inferences (conclusions based on partial information) as to the probable cause of death. Oh yes, there is one detail we forgot to mention: Leo and Moshia are fish. Does that help?

People often spin grand explanations and hypotheses based on sketchy details. Acting on inferences, people may act as though the "facts" clearly point to a specific conclusion. Determining the difference between a fact and an inference can help you more accurately use language to reach valid conclusions about what you see and experience.

What makes a fact a fact? Most students, when asked this question, respond by saying, "A fact is something that has been proven true." If that is the case, *how* has something been proven true? In a court of law, a **fact** is something that has been observed or witnessed. Anything else is speculation or inference.

"Did you see my client in your house, taking your jewelry?" asks the wise attorney.

"No," says the plaintiff.

"Then you do not know for a fact that my client is a thief."

"I guess not," the plaintiff admits.

The problem occurs when we respond to something as if it were a fact (something observed), when in reality it is an **inference** (a conclusion based upon speculation):

"It's a fact that your mother doesn't like me."

"It's a fact that you will be poor all of your life."

"It's a fact that you will fail this course."

Each of these statements, although it might very well be true, misuses the term *fact*. If you cannot recognize when you are making an inference instead of stating a fact, you may give your judgments more credibility than they deserve.

Being consciously competent about whether someone is reaching a conclusion based on facts or is speculating by drawing an inference can help you improve your information triage skill. An effective critical listener considers the quality of the factual evidence used to develop ideas and opinions. You can also more effectively respond and ask questions if you are aware of whether someone is drawing conclusions based on direct observation (facts) or partial information (inferences). Although people often reach conclusions based on inferences, being sensitive to the differences between how conclusions and observations are labeled can improve both critical listening and responding skills.

Improving Your Responding Skills

We've offered several strategies for responding to others when your goal is to comprehend information, empathize with others, or evaluate messages. Regardless of your communication goal, we'll now present several additional strategies to enhance your skill in responding to others. The timing of the response, usefulness of

fact. Something that has been directly observed to be true or can be proved to be true.

inference. Conclusion based on partial or available evidence.

When you are teaching some-one a new skill, the timing of your feedback is just as impor-tant as what you say. When should this grownup tell the child he is helping, how to im-prove his handstand? (Robert Harbison)

the information, amount of detail, and descriptiveness of the response are useful strategies to consider when responding to others.

Provide Well-Timed Responses

Feedback is usually most effective when you offer it at the earliest opportunity, par-ticularly if your objective is to teach someone a skill. For example, if you are teach-ing your friend how to make your famous egg rolls, you provide a step-by-step commentary as you watch your pupil. If he makes a mistake, you don't wait until the egg rolls are finished to tell him that he left out the cabbage. He needs immedi-ate feedback to finish the rest of the sequence successfully.

Sometimes, however, if a person is already sensitive and upset about something, delaying feedback can be wise. Use your critical thinking skills to analyze when feedback will do the most good. Rather than automatically offering immediate cor-rection, use the just-in-time (JIT) approach, and provide feedback just before the person might make another mistake. If, for example, your daughter typically rushes through math tests and fails to check her work, remind her right before her next test to double-check her answers, not immediately after the one she just failed. To provide feedback about a relationship, select a mutually agreeable place and time when both of you are rested and relaxed; avoid hurling feedback at someone "for his own good" immediately after he offends you.

Provide Usable Information

Perhaps you've heard this advice: Never try to teach a pig to sing. It wastes your time. It doesn't sound pretty. And it annoys the pig. When you provide information to someone, be certain that it is useful and relevant. How can you make sure your partner can use the information you share? Put yourself in your partner's mind-set.

Ask yourself, "If I were this person, how would I respond to this information? Is it information I can act on? Or is it information that may make matters worse?" Under the guise of effective feedback, you may be tempted to tell others your complete range of feelings and emotions. But research suggests that selective feedback is best. In one study, married couples who practiced selective self-disclosure were more satisfied than couples who told everything they knew or were feeling.[28] Immersing your partner in information that is irrelevant or that may be damaging to the relationship may be cathartic, but it may not enhance the quality of your relationship or improve understanding.

Avoid Unnecessary Details

When you are selecting meaningful information, also try to cut down on the volume of information. Don't overwhelm your listener with details that obscure the key point of your feedback. Hit only the high points that will benefit the listener. Be brief.

Be Descriptive Rather Than Evaluative

"You're an awful driver!" shouts Doris to her husband Frank. Although Doris may feel she has provided simple feedback to her spouse about his skills, Frank will probably not respond warmly or even listen closely to her feedback. If Doris tries to be more descriptive and less evaluative, then he might be inclined to listen: "Frank, you are traveling 70 miles an hour in a 50 miles an hour zone" or "Frank, I get very nervous when you zigzag so fast through the freeway traffic." is a less offensive comment. It describes Frank's behavior rather than render judgments about him that are likely to trigger a defensive, passive listening reaction.

Suggestions for Improving Responding Skills

Provide Well-Timed Responses	Sometimes immediate feedback is best; at other times provide a just-in-time (JIT) response when it will do the most good.
Provide Meaningful Information	Select information that your partner can act on, rather than making vague comments or suggestions that are beyond his or her capabilities.
Avoid Unnecessary Details	Avoid information overload; don't bombard the listener with too much information; keep your comments focused on major points.
Be Descriptive	Don't evaluate your listening partner; focus on behavior rather than personality.

Practicing Your Responding Skills

The purpose of this exercise is to help you practice your responding skills. Read each of the following paragraphs and then write each of the four types of responses, just as if you were talking to someone:

1. *Ask questions:* Probe for more information.

2. *Paraphrase content:* What is the essence of the message?

3. *Decentering response:* What is the other person thinking?

4. *Empathic response:* What is the other person feeling?

Now pair up with another person and compare your responses. If necessary, revise your responses to provide an accurate response in each of the four response styles.

Situation 1: "I'm not sure what to do. My life seems consumed with work. I'm trying to go to school, I work more than 20 hours a week, and when I get home I have the kids to take care of. I'm exhausted. But I can't quit my job; I need the money. And if I drop out of school, it just means I'll be stuck with a minimum-wage job longer. I have to take care of my kids—I can't just stop meeting their needs. But what about me? I'm exhausted, and I know I can't keep going on like this."

Situation 2: "I'm really struggling with what to do about my religion. When I was growing up, my family and I would always attend a very liberal church; there were few rules and no list of do's and don'ts. As I've grown older, my beliefs have changed. I need more structure in my life. I've started worshiping with another group that offers more fundamental views toward religion. The problem is that my parents, family, and even many of my friends believe I'm betraying them and my own heritage; my change

in worship habits is affecting my relationship with them. I just don't feel comfortable worshiping as I used to, but I also don't want to create conflict with my family and friends."

Situation 3: "I'm really not sure what to do about my relationship with Ben. We've been together for about a year now. I moved in with him a couple of months ago. But lately we've had more friction between us; we seem to disagree about more things. It seems to me that we want different things out of our relationship. I'm comfortable with just keeping things as they are, but Ben would like to make a more serious commitment. The increased conflict we're having makes me question whether our relationship will work out long term."

Source: Adapted from David W. Johnson, *Reaching Out: Interpersonal Effectiveness and Self-Actualization* (Boston: Allyn & Bacon, 2000), p. 234.

Summary

Listening effectively to others is the quintessential skill required for establishing other-oriented relationships. Listening, the process of creating meaning from verbal and nonverbal messages, includes selecting, attending, understanding, remembering, and responding to others. Preferred listening styles vary. Some of us are people-oriented listeners; some are action-oriented; others are content-oriented; and still others are time-oriented.

Most of us don't listen effectively because we are self-oriented instead of other-oriented. Barriers to effective listening include being self-focused, being distracted by emotional noise, criticizing the speaker, wasting the difference between speech rate and thought rate, and being distracted by information overload and external noise.

To become better listeners, we can pursue three seemingly simple steps: Stop, look, and listen. To stop means to avoid tuning in to our own distracting messages and to become mindful of what others are saying. To look is to observe and interpret unspoken messages. Nonverbal communication skills and principles are discussed in greater detail in the next chapter. After stopping and looking, we can then listen more effectively to others by focusing on details and the speaker's key ideas. Being other-oriented does not mean we should abandon our own convictions or values, but that we should make a conscious effort to pay attention to the needs and concerns of others. After we complete these three steps, we should ask questions and reflect content by paraphrasing.

We can further improve our ability to listen and respond empathically by seeking to understand our partner's feelings and paraphrasing his or her emotions. We can further improve our ability to listen and respond critically by looking for faulty logic and being consciously competent at distinguishing facts from inferences. And we can improve our skills at responding, regardless of the communication objective, by providing well-timed responses; providing usable information; avoiding unnecessary details; and being descriptive rather than evaluative.

For Discussion and Review

Focus on Comprehension

1. What are some differences between hearing and listening?
2. What are key listening barriers that keep people from listening well?
3. What strategies can we follow to respond with empathy?
4. What are some suggestions for effectively paraphrasing interpersonal messages?
5. What are reasoning fallacies? Provide examples.

Focus on Critical Thinking

6. Identify two situations during the past twenty-four hours in which you were an effective or ineffective listener. What factors contributed to your listening skill (or lack of skill)?
7. Miranda and Salvador often disagree about who should handle some of the child-rearing tasks in their home. When they have discussions about these issues, what are some effective listening skills and strategies that they could use to make sure they understand each other?
8. Jason and Chris are roommates. They both work hard each day and come home exhausted. What suggestions would you offer to help them listen effectively even when they are tired?

Focus on Ethics

9. Is it possible for paraphrasing and active listening to become a way to manipulate others? Support your answer.
10. Your friend asks you how you like her new dress. You really feel it is a bit too revealing and may embarrass your friend. But it is time to leave for your evening activity. Should you respond honestly even though it may mean that you and your friend will be late for important engagements?

11. Your roommate wants to tell you about his day. You are tired and really don't want to hear all the details. Should you fake attention so that you won't hurt his feelings, or simply tell your roommate you are tired and would rather not hear the details?

For Your Journal

1. Keep this checklist, first published in the *International Listening Association Newsletter,* with you one full day to monitor your listening problems.

   ### A Checklist for Listeners

   Today I . . .

   Interrupted other people _____ times.

   Misunderstood other people _____ times.

   Lost track of a conversation _____ times.

   Stopped making eye contact with a speaker _____ times.

   Asked someone to repeat himself/herself _____ times.

   Let my mind wander while listening to someone _____ times.

   Changed the subject in the middle of a conversation _____ times.

   Jumped to a conclusion about what someone was going to say _____ times.

   Reacted emotionally to what someone was saying before he or she finished _____ times.

   After keeping track of your personal listening statistics, what changes would you like to make in your listening behavior?

2. Monitor and then jot down notes about your own self-talk during a conversation with another person. What competing thoughts and ideas occurred to you while you were conversing with your partner? What did you do to refocus on the message?

Learning with Others

1. Place a check mark beside all the communication barriers that affect you. Identify the action you will take to manage the barrier. Discuss your results with your classmates.

   ### How Will You Overcome Listening Barriers?

Barrier	Action
Being self-absorbed	_____
	_____

Emotional noise

_____

_____

Criticizing the speaker

_____

_____

Speech rate versus thought rate

_____

_____

Information overload

_____

_____

External noise

_____

_____

2. Charting Your Listening Cycle

   Are you a morning person or an evening person? Use the chart shown here to plot your listening energy cycle. Draw a line starting at 6 A.M. showing the highs and lows of your potential listening effectiveness. For example, if you are usually still asleep at 6 A.M., your line will be at 0 and start upward when you awake. If you are a morning person, your line will peak in the morning. Or perhaps your line will indicate that you listen best in the evening.

   After you have charted your typical daily listening cycle, gather in small groups with your classmates to compare listening cycles. Identify listening strategies that can help you capitalize on your listening "up" periods. Also, based on the chapter and your own experiences, identify ways to enhance your listening when you traditionally have low listening energy.

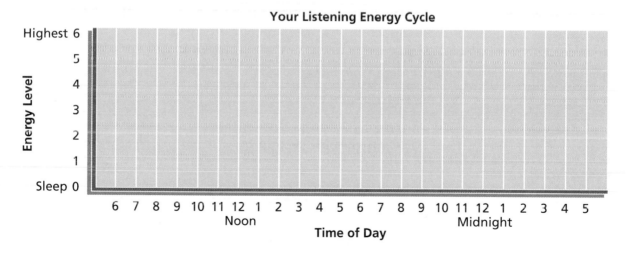

3. Assign one student from a group to speak very slowly on a difficult subject. Have the other members of the group write down short summaries during pauses in the speech, then compare their summaries.

4. Make a list of "red-flag" words that have derailed your listening ability in the past. Ask another student to make up a paragraph about an important issue, using these words, and read it aloud to you. Monitor your reactions to the words and see whether you can steer your internal conversations back to the issue. Also notice how you begin to feel about the speaker and what you do about those feelings.

Communicating Verbally

After you study this chapter

you should be able to ...

1. Describe the relationship between words and meaning.

2. Understand how words influence us and our culture.

3. Identify word barriers and know how to manage them.

4. Discuss how the words we use affect our relationships with others.

5. Understand supportive approaches to relating to others.

6. Understand how to confirm other people's sense of themselves.

● Understanding How Words Work

● Recognizing the Power of Words

● Avoiding Word Barriers

● Using Words to Establish Supportive Relationships

● Using Words to Value Others

Words can destroy. What we call each other ultimately becomes what we think of each other, and it matters.

JEANNE J. KIRKPATRICK

Words are powerful. Those who use them skillfully can exert great influence with just a few of them. Consider these notable achievements:

Lincoln set the course for a nation in a 267-word speech: the Gettysburg Address.

Shakespeare expressed the quintessence of the human condition in Hamlet's famous "To be, or not to be" soliloquy—363 words long.

Several of our great religions adhere to a comprehensive moral code expressed in a mere 297 words: the Ten Commandments.

Words have great power in private life as well. In this chapter we will examine ways to use them more effectively in interpersonal relationships. We'll investigate how to harness the power that words have to affect emotions, thoughts, and actions, and we'll describe links between language and culture. We will also identify communication barriers that may keep you from using words effectively and note strategies and skills for managing those barriers. Finally, we will examine the role of speech in establishing supportive relationships with others. In one of his pessimistic moments, the poet Robert Frost said, "Half the world is composed of people who have something to say and can't, and the other half who have nothing to say and keep on saying it." This chapter is designed to help you prove him wrong, to help you become a person who has something to say and can say it well.

Understanding How Words Work

As you read the printed words on this page, how are you able to make sense out of these black marks? When you hear words spoken by others, how are you able to interpret those sounds? Although several theories attempt to explain how people learn language and ascribe meaning to both printed and uttered words, there is no single universally held view that neatly clarifies the mystery.

Here's one thing that *is* known about words and meaning: *Meanings are in people, not in words.* As we noted in Chapter 1, one of the myths about communication is that words contain meaning. They don't. Meaning is created because words are

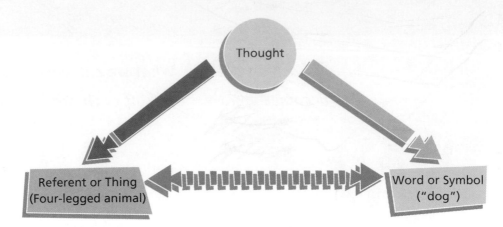

Figure 6.1

Triangle of Meaning

arbitrary symbols, used within a specific context, and interpreted within a cultural framework, with both denotative and connotative meaning. It's inaccurate to assume that a word means the same thing to everyone. The transactional nature of interpersonal communication suggests that meaning is co-created through the process of using and making sense out of words. People construct their reality based on how they use words to make sense out of the world. Words don't mean anything until someone interprets them and creates meaning. Now let's unpack that last sentence to gain a fuller appreciation of the transactional nature of words and meaning.

Words Are Symbols

As we noted in Chapter 1, words are **symbols** that represent something else. A printed or spoken word triggers an image, sound, concept, or experience. Take the word *cat,* for instance. The word may conjure up in your mind's eye a hissing creature with bared claws and fangs. Or perhaps you envision a cherished pet curled up by a fireplace.

The classic model in Figure 6.1 was developed by Ogden and Richards to explain the relationships between *referents, thought,* and *symbols.*[1] **Referents** are the things the symbols (words) represent. **Thought** is the mental process of creating an image, sound, concept, or experience triggered by the referent or the symbol. So these three elements, referents, thought, and symbols, become inextricably linked. Although some scholars find this model too simplistic to explain how people link all words to meaning, it does illustrate the process for most concepts, people, and tangible things.

Words Are Arbitrary

symbol. Word, sound, or visual device that represents an image, sound, concept, or experience.

referent. Thing that a symbol represents.

thought. Mental process of creating an image, sound, concept, or experience triggered by a referent or symbol.

In English, words arbitrarily represent something else. The word *dog,* for example, does not *sound* like a dog or *look* at all like a dog. There is no longer a logical connection between the beast and the symbol. Figure 6.2 shows the language tree that charts the evolution of, and links among, human languages. As you can see, the English language evolved from a mixture of Indo-European tongues. It will continue to evolve as people need to name and describe new phenomena. e-Connections: Cyber Shorthand (page 174) illustrates how the use of "words" continues to evolve.

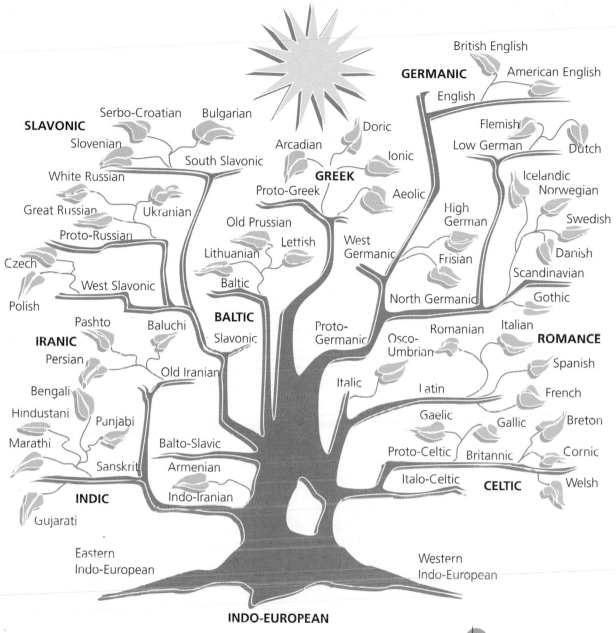

Figure 6.2

The "Language Tree," Caputo, et al., *Interpersonal Communication*, Kendall-Hunt, 1997.

Words Are Context Bound

Your English or speech communication teacher has undoubtedly cautioned you that taking something out of context changes its meaning. Symbols derive their meaning from the situation in which they are used. The phrase *old man* could refer to a male over the age of 70, your father, your teacher, your principal, or your boss. You need to know the context of the phrase in order to decipher its specific meaning. The transactional nature of communication emphasizes how meaning is created through discussion.

Words Are Culturally Bound

As you learned in Chapter 4, culture consists of the rules, norms, values, and mores of a group of people, which have been learned and shaped from one generation to the next. The meaning of a symbol such as a word can change from culture to culture. To a European, for example, a "Yankee" is someone from America; to a player on the Boston Red Sox, a "Yankee" is an opponent; and to someone from the American South, a "Yankee" is someone from the American North. A few years ago, General Motors sold a car called a Nova. In English, *nova* means bright star—an appropriate name for a car. In Spanish, however, the spoken word *nova* sounds like the words "no va," which translates, "It does not go." As you can imagine, this name was not a great sales tool for the Spanish-speaking market.

One measure of how words reflect culture is to consider the new words that become new entries in dictionaries. Here are some of the recent additions to *Webster's New World College Dictionary*, published at the start of the 21st century.

Bubba: A slang term that means *brother*

Pumped: Enthusiastic, confident

Viewbook: Richly illustrated booklet produced by a college or university for prospective students

Slamming: Switching someone's long-distance phone service without a person's knowledge

Megaplex: Many movie screens in a single place, which show different features

Racial profiling: Alleged to be a policy of police who stop vehicles that are driven by people from a particular racial or ethnic group

Face time: Time spent in the presence of someone

Hat hair: Hair that becomes matted after wearing a hat

The study of words and meaning is called *semantics.* One important body of semantic theory known as **symbolic interaction** suggests that a society is bound together by the common use of symbols. Originally developed by sociologists as a way of making sense out of how societies and groups are linked together,[2] the theory of symbolic interaction also illuminates how we use our common understanding of symbols to form interpersonal relationships. Common symbols foster links in under-

symbolic interaction. Theory that suggests societies are bound together through common use of symbols.

standing and therefore lead to satisfying relationships. Of course, even within a given culture people misunderstand each other's messages. But the more similar the cultures of the communication partners, the greater the chance for a meeting of meanings.

Words Have Denotative and Connotative Meaning

Language is the vehicle through which we share our sense of the world with others. Through language people translate experience into symbols and then use the symbols to share the experience. But as you learned in Chapter 1, the process of symbol sharing through language is not just a simple linear process of uttering a word and having its meaning clearly understood by another. Messages create both content and feelings. So language creates meaning on two levels: the denotative and the connotative.

high-context culture. Culture in which the meaning of messages is highly dependent on context and nonverbal cues.

low-context culture. Culture that relies primarily on language to communicate messages.

---

understanding diversity

High-Context and Low-Context Cultures

As you learned in Chapter 4, some cultures place great emphasis on the verbal context—the explicit importance of words—in a message. Others place more emphasis on the nonverbal context. Renowned anthropologist Edward T. Hall categorized these distinctions as **high context** (emphasis on the nonverbal) and **low context** (emphasis on the verbal).[3] The chart in Figure 6.3 depicts cultures arranged along a continuum from high to low context.[4]

Individuals from high-context cultures find nonverbal cues extremely important in helping them interpret the messages of others. Consequently, individuals from high-context cultures are usually more skilled at decoding nonverbal messages than individuals from

low-context cultures. In addition, because context plays a major role in communicating meaning, they may use fewer words and spend less time speaking than do individuals from low-context cultures.

Larry Samovar and Richard Porter found that individuals from high-context cultures often perceive those from low-context cultures as less attractive, knowledgeable, and trustworthy. They find typical low-context requests such as "Say what you mean," "Don't beat around the bush," and "Tell it to me straight" particularly annoying because they expect others to be as skilled as they are in interpreting unspoken, contextual cues.

Novelist Amy Tan notes,

I try to explain to my English-speaking friends that Chinese language is more strategic in manner, whereas English tends to be more direct; an American business executive may say, "Let's make a deal," and the Chinese manager may reply, "Is your son interested in learning about your widget business?" Each to his or her own purpose, each with his or her own linguistic path.[5]

High-Context Cultures

Japanese
Arab
Greek
Spanish
Italian
English
French
American
Scandinavian
German
German-Swiss

Low-Context Cultures

Figure 6.3

Cultures arranged along the high-context/low-context dimension.
Figure from Larry Samovar and Richard Porter, *Communication Between Cultures* (Belmont, CA: Wadsworth, 1991), 235.

The **denotative** meaning creates content. The denotation of a word is its restrictive or literal meaning. For example, here is one dictionary definition for the word *school*:

> An institution for the instruction of children; an institution for instruction in a skill or business; a college or a university.[6]

This definition is the literal or denotative definition of the word *school*; it describes what the word means in American culture.

The **connotative** meaning of language creates feelings. Words also have personal and subjective meanings. The word *school* to you might mean a wonderful, exciting place where you meet your friends, have a good time, and occasionally take tests and perform other tasks that keep you from enjoying your social life. To others, *school* could be a restrictive, burdensome obligation that stands in the way of making money and getting on with life. The connotative meaning of a word is more individualized. Whereas the denotative or objective meaning of the word *school* can be found in your Webster's, Funk and Wagnalls, or Oxford English Dictionary, your subjective, personal response to the word is probably not contained there.

Denotative and Connotative Meaning

Meaning	Definition	Examples
Denotative	Literal, restrictive definition of a word	Mother: the female person who gave birth to you
Connotative	Personal, subjective reaction to a word	Mother: the warm, caring woman who nurtured and loved you; or the cold, distant woman who always implied that you were not measuring up to her standards

Words Communicate Concrete or Abstract Meaning

Words can be placed along a continuum from abstract to concrete. People call a word *concrete* if they can experience its referent with one of their senses; if you can see it, touch it, smell it, taste it, or hear it, then it's concrete. If you cannot do these things with the referent, then the word is abstract. You can visualize the continuum from abstract to concrete as a ladder:

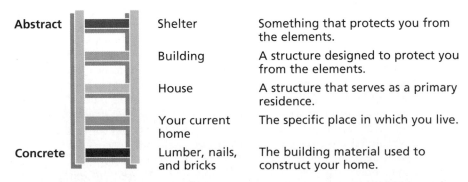

Abstract	Shelter	Something that protects you from the elements.
	Building	A structure designed to protect you from the elements.
	House	A structure that serves as a primary residence.
	Your current home	The specific place in which you live.
Concrete	Lumber, nails, and bricks	The building material used to construct your home.

denotative meaning. Restrictive or literal meaning of a word.

connotative meaning. Personal and subjective meaning of a word.

In general, the more concrete the language, the easier it is for others to understand.

Recognizing the Power of Words

Sticks and stones may break my bones,
But words can never hurt me.

This old schoolyard chant may provide a ready retort for the desperate victim of name-calling, but it is hardly convincing. With more insight, the poet Robert Browning wrote, "Words break no bones; hearts though sometimes." And in his book *Science and Sanity,* mathematician and engineer Alfred Korzybski argued that the words we use (and misuse) have tremendous effects on our thoughts and actions.[7] Browning and Korzybski were right. As we said at the beginning of this chapter, words have power.

Words Have Power to Create

"To name is to call into existence—to call out of nothingness,"[8] wrote French philosopher Georges Gusdorff. Words give you a tool to create our world by naming and labeling what you experience. You undoubtedly learned in your elementary science class that Sir Isaac Newton discovered gravity. Perhaps it would be more accurate to say that he labeled rather than discovered it. His use of the word *gravity* gave us a cognitive category; we now converse about the pull of the earth's forces that keeps us from flying into space. Words give us the symbolic vehicles to communicate our creations and discoveries to others.

When you label something as "good" or "bad," you are using language to create your own vision of how you experience the world. If you tell a friend that the movie you saw last night was vulgar and obscene, you are not only providing your friend with a critique of the movie; you are also communicating your sense of what is appropriate and inappropriate.

As we noted in Chapter 2, you create your self-worth largely with self-talk and with the labels you apply to yourself. Psychologist Albert Ellis believes that you also

Most of us can agree on the denotative meaning for the word "school." But the connotative meaning will be different for everybody. (Ellen Senisi/The Image Works)

create your moods and emotional state with the words you use to label your feelings.[9] If you get fired from a job, you might say that you feel angry and helpless, or you might declare that you feel liberated and excited. The first response might lead to depression, and the second to happiness. One fascinating study conducted over a thirty-five-year period found that people who described the world in pessimistic terms when they were younger were in poorer health during middle age than those who had been optimistic.[10] Your words and corresponding outlook have the power to affect your health. The concept of reframing that we discussed in Chapter 2 as a way to improve our self-concept is based on the power of words to "call into existence" that which we create with words.

Words Have Power to Affect Thoughts and Actions

How about some horse meat for supper tonight? Most of us find such a question disgusting. Why? Horse meat is not something we typically eat. Perhaps the reason horse meat is not a featured delicacy at the local supermarket is simply that we have no other word for it. Your butcher does not advertise pig meat or cow meat; labeling the meat as pork chops, ham, and sausage, or as steak and ribs, makes it sound more appetizing. Advertisers have long known that the way a product is labeled affects our propensity to purchase it.

Words also have power to affect policy and procedures. Consider the unsubstantiated story about a young FBI man who was put in charge of the supply department. In an effort to save money, he reduced the size of memo paper. One of the smaller sheets ended up on J. Edgar Hoover's desk. The director didn't like the small size and wrote on the narrow margin of the paper, "Watch the borders." For the next six weeks, it was extremely difficult to enter the United States from Canada or Mexico.

In the late 1960s a California sociology professor conducted an experiment to demonstrate that words have power to affect behavior.[11] He divided his class into two groups. To one group, he distributed a bumper sticker that boldly displayed the words "I support the Black Panthers." At that time, many members of the students' local community thought the Panthers were using unnecessary force to promote their agenda. Students in this first group had to drive around for a week with the stickers on their cars. The other group drove around as usual, without stickers.

It took only a few hours to prove the professor's point: Words do affect attitudes and behavior. Students who had the stickers were harassed by other motorists and issued traffic tickets at an alarming rate. The other group had no increase in hassles. By the end of the study, 17 days later, the "Panther" group had received 33 traffic citations.

Words Have Power to Affect and Reflect Culture

linguistic determinism. Theory that describes how use of language determines or influences thoughts and perceptions.

About a decade before the sociology professor's bumper sticker experiment, anthropologists Benjamin Whorf and Edward Sapir simultaneously began to refine a theory called **linguistic determinism,** which had originated in the 19th century.[12] Their version is based on a hypothesis of reciprocity: Language shapes your culture and culture shapes your language. To understand your culture, theorize these anthropologists, you should study the words you use. If an impartial investigator from

The "tech-speak" spoken here may help to create the special culture these individuals share. (Mark Richards/PhotoEdit)

another culture were to study a transcript of all of your spoken utterances last week, what would he or she learn about you and the culture in which you live? If you frequently used words like *MP3* and *download,* the investigator would know that these things are important to you. But he or she might not know what they mean if they are not also part of his or her culture.

Words not only reflect your culture; there is evidence that they mold it. When Wendell Johnson, a speech therapist, noticed that very few Indians in a certain tribe stuttered, he also found that their language had no word for stuttering.[13] He concluded that few people had this affliction because it never entered their minds as a possibility. Perhaps you've heard that Eskimos have 23 different words for snow. Even though they really don't have quite that many, there is evidence that they have more words for snow than someone native to Miami, Florida.[14]

These examples also show that the words people use and listen to affect their **world view**—how they interpret what they experience. If you were to don someone else's prescription glasses, the world would literally look different to you, and the glasses would either enhance or inhibit your ability to see the world around you. In a sense, your world view is your own set of prescription glasses, which you formulate over time, based on your experiences, attitudes, beliefs, values, and needs. The words you use to describe your view of the world reflect and further shape your perspective. And you, in turn, help to shape your culture's collective world view through your use of language.

Avoiding Word Barriers

According to theologian and educator Ruel Howe, a communication barrier is "something that keeps meaning from meeting." [15] Words have the power to create monumental misunderstandings as well as deep connections. Although it is true that meanings are in people, not in words, sometimes assumptions or inaccurate

world view. Culturally acquired perspective for interpreting experiences.

use of words hinders understanding. Let's identify some of the specific barriers to understanding that people sometimes create through language.

Bypassing: One Word, Two Thoughts

A student pilot was on his first solo flight. When he called the tower for flight instructions, the control tower asked, "Would you please give us your altitude and position?"

The pilot replied, "I'm five feet ten inches, and I'm sitting up front."

Bypassing occurs when the same words mean different things to different people.

Meaning is fragile. And the English language is imprecise in many areas. One researcher estimated that the 500 words used most often in daily conversations have over 14,000 different dictionary definitions. And this number does not take into

bypassing. Confusion caused by the same words meaning different things to different people.

---

considering others

The Talkaholic Scale

Are you a "talkaholic," or do you know someone who is? The simple description of a "talkaholic" is someone who talks more than most people. Being other-oriented means not only being a good listener, as we discussed in Chapter 5, but it means being sensitive to how much you talk. "Talkaholics" often oververbalize. They are sometimes insensitive to other's need for information. No, we're not suggesting that you should not contribute to the conversation, and at times it is appropriate and expected that you'll talk and others listen, but consider whether you may be a conversation dominator. Take the following test developed by communication researchers James McCroskey and Virginia Richmond to determine your "talkaholic" quotient. The higher your score, the higher your tendency to be a "talkaholic" when relating to others.

The Talkaholic Scale

Directions: The questionnaire below includes sixteen statements about talking behavior. Please indicate the degree to which you believe each of these characteristics applies to you by marking, on the line before each item, whether you (5) strongly agree that it applies, (4) agree that it applies, (3) are undecided, (2) disagree that it applies, or (1) strongly disagree that it applies. There are no right or wrong answers. Work quickly; record your first impression.

_____ 1. Often I keep quiet when I know I should talk.
_____ 2. I talk more than I should sometimes.
_____ 3. Often I talk when I know I should keep quiet.
_____ 4. Sometimes I keep quiet when I know it would be to my advantage to talk.
_____ 5. I am a "talkaholic."
_____ 6. Sometimes I feel compelled to keep quiet.
_____ 7. In general, I talk more than I should.
_____ 8. I am a compulsive talker.
_____ 9. I am not a talker; rarely do I talk in communication situations.
_____ 10. Quite a few people have said I talk too much.
_____ 11. I just can't stop talking too much.
_____ 12. In general, I talk less than I should.
_____ 13. I am *not* a "talkaholic."
_____ 14. Sometimes I talk when I know it would be to my advantage to keep quiet.
_____ 15. I talk less than I should sometimes.
_____ 16. I am *not* a compulsive talker.

Scoring: To determine your score on this scale, complete the following steps:
Step 1.   Add the scores for items 2, 3, 5, 7, 8, 10, 11, and 14.
Step 2.   Add the scores for items 13 and 16.
Step 3.   Complete the following formula:
          Talkaholic score =12 + total from step 1 – total from step 2.
A score of 40 or above suggests that you are a talkaholic.

Source: James C. McCroskey and Virginia P. Richmond, *Fundamentals of Human Communication: An Interpersonal Perspective* (Prospect Heights, IL: Waveland Press, 1996), 66.

account personal connotations. So it is no wonder that bypassing is a common communication problem.

Pavlov's dog salivated when he heard the bell that he learned to associate with food. Sometimes we respond to symbols the way Pavlov's dog did to the bell, forgetting that symbols (words) can have more than one meaning.

Bafflegab: High-Falutin' Use of Words

Do you suffer from bafflegab? Here is an example: Bafflegab is multiloquence characterized by consummate interfusion of circumlocution or periphrasis, inscrutability, incognizability, and other familiar manifestations of abstruse expatiation commonly used for promulgations implementing procrustean determinations by governmental bodies. Whew! What a mouthful. Why do some people use such highly abstract language? Perhaps they are just trying to dazzle their listener with evidence of their education, or they may simply not be other oriented. Bafflegabbers may be focused on impressing the receiver rather than on conveying meaning. Other-oriented speakers use clear words that the listener can understand: They adapt their choice of words to their listener.

e-connections
Avoiding Bafflegab

Uncertain of the meaning of a word that you find on the Internet? Look it up on the "Webopaedia." The following Web site will help you interpret words you don't understand:

http://www.pcwebopaedia.com/

Here's another site that can help you avoid Bafflegab. Here you'll find a comprehensive dictionary of technical jargon, especially computer jargon, that appears on the Web:

http://www.netmeg.net/jargon/

Lack of Precision: Uncertain Meaning

Alice Roosevelt Longworth writes about a merchant seaman who was being investigated under the McCarran Act. "Do you," asked the interrogator, "have any pornographic literature?"

"Pornographic literature!" the sailor burst out indignantly. "I don't even have a pornograph!"

At a ceremony in the Princeton University chapel, an old lady buttonholed an usher and commanded, "Be sure you get me a seat up front, young man. I understand they've always had trouble with the agnostics in the chapel!"

Each of these examples, along with the Far Side cartoon here, illustrates a **malapropism**—a confusion of one word or phrase for another that sounds similar to it. You have probably heard people confuse such word pairs as *construction* and *instruction,* and *subscription* and *prescription.* Although this confusion may at times be humorous, it may also result in failure to communicate clearly. So, too, can using words out of context, using inappropriate grammar, or putting words in the wrong order. Confusion is the inevitable result, as these sentences taken from a letter to the Philadelphia welfare department illustrate:

Ha ha ha, Biff. Guess what? After we go to the drugstore and the post office, I'm going to the vet's to get tutored.

> I want my money as quickly as I can get it. I've been in bed with the doctor for two weeks, and it didn't do me any good. If things don't improve, I will have to send for another doctor.

And the following statements appeared in church bulletins:

> The eighth-graders will be presenting Shakespeare's *Hamlet* in the church basement on Friday at 7 P.M. The congregation is invited to attend this tragedy.

> This afternoon there will be meetings in the north and south ends of the church— Children will be baptized on both ends.

These are funny examples, but in fact, incorrect or unclear language can launch a war or sink a ship. It is vital to remember that *meanings are in people, not in words.* We give symbols meaning; we do not receive inherent meaning *from* symbols. If you are other-oriented, you will assess how someone else will respond to

malapropism. Confusion of one word or phrase for another that sounds similar to it.

your message and try to select those symbols that he or she is most likely to interpret as you intend.

For most communication, the object is to be as correct, specific, and concrete as possible. Vague language creates confusion and frustration. Consider this example:

Derrick: Where's the aluminum foil?

Pam: In the drawer.

Derrick: What drawer?

Pam: In the kitchen.

Derrick: But where in the kitchen?

Pam: By the fridge.

Derrick: But which one? There are five drawers.

Pam: Oh, the second one from the top.

Derrick: Why didn't you say so in the first place?

Is it possible to be too precise? It is if you use a restricted code that has a meaning your listener does not know. A **restricted code** involves the use of words that have a particular meaning to a subgroup or culture. Sometimes we develop abbreviations or specialized terms that make sense and save time when we speak to others in our group. Musicians, for example, use special terms that relate to reading and performing music. Most computer hackers know that "a screamer" is someone who

restricted code. Using words that have meaning to a person, group, or culture.

sends messages in cyberspace in ALL CAPITAL LETTERS. Ham radio operators use codes to communicate over the airwaves. Yet in each instance this shorthand language would make little sense to an outsider. In fact, groups that rely on restricted codes may have greater cohesiveness because of this shared "secret" language or **jargon.** Whatever your line of work, guard against lapsing into phrases that can only be interpreted by a few.

When people have known one another for a long time, they may also use restricted codes for their exchanges. The *Blondie* cartoon is an example of how married couples can communicate using a code that no outsider could ever interpret.

Allness: The Language of Generalization

The tendency to use language to make unqualified, often untrue generalizations is called **allness.** Allness statements deny individual differences or variations. Statements such as "All women are poor drivers" and "People from the South love iced tea" are generalizations that imply that the person making the pronouncement has examined all the information and has reached a definitive conclusion. Although the world would be much simpler if we *could* make such statements, reality rarely, if ever, provides evidence to support sweeping generalizations.

For example, although research conclusions document differences between the way men and women communicate, it is inaccurate to say that all women are more emotional and that all men are task-oriented. Empathic, other-oriented speakers avoid making judgments of others based only on conventional wisdom or traditionally held attitudes and beliefs. If you respond to others (of a different gender, sexual orientation, or ethnicity) based on stereotypical concepts, you will diminish your understanding and the quality of the relationship.

One way to avoid untrue generalizations is to remind yourself that your use and interpretation of a word is unique. Saying the words "to me" either to yourself or out loud before you offer an opinion or make a pronouncement can help communicate to others (and remind yourself) that your view is uniquely yours. Rather than announcing, "Curfews for teenagers are ridiculous," you could say, "To me, curfews for teenagers are ridiculous."

Indexing your comments and remarks is another way to help you avoid generalizing. To index is to acknowledge that each individual is unique. Rather than announcing that all doctors are abrupt, you could say, "My child's pediatrician spends a lot of time with me, but my internist never answers my questions." This helps you remember that doctor number one is not the same as doctor number two.

Static Evaluation: The Language of Rigidity

You change. Your world changes. An ancient Greek philosopher said it best: "You can never step in the same river twice." A **static evaluation** is a statement that fails to recognize change; labels in particular have a tendency to freeze-frame our awareness. Ruby, known as the class nerd in high school, is today a successful and polished businessperson; the old label does not fit.

In addition, some people suffer from hardening of the categories. Their world view is so rigid that they can never change or expand their perspective. But the world is a technicolor moving target. Just about the time you think you have things neatly figured out and categorized, something moves. Your labels may not reflect the

jargon. Another name for restricted code: specialized terms or abbreviations whose meaning is known only to members of a specific group.

allness. Tendency to use language to make unqualified, often untrue generalizations.

indexing. Way of avoiding allness statements by separating one situation, person, or example from another.

static evaluation. Pronouncing judgment on something without taking changes into consideration.

buzzing, booming, zipping process of change. It is important to acknowledge that perception is a process, and to avoid trying to nail things down permanently into all-inclusive categories.

General semanticists use the metaphorical expression "the map is not the territory" to illustrate the concept of static evaluation. Like a word, a map symbolizes or represents reality. Yet the road system is constantly changing. New roads are built, old ones are closed. If you were to use a 1949 map to guide you on your cross-country tour from Washington, D.C., to Kansas City, Missouri, the interstate highway system would not even be on it, and you would probably lose your way. Similarly, if you use old labels and do not adjust your thinking to accommodate change, you will get lost semantically.

Perhaps you have a parent who still uses "old maps" when you come home to visit, expecting that you will be there for dinner each night and will still eat four helpings at every meal. Your parent may not understand that you have changed and that his or her old map does not function well in your new territory. You may have to help construct a new one.

To avoid static evaluation yourself, try dating your observations and indicate to others the time period from which you are drawing your conclusion. For example, if your second cousin comes to town for a visit, say, "When I last saw you, you loved to listen to Patti Smith." This allows for the possibility that your cousin's tastes may have changed during the last few years. But most importantly, try to observe and acknowledge changes in others. If you are practicing what you know about becoming other-oriented, you are unlikely to erect this barrier.

Polarization: The Language of Extremes

Describing and evaluating what you observe in terms of extremes, such as good or bad, old or new, beautiful or ugly, brilliant or stupid, is known as **polarization**. General semanticists remind us that the world in which we live comes not in black and white but in a variety of colors, hues, and shades. If you describe things in extremes, leaving out the middle ground, then your language does not accurately reflect reality. And because of the power of words to create, you may believe your own pronouncements.

"You either love me or you don't love me," says Jerome.

"You're either for me or against me," replies Lisa.

Both people are overstating the case, using language to polarize their perceptions of the experience.

Family counselors who listen to family feuds find that the tendency to see things from an either/or point of view is a classic symptom of a troubled relationship. Placing the entire blame on your partner for a problem in your relationship is an example of polarizing. Few relational difficulties are exclusively one-sided.

Biased Language: Insensitivity Toward Others

Using words that reflect your biases toward other cultures, ethnic groups, gender, sexual orientation, or people who are simply different from you can create a word barrier for your listeners. Because words, including the words used to describe

polarization. Describing and evaluating what you observe in terms of extremes such as good or bad, old or new, beautiful or ugly.

people, have power to create and affect thoughts and behavior, they can affect the quality of relationships with others. Although TV, radio, and magazine articles may debate the merits of political correctness, it is clear that sexist or racially stereotypical language can offend others. We'll address three issues in language use that can reflect poorly on the speakers and impact interpersonal relationships with others: sexist language, ethnic or racially biased language, and elitist language—language that assumes superiority.

Avoid Sexist Language

Sexist language is the use of words that reflect stereotypical attitudes or that describe roles in exclusively male or female terms.

Words such as congress*man*, mail*man*, and *man*kind ignore the fact that women are part of the workforce and the human race. Contrast these with *member of congress, letter carrier,* and *humankind,* which are gender neutral and allow for the inclusion of both men and women. Or, rather than eliminating the word *man* from your vocabulary, try to use appropriate labels when you know the gender of the subject. A male police officer is a policeman; a female police officer is a policewoman. Rather than salesperson, you could say salesman or saleswoman, depending on the gender of the seller.

O'Donnell found that even dictionaries fall into patterns of describing men and women with discriminatory language.[16] Included in the Oxford English Dictionary definition for *woman* are (1) an adult female being, (2) a female servant, (3) a lady-love or mistress, and (4) a wife. Men are described in more positive and distinguished terms: (1) a human being, (2) the human creation regarded abstractly, (3) an adult male endowed with many qualities, and (4) a person of importance of position.

Many of our social conventions also diminish or ignore the importance of women:

Sexist	Unbiased
I'd like you to meet Dr. and Mrs. John Chao.	I'd like you to meet Dr. Sue Ho and Dr. John Chao. They are husband and wife.
	or
	I'd like you to meet John Chao and Sue Ho. They're both doctors at Mercy Hospital.
Let me introduce Mr. Tom Bertolone and his wife Beverly.	Let me introduce Beverly and Tom Bertolone.

Language has, however, made more substantial progress in reflecting changes and changed attitudes toward women in the professional arena. Compare the terms used to describe workers now with those used in the 1950s:

Terms Used Today	Terms Used in 1950s
Flight attendant	Stewardess
Firefighter	Fireman
Police officer	Policeman
Physician	Female doctor
Women at the office	Girls at work
Ms.	Miss/Mrs.
People/humans	Mankind

e-connections

Avoiding Sexist Language

Although we've identified a rationale for avoiding biased language and offered several tips for using nonsexist language, you still may want additional strategies to help you using words that won't offend others. The following Web sites offer links to several sites that offer a wealth of strategies and suggestions for avoiding sexist language:

http://www.research paper.com/writing center/26.html

http://www.utexas.edu/student/lsc/handouts/1284.html

Consciously remembering to use nonsexist language will result in several benefits.[17] First, nonsexist language reflects nonsexist attitudes. Your attitudes are reflected in your speech, and your speech affects your attitudes. Monitoring your speech for sexist remarks can help you monitor your attitudes about sexist assumptions you may hold. Second, using nonsexist language will help you become more other-oriented. Monitoring your language for sexist remarks will reflect your sensitivity to others. Third, nonsexist language will make your speech more contemporary and unambiguous. By substituting the word *humankind* for *mankind,* for example, you can communicate that you are including all people, not just men, in your observation or statement. And finally, your nonsexist language will empower others. By eliminating sexist bias from your speech, you will help confirm the value of all the individuals with whom you interact.

In addition to the debate over language that reflects on one's gender, there is considerable and controversial discussion about the way in which people talk about someone's sexual orientation. Regardless of your personal view about sexual orientation, the principle of being other-oriented suggests that you can be sensitive to the way you speak of it. Your approval or disapproval of someone's sexual preferences should not undermine your goal of being an effective communicator. Labeling someone a *fag, queer,* or *dyke* may not only be offensive and hurtful to the person being labeled but may also reflect on the sensitivity of the person doing the labeling. In most circles, the preferred terms for someone who is homosexual are *gay* for men and *lesbian* for women. We're not suggesting that certain words be expunged from dictionaries or never be uttered; we are suggesting that when describing others, people should be sensitive to how they wish to be addressed and discussed.

Avoid Ethnic or Racially Biased Language

In addition to monitoring your language for sexual stereotypes, avoid racial and ethnic stereotypes. Using phrases such as "She's an Indian giver," or "I jewed him down" (to negotiate a price for goods or services), or "He doesn't have a Chinaman's chance" demonstrates an insensitivity to members of other cultural groups. Monitor your speech so that you are not, even unconsciously, using phrases that depict a racial group or ethnic group in a negative, stereotypical fashion.

Is Supreme Court justice Clarence Thomas Black or African American? Is labor leader Dolores Huerto Hispanic or Latina? Given the power of words, the terms we

The term "policeman" fails to account for the possibility illustrated here. A more inclusive term would be "police officer." (R. Sidney/The Image Works)

use to label ethnic groups reflect perceptions of culture and identity. Using the wrong word can result in someone's being labeled "politically incorrect" or worse, "bigot." In 1995, the U.S. Bureau of Labor Statistics surveyed 60,000 households, asking what ethnic label they like best. More than 44 percent of households then called "Black" by the government preferred the term "Black," and 28 percent preferred "African American." Twelve percent preferred "Afro-American" and a little more than 9 percent had no preference. In another ethnic category, "Hispanic" was the choice of 58 percent of those currently labeled "Hispanics," rather than terms such as "Latino" or the generic "of Spanish origin." More than 10 percent had no preference. The survey also reported that the label "American Indians" was the term of choice for slightly fewer than half of the respondents, whereas 37 percent preferred "Native American." Most of those currently designated "White" preferred that term, although 16 percent liked the term "Caucasian" and a very small percentage liked the term "European American."[18] Some of these preferences may surprise you, in that they may have changed in just the few years since this survey was conducted. A sensitive, other-oriented communicator keeps abreast of such changes and adopts the designations currently preferred by members of the ethnic groups themselves.

Avoid Language That Demeans One's Age, Ability, or Social Class

Language barriers are created not only when someone uses sexist or racially biased language, but also when someone disparages a person's age, mental or physical ability, or social standing. Calling someone a "geezer," "retard," or "trailer trash" may seem to some harmless or humorous, but may be perceived by others as disparaging.[19]

Discriminating against someone because of age is a growing problem in the workplace. In some occupations, as a worker moves into his or her fifties, it may be difficult to change jobs or find work. Despite laws designed to guard against age discrimination, such discrimination clearly exists. As we have noted, the language that people use has power to affect attitudes and behavior. That's why using negative terms to describe the elderly can be a subtle—or sometimes not-so-subtle—way of expressing disrespect toward the older generation.

Similarly, the way someone describes people with disabilities can negatively impact how they may be perceived. A study by researcher John Seiter and his colleagues found that when people with a disability were called demeaning or disparaging names, they were perceived as less trustworthy, competent, persuasive, and sociable than when the same people were described in more positive or heroic terms.[20] At the end of their study, the authors note, "communicators who want to be effective should avoid using derogatory language." Guard against calling attention to someone as a "cripple," "retarded," "dim-witted," or "mental"; these terms are offensive. As one common expression puts it: Much truth's spoken when you're just jokin'. Even though it may seem innocent to use such words to label others, it can alter your perceptions of others, as well as reflect poorly on you. Although there clearly are differences in ability among people, because of a variety of factors, be sensitive to your use of language. As suggested by communication researcher Dawn Braithwaite, the preferred terms are "disabled people" or "people with disabilities."[21]

Also monitor the way you talk about someone's social class. Although some societies and cultures make considerable distinctions among classes, it is nonetheless offensive today to use words that are intended to demean someone's social class. Terms such as "welfare recipients," "manual laborers," and "blue-collar workers" are often used derogatorily. Avoid labeling someone in such a way that shows disrespect toward the person's social standing, education, or socioeconomic status.

recap

Word Barriers

Barrier	Definition	Examples
Bypassing	Misinterpreting a word that evokes different meanings for different people	*W.C.* might mean *wayside chapel* to a Swiss and *water closet* to someone from England.
Bafflegab	Unnecessary use of many abstract words	"Please extinguish all smoking materials" instead of "No Smoking."
Lack of clarity	Words used inappropriately or in imprecise ways	Sign in Acapulco hotel: "The manager has personally passed all the water served here."
Allness	Lumping things or people into all-encompassing categories	All Texans drive pickup trucks and hang a rifle in their back windows.
Static evaluation	Labeling people, objects, and events without considering change	You call your 28-year-old nephew a juvenile delinquent because he spray-painted your fence when he was 11.
Polarization	Description in either/or terms—good or bad, right or wrong.	You're either for me or against me.
Biased language	Language that reflects gender, racial, ethnic, age, ability, or class biases	My mom is a mailman.

Using Words to Establish Supportive Relationships

"I'm going to win this argument."
"You're wrong and I'm right. It's as simple as that."
"You're going to do it my way or else!"

None of these statements is likely to result in a positive communication climate. All three are likely to result in debate rather than true dialogue. The words you hear and use are central to your establishing a quality or positive relationship with others. Author and researcher Daniel Yankelovich suggests that the goal of

Table 6.1

Debate and Dialogue Compared

Debate	Dialogue
There is one right answer, and you have it.	Many people have pieces of the answer; together you can find the best solution.
The goal is to win.	The goal is to seek common ground and agreement.
The focus is on combat; prove that you are right and the other person is wrong.	The focus is on collaboration; seek common understanding.
Search for weakness and errors in others' positions.	Search for strengths and value the truth in what others say.
Defend your views.	Use the contributions of others to improve your thinking.

Source: Adapted from Daniel Yankelovich, *The Magic of Dialogue: Transforming Conflict into Cooperation* (New York: Simon & Schuster, 1999), 39–40.

conversations with others should be to establish a genuine dialogue rather than to verbally arm-wrestle a partner in order to win the argument.[22] A true dialogue involves establishing a climate of equality, listening with empathy, and trying to bring assumptions into the open. Expressing equality, empathy, and openness is more likely to occur if you approach conversations as dialogue rather than debate. As shown in Table 6.1, in true dialogue people look for common ground rather than using a war of words to defend a position.

For more than three decades, Jack Gibb's observational research has been used as a framework for both describing and prescribing verbal behaviors that contribute to feelings of either supportiveness or defensiveness. His research, one of the most cited studies in communication textbooks in the past century, is so popular because he's identified practical strategies for developing supportive relationships with others—dialogue rather than debate—by the way we talk to each other.[23] Gibb spent several years listening to and observing groups of people in meetings and conversations, noting that some exchanges seem to create a supportive climate, whereas others create a defensive one.

Words and actions, he concluded, are tools we use to let someone know whether we support them or not. Now let's consider how you can use words to create a supportive climate rather than an antagonistic one.

Describe Your Own Feelings, Rather Than Evaluate the Behavior of Others

Most people don't like to be judged or evaluated. Criticizing and name-calling obviously can create relational problems, but so can attempts to diagnose others' problems or win their affection with insincere praise. In fact, any form of evaluation

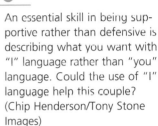

An essential skill in being supportive rather than defensive is describing what you want with "I" language rather than "you" language. Could the use of "I" language help this couple? (Chip Henderson/Tony Stone Images)

creates a climate of defensiveness. As British statesman Winston Churchill declared, "I am always ready to learn, although I do not always like being taught." Correcting others, even when we are doing it "for their own good" can raise their hackles.

One way to avoid evaluating others is to eliminate the accusatory *you* from your language. Statements such as "You always come in late for supper" or "You need to pick up the dirty clothes in your room" attack a person's sense of self-worth and usually result in a defensive reaction.

Instead, use the word *I* to describe your own feelings and thoughts about a situation or event: "I find it hard to keep your supper warm when you're late," or "I don't enjoy the extra work of picking up your dirty clothes." When you describe your own feelings instead of berating the receiver of the message, you are in essence taking ownership of the problem. This approach leads to greater openness and trust because your listener is less likely to feel rejected or as if you are trying to control him or her. Also, when you express your emotions, make sure you choose the right words to communicate your feelings. Building Your Skills: Practice Using "I" Language (page 192) will help you practice your skill in accurately expressing your feelings.

Solve Problems Rather Than Control Others

When you were younger, your parents gave you rules to keep you safe. Even though you may have resented their control, you needed to know what was hot, when not to cross the street, and not to stick your finger in a light socket. Now that you are an adult, when people treat you like a child, that often means they are trying to control your behavior, to take away your options. In truth, people have little or no control over someone else's behavior.

Most of us don't like to be controlled against our will. Someone who presumes to tell us what's good for us, instead of helping us puzzle through issues and problems, is likely to engender defensiveness. Open-ended questions, such as "What seems to be the problem?" or "How can we deal with the issue?" create a more supportive

building your skills

Practice Using "I" Language

An essential skill in being supportive rather than defensive is describing what you want with "I" language rather than "you" language. Rephrase the following "you" statements into "I" statements.

"You" Language	"I" Language
1. You are messy when you cook.	
2. Your driving is terrible.	
3. You never listen to me.	
4. You just lie on the couch and never offer to help me.	
5. You always decide what movie we see.	

climate than critical comments, such as, "Here's where you are wrong" or commands such as "Don't do that!"

Be Genuine Rather Than Manipulative

To be genuine means that you honestly seek to be yourself rather than someone you are not. It also means taking an honest interest in others and considering the uniqueness of each individual and situation, avoiding generalizations or strategies that focus only on your own needs and desires. A manipulative person has hidden agendas; a genuine person uses words to discuss issues and problems openly and honestly.

Carl Rogers, the founder of person-centered counseling, suggests that true understanding and dialogue occur when people adopt a genuine or honest positive regard for others.[24] If your goal is to look out only for your own interests, your language will reflect your self-focus. At the heart of being genuine is being other-oriented—being sincerely interested in those with whom you communicate. Although it's unrealistic to assume you will become best friends with everyone you meet, you can, suggests Rogers, work to develop an unselfish interest, or what he called an unconditional positive regard for others. That's hard to do. But the effort will be rewarded with a more positive communication climate.

Empathize Rather Than Remain Detached from Others

Empathy is one of the hallmarks of supportive relationships. As you learned earlier, empathy is the ability to understand the feelings of others and to predict the emotional responses they will have to different situations. Being empathic is the essence of being other-oriented. The opposite of empathy is neutrality. To be neutral is to be indifferent or apathetic toward another. Even when you express anger or irritation toward another, you are investing some energy in the relationship.

After an unsuccessful attempt to persuade his family to take a trip to Yellowstone National Park, Preston declared, "I don't care what you think; that's where we're going." His proclamation reflects a disregard for the feelings of others in his family. This insensitivity is self-defeating. The defensive climate Preston creates with his words will probably prevent the whole family from enjoying the vacation.

Be Flexible Rather Than Rigid Toward Others

Most people don't like someone who always seems certain that he or she is right. A "you're wrong, I'm right" attitude creates a defensive climate. This does not mean that you should have no opinions and go through life blithely agreeing to everything. And it doesn't mean that there is *never* one answer that is right and others that are wrong. But instead of making rigid pronouncements, you can use phrases such as "I may be wrong, but it seems to me ..." or "Here's one way to look at this problem." This manner of speaking gives your opinions a softer edge that allows room for others to express a point of view.

Present Yourself as Equal Rather Than Superior

You can antagonize others by letting them know that you view yourself as better or brighter than they are. You may be gifted and intelligent, but it's not necessary to announce it. And although some people have the responsibility and authority to manage others, "pulling rank" does not usually produce a cooperative climate. With phrases such as "Let's work on this together" or "We each have a valid perspective," you can avoid erecting walls of resentment and suspicion.

Also, avoid using bafflegab to impress others. Keep your messages short and clear, and use informal language. When you communicate with someone from another culture, you may need to use an **elaborated code** to get your message across. This means that your messages will have to be more explicit, but they should not be condescending. Two of your authors vividly remember trying to explain to a French exchange student what a fire ant was. First, we had to translate *ant* into French, and then we had to provide scientific, descriptive, and narrative evidence to help the student understand how these tiny biting insects terrorize people in the southern part of the United States.

recap   Use Words to Create a Supportive Climate

Describe your feelings instead of evaluating the behavior of others.

Keep the focus on problem solving, not on control.

Be genuine rather than manipulative in your approach.

Show that you understand another person's point of view instead of ignoring feelings.

Make it clear that you do not have all the answers rather than be perceived as a know-it-all.

Present yourself as an equal rather than as a superior.

elaborated code. Using many words and various ways of describing an idea or concept to communicate its meaning.

Expressing Your Emotions

Communication is enhanced if you can clearly express the emotions you are feeling to others. One way to communicate your emotions is to describe how you are feeling with a well-chosen word or phrase. The following list gives you several options for expressing your feelings in positive, neutral, or negative terms.

Positive:

		Negative:	
calm	hopeful	afraid	helpless
cheerful	hysterical	angry	horrible
comfortable	interested	annoyed	humiliated
confident	joyful	alone	intimidated
content	loving	bitter	listless
delighted	optimistic	confused	mad
ecstatic	passionate	defeated	mean
elated	peaceful	defensive	miserable
enthusiastic	playful	depressed	paranoid
excited	pleased	devastated	rebellious
flattered	refreshed	disappointed	regretful
free	romantic	disgusted	resentful
friendly	sexy	disturbed	restless
glad	tender	empty	shocked
grateful	warm	exhausted	suspicious
happy	willing	fearful	terrified
high	wonderful	frustrated	ugly
		furious	sad
		guilty	

Neutral:

amazed	hurried
ambivalent	lukewarm
apathetic	numb
bashful	possessive
bored	sentimental
detached	vulnerable

To practice expressing your emotions, consider using some of the words listed here to respond to the following situations. Write your response for each situation. Consider describing your response using either a single word or short phrase such as "I feel angry" or express your feelings in terms of what you'd like to do such as "I'd be so embarrassed I would sink through the floor," or "I would feel like leaving and never coming back to this house."

1. You have several thousand dollars charged to your credit cards, and you get fired from your job.

2. Your best friend, with whom you spend a lot of time, is moving to another country.

3. You have just learned that your aunt whom you adored died and left you a $35,000 inheritance.

4. Even though you do your best to keep your room clean, your roommate is complaining again about how you are a slob.

5. You have brought your 2-year-old son to a worship service but he continues to talk and run around during the service, and will not sit still. Other worshipers are looking at you with disapproval.

6. You arrive at your vacation hotel only to discover that they do not have a reservation for you, and you do not have your room confirmation number.

Using Words to Value Others

"I just don't feel appreciated any more," confides Jake during his counseling session. "My partner Pat just doesn't let me know he cares for me." One of the key skills in maintaining a long-term relationship is to know how to demonstrate that you value the other person. It's not just *nice* to know that someone cares about us; it is vital that we know others have genuine feelings of concern for us. In addition to acts of kindness, it is our words that let others know we appreciate them.

Researchers have identified ways people use language to confirm or disconfirm others.[25] A **confirming response** is a statement that causes others to value themselves more. Conversely, a **disconfirming response** is one that causes others to value themselves less.

Confirming Responses

The adage "People judge us by our words and behavior rather than by our intent" summarizes the underlying principle of confirming responses. Those who receive your messages determine whether they have the effect you intended. Formulating confirming responses requires careful listening and attention to the other person. Does it really matter whether we confirm others? Marriage researcher John Gottman used video cameras and microphones to observe couples interacting in an apartment over an extended period of time. He found that a significant predictor of divorce was neglecting to confirm or affirm one's marriage partner during typical, everyday conversation—even though couples who were less likely to divorce spent only a few seconds more confirming their partner than couples who eventually did divorce. His research conclusion has powerful implications: Long-lasting relationships are characterized by supportive, confirming messages.[26] We will describe several kinds of confirming responses here:

Direct Acknowledgment

When you respond directly to something another person says to you, you are acknowledging not only the statement, but also that the person is important.

Joan: It certainly is a nice day for a canoe trip.
Mariko: Yes, Joan, it's a great day to be outside.

Agreement About Judgments

When you confirm someone's evaluation of something, you are also affirming that person's sense of taste and judgment.

Nancy: I think the steel guitar player's riff was fantastic.
Victor: Yes, I think it was the best part of the performance.

confirming response. Statement that causes another person to value him- or herself more.

disconfirming response. Statement that causes another person to value him- or herself less.

Using Word Pictures to Express Your Feelings

A **word picture** is a short state-ment or story that dramatizes an emotion you experience. Using a visual image can add extra power in expressing your feelings where a simple descriptive word may not suffice.[27] Word pictures can be used to clarify how you feel, to offer praise or correction, as well as de-velop greater intimacy. A key goal of a word picture is to communi-cate your feelings and emotions. An effective way to express your emotions through a word picture is to use a simile. A simile, as you may remember from your English class, is a comparison that uses the word *like* or *as* to clarify the image you want to communicate. "When you forgot my birthday, I felt like crumbs swept from the table," exclaimed Marge to her forgetful husband. Or, after a hard day's work, Jeff told his family, "Have you seen a worn-out punching bag? That's just how I feel. I've been pounded time and time again, and now I feel torn and scuffed. I need a few minutes of peace and quiet before I join in the family conversation." His visual image helped communicate how exhausted he really felt. The best word pictures use an experience or image to which the listener can relate. To practice your skill, try to develop word pictures for the fol-lowing situations to express your feelings in a powerful and memo-rable way.

1. You have just learned that a cherished family pet has died.

2. You want to tell your friends how happy you are when you learn you received an A in a difficult course.

3. You've asked your sister not to leave empty milk cartons in the refrigerator, but you discover another empty carton in the fridge.

4. Your family is planning a vaca-tion but didn't ask you to be involved in the planning.

---

word picture. Short statement or story that illustrates or describes your emotions; word pictures often use a simile (a comparison using the words "like" or "as") to clarify the image.

🌑 Supportive Response

When you express reassurance and understanding, you are confirming a person's right to his or her feelings.

Lionel: I'm disappointed that I only scored a 60 on my interpersonal communication test.

Sarah: I'm sorry to see you so sad, Lionel. I know that test was important to you.

🌑 Clarifying Response

When you seek greater understanding of another person's message, you are confirming that he or she is worth your time and trouble. Clarifying responses also encourage the other person to talk in order to explore his or her feelings.

Larry: I'm not feeling very good about my family situation these days.

Tyrone: Is it tough with you and Margo working different shifts?

🌑 Expression of Positive Feeling

We feel confirmed or valued when someone else agrees with our expression of joy or excitement.

Lorraine: I'm so excited! I was just promoted to associate professor.

Dorette: Congratulations! I'm so proud of you! Heaven knows you deserve it.

Compliment

When you tell people you like what they have done or said, what they are wearing, or how they look, you are confirming their sense of worth.

Jean-Christophe: Did you get the invitation to my party?"
Manny: Yes! It looked so professional. I didn't know you could do calligraphy. You're a talented guy.

In each of these examples, note how the responder provides comments that confirm the worth or value of the other person. But we want to caution that confirming responses should be sincere. Offering false praise is manipulative, and your communication partner will probably sniff out your phoniness.

recap   Responses That Confirm Another Person's Self-Worth

Directly acknowledge something someone has said.

Agree with the person's judgments.

Be supportive; let the other person know you are trying to understand how he or she feels.

Ask questions to help clarify another person's statements if you are not sure you understand.

Express positive feelings to echo those of the other person.

Compliment the person, if you can be sincere.

building your skills

Supportive–Defensive Communication Charades

Divide into groups of two to four people. Each team or group should prepare a short play depicting one of the supportive or defensive communication responses described in this chapter. Perform your play for the class or another team to see whether they can identify the type of supportive or defensive communication behavior

your team is portraying. Consider one of the following situations or develop one of your own:

Speaking with a professor about a grade

Returning a broken item to a store

Talking with your child about his or her grades

Responding to a telemarketing salesperson who calls you during dinner

Talking with one of your employees who made a work-related mistake

Rebooking a flight because your flight was canceled by the airline

Taking an order from a customer at a fast-food restaurant

Receiving a complaint from a customer about poor service

Talking with someone who has knocked on your door, inviting you to his or her church

Asking someone to turn down the stereo or TV while you are trying to study

Variation: Instead of illustrating supportive and defensive communication, role-play an example of one of the confirming or disconfirming communication behaviors discussed in this chapter.

Disconfirming Responses

Some statements and responses can undermine another person's self-worth. We offer these categories so that you can avoid using them and also recognize when someone is trying to chip away at your self-image and self-esteem.

Impervious Response

When a person fails to acknowledge your statement or attempt to communicate, even though you know he or she heard you, you may feel a sense of awkwardness or embarrassment.

Rosa: I loved your speech, Harvey.
Harvey: (No response, verbal or nonverbal.)

Interrupting Response

When people interrupt you, they may be implying that what they have to say is more important than what you have to say. In effect, they could also be implying that they are more important than you are.

Anna: I just heard on the news that . . .
Sharon: Oh yes. The stock market just went down 100 points.

Irrelevant Response

An irrelevant response is one that has nothing at all to do with what you were saying. Chances are your partner is not listening to you at all.

Arnold: First we're flying down to Rio, and then to Quito. I can hardly wait to . . .
Peter: They're predicting a hard freeze tonight.

   The real message Peter is sending is "I have more important things on my mind."

Tangential Response

   A tangential response is one that acknowledges you, but that is only minimally related to what you are talking about. Again, it indicates that the other person isn't really attending to your message.

Richard: This new program will help us stay within our budget.
Samantha: Yeah. I think I'll save some bucks and send this letter by regular mail.

Impersonal Response

   A response that intellectualizes and uses the third person distances the other person from you and has the effect of trivializing what you say.

Diana: Hey, Bill. I'd like to talk with you for a minute about getting your permission to take my vacation in July.
Bill: One tends to become interested in recreational pursuits about this time of year, doesn't one?

Incoherent Response

   When a speaker mumbles, rambles, or makes some unintelligible effort to respond, it may leave you wondering if what you said was of any value or use to the listener.

Paolo: George, here's my suggestion for the merger deal with Antrax. Let's make them an offer of forty-eight dollars a share and see how they respond.

George: Huh? Well . . . So . . . Well . . . hmmm . . . I'm not sure.

🌑 Incongruous Response

When a verbal message is inconsistent with nonverbal behavior, people usually believe the nonverbal message, but they usually feel confused as well. An incongruous response is like a malfunctioning traffic light with flashing red and green lights—you're just not sure whether the speaker wants you to go or stay.

Sue: Honey, do you want me to go grocery shopping with you?

Steve: (Shouting) OF COURSE I DO! WHY ARE YOU ASKING?

Although it may be impossible to eliminate all disconfirming responses from your repertoire, becoming aware of the power of your words and monitoring your conversation for offensive phrases may help you avoid unexpected and perhaps devastating consequences.

Summary

The words we use have great power to affect our self-image and to influence the relationships we establish with others. English words are symbols that refer to objects, events, people, and ideas. They are arbitrary. We interpret their meaning through the context and culture to which they belong. Communication is complex because most words have both denotative (literal) meanings and connotative (subjective) meanings, and because words range from concrete to abstract.

The power of words stems from their ability to create images and to influence our thoughts, feelings, and actions. There is also an important link between the words we use and our culture. Language shapes culture and culture shapes language. Our view of the world is influenced by our vocabulary and the categories we have created with words.

Several word barriers can contribute to misunderstanding in interpersonal communication. Bypassing occurs when a word means one thing to one person and another to someone else. Our verbal expressions may lack clarity, either because we make language errors or because the meaning we want to convey is not clear to us. Allness statements can mislead and alienate listeners because the speaker falsely implies that he or she knows all there is to know about something. Another barrier, static evaluation, fails to take changes into account and uses outdated labels and categories. Polarization is the language of extremes; when someone thinks in black and white, many shades of meaning disappear. Finally, biased language that is insensitive to others creates noise that interferes with the meaning of a message.

The words you use can enhance or detract from the quality of relationships you establish with others. Supportive communication is descriptive rather than evaluative, problem-oriented rather than control-oriented, genuine rather than contrived or manipulative, empathic rather than neutral, flexible rather than rigid, and equal rather than superior. The words we use can either confirm or undermine another's sense of self-worth. If you directly acknowledge people, agree with their judgments, voice support when they feel bad, ask them to clarify their messages, affirm their positive feelings, and compliment them sincerely, then you may help them boost their self-images. Conversely, our responses can be disconfirming if we are impervious; interrupt someone; or use irrelevant, tangential, impersonal, incoherent, or incongruous messages.

For Discussion and Review

Focus on Comprehension

1. How do words create meaning for others?

2. What power do words have in our relationships with others?

3. What are some barriers to effective understanding, and what are strategies for overcoming these barriers?

4. What are the characteristics of a supportive communicator?

5. What are confirming communication responses? Describe a few.

6. What are disconfirming communication responses? Describe a few.

Focus on Critical Thinking

7. Marge and Paul are having an argument. Paul shouts, "You're constantly criticizing me! You don't let me make any important decisions!" How could Paul communicate how he feels in a more supportive way?

8. Alan asked Jessie to pick him up after work at the parking garage at 5:30 P.M. Jessie waited patiently at the parking garage on the other side of campus and finally went home at 6:30 P.M., having seen no sign of Alan. Alan was waiting at the parking garage behind his office rather than at the one on the other side of the campus. What word barriers do you think led to this misunderstanding?

9. Rephrase the following statements to use less biased language:

   a. I'd like to introduce Mr. Russell Browne and his wife, Muriel.

   b. In an office memo: "Several gals have been leaving their purses at their desks."

10. Rephrase the following statements, using the skill of indexing.

   a. All politicians want power and control over others.

b. All teachers are underpaid.

c. All Texans like to brag about how great their state is.

Focus on Ethics

11. If you really don't want to listen to your coworker go into detail about her latest vacation trip or provide details about the recent escapades of her children or grandchildren, is it appropriate to tell her that you'd rather not hear her "news"? Support your response.

12. Is it ethical to correct someone when he or she uses sexist language or makes a stereotyping remark about someone's race, gender or sexual orientation? What if that person is your boss or your teacher? Explain your answer.

13. Is it ethical to mask your true feelings of anger and irritation with someone by using supportive statements or confirming statements when what you really want to do is tell him or her "the truth" in no uncertain terms?

For Your Journal

1. Keep a log of examples of word barriers you experience or encounter. Note examples of bypassing, lack of precision in language, bafflegab, and other uses of words that inhibit communication. The examples could come from your own verbal exchanges or those that you observe in the conversations of others.

2. Make a list of words that are in your vocabulary today that were not in your vocabulary five years ago. Include new vocabulary words that you may have learned in school as well as words or phrases that were not generally used or that have been coined in the last half-decade (for example, Napster.com, 24/7).

3. Record a sample dialogue between you and a good friend that illustrates some of the confirming responses described on pages 195–197.

Learning With Others

1. Think of a bypass miscommunication that you've experienced. Share your recollection with a small group and compare your feelings and responses with those of others.

2. In your group, choose one person to play a recently divorced person whose spouse is not abiding by a child custody agreement and insists on seeing the children at odd hours. Another person should play the role of a trusted friend who only listens and responds. Ask the trusted friend to use the skills he or she learned in this chapter along with effective listening skills presented in Chapter 4. Then do a group evaluation of his or her response.

7

Communicating
Nonverbally

After
you study
this chapter

you should be able to . . .

1. Explain why nonverbal communication is an important and challenging area of study.

2. Describe the functions of nonverbal communication in interpersonal relationships.

3. Summarize research findings that describe codes of nonverbal communication behavior.

4. Describe three bases for interpreting nonverbal behavior.

5. Formulate a strategy for improving your ability to interpret nonverbal messages accurately.

- Why Learn About Nonverbal Communication?

- The Challenge of Interpreting Nonverbal Messages

- Nonverbal Communication Codes

- Interpreting Nonverbal Communication

- Improving Your Ability to Interpret Nonverbal Messages

Eddie: Lisa, will you get the telephone?
Lisa: Get it yourself!
Eddie: Hey! Why so testy? All I asked you
to do was answer the phone!

f you could view a videotape of Eddie and Lisa's interaction, perhaps you could more clearly see the source of the conflict. Eddie's tone of voice and his scowling facial expression might make his simple request seem more like an order.

As we noted in Chapter 1, communication has both content and relationship dimensions. Tone of voice, eye contact, facial expressions, posture, movement, vocal cues, appearance, use of personal space, manipulation of the communication environment, and other nonverbal clues reveal how people feel toward others. We can define **nonverbal communication** as behavior other than written or spoken language, that creates meaning for someone. In this chapter we focus on how nonverbal communication affects the quality of our interpersonal relationships. As we identify the functions and codes of nonverbal cues, we will also explore ways to improve skill in interpreting the nonverbal messages of others.

Why Learn About Nonverbal Communication?

hen you are sitting in a public place such as a shopping mall, airport, or bus stop, do you make assumptions about what other people might be like, as you observe their nonverbal behavior? Most of us are people watchers, and we rely on nonverbal communication clues to predict how others may feel about and react to us. Nonverbal communication plays a major role in relationship development because it is also the main channel we use to communicate our feelings and attitudes toward others. But because much of our nonverbal communication behavior is subconscious, most of us have only a limited awareness or understanding of it. We can begin examining nonverbal communication by looking at the ways we use it.

nonverbal communication.
Behavior other than written or spoken language, that creates meaning for someone.

205

Nonverbal Messages Communicate Our Feelings and Attitudes

Daryl knew that he was in trouble the moment he walked into the room. His wife Sandra gave him a steely stare. Her brow was furrowed, and her arms were crossed. On the table was a dish of cold lobster Newburg, extinguished candles burnt to nubs, and dirty dishes in all but one spot: his. Daryl was in the doghouse for forgetting the special meal his wife had prepared, and he needed no words to sense the depth of her displeasure.

Psychologist Albert Mehrabian concluded that as little as 7 percent of the emotional meaning of a message is communicated through explicit verbal channels.[1] The most significant source of emotional communication is our face—according to Mehrabian's study, it channels as much as 55 percent of our meaning. Vocal cues such as volume, pitch, and intensity communicate another 38 percent of our emotional meaning. In all, we communicate approximately 93 percent of the emotional meaning of our messages nonverbally. Although these percentages do not apply to every communication situation, the results of Mehrabian's investigation do illustrate the potential power of nonverbal cues in communicating emotion.[2]

When we interact with others, we base our feelings and emotional responses not on what our partner says, but rather on what he or she does. We also alter our nonverbal communication to suit different relationships. With good friends you let down your guard; you may slouch, scratch, and take off your shoes to show you trust them. But if you were interviewing for a job or meeting your fiancé's parents for the first time, your posture would probably be stiffer and your smiles more carefully controlled as you tried to convey the impression that you are mature, competent, and respectable.

Nonverbal Messages Are More Believable

"Honey, do you love me?" asks Brenda.

"OF COURSE I LOVE YOU! HAVEN'T I ALWAYS TOLD YOU THAT I LOVE YOU? I LOVE YOU!" shouts Jim, keeping his eyes glued to his morning newspaper.

Brenda will probably not be that reassured by Jim's pledge of affection. The contradiction between his spoken message of love and his nonverbal message of irritation and disinterest will leave her wondering about his true feelings.

Actions speak louder than words. This cliché became a cliché because nonverbal communication is more believable than verbal communication. Nonverbal messages are more difficult to fake. One research team concluded that North Americans use the following cues, listed in order of most to least important, to help them discern when a person is lying.[3]

- Greater time lag in response to a question
- Reduced eye contact
- Increased shifts in posture
- Unfilled pauses
- Less smiling
- Slower speech
- Higher pitch in voice
- More deliberate pronunciation and articulation of words

Because it is difficult to manipulate an array of nonverbal cues, a skilled other-oriented observer can see when a person's true feelings leak out. Social psychologists Paul Ekman and Wallace Friesen have identified the face, hands, and feet as key sources of nonverbal leakage cues.[4] Are you aware of what your fingers and toes are doing as you are reading this book? Even if you become expert at masking and manipulating your face, you may first signal disinterest or boredom with another person by finger wiggling or toe wagging. Or you may twiddle a pen or pencil. When you become emotionally aroused, the pupils of your eyes dilate, and you may blush, sweat, or change breathing patterns.[5] Lie detectors rely on these unconscious clues. A polygraph measures a person's heart and breathing rate, as well as the electrical resistance of the skin (called *galvanic skin response*), to determine whether he or she is giving truthful verbal responses.

Nonverbal Communication Plays a Major Role in Interpersonal Relationships

As you learned in Chapter 1, because of the ubiquitous nature of nonverbal communication you cannot *not* communicate; psychologist Raymond Birdwhistell suggests that as much as 65 percent of the social meaning in messages is based on nonverbal communication.[6] Of course, the meaning that others interpret from your behavior may not be the one you intended, and the inferences they draw based on nonverbal information may be right or wrong.

You learned in Chapter 3 that people begin making judgments about strangers just a fraction of a second after meeting them, based on nonverbal information. Within the first four minutes of interaction, you scope the other out and draw conclusions about him or her.[7] Another research team found that you may decide whether a date is going to be pleasant or dull during the first thirty seconds of meeting your partner, before your partner has had time to utter more than "Hello."[8] Nonverbal cues affect first impressions, accurate or not.

Nonverbal cues are important not only when people initiate relationships, but also as they maintain and develop mature relationships with others. In fact, the more intimate the relationship, the more people use and understand the nonverbal cues of their partners.

Portrait artists pay close attention to nonverbal cues such as posture, facial expression, and gesture to capture their subjects' personalities. What do the nonverbal cues reveal about this Spanish dancer? (John Singer Sargeant, "Belle Epoque." Erich Lessing/Art Resource)

Long-married couples spend less time verbalizing their feelings and emotions to each other than they did when they were first dating; each learns how to interpret the other's subtle nonverbal cues. If your spouse is silent during dinner, you may know that the day was a tough one, and you should give her a wide berth. And if, when you put on your new Kelly green pants, your husband grimaces as he asks, "New pants?" you may understand that he does not love them. In fact, all of us are more likely to use nonverbal cues to convey negative messages than to announce explicitly our dislike of something or someone. People also use nonverbal cues to signal changes in the level of satisfaction with a relationship. When we want to cool things off, we may start using a less vibrant tone of voice and cut back on eye contact and physical contact with our partner.

Even though we've discussed verbal messages and nonverbal messages in separate chapters in this book, verbal and nonverbal cues often work together to create meaning. Also keep in mind that interpersonal communication, especially the expression of nonverbal messages, is a transactional process. Meaning is created simultaneously between those communicating. **Interaction adaptation theory** describes the transactive process of how people adapt to the communication behavior of others.

Based on interaction adaptation theory, Judee Burgoon and her colleagues have concluded that nonverbal cues play a key role in how people adapt to others.[9] If, for example, your friend leans forward to tell a story, you may reciprocally lean forward to listen. Or if during a meeting you sit with folded arms, unconvinced of what you are hearing, you may look around the conference table and find others with similarly folded arms. Like an intricate dance, when we communicate, we relate to others by responding to movement, eye contact, gestures, and other nonverbal cues. Sometimes we relate by mirroring the posture or behavior of others. Or we may find ourselves gesturing in sync with someone's vocal pattern. The rhythm of life is often conveyed as we respond and adapt to others through our nonverbal behavior.

Although we rely heavily on nonverbal messages, they do not operate independently of spoken messages in our relationships. Instead, verbal and nonverbal cues work together in two primary ways to help us make sense of others' messages.

First, nonverbal cues substitute for, repeat, contradict, or regulate verbal messages. An extended thumb signals that a hitchhiker would like a ride. A circle formed by the thumb and index finger can either signal that everything is A-OK or convey an obscene message. When someone asks, "Which way did he go?" you can silently point to the back door. In these instances, you are substituting nonverbal cues for a verbal message.

You can also use nonverbal cues to repeat or reinforce your words. "Where is the personnel department?" asks a job applicant. "Three flights up. Take the elevator," says the security guard, pointing to the elevator. The guard's pointing gesture repeats her verbal instruction and clarifies the message.

"Sure, this is a good time to talk about the Henrikson merger," says the business executive, nervously looking at her watch, stuffing papers into her attaché case, and avoiding eye contact with her coworker. In this instance, the nonverbal cues contradict the verbal ones. And as we learned earlier, the nonverbal message is almost always the one we believe.

We also use nonverbal cues to regulate our participation in verbal exchanges. In most informal meetings it is not appropriate or necessary to signal your desire to speak by raising your hand. Yet somehow you are able to signal to others when you'd like to speak and when you'd rather not talk. How does this happen? You use eye contact, raised eyebrows, an open mouth, or perhaps a single raised index finger to signal that you would like to make a point. If your colleagues do not see

interaction adaptation theory. Theory suggesting that a predictor of how you interact with others is your tendency to adapt to what others are doing.

these signals, especially the eye contact, they may think you are not interested in talking.[10]

The second way in which nonverbal cues work together with verbal ones is in accenting and complementing emotional messages. "Unless we vote to increase our tax base," bellows Mr. Coddlington, "we will not have enough classroom space to educate our children." While delivering his impassioned plea to the school board, Mr. Coddlington also loudly slaps the lectern to accent his message and reinforce its intensity. A scolding mother's wagging finger and an angry supervisor's raised voice are other nonverbal cues that accent verbal messages.

Simultaneous and complementary verbal and nonverbal messages can also help to color the emotion we are expressing or the attitude we are conveying. The length of a hug while you tell your son you are proud of him provides additional information about the intensity of your pride. The firmness of your handshake when you greet a job interviewer can confirm your verbal claim that you are eager for employment.

recap   **Reasons to Study Nonverbal Communication**

1. Nonverbal communication is the primary way in which people communicate feelings and attitudes toward others.

2. Nonverbal messages are usually more believable than verbal messages.

3. Nonverbal communication plays a major role in relationship development.

   ● Nonverbal cues substitute for, repeat, contradict, or regulate verbal messages.

   ● Nonverbal cues accent and complement emotional messages.

The Challenge of Interpreting Nonverbal Messages

Even though we have made great claims for the value of studying nonverbal behaviors, it is not always easy to decipher unspoken messages. You have dictionaries to help interpret words, but there is no handy reference book to help decode nonverbal cues. Although the phrase "body language" is often used in casual conversation, there is no universal or agreed-on interpretation for body movements or gestures. To help you with the decoding process, we are going to classify some common types of nonverbal behaviors. But first you should be aware of some of the difficulties that hinder classification.

Nonverbal Messages Are Often Ambiguous

Most words carry a meaning that everyone who speaks the same language can recognize. But the meaning of nonverbal messages may be known only to the person displaying them. Perhaps even more importantly, that person may not intend for the behavior to have any meaning at all. And some people have difficulty expressing

their emotions nonverbally. They may have a frozen facial expression or a monotone voice. Or they may be teasing you, but their deadpan expressions lead you to believe that their negative comments are heartfelt. Often it is difficult to draw meaningful conclusions about another person's behavior, even if you know him or her quite well.

Nonverbal Messages Are Continuous

Words are discrete entities; they have a beginning and an end. You can circle the first word in this sentence and underline the last one. Nonverbal behaviors are not as easily dissected. Like the sweep of a second hand on a watch, nonverbal behaviors are continuous. Some, such as a slap or a hand clap, have definite beginnings and endings. But more often than not, nonverbal behavior unfolds without clearly defined starting and stopping points. Gestures, facial expressions, and even eye contact can flow from one situation to the next with seamless ease. Researchers have difficulty studying nonverbal cues because of this continuous stream, so trying to categorize and interpret them will be challenging for us as well.

Nonverbal Cues Are Multichanneled

Have you ever tried to watch two or more TV programs at once? Some televisions let you see as many as eight programs simultaneously so that you can keep up with three ball games and two soap operas and view commercials on the three other channels. Like the multichannel TV, nonverbal cues come to our perception center from a variety of sources simultaneously. And just as you can really watch only one channel at a time on your multichannel television—although you can move among them very rapidly—so too can you actually attend to only one nonverbal cue at a time. Social psychologist Michael Argyle suspects that negative nonverbal messages (frowns, grimaces, lack of eye contact) command attention before positive messages when the two compete.[11] Moreover, if the nonverbal message contradicts the verbal message, then you may have trouble interpreting either one correctly.[12]

Nonverbal Interpretation Is Culture Based

There is some evidence that humans from every culture smile when they are happy and frown when they are unhappy.[13] We also all raise or flash our eyebrows when

understanding
diversity

Cultural Differences in Interpreting Nonverbal Messages

Research investigating nonverbal communication in a variety of cultures confirms that individuals interpret nonverbal messages from their unique cultural perspective. Note the following conclusions:[14]

Facial Expressions One research team found that some facial expressions such as happiness, sadness, anger, disgust, and surprise were the same in 68 to 92 percent of the cultures examined. All humans probably share the same neurophysiological basis for expressing emotions, but learn different rules for sending and interpreting the expressions. For example, the Japanese culture does not reinforce the show of negative emotions; it is important for Japanese to "save face" and to help others save face as well.

Eye Contact There seems to be more eye contact in interpersonal interactions between Arabs, South Americans, and Greeks than between people from other cultures. There is evidence that some African Americans look at others less than do whites when sending and receiving messages. One of the most universal expressions among cultures appears to be the eyebrow flash (the sudden raising of the eyebrows when meeting someone or interacting with others).

Gestures Hand and body gestures with the most shared meaning among Africans, North Americans, and South Americans include pointing, shrugging, head nodding, clapping, thumbs down, waving hello, and beckoning. There are, however, regional variations within cultures; it is not wise to assume that all people in a given culture share the same meaning for certain gestures. The "okay" gesture made by forming a circle with the thumb and finger has sexual connotations for some South American and Caribbean countries. In France the "okay" sign means "worthless."

Space Arabs, Latin Americans, and Southern Europeans seem to stand closer to others than do people from Asia, India, Pakistan, and northern Europe. If you have been to Britain, you know that people queue or wait for buses in orderly straight lines. In France, however, queuing is less orderly, and individuals are more likely to push forward to be the next customer or get the next seat on the bus. As with gestures, however, there are regional variations in spatial preferences.

For a look at a comparison between Anglo and African American nonverbal communication, click on the following Web site:

http://www.nwsel.org/cnorse/booklets/ccc/table4.html

---

meeting or greeting others, and young children in many cultures wave to signal they want their mothers, raise their arms to be picked up, and suck their thumbs for comfort.[15] All this suggests that there is some underlying basis for expressing emotion. Yet each culture may develop unique rules for displaying and interpreting these gestures and expressions.

There is no common cross-cultural dictionary of nonverbal meaning. Consider the case of the Muslim woman who was arrested by suspicious policemen, when she strolled through a downtown skywalk in St. Paul, Minnesota. Her crime? She was wearing a veil. Revealing her face in public would violate her religious beliefs. If you grew up in a Seattle suburb, you might be startled when on a visit to New Orleans you stumble on a handkerchief-waving, dancing, exuberantly singing crowd, and discover that it is an African-American jazz funeral. What to the uninformed may seem like disrespect for the dead, others recognize as a joyous send-off to a better world. An American tourist in Russia might be puzzled to hear an audience break out in synchronized rhythmic hand clapping to express its appreciation of an act at the Moscow Circus.

Nonverbal Communication Codes

Keeping all these challenges to our understanding in mind, we can begin looking at the categories of nonverbal information that researchers have studied: movement and gestures, eye contact, facial expressions, use of space and territory, touch, and personal appearance. Although we will concentrate on the codes that fall within these categories in mainstream Western culture, we will also look at codes for other cultures and subcultures.

Body Movement, Posture, and Gestures

In 1771, when English explorer Captain Cook arrived in the New Hebrides, he didn't speak the language of the natives. His only way of communicating was sign language. Through gestures, pointing, and hand waving, he established contact with the natives. There is evidence that people have used gestures to communicate since ancient times—especially to bridge cultural and language differences. The first record of using sign language to communicate is found in Xenophon's *The March Up Country*, in which he describes unspoken gestures used to help the Greeks cross Asia Minor in about 400 B.C. Even when we do speak the same language as others, we use gestures to help us make our point.[16]

Kinesics is the study of human movement and gesture. Francis Bacon once noted, "As the tongue speaketh to the ear, so the hand speaketh to the eye." People have long recognized that movement and gestures provide valuable information to others. Various scholars and researchers have proposed paradigms for analyzing and coding these movements and gestures, as for spoken or written language.[17]

One paradigm identifies four stages of "quasi-courtship behavior."[18] The first stage is *courtship readiness.* When you are attracted to someone, you may suck in your stomach, tense your muscles, and stand up straight. The second stage includes *preening behaviors:* You manipulate your appearance by combing your hair, applying makeup, straightening your tie, pulling up your socks, and double-checking your appearance in the mirror. In stage three you demonstrate *positional cues,* using your posture and body orientation to be seen and noticed by others.

One researcher found 52 gestures and nonverbal behaviors that women use to signal an interest in men. Among the top unspoken flirting cues were smiling and surveying a crowded room with the eyes, and moving closer to the object of affection.[19] People intensify these cues in the fourth stage, *appeals to invitation,* using close proximity, exposed skin, open body positions, and eye contact to signal availability and interest. The classic Norman Rockwell painting at left shows teenagers illustrating typical

Can you identify the quasi-courtship behavior in this painting?

building your skills

Communicating Interest

Nonverbally play the roles of both a good listener and a bad listener. First, imagine that you are listening to someone talk. As a good listener, how would you communicate your interest in what the person is saying, without uttering a word? Note your posture, eye contact, presence or lack of hand movement. Are your arms and legs crossed?

Now role-play a poor listener—someone who appears to be bored or even irritated by what a speaker is saying. What are the differences in the cues you use? Use the spaces here, or write your responses on a sheet of paper, to describe the differences.

Nonverbal Behaviors of a Good Listener

Posture: _____

_____

_____

Body orientation: _____

_____

_____

Eye contact: _____

_____

_____

Gestures: _____

_____

_____

Movement: _____

_____

_____

Nonverbal Behaviors of a Poor Listener

Posture: _____

_____

_____

Body orientation: _____

_____

_____

Eye contact: _____

_____

_____

Gestures: _____

_____

_____

Movement: _____

_____

_____

appeals to invitation. Subjects in one study reported that they were aware of using all these techniques to promote an intimate relationship. In fact, people use these quasi-courtship behaviors to some extent in almost any situation in which they are trying to gain favorable attention from another.

Another team of researchers focused on nonverbal behaviors that prompt people to label someone warm and friendly, or cold and distant.[20] The team found that "warm" people face their communication partners directly, smile more, make more direct eye contact, fidget less, and generally make fewer unnecessary hand movements. "Cold" people make less eye contact, smile less, fidget more, and turn away from their partners.

Posture and body orientation reveal important information. Open body posture (uncrossed arms and legs) communicates that you are receptive and a responsive listener. When you are trying to decrease your contact with someone, say at a party or family gathering, you are likely to turn away from the individual you want to avoid. As you will find when you participate in Building Your Skills: Communicating Interest, your body orientation and posture provide important cues as to your interest and willingness to continue or end communication with someone.

Mehrabian has identified the nonverbal cues that contribute to perceptions of liking.[21] He found that an open body and arm position, a forward lean, and a relaxed posture communicate liking. When you are attempting to persuade someone,

kinesics. Study of human movement and gesture.

you typically have more eye contact and a more direct body orientation; you are more likely to lean forward and closer to others.

Ekman and Friesen classified movement and gestures according to their function. They identified five categories: emblems, illustrators, affect displays, regulators, and adaptors.[22]

🔹 Emblems

Nonverbal cues that have specific, generally understood meanings in a given culture and may actually substitute for a word or phrase are called **emblems.** When you are busy typing a report that is due tomorrow and your young son bounces in to ask for permission to buy a new computer game, you turn from your computer and hold up an open palm to indicate your desire for uninterrupted quiet. To communicate your enthusiastic enjoyment of a violin soloist at a concert, you applaud wildly. You want your children to stop talking in the library, so you put an index finger up to your pursed lips.

🔹 Illustrators

People frequently accompany a verbal message with **illustrators** that either contradict, accent, or complement the message. Slamming a book closed while announcing, "I don't want to read this anymore" or pounding a lectern while proclaiming, "This point is important!" are two examples of nonverbal behaviors that illustrate the verbal message. Typically, we use nonverbal illustrators at the beginning of clauses or phrases.[23] TV newscasters, for example, turn a page to signal that they are moving to a new story or topic. Most of us use illustrators to help us communicate information about the size, shape, and spatial relationships of objects. You probably even use them when you talk on the phone, although probably not as many as you use in face-to-face conversation.[24]

🔹 Affect Displays

Nonverbal movements and postures used to communicate emotion are called **affect displays.** As early as 1872, when Charles Darwin systematically studied the expression of emotion in both humans and animals,[25] people recognized that nonverbal cues are the primary ways to communicate emotion. Facial expressions, vocal cues, posture, and gestures convey the intensity of your emotions.[26] If you are happy, for example, your face will telegraph your joy to others. The movement of your hands, the openness of your posture, and the speed with which you move will tell others *how* happy you are. Similarly, if you are feeling depressed, your face will probably reveal your sadness or dejection, while your slumped shoulders and lowered head will indicate the intensity of your despair. When you are feeling friendly, you use a soft tone of voice, an open smile, and a relaxed posture.[27] When you feel neutral about an issue, you signal it by putting little expression on your face or in your voice. When you feel hostile, you use a harsh voice, frown with your teeth showing, and keep your posture tense and rigid.

🔹 Regulators

People use **regulators** to control the interaction or flow of communication between themselves and another person. When you are eager to respond to a message, you make eye contact, raise your eyebrows, open your mouth, raise an index finger, and lean forward slightly. In a classroom, you may raise your hand to signal overtly that you want to talk. When you do not want to be part of the conversation, you do the

---

emblems. Nonverbal cues that have specific, generally understood meanings in a given culture and may substitute for a word or phrase.

illustrators. Nonverbal behaviors that accompany a verbal message and either contradict, accent, or complement it.

affect display. Nonverbal behavior that communicates emotions.

regulators. Nonverbal messages that help to control the interaction or flow of communication between people.

opposite: avert your eyes, close your mouth, cross your arms, and lean back in your seat or away from the verbal action as attempts to regulate the interaction.

Adaptors

When you are cold, you reach for a sweater or wrap your arms around your chest to keep warm. When it's 102 degrees Fahrenheit in the shade without a breeze, you may reach for a fan to make your own breeze. These behaviors are examples of **adaptors**—nonverbal behaviors that help you satisfy a personal need and adapt to the immediate situation. When you adjust your glasses, scratch a mosquito bite, or comb your hair, you are using movement to help you manage your personal needs and adapt to your surroundings.

The Five Categories and Interpersonal Communication

How does understanding these five categories of nonverbal behavior help you understand interpersonal communication? It gives you a new and more precise way to think about your own behavior. By noting how often you use emblems instead of words to communicate a message, you can recognize how important emblems are in your relationships with others. The more you rely on emblems that have unique meanings for you and your partner, the more intimate the interpersonal relationship. Also, start to notice whether your nonverbal behavior contradicts what you say. Monitoring your use of illustrators can help you determine whether you are sending mixed signals to others. Be aware of how you display affect. Knowing that your face and voice communicate emotion, and that posture and gesture indicate the intensity of your feelings, can help you understand how others make inferences about your feelings and attitudes. If other people have difficulty interpreting your emotional state, you may not be projecting your feelings nonverbally. And finally, notice how you use adaptors. Individuals who do not learn the cultural norms of displaying adaptors can have a difficult time socially. For example, if you were never taught not to comb your hair or belch at the table, you may find you receive few dinner invitations.

Since nonverbal cues are ambiguous, it may not be a good idea to use them to achieve a specific objective. But as you have seen, people are more likely to respond in predictable ways if you use behaviors they can recognize and interpret easily.

adaptors. Nonverbal behaviors that satisfy a personal need and help a person adapt or respond to the immediate situation.

recap

Categories of Movement and Gestures

Category	Definition	Examples
Emblems	Behaviors that have specific, generally understood meaning	A hitchhiker's raised thumb.
Illustrators	Cues that accompany verbal messages and provide meaning for the message	A public speaker's pounding the podium to emphasize a point.
Affect displays	Expressions of emotion	Hugging someone to express love.
Regulators	Cues that control and manage the flow of communication between others	Looking at someone when you wish to speak.
Adaptors	Behaviors that help you adapt to your environment	Scratching, combing your hair.

Eye Contact

Subtle power. Whether you choose to look at someone or avert your gaze has an enormous impact on your relationship with that person. Researcher Adam Kendon has identified four functions for eye contact in interpersonal interactions.[28]

First, it serves a *cognitive* function because it gives you information about another person's thought processes. For example, if your partner breaks eye contact after you ask him or her a question, you will know that he or she is probably thinking of something to say.

Second, people use eye contact to *monitor* the behavior of others. You receive a major portion of the information you obtain through your eyes. You look at others to determine whether they are receptive to your messages. In fact, this search for feedback is implicit in the word for the center part of the eye, *pupil,* which comes from the Latin word *pupilla* or "little doll." When you look into someone's eyes, you can see a miniature reflection of yourself.[29]

Third, eye contact is one of the most powerful *regulatory* cues you use to signal when you want to talk and when you don't. We (your authors) have noticed that when we ask questions such as "Who can tell me the four functions of eye contact?" students quickly yet unobtrusively avert their eyes to signal, "Don't call on me." When you do want to communicate with others, say when standing in line at the bakery, you fix your eyes on the clerk to signal, "My turn next. Please wait on me."

Finally, the area around your eyes serves an *expressive* function. The eyes have been called the "mirror of the soul" because they reveal emotions to others. You may cry, blink, and widen or narrow your gaze to express your feelings.

As shown in Table 7.1, researchers Mark Knapp and Judith Hall have summarized conclusions on nonverbal communication that predict when you are most and least likely to have eye contact with someone.[30]

When people do establish eye contact with others, it may seem that their gaze is constant. Yet research suggests that they actually spend the majority of their time looking at something other than the person's eyes. One research team found that people focus on something else, including their partner's mouth, 57 percent of the time.[31] Not surprisingly then, facial expressions are another rich source of information in your communication with others.

Table 7.1

When Are You Most and Least Likely to Have Eye Contact with Someone?

You are more likely to have eye contact when you	You are less likely to have eye contact when you
• Like or love your partner	• Do not like your partner
• Are physically distant from him or her	• Are physically close to your partner
• Are discussing easy, impersonal topics	• Are discussing difficult, intimate topics
• Have nothing else to look at	• Have other things to look at
• Are interested in your partner's reactions	• Are not interested in your partner's reactions
• Are trying to dominate or persuade your partner	• Are not trying to dominate or persuade your partner
• Are from a culture that emphasizes eye contact	• Are from a culture that de-emphasizes eye contact
• Are an extrovert	• Are an introvert
• Have a high need to affiliate or to be included	• Have a low need to affiliate or do not need to be included
• Are dependent on your partner (and your partner is not responsive)	• Are more independent of your partner (and your partner is responsive to you)
• Are listening rather than talking	• Are talking rather than listening
• Are female	• Are male

Source: Adapted from Mark L. Knapp and Judith A. Hall, *Nonverbal Communication in Human Interaction* (Fort Worth, Texas: Harcourt Brace, 1997), 390–391.

recap **Functions of Eye Contact**

Cognitive Function	Provides cues about your thinking and thought processes
Monitoring Function	Provides information about how others are responding to you; you monitor to seek feedback
Regulatory Function	Manages the flow of communication; you use eye contact to signal when you do and do not want to interact with another person
Expressive Function	Provides information about feelings, emotions, and attitudes

Facial Expression

You tell your parents that you will not be able to spend the holidays with them because you have decided to take your children skiing. You present your fiancée with a new abstract art painting that you would like to hang in your bedroom after you

The face is an exhibit gallery for emotions. The messages you convey through thousands of different expressions are usually more powerful and direct than verbal ones. (Bob Daemmrich/Stock Boston)

are married. As the personnel director reviews your résumé, you sit in silence across from her desk. In each of these situations you would be eagerly awaiting some reaction from your partner. And what you would be scanning is his or her face. The face is the exhibit gallery for emotional displays. And although you often try to manipulate your facial cues to project a premeditated feeling, your face may still betray your true emotions to others.[32]

To interpret a partner's facial expressions accurately, you need to put your other-orientation skills to work, focusing on what the other person may be thinking or feeling. It helps if you know the person well, can see his or her whole face, have plenty of time to watch it, and understand the situation that prompted the emotion.[33] But it is also helpful to know the cues for "reading" facial expressions.

Your face is versatile. According to Ekman and Friesen, it is capable of producing over 250,000 different expressions.[34] Research suggests that women have greater variety in their emotional expressions and spend more time smiling than men.[35] But all facial expression can be grouped under six primary emotional categories; the following list describes the changes that occur on your face for each one.[36]

Surprise: Wide-open eyes; raised and wrinkled brow; open mouth.

Fear: Open mouth; tense skin under the eyes; wrinkles in the center of the forehead.

Disgust: Raised or curled upper lip; wrinkled nose; raised cheeks; lowered brow; lowered upper eyelid.

---

building your skills

Facial Expression Quiz

Students should divide into teams of two people. Person A selects one of the six primary emotions communicated by the face and attempts to display the emotion to person B. The six primary emotions are happiness, sadness, surprise, disgust, anger, and fear. Communicate all six emotions *in random order.*

Person B attempts to identify the emotions expressed by person A and list them in order below.

When person A has communicated all six emotions, he or she can reverse roles with person B.

1. _____

2. _____

3. _____

4. _____

5. _____

6. _____

e-connection

Japanese Turn E-mail "Smiley Faces" Right Side Up

Tokyo—When Yukihiro Furuse first began prowling international computer networks in the mid-1980s, he was perplexed to encounter emoticons, the strange combinations of punctuation and accent marks and letters that Westerners used in electronic mail to indicate happiness, sadness and other emotions.

But when Furuse and other network pioneers tried to incorporate symbols such as :-) into their domestic e-mail, their Japanese correspondents found the Western smiley—dare we say it—inscrutable.

"We had to write many times, 'If you tilt your head, you will see the face,'" said Furuse, who is director of the publications department at the

Center for Global Communications, a research institute affiliated with International University of Japan.

So in the latest example of Japan seizing upon a Western idea, adapting it to their culture and improving upon it, Japanese computer users have evolved a unique set of emoticons. The Japanese smileys are intricate in their design, somewhat ambiguous in their expression and, in what many here would argue is

a big advance, are right side up instead of sideways.

The basic smiley in Japan, (^_^), is much easier to recognize as a face than the Western version, but since the mouth doesn't curl upward (no character on the keyboard can do that), the Japanese smiley is somewhat harder to understand without knowing the context.

Source: Andrew Pollack, *The New York Times*

Japanese emoticons

Regular smile:	(^_^) (caret underscore caret)
Girl's smile:	(^.^) (caret . caret)
Banzai smiley:	\(^_^)/ backslash (caret underscore caret) /
Cold sweat:	(^^;) (caret caret ;)
Excuse me:	(^o^;>) (caret o caret ; greater than symbol)
Double-byte smiley:	(^__^) (caret long underscore caret)
Exciting:	(*^o*^) (asterisk caret o caret asterisk)

Anger: Tensed lower eyelid; either pursed lips or open mouth; lowered and wrinkled brow; staring eyes.

Happiness: Smiling; mouth may be open or closed; raised cheeks; wrinkles around lower eyelids.

Sadness: Lip may tremble; corners of the lips turn downward; corners of the upper eyelid may be raised.

You are undoubtedly familiar with emoticons, the computer "smiley faces" and other combinations of keyboard characters designed to communicate facial expression via e-mail. As e-Connections: Japanese Turn E-mail "Smiley Faces" Right-Side Up shows, the Japanese have adapted the use of emoticons to express emotions appropriate for their culture.

How accurately do people interpret emotions expressed on the face? Several studies have attempted to measure subjects' skill in identifying emotional expressions of others. They have found that reading facial expression is a tricky business. According to Ekman and Friesen, even though faces provide a great deal of information about emotions, people have learned how to control facial expressions.[37] In addition, facial expressions seem to be contagious. One researcher who showed his subjects video clips of President Reagan giving speeches discovered that they were likely to smile when Reagan smiled and frown when Reagan appeared angry or threatening.[38]

Vocal Cues

Try this. Say "John" to communicate the following emotions: anger, sadness, disgust, happiness, fear, surprise. If you are reading this in a public place, stop reading for a moment and give it a try even if you have to whisper. What happened to your voice? Like your face, your voice is a major vehicle for communicating your emotions. The pitch, rate, and volume at which you speak, and your use of silence, all provide important clues to your feelings.

Your voice is a primary tool for communicating information about the nature of relationships between you and others.[39] You use your voice to present one message on the surface (with words) and usually a more accurate expression of your feelings with your vocal quality. Say the following sentence out loud: "This looks great." Now say it sarcastically; you really don't think it looks great: "This looks great." Clearly, your vocal cues provide the real meaning.

Some vocal expressions of emotion are easier to identify than others. Expressions of joy and anger are obvious ones, whereas shame and love are the most difficult emotions to identify based on vocal cues alone.[40] People are also likely to confuse fear with nervousness, love with sadness, and pride with satisfaction. As an example of how the intonation of a single word can convey rich meaning, read the excerpt below from *A Lesson Before Dying*. In this story, a black schoolteacher is collecting money to buy a radio for a black man unfairly condemned to death by a white jury in Louisiana in the late 1940s.

Your voice also provides information about your self-confidence and your knowledge of the subject matter in your messages. Most of us would conclude that a speaker who mumbles, speaks slowly, consistently mispronounces words, and uses "uhs" and "ums" is less credible and persuasive than one who speaks clearly, rapidly, and fluently.[41] Even though mispronunciations and vocalized pauses ("ums" and "ahs") seem to have a negative effect on credibility, they do not seem to be a major impediment to attitude change. People may, for example, think that

---

I ate the food hungrily because I had not had dinner, and I sopped up the gravy with the light bread. Thelma watched me all the time. When I was finished, she put a wrinkled ten-dollar bill on the counter by my plate.

"Here."

It was the kind of "here" your mother or your big sister or your great-aunt or your grandmother would have said. It was the kind of "here" that let you know this was hard-earned money but, also, that you needed it more than she did, and the kind of "here" that said she wished you had it and didn't have to borrow it from her, but since you did not have it, and she did, then "here" it was, with a kind of love. It was the kind of "here" that asked the question, "When will all this end? When will a man not have to struggle to have money to get what he needs 'here'? When will a man be able to live without having to kill another man 'here'?"

I took the money without looking at her. I didn't say thanks. I knew she didn't want to hear it.

Ernest J. Gaines, *A Lesson Before Dying*

you are less knowledgeable if you stammer, but you may still be able to get your persuasive message across.

In addition to providing information about emotions, self-confidence, and knowledge, vocal cues, known as **backchannel cues,** can serve a regulatory function in interpersonal situations, signaling when we want to talk and when we don't. When we are finished talking, we may lower the pitch of our final word. When we want to talk, we may start by interjecting sounds such as "I . . . I . . . I . . ." or "Ah . . . Ah . . . Ah . . ." to interrupt the speaker and grab the verbal ball. We also may use more cues such as "Sure," "I understand," "Uh-huh," or "Okay" to signal that we understand the message of the other person and now we want to talk or end the conversation. These backchannel cues are particularly useful in telephone conversations when we have no other nonverbal cues to help us signal that we would like to get off the phone.

Sometimes it is not what we say, or even how we say it, that communicates our feelings. Being silent may communicate volumes. One researcher, in commenting about the importance of silence in speech, said, "Silence is to speech as white paper is to this print. . . . The entire system of spoken language would fail without [people's] ability to both tolerate and create sign sequences of silence–sound–silence units."[42]

Why are we sometimes at a loss for words? There are many possible reasons. We may simply not know what to say. Or there is evidence that when someone tells a lie, he or she may need a few moments to think of a credible ruse. We may be silent because we want to distance ourselves from those who are around us; we want to communicate that we really don't want to be involved in the conversation. Or perhaps we just need some time to think about what we want to contribute to the conversation. Silence, too, may be a sign of respect. Some children were raised with the message "Be seen and not heard." They were taught that those in authority should maintain control of the talking process. At other times we are silent with someone because words would diminish the experience we are sharing. Walking hand-in-hand on the beach, watching the sun set, or sitting on a balcony overlooking a spectacular mountain vista may call for silence; trying to translate the experience into words would diminish it.

Would you be comfortable just sitting silently with a good friend? Sidney Baker's theory of silence suggests that the more at ease you are when you share a silence with a close friend, the more comfortable you are with just being together and enjoying each other's companionship. People need to talk until there is nothing left to say; the uncertainty has been managed. In most long-term relationships, partners may not feel a need to fill the air with sound. Just being together to enjoy each other's company may be most fulfilling. Baker calls such moments "positive silence."[43] While watching a sunset with a close friend, for example, there may be no need to narrate what you are seeing—just to experience it.

Personal Space

Imagine that you are sitting alone in a booth at your local pizza parlor. As you sit munching your thin-and-crispy pepperoni pizza, you are startled when a complete stranger sits down in your booth directly across from you. With several empty tables and booths in the restaurant, you feel very uncomfortable that this unknown individual has invaded "your" area.

Normally, people do not think much about the rules they observe regarding personal space, but in fact every culture has fairly rigid ways of regulating space in social interactions. Violations of these rules can be alarming and, as in the preceding

backchannel cues. Nonverbal cues, typically vocal cues, that signal your wish to begin or end a conversation.

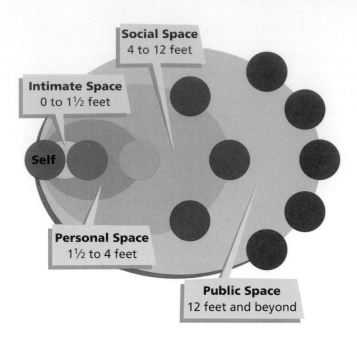

Social Space
4 to 12 feet

Intimate Space
0 to 1½ feet

Self

Personal Space
1½ to 4 feet

Public Space
12 feet and beyond

Figure 7.1
Edwin T. Hall's Four Zones
of Space

proxemics. Study of how close or far away from people and objects people position themselves.

intimate space. Zone of personal space most often used for very personal or intimate conversation, ranging from 0 to 1½ feet.

personal space. Zone of personal space most often used for conversation, ranging from 1½ to 4 feet.

social space. Zone of personal space most often used for group discussion, ranging from 4 to 12 feet.

public space. Zone of personal space most often used by public speakers or anyone speaking to many people, ranging beyond 12 feet.

scenario, even threatening. How close you are willing to get to others relates to how well you know them and to considerations of power and status.

One pioneer in helping people understand the silent language of personal space was Edward T. Hall. His study of **proxemics** investigated how close or how far away we arrange ourselves around people and things.[44] Hall identified four spatial zones that we unconsciously define for ourselves, as shown in Figure 7.1. When we are between 0 and 1½ feet from someone, we are occupying **intimate space.** This is the zone in which the most intimate interpersonal communication occurs. It is open only to those with whom we are well acquainted, unless we are forced to stand in an elevator, a fast-food line, or some other crowded space.

The second zone, which ranges from 1½ to 4 feet, is called **personal space.** Most conversations with family and friends occur in this zone. If someone you don't know well invades this space on purpose, you may feel uncomfortable.

Zone three, called **social space,** ranges from 4 to 12 feet. Most group interaction, as well as many professional relationships, take place in this zone. The interaction tends to be more formal than that in the first two zones.

Public space, the fourth zone, begins at 12 feet. Interpersonal communication does not usually occur in this zone, and many public speakers and teachers position themselves even more than 12 feet from their audience.

The specific space that you and others choose depends on several variables.[45] The more you like someone, the closer you will stand. We allow individuals with high status to surround themselves with more space than we allow for people with lower status. Large people also usually have more space around them than smaller ones, and women stand closer to others than men do.[46] All of us tend to stand closer to others in a large room than we do in a small room.

In a group, who's in charge, who's important, and who talks to whom are reflected by the spatial arrangement people select. The more dominant group members tend to select seats at the head of a table, while shyer individuals often select a corner seat at a rectangular table.[47]

Edward T. Hall's Classification of Spatial Zones

	Distance	Examples
Zone One	0 to 1½ feet	Communicating with our most intimate acquaintances
Zone Two	1½ feet to 4 feet	Conversing with good friends and family members
Zone Three	4 feet to 12 feet	Working with others in small groups and in professional situations
Zone Four	12 feet and beyond	Public-speaking situations

Territory

Territoriality is the study of how animals (including humans) use space and objects to communicate occupancy or ownership of space. You assumed "ownership" of the booth in the pizza parlor and the accompanying "right" to determine who sat with you, because you and your pizza were occupying the booth. In addition to invading your personal space, the intrusive stranger broke the rules that govern territoriality.

People announce ownership of space with territorial markers—things that signify the area has been claimed—much as explorers once planted a flag claiming uncharted land for the king. When you are studying at the library, for example, and need to hop up and check a reference at the computerized card catalog, you might leave behind a notebook or a pencil. In rural areas, landowners post signs at the borders of their property to keep hunters off their territory. Signs, locks, electronic security systems, and other devices secure home and office territories.

You also use markers to indicate where your space stops and someone else's starts. "Good fences make good neighbors," wrote the poet Robert Frost. When someone sits too close, you may try to erect a physical barrier, such as a stack of books or a napkin holder, or you might use your body as a shield by turning away.

territoriality. Study of how animals and humans use space and objects to communicate occupancy or ownership of space.

When you sit down at one end of a park bench how much of the bench do you consider to be your territory? When someone sits at the other end, is that an invasion of your space? (Richard Lord/The Image Works)

"Excuse me, sir. I am prepared to make you a rather attractive offer for your square."

If the intruder does not get the hint that "this land is my land," you ultimately resort to words to announce that the space is occupied.

Touch

Standing elbow to elbow in a crowded elevator, you may find yourself in physical contact with total strangers. As you stiffen your body and avert your eyes, a baffling sense of shame floods over you. If you are sitting at a conference table and you accidentally brush the toes of your shoes against your colleague's ankle, you may jerk away and even blush or apologize. Why do people react this way to unpremeditated touching? Normally, you touch to express intimacy. When intimacy is not our intended message, you instinctively react to modify the impression.

Countless studies have shown that intimate touching is vital to your personal development and well-being.[48] Infants and children need it to confirm that they are valued and loved. Many hospitals invite volunteers in to hold and rock newborns whose mothers cannot do it themselves. Advocates of breastfeeding argue that the intimate touching it entails strengthens the bond between mother and child.[49]

The amount of touch you need, tolerate, receive, and initiate depends on many factors. The amount and kind of touching you receive in your family is one big influence. If your mom or dad greets you with hugs, caresses, and kisses, then you probably do this to others. If your family is less demonstrative, you may be restrained yourself. Studies by researcher Nancy Henley show that most of us are more likely to touch people when we are feeling friendly, or happy, or under some of the following other specific circumstances:[50]

- When we ask someone to do something for us
- When we share rather than ask for information
- When we try to persuade someone to do something
- When we are talking about intimate topics
- When we are in social settings that we choose rather than in professional settings that are part of our job
- When we are thrilled and excited to share good news
- When we listen to a troubled or worried friend

Appearance

In all interactions with others, appearance counts. American culture places a high value on how much you weigh, the style of your hair, and the clothes you wear; these things are particularly important in the early stages of relationship development. Attractive females have an easier time persuading others than do those who are perceived as less attractive. In general, Americans think attractive people are more credible, happier, more popular, more sociable, and even more prosperous than less attractive people.[51]

In Chapter 2 we discussed the link between self-concept and personal appearance. The shape and size of your body also affects how others perceive you. Heavier and rounder individuals are often perceived to be older, more old-fashioned, less good-looking, more talkative, and more good-natured than thin people, who are perceived to be more ambitious, more suspicious of others, more uptight and tense, more negative, and less talkative. Muscular and athletically fit folks are seen as better looking, taller, and more adventurous. These perceptions are, in fact, so common

e-connections

How to Tell Others, Without Saying a Word, That You Want the Job

It's unlikely that you will interview for a job without speaking. But what you don't say may create the main impression of your poise, competence, and credibility. For an application of the nonverbal communication cues that can enhance the impression you make on others when interviewing for a job, click on the following Web site:

http://www.angelfire.com/co/bodylanguages/page6.html

that they have become easily recognizable stereotypes on which casting directors for movies, TV shows, and plays rely in selecting actors and actresses.

Aside from keeping you warm and within the legal bounds of decency, your clothes also affect how others perceive you. The clothes you wear are a way of communicating to others how you want to be treated. One classic study found that a man who jaywalked while dressed in nice clothes attracted more fellow violators than he could when he was shabbily attired.[52] Although studies have attempted to identify a "power" look, and magazines are constantly giving prescriptions for ways to be attractive and stylish, there is no formula for dressing for success.[53] Styles and expectations about appearances change. You have only to look at the clothing norms of the 1950s, 1960s, or 1970s to note how they differ from those of today.

recap   Codes of Nonverbal Communication

Movements and Gestures	Communicate information, status, warmth, credibility, interest in others, attitudes, liking
Eye Contact	Serves cognitive, monitoring, regulatory, and expressive functions
Facial Expressions	Express emotions
Vocal Cues	Communicate emotion through pitch, rate, volume, and quality; and modify the meaning of messages
Personal Space	Provides information about status, power, and intimacy
Territory	Provides cues to use, ownership, or occupancy of space
Touch	Communicates intimacy, affection, or rejection
Appearance	Influences perceptions of credibility and attraction

Interpreting Nonverbal Communication

So what does it all mean? How do you make sense out of the postures, movements, gestures, eye contact, facial expressions, uses of space and territory, touch, and appearance of others? Albert Mehrabian has found that people synthesize and interpret nonverbal cues along three primary dimensions: *immediacy, arousal,* and *dominance.*[54] These three dimensions provide a useful way to summarize how nonverbal cues may be interpreted.

Immediacy

immediacy. Feelings of liking, pleasure, and closeness communicated by such nonverbal cues as eye contact, forward lean, touch, and open body orientation.

Sometimes we cannot put a finger on the precise reason we find a person likable or unlikable. Mehrabian believes that **immediacy** cues are a likely explanation. Immediacy cues are behaviors that communicate liking and engender feelings of pleasure. The principle underlying immediacy is simple: We move toward persons and things we like and avoid or move away from those we dislike. Immediacy cues increase our sensory awareness of others. Not surprisingly, communication researcher Lois Hinkle found that spouses who reported high feelings of affection for their mates reported that their mates responded by expressing more immediacy cues toward them.[55] There is also evidence that when someone expresses immediate or pleasant nonverbal messages toward us, we reciprocate by responding in a pleasant manner. Researchers Judee Burgoon and Beth Le Poire found that people adapt their nonverbal messages to others.[56] When people express immediacy or liking toward you, you are more likely to reciprocate and express a similar sentiment toward them. Immediacy is contagious.

Use of space and territory is not the only cue that contributes to positive or negative feelings. Mehrabian has noted several other nonverbal cues that increase immediacy. One of the most powerful is touch; others include a forward lean, increased eye contact, and an open body orientation. The meaning of these behaviors is usually implied rather than explicitly spelled out in words.

In brief, to communicate that we like someone, we use these cues:[57]

Proximity:	Close, forward lean
Body orientation:	Direct, but could be side-by-side
Eye contact:	Eye contact and mutual eye contact
Facial expression:	Smiling
Gestures:	Head nods, movement
Posture:	Open, arms oriented toward others
Touch:	Cultural- and context-appropriate touch
Voice:	Higher pitch, upward pitch

e-Connections
Interpreting Nonverbal Messages

Is there a dictionary of nonverbal cues? Although there are no agreed-on standard meanings for gestures, there are some widely held interpretations of selected gestures. Click on to the following Web site:

http://members.aol.com/nonverbal12/diction.htm

Here you'll find a summary of several gestures with some common interpretations. After looking at gestures and their interpretations in the Web site, check the accuracy of this "dictionary" by seeing whether you and your friends or classmates agree with the interpretation presented.

Gender Differences and Nonverbal Communication

There is evidence that men and women display and interpret nonverbal cues differently.[58]

Eye Contact
Women usually have a more prolonged gaze with others than do men. Women, however, are less likely just to stare at someone; they break eye contact more frequently than men. In general, women receive more eye contact from others than do men.

Space
Men tend to have more space around them than do women. Women both approach and are approached more closely than men. And when conversing with others, women seem to prefer side-by-side interactions.

Facial Expression
Research suggests that women smile more than men. It is also reported that women tend to be more emotionally expressive with their faces than men; this is perhaps related to the conclusion that women are more skilled at both sending and interpreting facial expressions.

Gesture and Posture
Overall, women appear to use fewer and less expansive gestures than men. Women are more likely, for example, to rest their hands on the arms of a chair while seated; men are more likely to use gestures. Men and women cross their legs differently: women cross their legs at the knees or ankles while men are more likely to sit with their legs apart.

Touch
Men are more likely to initiate touch with others than are women. Women are touched more than men. Men and women also attribute different meaning to touch; women are more likely to associate touch with warmth and expressiveness than are men.

Vocal Cues
Vocal patterns may be more related to biological differences in the vocal register than other nonverbal behaviors. Women speak in both higher and softer tones than do men. Women also use their voice to communicate a greater range of emotions than do men. Women are also more likely to raise their pitch when making statements; some people interpret the rising pattern (as in asking a question) as an indication of greater uncertainty.

Arousal

The face, voice, and movement are primary indicators of **arousal.** If we see arousal cues, we conclude that another person is responsive to and interested in us. If the person acts passive or dull, we conclude that he or she is uninterested.

When you approach someone and ask whether he or she has a minute or two to talk, that person may signal interest with a change in facial expression and more animated vocal cues. People who are aroused and interested in you show animation in their face, voice, and gestures. Forward lean, a flash of the eyebrows, and a nod of the head are other cues that implicitly communicate arousal. Someone who says, "Sure, I have time to talk with you," in a monotone and with a flat, expressionless face is communicating the opposite. Think of arousal as an on-off switch. Sleeping is the ultimate switched-off state.

Dominance

The third dimension of Mehrabian's framework for implicit cues communicates the balance of power in a relationship. **Dominance** cues communicate status, position, and importance. A person of high status tends to have a relaxed body posture when interacting with a person of lower status.[59] When you talk to a professor, she

arousal. Feelings of interest and excitement communicated by such nonverbal cues as vocal expression, facial expressions, and gestures.

dominance. Feelings of power, status, and control communicated by such nonverbal cues as a relaxed posture, greater personal space, and protected personal space.

may lean back in her chair, put her feet on the desk, and fold her hands behind her head during the conversation. But unless your professor is a colleague or a friend, you will maintain a relatively formal posture during your interaction in her office.

Another dominance cue is the use of space. High-status individuals usually have more space around them; they have bigger offices and more "barriers" protecting them. A receptionist in an office is usually easily accessible, but to reach the president of the company you may have to navigate through several corridors, past several secretaries and administrative assistants who are "guarding" the door.

Other power cues that communicate feelings of dominance include use of furniture, clothing, and locations. You study at a table in the library; the college president has a large private desk. You may wear jeans and a T-shirt to class; the head of the university wears a business suit. Your dorm may be surrounded by other dorms; the president's residence may be a large house surrounded by a lush, landscaped garden in a prestigious neighborhood. People use space, territory, posture, and artifacts such as clothing and furniture to signal feelings of dominance or submissiveness in the presence of others.

British social psychologist Michael Argyle summarizes the nonverbal cues that communicate dominance:[60]

Use of space:	Height (on a platform or standing) Facing a group More space
Eye contact:	More when initially establishing dominance More when staring to establish power More when talking
Face:	No smile, frown, mature adult features
Touch:	Initiating touch
Voice:	Loud, low pitch, greater pitch range Slow, more interruptions, more talk Slight hesitation before speaking
Gesture:	Pointing at the other or at his or her property
Posture:	Standing, hands on hips, expanded chest, more relaxed

 recap | **Dimensions for Interpreting Nonverbal Behavior**

Dimension	Definition	Nonverbal Cues
Immediacy	Cues that communicate liking and pleasure	Eye contact, touch, forward lean, close distances
Arousal	Cues that communicate active interest and emotional involvement	Eye contact, varied vocal cues, animated facial expressions, forward lean, movement
Dominance	Cues that communicate status and power	Protected space, relaxed posture, status symbols

Improving Your Ability to Interpret Nonverbal Messages

As we have already cautioned, there are no universal dictionaries to which you can turn for help in interpreting specific nonverbal behaviors. People interpret messages of others based on their own experiences and cultural perspective. One theory that helps explain how to interpret nonverbal messages is called **expectancy violation theory.** Developed by Burgoon and several of her colleagues, this theory suggests that each of us enters a relationship with certain preconceived expectations as to how we expect others to behave.[61] For example, when meeting a business colleague for the first time, most North Americans would expect someone to smile, extend his or her hand, and say, "Hello, I'm Steve Beebe (or whatever *your* name is)." If, instead, the person clasps two hands together and bows demurely without uttering a word, the nonverbal behavior (or verbal behavior for that matter) is not what we expected. This violation of our expectation would result in us thinking about what the "violator" of our expectations might mean when bowing instead of offering to shake our hand. When our expectations are violated, we may feel uncomfortable. Research by communication researchers Beth Le Poire and Stephen Yoshimura found that we tend to adapt to the behavior of others, even when the behavior of others is not what we expected.[62] If someone behaves in a pleasant way to us by smiling, establishing eye contact, and maintaining an open body posture, we are more likely to reciprocate by displaying equally pleasant nonverbal messages. We interpret the messages of others by considering how we *expect* others to treat us and by adapting to others.

As you interact with others and make sense out of these interpersonal interactions, several principles and key skills can help you to interpret others' nonverbal messages more accurately.

Consider Nonverbal Cues in Context

Just as quoting an expert out of context can change the meaning of a statement, trying to draw conclusions from an isolated snatch of behavior or a single cue can lead to misinterpretations. Beware of looking at someone's folded arms and concluding that he or she does not like you or is not interested in what you are saying. It could be that the air conditioner is set too low and the person is just trying to keep warm.

Look for Clusters of Nonverbal Cues

Instead of focusing on a specific cue, look for corroborating cues that can lead you to a more accurate conclusion about the meaning of a behavior. Is the person making eye contact? Is he or she facing you? How far away is he or she standing from you?

Always consider nonverbal behaviors in conjunction with other nonverbal cues, the environment, and the person's verbal message.

expectancy violation theory.
Theory that you interpret the messages of others based on how you expect others to behave.

Consider Past Experiences When Interpreting Nonverbal Cues

"Familiarity may breed contempt," as the old saying goes, but familiarity with another person also increases your ability to interpret his or her nonverbal behavior. You may have learned, for example, that when your mother started crying when you played the piano, it meant she was proud of you, not melancholy. Family members can probably interpret one another's nonverbal cues more accurately than can those from outside the family. But after knowing someone over a period of time, you begin to increase your sensitivity to certain glances, silences, movements, and vocal cues that might be overlooked or misunderstood by others.

Check Your Perceptions with Others

You judge others by their behavior, not by their intent. As we discussed in Chapter 3, the only way to know what people intend is to ask them whether you have interpreted their behavior correctly. But before you blurt out a hunch, first consider the context and confirming cues; think about this person's previous behavior. Then, if you are still confused or uncertain about the meaning of a behavior, ask for clarification.

For example, if you receive a tremendous job offer that requires you to move to a new state, and your spouse greets your enthusiastic announcement with silence, you could ask, "Does your silence mean that you're opposed to the move, or are you speechless with excitement?" Then wait for a response.

Or suppose you work in the kitchen all day to make fish stew for your friend from Iowa. After her first bite you see her eyes open wide and her lips purse up. So you ask, "Does that mean you don't like it, or did you taste something new and different?"

This key skill is called **perception checking.** You can follow three steps to check your perception of someone's nonverbal behavior. First, observe the nonverbal cues, making a point to note such variables as eye contact, posture, use of gestures, facial expression, and tone of voice. Second, try to interpret what the individual is expressing through his or her nonverbal behavior. Finally, check your perception by asking him or her if it is accurate. Of course, we are not suggesting that you need to go through life constantly checking everyone's nonverbal cues. Overusing this skill would be irritating to most people. We are suggesting, however, that when you are uncertain of how someone feels, and it is important to know, a perception check may be in order. Consider this example:

Deonna: Hi, Mom. I'm sorry Erik and I missed the family reunion last week. It's been a hectic week. The kids had something goin' on every night, and we just needed to rest.

Muriel: (Frowns, makes little eye contact, folds her arms, and uses a flat voice.) Oh, don't worry about it.

Deonna: I know you said don't worry about it, Mom, but it looks like you are still upset. I know that look of yours. I also hear in your voice that you are not really pleased. Is it really OK, or are you still a little miffed?

perception check. Skill of asking someone whether your interpretation of his or her nonverbal behavior is accurate.

Muriel: Well, yes, to be honest, Dad and I were really looking forward to getting all the kids together.

Deonna: I'm sorry, Mom. We will make an effort to be at the next one. Thanks for sharing with me how you really felt.

Addressing your question to a specific nonverbal cue will help you interpret your partner's behavior in future interactions as well. As we noted earlier, evidence suggests that the longer couples are married, the more they rely on nonverbal behavior to communicate. One study claims that most couples spend less than eleven minutes a week in sustained conversation.[63] Even in marriages of fifty years, however, conversation is still required occasionally to clarify nonverbal responses.

recap   How to Check Your Perceptions of Others' Nonverbal Cues

Steps	Consider
1. Observe their nonverbal behavior.	Are they frowning?
	Do they have eye contact?
	Are their arms crossed?
	What is their tone of voice?
	What is their posture?
2. Form a mental impression of what you think they mean.	Are they happy, sad, angry?
	Is the nonverbal message contradicting the verbal message?
3. Ask to check whether your perception is accurate.	"Are you upset? You look angry."
	"Your expression and your voice suggest you don't believe me. Do you think I'm lying?"
	"The look on your face tells me you really like it. Do you?"

Be Aware That the Nonverbal Expression of Emotion Is Contagious

emotional contagion theory
Theory that emotional expression is contagious; people can "catch" emotions just by observing each other's emotional expressions.

Have you ever noticed that when you watch a funny movie, you are more likely to laugh out loud if other people around you are laughing? That when you are around people who are sad or remorseful, you are more likely to feel and express sadness? There's a reason this happens. Nonverbal emotional expressions are contagious. People often display the same emotions that a communication partner is displaying. **Emotional contagion theory** suggests that people tend to "catch" the emotions of others.[64] Interpersonal interactions with others can affect your nonverbal expression of emotions. The ancient Roman orator Cicero knew this when he gave advice to public speakers. He said if you want your audience to experience joy, you must be a joyful speaker. Or, if you want to communicate fear, then you should express fear when you speak. Knowing that you tend to catch or imitate the emotions of others can help you interpret your own nonverbal messages and those of others; you may be imitating the emotional expression of others around you.

Look for Cues That May Communicate Lying

"Look at me, young man. I know you're not telling the truth." Sometimes parents just seem to know whether kids are telling the truth or lying. How do they know? It may not be the "story" but the nonverbal message that gives the kids away. Several researchers have been interested in identifying those nonverbal cues that indicate deceit.[65] As we've emphasized several times, because of the transactional nature of interpersonal communication, meaning is created as people communicate with others; behaviors do not have a fixed interpretation. Also, remember not to place too much emphasis on a single cue. As we've just noted, look for clusters of cues rather than pointing your finger when someone has less eye contact and saying, "Ah ha! Now I know you're a liar!" Figure 7.2 summarizes research conclusions about nonverbal messages, comparing liars and those who are telling the truth.[66]

Honest Communicators	Lying Communicators
Voice	
Have fewer pauses when they talk	Pause more; they are thinking about what "story" they want to give
Speak fluently, smoothly	Use more nonfluencies ("ah," "er," "um")
Speak at a normal speaking rate	Speak a bit faster than normal
Facial Expression	
Smile genuinely and sincerely	Display a plastered-on, phony smile May smile a bit too long
Gestures	
Are less likely to play with objects	Are more likely to play with objects, such as twiddle a pencil
Use fewer gestures	Use more gestures, more self-adaptors, and touching of their face and body
Are not likely to shift body weight	Are more likely to shift their posture
Generally display less nervousness	Display increased nervousness
Eye Contact	
Maintain normal eye contact—a steady, natural gaze	May look away, maintain less direct eye contact
Have an eye blink rate that is normal—no increase in eye blink	Have an increased eye blink rate—a sign of increased anxiety

Figure 7.2

Who's Telling the Truth? Differences Between Honest and Lying Communicators

Checking Perceptions

Practice checking your perceptions of nonverbal information by asking questions.
Look at the following photographs. Then formulate the perception-checking
question requested next to each photograph.

Photo 1:
Perception-checking question the teacher could ask her student:

_____

_____

_____

_____

_____

_____

Photo 2:
Perception-checking question the father could ask his son:

_____

_____

_____

_____

_____

Photo 3:
Perception-checking question the salesperson could ask his customer:

_____

_____

_____

_____

_____

_____

Summary

Unspoken messages have a major effect on interpersonal relationships. The primary way in which you communicate feelings, emotions, and attitudes is through nonverbal cues. When there is a contradiction between your verbal and nonverbal messages, others almost always believe the nonverbal one. But nonverbal messages are usually more ambiguous than verbal messages. Although some nonverbal messages have a definite beginning and ending, most are part of a seamless flow of movement, gestures, glances, and inflections. Also, there are culture-based differences in the way people learn and interpret unspoken messages.

Nonverbal cues can be categorized and studied to reveal the codes to our unspoken communication. Movement, posture, and gestures communicate both content and expressive information when we use them as emblems, illustrators, affect displays, regulators, and adaptors. Eye contact is an important code for regulating interaction in interpersonal exchanges. Facial expressions and vocal cues provide a wealth of information about our emotions. Our use of personal space and territory communicates a variety of messages relating to power, status, and other relational concerns. Touch is one of the most powerful cues to communicate liking; and our appearance telegraphs to others how we wish to be treated and how we perceive our role in relation to them.

One of the prime fascinations with nonverbal messages is the potential to understand hidden meaning communicated through unspoken codes. It is difficult to read nonverbal cues as easily as reading the words on this page, but there is a general framework that can help you assess the nonverbal messages of others, as well as your own nonverbal expressions. Researchers have identified three primary dimensions for interpreting nonverbal messages: Immediacy cues provide information about liking and disliking. Arousal cues tip others off as to your interest and level of engagement with them; and position, power, and status are often communicated through dominance cues.

To enhance your skill in interpreting nonverbal messages, always consider the context in which you observed the cues, and look for clusters of nonverbal behaviors. The longer you have known someone, the easier it is to interpret his or her unspoken messages. But to verify whether you understand someone's nonverbal behavior, ask whether your interpretation is accurate.

For Discussion and Review

Focus on Comprehension

1. What is nonverbal communication?

2. Why is it important to study nonverbal communication?

3. Describe nonverbal emblems, illustrators, affect displays, regulators, and adaptors.

4. What are the nonverbal communication codes presented in this chapter?

5. What are the nonverbal cues that communicate immediacy, arousal, and power?

6. Which nonverbal cues communicate that someone may not be telling the truth?

🌑 Focus on Critical Thinking

7. Sasha has had difficulty getting hired as a manager. One of her best friends suggests that she pay more attention to her nonverbal behavior when she is interviewed for a job. What advice would you give Sasha to ensure that she monitors her nonverbal interview behavior?

8. Greg has been told that he sometimes comes across as cold, aloof, and stand-offish. What could Greg do to communicate his sincere desire to be inter-personally warm and approachable?

🌑 Focus on Ethics

9. Donald really wants to be hired as a salesperson. He hires a fashion consultant to recommend what he should wear and determine how he should look when he interviews for a job. In general, is it ethical to manipulate your appearance so that you can impress others?

10. Is it appropriate to draw definitive conclusions about another's personality and attitudes based only on a "reading" of his or her other nonverbal cues? Support your answer.

11. Is it ethical for salespeople, politicians, and others who wish to make favorable impressions to alter their nonverbal messages to get you to like them, vote for them, or buy their products? Explain your answer.

For Your Journal

1. Videotape 15 minutes of a TV drama or situation comedy. View the program with the sound turned off. Using the four principles of interpreting nonverbal messages, describe the meaning of the nonverbal messages you watch. After you have made written observations in your journal, view the program with full sound and determine how accurate your interpretations were.

2. Mehrabian has suggested that people convey 55 percent of their emotional meaning through facial expressions, 38 percent through vocal cues, and only 7 percent through verbal statements. Spend thirty minutes observing four or five people in a public place, such as a mall, airport, or student center, and attempt to prove or disprove Mehrabian's conclusions. Before you begin your people watching, design a method for recording your observations in your journal.

Learning with Others

1. Go on a nonverbal communication scavenger hunt. Your instructor will ask you to observe your family members and friends to find one or more of the following sets of nonverbal communicators:

   a. Examples of emblems, illustrators, affect displays, regulators, and adaptors.

   b. Examples of how people use the four zones of personal space.

   c. Examples of pleasure, arousal, and dominance.

   d. Examples of the cognitive, monitoring, regulatory, and expressive functions of eye contact.

   e. Examples of clothing that reveals intentions or personality traits.

2. Spend some time observing people in a public place, such as a restaurant, airport terminal, student center, or bar, and write examples of quasi-courtship behavior as discussed in this chapter on page 212. List the four phases we described (courtship readiness, preening, positional cues, appeals to invitation) on a sheet of paper, and describe several examples to illustrate each of these phases.

3. Divide into groups of three or four people. Use the following evaluation form to evaluate a room or public space. Each person in your group should evaluate the same room. It could be your own room, a cafeteria, classroom, fast-food restaurant, or even a hotel lobby. Compare your answers with other group members. You could also give a report to the class on your results.

   a. Briefly describe the environment you analyzed. Describe the size, furniture or other movable objects, predominant colors, lighting, sounds, decor.

   b. Rate the room you observed, using the following scales:

Formal	___	___	___	___	___	___	___	Informal
Warm	___	___	___	___	___	___	___	Cold
Pleasant	___	___	___	___	___	___	___	Unpleasant
Useful	___	___	___	___	___	___	___	Not useful
Beautiful	___	___	___	___	___	___	___	Ugly

   c. Describe the probable effects the room design has on communication interaction patterns. (For example, does it encourage or discourage communication?)

   _____

   _____

   _____

   d. Based on your observations, is the room appropriately designed for its intended use? Explain.

   _____

   _____

   _____

Conflict Management Skills

you should be able to . . .

1. Define conflict.

2. Compare and contrast three types of interpersonal conflict.

3. Identify commonly held myths about interpersonal conflict.

4. Describe differences between destructive and constructive approaches to managing conflict.

5. List and describe five stages of conflict.

6. Describe three types of conflict management styles.

7. Identify and use conflict management skills to help manage emotions, information, goals, and problems when attempting to resolve interpersonal differences.

T his house stinks," said Paolo, wrinkling up his nose. "It smells like day-old garbage."

"Take it out yourself. It's your job," said Anya, turning her back on him to scrub furiously at an imaginary morsel of food on a frying pan that was already polished clean.

"Hey, hey," said Paolo, holding up both hands in front of him, "I wasn't accusing you. I just said it smelled bad in here. Don't be so touchy."

"Oh, no? Well, you're always criticizing me. You think just because you have a big important job that you can come in here and say anything you like. And I come home from work feeling tired, too, you know, but you don't do anything to help, not even the things you agree to!" shouted Anya, turning around to confront her mate, planting her soapy hands on her hips.

"Well, you're always hocking me for no reason. I'm not putting up with this bad treatment from you anymore," snarled Paolo. As he turned on his heel to stalk out of the kitchen, Anya burst into tears.

Why have Paolo and Anya reached an impasse in their attempt to communicate?

Eventually, all relationships experience conflict. Paolo and Anya's exchange is complicated, seething with conflicting goals and underlying resentments. How can you avoid the same kind of outcome in your own complicated exchanges?

Conflict management is not a single skill but a set of skills. But to manage conflict effectively involves more than learning simple techniques.

The best route to success in resolving conflict effectively is acquiring knowledge about what conflict is, what makes it happen, and what we can do about it. We will begin by defining conflict, then examine some of the myths about it and focus on some of its constructive functions. We will also discuss the relationship among conflict, power, and conflict management styles.

In addition, we will discuss how learning about your typical style of managing conflict can give you insight into managing interpersonal differences. And finally, we will build on the skills of listening and verbal and nonverbal communication that we discussed in the previous chapters, to help manage the inevitable interpersonal conflicts that arise in the best of relationships.

What Is Conflict?

Simply stated, **interpersonal conflict** is an expressed struggle that occurs when two people cannot agree on a way to meet their needs. If the needs are incompatible, if there are too few resources to satisfy them, or if the individuals opt to compete rather than cooperate to achieve them, then conflict occurs. The intensity level of a conflict usually relates to the intensity of the unmet needs. Sam Keltner developed the "struggle spectrum," shown in Figure 8.1, to describe conflicts ranging from mild differences to fights.[1] But at the bedrock of all conflict are differences— different goals and experiences.

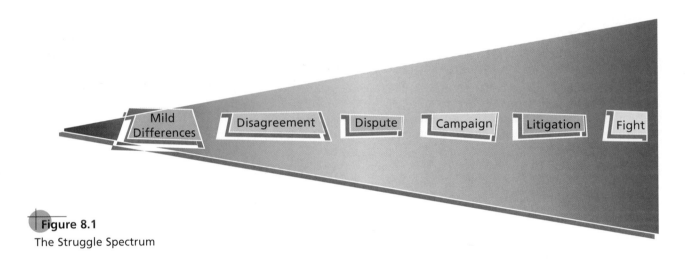

Figure 8.1
The Struggle Spectrum

Goals and Conflict

Psychologists agree that we are need-driven, goal-oriented individuals. Because most of what we do is based on achieving a desirable goal, it is not surprising that most conflict is goal driven. You want something; your partner wants something else. If your partner interferes with your achievement of your goal, there may be a fight.

Suppose you are trying to find a parking spot in a busy shopping center. Just as you find one, another shopper zips into "your" space. Your blood boils, and you get out of your car fighting mad. Or suppose you have had a difficult day at work. All you want to do is hunker down with a bowl of popcorn and watch MTV. But your spouse announces that a friend and his 6-year-old son are coming over for dinner. "That's not what I feel like doing tonight. Why didn't you ask me before you invited them?" you shout. In both instances, your goals are colliding head-on with someone else's, and you feel as if you have lost control of the situation.

interpersonal conflict.
Struggle that occurs when two people cannot agree on a way to meet their needs or goals.

Experiences and Conflict

Our inherent differences, coupled with our experiences, provide fuel for conflict. Consider the conflict that newlyweds Christy and Matt are having about how to celebrate the upcoming winter holidays. They have only two days to spend in their parents' town before returning to their new home in another city. Christy's family always exchanges presents and has a huge gathering on Christmas Eve and a family dinner on Christmas Day. Matt's family is Jewish. They celebrate Hanukkah quietly and do not feel comfortable trying to fit in at someone else's traditional celebration. Matt would like to celebrate Hanukkah at his parents' house, but Christy cannot understand why his family does not want to join her family's festivities. The conflict between Christy and Matt is not based on different goals: They both want to see each set of parents and both want to celebrate the holidays. The conflict stems from their different backgrounds and experiences.

Myths About Conflict

Although not all conflict is destructive to relationships, many cultures have taboos against displaying it in public. According to one researcher, many of us were raised with five conflict myths that contribute to our negative feelings about conflict.[2] As you read the following sections, you may shake your head and say, "That's not where I came from." In some American families, conflict is expressed openly and often. But even if your experience has been different, reading about these prevailing myths may help you understand your emotional responses to conflict or your partner's response when conflict occurs.

Myth 1: "Conflict Is Always a Sign of a Poor Interpersonal Relationship"

It is an oversimplification to assume that all conflict is rooted in underlying relational problems. Conflict is a normal part of any interpersonal relationship. Although it is true that constant bickering and sniping can be symptomatic of deeper problems, disagreements do not necessarily signal that the relationship is on the rocks. All relationships experience conflict. In fact, overly polite, stilted conversation is more likely than periodic disagreements to signal a problem. The free expression of honest disagreement is often a hallmark of healthy relationships. Assertively expressing honest ideas may mean that a person feels safe and comfortable enough with his or her partner to disagree. As we will discuss later, conflict in interpersonal relationships can play a constructive role in focusing on issues that may need attention. The ebb and flow of interpersonal psychological intimacy and separation inevitably leads to some degree of conflict in any relationship. When conflict happens in your relationships, don't immediately assume that the relationship is doomed.

Myth 2: "Conflict Can Always Be Avoided"

"If you can't say anything nice, don't say anything at all." Many of us learned early in our lives that conflict is unnatural and that we should eliminate it from our conversations and relationships. Yet evidence suggests that conflict arises in virtually every relationship. Because each of us has a unique perspective on our world, it would be extraordinary for us *always* to see eye-to-eye with another person. Research suggests that contentment in marriage relates not to the amount of conflict, but to the way in which partners manage it.[3] Conflict is also a normal and productive part of interaction in group deliberations.[4] It is a myth that we should view conflict as inherently unproductive and something to be avoided. It happens, even in the best of relationships.

Myth 3: "Conflict Always Occurs Because of Misunderstandings"

"You just don't understand what my days are like. I need to go to sleep!" shouts Janice as she scoops up a pillow and blanket and stalks off to the living room. "Oh, yeah? Well, you don't understand what will happen if I don't get this budget in!" responds Ron, who is hunched over the desk in their bedroom. It is clear that Ron and Janice are having a conflict. They have identified the cause of their problem as a lack of understanding between them, but in reality they *do* understand each other. Ron knows that Janice wants to sleep; Janice knows he wants to stay up and work. Their problem is that they disagree about whose goal is most important. This disagreement, not lack of understanding, is the source of the conflict.

Myth 4: "Conflict Can Always Be Resolved"

Consultants, corporate training experts, and self-help book authors often offer advice about how to eliminate conflict so that all will be well and harmony will prevail. Some people claim that with the application of a few skills and how-to techniques, conflicts can disappear, much like a stain from a shirt laundered with the right kind of detergent. This is simply not true. Not all differences can be resolved by listening harder or paraphrasing your partner's message. Some disagreements are so intense and the perceptions so fixed that individuals may have to agree to disagree and live with it.

Myth 5: "Conflict Is Always Bad"

It's a common fantasy to dream of eliminating all interpersonal conflict from relationships. It would be bliss, we think, if we could live without disagreement, hassle, haggling, and tension. But conflict is a healthy component of relationships. In fact, if a relationship is conflict-free, the individuals are probably not being honest with each other. Although it can be destructive, conflict can also help us identify issues that need further discussion and lead to negotiations that give us fresh insights into the relationship.

recap   Conflict Myths

Myth 1:	"Conflict is always a sign of a poor interpersonal relationship."
Myth 2:	"Conflict can always be avoided."
Myth 3:	"Conflict always occurs because of a misunderstanding."
Myth 4:	"Conflict can always be resolved."
Myth 5:	"Conflict is always bad."

Types of Conflict

At some time or another, many close relationships go through a conflict phase. "We're always fighting," complains a newlywed. But if she were to analyze these fights, she would discover important differences among them. According to communication researchers Miller and Steinberg, most conflicts fit into three different categories: (1) **pseudoconflict**—triggered by a lack of understanding; (2) **simple conflict**—stemming from different ideas, definitions, perceptions, or goals; and (3) **ego conflict**—which occurs when conflict gets personal.[5]

Pseudoconflict: Misunderstandings

Will: Let's walk to the store.

Sean: No, it's too far. Let's drive.

Will: But the store is close.

Sean: No, it's not.

pseudoconflict. Conflict triggered by a lack of understanding and miscommunication.

simple conflict. Conflict that stems from different ideas, definitions, perceptions, or goals.

ego conflict. Conflict that is based on personal issues; conflicting partners attack each other's self-esteem.

understanding

diversity

Gender and Conflict

Research suggests distinctions between feminine and masculine styles of responding to conflict. The feminine style is more likely to focus on relationship issues, whereas the masculine style typically focuses on tasks.[6] The feminine style often interacts with others to achieve intimacy and closeness, but the masculine style interacts to get something done or to accomplish something apart from the relationship. Those employing a masculine style are often more aggressive and assertive than those employing a feminine style when pursuing a goal or conquest.[7] The following list summarizes key differences that researchers have observed between feminine and masculine styles of responding to conflict. Note that individuals of either sex may employ some characteristics of both feminine and masculine gender styles.

Perceived Gender Differences in Responding to Conflict[8]

Feminine Styles	Masculine Styles
Concerned with equity and caring; connect with and feel responsible to others	Concerned with equality of rights and fairness; adhere to abstract principles, rules
Interact to achieve closeness and interdependence	Interact for instrumental purposes; seek autonomy and distance
Attend to interpersonal dynamics to assess relationship's health	Are less aware of interpersonal dynamics
Encourage mutual involvement	Protect self-interest
Attribute crises to problems in the relationship	Attribute crises to problems external to the relationship
Are concerned with the impact of the relationship on personal identity	Are neither self- nor relationship-centered
Respond to conflict by often focusing mainly on the relationship	Respond to conflict by often focusing on rules and being evasive until a unilateral decision is reached

Will: Yes, it is. It's just off Market Street.

Sean: Oh, you mean the convenience store.

Will: Sure, that's exactly what I mean.

Sean: Oh, no problem.

Pseudo means false or fake. Pseudoconflict occurs when we simply miss the meaning in a message. But unless we clear up the misunderstanding by asking for more information, a real conflict might ensue. Note that in this example, Will offers helpful information ("It's just off Market Street") and Sean checks it with feedback ("Oh, you mean the convenience store").

How can you avoid pseudoconflict? A key strategy is to clarify the meaning of words and expressions that you don't understand. Keep the following strategies in mind to minimize misunderstandings before they occur:

● *Check your perceptions:* Ask to clarify what you don't understand; seek to determine whether your interpretation is the same as your partner's.

● *Listen between the lines:* Look for puzzled or quizzical facial expressions of your partner. People may not voice their misunderstanding, but may express their uncertainty nonverbally.

● *Establish a supportive rather than a defensive climate for conversation:* Avoid evaluating, controlling, using manipulative strategies, being aloof, acting superior,

Although these findings provide a starting point for analyzing our conflicts with members of the opposite sex, we caution you against lapsing into "allness" statements such as "Oh, you're just like all women. That's why you disagree with me." Or "You're just like all men. You never want to focus on how I feel." Even thinking in these ways can prevent you from listening to what your partner is saying.

The most recent perspective on analyzing gender differences is called the *partnership perspective.* Rather than viewing gender differences as a gulf between people who live on different planets, this perspective suggests that men and women are not locked into particular styles or approaches.[9] The partnership approach emphasizes the importance of keeping channels open and avoiding the tendency to stereotype communication styles by gender.

Culture and Conflict

An individual's culturally learned assumptions influence his or her conflict behavior. In some cultures, most of the conflict is **expressive**; it focuses on the quality of relationships, and on managing interpersonal tension and hostility. In other cultures, conflict is more **instrumental.** It centers less on relationships and more on achieving a specific goal or objective.[10] One researcher noted that for people from low-context cultures, (those who derive more meaning from words than from the surrounding context), conflicts are most often instrumental.[11] Most North Americans come from low-context cultures. Many Asian cultures, in contrast, are high-context cultures. They are also collectivist: they value group effort over individual achievement. For people from these cultures, conflicts often center on expressive,

relational concerns. Keeping peace in the group or saving face is often a higher priority than achieving a goal.

Managing culture-based conflict requires a strong other-orientation. One research team suggests that Anglo-Americans of European descent receive little training in how to develop solutions to problems that are acceptable to an entire group.[12] They are often socialized to stick up for their own rights at any cost, and they approach conflict as a win–lose situation. In contrast, people from collectivist cultures approach conflict management situations from a win–win perspective; it is important that both sides save face and avoid ridicule. Such differences in approaches provide a double challenge. In addition to disagreeing over the issue at hand, people from different cultures may also have different strategies for reaching agreement.

or rigidly asserting that you're always right. These classic behaviors are like pushing the button to increased defensiveness and misunderstanding.

Simple Conflict: Different Stands on the Issues

Simple conflict stems from differences in ideas, definitions, perceptions, or goals. You want to go to Disney World for your vacation; your spouse wants to go to Washington, D.C. Your spouse wants to fly; you would rather take the train. You understand each other, but you disagree.

A key to unraveling a simple conflict is to keep the conversation focused on the issues at hand so that the expression of differences does not deteriorate into a battle focusing on personalities.

The following exchange between Mark and Nick illustrates a conflict over a simple difference of opinion; notice how both partners stick to the issues and figure out a way to resolve their differences.

Mark: I want to watch *The Simpsons* tonight. It's their Christmas show.

Nick: No way, man. I have to watch a documentary about textiles for my history class. It's an assignment.

expressive conflict. Conflict that focuses on issues about the quality of the relationship and managing interpersonal tension and hostility.

instrumental conflict. Conflict that centers on achieving a particular goal or task and less on relational issues.

You can avoid pseudo or false conflict if you ask for clarification, listen between the lines, and work to establish a supportive climate. (B. Daemmrich/The Image Works)

Mark: But I've worked all weekend. I'm beat. The last thing I want to watch is some stuffy old documentary on the history of weaving.

Nick: Tell you what. Go ahead and watch *The Simpsons.* I'll videotape the documentary and watch it later. Deal?

Mark: Okay. Thanks. And I'll go grill some burgers so we can have supper together first.

This next exchange between Sue and Nadiya is a bumpier one. What starts as a simple conflict deteriorates into a series of personal attacks.

Nadiya: Sue, can I borrow your skirt? I have a date tonight. It would look great with my new jacket.

Sue: Sorry, Nadiya. I'm going to wear it tonight. I've got to give a presentation to the school board about our new mentor program.

Nadiya: In case you don't remember, when you brought it home you said I could borrow it anytime. Besides, you haven't paid back the twenty bucks I loaned you to buy it.

Sue: Yes, but I bought the skirt especially for this occasion.

Nadiya: Well, don't ask to borrow anything from me ever again. You're just plain selfish.

Sue: Oh, yeah? Well *you're* the one who hogs all the space in the refrigerator. Talk about someone who's selfish. If that's not the pot calling the kettle black!

Nadiya: All right, now that we're being honest about who hogs what, *you're* the one who monopolizes the bathroom in the morning.

And so it escalates. The original disagreement about the skirt is forgotten, and egos become attacked and bruised.

To keep simple conflict from escalating into personal vendettas, consider the following strategies:

● *Clarify your and your partner's understanding of the issues and your partner's understanding of the source of the disagreement.*

● *Keep the discussion focused on facts and the issue at hand, rather than drifting back to past battles and unrelated personal grievances.*

● *Look for more than just the initial solutions that you and your partner bring to the discussion; generate many options.*

● *Don't try to tackle too many issues at once:* Perform "issue triage"—identify the important issues and work on those.

● *Find the kernel of truth in what your partner may be saying:* Find agreement where you can.

● *If tempers begin to flare and conflict is spiraling upward, cool off:* Come back to the discussion when you and your partner are fresh.

Ego Conflict: Conflict Gets Personal

As you can see from the preceding example between Sue and Nadiya, a personal attack puts your partner on the defensive, and many people behave according to the adage "The best defense is a good offense." When you launch a personal attack, you are "picking a fight." And as Sue and Nadiya's exchange illustrates, fights that begin as pseudo- or simple conflicts can easily lapse into more vicious ego conflicts. Here's another example:

Shasta: I've told you before. I think we should split the expenses 50–50. You never listen to me. You always want everything to go your way. I'm tired of you trying to boss me around.

Carol: Face it, Shasta, you just can't take constructive criticism. You've never liked me since I moved in here to help you out by sharing some expenses.

Shasta: It's just that I don't like a bully. You try to dictate what we're supposed to have for dinner, what TV show to watch, and what music to hear. Well, you're not the boss of me!

Carol: What an ungrateful attitude! After all I've done to help you out, and now you're complaining about such petty stuff. You're a real piece of work, Shasta.

Note that as each person in the conflict becomes more defensive about his or her position, the issues become more tangled.

Remember Paolo and Anya's argument about taking out the garbage at the beginning of this chapter? It started with what was probably an offhand remark and escalated into a major argument because both participants began attacking each other and bringing up other sensitive issues instead of focusing on the original comment.

If you find yourself involved in ego conflict, try to refrain from hurling personal attacks and emotional epithets back and forth. Instead, take turns expressing your feelings without interrupting each other, then take time to cool off. It is difficult to use effective listening skills when your emotions are at a high pitch.

Here are additional strategies to consider when conflict becomes personal:

- *Try to steer the ego conflict back to simple conflict:* Stay focused on issues rather than personalities.

- *Make the issue a problem to be solved rather than a battle to be won.*

- *Write down what you want to say:* It may help you clarify your point, and you and your partner can develop your ideas without interruption. A note of caution: Don't put angry personal attacks in writing. Make your written summary rational, logical, and brief rather than emotion-laden.

- *When things get personal, make a vow not to reciprocate:* Use "I" messages that we talked about in Chapter 5 ("I feel uncomfortable and threatened when we yell at each other" rather than "you" messages ("You're such a creep. You never listen.") to express how you are feeling.

recap

Types of Conflict

	Pseudoconflict	Simple Conflict	Ego Conflict
What It Is	Individuals misunderstand each other.	Individuals disagree over which action to pursue to achieve their goals.	Individuals feel personally attacked.
What to Do	Check your perceptions.	Clarify understanding.	Return to issues rather than personal attacks.
	Listen between the lines; look for nonverbal expressions of puzzlement.	Stay focused on facts and issues.	Talk about a problem to be solved rather than a fight to be won.
	Be supportive rather than defensive.	Generate many options rather than arguing over one or two options.	Write down rational arguments to support your position.
	Listen actively.	Find the kernel of truth in what your partner is saying; emphasize where you agree.	Use "I" messages rather than "You" messages.

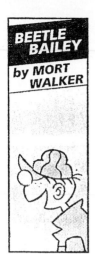

Conflict as a Process

Cathy was reading the Sunday paper, enjoying a second cup of coffee, and listening to her favorite classical music station. All seemed well. Suddenly, for no apparent reason, her roommate Barb brusquely stormed into the room and shouted, "I can't stand it anymore! We have to talk about who does what around here." Cathy was taken completely off guard. She had no idea her roommate was upset about the division of household chores. To her, this outburst seemed to come out of the blue; in reality, however, several events had led up to it.

Most relational disagreements have a source, a beginning, a middle, an end, and an aftermath.[13] Let's find out how they function.

Source: Prior Conditions

The first phase in the conflict process is the one that sets the stage for disagreement; it begins when you become aware that there are differences between you and another person. The differences may stem from role expectations, perceptions, goals, or resources. In the previous example, Barb perceived that she and Cathy played different roles in caring for the household.

In interpersonal relationships, *many* potential sources of conflict may be smoldering below the surface. It may take some time before they flare up into overt conflict. Moreover, they may be compounded with other concerns, making them difficult to sort out.

Beginning: Frustration Awareness

At this stage, at least one of you becomes aware that the differences in the relationship are increasingly problematic. You may begin to engage in self-talk, noting that something is wrong and creating frustration. Perhaps you realize that you won't be able to achieve an important goal or that someone else has resources you need to achieve it. Or you may become aware of differences in perceptions. Barb knew that Cathy's family always used weekends for relaxation. All the members of Barb's family, in contrast, pitched in on weekends to get household chores done for the week. Barb may have recognized that difference, even as her frustration level rose.

Becoming aware of differences in perception does not always lead to increased frustration. But when the differences interfere with something you want to accomplish, then your frustration level rises. In Barb's case, she wanted to get the house clean so she could turn her attention to studying for a test she had the next day. Cathy's apparent indifference to helping Barb achieve that goal was a conflict trigger.

Middle: Active Conflict

When you bring your frustration to the attention of others, a conflict becomes an active, *expressed struggle.*[14] If frustrations remain only as thoughts, the conflict is passive, not active. Active conflict does not necessarily mean that the differences are expressed with shouting or emotional intensity. An expression of disagreement may be either verbal or nonverbal. Calmly asking someone to change an attitude or behavior to help you achieve your goal is a form of active conflict; so is kicking your brother under the table when he starts to reveal your secret to the rest of the family.

Cathy was not aware of the division of labor problem until Barb stormed into the room demanding a renegotiation of roles. Barb had been aware of her frustration for some time, yet had not acted on it. Many experts advocate that you do not wait until your frustration level escalates to peak intensity before you approach someone with your conflict. Bottled-up frustration tends to erupt like soda in a bottle that has just been shaken. Intense emotions can add to the difficulty of managing a conflict.

End: Resolution

When you begin to try to manage the conflict, it has progressed to the resolution stage. Of course, not all conflicts can be neatly resolved. Couples who divorce, business partners who dissolve their corporation, or roommates who go their separate ways have all found solutions, even though they may not be amicable.

After Barb's outburst, she and Cathy were able to reach a workable compromise about the division of their household labor. Cathy agreed to clean the house every other week; Barb promised not to expect her to do it on weekends.

Aftermath: Follow-Up

As Yogi Berra once said, "It ain't over 'til it's over." After a conflict has been resolved, the follow-up stage involves dealing with hurt feelings or managing simmering grudges, and checking with the other person to confirm that the conflict has not retreated into the frustration awareness stage. As we noted in Chapter 1, interpersonal relationships operate as transactive processes rather than as linear, step-by-step functions. Conflict does progress in stages, but your resolutions can backslide unless you confirm your understanding of the issues with your partner.

The Friday after their discussion, Cathy proudly showed off a spotless apartment to Barb when she came home from class. Barb responded with a grin and a quick hug and privately resolved to get up early on Sunday morning so that she could go out to get Cathy pastries and the Sunday papers before she awoke. This kind of mutual thoughtfulness exemplifies a successful follow-up in a conflict.

Understanding Conflict as a Process

Prior Conditions Stage	The stage is set for conflict because of differences in the individuals' actions or attitudes.
Frustration Awareness Stage	One individual becomes aware that the differences are problematic and becomes frustrated and angry.
Active Conflict Stage	The individuals communicate with each other about the differences; the conflict becomes an expressed struggle.
Resolution Stage	The individuals begin seeking ways to manage the conflict.
Follow-Up Stage	The individuals check with themselves and each other to monitor whether both are satisfied with the resolution.

Understanding the stages of conflict can help you better manage the process. You'll also be in a better position to make the conflict a constructive rather than a destructive experience. Conflict is **constructive** if it helps build new insights and establishes new patterns in a relationship. Airing differences can lead to a more satisfying relationship in the long run. David W. Johnson lists the following as benefits of conflict in interpersonal relationships. Interpersonal conflict

- Focuses attention on problems that may have to be solved
- Clarifies what may need to be changed
- Focuses attention on what is important to you and your partner

constructive conflict. Conflict that helps build new insights and establishes new patterns in a relationship.

By focusing on the problem at hand rather than assuming a defensive attitude, this machinist and foreman may reach a constructive solution to their conflict. (Richard Pasley/Stock Boston)

- Clarifies who you are and what your values are
- Helps you learn more about your partner
- Keeps relationships interesting
- Strengthens relationships by increasing your confidence that you can manage disagreements[15]

Although conflict can be constructive, we don't want to oversell the value or function of conflict in relationships with others. Conflict can also be **destructive.** The hallmark of destructive conflict is a lack of flexibility in responding to others.[16] Conflict can become destructive when people view their differences from a win–lose perspective, rather than looking for solutions that allow both individuals to gain. If the combatants assume that one person will lose, the resulting competitive climate precludes cooperation and flexibility.

One way to minimize destructive conflict cycles is to understand the sequence of conflict-triggering causes so that you can address them at an early stage. It's important to perceive interpersonal conflict not just as something you react to once an issue has surfaced; becoming aware of underlying frustrations before they blossom into active expressions of conflict can help maintain both honesty and trust in a relationship. Also, diagnosing whether the conflict is a misunderstanding, a simple disagreement, or a personal vendetta can give you insight into managing disagreements before they move closer to a fight on the struggle spectrum.

Conflict Management Styles

What's your approach to managing interpersonal conflict: fight or flight? Do you tackle conflict head-on or seek ways to remove yourself from it? Most of us do not have a single way of dealing with differences, but we do have a tendency to manage conflict by following patterns that we have used before. The pattern we choose depends on several factors: our personality, the individuals with whom we are in conflict, the time and place of the confrontation, and other situational factors. For example, if your boss gives you an order, you respond differently from the way you do if your spouse gives you an order. Virginia Satir, author of *Peoplemaking,* a popular book about family communication, suggests that we learn conflict response patterns early in life.[17]

Several researchers have attempted to identify the patterns or styles of conflict.[18] One widely accepted approach organizes conflict styles into three types: (1) nonconfrontational (avoiding, withdrawing, being indirect); (2) confrontational (attempting to use power strategies to control or manipulate outcomes); and (3) cooperative (seeking a solution that both individuals will find acceptable).[19] Before you read the following sections, try Building Your Skills: Identifying Your Conflict Management Style, pages 254–255, to see what style you typically use in managing conflict.

Nonconfrontational Style

One approach to handling conflict is to back off, avoiding the conflict. Placating, distracting, computing, withdrawing, and giving in are responses that typify a **nonconfrontational style.**

destructive conflict. Conflict that dismantles relationships without restoring the relationship.

nonconfrontational style. Style of managing conflict that includes placating, distracting, computing, withdrawing, and giving in.

A *placating* response is an attempt to please; generally placaters are uncomfortable with negative emotions and may adopt this approach because they fear rejection if they rock the boat. Typically, they seek approval and try to avoid threats to their self-worth. Placaters never seem to get angry, are so controlled that they seem unresponsive to the intensity of the situation, quickly agree with others to avoid conflict, and try to avoid confrontation at all costs. They appear to be other-oriented, but in fact they are simply seeking self-protection. Satir describes them as "syrupy, martyrish, and bootlicking." In the following exchange, note Hillary's placating response to Leslie's complaint:

Leslie: Hillary, I'm not in agreement with you on the QCN merger. I think the merger should be called off.

Hillary: Okay. Whatever you think is best. I just want you to feel good about your decision.

A second nonconfrontational response that Satir identifies is *distracting.* Distracters attempt to change the subject and avoid conflict or stress, rather than face issues directly. They hope that eventually the problem will just go away if it can be put off long enough.

A third nonconfrontational response is called *computing;* computers remove themselves from conflict by remaining aloof and cool. They avoid emotional involvement and refuse to be provoked or ruffled, even under intense pressure. This detachment allows them to avoid expressing genuine feelings about issues and ideas. Instead, they respond to emotional issues with impersonal words and phrases, such as "One would tend to become angry when one's car is dented, wouldn't one?" The computing style is characterized by low empathy and minimal involvement with the issues at hand.

Withdrawing from conflict, either physically or psychologically, is another nonconfrontational approach. Typical responses from someone who uses this style are "I don't want to talk about it," "It's not my problem," "Don't bother me with that now," or "I'm not interested in that."

Finally, some people consistently *give in* when faced with conflict. They are so uncomfortable that they surrender before the conflict escalates. Reggie hates westerns. Yet when Pam wants to rent *How the West Was Won,* Reggie says, "Okay, fine," just to avoid a confrontation.

Confrontational Style

"You're wrong!" shouts Ed. "Here's how to get our project in on time. We can't waste time in the library. We just have to write up what we have."

"But Ed," suggests Derrick, "the assignment calls for us to have three library sources."

"No. We don't have time. Just do it," Ed insists.

Ed wants to *control,* not *collaborate.*

Each of us has some need to control and be controlled by others. But some people almost always want to dominate and make sure that their objectives are achieved. In managing conflict, **confrontational** people have a win–lose philosophy. They want to win at the expense of the other person, to claim victory over their opponents. They want to control others. They are focused on themselves and usually ignore the needs of others.

confrontational style. Style of managing conflict motivated by a desire to dominate. Behaviors include blaming, threatening, warning, and other forms of verbal abuse.

Identifying Your Conflict Management Style

We each learn to manage conflict in different ways. This exercise helps you increase your awareness of your conflict management style.

1. Complete the following questionnaire, "What Would I Do in a Conflict?"

2. After you've completed and scored the questionnaire, rank-order the five conflict strategies from the one you use most, to the one you use least.

3. Your instructor may ask you to discuss your results with another person or with a group of your classmates. Think of examples that illustrate each of the conflict styles.

What Would I Do in a Conflict?

1. You and a classmate both want to use the computer at the same time.

   a. I would give up wanting it and give up on the classmate as a friend.

   b. I would try to force the classmate to let me use the computer first.

2. You and a classmate both want the same library book at the same time.

   a. I would give up on wanting it and give up on the classmate as a friend.

   b. I would listen carefully to why my classmate needed the book, and if his reasons were more important than mine, I would let him have it. because a good friend is important.

3. You and a classmate both want to sharpen your pencil at the same time.

   a. I would let the classmate go first and give up on her as a friend.

   b. I would ask for us to solve the problem by one person sharpening both pencils so both of us have to wait an equal amount of time.

4. You and a classmate both want to be first in the lunch line.

   a. I would let the classmate go first and give up on him as a friend.

   b. I would compromise by agreeing to alternate who goes first for an equal number of days.

5. You and a classmate both want the same chair at your favorite table in the library.

   a. I would try to force the classmate to let me have the chair, not caring if she was angry or upset with me.

   b. I would listen carefully to why my classmate wanted the chair, and if her reasons were more important than mine, I would let her have it, because a good friend is important.

6. You and a classmate are working on a group project. Both of you want to draw the illustrations, and neither wants to write the report.

   a. I would try to force the classmate to let me draw the illustrations, not caring if he was angry or upset with me.

   b. I would compromise by agreeing for each of us to draw half of the illustrations and write half of the report.

7. You and a classmate have been playing ball. Neither of you wants to put the equipment away.

   a. I would try to force the classmate to do it, not caring if she was angry or upset with me.

Confronters often resort to *blaming*, or seeking a scapegoat, rather than assuming responsibility for a conflict. "I didn't do it," "Don't look at me," and "He made me do it" are typical blaming statements.

If these strategies do not work, confronters may try *threats* and *warnings*. *Threats* refer to actions they can actually carry out.[20] *Warnings* are negative prophecies they cannot actually control. The boyfriend who says, "If you don't stop calling me names, I'm going to leave you," has issued a threat; he has the power to leave. If he were to say, "Don't call your parents names or they'll write you out of their will," that would be a warning. In reality, he has no control over his girlfriend's parents.

b. I would ask for us to solve the problem by putting the equipment away together.

8. You and a classmate are making a video. Both of you want to run the camera, and neither wants to narrate.

   a. I would listen carefully to why my classmate wanted to do the filming, and if his reasons were more important than mine, I would let him do it, because a good friend is important.

   b. I would ask the classmate to compromise so that each of us filmed half of the time and each narrated half of the time.

9. You told a classmate a secret, and she told it to several other people.

   a. I would listen carefully to why my classmate told my secret, and if her reasons were more important than mine, I would forgive her, because a good friend is important.

   b. I would try to solve the problem by asking my classmate what happened and by working out an agreement about keeping secrets in the future.

10. You and a classmate both believe you did most of the work on a joint report.

    a. I would compromise by agreeing that we both did half.

    b. I would try to solve the problem by reviewing each aspect of the paper and decide who did how much on that aspect.

Scoring Procedure

Circle the letters below that you circled on each question. Then total the number of letters circled in each column.

Question	Withdrawing	Forcing	Smoothing	Compromising	Negotiating
1.	a	b			
2.	a		b		
3.	a			b	
4.	a				b
5.		a	b		
6.		a		b	
7.		a			b
8.			a	b	
9			a		b
10.				a	b
Total	_____	_____	_____	_____	_____

You score for withdrawing reflects your *nonconfrontational* approach to conflict. If you scored high on forcing, you may tend to have a more *confrontational* style. If you scored high on smoothing, compromising, and negotiating, you are more likely to seek *cooperative* ways of managing conflict. Remember: There is no one best style to use all of the time. Although the cooperative approach is more likely to result in dialogue, there are times when it is best to be nonconfrontational. And in some situations it may be appropriate and ethical to confront the issues. Throttling up your listening skills is important when forcing or confronting issues.

Source: David W. Johnson, *Reaching Out: Interpersonal Effectiveness and Self-Actualization* (Allyn & Bacon, 2000), 253–255.

Obviously, threats are more powerful than warnings in changing behavior, and then only if the other person would genuinely find the threatened actions punishing or disruptive. If a parent threatens a spanking, a child will take the threat seriously only if he or she knows the parent will carry it out. If the parent has administered only light raps on the wrist in the past, the child will probably not pay much attention to the threat.

Why are some people verbally aggressive? There may be any of several reasons.[21] As noted in Chapters 1 and 2, recent research emphasizing what is called the "communibiological approach to communication" suggests that we are each born with

certain traits or characteristics.[22] It's just some people's nature to be **verbally aggressive.** Being verbally aggressive is also closely linked to the concept of seeking power in a relationship.[23] Verbally aggressive people often use hurtful language as a way of gaining or maintaining power over others. They may learn that they can get what they want by bullying others. As long as they continue to get what they want and are reinforced for their heavy-handed verbal aggressiveness, they will continue to do it. Still other people are verbally aggressive as a way of expressing bottled-up emotions and frustrations. And finally, verbal aggressiveness is contagious. When one person is verbally aggressive, the other person is likely to reciprocate.[24]

What should you do if you are a victim of verbal aggressiveness? The simple and obvious answer is to avoid relationships with people who are verbally aggressive. The verbally aggressive person may need more power and confirmation of his or her own worth; trying to find constructive strategies to let the aggressor know he or she is valued may help. But if long-held patterns of being verbally aggressive are present, don't expect quick or dramatic changes in the aggressive person by just offering him or her compliments. Verbally aggressive comments by others are often triggered by anger. Later in the chapter we offer specific strategies to manage anger and other emotions during conflict.

Cooperative Style

People who take a **cooperative approach** to conflict management view conflicts as a set of problems to be solved, rather than games in which one person wins and another loses. They use other-oriented strategies and foster a win–win climate by using the following techniques.[25]

Separate the people from the problem. They leave personal grievances out of the discussion, describing problems without making judgmental or evaluative statements about personalities.

Focus on shared interests. They ask questions such as "What do we both want? What do we both value? Where are we already agreeing?" to emphasize common interests, values, and goals.

Generate many options to solve the problem. They use brainstorming and other techniques to generate alternative solutions. (You will learn more about problem-solving techniques later in this chapter.)

verbal aggressiveness. Using words in a way that causes pain and attacks another person's self-concept.

cooperative style. Style of managing conflict that seeks win–win solutions to problems. Cooperative people separate the people from the problem, focus on shared interests, generate multiple solutions, and base decisions on objective criteria.

Assessing Your Verbal Aggressiveness

The following scale is designed to assess your verbal aggressiveness. Use the following scale:

1 = Almost never true
2 = Rarely true
3 = Occasionally true
4 = Often true
5 = Almost always true

How Verbally Aggressive Are You?

_____ 1. I am extremely careful to avoid attacking individuals' intelligence when I attack their ideas.

_____ 2. When individuals are very stubborn, I use insults to soften the stubbornness.

_____ 3. I try very hard to avoid having other people feel bad about themselves when I try to influence them.

_____ 4. When people refuse without good reason to do a task I know is important, I tell them they are unreasonable.

_____ 5. When others do things I regard as stupid, I try to be extremely gentle with them.

_____ 6. If individuals I am trying to influence really deserve it, I attack their character.

_____ 7. When people behave in ways that are in very poor taste, I insult them in order to shock them into proper behavior

_____ 8. I try to make people feel good about themselves even when their ideas are stupid.

_____ 9. When people simply will not budge on a matter of importance, I lose my temper and say rather strong things to them.

_____ 10. When people criticize my shortcomings, I take it in good humor and do not try to get back at them.

_____ 11. When individuals insult me, I get a lot of pleasure out of really telling them off.

_____ 12. When I dislike individuals greatly, I try not to show it in what I say or how I say it.

_____ 13. I like poking fun at people who do things which are very stupid in order to stimulate their intelligence.

_____ 14. When I attack a person's ideas, I try not to damage his or her self-concept.

_____ 15. When I try to influence people, I make a great effort not to offend them.

_____ 16. When people do things that are mean or cruel, I attack their character in order to help correct their behavior.

_____ 17. I refuse to participate in arguments when they involve personal attacks.

_____ 18. When nothing seems to work in trying to influence others, I yell and scream in order to get some movement from them.

_____ 19. When I am not able to refute others' positions, I try to make them feel defensive in order to weaken their positions.

_____ 20. When an argument shifts to personal attacks, I try very hard to change the subject.

Here's how to compute your verbal aggressiveness score:

Step 1: Add the scores on items 2, 4, 6, 7, 9, 11, 13, 16, 18, 19.

Step 2: Add the scores on items 1, 3, 5, 8, 10, 12, 14, 15, 17, 20.

Step 3: Subtract the score from step 2 from 60.

Step 4: Add the score from step 1 to the score you obtained from step 3.

Here's what the scores mean:
Score
59–100: You are highly verbally aggressive.
39–58: You are moderately verbally aggressive.
20–38: You are rarely verbally aggressive.

Questions for reflection:
1. Does your score seem to fit your understanding of yourself?
2. Ask others who will be honest with you about their perceptions of your verbal aggressiveness? Do their perceptions fit your score on this test?
3. If you are highly verbally aggressive, what are some alternative ways of communicating your ideas without always being overly aggressive?

Source: Dominic Infante and C. J. Wigley, "Verbal Aggressiveness: An Interpersonal Model and Measure," _Communication Monographs,_ 53 (1986): 61–69.

Base decisions on objective criteria. They try to establish standards for an acceptable solution to a problem—these standards may involve cost, timing, and other factors. Suppose, for example, that you and your neighbor are discussing possible ways to stop a nearby dog from barking endlessly into the night. You decide on these criteria: The solution must not harm the dog; it must be easy for the owner to implement; the owner must agree to it; it should not cost more than fifty dollars; and it must keep the dog from disturbing the sleep of others. Your neighbor says, "Maybe the dog can sleep in the owner's garage at night." This solution meets all but one of your criteria, so you call the owner, who agrees to put the dog in the garage by 10 P.M. Now everyone wins, because the solution meets a sound, well-considered set of objective criteria.

recap   Conflict Management Styles

Nonconfrontational Style	Avoids conflict by placating (agreeing), distracting, computing (becoming emotionally detached), or withdrawing from the conflict
Confrontational Style	Manipulates others by controlling, blaming, and making threats and warnings and being verbally agressive; sets up win–lose framework
Cooperative Style	Seeks mutually agreeable resolutions to manage differences

Works within an other-oriented, win-win framework:
- Separates people from the problem
- Focuses on shared interests
- Generates many options to solve problems
- Bases decisions upon objective criteria

Conflict Management Skills

A s we saw in the previous section, the nonconfrontational and confrontational styles of conflict management do not always solve problems effectively, nor do they foster typically healthy long-term relationships. The skills we will review here are those we touched on in our discussion of the cooperative style.[26]

Managing conflict, especially emotion-charged ego conflict, is not easy. Even with a fully developed set of skills, you should not expect to melt tensions and resolve disagreements instantaneously. The following skills can, however, help you generate options that promote understanding and provide a framework for cooperation.

Manage Your Emotions

For weeks you have been working on a brochure with a tight deadline. You turned it over to the production department with instructions two weeks ago. Today you call to check on its progress, and you discover that it is still sitting on the produc-

considering others

Empathy Can Span the Abyss

Intergenerational conflicts and misunderstandings can cause pain and emotional bruises. Instead of finding nurturing and love within the family circle, some people encounter exactly the opposite.

For example, a Nebraska man writes: "I don't look forward to family gatherings because I come back with my self-esteem reduced to zero and feeling like a stereotypical old geezer. I'm rebuffed by my own children, giggled at, and made to feel my thoughts aren't important."

An Indiana reader describes in detail a truly unhappy situation. "I gave my money to my children, trusting them to take care of my needs when I grew older. But now that I have no money left, they have discarded me. How stupid I was not to take care of my security! I'm alone now, really alone. I need to understand what I did wrong. I guess I gave too much, cared too much."

Many letters from elderly people tell similar stories. I also hear from their sons and daughters, members of the so-called sandwich generation, whose reports have a different focus. A 54-year-old woman writes from New York about the "hard burden" she bears in caring for her 88-year-old mother: "I'm angry that I am increasingly having to be a parent to someone whose self-centeredness and narcissism made her unable to be a mother to me. The simple, awful fact is that I respect my mother and love her as my flesh and blood, but I don't like her and I wish she weren't in my life. My fear is that she's going to live on and on, growing more and more needful of my 'parenting,' and that I won't be free of her presence until I'm approaching seventy myself."

Another letter from a member of the sandwich generation comes from Arizona: "My challenge involves my relationship with my mother-in-law of twenty-nine years. She's 89. She has lost all semblance of a positive outlook. She speaks only of her aches and pains and the bleakness of her life. I cannot deal with this negative approach to living. Whatever I try to do for her, nothing is ever right."

Reflecting on these letters, I find the key word for what both sides need is empathy—which the dictionary defines as identification with and understanding of the situation, feelings, and motives of another person. Without this empathy, a great abyss can exist where there should be communication. Can we overemphasize that there's no substitute for honest communication between people? *Tell* others what you feel! Try to explain *why* you feel as you do. This can lead to real understanding.

A woman in New Jersey offers a promising, creative role model for others: "Sometimes I'm not delighted to hear what my mother needs and wants because it impinges on my time and energy. However, I prefer to know what she's thinking and feeling, even if it results in conflict. The resolution of such conflicts has strengthened our friendship and the community that is our family. Love, I believe, is being open and seeking a resolution that may require mutual sacrifice."

An extremely helpful, sound definition. Speaking of love, a Florida reader writes: "Many years ago my mother gave me a book that set my life on a self-respecting, self-valuing course. It says it's quite okay to love yourself. If you don't, how can anyone else love you? If you think you're not worth loving, then, by cracky, you're not. If you think you're not worth much, you will always be a problem—if not a pain—to be around. Is that what you want for yourself? Not I."

A final intergenerational note from Florida: "My life was lonely after I lost my husband," a woman writes. "I volunteered at the hospital, bowled twice a week, was active at my church and kept my home. But there was still a terrible void in my life. Then my 23-year-old granddaughter told me to keep Wednesday evenings open for her. We take turns cooking, or sometimes we go out. You have no idea what this has done for me. We share a meal, talk, and just enjoy our friendship. Our talk may be about her work or what I've done the past week—just nice conversation. We sometimes cry together. But we laugh together as well."

This grandmother and granddaughter have found a happy way to bridge the generation gap. Others could profit from their example.

Source: Malcolm Boyd, *Modern Maturity.* Reprinted with permission from Modern Maturity. Copyright 1992, American Association of Retired Persons.

tion coordinator's desk. You feel angry and frustrated. How should you respond? You may be tempted to march into the production coordinator's office and scream at her, or to shout at her supervisor.

Try to avoid taking action when you are in such a state. You may regret what you say, and you will probably escalate the conflict.

Often the first sign that we are in a conflict situation is a feeling of anger, frustration, fear, or even sadness, which sweeps over us like an ocean wave. If we feel powerless to control our own fate, then we will have difficulty taking a logical or rational approach to managing the conflict. Expressing our feelings in an emotional outburst may make us feel better for the moment, but it may close the door to logical, rational negotiation.

When we are emotionally charged, we experience physical changes as well. One researcher found that

> . . . our adrenaline flows faster and our strength increases by about 20 percent. The liver, pumping sugar into the bloodstream, demands more oxygen from the heart and lungs. The veins become enlarged and the cortical centers where thinking takes place do not perform nearly as well. . . . the blood supply to the problem-solving part of the brain is severely decreased because, under stress, a greater portion of blood is diverted to the body's extremities.[27]

Such changes fuel our fight–flight responses. If we choose to stay, verbal or physical violence may erupt; if we flee from the conflict, we cannot resolve it. Until we can tone down (not eliminate) our emotions, we will find it difficult to apply other skills. Let's look at some specific strategies that you can draw on when an intense emotional response to conflict clouds your judgment and decision-making skills.[28]

Be Aware That You Are Becoming Angry and Emotionally Volatile

One characteristic of people who "lose it" is that they let their emotions get the best of them. Before they know it, they are saying and doing things that they later regret. Unbridled and uncensored emotional outbursts rarely enhance the quality of an interpersonal relationship. An emotional purge may make you feel better, but your partner is likely to reciprocate, which will only escalate the conflict spiral.

Before that happens, become aware of what is happening to you. As we described earlier, your body will start to react to your emotions with an increased heart rate. Be mindful of such changes. Be sensitive to what is happening to you physically.

Seek to Understand Why You Are Angry and Emotional

Understanding what's behind your anger can help you manage it. Realize that it is normal and natural to be angry. It's a feeling everyone experiences. You need not feel guilty about it. Anger is often expressed as a defense when you feel violated. Two powerful anger triggers are (1) you don't think you have been treated fairly, and (2) you feel entitled to something that you are being denied. Think about the last time you became very angry. Chances are your angry outburst stemmed from a sense that you were not treated fairly or that someone denied you something you were entitled to. Often there is a sense of righteous indignation when you are angry. You are being denied something you feel you should have.

Select a Mutually Acceptable Time and Place to Discuss a Conflict

If you are upset, or even tired, you are at risk for an emotion-charged shouting match. If you ambush someone with an angry attack, don't expect him or her to be in a productive frame of mind. Instead, give yourself time to cool off before you try to resolve a conflict. In the case of the lapsed deadline mentioned earlier, you could call both the production coordinator and her boss and schedule an appointment to meet with them later in the day. By that time, you could gain control of your feelings and also think the issue through. Of course, issues sometimes need to be discussed on the spot; you may not have the luxury of waiting. But whenever practical, make sure the other person is ready to receive you and your message.

🔵 Plan Your Message

If you are approaching someone to discuss a disagreement, take care to organize your message. Identify your goal and determine what outcome you would like; do not barge in and pour out your emotions.

🔵 Make a Conscious Decision About Whether to Express Your Anger

Rather than just letting anger and frustration build and erupt out of control, make a conscious choice about whether you should express your frustration and irritation. We're not denying that there are valid reasons for you to express anger and frustration or suggesting that you should not express your feelings. Sometimes there is no way to let someone know how important an issue is to you other than by forcefully expressing your irritation or anger. As these lines from William Blake illustrate, sometimes the wisest strategy is to be honest with others and express how you feel.

> I was angry with my friend:
> I told my wrath, my wrath did end.
> I was angry with my foe:
> I told it not, my wrath did grow.

If you do decide to express your anger, don't lose control. Be direct and descriptive. The guidelines for listening and responding that we provided in Chapter 5 can serve you well. Keep your anger focused on issues rather than personalities.

🔵 Breathe

One of the simplest yet most effective way to avoid overheating is to breathe. As you become aware that your emotions are starting to erupt, take a slow, deep, calm, unnoticeable breath. Then breathe again. This can help calm you and manage the physiological changes that adrenaline creates. Deep breathing—the prime strategy women use to manage the pain of childbirth—can powerfully help restore calmness to your spirit. Focusing on your breathing is also one of the primary methods of meditation. We're not suggesting that you hyperventilate. But unobtrusively breathing, a deep, slow breath that not just fills your upper lungs, but starts in your diaphragm—the muscles that support your lungs—is an active strategy to help you regain rational control.

You might also consider talking with a trusted friend or colleague. A good friend with empathic listening skills can help you clarify the issues in the conflict. If you don't talk with a friend, consider writing down the key ideas you want to express to help you prepare for your face-to-face discussion. The purpose of the notes is not to deliver a speech when you meet your conflict partner. But taking time to plan your message with a friend or in writing can help you frame the issues of the disagreement.

🔵 Monitor Nonverbal Messages

As you learned in Chapter 7, your actions play a key role in establishing the emotional climate in any relationship. Monitoring your nonverbal messages can help to de-escalate an emotion-charged situation. Speaking calmly, using direct eye

considering
others

Managing Anger During Conflict

One of the most typical emotional responses you may experience during conflict is anger.[29] Anger occurs when you feel someone is keeping you from what you want, someone is unjustly blaming you for something you didn't do, or someone is attacking you. Some people may tell you it is a good idea to express your anger to the person who is making you angry; get your anger out; don't keep it bottled up. There are times when expressing your anger is appropriate. Being assertive in expressing what bothers you is appropriate when the other person is not aware of what is bothering you. But uncensored angry words can escalate the anger you feel and also increase others' anger.[30] One research team offers these prescriptions for helping you manage your anger during conflict.[31]

1. *Be determined not to get angry yourself.* If you know you are going to face someone who is likely to tick you off, prepare yourself before you meet with him or her. Assertively express your feelings, but make yourself promise not to "lose it" by degenerating into a loud shout fest.

2. *Get on the same physical level as the other person.* One person should not be standing and the other sitting. Try to face each other eye-to-eye. You can also build rapport by trying to mirror the posture of the other person. We're not suggesting that you mimic your partner (this would probably make him or her more angry), but try to adopt a similar communication position.

3. *Be silent.* If you are angry and afraid you might say something you'll regret, just be quiet and listen.

4. *Express your concern nonverbally.* Because much of the emotional message is communicated nonverbally, use your facial expression and eyes to let the other person know you care about him

or her. Your communication partner will believe what you do, more than what you say.

5. *Make an appropriate empathic statement.* Saying "I would probably feel angry if I had experienced what you experienced" or "I think I can see why you are so upset" may help. But be careful not to say, "I know just how you feel" or "I know where you're coming from." For many people, those statements can seem patronizing.

6. *Remind yourself that no one can make you angry. You control your own emotions.* Even though others may do and say things that can upset you, you are the only person who can control you and your response to others. Try to respond to others rather than just emotionally react to them.

7. *Recognize that angry emotional outbursts rarely change someone's mind.* Exploding in an angry tirade may make you feel better for a moment by getting it "off your chest," but it usually does little to advance understanding and manage the issues at hand.

contact, and maintaining a natural facial expression will signal that you wish to collaborate rather than control. Your nonverbal message should also support your verbal response. If you say you are listening to someone, but you continue to read the paper or work on a report, you are communicating a lack of interest in the speaker and the message.

🔴 Avoid Personal Attacks, Name-Calling, and Emotional Overstatement

Using threats and derogatory names can turn a simple conflict into an ego conflict. When people feel attacked, they will respond by protecting themselves. Also try to avoid exaggerating your emotions. If you say you are irritated or annoyed rather than furious, you can still communicate your feelings, but you take the sting out of your description.

Avoid the bad habit of **gunny-sacking.** This occurs when you dredge up old problems and issues from the past, like pulling them out of an old bag or gunny sack, to use against your partner. Keep your focus on the issues at hand, not on old

gunny-sacking. Dredging up old problems and issues from the past, like pulling them out of an old bag or gunny sack, to use against your partner.

What strategies do this mother and daughter seem to have drawn on to manage their conflicts? (Bruce Ayres/ Tony Stone Images)

hurts from the past. Gunny sacking usually succeeds only in increasing tension, escalating emotions and reducing listening effectiveness. See the list of "fair fighting" strategies on page 275 to help keep your discussions productive rather than allow them to degenerate into emotional shouting matches.

Use Self-Talk

When Kosta was chairing the committee meeting, Monique accused him of falsifying the attendance numbers at the last fine arts festival. Instead of lashing back at Monique, he paused, took a slow, deep, yet unnoticed breath, and thought, "I'm tired. If I snarl back, all we will do is escalate this issue out of proportion. I'll talk with Monique later after we have both cooled down." Perhaps you think that talking to yourself is an eccentricity. Nothing could be further from the truth. As you saw in Chapter 2, thoughts are directly linked to feelings,[32] and the messages we tell ourselves play a major role in how we feel and respond to others. Ask yourself whether an emotional tirade and an escalating conflict will produce the results you want. When Eleanor Roosevelt noted that "No one can make you feel inferior without your consent," she was acknowledging the power of self-talk in affecting your emotional response to what others say and do.

Manage Information

Because uncertainty, misinformation, and misunderstanding are often byproducts of conflict and disagreement, skills that promote mutual understanding are an important component of cooperative conflict management. Based on the listening, and responding skills discussed in Chapter 5, the following specific suggestions can help you reduce uncertainty and enhance the quality of communication during conflict.

🍥 Clearly Describe the Conflict-Producing Events

Instead of just blurting out your complaints in random order, think of delivering a brief, well-organized minispeech. Offer your perspective on what created the conflict, sequencing the events like a well organized story. Describe the events dispassionately so that the other person shares your understanding of the problem.

When Marsha almost had a car accident, she came home and told her husband, "Last week you said you would get the brakes fixed on the car. On Monday, when you still hadn't taken the car in, you said you would do it on Wednesday. Now it's Friday, and the brakes are in even worse shape. I had a close call this afternoon when the car almost wouldn't stop. We've got to get those brakes fixed before anyone drives that car again."

🍥 "Own" Your Statements by Using Descriptive "I" Language

"I feel upset when you post the week's volunteer schedule without first consulting with me," reveals Katrina. Her statement is an example of **"I" language.** "I" language expresses how a speaker is feeling. The use of the word "I" conveys a willingness to "own" one's feelings and statements about them.

If Katrina had said, "You always prepare a schedule without telling anyone first. All of us who volunteer are mad about that," her statement would have had an accusatory sting. Beginning the statement with "you" sets the listener up for a defensive response. Also, notice that in the second statement, the speaker does not take responsibility for the problem; she suggests that it belongs to several unidentified people as well. If you instead narrow the issue down to a conflict between you and the other person, you put the conflict into a more manageable framework.

🍥 Use Effective Listening Skills

Managing information is a two-way process. Whether you are describing a conflict situation to someone, or that individual is bringing a conflict to your attention, good listening skills will be invaluable.

Give your full attention to the speaker and make a conscious point of tuning out your internal messages. Sometimes the best thing to do after describing the conflict-producing events is simply to wait for a response. If you don't stop talking and give the other person a chance to respond, he or she will feel frustrated, the emotional pitch will go up a notch, and it will become more difficult to reach an understanding.

Finally, focus not only on the facts or details, but also analyze them so you can understand the major point the speaker is making. Try to use your understanding of the details to interpret the speaker's major ideas. Remember to stay other-oriented, and "seek to understand rather than to be understood."[33]

🍥 Check Your Understanding of What Others Say and Do

Respond clearly and appropriately. Your response and that of your conflict partner will confirm that you have understood each other. Checking perceptions is vital when emotions run high.

If you are genuinely unsure about facts, issues, or major ideas addressed during a conflict, ask questions to help you sort through them instead of barging ahead with solutions. Then summarize your understanding of the information; do not parrot the speaker's words or paraphrase every statement, but check key points to ensure that you have understood the message. Note how Ted adeptly paraphrases to check his understanding:

"I" language. Expresses with the word "I" how the speaker is feeling.

Maggie: I don't like the conclusion you've written to the conference report. It doesn't mention anything about the ideas suggested at the symposium. I think you have also misinterpreted the CEO's key message.

Ted: So, if I understand you, Maggie, you're saying the report missed some key information and may also include an inaccurate summary of the CEO's speech.

Maggie: Yes, Ted. Those are the concerns I have.

Manage Goals

As we have seen, conflict is goal-driven. Both individuals involved in an interpersonal conflict want something. And for some reason, be it competition, scarce resources, or lack of understanding, the goals appear to be in conflict. To manage conflict, it is important to seek an accurate understanding of these goals and to identify where they overlap.

Identify Your Goal and Your Partner's Goal

After you describe, listen, and respond, your next task should be to identify what you would like to have happen. What is your goal? Most goal statements can be phrased in terms of wants or desires. Consider the following examples:

Problem	Goals
Your boss approaches you and wants you to work overtime; you need to pick up your son from day care	You want to leave work on time; your boss wants the work completed ASAP.
Your spouse wants to sleep with the window open; you like a warm room and sleep better with the window closed.	You want a good night's rest; your spouse wants a good night's rest.
Your 6-year-old son wants to go to a swim party with no lifeguards.	You want your son to be safe; your son wants to have a good time.

Often in conflicts you will face balancing your goal against the goal of maintaining the relationship that you have with your partner. Eventually, you may decide that the latter goal is more important than the substantive conflict issue.

Research by Charles Pavitt and Bradley Kemp confirms the significant role of using positive goals in conflict and negotiation situations.[34] If you're negotiating with someone you like, you will expect your negotiation partner to use more positive approaches to achieve the goal. Conversely, if you're negotiating with someone you don't like, you will expect that person to use more threats and demands, and be more obstinate.

Next, it is useful to identify your partner's goal. In each problem on the preceding list, in order to manage the conflict, you would need to know what the other person wants. Use effective listening, and responding skills to determine what each of you wants and to verbalize your goals. Obviously, if you both keep your goals hidden, it will be difficult to manage the conflict.

Identify Where Your Goals and Your Partner's Goals Overlap

Authors of the best-selling book *Getting to Yes,* Roger Fisher and William Ury, stress the importance of focusing on shared interests when seeking to manage differences.[35] Armed with an understanding of what you want and what your partner wants, you can then determine whether the goals overlap. In the conflict over whether the window should be open or closed, the goal of both parties is the same: each wants a good night's sleep. Framing the problem as "How can we achieve our mutual goal?" rather than arguing over whether the window should be up or down, moves the discussion to a more productive level.

If you focus on shared interests (common goals) and develop objective, rather than subjective, criteria for the solution, there is hope for finding a resolution that will satisfy both parties.

Manage the Problem

If you can structure conflicts as problems to be solved rather than battles to be won or lost, you are well on your way to seeking strategies to manage the issues that confront you and your partner. Of course, as we have stressed earlier, not all conflicts can be resolved. However, approaching the core of a conflict as a problem to be managed can provide a constructive way of seeking resolution. Structuring a conflict as a problem also helps to manage the emotion and keeps the conversation focused on issues (simple conflict) rather than personalities (ego conflict). The problem-solving structure we suggest here is straightforward: Define the problem, analyze the problem's causes and effects, determine the goal you and your partner seek, generate many possible options, then select the option that best achieves the goals of both you and your partner.

Define the problem

You can apply all the skills described so far to pursue a proven method for problem solving, which is shown in Table 8.1. First, *define the problem.* Most problems boil down to something you want more or less of.

Cara and Vaughn have been going together for over a year. Lately they have been fighting over small issues, so they decide to spend some time talking about what is wrong and trying to understand one another. At the root of their conflicts, they

Table 8.1

**Solving Problems: One Method of
Organizing Problem-Solving Discussions**

1. Define the problem.	Determine the question about which you disagree on the answer.
2. Analyze the problem.	Determine the causes, symptoms, effects, and obstacles.
3. Determine the goals.	Determine what you want. Determine what your partner wants. How do the goals overlap?
4. Generate many solutions.	List many options, rather than debating one or two strategies for achieving the goal.
5. Select the best solution and try it.	Eliminate options that are not mutually agreeable. If possible, take the best ideas from several generated to reach an amicable resolution.

discover, is a basic problem: Cara wants to get married to Vaughn now. Vaughn wants to stay with Cara, but he wants to wait until he feels ready for marriage. He also wants to feel financially secure before he marries.

Analyze the Problem

Next, *analyze the problem.* To analyze is to break something down into its components. With your partner, begin by describing the conflict-producing events in chronological order (see page 264). Then decide whether it is a pseudo conflict, a simple conflict, or an ego conflict (see page 243). Attempt to ferret out symptoms, effects, and obstacles; decide whether the conflict stems from several subproblems or from one major issue. As you proceed with your analysis, you and your partner may decide that you need more information to help clarify the issues.

After some discussion, Cara and Vaughn analyze the problem. They realize they come from different family backgrounds and have different expectations about marriage. Cara's folks were high school sweethearts and got married when they were 18. Vaughn's parents are older; they met after each of them had been divorced, and they married after a long, slow-paced relationship. Cara and Vaughn's different frames of reference help explain their feelings about the timing of marriage.

Determine the Goals

The next step in managing the problem is to *determine the goals* of you and your partner, following the suggestions on page 265. Also, generate objective criteria for a solution (see page 258). The more measurable, verifiable, and objective the criteria, the greater the likelihood that you and your partner will be able to agree when the criteria have been met. Cara and Vaughn decide that, ultimately, they have the same goal: to get married. The issue boils down to timing. So they decide to seek a course of action that will make them both feel secure.

✱ 🔵 Generate Multiple Solutions

Their next step is to *generate multiple solutions.* Simply understanding the issues and the causes, effects, symptoms, and history of a problem will not enable you to manage a conflict. It takes time and creativity to find mutually satisfactory solutions to most problems. It stands to reason that the more solutions you generate, the greater the probability that you can manage the conflict constructively. One way to generate options is through brainstorming. To use brainstorming, try the following suggestions:

1. Make sure the problem and the goals are clear to both of you.

2. Try to suspend judgment and evaluation temporarily; do not censor your thoughts.

3. Specify a certain time period for brainstorming.

4. Consider having each partner brainstorm ideas separately before a meeting, or write ideas down before verbalizing solutions.

5. Try to develop at least one unique or far-out idea. You can always tame wild ideas down later.

6. Piggyback off the ideas of your partner. Encourage your partner to use or modify your ideas.

7. Write down all the ideas suggested.

8. Review each idea, noting ways to combine, eliminate, or extend them.

If the goal is to find the best way to manage the difficulty, it may take only one good idea to help move the conflict forward to a constructive resolution.

When they brainstorm, Cara and Vaughn generate the following options: Save money for a year and then get married; take turns going to college; take turns working to support the family while the other gets a degree; get married now, get jobs, and postpone college; get married now and take out college loans.

🔵 Select the Best Solution

Finally, Cara and Vaughn decide to *select the best solution.* Sometimes it may take several attempts at defining, analyzing, goal setting, and generating multiple ideas before a mutually agreeable solution emerges. It is always appropriate to recheck your understanding of the issues and goals. Cara and Vaughn decide to combine the best of several ideas. They agree to get engaged, but not to set a date. Instead, they set a financial goal of $5,000 in savings. When they hit that goal, they will set a wedding date. If they are both attending college, they will get part-time jobs so that they have income, and they will also apply for college loans.

If, after repeated attempts, you cannot arrive at a mutually acceptable solution, you may decide to keep trying. Or you may agree to take the issue to an impartial person who can help you identify conflict management strategies and solutions. At work, your immediate superior may be called in to help settle the matter. Or, occasionally, you may agree to disagree and drop it.

The goal of managing conflict is not just to solve a problem, but to help manage relational issues with your partner, especially if your partner thinks he or she has "lost" the conflict. When seeking a solution to interpersonal problems, try to find

Practicing Conflict Management Skills

In this activity you will be paired with another person and invited to role-play a conflict that you have had with that person. A third person will observe and provide feedback about the communication skills you use to manage the conflict.

Person A:

Think about a recent incident in which someone offended you. Make a few notes about the conflict. Then approach person B, who will play the person who has offended you. Describe the conflict, remembering to manage your emotions.

Person B:

You have offended person A. Your job is to listen, reflect, and help to manage the conflict. Start a dialogue to identify each other's goals and see how they overlap; then try to generate strategies to achieve the goals.

Person C:

Your job is to observe the role play. Use the following checklist to help you evaluate the participants. When the role play is over, tell the participants what they did well. Ask them how they could improve, and offer suggestions as well.

If time permits, switch roles and conduct another role play.

Conflict Management Role Play Checklist

Managing Emotions	Person A	Person B
Makes direct eye contact	_____	_____
Maintains open body posture	_____	_____
Uncrosses arms and legs	_____	_____
Leans slightly forward	_____	_____
Speaks in a calm voice	_____	_____
Uses reinforcing head nods	_____	_____
Has appropriate facial expression	_____	_____
Managing Information		
Paraphrases content accurately	_____	_____
Paraphrases feelings accurately	_____	_____
Clearly describes the problem	_____	_____
Managing Goals		
States the goals clearly	_____	_____
Identifies how goals overlap	_____	_____
Managing the Problem		
Identifies several options	_____	_____

ways for your partner to "win" while you also achieve your goal. Help your partner save face. The concept of **face,** attributed to sociologist Erving Goffman, is the self-image or self-respect that you and your partner seek to maintain.[36] Communication researcher Stella Ting Toomey has conducted research studies that emphasize the importance of face-saving or maintaining a positive image, especially in collectivist

face. Self-image or self-respect that you and your partner seek to maintain.

cultures such as Asia, where maintaining face is especially important.[37] Sometimes after you have found a solution to a problem, the goal then becomes to help your partner save face. How do you help someone save face and avoid embarrassment? Sometimes you can offer genuine forgiveness. Or you can offer explanations that help reframe the differences, perhaps suggesting that it was really just a misunderstanding that led to the disagreement. After a tough-fought football game, a victorious, well-mannered coach may say, "They were great opponents. I have much admiration for the way they played." Such face-restoring comments can help mend bruised egos. Such is also the case during interpersonal conflict. Finding ways to be gracious or allow your partner to save face is an important other-oriented approach to dealing with people.

Even though we have presented these conflict management steps as prescriptive suggestions, it is important to remember that *conflict rarely follows a linear, step-by-step sequence of events.* These skills are designed to serve as a general framework for collaboratively managing differences. But if your partner does not want to collaborate, your job will be more challenging.

In reality, you don't simply manage your emotions and then move neatly on to developing greater understanding with another person. Sorting out your goals and your partner's goals is not something you do once and then put behind you. It will take time and patience to balance your goal of maintaining a relationship with your immediate achievement goals. In fact, as you try to manage a conflict, you will more than likely bounce forward and backward from one step to another. This framework gives you an overarching perspective for understanding and actively managing disagreements, but the nature of interpersonal relationships means that you and your partner will respond—sometimes in unpredictable ways—to a variety of cues (psychological, sociological, physical) when communicating. Think of the skills you have learned as options to consider, rather than as hard-and-fast rules to follow in every situation.

When Others Aren't Other-Oriented: How to Be Assertive

Even if you master collaborative conflict management skills, others may make irrational, inappropriate demands that create conflict and tension. In these instances, you will need to assert yourself, especially if someone has aggressively violated your rights.

Assertiveness Defined

Assertiveness was defined in Chapter 1 as the tendency to make requests, ask for information, and generally pursue one's own rights and best interests. Assertive people let their communication partners know when a behavior or message is infringing on their rights. Each individual has rights. In interpersonal communication, you have the right to refuse a request someone makes of you, the right to express your feelings as long as you don't trample on the feelings of others, and

assertiveness. Pursuing your best interests without denying your partner's rights.

 By using assertive "I-messages" this couple may be able to resolve their conflict without taking an aggressive stance. (Jonathan Nourok/PhotoEdit)

the right to have your personal needs met if they don't infringe on the rights of others.

Some people confuse the terms *assertiveness* and *aggressiveness*. **Aggressiveness** means pursuing your interests by denying the rights of others. Assertiveness is other-oriented; aggressiveness is exclusively self-oriented. Aggressive people are coercive. They blame, judge, and evaluate to get what they want. They use intimidating non-verbal cues such as steely stares, a bombastic voice, and flailing gestures. Assertive people can ask for what they want without judging or evaluating their partner.

As we noted earlier in the chapter, you can use "I" messages to express your thoughts and feelings rather than "you" messages. "You creep! You ate the last breakfast taco" is an aggressive "you" statement. "I asked you to save one taco for me; now I won't have anything to eat for breakfast" is an assertive statement of your rights and describes the consequences of violating them.

 recap   **Assertiveness versus Aggressiveness**

Assertiveness	Aggressiveness
Expresses your interests without denying the rights of others	Expresses your interests and denies the rights of others
Is other-oriented	Is self-oriented
Describes what you want	Evaluates the other person
Discloses your needs, using "I" messages	Discloses your needs, using "you" messages

aggressiveness. Expressing your interests while denying the rights of others by blaming, judging, and evaluating the other person.

How to Assert Yourself If You Are Sexually Harassed

What Is Sexual Harassment?

Any unwelcome sexual advances, requests for sexual favors, or other inappropriate verbal or physical behavior of a sexual nature may be classified as sexual harassment. Examples include

- Repeated and unwanted requests for dates, sexual flirtations, or propositions of a sexual nature
- Unwanted sexual remarks or questions about a person's clothing, body, or sexual activity
- Unnecessary touching, patting, hugging, or brushing against a person's body
- Direct or implied threats that failure to submit to sexual advances will affect employment, work status, grades, letters of recommendation, or residential choice
- Physical assault
- A pattern of conduct that causes humiliation or discomfort, such as inappropriate terms of greeting; sexually explicit or sexist comments, questions, or jokes; or leering at a person's body

What to Do if You Are Sexually Harassed

- Be direct and candid with the person.
- Use "I" messages (for example, "I don't like those kinds of jokes made about me").
- Avoid being overly dramatic; remain confident that the incident will be dealt with.
- If the incident happens at school or work, use the grievance procedure.
- Report the harasser to your supervisor, department chair, or dean.
- If the harasser is your supervisor or an administrative official, report the incident to his or her supervisor.
- Report the harassment immediately after it occurs. The longer you wait, the less credible your story will be.
- When the harassment occurs, write down important facts.
- Report the incident as if you were a journalist: give the who, what, when, where, and how. Keep to the facts.
- Be prepared to give the interviewer names of witnesses.
- Put aside your anger and be thorough when telling the story.

Source: Information adapted from Southwest Texas State University policy and procedure statement on sexual harassment and Vicki West, "Sexual Harassment: Identify, Stop, and Prevent" seminar.

Five Steps in Assertive Behavior

Many people have a tendency to withdraw in the face of controversy, even when their rights are being violated or denied. But you can develop skill in asserting yourself, by practicing five key suggestions.[38]

Describe

Describe how you view the situation. To assert your position, you first need to describe how you view the situation. You need to be assertive because the other person has not been other-oriented. For example, Doug is growing increasingly frustrated with Maria's tardiness at the weekly staff meeting. He first approaches Maria by describing his observation: "I have noticed that you are usually fifteen minutes late to our weekly staff meetings." A key to communicating your assertive message is to monitor your nonverbal message, especially your voice. Avoid sarcasm or excessive vocal intensity. Calmly yet confidently describe the problem.

Disclose

Disclose your feelings. After describing the situation from your perspective, let the other person know how you feel.[39] Disclosing your feelings will help to build empathy and avoid lengthy harangues about the other person's unjust treatment. "I feel you don't take our weekly meetings seriously," continues Doug as he asserts his desire for Maria to be on time to the meeting. Note that Doug does not talk about how others are feeling ("Every member of our group is tired of your coming in late"); he describes how *he* feels.

Identify Effects

Identify effects. Next, you can identify the *effects* of the other person's behavior on you or others. "When you are late, it disrupts our meeting," says Doug.

Be Silent

Wait. Then you can simply wait for a response. Nonassertive people find this step hard. Again, be sure to monitor your nonverbal cues. Make sure your facial expression does not contradict your verbal message. Delivering an assertive message with a broad grin might create a double bind for your listener, who may not be sure what the primary message is—the verbal one or the nonverbal one.

Paraphrase

Paraphrase content and feelings. After the other person responds appropriately, paraphrase both the content and feelings of the message. "Oh, I'm sorry. I didn't realize I was creating a problem. I have another meeting that usually goes overtime. It's difficult for me to arrive at the start of our meeting on time," says Maria. Doug could respond, "So the key problem is a time conflict with another meeting. It must make you feel frustrated to try to do two things at once."

If the other person is evasive, unresponsive, or aggressive, you'll need to cycle through the steps again: Clearly describe what the other person is doing that is not acceptable; disclose how you feel; identify the effects; wait; then paraphrase and clarify as needed. A key goal of an assertive response is to seek an empathic connection between you and your partner. Paraphrasing feelings is a way of ensuring that both parties are connecting.

If you tend to withdraw from conflict, how do you become assertive? Visualizing can help. Think of a past situation in which you wished you had been more assertive and then mentally replay the situation, imagining what you might have said. Also practice verbalizing assertive statements. When you are appropriately assertive, consciously congratulate yourself for sticking up for your rights. To sharpen your assertiveness skills, try Building Your Skills: How to Assert Yourself.

building your skills

How to Assert Yourself

Working with a partner, describe a situation in which you could have been more assertive. Ask your partner to assume the role of the person toward whom you should have been more assertive. Now replay the situation, using the following skills:

1. *Describe:* Tell the other person that what he or she is doing bothers you. Describe rather than evaluate.

2. *Disclose:* Then tell the other person how you feel. For example, "I feel *X*, when you do *Y*."

3. *Identify effects:* Tell the other person the effects of his or her behavior on you or your group. Be as clear and descriptive as you can.

4. *Wait:* After you have described, disclosed, and identified the effects, wait for a response.

5. *Paraphrase:* Use reflective listening skills: Question, paraphrase content, paraphrase feelings.

Observation of Assertiveness Skills

Ask your classmates to observe your role play and provide feedback, using the following checklist. When you have finished asserting your point of view, reverse roles.

_____ Clearly describes what the problem was

_____ Effectively discloses how he or she felt

_____ Clearly describes the effects of the behavior

_____ Pauses or waits after describing the effects

_____ Uses effective questions to promote understanding

_____ Accurately paraphrases content

_____ Accurately paraphrases feelings

_____ Has good eye contact

_____ Leans forward while speaking

_____ Has an open body posture

_____ Has appropriate voice tone and quality

Fighting Fairly

Consider the following suggestions to keep you focused on issues rather than personalities when you experience interpersonal conflict:

1. Be specific when you introduce a complaint.

2. Don't just complain; ask for a reasonable change that will make the situation better.

3. Give and receive feedback about the major points of disagreement to make sure you are understood by your partner.

4. Try tolerance. Be open to your own feelings, and equally open to your partner's feelings. Openness means that you accept change and can verbalize that attitude to your partner.

5. Consider compromise if appropriate. Many conflicts involve issues that are neither right nor wrong. Your partner may even have some good ideas.

6. Deal with one issue at a time.

7. Don't "mind rape." Don't assume to tell your partner what he or she knows or feels. Never assume you know what your partner thinks. Ask.

8. Attack the issue, not each other.

9. Don't call each other names or use sarcasm.

10. Don't "gunny-sack." Just as farmers use a gunny sack to carry feed, many people carry past hurts into the conflict and then unleash them from the "gunny sack." Forget the past and stay with the issue at hand.

11. Don't burden your partner with too many issues.

12. Think about your thoughts and feelings before speaking.

Source: Adapted from George R. Bach and Ronald M. Deutsch, *Pairing* (New York: Peter Wyden, 1970).

 How to Assert Yourself

Step	Example
1. Describe.	"I see you haven't completed the report yet."
2. Disclose.	"I feel the work I ask you to do is not a priority with you."
3. Identify effects.	"Without that report, our team will not achieve our goal."
4. Be silent.	Wait for a response.
5. Use reflective listening	
Question.	"Do you understand how I feel?"
Paraphrase content.	"So you were not aware the report was late."
Paraphrase feelings.	"Perhaps you feel embarrassed."

Summary

Interpersonal conflict is an expressed struggle that occurs when two people cannot agree on a way to meet their needs or goals. At the root of all conflicts are our individual perspectives, needs, and experiences.

Many people hold myths about the conflict management process, such as that conflict should always be avoided, that conflict always occurs because of misunderstandings, that conflict always occurs because of a poor interpersonal relationship, and that conflict can always be resolved. But conflict in interpersonal relationships is inevitable and is not always destructive. It can actually play a constructive role by identifying areas that need attention and transformation.

Conflict can result from misunderstanding someone (pseudoconflict), or it can stem from a simple difference of opinion or viewpoint (simple conflict). Ego conflict occurs when personalities clash; the conflict becomes personal and you may feel a need to defend your self-image.

Although conflict seems to erupt suddenly, it often originates in events that occur long before the conflict manifests itself. It evolves from these prior conditions into frustration awareness, active conflict, solution, and follow-up stages. Understanding conflict as a process also involves recognizing how people seek and are given control over others.

Nonconfrontational approaches to conflict include placating, distracting, computing, and withdrawing. Confrontational approaches can employ blaming, controlling, threats and warnings, and verbal aggressiveness. Cooperative approaches involve separating the person from the problem, focusing on shared interests, generating many options to seek a solution, and basing the decision on objective rather than subjective criteria. Skills for managing conflict focus on managing emotions, information, and goals and ultimately on managing the problem. Even if you master collaborative conflict management skills, in some instances you may need to assert yourself firmly.

The goal of this chapter is not to eliminate conflict from your interpersonal relationships; that would be unrealistic and even undesirable. But knowing principles and skills for bridging differences can give you greater flexibility in maintaining satisfying relationships with others.

For Discussion and Review

Focus on Comprehension

1. What are five myths about conflict?

2. What are pseudo-, simple, and ego conflict?

3. What are the five stages of the conflict management process?

4. What are the four essential skills for managing conflict?

Focus on Critical Thinking

5. Richard has an explosive temper. He consistently receives poor performance evaluations at work because he lashes out at those who disagree with him. What strategies might help him manage his emotional outbursts?

6. Melissa and Jake always seem to end up making personal attacks and calling each other names when they get into a disagreement. What type of conflict are they experiencing when they do this, and how can they avoid it?

7. Analyze the opening dialogue in this chapter. What are Anya and Paolo doing wrong in managing their differences? Are they doing anything right?

Focus on Ethics

8. Is it ethical to mask your true emotions in order to get along with others? Is honesty in a relationship always the best policy? Explain your response.

9. When a conflict arises between two people, are certain types of power more ethical to draw on than others? Explain your answer, describing conditions that would justify the use of certain types of power.

10. Are there situations in which you should *not* assert your point of view? Provide an example to support your answer.

For Your Journal

1. Analyze several recent conversations in which you were trying to convince someone to do something. Discuss the types of power you used in your efforts.

2. Consider a recent conflict you have had with someone. Determine whether it was a pseudo-, simple, or ego conflict. Describe the strategies you used to manage the conflict. Now that you have read this chapter, discuss the other strategies you could have used to help manage the disagreement.

3. Identify a current or recent conflict you are having or have had with a friend or acquaintance. Use the problem-solving steps presented in this chapter to seek a solution to the problem that is creating the conflict. Define the problem: Identify the issues. Analyze the problem: What are the causes, symptoms, effects, and obstacles that keep you from achieving your goal? Determine your goal: What do you want? What does your partner want? Generate many possible solutions to the problem. Finally, select the solution(s) that would permit each person to achieve his or her goal.

4. Briefly describe a conflict during which you did not do a good job of managing your emotions—that is, one in which you became angry and upset and lost your cool. Respond to the following questions: Why did you lose control of your emotions? If you could go back in time, what would you do differently to better manage your emotions before and during the conflict? Consider incorporating some of the suggestions discussed in this chapter.

Learning with Others

1. Win as Much as You Can[40]

   This activity is designed to explore the effects of trust and conflict on communication. You will be paired with a partner. There will be four partner teams working in a cluster.

4 Xs: Lose $1 each
3 Xs: Win $1 each 1 Y: Lose $3
2 Xs: Win $2 each 2 Ys: Lose $2 each
1 X: Win $3
3 Ys: Lose $1 each 4 Ys: Win $1 each

   Directions: Your instructor will provide detailed instructions for playing this game. For ten successive rounds, you and your partner will choose either an X or a Y. Your instructor will tell all partner teams to reveal their choices at the same time. Each round's payoff will depend on the decision made by others in your cluster. For example, according to the scoring chart shown above, if all four partner teams mark X for round one of this game, each partner team loses $1. You are to confer with your partner on each round to make a joint decision. Before rounds 5, 8, and 10, your instructor will permit you to confer with the other pairs in your cluster. Keep track of your choices and winnings on the following score sheet. When you finish the game, compare your cluster's results with those of others. Discuss the factors that affected your balances. There are three key rules:

   1. Do not confer with the other members of your cluster unless you are given specific permission to do so. This applies to nonverbal and verbal communication.

   2. Each pair must agree on a single choice for each round.

   3. Make sure that the other members of your cluster do not know your pair's choice until you are instructed to reveal it.

Round	Time Allowed	Confer with	Choice	$ Won	$ Lost	$ Balance	
1	2 min.	Partner	_____	_____	_____	_____	
2	1 min.	Partner	_____	_____	_____	_____	
3	1 min.	Partner	_____	_____	_____	_____	
4	1 min.	Partner	_____	_____	_____	_____	
5	3 min.	Cluster					Bonus Round:
	1 min.	Partner	_____	_____	_____	_____	Pay × 3
6	1 min.	Partner	_____	_____	_____	_____	
7	1 min.	Partner	_____	_____	_____	_____	
8	3 min.	Cluster					
	1 min.	Partner	_____	_____	_____	_____	Pay × 5
9	1 min.	Partner	_____	_____	_____	_____	
10	3 min.	Cluster					
	1 min.	Partner	_____	_____	_____	_____	Pay × 10

2. Agree/Disagree Statements About Conflict

Read each statement once and mark whether you agree (A) or disagree (D) with it. Take five or six minutes to do this.

_____ 1. Most people find an argument interesting and exciting.

_____ 2. In most conflicts someone must win and someone must lose. That's the way conflict is.

_____ 3. The best way to handle a conflict is simply to let everyone cool off.

_____ 4. Most people get upset at a person who disagrees with them.

_____ 5. If people spend enough time together, they will find something to disagree about and will eventually become upset with each other.

_____ 6. Conflicts can be solved if people just take the time to listen to one another.

_____ 7. If you disagree with someone, it is usually better to keep quiet than to express your personal difference of opinion.

_____ 8. To compromise is to take the easy way out of conflict.

_____ 9. Some people produce more conflict and tension than others. These people should be restricted from working with others.

After you have marked the preceding statements, break up into small groups and try to agree or disagree unanimously with each statement. Especially try to find reasons for differences of opinion. If your group cannot reach agreement or disagreement, you may change the wording in any statement to promote consensus. Assign one group member to observe your group interactions. After your group has attempted to reach consensus, the observer should report how effectively the group used the guidelines suggested in this chapter.

Part Three

Interpersonal Communication In Relationships

The next three chapters focus specifically on interpersonal communication within the context of relationships. Interpersonal communication is examined in terms of how it can be used to initiate, develop, maintain, and terminate relationships with other people. In the previous chapters you have learned about some of the fundamental skills of interpersonal communication; now you will see them applied within the context of relationships. Chapter 9 introduces you to some of the qualities that affect your relationships, such as trust, self-disclosure, attraction, intimacy, and power; we also present a model of relational development and discuss the forces that move you through relationships. Chapter 10 presents communication skills and principles that you can apply to managing your relationships. Chapter 11, our final chapter, applies interpersonal communication principles and skills to our interactions with family and co-workers and in computer mediated relationships.

chapter 9

Understanding Interpersonal Relationships

After you study this chapter

you should be able to ...

1. Explain how relationships are systems.

2. Differentiate between relationships of choice and circumstance.

3. Explain how trust and self-disclosure relate to relational development.

4. Describe the elements that contribute to interpersonal attraction.

5. Describe the patterns of power in relationships and the types of power.

6. Explain the stages of relational escalation and de-escalation.

7. Describe two theories that explain how relationships develop.

● An Interpersonal Relationship as a System and a Process

● Relationships of Circumstance and Relationships of Choice

● Interpersonal Trust and Self-Disclosure in Relationships

● Attraction and Intimacy in Relationships

● Interpersonal Power in Relationships

● Stages of Interpersonal Relationships

● Interpersonal Relationship Development Theories

You can hardly make a friend in a
year, but you can lose one in an hour.

CHINESE PROVERB

Pat: Hi, aren't you in my communication course?

Chris: Oh, yeah, I've seen you across the room.

Pat: What do you think about the course so far?

Chris: It's okay but I feel a little intimidated by some of the class activities.

Pat: I know what you mean. It gets kind of scary to talk about yourself in front of everyone else.

Chris: Yeah. Plus some of the stuff you hear. I was paired up with this one student the other day who started talking about being arrested last year on a drug charge. It made me feel uncomfortable.

Pat: Really? I bet I know who that is. I don't think you have to worry about it.

Chris: Don't mention that I said anything.

Pat: It's okay. I know that guy, and he just likes to act big.

This interaction between Pat and Chris illustrates the reciprocal nature of interpersonal communication and interpersonal relationships. As you learned in Chapter 1, **interpersonal relationships** are connections that we develop with other people as a direct result of our interpersonal communication with them. The character and quality of interpersonal communication is affected, in turn, by the nature of the relationship.

The conversation between Pat and Chris begins with a casual acknowledgment but quickly proceeds to a higher level of intimacy. Chris confides in Pat. Pat, an other-oriented listener, offers confirmation and support; this response encourages Chris to confide even more. In this brief encounter, Pat and Chris have laid the groundwork for transforming their casual acquaintanceship into an intimate relationship.

In the next three chapters, we explore the dynamic link between interpersonal communication and interpersonal relationships. Drawing from the understanding of communication you have acquired from the first eight chapters, you will learn about the nature of relationships, their development from initiation to termination, and the specific communication skills you can apply to maintaining them.

In this chapter we examine the nature of interpersonal relationships and the principles of how relationships work, building on the descriptions presented in Chapter 1.

An Interpersonal Relationship as a System and a Process

Interpersonal relationships are transactional just like interpersonal communication. This means that each person in a relationship affects the other person. Actually, relationships are affected by a wide range of factors that can best be understood by thinking of a relationship as a system. Systems theory was created originally to explain changes that occur in plant life,[1] but it also has proven valuable in explaining a variety of other phenomena including interpersonal relationships.

A **system** is a set of interconnected elements often described in terms of their relationships as *inputs*, *throughputs* (or *process*), and *outputs*. The most fundamental notion in systems theory is that a change in any system element affects all the other elements. Relationships can be thought of as a kind of system, which means that a change in one element of the relationship affects the other elements. For example, a change in your best friend's mood or behavior affects your mood and behavior as well. The more interdependent we are, the more impact each partner has on the other partner, and the more a change in one affects the other. Married couples can be classified according to how interdependent their relationship is (this is covered in more detail in Chapter 11) and thus how much they are like a system.

One difficulty in analyzing a relationship as a system is deciding what elements are part of the system; that is, what are its boundaries. Is your job, your relationship with your father, your boss's mood, or your communication teacher an element of your relationship with your best friend? Certainly each of these can affect you, and thus can affect your relationship. If your communication instructor acts particularly nasty to you in class one day (this is just hypothetical, because we know how great communication instructors are), that might affect how you feel about yourself and

system. A set of interconnected elements in which a change in one element affects all the other elements.

In an intimate, trusting relationship, we can feel safe in telling our deepest secrets to another person. (Peter Cade/Tony Stone Images)

influence your interaction with your best friend. For the purposes of this text, you don't need to worry about deciding what is in and what is out of the system; simply recognize that lots of factors affect your relationships, including ones of which you are unaware.

When one element of a system changes, the other elements also change, to adapt and to maintain balance. From a relational perspective, this might mean that you will counter your roommate's bad mood by attempting to provide comfort or diversion. Chapter 10 suggests a number of ways you can maintain relationships. Essentially, maintaining relationships requires you to develop strategies to counter efforts to escalate or de-escalate the relationships. Suppose you are dating someone but aren't interested in becoming very intimate; however, your partner wants to spend more time with you. What do you do? Your partner's actions represent a change in your relational system that affects you and your behavior. You can either choose to spend more time with this person, or engage in behaviors to avoid that increase.

Systems represent a process in that they are constantly changing, evolving, and are dynamic. As a process, relationships are always moving to a new place, changing, and being redefined. The changes might not be enormous, but because it's a system you change too. Part of the change is simply due to the fact that relationships are ongoing, they exist over a period of time. Existing over the passage of time means that relationships develop a history; they are accumulative. As you interact with a person, you gain a history together that becomes part of the relationship and affects each subsequent interaction. In the movie *When Harry Met Sally*, the two friends seem to initiate a relationship three different times. However, their first interaction has a direct impact on how they behave in their second interaction, and their second interaction affects the third. The accumulative nature of process means we can't undo something that has been done. Harry and Sally can't undo the impact they had on each other in their first interaction. However, this doesn't mean they can't overcome any negative impression they might have formed about each other.

Relationships of Circumstance and Relationships of Choice

In Chapter 1 we defined an **interpersonal relationship** as an ongoing connection with another person that we carry in our minds (and, metaphorically, in our hearts), whether the other person is present or not. These ongoing connections can be formed either because of unintentional circumstances or because of intentional choice. **Relationships of circumstance** form not because we choose them, but simply because our lives overlap with others' in some way. Relationships with family members, teachers, classmates, and coworkers fall into this category. In contrast, when we seek out and intentionally develop relationships, those are **relationships of choice.** These relationships might include friends, lovers, spouses, and counselors. Von Giebel says,

> "It is chance that makes brothers but hearts that make friends."

We act and communicate differently in these two types of relationships because the stakes are different. The effect of the same interpersonal communication behavior on different relationships can be dramatic. If we act in foolish or inappropriate

interpersonal relationship.
A connection you make with other people through interpersonal communication.

relationship of circumstance.
Interpersonal relationship that exists because of the circumstances in which you are born, circumstances in which you work or study, and so on.

relationship of choice.
Interpersonal relationship you choose to initiate, maintain, and terminate.

Whom Do You Trust?

Create a list of names of those people with whom you have ongoing relationships: family members, coworkers, boss, friends, teachers, and so on. For each person on your list, write down the type of trust that characterizes your relationship: trust in ability, trust in regard for your welfare, trust in protecting privileged information, or trust in commitment to the relationship. You can put down more than one type for each person. Next, assign a number from 1 to 10 for the amount of trust you have in each person, with 1 being very little, and 10 being a lot.

Are your rankings consistently high or consistently low? What general observations can you make about how trusting you are of others?

Who Trusts You?

How trustworthy are you? Use the list of names of those whom you trust to protect privileged information and/or maintain a relational commitment. Using the same scale of 1 to 10, write down a number to indicate how much trust you believe the other person has in you.

How do your scores match up with those for "Whom Do You Trust"? What are some of the reasons for the similarities and differences? In what kinds of relationships do you share a high degree of mutual trust? In what kinds is there a large imbalance in the levels of trust?

ways, our friends might end the relationships. If we act the same way within the confines of our family, our relatives may not like us much, but we will still remain family.

Of course, these categories are not mutually exclusive. Relationships of circumstance can also be relationships of choice: Your brother or sister can also be your best friend. You can break off interacting with family members or quit your job to sever your relationships with fellow employees. In addition, the other individual can define and redefine the relationship. Your boss might fire you, a relative might cut you off, or a lover might desert you.

Interpersonal Trust and Self-Disclosure in Relationships

Think about the kind of trust you have in people who are important to you. What does it mean to trust your doctor? Your lover or spouse? Your accountant? More than likely, each of these relationships involves a different kind of trust, as shown in Table 9.1.

Our concern in this text is primarily with the kind of trust that contributes to relational development called interpersonal trust. **Interpersonal trust** is the belief that you can feel safe in disclosing personal information to another person. Establishing trust in a relationship is part of the process that leads to intensifying the

interpersonal trust. Belief that it is safe to disclose personal information to another person.

Table 9.1

Types of Trust

Types of Trust	Explanation	Example
Trust in someone's ability	You believe that the person has the skill, knowledge, will, and ethical standards to do a good job or fulfill some role expectation.	Your accountant
Trust in someone's regard for your welfare	You believe that this person will not cause you harm as you place your health, welfare, resources, and security in his or her hands.	Your doctor
Trust in someone's regard for privileged information	You believe that the person to whom you have disclosed personal information will not use this information against you.	Your counselor or a friend
Trust in someone's relational commitment	You believe that when you disclose personal information, the other will acknowledge your feelings and vulnerability, will not exploit you, and will remain in the relationship.	Your lover or partner

relationship. As relationships develop, people look for trustworthiness from their partners.

As noted in the last *Building Your Skills* activity, a person who is **trustworthy** accepts personal information about you and doesn't exploit it, protects your vulnerabilities, and remains committed to the relationship. But how can you know if your partner is trustworthy? You watch for behaviors that are consistent with this attribute such as not cheating, keeping your secrets, not using information against you that you have shared, maintaining the same level of the relationship even when you disclose negative or threatening information, and displaying trust in you by reciprocating disclosures. Your partner, in turn, expects the same from you. To sustain a close interpersonal relationship, both participants need to exhibit and expect trusting and trustworthy behavior.[2]

As trust builds, so does disclosure of personal information; and the more people self-disclose, the more trust that is built. In Chapter 2 you learned that **self-disclosure** occurs when you purposefully provide information to others about yourself that they would not learn if you did not tell them. Self-disclosure is necessary for relationships to reach intimacy, although simply disclosing information about yourself is no guarantee that your relationship will become intimate.[3]

Self-disclosing is often associated with relational development. In Chapter 2 you read about how self-disclosure relates to your self-concept. You read about how Altman and Taylor's social penetration theory proposes that you move toward intimacy as you increase the breadth and depth of your disclosures. Their model of the self looks like a pie, with the pieces of pie reflecting your breadth and concentric circles representing the depth of information about yourself that you disclose. You have seen several illustrations that represented how relationships differ in terms of the breadth and depth of disclosures. Besides differentiating among relationships, we can examine how self-disclosure changes as a given relationship moves toward intimacy.

trustworthiness. Being capable of being trusted to accept personal information without exploiting it, support vulnerabilities, and remain in a relationship.

self-disclosure. Providing information about yourself that other people would not learn if you did not tell them.

As we develop a relationship we reveal more of ourselves, removing the masks that we routinely use with strangers. (Sandra Rice)

As relationships move toward intimacy, they typically include periods of high self-disclosure early in the relationship. However, the *amount* of information that is disclosed decreases as the relationship becomes more and more intimate. In other words, there is generally more self-disclosing activity earlier in a relationship than later. As a relationship proceeds, we begin sharing low-risk information fairly rapidly, move on to share higher-risk information, and then finally, to share our most personal disclosures. The more intimate the relationship becomes, the more intimate the information that is disclosed. The sculpture in the photo represents the way we reveal ourselves when we are with close friends. Holding back from sharing intimate information signals a reluctance to escalate the relationship. The amount of information that we have to share about ourselves is finite, so we slow down as we have less left to disclose.

Graph A in Figure 9.1 illustrates a typical disclosure pattern over the course of a long and intimate relationship. The peaks and valleys represent periods of variable disclosure. Note that most of the disclosure takes place in the beginning of the relationship. Not all relationships progress this way, however. The relationship in graph B represents two individuals who started to get to know each other but were interrupted before they became close friends. They might have stopped because of some conflict, indecisiveness about pursuing the relationship, or external circumstances that limited opportunities for interacting. When the disclosure resumed, it became more intense. Graph C represents two individuals who probably knew each other as acquaintances for some time but never really had the opportunity or inclination to self-disclose. Once they did begin to escalate the relationship, however, there was a steep rise in self-disclosure. This graph might represent two coworkers who eventually start dating, or two students who have shared a class or two together before striking up a friendship.

Generally, a dramatic increase or decrease in self-disclosure reflects some significant change in the relationship. Even long-term relationships have significant increases and decreases in disclosure that signify changes. Before the birth of a first

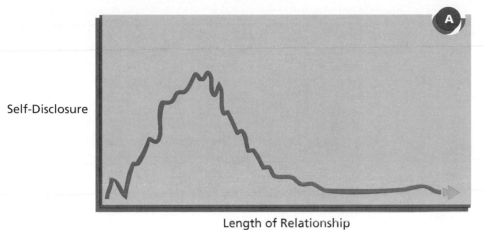

A long and intimate relationship

Self-Disclosure

Length of Relationship

Two individuals who started to get to know each other, but were interrupted before finally becoming friends.

Self-Disclosure

Length of Relationship

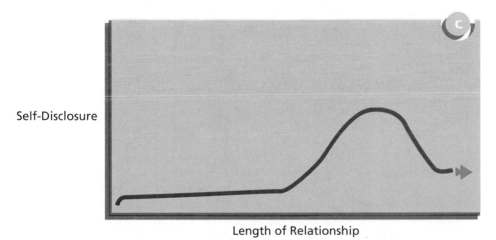

Two individuals who knew each other as acquaintances before the relationship started to escalate.

Self-Disclosure

Length of Relationship

Figure 9.1
Self-Disclosure and
Relational Development

Self-Disclosure Patterns

Think about two of your current relationships and draw a graph like those in Figure 9.1 to show how the self-disclosure has progressed in each of them. How do the patterns compare? What do the differences or similarities reflect about the two relationships? What caused the peaks and valleys? Were there times when you or your partner tried to increase the rate of self-disclosure, and the other person rejected that attempt? What happened?

child, for example, both parents might disclose their fears and expectations about child rearing, and the information might have a profound effect on the relationship.

Interpersonal relationships cannot achieve intimacy without self-disclosure. Without true self-disclosure, we form only superficial relationships. You can confirm another person's self-concept, and have your self-concept confirmed, only if both you and your partner have revealed yourselves to each other.

Attraction and Intimacy in Relationships

In addition to the development of trust in interpersonal relationships, people also develop feelings of attraction and liking toward the other person. Attraction exists whenever you feel a positive regard for another person, or when you like someone; however, the intensity or strength of that attraction varies from relationship to relationship. Think about your feelings or liking for those people you regard as casual friends, and those you regard as best friends. You like your best friends more—you have greater attraction toward your best friends. There is a strong correlation between the level of intimacy in a relationship, and level of attraction. Feelings of attraction continually change as relationships change.

People are often led to initiate relationships because of some preliminary attraction toward another person; as the relationship becomes more intimate, so do the feelings of attraction. **Interpersonal attraction** is the degree to which you

interpersonal attraction.
Degree to which you desire to form or maintain an interpersonal relationship.

Dating Customs Around the World

The description of relational escalation described in this chapter describes the general pattern within the United States; however, the development of relationships varies from culture to culture. The following list describes some of the dating behaviors from cultures throughout the world.

These are some of the ways teens date in other countries of the world.

Afghanistan
Dating is rare because most marriages are arranged by parents, and schools are separate for boys and girls. Opportunities to meet are rare. Girls have a 7 P.M. curfew, wheareas boys have an 11 P.M. curfew.

Australia
Most teens go out in large groups and don't pair off until they are 18 or 19 years old. Girls often ask boys out, and pay for the date, too. Couples often go to dinner parties, barbecues, or the beach.

Central and South America
Dating is not allowed until the age of 15. When of age, most boys and girls date in large groups, going out together to weekend dance parties.

When not dancing, teens gather at local clubs to eat and talk.

Europe
Dating is usually a group event. In Finland, as many as thirty teens may attend a movie together. Slumber parties are common in Italy and Switzerland, where teens gather for parties at a home and sleep there when the party is over.

In Spain teens join a *pandilla,* a club or a group of friends with the same interests, such as cycling or hiking. Dating is done one-to-one, and both girls and boys ask each other out and split the cost of the evening's entertainment.

In Russia dates take place at dances or at clubs where teens eat or chat with friends. In small towns, teens meet in the streets downtown or gather around a fountain.

Iran
It is against the law to date. Teens are separated until they are of marrying age; then their families introduce them to each other and sometimes a courtship follows.

Japan and Korea
Most high school students don't date or go to parties, but spend their time studying instead. Dating begins in college, when only boys do the asking and pay for the dates.

Source: "Dating Customs Around the World." FactMonster.com. © 2000 The Learning Network Inc. *http://www.factmonster.com/ipka/A0767654.html* (Sept. 26, 2000).

In Russian small towns, teens often meet in the streets downtown to socialize together. How does this compare with your experiences? (Jeff Greenberg/PhotoEdit)

want to form or maintain an interpersonal relationship. As you move closer to intimacy, that desire increases. In everyday usage, intimacy is often associated with sexual activity, however, interpersonal intimacy has a broader meaning that is generally independent of sexual intimacy. **Interpersonal intimacy** is a quality of a relationship represented by the degree to which each person's sense of self is confirmed and accepted by their partner; in essence, it means being able to be yourself and still be accepted by your partner. You can measure the intimacy of a

interpersonal intimacy.
Quality of a relationship represented by the degree to which a person's sense of self is accepted and confirmed by another person.

relationship by the extent to which other people let you know that they see you the same way you see yourself while expressing positive feelings toward you. In essence, they love you in spite of your flaws and you don't have to hide those flaws from them.

One of the reasons this text includes a chapter on self is because the self is inextricably linked to intimate relationships. We depend on intimate relationships to provide us information about ourselves (as exemplified in the Johari window) and to bolster our self-confidence. The more intimate the relationship, the more we depend upon others for acceptance and confirmation of our self-image.[4] During periods when we might not have very intimate relationships, it is sometimes hard to maintain a strong positive self-image. Research confirms that having strong social support networks is related to subjective well-being.[5]

By now you have probably recognized the interactive nature of the qualities of interpersonal relationships about which you have been reading. A person becomes attracted to someone, and that can lead to interacting and developing trust, and that can lead to greater self-disclosing and attraction, and that can lead to intimacy. As relationships move toward greater intimacy, a number of changes occur in our communication and behaviors toward our partners (you'll read more about relationship stages later in this chapter). We directly and indirectly communicate our sense of intimacy through our words and actions. We might tell another person how we feel about him or her and how much we value the relationship. We might also use a variety of nonverbal cues, such as close physical proximity, eye contact, words of endearment, tone of voice, physical contact, and the amount of time we commit to the interacting.

Short-Term Initial Attraction and Long-Term Maintenance Attraction

Interpersonal attraction occurs in the early stages of relational development as short-term initial attraction, and in the later stages of relational development as long-term maintenance attraction. You can understand the difference between the two by looking at your own relationships. Think of the dozens of people whom you initially found attractive but with whom you never developed an intimate relationship. **Short-term initial attraction** is the degree to which we sense a *potential* for developing an interpersonal relationship. For instance, you might find one of your classmates to be physically attractive, but never move to introduce yourself. The information you gather in your first interaction with someone can also generate a short-term initial attraction for a relationship, which you may or may not pursue, depending upon the circumstances. **Long-term maintenance attraction,** in contrast, is the type that sustains relationships like your best friendships. It refers to a level of liking or positive feeling that motivates us to maintain or escalate a relationship. Short-term attraction gives way to long-term attraction as a relationship develops through the stages presented later in this chapter.

Think about your best friend. How did that relationship start? Perhaps it was because he or she was physically attractive, or perhaps you observed your friend laughing and joking with others and found that quality attractive. Why are you still friends with this person? Rarely (except in some movies or TV shows) do we commit to, and maintain, a long-term intimate relationship such as marriage or enduring friendship solely because we find another person physically attractive.[6] Perhaps you have discovered that you and your friend have a lot in common, or that you

short-term initial attraction. Degree to which you sense a potential for an interpersonal relationship.

long-term maintenance attraction. A liking or positive feeling that motivates you to sustain a relationship.

complement each other's personalities. For instance, your friend's calm, even disposition might balance your fiery temper.

Elements of Interpersonal Attraction

Why do you feel attracted to some people and not to others? The explanations are complex, but researchers have identified seven elements that influence our feelings of attraction. As you read about them, try to analyze your own feelings about people you find attractive.

Physical Attraction

The degree to which you find another person's physical appearance appealing represents your **physical attraction** to him or her. That appeal might be based on size, height, clothing, hairstyle, makeup, jewelry, vocal qualities, gestures, and so forth. The old adage "Beauty is in the eye of the beholder" is particularly true in terms of explaining physical attraction. Each culture has its own definition of the physical ideal, which it teaches and perpetuates. In the United States, for instance, advertisements and TV programs promote an ideal of slenderness for both males and females. This certainly contributes to the American fixation on losing weight and staying fit. However, in some cultures, and at various times throughout history, physical attractiveness was synonymous with bulkiness.

Physical attractiveness acts as a convenient filter to reduce relationship possibilities.[7] In general, people tend to seek out individuals who represent the same level of physical attractiveness as themselves. Suppose you are really into physical conditioning and have a personal philosophy about good eating habits, exercising, avoiding drugs, and not smoking. You will probably seek out and attract a physically fit person to be your partner. To a certain degree, the physical image a person presents can reflect more substantive qualities. For example, there is a good possibility that a physically fit individual's philosophy about eating and exercise would be similar to yours. That similarity might serve as the basis for a long-term maintenance attraction. As you learned in Chapter 3, people use superficial information to make inferences about personality with varying degrees of accuracy, but whether they decide to escalate a relationship depends on what happens in the initial interaction and subsequent interactions.

physical attraction. The degree to which you find another person's physical appearance appealing.

Credibility, Competence, and Charisma

Most of us are also attracted to individuals who seem competent and credible. We like those who are sure of themselves, but not full of themselves. We assume they are competent if they seem skilled, knowledgeable, and experienced. We find people credible if they display a blend of enthusiasm, trustworthiness, competence, and power. Competence, credibility, and sometimes physical attractiveness are all important elements in the composite quality called *charisma*, which inspires strong attraction and allegiance. Political and other types of leaders often depend on their charisma to attract supporters who are motivated to form relationships with them and willing to devote themselves to a chosen cause.

Proximity

People are more likely to be attracted to people who are physically close than to those who are farther away. In this class, you are more likely to form relationships with classmates sitting on either side of you than with someone seated at the opposite end of the room. This is partly because physical **proximity** increases communication opportunities. We tend to talk with someone on a casual, offhand basis because he or she is right next to us. We are more likely to talk, and therefore to feel attracted to, neighbors who live right next door than to those who live down the block. Any circumstance that increases the possibilities for interacting is also likely to increase attraction.

In impromptu surveys of students in our classes over the years, your authors have found a high percentage form close friendships with dormitory roommates who were randomly assigned. There is a good chance that two individuals will become good friends simply because they share living accommodations. In one study on atraction, a researcher told pairs of people about each other, describing to each the other's dissimilar attitudes on a particular topic.[8] The participants were then asked to rate their attraction to the other person. All the ratings were low. Then the partners were introduced to one another and allowed to interact. Even when they discussed only the attitude on which they disagreed, they had significantly more attraction for one another. Clearly, the information exchange that communication affords, increases our ability to make an informed decision about pursuing a relationship. In addition, in both of these examples, the interaction was between two college students—two individuals who already have a great deal in common. That commonality is the source of the next form of attraction.

Similarity

In general, we are attracted to people whose personality, values, upbringing, personal experiences, attitudes, and interests are **similar** to ours. We seek them out through shared activities. For example, you may join a folk dance group because you know the members share a dance interest with you. Within the group, you would be especially attracted to those who have a similar sense of humor, who share the same attitudes on certain issues, or who enjoy some of the same additional activities that you do. As we interact, we discover both similarities and differences between ourselves and others. We assess the relative weight of those similarities and differences and arrive at a level of attraction that may change over time as we continue to discover more information.

In the initial stages of a relationship, we try to emphasize positive information about ourselves to create a positive and attractive image. We reveal those aspects of ourselves that we believe we have in common with the other person, and the other person does the same.[9] Think about your initial interactions with strangers; typically, you spend the first few minutes trying to find topics of mutual interest. You discover that the person is from a place near your hometown, has the same musical tastes, likes the same sports, frequents the same restaurants, has been to your favorite campground, has the same attitude about school, has had the same instructor for history class, and on and on. But the depth of this information is limited. You save

proximity. Quality that promotes attraction because of being physically close to another and therefore in a position to communicate easily.

similarity. Quality that promotes attraction because people share comparable personality, values, upbringing, personal experiences, attitudes, and interests.

your revelations about important attitudes and issues for a later stage in the relational development process.[10] Attitude similarity is more likely to be a source of long-term maintenance attraction than of short-term initial attraction.

Complementary Needs

You have heard the adage "Opposites attract." Although we like people with whom we have much in common, most of us wouldn't find it very exciting to be stuck for the rest of our lives with someone who has identical attitudes, needs, values, and interests. Most of us look instead for someone with **complementary needs**; essentially, a matching of needs such that one partner contributes something to the relationship that the other partner needs. As we discussed in Chapter 2, Schutz identified three interpersonal needs that motivate us to form and maintain relationships with others: inclusion, control, and affection.[11] *Inclusion* represents the need to include

complementary needs. A matching of needs such that one partner contributes something to the relationship the other partner needs; one person's weakness is the other person's strength.

building your skills

Are Your Needs Complementary?

Evaluate your level of interpersonal needs for each of the following by putting your first initial along the rating scale.

1. How much do you like to include others in the activities you do?
   Very little 1   2   3   4   5   6   7   8   9   10 A great deal

2. How much do you like to be included by others when they are involved in activities?
   Very little 1——2——3——4——5——6——7——8——9——10 A great deal

3. How much do you like to take responsibility for decision making?
   Very little 1——2——3——4——5——6——7——8——9——10 A great deal

4. How much do you like to let others make decisions for you?
   Very little 1——2——3——4——5——6——7——8——9——10 A great deal

5. How much do you feel a need to be accepted and loved by others?
   Very little 1——2——3——4——5——6——7——8——9——10 A great deal

6. How much do you feel a need to accept others and to give love to others?
   Very little 1——2——3——4——5——6——7——8——9——10 A great deal

Now think of two close friends. Go back and place their first initials along each rating scale to indicate how much each item applies to them. Or ask your friends to initial the scale for themselves. Compare your ratings with those of your friends. Are there areas where you are similar? Complementary? Are there differences that cause difficulties in the relationship—for example, you both want to make decisions rather than accept others' decisions?

others in our activities, or to be included in theirs. *Control* represents the need to make decisions and take responsibility, or the willingness to accept others' decision making. *Affection* represents the need to be loved and accepted by others, or the willingness to give love and acceptance to others.

If you have a high need to control and make decisions, and little respect for others' decision making, you will be more compatible with someone who does not have similar needs—someone who wants others to make decisions for him or her. In essence, we can view pairs of individuals as a team in which both sides complement the other side's weaknesses. If you're not very good at keeping track of your bills and balancing your checkbook, you might pair up with someone who is good at maintaining a budget to create a strong personal finance team. In reality, there are no "perfect" matches, only degrees of compatibility relative to needs.

Relationship Potential

We need interpersonal relationships to confirm our self-image. **Predicted outcome value theory** claims that we assess the potential for any given relationship to meet this relational need and then weigh that assessment against the potential costs.[12] We are attracted to others with whom a relationship may yield a high outcome value (the rewards might exceed the costs). Over time, our assessments may change. In the movie *When Harry Met Sally,* for example, the main characters both thought initially that their relationship had little potential for meeting their needs. Over time, Harry and Sally developed a friendship that did meet certain needs. At that point they both thought the relationship had gone as far as it could. In the end, however, they discovered that they could have a more intimate relationship with a high outcome value.

Like Harry and Sally, most of us begin predicting outcome values in initial interactions and continually modify our predictions as we learn more and more about the other person. We pursue attractions beyond the initial interaction stage if we think they can yield positive outcomes, and generally avoid or terminate relationships for which we predict negative outcomes.[13]

Reciprocation of Liking

Reciprocation of liking simply means that we like people who like us. One way to get other people to reciprocate is to show that we like them. However, in initial interactions we are often reluctant to let other people know that we are attracted to them. We may hold back from showing our interest because we fear rejection or fear that we may give the other person a certain amount of power over us.

A study conducted by one of your authors and a colleague found that we often underestimate how much a new acquaintance is attracted to us.[14] Pairs of male and female college students interacted for the first time and then indicated their level of attraction for their partner, as well as their perception of how attracted their partner was to them. Most of the students significantly underestimated the amount of attraction the other person felt for them. It is unclear whether we underestimate because we don't have much confidence that others will like us as much as we like them, or because we, as Americans, in general do not communicate effectively our level of attraction for others. Even in long-term relationships, people sometimes repress their continued attraction for their friends or mates. As you interact with new acquaintances, keep in mind that they probably are more attracted to you than you realize, so you might want to adapt your decision making accordingly.

relationship potential (predicted outcome value theory). People are most attracted to those relationships that potentially have greater rewards or benefits than costs.

reciprocation of liking. We like people who like us.

Interpersonal Power in Relationships

As relationships move toward intimacy, people often struggle with issues of who's calling the shots in the relationship, who's making the decisions and who's in control. These are issues of power, and they play a significant role in the development and health of a relationship. Power and control have been defined in a variety of ways,[15] but for our purposes **interpersonal power** means the ability to influence another person in the direction you desire—to get another person to do what you want. Distributing power in a relationship requires a lot of subtle and not so subtle negotiation and agreement. The ability to successfully resolve power issues is a major factor in achieving and maintaining intimate relationships.

Power is present in each interpersonal interaction, and generally power is processed rather smoothly. For the power management to go smoothly, both parties must be willing to accept the way power is being played out. For example, you go into an office, approach the receptionist, and ask, "May I see Dr. Washington?" Initially, you are attempting to exert a small degree of power, because you initiated the interaction. By asking a question, you are also attempting to influence the receptionist. What if the receptionist looks up at you and doesn't reply? At that point, the receptionist might be resisting your attempt at influence. You've probably been in situations where someone has asked you a question and you have refused to answer. This usually results in an aggravated encounter that reflects some degree of power struggle.

Types of Power Relationships

In the discussion of attraction, you read about how one person who likes to make decisions would make a good partner with another person who likes other people to make decisions for him or her. This complementarity of needs is one form of attraction. This reflects one of the three patterns that characterize relationship power. In **complementary relationships,** one partner usually dominates and the other usually submits: One likes to talk, the other to listen; one likes to lead, the other to follow. You might find such a relationship undesirable to your own interests, but for many people such a relationship works to the satisfaction of both partners.

What happens when both partners want to call the shots, when both want to make the decision? Having both partners behaving in similar ways creates **symmetric relationships.**[16] Sometimes both partners want to dominate, and sometimes both want to be submissive. A **competitive symmetric relationship** exists when both partners are vying for control or dominance over the other person. For example, each might try to control which TV program they watch, or might insist on participating in every spending decision. Competition in such relationships often increases the amount of conflict and negotiation associated with decision making. At times neither partner wants to take control or make a decision, and this creates a **submissive symmetric relationship.** The following is an example of submissive symmetry (does it sound familiar to you?):

interpersonal power. Ability in a personal relationship to influence another person in the direction that person desires.

complementary relationship. Relationship in which the power is represented by one partner dominating and the other person submitting.

symmetric relationship. Relationship in which the power is represented by both partners attempting to have the same level of power.

competitive symmetric relationship. Relationship in which both partners vie for control or dominance of the other.

submissive symmetric relationship. Relationship in which neither partner wants to take control or make decisions.

Bea: What movie do you want to rent?

Vic: Oh, I don't care. You decide.

Bea: No, you decide. I don't care either.

Most relationships, however, are neither purely complementary nor purely symmetrical; they are parallel. **Parallel relationships** involve a shifting back and forth of the power between the partners depending on the situation. For example, if Janene knows more about computers than her husband, Justin, then he might defer to her the decision about what new computer to purchase. However, Janene might defer to her husband to plan their upcoming vacation because of his travel-planning

parallel relationship. Relationship in which power shifts back and forth between the partners depending on the situation.

Power in Your Relationships

Think of one of your close relationships as you answer the following questions. Try this with several relationships such as your best friend, romantic partner, sibling, or parent.

Cp1.	I let my partner make most decisions.	Yes	No
Cp2.	I'm comfortable with the decisions my partner makes about our relationship.	Yes	No
Cp3.	I like how my partner plans our time together.	Yes	No
C1.	I make most of the decisions in the relationship.	Yes	No
C2.	My partner likes that I am the one who makes decisions in our relationships.	Yes	No
C3.	I'm usually the one who decides what we're going to do.	Yes	No
Sc1.	My partner and I both are pretty assertive about what we want.	Yes	No
Sc2.	There are times where both my partner and I want to make the decision.	Yes	No
Sc3.	We sometimes struggle because each of us wants to decide things.	Yes	No
Ss1.	Usually neither my partner nor I want to make the decision.	Yes	No
Ss2.	We get stuck sometimes because neither of us wants to decide.	Yes	No
Ss3.	Neither of us wants to be pushy, so we tend to be laid-back about decisions.	Yes	No
P1.	Sometimes I make decisions, and sometimes my partner makes them.	Yes	No
P2.	We each have areas where we defer to the other person's judgment.	Yes	No
P3.	If I can't decide something my partner will, and vice versa.	Yes	No

Look at your scoring for the five sets of items. Which ones have the most "Yes" responses? The "Cp" set reflects a complementary relationship in which your partner dominates as compared to the "C" set in which you are the dominant member. The "Sc" items reflect a symmetric relationship in which you and your partner compete for control. The "Ss" items cover a more submissive style of symmetric relationship. The "P" items are typical of the statements made in relationships that handle power within a parallel relationship.

experience. Establishing who has power in various situations is a point of contention in developing relationships and takes time for the parties involved to resolve. Power in any relationship changes as individuals change. As Justin gains computer savvy, he might want more say in purchasing a new system. Having knowledge or expertise is one way we hold power over another person.

Types of Power

Why does one person in a relationship have power over the other? There are many explanations; one that works well identifies five sources of power: legitimate (or position power), referent power, expert power, reward power, and coercive power.[17]

Legitimate power is power that comes because of respect for a position that another person holds. Teachers, parents, law officers, store managers, and company presidents all have power because of the position they hold relative to other people. When a police officer tells you to pull off to the side of the road you respond to this enactment of power by obeying the officer's command.

Referent power is power that comes from our attraction to another person, or the charisma a person possesses. We let people we like influence us. We change our behavior to meet their demands or desires because we are attracted to them.

Expert power is based on the influence derived from a person's knowledge and experience. We convey power on those who know more than we do, or have some expertise we don't possess. This knowledge can even include knowledge about how to manage a relationship effectively. We grant power to partners who have more experience in relationships. There were frequent episodes of the *Seinfeld* TV series in which the characters defer to the expertise of their friends when it came to how to handle various relational crisis.

Reward power is based on another person's ability to satisfy your needs. There are obvious rewards, such as money and gifts, but most rewards are more interpersonal in nature. In Chapter 2 we talked about the interpersonal needs of control, affection, and inclusion. The degree to which another person is able to satisfy these needs gives them a certain power. For example, those people who are able to help us meet your need to be included in social activities have power over you. You will do what they ask if you see that your need will continue to be met. Reward power is probably the most common form of power in interpersonal relationships. Withholding rewards is actually a form of punishment, or what is called coercive power.

Coercive power involves the use of sanctions or punishment to influence others. Sanctions include holding back or removing rewards. If you have a high need for physical affection, your partner might threaten to hold back that affection if you do not comply with a given request. You might threaten to end the relationship as a sanctioned form of power in order to accomplish a given goal. Punishment involves imposing something on another person that he or she does not want. Coercive power exists in relationships when one partner has the ability to impose the sanction or punishment on another. Your parents had the power to take away your allowance when you were younger, and therefore you did the chores they requested. However, once you have your own source of income, your parents no longer have this source of power over you.

legitimate power. Type of power that comes from respect for a position that another person holds.

referent power. Type of power that comes from our attraction to another person, or the charisma a person possesses.

expert power. Type of power based on a person's knowledge and experience.

reward power. Type of power based on a person's ability to satisfy our needs.

coercive power. Type of power based on the use of sanctions or punishments to influence others.

recap   Types of Power

Type	Definition	Examples
Legitimate power	Comes because of respect for a position that another person holds	Teachers, parents, officials, law officers, clergy
Referent power	Comes from our attraction to another person, or the charisma a person holds	Professional athletes, rock stars, evangelists, cult leaders
Expert power	Derives from a person's knowledge or experience	Scientists, consultants, senior members of an organization
Reward power	Comes from another person's ability to satisfy our needs	Bosses (giving money), friends (giving love or companionship)
Coercive power	Stems from the use of sanctions or punishment to influence others	Boss (threatening to fire), parent (taking away privileges)

Stages of Interpersonal Relationships

Although researchers use different terms and different numbers of stages, all agree that **relational development** does proceed in discernible stages. Understanding these stages is important to your studies because interpersonal communication is affected by the stage of the relationship. Individuals in an intimate stage discuss topics and display nonverbal behaviors that do not appear in the early stages of a relationship. We use interpersonal communication to move a relationship forward as we proceed from being strangers to acquaintances to friends. Outsiders usually can tell what stage a relationship is in by observing the interpersonal communication.

You can think of the stages, from first meeting to intimacy, as the floors in a high rise. Relational development is like an elevator that stops at every floor. As you get to each floor, you might get off and wander around for a while before taking the elevator to the next floor (see Figure 9.2). Each time you get on, you don't know how many floors up the elevator will take you, or how long you will stay at any given floor. In fact, sometimes you never get back on the elevator, electing instead to stay at a particular stage of relational development. But, if you fall head over heels in love, you might want to move quickly from floor to floor toward intimacy. Part of the time you share this elevator with your partner, and the two of you make decisions about how high you will ride the elevator, how long to stay at each floor, and when and whether to ride the down elevator.

Just as there are lights on a panel to let you know the elevator has moved from one floor to another, markers signal a move from one stage to another. These markers are called turning points. **Turning points** are specific events or interactions that are associated with positive or negative changes in a relationship.[18] A first meeting, first date, first kiss, first sex, saying "I love you" for the first time, meeting

relational development. Process of moving from one stage to another as a relationship moves toward or away from greater intimacy.

turning point. Specific event or interaction associated with positive or negative changes in a relationship.

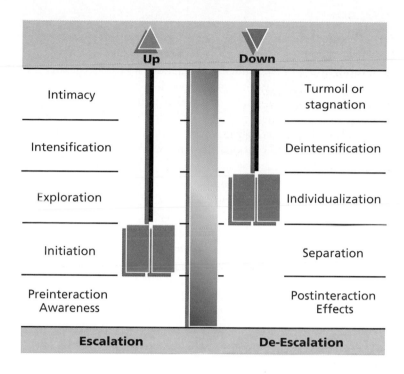

Figure 9.2
Model of Relational Stages

a partner's family, going away together somewhere, making up after a conflict, moving in together, providing help in a crisis, or providing a favor or gift might all be turning points that indicate a relationship is moving forward. A pair of researchers found that 55 percent of the time, these turning points inspired a discussion about the nature of the relationship.[19] Such discussion helps the partners reach mutual agreement about the definition of the relationship.

e-connection
Relationship Style

The development of relationships is highly dependent on your attitude and approach to relationships. According to attachment theory, people differ in terms of their general orientation toward intimate relationships. The theory derived from the study of how infants connected with their caregivers. Current theory identifies four relationship styles: *secure* (is comfortable in relationships and doesn't fear abandonment), *preoccupied* (wants relationships but fears scaring others away, *dismissing* (avoids relationships as a way of maintaining self-reliance and independence), and *fearful* (avoids relationships because of a fear of being hurt). The following Web site allows you to take a self-scoring assessment of your relationship style.

http://psyweb.ucdavis.edu/Shaver/fraley/CRQ2.htm

Relational Escalation

Relational escalation is the movement of a relationship toward greater intimacy. This movement usually goes through a series of discernible stages: preinteraction awareness, initiation, exploration, intensification, and intimacy. Movement upward from one stage to another represents an increase in the amount of intimacy that exists between two people. Each stage is accompanied by specific communication patterns, turning points, and relational expectations.

Preinteraction Awareness

As you can see in the model in Figure 9.2, the first floor is the *preinteraction awareness stage.* Here, you might observe someone or even talk with others about him or her without having any direct interaction. Gaining information about others without directly interacting with them is a *passive strategy* for acquiring knowledge.[20] Through your passive observations, you form an initial impression. You might not move beyond the preinteraction awareness stage if that impression is not favorable or the circumstances aren't right.

Initiation

If you are attracted to the other person and the circumstances are right, you might proceed to the *initiation stage,* one of the first turning points in a relationship. In this stage, the interaction typically is routine; you might each respond to a large number of standard questions during the first four minutes of conversation,[21] sticking to safe and superficial topics, and presenting a "public self" to the other person. Your partner is now riding on the elevator with you, and any decision about whether the elevator should go up, down, or nowhere is a mutual one for the rest of the ride. You can never return to the initiation stage. Once you make an initial contact, you have created a relational history on which you will continue to build.

Exploration

If you decide to go to the next floor, *exploration,* you will begin to share more in-depth information about yourselves. But you will have little physical contact, maintain your social distance, and limit the amount of time you spend together. This stage can occur in conjunction with the initiation stage.

Intensification

If you proceed to the *intensification stage,* you will start to depend on each other for self-confirmation and engage in more risky self-disclosure. You will spend more time together, increase the variety of activities you share, adopt a more personal physical distance, engage in more physical contact, and personalize your language. Also, you may discuss and redefine the relationship often in this stage, perhaps putting a turning-point label on yourselves, such as "going steady," "good buddies," or "best friends." Other turning points associated with this stage include decisions to date each other exclusively, to become roommates, or to spend time with each other's families.

Intimacy

The top floor in the building is the *intimacy stage.* In this stage the two partners turn to each other for confirmation and acceptance of their self-concept. Their

relational escalation. Upward movement of a relationship toward intimacy through five stages: preinteraction awareness, initiation, exploration, intensification, and intimacy.

As couples proceed from exploration to intensification, they have more physical contact and begin sharing more activities and confidences. Does it seem as if this couple is heading into the intensification stage? (Sandra Rice)

communication is highly personalized and synchronized. They talk about anything and everything. There is a free flow of information and self-disclosure. There is a commitment to maintaining the relationship that might even be formalized through marriage or some other agreement. The partners share an understanding

Graphing Your Relationship Changes

Think of an interpersonal relationship that you have had for at least a year. On the graph at right, plot the development of that relationship from stage to stage, reflecting the relative amount of time you spent in each stage. You can also indicate whether you backed up to a previous stage at any point.

If possible, have your relational partner fill out a similar graph and

compare your perceptions of how the relationship has developed. What differences are there and why?

You also might want to share your graph with those of classmates

to compare how different relationships develop. What can you tell from the graphs about the nature of their relationships?

Intimacy

Intensification

Exploration

Initiation

Preinteraction Awareness

Time

of each other's language and nonverbal cues, and have a great deal of physical contact. They use fewer words to communicate effectively, and they have a clearer definition of their roles and of the relationship. Reaching this stage takes time—time to build trust, time to share personal information, time to observe each other in various situations, and time to build a commitment and emotional bond.

Relational De-Escalation

Relational de-escalation is the movement that occurs when a relationship decreases in intimacy. Our model identifies five stages in this process: turmoil or stagnation, deintensification, individualization, separation, and postinteraction. These stages can be observed when an intimate relationship moves to termination. The process of ending a relationship is not as simple as going down the same elevator you came up on: It is not a reversal of the formation stage.[22] However, relational de-escalation can also involve only one or two of the stages. For example, a relationship might move from being a good friend to a more casual friendship.

Turmoil or Stagnation

When an intimate relationship is not going well, it usually enters either the *turmoil* or *stagnation* stage. Turmoil involves an increase in conflict, as one or both partners tend to find more faults in the other. The definition of the relationship seems to lose its clarity, and mutual acceptance declines. The communication climate is tense and exchanges are difficult.

Stagnation occurs when the relationship loses its vitality and the partners become complacent. Communication and physical contact between the partners decrease; they spend less time together, but do not necessarily fight. Partners in a stagnating relationship tend to go through the motions of an intimate relationship without the commitment; they simply follow their established relational routines.

As with the up elevator, individuals can stop at this point on the down elevator and decide to quit descending. The relationship can remain in turmoil or stagnate for a long time, or the individuals can repair, redefine, or revitalize the relationship and return to intimacy.

Deintensification

If the turmoil or stagnation continues, however, the individuals might move down to the *deintensification stage,* decreasing their interactions; increasing their physical, emotional, and psychological distance; and decreasing their dependence on the other for self-confirmation. They might discuss the definition of their relationship, question its future, and assess each partner's level of satisfaction or dissatisfaction. The relationship can be repaired and the individuals can move back up to intensification and intimacy, but that is more difficult to accomplish now.

Individualization

On the next floor down, the *individualization stage,* the partners tend to define their lives more as individuals and less as a couple. Neither views the other as a partner or significant other anymore. Interactions are limited. The perspective changes from "we" and "us" to "you" and "me," and property is defined in terms of "mine" or "yours" rather than "ours." Both partners turn to others for confirming their self-concepts.

relational de-escalation.
Downward movement of a relationship away from intimacy through five stages: turmoil or stagnation, deintensification, individualization, separation, and postinteraction.

Separation

In the *separation stage,* individuals make an intentional decision to eliminate further interpersonal interaction. If they share custody of children, attend mutual family gatherings, or work in the same office, the nature of their interactions will change. They will divide property, resources, and friends. Early interactions in this stage are often tense and difficult, especially if the relationship has been intimate. For relationships that never went beyond exploration or intensification, however, the negotiation is often relatively painless.

For former intimates, one of the awkward things about separating is their extensive personal knowledge about one another. Their talk is limited to superficial things, although they still know a lot about each other. This tends to make the interactions fairly uncomfortable. Over time, of course, each partner knows less about who the other person has become. For example, even after spending just a few years away from your high school friends, you might have difficulty interacting with them because the knowledge you both share is out of date.

Postinteraction

Although interaction may cease altogether, the effect of the relationship is not over. The relational-stages high rise is like something out of the old TV series, *Twilight Zone*: Once you enter it, you can never leave it. The bottom floor on the down elevator, where you remain, is the *postinteraction stage.* This floor represents the lasting effects the relationship has on your self, and therefore on your other interactions and relationships. Steve Duck claims that in this final stage of terminating relationships we engage in "grave-dressing."[23] We create a public statement for people who ask why we broke up and also come to grips with losing the relationship.

---

considering others

A New Friend a Day Keeps a Cold Away

Fighting a cold? You need a friend—and not just to bring you chicken soup. The more diverse your set of relationships—friends, relatives, co-workers, neighbors—the less likely you are to catch a cold, according to a study.

People with six or more types of relationships fought off colds best after being dosed with a virus, the study of 300 healthy volunteers found. They had less than one-fourth the risk of becoming sick of those who had only one to three types of relationships.

"The notion of 'get a life' applies here," said Sheldon Coehn, professor of psychology at Carnegie Mellon University in Pittsburgh, and lead author of the federally financed study in the current *Journal of the American Medical Association.*

Part of a growing field known as psychoneuroimmunology—or the study of how such things as stress and social support affect the immune system and overall health—the study is being welcomed by specialists as an important contribution.

Other studies have found less depression and lower overall mortality among people with a broad social network or who are experiencing the least stress. But this work is "the first to show that there is a direct tie in terms of a health outcome, by actually infecting people with a cold virus and then asking, 'Did people who get colds differ in terms of social ties?'" said Janice Kiecolt-Glaser, a professor of psychiatry at Ohio State University Medical Center.

While research cannot yet explain how social support affects health, Benson said, "One possibility is that social ties decrease stress, and stress liberates hormones that lower one's resistance."

Source: Des Moines Register, June 25, 1997, p. 1

Sometimes our sense of self gets battered during the final stages of a relationship, and we have to work hard to regain a healthy sense of self.

Of course, we are all aware of people who hop on an express elevator to get out of a relationship, bypassing all the normal stages of decline. One study found that of the various ways to terminate a relationship, abandoned partners most dislike the quick exit without discussion.[24]

Interpersonal Relationship Development Theories

The model of relational stages provides a description of the stages you can expect to experience as you move through interpersonal relationships. However, it doesn't really provide an explanation of what motivates you to move from one stage to another. Think about some of your closer relationships. How did you move from acquaintanceships to being close friends? The earlier description of attraction theories provides a partial answer to this question by offering explanations of what evokes your interest in another person. However, they don't adequately explain why you might stay at one stage, back down from a stage, or move forward to the next. Noted relationship scholar Steve Duck suggests we go through a process of "filtering" in which we apply criteria at each stage of relational development that a potential close friend must pass.[25] In essence, a move from one stage to another toward intimacy means that a person has passed through another, finer screen filter. These screens represent decision points in which we make some assessment of the relationship and decide how we want to proceed. We can either choose to escalate, maintain, or de-escalate the relationship. Two theories reflect the kind of decision making that might be taking place: social exchange theory and dialectical theory (or dialectics).

Social Exchange Theory

social exchange theory. A theory that claims people make decisions on the basis of assessing and comparing the costs and rewards.

immediate costs and rewards. Those costs and rewards that are associated with a relationship at the present moment in time.

forecasted costs and rewards. The costs and rewards that an individual assumes will occur on the basis of projection and prediction.

Social exchange theory is an economic model of human behavior that has been used to explain how people arrive at decisions in a variety of situations. **Social exchange theory** posits that people seek the greatest amount of reward with the least amount of cost. You've probably been in a difficult relationship where you have asked yourself, "Is this relationship really worth it?" What you are asking is whether the rewards you are gaining from the relationship are worth the trouble or expense necessary to sustain the relationship (the costs). Students frequently tell us about breaking up from long-distance relationships because the expense (driving time, telephone calls, missing activities where you live, and so on) ends up being greater than the rewards of the intermittent contact. Fortunately for some, the rewards associated with long-distance relationships remain greater than the costs, and those relationships continue to prosper.

Relationships can be evaluated in terms of immediate, forecasted, and cumulative rewards and costs.[26] **Immediate rewards and costs** occur in a relationship at the present moment in time. You can think about your current relationships and assess their present value. **Forecasted rewards and costs** are based on projection or prediction. We make guesses about the potential or future outlook of a relationship (communication scholar Michael Sunnafrank calls this predicted outcome value)[27] When you meet someone and begin to talk, you go through an initial assessment about whether a relationship with this person would be rewarding. You use forecasting to decide whether to remain in existing relationships during troubled times (costs escalate or rewards deteriorate). However, you don't immediately abandon long-term relationships at the first sign of trouble (low immediate rewards/high immediate costs) if you believe that things will improve (forecasted rewards).

Another reason people remain in ongoing relationships during periods of low immediate rewards has to do with cumulative rewards and costs. **Cumulative rewards and costs** represent the total rewards and costs accrued during the duration of the relationship. Just as with your finances, when you have greater income than expense, you put your extra money in savings. Analogously, you build up a relational savings account of the extra rewards. You can draw on that savings account during times when the relationship is not paying off well. You hold on to a relationship because you have invested a lot in it and have gotten a lot out of it. However, just as your savings account can run out of money, so can cumulative rewards, and at that point you might decide to terminate the relationship.

You can also consider rewards and costs in terms of their magnitude and the ratio. Suppose you have two friends, Kelsey and Moira. Kelsey makes you feel good about yourself, is helpful, and is lots of fun (rewards) but she is very needy and demanding (costs). Moira is lots of fun and helpful, but she is also needy. Which friendship would you pursue more? You might be inclined to pursue the relationship with Kelsey, because she is helpful, fun, and makes you feel good, whereas Moira is only fun and helpful. The magnitude of the rewards is greater with Kelsey than Moira. However, you might pursue a relationship with Moira because that relationship has a better ratio of rewards to costs (two rewards to one cost compared to Kelsey's three rewards to two costs). You might think that further developing a relationship with Moira might result in increased rewards with the same costs. However, relationships seem to have some point where there is maximum return for the investment; that is, a point where no matter how much you invest either the reward does not increase further or the costs increase significantly. Suppose you have a casual friend with whom your only shared interest is movies. Once a week you have a very rewarding visit with this friend about the latest releases. You decide to spend more time with this friend (cost) and find awkward dead spots in the conversation because there isn't really anything else of mutual interest to talk about (reward). In terms of your relationship with Moira, this means that having fun with her and getting her help is the only reward you will gain regardless of how much you invest in the relationship.

Finding that point where you maximize your rewards while minimizing costs is one challenge of relational development. You've probably been confronted with trying to decide whether to date someone whom you regarded as a friend. Your decision was probably a desire to see if you could increase the amount of reward. You or your partner might have been hesitant to change the relationship for fear that you might lose everything (similar to going bankrupt because of a bad investment). Decisions to spend more time with a given individual are usually attempts to garner more rewards; if we find the costs increase as well, we might reduce the time together.

The example of deciding between time with Kelsey or Moira reflects how people apply social exchange principles to relational decision-making by comparing relationships. We can compare a current relationship to previous relationships, ideal

cumulative costs and rewards.
The total costs and rewards accrued during the duration of a relationship.

relationships, and potential relationships.[28] We hate to hear someone tell us, "You're just like my previous boyfriend" or "You're different from my last girlfriend, she was wild." Most of us are sensitive enough not to voice such comparisons, but nonetheless it seems to be a natural thing to do. One way to judge the value of a relationship is in terms of how it stacks up with other relationships you have experienced. You might savor a particular friendship because it is more rewarding than any other relationship you have had.

People seem to construct templates in their minds for what relationships should be like. **Expected costs and rewards** represent expectations and ideals about how rewarding a relationship should be relative to its costs. We have a model of the ideal friend, the ideal lover, the ideal coworker, and so on. We use the expected costs and rewards associated with these ideals to assess current relationships. We might abandon a relationship if we don't think it matches or has the potential to match our ideal. In essence, we set standards or criteria for our relationships by which we assess the desirability of a given relationship. Like Duck's filtering process, ideal images allow you to sort through relationships and focus on those that are closest to or exceed your ideal. The major difficulty associated with such comparisons rests in setting reasonable standards or ideals. For example, some parents adopt a philosophy of never arguing in front of their children. As the children become adults, they may have an expectation that happy marriages are ones that have no conflicts and thus evaluate their own marriages as a failure to reach their ideal. Continual disappointment in the ability to find relationships that measure up to your ideals suggests that you may need to reassess your standards.

Finally, we compare our current relationships to the rewards and costs we forecast for other potential relationships—this is where we leave someone for another person. We reduce our time spent with one friend when we believe we can have a more rewarding relationship with another person. Although we all dislike having someone "dump" us for another person, one way we assess the value of a given relationship is how it compares to other prospects. You choose to spend time with some friends more than others because of how those relationships compare. You try to spend the most time with those relationships that have the best relative outcomes.

All these comparisons work in concert with one another. We compare our current relationships to previous ones, to the ideal, and to potential ones. For example, communication researchers Gerald Miller and Malcolm Parks have proposed that we will move quickly to terminate a relationship if it falls below our expectations and we think we have an opportunity to develop a new relationship that has the potential to exceed all of our expectations.[29]

Dialectical Theory

Dialectical theory looks at the human condition in terms of a set of opposing forces. When applied to interpersonal relationships, we can identify forces pulling us toward intimacy and opposing forces pulling us toward independence. Researcher Leslie Baxter has identified three dialectical tensions that have been widely used in interpersonal research.[30]

Connectedness versus autonomy. We desire to connect with others and to become interdependent at the same time we have a desire to remain autonomous and independent. In one study of married couples, these desires to be connected and autonomous were found to be the most frequently occurring of the dialectical tensions.[31]

expected costs and rewards. The templates we have for how much reward we should get from a given relationship in comparison to its costs.

dialectical theory. A theory that says relational development occurs in conjunction with various tensions that exist in all relationships, particularly connectedness versus autonomy, predictability versus novelty, and openness versus closedness.

Predictability versus novelty (certainty versus uncertainty). Knowing what to expect and being able to predict the world around us helps us reduce the tension that occurs from uncertainty. At the same time, we get bored by constant repetition and routine and therefore are attracted to novelty and the unexpected. This might explain why people relish horror movies where the unexpected jumps out at them. Fright becomes joyful because it meets a need for the unexpected.

Openness versus closedness. We wish we could disclose information to others and to hear those we are attracted to disclose to us. One ideal we seem to have in relationships is the ability to be totally open with our partner. However, we also value our privacy and feel a desire to hold back information. Research conducted by one of your authors has found that the number one way that people adapt content in interactions is to hold back or modify information.[32] This tension was identified in the study of married couples mentioned earlier as the most important of the three tensions, although it did not occur as often as the other two tensions.[33]

According to the dialectical theory, each pair of tensions is present in every relationship but the impact of each polar force changes as a relationship progresses. Movement in relationships can be seen as a shift that occurs in the relative pull of one tension. For example, when you begin developing a new friendship, one issue you have to address is whether you want to give up some of your autonomy (freedom to do your own things) in order to spend time with this other person (connectedness). Notice how this is similar to social exchange theory in that you weigh costs (giving up autonomy) against rewards (becoming connected).

Dialectical theory posits that a tension exists between our desire for predictability and our attraction to the unexpected. (Private Collection/ Christian Pierre/Superstock)

Both forces of autonomy and connectedness can be found even in close relationships.[34] Even though long-married couples have usually settled the issues of interdependence versus independence, dialectical theory asserts (and the research mentioned earlier supports) tension is present from these forces. Generally, such tension diminishes as we become more intimate; however, many an engagement has been called off at the last minute because of the inability of the bride or groom to resolve this tension. This tension represents the challenge faced by individuals forming close relationships who are faced with maintaining their own identities while at the same time, melding their identity with another person.

Movement in relationships can be seen as moments during the developmental process in which some element of tension has been resolved or overcome.[35] For example, during the initial stages of a relationship you are restrained in your self-disclosures (closedness). As long as you remain closed, the relationship can only progress so far. You are confronted with the question of whether or not you should share information and increase the level of intimacy in the relationship. Thus a tension exists until you make your decision. Once you have decided, some of the tension is relieved. Thus if you decide on more openness, the reduction in tension is accompanied by a change in the relationship.

Assessing Dialectical Tensions

Think of three relationships you have; one that is escalating, one that is de-escalating, and one that is stabilized. Evaluate how each of the three sets of tensions is affecting each of these relationships. Compare each relationship in terms of each tension; that is, how do they compare in terms of connectedness/autonomy, predictability/novelty, and openness/closedness? In what ways have changes in these tensions resulted in changes in the relationships?

Summary

As a system, an interpersonal relationship is a set of interconnected elements in which a change in one element affects all the others. The process nature of relationships means they are constantly changing. They can be considered relationships of circumstance when they occur, because surrounding conditions cause you to interact with someone. In contrast, you create relationships of choice when you intentionally seek to establish a relationship you could otherwise avoid.

Several types of trust are exhibited in relationships. Interpersonal trust is the degree to which you feel safe disclosing personal information to another person. Trust is a key element in your willingness to self-disclose. The amount and depth of your self-disclosure varies as relationships develop but is critical if you are to reach an intimate relationship. Intimacy itself varies among relationships and depends on how attracted you are to others. Interpersonal attraction is the degree to which you desire to form or maintain an interpersonal relationship. Within each relationship, interpersonal intimacy is reflected in how much you can be yourself and be accepted by your partner.

Before you interact with a stranger or during your first interactions, you might experience short-term initial attraction, but as a relationship develops you form more long-term maintenance attraction. Elements that influence feelings of attraction include physical appeal, proximity, similarity, complementary needs, relationship potential, reciprocation of liking, as well as credibility, competence, and charisma.

Your ability to influence other people in the direction you desire—interpersonal power—is an important factor in the development and success of relationships. The pattern of power in relationships can either be complementary (one dominates and the other submits), symmetrical (both have the same amount of power, which is competitive when both are strong, or submissive when both are weak), and parallel (changes from situation to situation). Five types of power often found in relationships include legitimate, referent, expert, reward, and coercive.

Specific stages of relationships can be identified as relationships escalate toward intimacy or de-escalate away from it. Each stage is marked by turning points, differences in self-disclosure, and specific verbal and nonverbal communication patterns. Escalation patterns move through the following stages: preinteraction awareness, initiation, exploration, intensification, and intimacy. Relationships that move from the intimate to the severing of all ties go through these stages: turmoil or stagnation, deintensification, individualization, separation, and postinteraction effects.

Two theories that explain relationship development are social exchange theory and dialectical theory. Social exchange theory posits that we make decisions about becoming more or less intimate on the basis of the rewards and costs associated with the relationship. This decision is done in concert with forecasted and cumulative rewards and costs as well as in comparison with previous, potential, and ideal relationships. Dialectical theory sees our decisions being based on resolution of competing forces in our lives, particularly connectedness versus autonomy, predictability versus novelty, and openness versus closedness. As these forces are addressed, we move either toward or away from intimacy in our relationships.

For Discussion and Review

Focus on Comprehension

1. Distinguish relationships of circumstance from relationships of choice.

2. Define interpersonal trust, intimacy, and interpersonal power.

3. Identify the five stages of relational escalation and five stages of de-escalation.

4. What are the elements of social exchange theory that people use in evaluating relationships?

5. What are the tensions that exist in relationships, according to dialectical theory?

Focus on Critical Thinking

6. Under what circumstances is it appropriate for a person to use the power he or she has over another person to satisfy personal goals?

7. What is the relationship between interpersonal attraction and self-disclosure?

8. Trace two close relationships that you have had—one with a friend of the same sex, and one with a friend of the opposite sex—through the applicable stages of relational escalation and de-escalation. What differences and similarities do you find at each stage? How can you explain them?

9. Explain how social exchange theory relates to dialectical theory.

10. How can you judge whether information that has been disclosed to you is privileged and private information not to be shared with others? When is it okay to tell other people what you know about someone?

11. Under what conditions is it ethical or unethical to approach (a) a coworker, (b) a subordinate, or (c) a superior for the purposes of developing an interpersonal relationship because you feel attracted to him or her?

For Your Journal

1. Monitor a face-to-face conversation between two or three of your friends that is at least four minutes long. You should play the role of a quiet observer. Write down all the ways in which your friends attempted to gain or concede power during the interaction. Include examples of the language they used and the nonverbal cues they exchanged.

2. At the end of a day, reflect on your interactions with others. For each interaction you can recall, write down what you disclosed. What factors affected what you chose to disclose? How did the differences in your relationships with the various people involved affect your decisions about self-disclosure?

Learning with Others

1. Create two lists of names: those people you regard as casual friends and those you regard as close friends. Identify what attracts you to the people on your list. Compare what attracts you to casual friends and close friends with other students. How does your list fit with the categories for attraction identified in the text? What's different? What's the same?

2. In groups of three or four, develop a rating system for calculating the costs and rewards of relationships. Use this system to determine the value of the relationships you are in or that you have ended. Compare your ratings with the other group members to determine the relative value of the relationships you have identified.

3. In class, form at least five pairs of students. Each pair should choose a particular stage of relational development without telling the rest of the class. Then each pair should spend two minutes discussing plans for the upcoming weekend in a way that communicates the stage they have chosen. The rest of the class should write down what stage they think each pair is portraying. After all the pairs have finished their dialogues, score each others' responses. Which stage was easiest to portray and identify? Which stage was most difficult? How easy is it to see differences in communication behavior at various stages?

4. In small groups, brainstorm some of the turning points that each of you has experienced in important relationships. Identify the relational stages that they led to. Which stages crop up most often? Least often? What does the frequency tell you about those stages?

10 Developing Interpersonal Relationships

After you study this chapter

you should be able to ...

1. Discuss the skills for starting relationships.

2. Explain the difference between friends and lovers.

3. Explain how friendships change during our lifetimes.

4. Describe the six different types of love.

5. Identify and explain skills and strategies for escalating and maintaining relationships.

6. Discuss the potential responses to relational problems.

7. Identify some of the causes for relational de-escalation and termination.

8. Describe the model of ending relationships.

9. Discuss strategies for ending relationships.

- Skills for Starting Relationships

- Escalating and Maintaining Relationships with Friends and Lovers

- Skills and Strategies for Escalating and Maintaining Relationships

- De-Escalating and Ending Relationships

Love is not only something you feel. It is something you do.

DAVID WILKERSON

Scenario 1: Josh and Nona are strangers standing at a bus stop.

Josh: Hi. I noticed your T-shirt says Michigan Tech. Are you a student there?

Nona: Huh, oh, no, I just picked this up at a T-shirt clearance sale. I just thought it looked cool—I liked the husky on it. Are you from Michigan Tech?

Josh: My family used to vacation near there and we've visited the campus.

Nona: Where exactly is it?

Josh: It's in Houghton, Michigan, which is way up in northern Michigan. Have you ever been in northern Michigan?

Nona: No, but I've been in lower Michigan. I went skiing there once with some friends from school.

Scenario 2: Several months later:

Nona: Hey Josh, I was thinking that maybe you'd like to go home with me over break and meet my family and friends. How about it?

Josh: Wow. It's really nice that you'd like me to meet your family and all, but I really don't think I'd be very comfortable doing that.

Nona: Oh. Okay, I guess. I just wanted them to meet you, but if you don't want to . . .

Josh: Don't be angry. I just think it's a little early for us to be meeting each other's families. Maybe we can make the trip another time.

Scenario 3: A couple months later:

Josh: Nona, where do you want to go to eat?

Nona: I'm not really up for going out, but you go ahead. I'll see you tomorrow.

Josh: What's wrong?

Nona: I don't know, Josh. I'm just feeling the need to cool things in our relationship right now. I think I just need more from a relationship.

Josh: Oh. I'm sorry if I haven't been able to give you what you want. I guess I've been feeling a little distant in our relationship too.

Nona: I do like you, Josh, and I really value your friendship. You've really become like a big brother to me.

315

These three scenarios illustrate many of the principles discussed in the last chapter and reflect some of the skills and concepts discussed in this chapter. The first scenario reflects some of the ways that you can go about initiating interactions with another person. Nona responds to Josh's initial comments in a way that signals her willingness to interact. Scenario 2 involves an attempt by Nona to move the relationship to another stage of intimacy, while Josh attempts to keep the relationship at its current level. The final scene shows Josh and Nona recognizing that the relationship has begun to de-escalate and that it needs to be redefined. Will Josh and Nona remain friends, or are they just being nice to each other?

Skills for Starting Relationships

J osh used the "free" information that was available on Nona's T-shirt as a way to open a conversation with her. This is one of the techniques you can use to begin conversations and initiate relationships. In the initiation stage of relational development, people generally follow a script that helps both parties reduce their level of anxiety about interacting with a stranger. They also stick to safe topics and disclose only descriptive information about themselves as they begin to build the foundations for a potential relationship. The following sections explain some of the principles to follow as you interact with others for the first time.

We can learn the skills that can help us reduce the interpersonal tensions that most of us feel at the start of a relationship. (B. Daemmrich/The Image Works)

Gather Information to Reduce Uncertainty

Meeting strangers and starting relationships is rarely easy. We all seem to share a fear of the unknown, which includes interacting with strangers whose behavior we cannot predict. The research team of Charles Berger, Richard Calabrese, and James Bradac developed a theory to explain relational development.[1] Their **uncertainty reduction** theory is based on one basic cause–effect assumption: We like to have control and predictability in our lives; therefore, when we are faced with uncertainty, we are driven to gain information to reduce that uncertainty. Reducing uncertainty requires using a number of skills we have already covered, but primarily depends on effective perception and active listening. You need to gather as much information as you can about your partner to increase predictability and reduce anxiety.

We all are most comfortable in predictable situations, because we can call on familiar strategies to handle the situation. In initial interactions we often follow predictable, scripted behavior that reduces uncertainty. What if you approached a stranger and said, "Hello," and the stranger responded by saying, "Bananas"? You would probably feel a little leery. You would feel even more uneasy if you then asked for the stranger's name, only to get the same reply, "Bananas." At this point you'd probably look for the nearest exit. If a person's response does not follow the normal initiation script, it might create so much anxiety that you will stop interacting.

Usually, however, we reduce uncertainty by gathering either cognitive or behavioral information about others.[2] Cognitive information relates to thoughts, attitudes, and opinions. Behavioral information relates to reactions and remarks in various situations. As you have seen, you gather some of this information during the preinteraction stage of a relationship through observations and conversations with others who know the person. Later, you can directly observe the other's behaviors in interactions with him or her, and also ask direct questions. Usually people gather behavioral information through observation and cognitive information through interactions.

uncertainty reduction theory. A theory that claims people seek out information in order to reduce uncertainty, thus providing control and predictability.

building your skills

Anxiety Level and Familiarity

Write down at least ten different social situations you can recall having been in, such as attending weddings, funerals, or ball games; going to your grandmother's for dinner; visiting your best friend's parents for the first time; or meeting your new roommate. Next to each one, indicate how nervous you felt in that situation. Use a scale from 1 to 10, with 1 being calm and cool, and 10 being highly apprehensive. After you have rated each situation, go back and rate each one on how familiar or unfamiliar the situation was. Again use a scale of 1 to 10, with 1 being very familiar and 10 being very unfamiliar.

According to uncertainty reduction theory, there should be a strong correlation between your level of anxiety and the level of familiarity. Which situations caused the most anxiety? To what degree did your unfamiliarity with the situation affect your level of anxiety? What were you most uncertain about in each situation? In which situations were you most comfortable and why? Did you feel uncomfortable under some circumstances even though the situation was familiar? Why?

We are particularly motivated to gain information early in a relationship when uncertainty is greatest, and when we are trying to evaluate the predicted outcome value.[3] We also are likely to seek out information if others behave in an unexpected way.[4] If your close friend who watches *South Park* every night suddenly begins reading during that time slot, you will probably ask why. Whether the friend shares with you what is going on will depend on how comfortable he or she is in revealing information about him or herself.

Adopt an Other-Oriented Perspective

When you were frightened by an encounter with a wild animal or a neighbor's pet as a child, your parents probably told you, "It's just as afraid of you as you are of it." These words reflect an other-orientation and are useful to remember when we encounter new people as well. For all of us, meeting someone for the first time generally produces some degree of anxiety. When this happens to you, try to remember what other people did to make you comfortable in past encounters. They probably smiled a lot, actively listened, showed interest in you but didn't put you on the spot, disclosed information about themselves, and kept the conversation light. Try to use these techniques yourself to put your partner at ease.

Also, try to think about how you appear to the other person. For instance, if you are speaking to someone you just hired, he or she may feel nervous and uncomfortable because of the power and status differences between you. Do your best to minimize the differences; for example, sit in chairs that face each other without a desk between them. In general, try to apply all the information you have and that you observe about the other person to make decisions about your own behavior. Don't just react; take the initiative to make the first interaction pleasant and satisfying to you both.

Observe and Act on Approachability Cues

Subway riders in New York learn to avoid eye contact because it is a signal for approachability. Other ways we can signal approachability include turning toward another person, smiling, being animated (versus sitting very still), taking an open body posture, winking, and waving. In the absence of these cues, we generally conclude that a person wants to be left alone.

Sometimes circumstances prevent us from exchanging approachability cues. The seating arrangements in your class, for example, might hamper the use of nonverbal cues. So instead, you may try to develop some sensitivity to the way other people respond to your greetings. Saying "Hello" lets people know that you are approachable, and it tests approachability. If the other person responds with a warm smile and a few words, such as "Have you finished today's assignment yet?" then the door might be open for further interaction. But if the person gives you a silent half smile and hurries on, you can take this as a signal that the door is closed.

Identify and Use Conversation Starters

Like Nona in the opening scenario of this chapter, we all give off a certain amount of "free" information that others can easily observe. You can use that information as a starting point for a conversation. When Josh noted that Nona was wearing a

Michigan Tech T-shirt, he asked whether Nona was a student there. You can apply the same approach. If someone is walking a dog of the same breed as your childhood pet, you open a conversation by offering an observation about some peculiarity of the breed. If someone is carrying a book from a class you took last semester, ask him or her how the course is going. For example, "Hi; isn't that book you're carrying the one for the dreaded Dr. Bellfinger's class? I really had to work my tail off in that class."

Follow Initiation Norms

Many of the initial interactions in a relationship are almost ritualistic, or at least scripted. In the United States, when two strangers meet for the first time they typically follow this pattern of conversation:[5]

Greetings: Say "Hello," "Hi," or "Howdy."

Introductions: Exchange names and pleasantries.

Topic 1: Discuss the present situation or weather.

Topic 2: Discuss current or past residences (where they live, hometown, and so on).

Topic 3: Determine whether they know people in common.

Topic 4: Discuss their educational backgrounds or occupations.

Topic 5: Discuss general topics such as TV, movies, music, family, sports, books, and/or travel.

Discuss further meeting (optional): Say something like "Let's get together sometime."

Exchange pleasantries: Say, "Nice to meet you," "Hope to see you again," and so on.

Close Conversation: Indicate the intent to end the conversation with such statements as, "See you later," "Got to go to class now," or "Give me a call."

Goodbyes: Make final statements, say "Bye," and move in different directions.

Following the script provides some comfort and security because both partners can thus reduce the level of uncertainty. If you deviate too much from this script, you might undermine your partner's sense of security and discourage him or her from pursuing a relationship. For example, after an initial greeting how would you react to a stranger deviating from the script by saying, "Nice to meet you, too. Did you know that television is becoming the vast wasteland of American intellect, draining the very life blood of our youth?" Most of us would be a bit leery of jumping directly into a discussion of some issue with a person we just met.

As you follow the script, however, you should take advantage of opportunities to expand and develop the conversation in safe ways. Listen for details about the person's background and interests that you can inquire about, and share information about your own interests.

Provide Information About Yourself

Disclosing information about yourself allows the other person to make an informed decision about whether or not to continue the relationship. Remember, both of you need to be in a position to make such a decision. You may have found out what you want and decided that you have a lot in common with the other person, but he or she may not have reached that same point. However, be careful not to violate the script or cultural expectations about what is appropriate to disclose in an initial conversation. You have probably had the experience of someone you have just met telling you his or her problems. Such disclosures usually alienate the other, rather than advancing the relationship.

Present Yourself in a Positive Way

Presenting yourself positively may seem like a pretty obvious strategy. People tend to find others attractive who have positive self-images. And as we have mentioned, it is also against our cultural norms to disclose negative information early on in a relationship. But this doesn't mean you should act cocky or try to act ebullient if you are not that way by nature. Do not provide false information about yourself; simply be selective about the information you share. Also keep in mind that we all have weaknesses and foibles, so the person interacting with you is probably also attempting to present a positive image. Practice the social decentering process you learned in Chapters 3 and 4 to think about the other person's thoughts and feelings as you listen to what he or she puts forward for your consideration. Being kind and responsive will win you more points than trying to act sarcastic and clever.

You can increase the likelihood of a positive response from other people toward you by engaging in appropriate nonverbal cues that communicate a friendly attitude. Such cues include the following:[6]

Proximity:	Move closer and lean forward if you are seated.
Orientation:	Sit directly in front of or closely beside the person.
Gaze:	Look the person in the eyes, especially when he or she looks at you.
Facial expression:	Smile.
Gestures:	Nod your head; use lively movements.
Posture:	Keep an open posture, with your arms stretched toward the other person, rather than placing your arms on your hips or folding them.
Touch:	Touch the person in a friendly, nonsexual way.
Tone of voice:	Raise your pitch; speak with a rising inflection and clear, pure tone.

Ask Questions

Asking questions will accomplish two goals: First, it will help you learn about the other person; and second, it will let the other person know you are interested in her or him. As you begin the conversation, you might ask whether the person has had a particular experience or knowledge, to which he or she might simply reply yes or no. You should follow up with more open questions that invite more elaborate answers, but don't be too invasive—don't interrogate the person.

People are usually open to questions concerning the circumstances surrounding them. The following examples include both general questions and questions related to a circumstance.

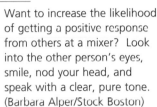

Want to increase the likelihood of getting a positive response from others at a mixer? Look into the other person's eyes, smile, nod your head, and speak with a clear, pure tone. (Barbara Alper/Stock Boston)

Circumstance 1: The other person is a student.

- "What's your major?" "Why did you choose that?" "What kind of job are you interested in after graduation?"

Circumstance 2: Standing at a bus stop.

- "How well do the buses follow the posted time schedule?" "How easy is it to get around town on the buses?" "When are the buses most crowded?"

Circumstance 3: Standing in line to purchase tickets to a rock concert.

- "How did you get interested in (name of the group)?" "Which song of theirs do you like best?" "What other groups have you gone to?"

In each of these instances, be flexible and ask follow-up questions related to the answers you get. Be open and provide information about yourself that is relevant to the questions. Usually the other person will ask you questions. If the other person gives short responses without any reciprocal questions that may be a signal that he or she is not particularly interested in interacting. If so, you may be better served by not pursing the interaction any further.

You might ask a question that you believe is safe and appropriate, such as "What does your father do for a living?" to which the stranger sheepishly responds, "I haven't heard from him since I was 5." Unknowingly, you may have evoked uncomfortable feelings and memories. Some questions should obviously be avoided because of their inappropriateness in an initial interaction; however, almost any seemingly simple question can sometimes evoke a negative reaction. Other-centered communication skills can help you manage sensitive situations. Having little information about a stranger on which to base your communication decisions means you need to monitor the interaction carefully. Recognize that the experiences and feelings evoked by your questions differ from person to person. A question you find easy and comfortable to answer may not be for others. Be sensitive to how the other person responds to your questions, and be prepared to adapt your comments appropriately. Put yourself in the other person's shoes. If you were a person who hadn't seen his or her father since you were 5, what would you most like to be said next?

Don't Expect Too Much from the Initial Interaction

Initial interactions do not necessarily determine the future of a relationship. In movies, such as *The Matrix,* initial interactions between the hero and the heroine are often brusque and unfriendly, but after sharing traumatic experiences, they eventually find love. Although real life does not usually work this way, keep in mind that the scripted nature of an initial interaction limits the opportunity for you and your partner to achieve an in-depth understanding of one another. Relax and arrange another meeting if you feel the spark of attraction. It will probably take a few interactions before you can make a sound cost-benefit analysis of the relationship.

Initiating conversation is only one step in the process of developing an interpersonal relationship. Next we examine ways to escalate a relationship once it gets started, and in Chapter 11 we offer strategies for strengthening relationships with family members and colleagues.

Escalating and Maintaining Relationships with Friends and Lovers

Successful first encounters move relationships from the initiation stage to exploration, intensification, and possibly intimacy. In the second opening scenario of this chapter, Nona and Josh's relationship has escalated beyond the initiation stage. Nona seeks to move the relationship to greater intimacy, while Josh seeks to maintain the relationship at its current level. We engage in one set of strategies and behaviors that move our relationships to greater intimacy (Nona's effort) and another set of strategies and behaviors that help us maintain relationships at the levels at which we are most comfortable (Josh's response).

Two of the most important categories of interpersonal relationships that we develop are friends and lovers. We use these two terms to distinguish relationships that differ in terms of their level of intimacy and sexuality. Both types of relationships are important. Our friendships are one of our most valuable sources of support. In a survey of more than 100,000 men and women, single women rated friends and social life as the most important source of happiness in their lives. Single men rated friends second only to their job duties.[7] Generally, lovers can be classified as relationships in which there is both a high degree of intimacy and attachment as well as sexual activity and/or attraction.[8] Historically, marriage was considered the most intimate relationship, rooted in the goal of procreation and forming a family.[9] Today, gay and lesbian relationships also reflect a form of intimate romantic relationships with relational dynamics similar to heterosexual relationships, including marriage and child rearing.

Friends

A friend is someone we like and who likes us. We trust our friends. We share good and bad times with them. We want to be with them and we make time for that

Questions to Keep the Conversation Going During a Date

1. Have you ever been here (the restaurant or other setting the two of you are in) before? (Discuss aspects of the facility such as food, amenities, and so forth.)

2. Do you live in (name of town or city)? How long have you lived in the area? How do you like it here? (This can lead into a discussion of area politics and other local issues.)

3. Have you visited the local (park, library, shopping center)? (Talk about the special attractions of your town.)

4. Did you grow up here? (If not,) Where did you live before this? What was it like there? How does this area compare with that one?

5. Does the rest of your family live nearby? (Parents, grandparents, aunts, uncles?)

6. What do you like most about the area?

7. What kind of movies do you like? What is the worst movie you ever saw? Who is your favorite actor/actress?

8. What is your favorite TV show? What is your least favorite?

9. Did you catch the academy awards (or that new show, or the game, etc.) last night?

10. What kind of music do you enjoy? Who is your favorite performer/group/band? Who do you think is the hottest this year? Do you think they still will be next year?

11. What is your favorite type of reading matter? Who is your favorite author? What's the best book you've read recently? Do you subscribe to magazines?

12. Do you belong to any local clubs or organizations?

13. Are you a morning person, or do you find yourself at your peak later in the day? (For young people): What kind of career are you interested in? Or What are your career goals?

14. What do you like to do in your spare time? Hobbies, interests . . . ?

15. How did you get involved in your hobby? What do you like most about it?

This isn't nearly everything you and your date can talk about, of course. If you're young, school is an excellent subject for conversation, and can provide an endless supply of topics. If your date is employed, work can be a good source for conversation. Here are some additional tips for keeping the conversation going:

Discuss events in the news.
Maybe the other person isn't real up on current events. But there's an easy way to find out. When the other person says something that reminds you of something you read or heard on the news, use this natural tie-in and see if it gets a good reaction: Speaking of politics, did you hear about the new crime bill they're trying to put into law? If the other person isn't up on current events, he or she may really be into celebrity news or pop culture. So study up a bit on feature articles in newspapers and magazines before you go on the next date.

Talk about the situation that brought you together.
The friend who introduced you or the place where the two of you met is a perfectly natural topic of conversation.

Talk about the present situation.
That salad looks delicious. What's in it?
Look at all the bicyclists out today! Do you yourself enjoy riding?
I'm really looking forward to that movie tonight. Have you caught any of Arnold Schwarzenegger's previous films?

Raise hypothetical questions.
These are the old stand-bys:
"If you had to spend a month in the hospital, what famous person would you most like to share the same room with, and why?"
"If you knew you would be stranded on a desert island, for a year, what three books would you bring with you?"

By Tim Arends, retrieved on December 20, 2000 from http://dating.about.com/people/dating/gi/dynamic/ offsite.htm?site=http%3A%2F%2Fwww.life-n-leisure.com%2Fdating%2Farticles%2Fquestions.htm Used by permission of the author.

purpose. Or, as one armchair philosopher observed, a real friend is one who will continue to talk to you over the back fence even though he knows he's missing his favorite television program.

Friendship is a relationship that exists over time between people who share a common history.[10]

Here's a list of some of the qualities of friendship identified in a variety of research studies.[11] Which ones do you feel apply to your conception of what makes a friend?

Self-disclosure/feeling free to express intimate information

Openness/honesty/authenticity

Compatible/similarity

Ego-reinforcing/self-concept support

Accepting one's individuality

Respect

Helping behavior

Positive evaluation

Trust

Concern and empathy

We each have our own expectations of friendship that include some of the items from this list as well as additional qualities. How well a given person meets these expectations is one factor that we use in making a choice about whether to establish a friendship. As discussed in Chapter 9, friends represent relationships of choice; as one researcher suggests, "Chance makes our parents, but choice makes our friends." Friendship develops naturally into an interdependent relationship that is different from other interpersonal relationships. In friendship, we have no external constraints that keep us together, such as a job, school, or family, even though we often make friends with people in these situations. Usually we form friendships with our equals, whereas we often form other types of relationships with people of different ages or social backgrounds.[12]

Besides helping us enjoy a healthy life, friends help us cope with stress, take care of physical needs, and even help in the development of our personality. Friends also help shape our attitudes and beliefs. Especially during periods of change and crisis in our lives, such as adolescence and retirement, friends help us cope with uncertainty and have a profound influence on our behavior.[13]

One of the most important functions that friends perform is to help us manage the mundane. Most friendships are not based on unusual activities. On the contrary, most of us seek out friends just to talk, have a meal, or be entertained together.

How many friends do we need? Typically, people have up to five close friends, fifteen other friends, twenty or more members in a social network (which could include family members), and many more people who are simply acquaintances.[14] In all our social interactions, we are happiest when we are in the company of our friends. Perhaps the ancient Roman orator Cicero said it best: A friend multiplies our joys and divides our sorrows.

Friends also perform other functions, such as bolstering our self-esteem. Most of us need people who provide encouragement and tell us that we are decent and likable. It is confirming to have a friend become indignant for us when we have experienced an injustice. Friends can help keep a stream of positive acceptance flowing to counteract the numerous nicks and bruises that our self-worth suffers in the course of daily living.

Friends also provide material help when we need it. When you are away on vacation, you might ask a friend to feed your cat and water your plants. If you run out of gas, you might call a friend to bring you some or pick you up.

● Friendships at Different Stages in Life

As we saw in Chapter 9, establishing intimacy with another person takes time, so most of us have a limited number of intimate relationships. We also have different needs for intimacy at various stages of our lives. Relationship scholars W. J. Dickens and D. Perlman examined the differences among friendships at four stages in life: childhood, adolescence, adulthood, and old age.[15]

Childhood Friendships

At about the age of 2, when we start to talk, we begin parallel play with others. As toddlers we perceive our playmates as others who can help meet our needs. Our first friendships are usually superficial and self-centered. Childhood friendships can be categorized into five sometimes overlapping stages.[16] From ages 3 to 7, we have *momentary playmates*—we interact with those in our presence. From ages 4 to 9, we have *one-way assistance*. We still view friendships from a "take" perspective, as instruments to help meet our needs, rather than from a "give" or "give-and-take" perspective.

The third stage, ages 6 to 12, is the *fair-weather friend* stage. There is more give and take in friendships, but the reciprocity occurs when things are going well; the relationship is likely to end if problems and conflicts develop. The fourth stage, ages 9 to 15, is called *mutual intimacy*. With the closeness that develops, relationships become more possessive. The last stage (12 through adulthood) allows for more *independence* in friendships, as well as deepening interdependence with friends that permits greater levels of intimacy and sharing.

Adolescent Friendships

During adolescence, beginning with the onset of puberty around age 12, we move away from relationships with parents and other adults and toward greater intimacy with our peers. During adolescence, peer relationships are the most important social influence on our behavior. We develop cliques of friends and form friendship networks. Boys are more likely to join groups which may be socially acceptable groups such as a sports or debate team, or less socially desirable groups bent on violence and destruction of property. Girls are more likely to develop intimate relationships with one or two good friends. Friendship relationships usually peak in late adolescence and early adulthood, before we select a mate.[17]

During adolescence boys seem to have more friends, whereas girls appear to develop closer, more intensive and intimate relationships. The patterns of making and keeping friends we learn as children continue to affect the formation of friendships during adolescence.

Here is how one researcher described the nature of teenage friendships:

> There is order in the chaos and chaos in the order, of teenage friendships. We want to hang out with the gang, but we want to be close to somebody too. We want to be close to somebody, but we don't want to shut anybody out, either. We want to trust fully, but discover that people let you down—while at the same time we are ready to drop the friendship if our needs aren't being met.[18]

Adult Friendships

Adult friendships are among our most valued relationships. Minister, poet, and essayist Henry Van Dyke summarized the virtues of developing a trusting, intimate relationship with a friend when he wrote the following:

> But, after all, the very best thing in good talk, and the thing that helps most, is friendship. How it dissolves the barriers that divide us, and loosens all constraint, and diffuses itself like some fine old cordial through all the veins of life—this feeling that we understand and trust each other, and wish each other heartily well. Everything into which it really comes is good.[19]

Despite the value people place on friendships during adulthood, those friendships may still dissolve, for at least four reasons.[20] First, they may cool because of physical separation. One person may move to a new community, or even if the person hasn't moved, he or she may no longer travel in the same social circles. Second, new friends may replace old. Changing jobs, joining a new club or religious organization, or having new neighbors move in next door, may diminish the amount of time you can spend with former friends. A third and obvious reason for ending a friendship is that you may simply dislike something your friend did. Perhaps he or she did not help you in a time of need, betrayed a confidence, or violated another friendship rule. And, finally, if and when we begin the process of selecting a mate for life, our friendship relationships may change.

Friendships can sometimes have an adverse effect on a couple if one partner feels that the other's friends are competing for time and intimacy. If one partner's desire to go out alone with friends becomes more important than marriage and family, then conflict flares up.

The Elderly and Friendships

Although the elderly make new friends, they value old ones most. During retirement, when individuals have more time for socializing, friendships become increasingly important; but older adults form fewer new friendships. Instead, they tend to maintain a small, highly valued network of friends.

Psychologist Howard Markman and his colleagues found that self-disclosure, one of the most important components of friendship, did not seem to change in either

Elderly people may make new friends, but they usually rely most on their spouses and oldest friends to fulfill their need for companionship. (Sandra Rice)

depth or amount from young adulthood through age 91.[21] They did report, however, that as friends get older, there is more negative self-disclosure; we are more willing to tell our friends less positive things about ourselves rather than limiting our disclosures to information that makes us "look good."

Yet other research suggests that changes occur in marital relationships as couples get older. Self-disclosure declines, yet retired couples tend to have fewer marital problems than younger couples. Research also suggests that, in general, older individuals express negative attitudes less frequently than younger individuals during problem-solving discussions, except during discussions in which the issue is very important. If the conflict is about an important topic, the older individuals tend to have more heated, intense disagreements with others than do younger individuals.[22]

Friendships at Different Life Stages

Childhood Friendships	Self-focused and often superficial.
Adolescent Friendships	Peers influence social behavior. Boys often associate with others in groups, whereas girls develop deep friendships with a smaller circle of friends.
Adult Friendships	Other relationships may change if selection of a lifelong mate begins.
Elderly Friendships	Old friends are valued, and friendship networks often shrink.

Intergenerational, Intercultural, and Interracial Friendships

Most of our friendships are with people who are fairly similar to us. Similarity makes it easier to communicate effectively and to reach mutual understanding. The more we differ from other people, the greater the challenges that must be overcome to maintain a relationship, as was discussed in Chapter 4. However, we do develop both friendships and romantic relationships with people who differ from us in terms of culture, age, and race. Part of the success of these relationships depends on whether the difference is more superficial than profound. For example, the impact of a ten-year age difference between you and another person is likely to be minimal if you both have the same interests in activities and similar values. However, someone forty years older might have a very different outlook on life from yours. Usually, the older people become, the less impact age differences have on them.[23] A 15-year-old interacting with a 30-year-old represents a very different kind of relationship from a 30-year-old talking to a 45-year-old.

Think about your relationships with people older or younger than you. How do these relationships differ from relationships with people close to your age? First of all, how many close relationships do you have with anyone significantly older or younger? Developing and sustaining such relationships often requires special effort by the participants. We are probably more likely to have casual intergenerational relationships. One study compared close friendships with peers of similar age and with others who were at least ten years different in age.[24] The sample included participants who ranged from 18 to 76 years of age. Close relationships with peers, as compared to relationships with those who were age discrepant, were seen as providing more companionship, satisfaction, intimacy, and nuturance, and being more likely to continue in the future. Casual relationships with those who were similar in age and with those who were different in age did not differ on these qualities. The only difference in the casual relationships was that those who differed in age were admired more than peers.

Age is only one of the differences that impacts relationships. Cultural and ethnic differences also come into play. One of the major elements affecting intercultural and interethnic friendships is that the qualities and expectations associated with being a friend differ from culture to culture (see Understanding Diversity: Friendship and Culture). This means you might engage in behavior that you think is appropriate in your friendship with a person from another culture, only to find that you have offended your friend by violating his or her culturally based expectations. In fact, one study that examined the qualities associated with friendship by various ethnic groups in the United States found that "Latinos emphasized relational support, Asian Americans emphasized a caring, positive exchange of ideas, African Americans emphasized respect and acceptance, and Anglo Americans emphasized recognizing the needs of the individual."[25] Realize, of course, that such generalities may not be specifically valid for a particular member of an ethnic group. However, the study also found that in developing interethnic relationships, individuals seemed unaware of cultural or ethnic differences; in essence, they developed a unique relationship de-

understanding
diversity

Friendship and Culture

The following lists show qualities associated with friendship and their importance for three cultures. These qualities reflect inherent values for each culture, which, as you can see, vary widely.

United States	*Korea*	*Nigeria*
Trust (high)	Congeniality (moderate)	Tolerance (high)
Respect (high)	Sympathy (moderate)	Honesty (high)
Authenticity (high)	Unselfishness (moderate)	Caring (high)
Psychological support (low)	Responsibility (moderate)	Trust (high)
	Honesty (moderate)	Humor (low)
	Generosity (high)	Intelligence (low)
	Intelligence (high)	Responsibility (moderate)

Source: A. M. Nicotera, "Summary of Studies on the Theory of Friendship and Consideration of Implications" in *Interpersonal Communication in Friend and Mate Relationships,* edited by A. M. Nicotera and Associates (Albany: University of New York Press, 1993), 125–135.

fined by their own relational rules rather than cultural rules.[26] This is similar to the notion of developing a third culture that was discussed in Chapter 4.

Interethnic and interracial relationships are faced with the typical problems associated with any other relationship; but in addition, they often must address the reaction of members of each partner's ethnic or racial group. Before the U.S. Supreme Court decision on this issue in 1967, there were still some states in which interracial marriages were illegal. Even today, an African American who marries an Anglo American in the United States may still face strong negative reactions and opposition.[27] Interracial friends might also experience negative reactions from members of their community. The fear of facing negative reactions probably reduces some people's inclination even to initiate interracial relationships. The level of negative reaction to an interracial relationship varies depending on the social context. Fortunately, negative reaction to interracial and interethnic relationships in the United States seems to be declining, as evidenced by a continuing increase in the number of interracial marriages. The number of marriages between individuals from different racial and ethnic backgrounds reportedly doubled between 1980 and 1999.[28]

You probably have your own views about what is important in a friendship that may or may not be in concert with those of your racial or ethnic group. In interacting with people, you should primarily focus on working toward a mutual understanding and acceptance of what your expectations are for your friendship. There is great value in forming relationships with individuals who are different from you; not only can you learn about other people, but you can also gain a better sense of yourself. Learning how another person's race, ethnicity, or religion affects his or her values, thoughts, and behaviors can increase your awareness of how those factors have influenced you.

Lovers: Romantic Relationships

We use the term "lovers" to describe people who are involved in a romantic relationship. Certainly we can love our friends, but that type of love is different from that of a romantic attachment. Romantic relationships fill particular needs that differ from those friendships fill. People usually think of their lovers as also being their best friends, but romantic, loving relationships differ in quality from friendships. One pair of researchers suggests that love differs from friendship "in the identity of interest that the partners share. Love exists to the extent that the outcomes enjoyed or suffered by each are enjoyed or suffered by both."[29]

Another key difference between friends and lovers lies in how they talk about their relationship. Friends are less likely to talk about what attracted them to each other than are lovers. Friends are also less likely to celebrate anniversaries and mark the passage of time in formal ways, such as with a card or a special dinner. Love involves an increase in a sense of "we-ness," of passionate solidarity and identification with the other.

Zick Rubin, a lawyer and social psychologist, attempted to identify differences between love and friendship by developing two scales—one to measure love and the other to measure liking.[30] He found that people made distinctions between love and liking based on these scales. Love relationships are more passionate and intimate than friendships, but interestingly, people like their lovers only slightly more than they like their friends. And women make greater distinctions between loving and liking than do men.

The closest relationship you develop with another human being will probably be a romantic one. When one research team asked a group of students, "With whom do you share your closest relationship?" 47 percent said it was with a romantic partner.[31] And 36 percent said they were closest to their friends, 14 percent said they were closest to a family member, and 3 percent reported "other."

The **triangular theory of love** identifies three dimensions that can be used to describe variations in our loving relationships: intimacy, commitment, and passion.[32] In this model, intimacy includes such attributes as trust, caring, honesty, supportiveness, understanding, and openness (many of the qualities of intimacy discussed in Chapter 9). The second dimension, commitment includes loyalty, devotion, putting the other first, and needing one another. The final dimension, passion includes excitement, sexual interest and activity, and extreme longing. Passion has been identified as the most important dimension for developing romantic relationships.[33] Despite controversy over how valid this theory is, recent research has found relationship satisfaction to be related to variations among the three dimensions.[34] These dimensions provide a valuable way of thinking about how love might manifest itself in relationships. Under the triangular theory of love, the presence and strength of each of these three dimensions varies from relationship to relationship, with each combination defining a style of love.

Sociologist John Alan Lee created a similar scheme that defined six types of love found in both romantic and nonromantic relationships: eros, ludis, storge, mania, pragma, and agape.[35] As you read the descriptions of these types, see which best describes the types of love you find in your relationships.

Eros is sexual love based on the pursuit of beauty and pleasure. The physical need for sex brings many couples together. Erotic lovers crave sexual intimacy and passionately seek sexual activity to satisfy their need. Sexual attraction brings special needs and emotions to a relationship, sometimes obscuring other concerns. Shakespeare described this phenomenon when he wrote, "But love is blind, and lovers cannot see the petty folly that themselves commit."

Ludis describes love as a game, something to pass the time. Ludic lovers are not seeking long-term relationships; rather, they seek immediate gratification and to win their partner's affection. Their goal is to be in love and to enjoy their partner rather than to achieve a sexual victory.

Early dating relationships are often of the ludic type. Going on a date to a junior high dance is a casual pleasure, not a prelude to a lifelong commitment. Ludis lasts as long as the couple has fun and finds the relationship mutually satisfying.

Storge is the sort of love we find in most friendships and in relationships with siblings and other family members. Sexual consummation is not a factor in this sort of love, although sexual attraction may be present. A storgic relationship usually develops over a long period of time, and it is solid and more resistant to change than erotic love. Trust, caring, and compassion are high. Selfishness is low.

Mania describes a relationship that swings wildly between extreme highs and lows. A manic lover is one who is obsessed with the relationship with the other person. Each of the lovers may have an insatiable need for attention, often fueled by a low self-concept.

Pragma is the root word for *pragmatic*. This kind of relationship works because the partners' personal requirements, personalities, backgrounds, likes, and dislikes are compatible. In some cultures, parents prearrange marriages because of pragmatic concerns, and if the children are lucky, passion develops later on, as the relationship takes its course.

triangular theory of love. A theory that purports that all loving relationships can be described according to three dimensions: intimacy, commitment, and passion.

eros. Sexual, erotic love based on the pursuit of physical beauty and pleasure.

ludis. Game-playing love based on the enjoyment of others.

storge. Solid love of friendship based on trust and caring.

mania. Obsessive love driven by mutual needs.

pragma. Practical love based on mutual benefits.

Agape love is based on a spiritual ideal of love. It involves giving of yourself and expecting nothing in return. The famous passage in 1 Corinthians 13 describes this love:

> Love is patient, love is kind. It does not envy, it does not boast, it is not proud. It is not rude, it is not self-seeking. It is not easily angered, it keeps no record of wrongs. Love does not delight in evil but rejoices with the truth. It always protects, always trusts, always hopes, always perseveres. Love never fails.[36]

This kind of "pure" love may characterize the relationship between a parent and a child, or the relationship between a spiritual leader and his or her followers.

Most relationships do encompass more than one kind of love. And relationships evolve. A relationship based on storgic love may evolve into an erotic relationship, for example. Several studies have found that men and women have different styles of loving. Men gravitate toward ludic and erotic relationships, whereas women are more likely to be manic, storgic, or pragmatic. Clyde and Susan Hendrick found that most people consider eros, agape, and storge the most important kind of love for them.[37] Manic and pragmatic were next in importance, and ludic love was the least important. The Hendricks also report that

> Men fell in love more easily than women (eros), who were more cautious about entering relationships (pragma). Once involved in a love relationship, men were less likely than women to break it off, and it was easier for women to remain friends after the breakup (storge).[38]

Passion and love are such highly individual phenomena that we will not presume to teach you a set of skills to cultivate them. We do, however, urge you to keep in mind the skills and principles that we have emphasized throughout the book for initiating and maintaining healthy interpersonal relationships. Become other-oriented by stopping, looking, and listening to your partner. Consider his or her feelings, and try to decenter and empathize. Understand how people develop relationships through conversation. Also be mindful of the typical patterns that most meaningful relationships follow. In general, the ability to develop loving relationships with others requires sensitivity to their unique needs and personalities.

 Types of Love

Eros	Sexual, erotic love based on the pursuit of beauty and pleasure
Ludis	Playful, game-playing love based on immediate gratification and enjoyment
Storge	Solid love found between friends or with family based on trust and caring
Mania	Obsessive love driven by the mutual needs of both partners
Pragma	Practical love based on mutual benefits for both partners
Agape	Selfless love based on giving of oneself for others

agape. Selfless love based on giving of yourself for others.

Interracial Relationships: Hollywood Style

By Kimberly Hohman

What do Whoopi Goldberg, Woody Allen and Puff Daddy have in common? The same hairstylist or fashion designer, maybe? Not quite. But they are all currently involved in interracial relationships. Interracial couples are nothing new in Hollywood. From early pairings like Dorothy Dandridge and Jack Dennison to the abundance of interracial couples gracing today's awards shows and magazine pages, interracial couples have made their mark in tinsel town. So if real-life Hollywood couples are comfortable enough with mixed relationships, why isn't art imitating life?

Hollywood's portrayal of interracial relationships, on the big and small screens, are few and far between. And it seems when they are represented, it is too often met with controversy. Recently David E. Kelly, the creator of the hit Fox show *Ally McBeal* came under fire for what he calls his "consciously colorblind show." In the series, the lead character, played by Calista Flockhart, had an ongoing relationship with a black man. Two other main characters have had an interracial relationship, as well. Ling and Richard, characters played by Lucy Liu and Greg Germann, also have carried on a relationship throughout much of the recent seasons. The onscreen interracial relationships have since ended, but not before a flurry of criticism from those who thought Kelly's angst-less portrayals of interracial relationships resemble a fairy tale more than real life.

And speaking of fairy tales, perhaps that is one place where it is safe to cast characters in interracial relationships. In the Disney remake of Rodgers and Hammerstein's *Cinderella* starring Brandy and Whitney Houston, diversity was the theme of the day. With Whoopi Goldberg and Victor Garber pairing up as the king and queen and Brandy playing Cinderella to Paolo Montalban's prince, interracial couples abounded. This piece of work was actually praised by the critics for its multicultural cast. But then, I suppose it's easier to believe that mixed marriages can work in a world where pumpkins can turn into carriages.

Another show that has tackled the interracial relationship issue head on is ABC's *Boy Meets World.* On this show, Rider Strong and Trina McGee-Davis play a college-aged couple in an interracial relationship with all the typical pains of young love—except the racial ones. In fact, the show's executive producer, Michael Jacobs, made a point of informing the actors that the race issue would not be addressed. McGee-Davis, for one, is all for the representation of interracial couples on prime time. She even went as far as to come to David E. Kelly's

Skills and Strategies for Escalating and Maintaining Relationships

Developing friendships and romantic relationships can be facilitated by the application of a variety of interpersonal communication skills and strategies. Moving relationships through the stages of escalation involves such skills as tactful self-disclosure, active listening, and adapting. We can also use a variety of strategies to enhance relational development such as indirectly communicating our interest in the other person. There are also skills and strategies for maintaining relationships that have stabilized at a given stage. For example, to maintain a loving relationship requires such skills as effectively expressing your emotions, showing tolerance and restraint, and engaging in relationship talk.

defense when critics attacked *Ally McBeal.* In a letter to the *Los Angeles Times,* Ms. McGee-Davis eloquently commended Kelly's approach to the relationship on his show. She went on to refer to the uncomplicated interracial relationships on television as "search engines" and "portals" to the future.

But not all actors are so hip to the idea of interracial relationships on the tube. Eriq LaSalle of NBC's hit drama *ER* had a problem with it. LaSalle's character, Dr. Peter Benton, had an ongoing relationship with Alex Kingston's character, Dr. Elizabeth Corday, on the show. LaSalle reportedly pushed for an end to their characters' interracial relationship as it was something he was "not comfortable" with. LaSalle's character had a string of dysfunctional relationships with black women. In the interracial relationship, however, he felt his character was written to be more warm and loving than in the previous ones. He felt it was sending the wrong message to African-American viewers;

that interracial relationships allowed black men to be more tender than relationships with black women. Kingston, on the other hand, felt the characters' relationship was "a wonderful thing."

As rare as interracial relationships are on primetime television, the big screen tends to have even fewer examples of interracial couples. *Guess Who's Coming to Dinner* is an obvious example of a Hollywood classic with an interracial theme, but since its 1967 release, there haven't been many to follow. Spike Lee took a stab at the issue in his *Jungle Fever,* but this film wasn't a huge box office draw. There are higher expectations for the recently released *Snow Falling on Cedars,* based on a novel by David Guterson. This film follows the forbidden relationship of a white man and a Japanese woman in the 1950s.

In an article called "Black Men Can't Kiss" E! Online addressed the issue of interracial relationships in the movies. The author, Ken Neville,

raises the question of why black men and white women who are paired up in films like *The Pelican Brief* and *Kiss the Girls* don't develop the sexual relationships that viewers have come to expect of similar pairings of same-race couples. Neville defers to the author of a book on the subject of race in the movies who was quoted by the *New York Post* as saying, "Who is this a taboo for? Not for regular people. It's just a taboo for people in Hollywood who are shaping these images." With interracial marriages continuing to rise, perhaps it's time for Hollywood television and film producers to take their cues from society.

Communicate Attraction

When we are attracted to people, we use both indirect and direct strategies to communicate our liking through nonverbal and verbal cues. Nonverbal immediacy represents those nonverbal cues we display when we are attracted to someone. For instance, we tend to reduce the physical distance between us; increase our eye contact and use of touch; lean forward; keep an open body orientation; and smile. We also use the courtship readiness behaviors, preening behaviors, positional cues, and appeals to invitation described in Chapter 7.

We also indirectly communicate our attraction verbally. We use informal and personal language, addressing the person by his or her first name and often referring to "you and I," and "we." We ask questions to show interest, probe for details when our partner shares information, listen responsively, and refer to information shared in past interactions. All these behaviors confirm that we value what the other person is saying.

We can also directly communicate our attraction verbally. Most of us don't do this very often. But think about how you feel when a friend tells you that he or she likes you. It raises your self-esteem; you feel valued. You can make others feel that way by communicating your liking for them, although in the early stages of relational development, there are social mores against doing so. We verbally communicate liking in other, more subtle ways as well. We might tell someone that we like a particular trait or ability, such as the way she tells jokes, or the way he handled an irritating customer. Or we might compliment someone's outfit, hairstyle, or jewelry. Each of these messages communicates attraction for the other person and is likely to elicit a positive response from him or her.

We also use **affinity-seeking strategies** to get people to like us. Table 10.1 summarizes strategies identified by the research team of Bell and Daly.[39] Deciding to display nonverbal immediacy cues or to provide verbal self-confirmation are not only ways we communicate our attraction toward other people, they are also ways of getting other people to like us. Other affinity-seeking strategies include establishing mutual trust, being polite, showing concern and caring, and involving people in our activities. Apparently, these strategies do work. Bell and Daly found that individuals who seemed to use many affinity-seeking strategies were perceived as likeable, socially successful, and satisfied with their lives.[40]

Be Open and Self-Disclose Appropriately

In Chapters 2 and 9 we wrote about self-disclosure being a critical element for movement toward intimacy. People cannot form truly intimate relationships without mutual self-disclosure. Restricting the amount of self-disclosure is one way to control the development of a relationship. If a relationship is moving too fast you might choose to reduce how much you are self-disclosing, as a way to slow the progression of the relationship. The level of self-disclosure needs to be appropriate to the level of development, and both partners must be sensitive to the timing of the disclosures. Failing to disclose or disclosing the wrong thing at the wrong time can damage a relationship.

building your skills

Affinity-Seeking Observation

Put yourself in a place where you can observe strangers interacting, such as a party or a student center. Without violating anybody's privacy, see if you can observe affinity-seeking behaviors or hear what is being said that communicates attraction between interactants. Which of the affinity-seeking strategies seem to be used the most? The least? How do people seem to respond to the affinity-seeking behaviors of their partners?

affinity-seeking strategies.
Ways of getting other people to like you.

Table 10.1

Affinity-Seeking Strategies

	Strategies	Examples
1. Control	Present yourself as in control, independent, free-thinking; show that you have the ability to reward the other person.	• "I'm planning on going to grad school, and after that I'm going to Japan to teach English." • "You can borrow my notes for the class you missed if you'd like."
2. Visibility	Look and dress attractively; present yourself as an interesting, energetic, and enthusiastic person; increase your visibility to the other person.	• "Wow, that was a great show about Chinese acrobats. I do gymnastics too. Would you like to come watch me next week in our dual meet?"
3. Mutual Trust	Present yourself as honest and reliable; display trustworthy behaviors; show that you trust the other person by self-disclosing.	• "That guy you're having problems with called me and asked about you. I told him I didn't have anything to say." • "I've never told anyone this, but I've always hoped I could find my birth parents."
4. Politeness	Follow appropriate conversational rules; let the other person assume control of the interaction.	• "I'm sorry. I interrupted. I thought you were done. Please, go on." • "No, you're not boring me at all; it's very interesting. Please tell me more about it."
5. Concern and Caring	Show interest in and ask questions about the other person; listen; show support and be sensitive; help the other person accomplish something or feel good about him- or herself.	• "How is your mother doing after her operation?" • "I'd like to help out at the benefit you're chairing this weekend." • "That must have been really hard for you, growing up under those conditions."
6. Other-Involvement	Put a positive spin on activities you share; draw the other person into your activities; display nonverbal immediacy and involvement with the other person.	• "This is a great party, I'm glad you came along." • "A group of us are going to get a midnight snack; how about coming along?"
7. Self-Involvement	Try to arrange for encounters and interactions; engage in behaviors that encourage the other person to form a closer relationship.	• "Oh hi! I knew your class ended at two, so I thought I'd try to catch you." • "It would really be fun to go camping together this summer; I have this favorite place."
8. Commonalities	Point out similarities between yourself and the other person; try to establish equality (balanced power); present yourself as comfortable and at ease around the other person.	• "I've got that computer game too. Don't you love the robots?" • "Let's both work on the project together. We're a great team." • "It's so easy to talk to you. I really feel comfortable around you."

Source: Adapted from R. A. Bell and J. A. Daly, "The Affinity Seeking Function of Communications," *Communication Monographs,* 51 (1984): 91–115.

You expect that you can disclose your most private secrets to your intimate partners. You also expect your intimate partners to listen and provide confirming responses to you when you make such disclosures. Imagine what effect it would have on an intimate relationship if your partner turned away from you every time you tried to self-disclose highly personal information. You would become frustrated and disenchanted. The relationship would lose value. You must also be willing to accept your partner's disclosures.

Express Emotions

Expressing emotions is a particular form of self-disclosure and is a skill that can be improved, as discussed in Chapter 6. Many of us are embarrassed about expressing our feelings, yet sharing feelings at the appropriate time during relational development is one way to continue its escalation. Conversely, sharing the wrong feelings at the wrong time can have a detrimental effect.

There are two ways we share feelings with our partners. The first includes disclosing information about our past or current emotional states, such as sadness about the death of a family member, or fear about what we will do after we graduate. The second way we share emotions is the direct expression of emotions such as expressing attraction, love, or disappointment toward our partner. As relationships become more intimate, we have a greater expectation that our partner will disclose emotions openly. The amount of risk associated with such emotional disclosures varies from person to person. Most of us are comfortable sharing positive emotions such as happiness and joy, but are more reserved about sharing negative emotions such as fear or disappointment. We may think expressing negative emotions makes us appear weak or vulnerable. However, in a study of forty-six committed, romantic couples, researchers found that the number one problem was the inability to talk about negative feelings.[41] For example, partners often made the following types of observations: "When she gets upset, she stops talking"; "He never lets me know when he's upset with something he doesn't like"; and "He just silently pouts." We generally want to know how our partners in intimate relationships are feeling, even if those feelings are negative.

However, a constant barrage of negative expressions can also alienate our partner. Research has found that marital satisfaction rises with the number of positive feelings the partners disclose, not with the number of negative ones.[42] A balance has to be found that includes expressing both positive and negative emotions at the right time in a constructive and confirming manner.

Engage in Relationship Talk

Relationship talk is talking about the nature, quality, direction, or definition of a relationship. Relationship talk is generally considered inappropriate in the early stages of a relationship. A relationship might be prematurely terminated if one partner tries to talk about the relationship too early. Willingness to talk about the relationship is one way to implicitly signal your partner about your level of interest and commitment to the relationship. As relationships move toward greater intimacy, however, the amount of direct relationship talk increases. As the relationship escalates, we should be prepared to discuss our thoughts and feelings about it. In more intimate relationships, relationship talk helps the partners resolve differences

relationship talk. Talking about the nature, quality, direction, or definition of a relationship.

in their perceptions of the relationship that might be contributing to conflict and dissatisfaction. Unwillingness to talk about the relationship in an intimate relationship can ultimately drive a partner away.

Monitor Your Perceptions

You need to be aware of your perceptual biases that affect your reactions to your partner. Such biases might inhibit the growth of a relationship because of an inaccurate inference. Effective perception can enhance your ability to understand and adapt to your partner as a relationship escalates. Perception checking helps you reach a more accurate understanding of your partner, and thus provides you with better information about whether to continue the relationship. Directly asking your partner for explanations about things you have perceived can potentially lead to more effective relationship management. For example, suppose you are interacting with Miguel, whom you don't know very well. During the conversation, every time you start to talk about a mutual friend of yours, Sandra, Miguel changes the subject. One interpretation of this perception is that Miguel is rude and impolite, and therefore you might decide to abandon the relationship. Or you might ask Miguel about your perception. The explanation might be that he and Sandra recently had a fight and he prefers not to talk about her. A hasty inference in this case might have precluded the development of a potentially satisfying relationship.

Listen Actively and Respond Confirmingly

Listening skills are also crucial for developing and maintaining relationships. Listening clues you into others' needs, wants, and values and it enables you to respond to them in appropriate ways. In the initial stages of a relationship, partners share a great deal of information. The amount of information tapers off in the later stages and as a relationship continues over time. This tapering off creates the illusion that you don't have to listen as much or as well as you did early on. But listening is a way to demonstrate ongoing interest in another person. Even in long-term relationships, you do not know everything your partner has to say. It is still important to stop, look, and listen—to put down the newspaper or turn off the radio when your close friend begins talking to you.

You also need to listen actively and provide confirming responses. In Chapter 5 we discussed the notions of confirming and disconfirming responses. Using confirming responses increases your partner's sense of self-worth and communicates the value you place on him or her. In addition, if you can develop an awareness of the biases that prevent you from responding with empathy, you can deliberately work to overcome them as you ask questions and paraphrase your partner's messages.

Socially Decenter and Adapt

The skills covered in Chapter 4 for social decentering, empathizing, and adapting to others enhances both the escalation and maintenance of relationships. Social

Well-adjusted couples display support and affection for each other through positive non-verbal cues. (PhotoDisk, Inc.)

decentering helps you better understand your partner, which provides you with a basis for choosing the most effective strategies for accomplishing your communication goals. We have been discussing the notion of "appropriateness" of your behaviors to the effective advancement and maintenance of your relationships. Determining appropriateness depends on your ability to read the situation and your partner, and then to adapt or choose the best behaviors. Essentially, you can either consider what your partner is thinking now, or will think in response to your actions—put yourself in your partner's shoes. For example, suppose you are on a first date and trying to decide

considering others

More Talk Doesn't Mean More Satisfaction

"What we have here is a failure to communicate."

That cliche, from the movie *Cool Hand Luke,* has been quoted for years as a testament to the importance of good communication skills. If only we all knew how to talk with and listen to each other, the world would be brimming with brotherhood and amity.

Not so, say more and more researchers.

"What we really have here is a lot of talk that makes things worse," says David Stiebel, a conflict resolution consultant in California who contends that, more often than not, we understand each other perfectly well. We just don't agree.

Nowhere has the value of communication been more oversold than in marital relationships, says Brant Burleson, a professor of communication at Purdue University.

Studies show that when one or both spouses are dissatisfied, the better the communication skills, the less satisfied they are. Why? They're using their nifty skills to stick it to each other.

Skilled communicators take the perspective of the other person, Burleson says. They know not only what will help that person but "exactly where to put the knife and twist it as well."

But what about all those "mirroring" exercises we've been drilled in? The ones in which we listen nondefensively while our partner says stuff like, "I feel embarrassed when you wear your leopard-print leggings to church."

"Mirroring can be useful if the problem is lack of clarity or people not understanding each other," Burleson says. "But not all problems in marriages are communication-related. People have affairs, spend too much money, disagree over how kids ought to be raised.

"Bad communication can exacerbate those problems, but there's no guarantee that good communication is going to solve those problems."

However, talking things out can succeed—if there's a real disagreement, and if you have a problem-solving strategy. That's the thesis of Stiebel's book, *When Talking Makes Things Worse.*

Talk It Out
Talking can help, Daniel Stiebel writes in *When Talking Makes Things Worse.* The key is to use "strategic communication," which Stiebel swears is not about manipulating your opponent. Here are the four steps:

- Decide whether you have a misunderstanding or a true disagreement.

- Create the other person's next move. Ask yourself, "What do I want this person to do?" Focus on the most he or she is willing and able to do for you right now, Stiebel suggests.

- Use other people's perceptions to persuade them to budge.

- Predict the other person's response. Learn to anticipate how the other person is likely to respond to your next move and adjust your approach accordingly.

Source: Lorraine O'Connell, *Orlando Sentinel,* May 11, 1997.

whether to tell your partner about a very intimate relationship you had, which just ended. Put yourself in the other person's shoes. Would you want to hear on a first date about someone's recent breakup? What information do you have about your date that can help you determine your date's reaction? As relationships become more intimate, you receive more and more information that can improve decentering and adaptation.

Gaining information about your partners is one way you will be able to make decisions about how to help them in distressing situations. One pair of researchers, Ruth Ann Clark and Jesse Delia, studied how people wanted to be treated by their friends in response to six different distressing situations.[43] Clark and Delia found that there was not a strong desire to talk about the situation and a lot of variation in how people wanted their friends to approach it. When people were distressed, they wanted to be the ones to decide whether to bring up the issue or not. This means that rather than a formulaic approach to distressed friends, you should use

considering others

Managing Intimate Relationships

One technique for managing intimate relationships is to back off occasionally—periods of closeness must be balanced by periods of distance. We need time to ourselves in order to recharge and gain perspective. The following excerpt reflects the use of decentering, restraint, and effective conflict management to maintain intimate relationships.

The kinds of things we get upset about in intimacy tend to follow certain themes. Basically, we become hurt or resentful because we're getting "too much" or "too little" of something. Too many demands, too much criticism, too much domination. Or the converse, too little affectional, conversational, or sexual attention (which translates into "you don't feel I'm important" or "you don't love me"). Insufficient empathy is usually voiced as "you don't understand me," and

too little responsibility translates into failure to take one's share of household and/or financial tasks. All these complaints require some attention, action, or retreat.

SHIFTING GEARS: It's not enough to identify the source of personal concern. You have to present your concerns in a way your partner can hear. If I say directly to my partner, "I'm afraid you're going to leave me," he has the opportunity to respond, "Darling, that's not true. What gave you that idea?" I get the reassurance I need. But if I toss it out in an argument, in the form of "you don't care about me," then my partner's emotional arousal keeps him from hearing me. And he is likely to back away—just when I need reassurance most.

If people were aware that intimate relationships are by nature characterized by ambivalence, they would understand the need to negotiate occasional retreats. They wouldn't feel so threatened by the times when one partner says, "I have to be by myself because I need to think about my life and where I'm going." Or "I need to be with my friends and spend time playing." If people did more backing off into constructive activities, including

time to meditate or play, intimate relationships would be in much better shape today.

If couples could be direct about what they need, then the need for retreat would not be subject to the misrepresentation that now is rampant. The trouble is, we don't talk to each other that openly and honestly. What happens if one partner left behind doesn't know what the withdrawal means. But he or she draws on a personal history which provides room for all sorts of negative interpretations, the most common being "he doesn't care about me."

No matter how hard a partner tries to be all things to us, gratifying all of another's needs is a herculean task—beyond the human calling. Criticism, disappointment, and momentary rejection are intrinsic parts of intimate life; developing thicker skin can be healthy. And maintaining a life apart from the relationships is necessary. Energy invested in other people and activities provides a welcome balance.

Source: Geraldine K. Piorkowski, *Psychology Today.* Reprinted with permission from *Psychology Today* magazine, copyright © 1995. 28(1): 50, (Sussex Publishers, Inc.).

---

your ability to socially decenter and adapt to each one's particular needs. The abilities to provide comfort, social support, and ego support have been found to be associated with being a best friend.[44]

Be Tolerant and Show Restraint

The most satisfying relationships are those in which both partners refrain from continually disagreeing, criticizing, and making negative comments to each other. Both individuals learn to accept the other and do not feel compelled to continually point out flaws or failures. One study found that well-adjusted couples focus their complaints on specific behaviors, whereas maladjusted couples complain about each other's personal characteristics. Well-adjusted couples are also kinder and more positive, and have more humor in their interactions. They tend to agree with each other's complaints, whereas the partners in maladjusted relationships launch countercomplaints.[45] In addition, happy couples, when compared to unhappy couples, display more affection through positive nonverbal cues, display more supportive behaviors, and make more attempts to avoid conflict.[46]

Maintaining a relationship requires tolerance. You must learn to accept your partners for who they are and put up with some things you dislike. When couples lose their tolerance, they begin focusing on and criticizing characteristics that they used to accept. Then relationships begin to deteriorate.

Manage Conflict Cooperatively

Conflicts are inevitable in interpersonal relationships. As relationships develop, the individuals share more personal information and spend more time together, so the likelihood for conflict increases. The key to successful relational development and maintenance is not to avoid conflict altogether, but rather to manage it effectively. As we discussed in Chapter 8, a cooperative management style can actually transform conflict into an experience that strengthens a relationship. It can clarify the definition of a relationship, increase the exchange of information, and create a cooperative atmosphere for problem solving.

Seek Compliance

The final skill for developing and maintaining relationships might seem somewhat contrary to the ones we have been discussing. Strictly speaking, **compliance gaining** involves the use of persuasive strategies to accomplish your personal goals—that is, to get your own way. We are not urging you to force your will on others. We are, however, suggesting that it is sometimes ethical and moral to persuade others to go your way. In an ideal situation, the resulting interactions will fulfill both partners' goals.

You need compliance-gaining strategies if you encounter resistance to fulfilling your goal. For example, suppose you want to go out to a movie and you need to borrow money from one of your friends to pay for it. You may simply ask, "Can I borrow eight dollars so I can go to a movie?" If your friend says, "Sure," the interaction is completed. If your friend says, "No, you haven't paid me back from last time," however, you will probably use some compliance-gaining strategy.

Compliance-gaining strategies are responsive to the ongoing, transactive nature of interpersonal relationships.[47] We plot strategies that develop over a number of interactions and modify them in accordance with others' responses. For example, before you ask to borrow money from your friend, you might first do a few favors for her during the day. Then if your friend says no, you might remind her that she owes you for all you've done for her. If she still says no, you might offer to help her over the weekend with her class project. The type of relationship you have established with the other person will affect your strategy selection. Often we face little resistance to our requests from our partners, so we have no need for any compliance-gaining strategy.

compliance gaining. The use of persuasive strategies to accomplish interpersonal goals.

De-Escalating and Ending Relationships

Given the process nature of relationships discussed in Chapter 9, you know that relationships are always changing. Sometimes the change is to a less intimate level, and sometimes it's the complete termination of the relationship. Part of effective relationship management involves being sensitive to cues that signal relational problems or change. As Understanding Diversity: Gender and Ending Relationships on page 343 indicates, women usually sense trouble in a relationship earlier than do men—but what exactly do they sense? Because each stage in a relationship has unique communication qualities, specific verbal and nonverbal cues can tip us off when a relationship begins to de-escalate.[48] There is a decrease in touching and physical contact (including less sexual activity), physical proximity, eye contact, smiling, vocal variety in the voice, and ease of interaction. In addition, there is a decrease in the amount of time spent together, an increase in time between interactions, and more separation of possessions. The interactions become less personal, and so does the language.

Couples use fewer intimate terms; they use less present tense and more passive language; they make fewer references to their future in the relationship; they use more qualified language ("maybe," "whatever," "we'll see"); make fewer evaluative statements; and spend less time discussing any given topic. They fight more, and

e-connection
Breaking Up

The end of a romantic relationship has many effects, from emotional upheaval to lengthy introspection. A person's experiences in ending relationships obviously differ a great deal if he or she is the one choosing to end the relationship, rather than a partner choosing to end it. One way people work through their feelings is by writing about their experiences and even to share those with others. The Internet is becoming a wonderful place where people can be expressive and share their experiences in a fairly safe environment. The following Web address accesses a site about teenagers:

    http://teenwriting.about.com/

After you log on to the site, type the words "breaking off relationships" into the search engine for a sampling of hundreds of poems written by teenagers about the ending of close relationships. You can also search this site for other writings on starting a new relationship, finding a new love, and a variety of other relational events. Even if you are beyond your teenage years, you may appreciate the feelings and thoughts expressed by people exploring the challenges of interpersonal relationship management.

understanding

di ve r ʃ i ty

Gender and Ending Relationships

en and women differ when it comes to dating and marital breakups. Women tend to be stronger monitors of the relationship, so they usually detect trouble before men do. Women's sensitivity to the health of the relationship may be one factor that makes them more likely to initiate the termination of a relationship as well.[56] However, when some men want out of a relationship, men engage in behaviors that women find totally unacceptable. This allows both partners to feel as if they were the ones who initiated the breakup and therefore lets them "save face."

Relationship ending problems are sometimes associated with behaviors that appear early in a relationship. Marriages in which the men avoid interaction by stonewalling and responding defensively to complaints are more likely to end in divorce.[57]

In one study of divorce, men tended to see the later part of the process as more difficult, whereas the women said the period before the decision to divorce was more difficult. In addition, two-thirds of the women were likely to discuss marital problems with their children as compared to only one-fourth of the men; and men were twice as likely to say that no one helped them during the worst part of the process.[58]

they disclose less. If one person becomes less open about discussing attitudes, feelings, thoughts, and other personal issues, he or she is probably signaling a desire to terminate or, at least, redefine the relationship. Can you pick up the signals of the couple's difficulty reflected in the photograph on page 347?

Responses to Relational Problems

When you pick up signals of relational problems, you have three choices: just wait and see what happens; make a decision to redefine or end the relationship; or try to repair the relationship. Repairing the relationship involves applying all the maintenance skills we talked about earlier. Some of the strategies for dealing with conflict that you learned in Chapter 8 will also help you. Underlying the success of any repair effort, however, is the degree to which both partners want to keep the relationship going. The nature of the problem, the stage of the relationship, and the commitment and motivation of the partners all affect the success of repair efforts. There is no single quick solution to relational problems because so many factors influence each one. You need to focus on the specific concerns, needs, and issues that underlie the problem; then adapt specific strategies to resolve it. Professional counseling may be an important option.

What if it is your partner who wants to end the relationship? There is no pat answer for addressing this situation. If a friend stops calling or visiting, should you just assume the relationship is over and leave it alone, or should you call and ask what's up? People lose contact for a myriad of reasons. Sometimes it is beneficial to ask an individual directly if he or she is breaking off the relationship, although such direct requests place your self-concept on the line. How should you react if your friend confirms a desire to end the relationship? If possible, try to have a focused discussion on what has contributed to his or her decision. You might get information you need to repair the relationship. Or you might gain information that will help you in future relationships.

The Decision to End a Relationship

If you do choose to end the relationship, consider your goals. Do you want to continue the relationship at a less intimate level, or terminate it altogether? Do you care enough about the other person to want to preserve his or her self-esteem? Are you aware of the costs involved in ending the relationship? There is no one correct or best way to end a relationship. Ending relationships is also not something you can practice in order to improve. But you can practice the effective relational management skills such as decentering and empathy, adaptation, and compliance gaining. These skills will also help you in ending relationships.

We rely on our social networks for support and self-confirmation when an intimate relationship comes to an end. Advice about how to handle the loss of a close relationship is plentiful, but basically each person must find a way to compensate for the loss of intimacy and companionship. The loss of an important relationship hurts, but it need not put us out of commission if we make the most of our friends and family.

The de-escalation and termination of a relationship is not inherently bad. Not all relationships are meant to endure. Ending a relationship can be a healthy move if the relationship is harmful, or if it no longer provides confirmation of the self or satisfies interpersonal needs; it also can open the door to new relationships. Sometimes we choose not to end a relationship, but rather to de-escalate to a less intimate stage where there is a better balance between benefits and costs.

Breaking up an intimate relationship is hard because of the degree to which we become dependent on the other person to confirm our sense of self. When a relationship ends, we may feel as if we need to redefine who we are. The most satisfying breakups are those that confirm both partners' worth rather than degrade it. "I just can't be what you want me to be"; "I'll always love you but . . ."; or "You're a very special person, but I need other things in life" are all examples of statements that do not destroy self-esteem.

The process of ending a relationship is considerably different when only one party wants out of the relationship (unilateral) from when both are agreeable to it (bilateral).[49] In **bilateral dissolutions,** both parties are predisposed to ending the relationship; they simply need to sort out details such as timing, dividing possessions, and defining conditions for the contact after the breakup. In a **unilateral dissolution,** the person who wants to end the relationship must use compliance-gaining strategies to get his or her partner to agree to the dissolution. Sometimes, however, people simply walk out of a relationship.

How Relationships End

bilateral dissolution. Ending a relationship when both parties are agreeable.

unilateral dissolution. Ending a relationship when only one party is agreeable.

fading away. Ending a relationship by slowly drifting apart.

A declining relationship usually follows one of several paths. Sometimes a relationship loses steam and runs down like a dying battery. Instead of a single event that causes the breakup, the relationship **fades away**—the two partners just drift further and further apart. They spend less time together, let more time go by between interactions, and stop disclosing much about themselves. You've probably had a number of friendships that ended this way—perhaps long-distance relationships. Long-distance relationships require a great deal of effort to maintain, so a move can easily decrease the level of intimacy.

Empathy and Sexual Orientation

One of your authors once volunteered as a crisis phone counselor in a large metropolitan area. We were trained to use effective counseling skills, such as empathy, in relating to the callers' crises. One night, a call came in from a very distressed and depressed man about his breakup with his homosexual partner, with whom he had a long-term intimate relationship. At first I was uncomfortable dealing with the situation. Despite extensive training and role-playing, I wondered how I, as a heterosexual male, could empathize with or relate to this caller. However, I continued to ask questions about how he felt, what he saw as his needs, and his perception of the problems. The more we talked, the more empathic I became, because I realized that his description was very familiar. I had been divorced some four years earlier, and this caller's descriptions of his feelings matched the feelings I experienced during that time. I was able to talk about some of the feelings I had experienced, and this seemed to help him understand his own situation. I realized that though the sex of our partners was different, the overriding issue was the loss of an intimate relationship. I grew a little wiser that night.

Some relationships end in sudden death.[50] As the name suggests, **sudden death** moves straight to separation. One partner might move away or die, or more frequently, a single precipitating event such as infidelity, breaking a confidence, a major conflict, or some other major role violation precipitates the breakup. Sudden death is like taking an express elevator from a top floor to ground level.

In between fading away and sudden death lies incrementalism. **Incrementalism** is the process by which conflicts and problems continue to accumulate in the relationship until they reach a critical mass that leads to the breakup; the relationship becomes intolerable or, from a social exchange perspective, too costly. "I just got to a point where it wasn't worth it anymore," and "It got to the point where all we did was fight all the time" are typical statements about incremental endings.

Causes of De-Escalating and Terminating Relationships with Friends and Lovers

The reasons for ending an interpersonal relationship are as varied as relationships themselves. In general, we end relationships when they cost us more than they reward us. This does not mean that as soon as a relationship becomes difficult, we dump it. Relationships are somewhat like savings accounts. If the relationship is profitable, you deposit your excess rewards into an emotional savings account. Then at times when the costs exceed the rewards, you draw from your savings account to make up the deficit. In other words, if you have had a strong, satisfying relationship with someone for a long period of time, you will be more inclined to stay in the relationship during rough times. There might be a point, however, at which your savings account will run out, and you will decide to close your account—end the relationship. Of course, if you can foresee that you will reap more benefits in the future, you might decide to keep the account open, even when it is overdrawn. In addition, if you have had even less satisfying relationships in the past, or if your alternatives seem more dismal than your current relationships, you

sudden death. Ending a relationship abruptly and without preparation.

incrementalism. Ending a relationship when conflicts and problems finally reach a critical mass.

Table 10.2

Reasons Given for Breakups

Faults

I realized that he/she had too many personality faults.

He/she behaved in ways that embarrassed me.

His/her behaviors were more to blame for the breakup than anything else.

Unwillingness to Compromise

I realized she/he was unwilling to make enough contributions to the relationship.

I felt that he/she no longer behaved toward me as romantically as she/he once did.

I felt that he/she took me for granted.

I felt that he/she wasn't willing to compromise for the good of the relationship.

Feeling Constrained

I felt that the relationship was beginning to constrain me, and I felt a lack of freedom.

Although I still cared for him/her, I wanted to start dating other people.

Although this relationship was a good one, I started to get bored with it.

He/she made too many contributions, and I started to feel suffocated.

Source: Adapted from M. J. Cody, "A Typology of Disengagement Strategies and an Examination of the Role Intimacy and Relational Problems Play in Strategy Selection," *Communication Monographs,* 49(3), 1982, 162.

might decide to stick it out.[51] Of course, under those relational circumstances, when attractive alternatives do appear, relationships often suffer a sudden death.

According to researcher Michael Cody, the responses of students as to what caused their intimate heterosexual relationships to break up can be put into three categories.[52] As Table 10.2 shows, "faults" are the number one cause. These are problems with personality traits or behaviors that one partner dislikes in the other. The number two cause, "unwillingness to compromise," represents a variety of failings on the part of one or both partners, including failure to put enough effort into the relationship, a decrease in effort, or failure to make concessions for the good of the relationship. The final cause, "feeling constrained," reflects one partner's desire to be free from the commitments and constraints of a relationship. But a variety of other elements can contribute to the breakup of both romantic and nonromantic relationships, including loss of interest in the other person, desire for independence, and conflicting attitudes about the definition of the relationship in areas such as sexual conduct, marriage, and infidelity.

Just as there are behavioral rules for making and maintaining friends, there are behaviors that, if you pursue them, will almost certainly cost you a friendship. Listed in order of offensiveness, they are as follows.[53]

1. Acting jealous or being critical of your relationship

2. Discussing with others what your friend said in confidence

3. Not volunteering help in time of need

4. Not trusting or confiding in your friend

5. Criticizing your friend in public

6. Not showing positive regard for your friend

7. Not standing up for your friend in his or her absence

8. Not being tolerant of your friend's other friends

9. Not showing emotional support

10. Nagging your friend

In Chapter 9 we saw how relationships intensify and sometimes become less intense in predictable stages. Relationship dissolution is not an event but a process. Love relationships usually end more abruptly and with more emotional intensity than friendships. When one researcher asked individuals to identify why their friendships with a friend of the same sex ended, first on the list was physical separation.[54] Moving away from our friends apparently takes a toll on the intensity of the relationship. Second, subjects reported that new friends replace old friends as circumstances change. Third, people often just grow to dislike a characteristic of the friend's behavior or personality. And finally, interference from dating or a couple's relationship often contributes to the decay of a friendship. It should come as no surprise that casual friendships are more likely to end than are those with close or intimate friends. Close friendships are better able to withstand change, uncertainty, and separation.

Which of the three types of relationship termination do you think is evident here: fading away—where the partners drift slowly apart, sudden death—where separation is immediate, or incrementalism—where the conflicts gradually build until they reach the breaking point? (Donna Day/Tony Stone Images)

A Model of Ending Relationships

Steve Duck developed a model to show stages in ending a relationship.[55] As Figure 10.1 shows, first one partner reaches some threshold of dissatisfaction that prompts him or her to consider ending the relationship. In this **intrapsychic phase,** we focus on evaluating our partner's behaviors, often focusing on the rea-

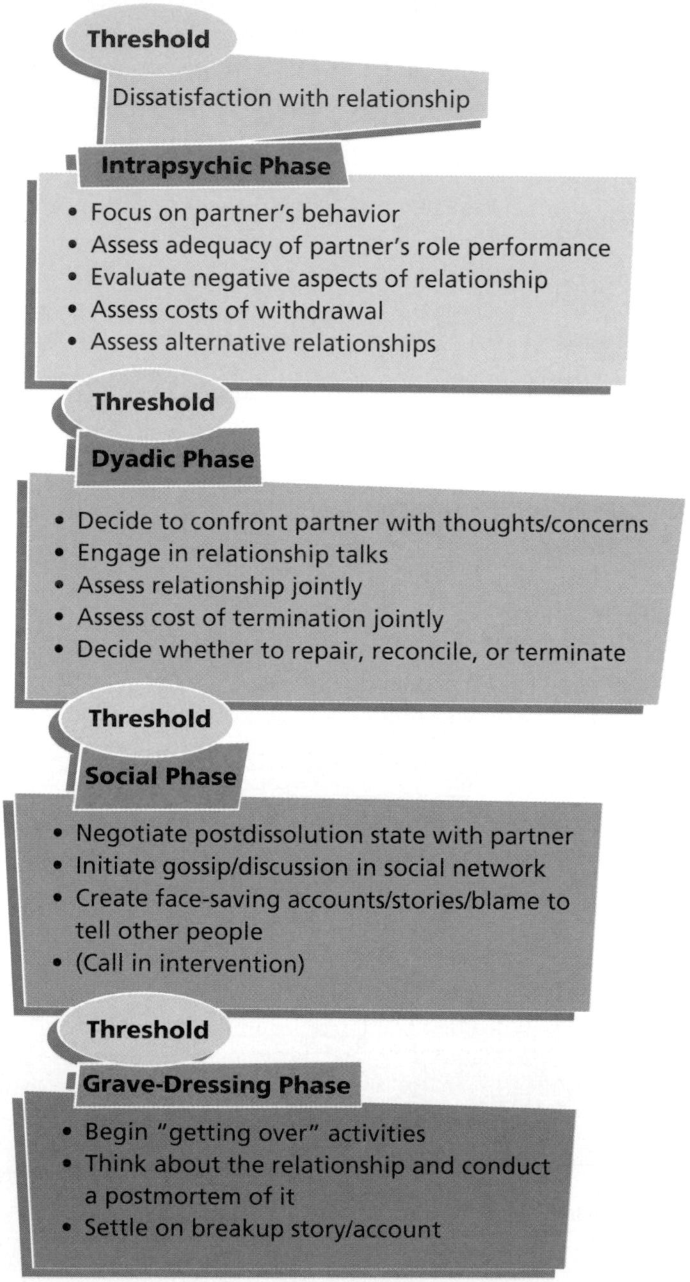

Threshold

Dissatisfaction with relationship

Intrapsychic Phase

- Focus on partner's behavior
- Assess adequacy of partner's role performance
- Evaluate negative aspects of relationship
- Assess costs of withdrawal
- Assess alternative relationships

Threshold

Dyadic Phase

- Decide to confront partner with thoughts/concerns
- Engage in relationship talks
- Assess relationship jointly
- Assess cost of termination jointly
- Decide whether to repair, reconcile, or terminate

Threshold

Social Phase

- Negotiate postdissolution state with partner
- Initiate gossip/discussion in social network
- Create face-saving accounts/stories/blame to tell other people
- (Call in intervention)

Threshold

Grave-Dressing Phase

- Begin "getting over" activities
- Think about the relationship and conduct a postmortem of it
- Settle on breakup story/account

Figure 10.2

A Model of Ending Relationships

Source: S. Duck, "A Typography of Relationship Disengagement and Dissolution," from *Personal Relationships, 4: Dissolving Relationships,* edited by S. Duck (Academic Press: London), p. 16.

sons in Table 10.2 to justify withdrawing. We don't intentionally communicate these thoughts to our partner, however, and we often decide not to dissolve the relationship. From time to time we all become frustrated with a relationship that we consider terminating, but never proceed further than this phase. However, we might "leak" our thoughts and feelings through our communication, displaying such emotions as hostility, anxiety, stress, or guilt. We might decide to confide to a third party about our dissatisfaction. We might consider various strategies for ending the relationship.

At some point we might decide to move from our internal contemplations about the relationship to confronting our partner. This is the **dyadic phase** in the model. If our partner feels challenged and intimidated by our desire to end the relationship, we might have to justify our thoughts and feelings. Our partner might also criticize our behavior and identify our failings. He or she might raise issues that cause us to reevaluate the relationship, our partner, and the costs of dissolving the relationship. We might decide instead to work on improving and repairing the relationship.

If we agree to end the relationship, we enter the **social phase** and begin making the information public. Sometimes a person's social network will mobilize to preserve the relationship. Friends might act as mediators, encouraging reconciliation and suggesting ways to repair the relationship. Of course, friends can also reinforce a decision to separate. Rumors and stories about what happened and what is happening can fuel bad feelings and hasten the end of the relationship.

In the **grave-dressing phase,** one or both partners may attempt to place flowers on the grave of their relationship to cover up the hurt and pain associated with its death. They need a public story that they can share with others about what happened: "We still love each other; we just decided we needed more in our lives." Such a story often places blame on the other partner: "I knew he had his faults, but he thought he could change, and he just wasn't able to." During this phase, our friends encourage us to get back into social activities; they might even try to fix us up with dates. Most importantly, we go through an internal stage in which we come to accept the end of the relationship. We let go of feelings of guilt, failure, and blame.

Strategies for Ending Relationships

When the vitality in long marriages fades away over a period of years, the individuals move slowly through the de-escalation stages before finally divorcing. Brand new relationships are far more likely to end abruptly. As you saw in Chapter 9, the farther up the relational high rise you take the elevator, the longer the ride down.

But no matter what stage a relationship is in, partners use both direct and indirect strategies when they wish to end it. **Indirect strategies** represent attempts to break up a relationship without explicitly stating the desire to do so. **Direct strategies** involve explicit statements. The strategy that a person chooses will depend on level of intimacy in the relationship, level of desire to help the partner save face, degree of urgency for terminating the relationship, and the person's interpersonal skills. The Cathy cartoon on page 350 illustrates the difficulties we all face in coming up with a unique and nonthreatening strategy for ending a relationship.

intrapsychic phase. The first phase in a model of relationship termination: an individual engages in an internal evaluation of the partner.

dyadic phase. The second phase in a model of relationship termination: the individual discusses termination with the partner.

social phase. The third phase in a model of relationship termination: members of the social network around both parties are informed and become involved.

grave-dressing phase. The final phase in a model relationship termination: the partners generate public explanations and move past the relationship.

indirect relational termination strategies. Attempts to break up a relationship without explicitly stating the desire to do so.

direct relational termination strategies. Explicit statements of a desire to break up a relationship.

Indirect Strategies

One researcher identifies three strategies that people use to indirectly disengage: withdrawal, pseudo-de-escalation, and cost escalation. *Withdrawal* involves reducing the amount of contact and interaction without any explanation.[59] This strategy is the most dissatisfying for the other partner.[60] Withdrawal represents an attempt to avoid a confrontational scene and to save face.

In *pseudo-de-escalation* one partner claims that he or she wants to redefine the relationship at a lower level of intimacy, but in reality, he or she wants to end the relationship. Statements such as "Let's just be friends" or "I think of you as more of a sister" may be sincere, or they may reflect an unspoken desire to disengage completely. When both parties want to end the relationship, they sometimes use mutual pseudo-de-escalation and enter into a false agreement to reduce the level of intimacy as they move to disengagement.

Cost escalation is an attempt to increase the costs associated with the relationship in order to encourage the other person to terminate it. A dissatisfied partner may ask for an inordinate amount of the other person's time, pick fights, criticize the other person, or violate relational rules. As Understanding Diversity: Gender and Ending Relationships (page 343) indicates, men apparently use this strategy more often than women do.

Direct Strategies

The same researcher also identified four direct strategies that we use to terminate relationships: negative identity management, justification, de-escalation, and positive tone.[61] *Negative identity management* is a direct statement of the desire to terminate the relationship. It does not take into account the other's feelings, and it may even include criticisms. "I want out of our relationship," "I just can't stand to be around you anymore," and "I'm no longer happy in this relationship and I want to date other people" reflect negative identity management.

Justification is a clear statement of the desire to end the relationship, accompanied by an honest explanation of the reasons. Justification statements may still hurt the other person's feelings: "I've found someone else that I want to spend more time with who makes me happy" and "I feel as if I've grown a great deal and you haven't." But a person who uses justification does not fault the other person, and he or she makes some attempt to protect both parties' sense of self. One researcher found that most people on the receiving end like this strategy best.[62]

De-escalation is an honest statement of a desire to redefine the relationship at a lower level of intimacy or to move toward ending the relationship. One partner might ask for a trial separation so that both people can explore other opportunities and gain a clearer understanding of their needs:[63] "Neither of us seems to be too happy with the relationship right now, so I think we should cool it for a while and see what happens."

Positive tone is the direct strategy that is most sensitive to the other person's sense of self. This strategy can seem almost contradictory because the initiator tries to affirm the other's personal qualities and worth at the same time that he or she calls a halt to the relationship. "I love you; I just can't live with you"; "I'm really sorry I've got to break off the relationship"; and "You really are a wonderful person, you're just not the one for me" are examples of positive tone statements.

Strategies for Ending Relationships

	Term	Explanation
How Relationships End	Fading away	The relationship dissolves slowly as intimacy declines.
	Sudden death	The relationship ends abruptly, usually in response to some precipitating event
	Incrementalism	Relational conflicts and problems accumulate until they become intolerable, then the relationship ends.
Indirect Strategies	Withdrawal	Reducing the amount of contact, without any explanation.
	Pseudo-de-escalation	Claiming a desire for less intimacy, when you really want out.
	Cost escalation	Increasing relational costs to encourage the other to end the relationship.
Direct Strategies	Negative identity management	Directly stating a desire to end the relationship, without concern for the other person's feelings.
	Justification	Directly stating a desire to end the relationship, with an explanation of the reasons.
	De-escalation	Directly stating a desire to lower the level of intimacy or move toward termination.
	Positive tone	Directly stating a desire to end the relationship, while affirming the other person's value.

building your skills

How Your Relationships Have Ended

Identify two relationships that you have ended and two relationships that the other person ended. For each relationship, try to determine which of the indirect or direct strategies were used to end the relationship. What differences were there in how the relationships ended? What effects do you think the choice of strategy had on you and your partner?

Conduct a survey of your friends by asking them these same questions. What conclusions can you draw about how people feel concerning different relationship termination strategies?

Summary

People use a variety of skills and strategies to initiate, escalate, maintain, de-escalate, and terminate interpersonal relationships. Effective initiation of a relationship can be aided by gathering information to reduce uncertainty, adopting an other-oriented perspective, observing and acting on approachability cues, identifying and using conversation starters, following initiation norms, providing information about ourselves, presenting ourselves in a positive way, and asking questions. We should also be careful not to expect too much from an initial interaction.

Successful initial interactions set the stage for the development of friendships and romantic relationships. Friends (people we like, who like us) play an important part in our lives by providing support, helping us manage the mundane and cope with stress, shaping our personality, and providing material help. Our friendships change as we move from childhood, to adolescence, to adulthood, and when we become elderly. A variety of factors influence our friendships with those who differ from us in age, culture, race, and ethnicity. These relationships require a special sensitivity to how the differences affect our partners and these relationships.

Romantic relationships with lovers differ from friendships because lovers expect more, talk more about the relationship and are more passionate, more intimate, and more committed. Our relationships with lovers vary according to three dimensions (passion, intimacy, and commitment) that make up the triangular theory of love. Quality variations in love can be categorized as eros, ludis, storge, mania, pragma, and agape.

People can react to relational problems by either ignoring them, trying to address and repair them, or by choosing to redefine or end the relationship. In a bilateral dissolution, both parties want to end the relationship, whereas in a unilateral dissolution one person wants to end the relationship and the other wants to maintain it. Relationships typically end in one of three ways: by fading away, through sudden death, or incrementally.

In general, relationships seem to end when the costs exceed the rewards over some period of time. The causes given for ending a relationship fall into three categories: faults, unwillingness to compromise, and feeling constrained.

One model for ending relationships has four phases: intrapsychic, dyadic, social, and grave-dressing. First, we internally assess the value of the relationship and consider termination; then we discuss it with our partner; we proceed by announcing the termination and interacting with friends and family; and finally, we come to grips with the consequences of separation.

We can use direct or indirect strategies to bring a relationship to an end. Indirect strategies to terminate a relationship include withdrawal, pseudo-de-escalation, and cost escalation. Among the direct strategies we can use to end a relationship are negative identity management, justification, de-escalation, and positive tone.

For Discussion and Review

● Focus on Comprehension

1. What skills are associated with starting a relationship?

2. What are the attributes of friendships at different stages in life (for example, during childhood, adolescence, adulthood, and old age)?

3. Describe the six types of love.

4. What interpersonal skills are associated with maintaining and escalating relationships?

5. What are the four phases of the model of ending relationships?

6. What are direct and indirect strategies for ending relationships?

● Focus on Critical Thinking

7. Which two skills are probably the most important for starting a relationship, and which two are the least important? Why?

8. How do the strategies for escalating and maintaining a relationship relate to the indirect and direct strategies for terminating a relationship?

9. What strategies for escalating and maintaining a relationship are probably most important for a friendship? For a romantic relationship? Why?

Focus on Ethics

10. You are in a romantic relationship that has become physically intimate. How ethical is it for you to say, "I love you" if you really aren't sure you do? If your partner says "I love you," should you say, "I love you too," even if you don't mean it?

11. How ethical is it for a person who is very skilled at compliance gaining to convince another person to escalate the relationship if that person has a strong initial resistance to escalation?

12. Under what circumstances might it be ethical for a person in an intimate relationship to use sudden death withdrawal as a strategy for ending a relationship? Under what circumstances would it be unethical?

13. Lynn and Chris have had an intimate relationship and have been living together for over a year. The relationship has seemed to be comfortable for both of them. One day Lynn comes home from work and finds that all of Chris's belongings are gone. A note from Chris says, "I couldn't bring myself to tell you I'm leaving. Sorry. Good-bye." Is Chris's behavior ethical?

For Your Journal

1. At the end of each day for three or four days, stop and assess which of the interpersonal communication skills you used the most in your interactions that day. Try to see if there is a consistent pattern in the skills you rely on. What skills do you seem to use the most? What skills do you use the least? How might using other skills affect your interactions and relationships?

2. Think about a close relationship you had that you ended. What strategy did you first use? How well did this strategy work? What was your partner's reaction to this strategy? How did you feel using this strategy? What other strategies were used, if any? What were the reactions to those? If you had it to do over again, what other strategy might you have chosen to use? How do you think your partner would have reacted to that strategy? Why? If you can't think of any relationship that you have ended, use one in which your partner has ended the relationship, and adapt the questions accordingly.

Learning with Others

1. Write down all the qualities you can think of that you associate with someone you would call your "friend." Now write down the qualities you associate with someone you would call your "lover." Get together in groups of four or five students, and compare your lists. What qualities have you listed that nobody else has? Why? What qualities does the group share? To what degree are the qualities defined by your culture? In what way are the qualities for friends the same as for lovers? In what ways are they different?

2. Divide into groups of four or five students. As you go around your group, have each student respond to the following request: Describe the most successful conversation starter that has been used with you, or which you have used. What made it successful? What did you like about it? What was the outcome? Next, go around and describe the worst conversation starter that has been used on each of you, or by each of you. What made it the worst? What was the outcome?

3. Working in groups of four or five students, use your own experiences to develop an answer to the following question: Do the reasons for breaking up a relationship change as the relationship becomes more intimate? To answer this question, start with casual relationships and identify reasons that people end those relationships. Next, talk about friendships, and discuss reasons for ending them. And finally, talk about intimate relationships and the reasons they break up. What are the similarities and differences among these different types of relationships and why they break up?

11 Interpersonal Relationships at Home, at Work, and on the Internet

After you study this chapter

you should be able to ...

1. Define the term family and describe four types of families.

2. Briefly describe the communication in different family relationships.

3. Identify and describe the communication characteristics of a healthy family.

4. Describe principles of upward, downward, horizontal, and outward communication.

5. Identify the characteristics of an effective leader and follower in an organization.

6. Distinguish among the different types of computer-mediated communication.

7. Compare face-to-face communication with computer-mediated communication.

8. Describe principles for using computer-mediated communication to initiate relationships.

9. Describe principles for using computer-mediated communication to maintain existing relationships.

- Interpersonal Relationships at Home

- Interpersonal Relationships at Work

- Interpersonal Relationships on the Internet

People who have good relationships at home are more effective in the marketplace.

ZIG ZIGLAR

Debbie logs on to her AOL e-mail account and a chirpy voice says, "You've got mail!" The first message is from her dad:

It was great seeing you this weekend. Your mom and I always appreciate it anytime you can get home during the semester. As to your changing majors, I want you to know that whatever decision you make is okay with me. Don't worry about having to stay an extra semester to finish up—the world will still be here when you graduate. That communication course you're taking on how to interact with people sounds like a lot of fun—maybe I could take one like it too. Well, I've got to get back to work. Just wanted you to know how nice it was to have you home for a couple days. Write when you get a chance, Love Dad.

Debbie clicks on the Reply button and quickly writes her dad a friendly response. Next she opens an e-mail from Tyrone, one of her coworkers:

Man, you picked a great weekend not to work. Harry went ballistic with all the employees—he yelled his head off, accusing everyone of being lazy and good for nothing before storming out. It was quite the scene. He came back a couple hours later and apologized, but everyone still felt tense. Be prepared when you come in today. How was your visit with your folks? I haven't seen my family all term. I'm looking forward to break so I can fill up on my mom's baking. See you at work, Ty.

Suddenly a small box appears on the screen with an Instant Message from Maria:

Maria: What's up girl?

Debbie: *(replies)* Not much, just got back into town.

Maria: Whoa, I forgot. You missed a big blowup at work.

Debbie: Yea, Tyrone e-mailed me about it.

Maria: Tyrone? I didn't know you two were an item—cooooooooooool.

Debbie: We're just friends, you jerk : -)

Computer-mediated communication is quickly adding another tool to use in interacting with friends and families. The interactions just described illustrate three specific contexts that are the focus of this chapter: the family, the workplace, and cyberspace. Each of these contexts has unique characteristics and demands that make them special forms of interpersonal communication. Interactions at home and at work are often within the context of relationships of circumstance—those relationships that are created not by choice, but because of the situation. In Chapter 9 you read about how these relationships can become relationships of choice when people decide to create friendships and more intimate relationships with family members or coworkers.

E-mail messages convey information about the nature of the relationships among the correspondents. In the preceding e-mails you can tell that Debbie has formed friendships with at least two of her coworkers, Maria and Tyrone. Debbie's father expresses his feelings about her weekend visit and confirms his support for the decisions she's making. Tyrone's e-mail contains information about work, includes personal disclosures, and lets Debbie know he values her friendship. Maria's comments reflect an easy and relaxed interactive style typical of close friends. In each instance, computer-mediated communication supplements face-to-face relationships. It is also possible to develop and maintain relationships over the Internet without ever meeting face to face.

Interpersonal Relationships at Home

Families have changed since your parents were children. In the 1950s a majority of American families were like the Cleavers from the TV sitcom *Leave it to Beaver*; almost two-thirds consisted of a working father, stay-at-home mother, and at least two biological children. Today, according to the U.S. Bureau of the Census, fewer than 7 percent of all American families fit that description. Divorce, single-parent families, mothers with careers outside the home, the longer wait to start families, the move from an agrarian to an industrial society, and mobility all have dramatically altered the very nature of American families. Communication within the family has changed too. The way family members interact with one another has been altered by a variety of social influences. Most research on family communication tends to be descriptive; it describes how different types of families interact. We can offer suggestions on how to improve or enhance communication in families but *there is no single best way to communicate in families.* Each unique family comes with its own particular challenges for understanding and improving communication.

Families are a basic cultural unit. Experiences in families provide people with their fundamental understanding of culture. This means the rules and behaviors exhibited by a family are culture-bound—what applies to a family in one culture is not necessarily true in another. Families are often at the forefront of change, creating co-cultures through intercultural marriages. Many families go through a process of blending different aspects of each parent's culture. For example, a family with a Jewish father and a Catholic mother may have to come up with unique ways to celebrate Hanukkah and Christmas. In what ways does your family represent a blend of cultures?

Our discussion in this chapter focuses on the American family. Like many other entities talked about in this text, families are dynamic and changing. Because the members of a family get older, roles and relationships change over time. In addition, families add members and lose others. As new children are born, or as a member moves out of the home, the dynamics of the family changes. Ultimately, what is true at one moment of time for a family may not hold true later. As you consider your own family experiences and apply the principles we discuss in this chapter, remember above all to continually monitor your family relationships and adapt accordingly. By now you have already experienced the kinds of change that takes place in families as you have become older and gone from being very dependent on your parents to becoming more independent. As you get older, you may discover that your relationship with your parents moves from their providing care for you, to you providing care for them.

There are two ways to examine your interactions with family members. First, **communication *among* family members** involves looking at the totality of communication within a family, at communication in the entire family. Various typologies have been created to label different types of families and identify the associated communication patterns.[1] Second, **communication *between* family members** focuses on the individual relationships between members of the family: husband to wife, mother to daughter, brother to sister, grandmother to grandchild, and so on. These are relationships of circumstance, but as discussed in Chapter 9, they can also be relationships of choice. You can choose to develop friendships with any of your family members. Regardless of whether you form relationships of choice with family members, unique and interesting dynamics still affect the way you relate to specific family members.

Family Defined

You might think that because families are basic to human existence, people do not need a formal definition of a family, and considerable controversy exists as to what constitutes a family. Traditional definitions of a family focus on the roles of husbands, wives, and children who all live together under one roof. Here is one definition written by sociologist George Murdock in 1949:

> The family is a social group characterized by common residence, economic cooperation, and reproduction. It includes adults of both sexes, at least two of whom maintain a socially approved sexual relationship, and one or more children, of one's own or adopted, of the sexually cohabitating adults.[2]

More recently, sociologists Nass and McDonald defined a family as

> a social group having specified roles and statuses (e.g., husband, wife, father, mother, son, daughter) with ties of blood, marriage, or adoption who usually share a common residence and cooperate economically.[3]

Other definitions of a family deemphasize the traditional role of mother, father, and children, placing more emphasis on interpersonal relationships and personal commitment. In 1982, the New York Supreme Court ruled that it is legal for a man to adopt his older homosexual lover as a son. The court stated,

> The best description of a family is a continuing relationship of love and care, and an assumption of responsibility for some other person. Certainly, that is present."[4]

In a survey conducted a few years later, more than 30 percent of unmarried couples believed that homosexual couples should have the same legal rights as do married couples. Art Bochner's definition of a family echoes this relational emphasis. For him, the family is

> an organized, naturally occurring relational interaction system, usually occupying a common living space over an extended time period, and possessing a confluence of interpersonal images which evolve through the exchange of messages over time.[5]

For our purposes in this chapter, we synthesize these perspectives to define the **family** as a self-defined unit made up of any number of persons who live in relationship with one another over time in a common living space, and who are usually, but not always, united by marriage and kinship.

Family Types

Virginia Satir, a well-known expert in family therapy, has identified four types of families: natural, blended, single-parent, and extended.[6] The traditional family—a mother and father and their biological children—is often considered to be the **natural family,** or nuclear family. But because changes in culture, values, economics, and other factors have rendered this family type no longer typical, the traditional family is sometimes called an idealized natural family.

An increasingly common family type today is the **blended family.** This family type consists of two adults and their children. But because of divorce, separation, death, or adoption, the children may be the product of other biological parents or of just one of the adults who is raising them.

The **single-parent family** is self-explanatory. This type of family has one parent and at least one child. Divorce, unmarried parents, separation, desertion, and death make single-parent families the fastest growing type of family unit in the United States today.

The **extended family** typically refers to the relatives—aunts, uncles, cousins, or grandparents—who are part of the family unit. Some extended families also include individuals who are not related by marriage or kinship but are treated like family or share a common identity with the family. These surrogate family members may even be called Mom, Dad, Aunt, or Uncle, honoring them as part of the family circle.

In addition to Satir's categories, at least one other can encompass any of her definitions. The family in which you were raised—no matter what type it is—is your **family of origin.** It is in your family of origin that you learned the rules and skills of interpersonal communication and developed your basic assumptions about relationships. You may have had more than one family of origin if you come from a blended family; due to divorce, separation, or death of a parent, you may have been reared in more than one intact family of origin.

Families come in all sizes, types, and forms. A gay or lesbian couple may decide to live together and form a family and raise a child or children. At the heart of our definition of a family is the concept that it includes people who live in relationship with one another. A family is a family if it thinks it's a family.

A Model of Family Interaction

Regardless of the type of family you have, communication plays a major role in determining the quality of family life. As shown in Figure 11.1, one research team

family. Unit made up of any number of persons who live in relationship with one another over time in a common living space who are usually, but not always, united by marriage and kinship.

natural family. Mother, father, and their biological children.

blended family. Two adults and their children. Because of divorce, separation, death, or adoption, the children may be the product of other parents, or of just one of the adults who is raising them.

single-parent family. One parent raising one or more children.

extended family. Relatives such as aunts, uncles, cousins, or grandparents who are part of the family unit.

family of origin. Family in which you were raised.

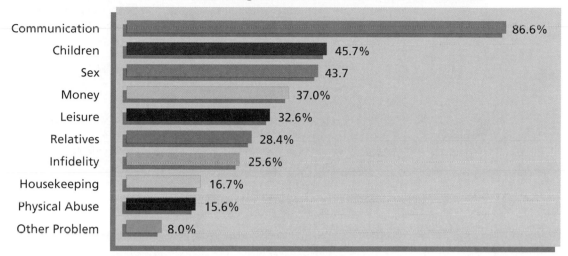

Figure 11.1

Sources of Family
Difficulties

found that over 86 percent of the families who reported family difficulty and stress said that communication was the key source of the problem.[7] Virginia Satir thinks good family communication is so important that she calls it "the largest single factor determining the kinds of relationships [we make] with others."[8] Psychologist Howard Markman found that the more positively premarital couples rated their communication with their partner, the more satisfied they were with their marriage relationships more than five and one-half years later.[9]

More than a century ago, the Russian author Leo Tolstoy observed, "All happy families are alike. Each unhappy family is unhappy in its own way." More recently, a pair of family therapists observed, "Unhappy people came from families where there were a lot of other unhappy people."[10] As they attempted to identify causes for the problems in dysfunctional families, the therapists discovered that usually the major source of a family problem "was not buried in the deep complexes and superegos and egos of the individuals, but was evident in plain daylight to the therapists. It lay in the family system: in the way the family was organized; in the way its members communicated; in the way they worked out their daily interactions."[11]

Another team of researchers have developed a model called the **circumplex model of family interaction** to explain the dynamics of both effective function and dysfunction within family systems.[12] The model's three basic dimensions, as indicated in Figure 11.2, are adaptability, cohesion, and communication. **Adaptability,** shown on the model ranging from chaotic to rigid, is the family's ability to modify and respond to changes in its own power structure and roles. For some families, tradition, stability, and historical perspective are important to their sense of comfort and well-being. Other families that are less tradition-bound are better able to adapt to new circumstances.

The term **cohesion** refers to the emotional bonding and feelings of togetherness that families experience. Family cohesion ranges from excessively tight, or enmeshed, to disengaged. Because family systems are dynamic, families usually move up and down the range from disengaged to enmeshed. The three poems that follow to characterize families who are disengaged, enmeshed, and balanced, respectively.

circumplex model of family interaction. Model that shows the relationships among family adaptability, cohesion, and communication.

family adaptability. A family member's ability to modify and respond to changes in the family's power structure and roles.

family cohesion. The emotional bonding and feelings of togetherness that families experience.

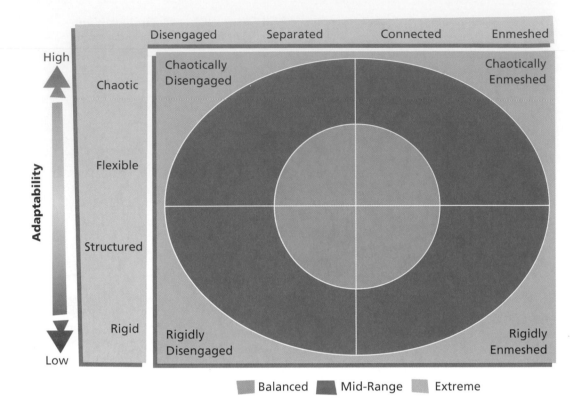

Figure 11.2

A Circumplex Model of Family Systems
Source: Adapted from David Olson and Hamilton I. McCubbin,
Families: What Makes Them Work (Newbury Park: Sage, 1983).

Use what you know about the Circumplex model and the cues you see in this photo to describe the relationships in this family. (Bob Daemmrich/The Image Works)

Circumplex Model of Family Systems

Disengaged:

If a man does not keep pace with his companions,
perhaps it is because he hears a different drummer.
Let him step to the music which he hears,
however measured or far away.

Henry David Thoreau

Enmeshed:

We do our thing together
I am here to meet all your needs and expectations
And you are here to meet mine
We had to meet, and it was beautiful
I can't imagine it turning out any other way.

Jerry Gillies

Balanced:

Sing and dance together and be joyous,
but let each one of you be alone
Even as the strings of a lute are alone
though they quiver with the same music
And stand together yet not too near together;
For the pillars of the temple stand apart,
And the oak tree and the cypress grow
not in each other's shadow
But let there be spaces in your togetherness
And let the winds of the heavens dance between you.

From *The Prophet* by Kahlil Gibran. Copyright 1923 by Kahlil Gibran and renewed 1951 by Administrators C T A of Kahlil Gibran Estate and Mary G. Gibran. Reprinted by permission of Alfred A. Knopf, a Division of Random House.

The third key element in the model—and the most critical one—is communication. It is not labeled in the model because *everything* in the model is influenced by communication. Through **communication** families can adapt to change and maintain either enmeshed or disengaged relationships. Communication determines whether families are cohesive or adaptable. Communication keeps the family operating as a system.

The circumplex model helps us understand relationships among family cohesiveness, adaptability, and communication at different stages of family development. In general, families with balanced levels of cohesion and adaptability function better across the entire family life cycle than do those at the extremes of these dimensions. A balanced family has a moderate amount of cohesion and adaptability—represented by the center circle on the model. Balanced families can often better adapt to changing circumstances and manage stressful periods, such as the children's adolescence. Not surprisingly, these balanced families usually have better communication skills.

family communication. Way in which family members mutually influence one another.

As we have already emphasized, however, research suggests that *there is no single best way to be a family*. At some stages of family life, the balanced ideal of the circumplex model may not apply. Older couples, for example, seem to operate more effectively when there is more rigid structure and a lower level of cohesiveness. Families with younger children seem to function well with high levels of both cohesion and adaptability. Only one thing is constant as we go through family life: Effective communication skills play an important role in helping families change their levels of cohesiveness or adaptability. These skills include active listening, problem solving, empathy, and supportiveness. Dysfunctional families—those that are unable to adapt or alter their levels of cohesion—invariably display poor communication skills. Family members blame others for problems, criticize one another, and listen poorly.

● Communication Between Family Members

The circumplex model provides a sense of what the overall communication is like in a family—communication among family members. We can gain further understanding of family communication by looking at the interactions between any two members of the family. Scholars often examine these dyadic relationships because of their unique communication characteristics. The interaction between wives and husbands has been the most widely examined, because of its centrality to the traditional model of families. Parents and their children share very special relationships that evolve over the course of their lives. You probably recognize the impact that your parents have had on the development of your interpersonal communication skills. Finally, siblings often provide the first opportunities to interact interpersonally with a peer. Siblings often develop relationships of choice such that they remain lifelong friends.

● Husbands and Wives

You've already read about the nature of intimate and loving relationships, information that applies to married couples as well. However, the formal recognition and approval by a culture through the ritual of marriage adds additional meaning and challenges to that relationship. This is one reason some gay and lesbian couples seek public and legal recognition of their relationships through marriage. Most of us take the commitment of marriage very seriously (despite a few TV executives turning it into a game event of marrying a millionaire). When two people enter into marriage, they spend a lot of time defining their roles and working through the trials of cohabitation. The nature of their relationship depends on a variety of factors, such as how they distribute power and make decisions (symmetric, complementary, or parallel) and what roles they each assume. Despite the variety of differences, couples can be classified according to how the partners communicate with one another.

Researcher Mary Anne Fitzpatrick has identified four types of married couples that she believes can be found in American society: traditional, independent, separate, and mixed.[13] According to Fitzpatrick, **traditionals** are interdependent, exhibit a lot of sharing and companionship in the shared space and time, follow a daily schedule, are not assertive, have conflicts, emphasize stability over spontaneity, and follow traditional community customs (such as the wife taking the husband's last name). **Independents** share and exhibit companionship but allow each other individual space; they believe the relationship should not limit their individual freedoms. They are psychologically interdependent but have a hard time matching schedules, and also engage in conflict. **Separates** hold somewhat opposing values; on the one

traditionals. Married partners who are interdependent and who exhibit a lot of sharing and companionship in shared space and time.

independents. Married partners who exhibit sharing and companionship but allow each individual space while being psychologically interdependent.

separates. A type of married couple who support the notion of marriage and family but stress the individual over the couple.

Research shows that "traditional" married couples are the most satisfied. (Maureen Fergusin/PhotoEdit)

hand, they support traditional marriage and family values; on the other hand, they stress the individual over the couple. They have low interdependence and avoid conflict. This means that by maintaining their autonomy, they display less companionship and sharing than the other couple types, but they still try to keep a daily schedule. Each of the preceding three types occurs when both the wife and husband share the same perspective about the nature of their relationship. When the husband and wife have divergent perspectives on their roles, they are a **mixed couple** (the fourth type). There are six possible combinations of the three other types that make up the mixed category: husband independent, wife traditional; husband separate, wife traditional, husband traditional, wife independent, wife independent, husband traditional, wife separate, husband traditional, and wife separate, husband independent.

Before you decide that the separate style sounds appealing, you should know that research shows traditional couples are the most satisfied, while separates are the least.[14] One explanation for this is that traditional partners are the most likely to meet each other's relational expectations.[15] In a survey of more than 700 couples, Fitzpatrick and her colleagues found the following percentages of couple types: traditionals, 20 percent; independents, 22 percent; separates, 17 percent, and mixed, 30 percent (fairly equally distributed among the six types 6–9 percent).[16] These data are from the late 1970s and early 1980s and therefore may not reflect marriage types today. What types do you think may have increased or decreased in the last twenty years? What type would you most prefer?

Parents and Children

A lot of study has been done on the nature of the interaction between parents and their children. Most studies focus on identifying the most effective ways for parents to communicate with their children or describing the nature of parent–child interactions. And some studies have examined the impact that a parent's communication with the child has on the development of the child's communication skills as an adult.

mixed. Those married couples in which the husband and wife each adopt a different perspective (traditional, independent, separate) about the nature of the marriage.

building your skills

Origins of Your Interpersonal Communication Skills

Throughout this text you have had the opportunity to assess your interpersonal communication skills. Take a moment now to think about the role your parents or other adult relatives have played in the development of those skills. Does the way you interact with others match your mother or father's style? What skills have you developed by modeling your parents' behavior? What skills are the result of adapting or accommodating to your parents' communication style (for example, your father was very emotional, so you learned how to provide effective support and comfort to others)?

The way your parents interacted with you has had an impact on your behavior and attitudes, although the impact is not always straightforward. One study found a correlation between self-reports of mothers' aggressive communication style and that of their college-aged children, but did not find such a relationship between fathers and their children.[17] Another study found that seventh graders' responses were similar to their mothers' views on openness in sharing thoughts and feelings and to their fathers' views on conformity and authority. By the eleventh grade, however, children's views on openness matched their fathers', whereas their views on conformity matched their mothers'.[18] Students' views on sex and alcohol use were not found to correlate with their parents' attitudes, but the more open the communication in the family was about sex and alcohol, the more likely students were to engage in safe behavior.[19] The exact effects of your parents' communication style on you, and the effect you will have on your children are obviously unclear; however, it is clear there are effects. Many of the interpersonal communication skills and principles covered throughout this text can be applied to interactions with your parents and your own children. Whether you are using good listening skills, providing confirming responses, managing conflict constructively, being other-oriented, or clarifying perceptions, your parent–child relationships can be enhanced.

Siblings

Making generalizations about communication between siblings is difficult, because so many factors influence the nature of the relationship, most notably the sex and age differences between the siblings. Just as your relationship with your parents changes over time, so do your relationships with your siblings. During childhood, sibling rivalry often occurs as children vie for their parents' love or compete with one another. This rivalry can last throughout the siblings' lifetime. Sibling rivalry is only one issue that leads to conflict among children in the same family. However, there is a positive side to sibling relationships. Siblings can often provide warmth and support to each other, both as children and as adults. One study found that young adults were more likely to turn to their siblings than to their parents to discuss such things as their dating experiences and negative experiences.[20] In addition, young adults preferred being able to talk to a same-sex sibling about sexual matters than to any other family member.[21] The authors of this study found that such disclosures occurred because there was less fear of evoking disappointment or disapproval from a sibling than from a parent.

When people are children, brothers and sisters are often their first playmates. They gain valuable psychosocial skills through interactions with siblings that translate into how they interact with friends and peers. Some learn parenting skills when there is such a large age difference between siblings that the older ones play a nurturing role. The relationships siblings have are influenced by the overall family dynamics (as reflected in the circumplex model) and particularly by the parents. The way parents define the relationships among siblings, the way parents manage sibling conflict and rivalry, and the other rules established and enforced by parents affect the resulting sibling relationship. The various family types described earlier reflect not only the relationships between the parents and children, but among the children as well.

Improving Family Communication

Wouldn't it be fantastic if you could learn special secrets guaranteed to enrich your family life? But, alas, there are no sure-fire prescriptions for transforming your family system into one that a TV sitcom family would envy. Instead, we can pass on some skills and principles that researchers have either observed in healthy families or applied successfully to improve dysfunctional ones.

Virginia Satir found that in healthy families "the members' sense of self-worth is high; communication is direct, clear, specific, and honest; rules are flexible, humane, and subject to change; and the family's links to society are open and hopeful."[22] In such families, she notes, people listen actively; they look *at* one another, not *through* one another or at the floor; they treat children as people; they touch one another affectionately regardless of age; and they openly discuss disappointments, fears, hurts, angers, and criticism, as well as joys and achievements.[23]

A study by Judy Pearson entitled *Lasting Love: What Keeps Couples Together* also sought to identify what explains marital satisfaction and stability.[24] Pearson interviewed several couples who had been together from forty to seventy years. She reports the following eight factors as hallmarks of happily married couples: (1) lowered

expectations (realistic understanding of what being married means); (2) unconditional acceptance of each other; (3) seeing others in a positive way (what Pearson calls positive distortion); (4) viewing themselves as a united team (becoming one); (5) remaining separate, unique individuals (remaining two); (6) mutually satisfying sexual relations; (7) the skills to manage conflict; and (8) persistence.

These studies are descriptive rather than prescriptive. They report what satisfied married couples *do*, rather than recommend specific actions or suggestions. Perhaps you have noticed, however, that several communication-related behaviors keep cropping up in these reports. Let's explore their usefulness as skills.

Take Time to Talk About Relationships and Feelings

Healthy families talk.[25] The sheer quantity of communication depends on family members' needs, expectations, careers, and activities. But the talking extends beyond idle chatter to focus on issues that help the family adapt to change and maintain a sense of cohesiveness.

Often, because of the crush of everyday responsibilities and tasks, family members may lapse into talking only about the task-oriented, mundane aspects of making life work: yard mowing, grocery shopping, errand running, and other uninspiring topics. Healthy families communicate about much more: their relationships, how they are feeling, and how others are feeling. They make time to converse, no matter how busy they are. They have an other-orientation in these conversations, instead of focusing on themselves. In addition, they enjoy one another and don't take themselves too seriously.[26]

Navaran found that couples who are more satisfied with their marriages take time to talk.[27] In satisfied marriages, couples are more likely to

1. Talk over pleasant things that happened during the day.

2. Feel they are understood by their spouse.

3. Discuss shared interests.

4. Avoid pouting and breaking off communication.

5. Talk with each other about personal problems.

6. Use words that have a private meaning for the couple.

7. Talk most important things over together.

8. Be sensitive to each other's feelings and make adjustments to take these into account when they speak.

9. Discuss intimate issues without restraint or embarrassment.

10. Tell what type of day their spouse had without asking.

11. Intentionally communicate nonverbally to a greater degree; they express affection nonverbally in meaningful ways.

Listen Actively and Clarify the Meaning of Messages

Because talking about relationships is important in healthy families, it is not surprising that effective listening is also important. In the often stressful context of family life, good listening skills are essential.

Good listening requires an other-orientation. In Chapter 5, we presented fundamental skills for listening and responding to messages. Family members will com-

"Good" Apology Can Mend a Marriage

The skills of being able to make a genuine, solid apology—and being able to gracefully accept one—go a long way toward achieving a successful relationship.

"A bad apology will erode intimacy. A good apology will help restore intimacy, perhaps even deepen it," says Howard Markman, a marital researcher who is professor of psychology at the University of Denver. He is also an author of *Fighting for Your Marriage* (Jossey-Bass).

"OK, I'm sorry. Can you please just drop it now?" is a bad apology. Also, "I'm sorry I did that, but I wouldn't have if you hadn't . . . "

"A bad apology is one that's not wanting to deal with whatever the source of the problem is," Markman says, "and it usually rests with the person trying to do the apologizing."

John Gottman, professor of psychology at the University of Washington in Seattle, has long studied what makes marriages successful. "Being able to accept influence from one's partner is significant," Gottman says, and being able to apologize is part of this.

Men in violent marriages won't accept any suggestions from their wives that something be done differently—it's as if they're in a bat-

ting cage, hitting back ball after ball, Gottman says. But in marriages that work, husbands accept suggestions all the time.

"In long-term happy marriages, that's a lot of what people are doing, being very respectful in the way they try to influence one another," Gottman says.

"Somebody who could really say, 'I was wrong,' or at an even higher level, 'I'm really sorry I hurt you. It hurts me that I hurt you. I don't want to hurt you,' and to really mean it—that's a very powerful interaction," says Gottman, who is author of *Why Marriages Succeed or Fail.*

Source: Mary Jo Kochakian, *The Hartford Courant,* April 7, 1996.

municate with greater accuracy if they learn to stop, look, and listen. Stop: minimize mental and outside distractions; don't try to carry on a conversation over a TV blaring, a video game bleeping, or a stereo's distracting rhythmic pulse. Look: Constantly monitor the rich meaning in nonverbal messages; remember that the face and voice are prime sources for revealing emotional meaning; body posture and gestures provide clues about the intensity of an emotion. Listen: Focus on both details and major ideas. Asking appropriate follow-up questions and reflecting content and feelings are other vital skills for clarifying the meaning of messages. And remember the importance of checking your perceptions of the meaning of nonverbal messages.

Good listeners try to understand the feelings behind another person's words—to read between the lines. One pair of researchers suggests that you should try to interpret messages according to the sender's code system, not your own. Because you are in intimate daily contact with other family members, you have every reason and opportunity to learn their code systems. Then you can avoid becoming involved in diversionary arguments about the proper meaning of a word, phrase, or gesture.[28] Of course, after you attempt to understand your partner's meaning, you then need to relate the message to your own system of meaning.

Support and Encourage One Another

A smoothly functioning family can be a supportive, encouraging sanctuary from everyday stresses. Through communication, people can let others know that we support and value them. Satir suggests that many, if not most, sources of dysfunction in families are related to feelings of low self-worth.[29] Healthy families take time to nurture one another, express confirming messages, and take a genuine interest in each person's unique contributions to the family. It is important to learn the

Wise parents use support and encouragement rather than coercion as a primary strategy for shaping their children's behavior. The challenge is to find a middle ground that tempers support with appropriate control. (John Lei, Jr./Stock Boston)

guidelines we discussed in Chapters 6 and 7 concerning the types of messages—verbal and nonverbal—that help establish positive, supportive relationships and an open climate for conversation.[30] It is also important to remember, however, to be selective in providing feedback and disclosing your feelings and attitudes about other family members.[31] As you saw in Chapter 9, although trust is important in developing support, total honesty and candidness, however well intended, will not necessarily strengthen your relationships. After a point, too much disclosure can lower satisfaction.[32]

Parents have a special obligation to disclose responsibly to their children. Too much negative and controlling feedback can cause permanent damage.[33] On the one hand, researchers have found that supportive messages—those that offer praise, approval, help, and affection—can lead to higher self-esteem in children, more conformity to the wishes of the parent, higher moral standards, and less aggressive and antisocial behavior.[34]

Parents frequently deliver control messages to get children to do what the parents want. Often these messages involve coercion or threats. One research team found control messages are effective in shaping a child's behavior up to a point; an overemphasis on control often results in rebellion.[35] The challenge is for parents to strike a balance between genuine support and appropriate control. Kahlil Gibran's timeless advice to parents (see the poem on the next page) suggests that children need a balance of control and support as they seek their independence from parents.

Jane Howard, who traveled extensively in search of a "good family," found that "good" families have a sense of valuing and supporting each other.[36] In addition:

1. They have a chief, heroine, or founder—someone around whom others cluster.

2. They have a switchboard operator—someone who keeps track of who is doing what.

3. They maintain strong bonds within the family, but have other group associations as well.

4. They are hospitable.

5. They deal directly with stress and tragedy.

6. They cherish family rituals and traditions.

7. They express affection in a way that is meaningful to other family members.

8. They have a sense of place.

On Parenting

Your children are not your children.
They are the sons and daughters of Life's longing for itself.
They come through you but not from you,
And though they are with you, yet they belong not to you.
You may give them your love but not your thoughts,
For they have their own thoughts.
You may house their bodies but not their souls,
For their souls dwell in the house of tomorrow,
    which you cannot visit, not even in your dreams.
You may strive to be like them, but seek not to make them like you,
For life goes not backward nor tarries with yesterday.
You are the bows from which your children as living arrows are sent forth.
The Archer sees the mark upon the path of the infinite,
    and He bends you with His might that
    His arrows might go swift and far.
Let your bending in the Archer's hand be for gladness;
For even as He loves the arrow that flies,
    so He loves also the bow that is stable.

From *The Prophet* by Kahlil Gibran. Copyright 1923 by Kahlil Gibran and renewed 1951 by Administrators C T A of Kahlil Gibran Estate and Mary G. Gibran. Reprinted by permission of Alfred A. Knopf, a Division of Random House.

9. They find some way to connect with future generations.

10. They honor their elders.

Use Productive Strategies for Managing Conflict, Stress, and Change

All too often parents resort to violence when their children balk at their orders. The Family Violence Almanac on page 372 includes statistics and research conclusions about the increase in child abuse and violence in today's families. Actor Tom Cruise has disclosed how his father physically abused him as a child. "As a kid," says Tom, "I had a lot of hidden anger about that. I'd get hit, and I didn't understand it." When his father was dying of cancer, Cruise said, he was finally able to address the issue directly with his dad.

Learning to manage conflict with siblings is also a challenge in many families. It is with our siblings that we first learn how to manage the complexities of relationships and especially how to manage conflict. One study reported that more than half of all adolescent conflicts are between siblings.[37] The most typical method of managing sibling conflict is withdrawal. However, some siblings resort to violence when they run out of things to say. One survey found that 62 percent of senior high students said they had hit a brother or sister within the past year.[38] Sibling conflicts, as well as other family conflicts, often have a special intensity. Maybe that is because we drop our guard in the privacy and security of a family; we know our family members will love us no matter what, so we may express our feelings with an intensity that would be inappropriate in other social settings. Another reason conflict flares

Family Violence Almanac

When words are not enough to communicate anger and frustration, physical violence often takes their place in today's families. Consider the following statistics and research conclusions about family violence.[39]

From Surveys of Research on Family Violence:

Percentage of families in which one spouse assaulted the other: 16

Percentage of children who were physically abused by a parent: 11

Percentage of children who have hit a parent: 20

Percentage of parents between the ages of 18 and 30 who have at least one child and use some form of physical aggression to discipline their children: 70

Percentage of husbands and wives who use physical means to resolve a conflict: 30

From a Study on the Effects of Family Violence:

Question: Do parents who use physical violence increase or decrease aggressive behavior in their children?

Answer: They increase it.

From a Leading Family Researcher:

"People are more likely to be hit, beat up, or even killed in their own homes by another family member than anywhere else, or by anyone else, in our society."

From a Study of Family Aggression:

Teenagers who see one parent hitting another parent are much more likely to beat their own spouse.

---

up is that we often communicate with family members when we are tired and stressed, so emotions are less controlled.

As we saw in Chapter 8, all close relationships undergo periods of conflict and stress, so families should be prepared to handle them. Satisfied couples report just as many conflicts as dissatisfied couples. The difference is that satisfied couples have learned skills and strategies for managing interpersonal differences. D. A. Infante and his colleagues found that couples who lack constructive argumentation skills are those who resort to verbal aggression (attacking their partner's self-worth to inflict psychological pain)[40] and even physical violence.[41]

John Gottman, who studied couples relationships for over twenty years, identified four categories of communication behavior that indicate increasing problems in a marriage.[42] These behaviors undermine effective communication between couples and can lead to ending the relationship. The first warning sign is criticism or attacks on someone's personality. The second sign is the display of contempt through insults and psychological abuse. The third sign is defensive behavior such as denying responsibility, making excuses, whining, and countercomplaining. The final communication behavior that undermines a marriage is stonewalling, in which the partners withdraw, quit responding to each other, and become minimally engaged in the relationship. Among the four, stonewalling is the single best predictor of divorce. If all four signs are consistently present, there is a 94 percent chance the couple will eventually divorce.[43] Most couples experience some of these behaviors, but happy couples develop effective communication patterns to overcome them.

Gottman has developed a set of suggestions for handling conflict between couples, some of which apply equally to parent–child and sibling conflicts as well.[44] Many of his suggestions reflect recommendations made in Chapter 8 on managing conflict. In approaching an issue, he suggests picking your battles carefully, scheduling the discussion, employing a structure (build an agenda, persuade and argue, resolve), and moderating your emotions. In dealing with your partner, acknowledge his or her viewpoint before presenting your own, trust your partner, communicate nondefensively, and provide comfort and positive reinforcement. Enhance the romance and find enjoyment in having the relationship. He further suggests taking stock of the relationship and knowing when to seek help or to end the relationship.

No list of do's and don'ts will miraculously manage all differences in a family relationship. The suggestions offered here provide only a starting point. As we have emphasized, you will need to adapt these skills and suggestions to the context of your unique family system. But research consistently shows that listening skills and empathy are strong predictors of family satisfaction.

recap   How to Improve Family Relationships

Take time to talk about relationships and feelings.
- Be other-oriented in your focus.
- Don't take yourself too seriously.

Listen and clarify the meaning of messages.
- Learn and interpret messages according to the sender's code system.
- Check your interpretation of messages.

Support and encourage one another.
- Use confirming messages.
- Be selective in disclosing your feelings.

Use productive strategies for managing conflict, stress, and change.
- Watch for communication warning signs.
- Learn to renegotiate role conflicts.

Interpersonal Relationships at Work

What does interpersonal communication have to do with the workplace? Obviously, communication is important in any organization, but is *interpersonal* communication at work really important? In the article on page 375 you'll see what skills employers report they look for in the ideal candidate. At the top of the list are interpersonal skills, followed by teamwork and verbal communication skills. More and

Interpersonal communication skills help us in our interactions with coworkers. Developing satisfying interpersonal relationships in an organization is often a rewarding part of a job. (D. Young-Wolff/PhotoEdit)

more, organizations are looking for employees who can effectively relate to other people—bosses, subordinates, peers, and clients. These reflect the four directions of organizational communication: upward (to bosses), downward (to subordinates), horizontal (to peers), and outward (to clients). All the skills you have been studying throughout this text can improve your effectiveness in dealing with organizational relationships.

Your interactions in the workplace typically vary according to their degree of task versus social orientation. This variation is the source of both personal satisfaction and conflict. After you graduate, the workplace becomes a major source for developing interpersonal relationships. You make friends with the people with whom you work. You will socialize both on and off the job with various people from the organization. Conflicts arise when job-related decisions affect personal relationships, and vice versa. As a manager, you might become friends with some of your subordinates, but if the work performance of one of those subordinates falls below a satisfactory level, the friendship could interfere with your ability to address that problem. Many companies used to have policies prohibiting socializing among employees; however, this policy created strong dissatisfaction and discontent. Organizational policies that nurture relationships among employees build camaraderie and a supportive work atmosphere.[46]

Friendships at work are like any other relationships in terms of relational dimensions and development. One study, in which coworkers were extensively interviewed, identified three distinct transitions: acquaintance to friend, friend to close friend, and close friend to "almost best" friend.[46] Interestingly, the researchers found respondents hesitant to refer a coworker as "best" friend, opting instead for "best friend at work" or "very close." The initial development of workplace friendships occurred for a variety of reasons, such as proximity, sharing tasks, sharing a similar life event, or perceiving similar interests.[47] As the relationships developed, the changes identified in this study were similar to those typically found in any developing friendship—easier and more flexible communication, increased self-disclosing, more frequent interactions, more socializing, and increased discussion of both work problems and nonwork topics.[48]

The challenge of workplace interpersonal relationships is to maximize the satisfaction that comes from healthy relationships, while minimizing the negative impact. Relationships often result in conflicts among the participants as they move through the relational development stages. They must resolve issues and establish rules regarding their workplace roles and interpersonal roles. The participants are expected to perform their required work in the face of these interpersonal struggles. Power is one of the most challenging factors that must be addressed in workplace interpersonal relationships. The position power of a manager over a subordinate can result in a harassment situation in which the subordinate feels forced into an undesirable interpersonal relationship. Power is defined by the organizational roles that each person plays and is thus a defining factor of workplace interpersonal relationships.

Ideal Candidate Has Top-Notch Interpersonal Skills, Say Employers

Bethelem, PA—Job candidates who have good interpersonal skills have a significant advantage over their loutish competitors, say 435 employers responding to Job Outlook 2000, an annual survey conducted by the National Association of Colleges and Employers (NACE).

With a rating of 4.54 on a five-point scale (1 = not important and 5 = very important), interpersonal skills topped the list of skills employers deem important in a job candidate, just edging out teamwork skills and verbal communication skills, which both earned ratings of 4.51. (See Figure 11.3.)

Employers also were asked to name the top 10 personal qualities they seek in job candidates. Communication skills topped the list, followed by motivation/initiative, teamwork skills, leadership abilities, and academic achievement. (See Figure 11.4.)

"If you look at the crossover between the skills and qualities employers say are important, you can see that the skills that help people work together effectively come out on top," says Marilyn Mackes, NACE executive director. "Employers believe that candidates best suited to today's workplace are those who have the skills needed to excel in a team-oriented environment."

While employers included academic achievement/GPA, computer skills, and technical skills on their wish lists, they placed these attributes below "working together" skills. Says Mackes, "It's not enough for a candidate to have knowledge— the candidate has to be able to share that knowledge effectively and tactfully in order for the company to succeed."

The Job Outlook survey is an annual forecast of the hiring intentions of employers as they relate to new college graduates. Each year, the National Association of Colleges and Employers surveys its employer members about hiring plans, starting salary data, and other issues related to the employment of new college graduates. For Job Outlook 2000, 1,743 NACE employer members were surveyed; 435, or 25 percent, responded.

Source: January 18, 2000. Copyright © National Association of Colleges and Employers. Retrieved from www.jobweb.org/joboutlook/candidate.htm.

Figure 11.3

Employers Rate New Hire Skills
(5-point scale: 1 = not at all important, 5 = very important)

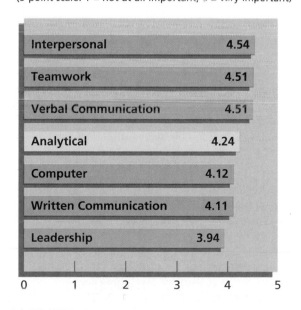

Interpersonal	4.54
Teamwork	4.51
Verbal Communication	4.51
Analytical	4.24
Computer	4.12
Written Communication	4.11
Leadership	3.94

Figure 11.4

Top 10 Personal Qualities Employers Seek

1. Communication skills
2. Motivation/initiative
3. Teamwork skills
4. Leadership skills
5. Academic achievement/GPA
6. Interpersonal skills
7. Flexibility/adaptibility
8. Technical skills
9. Honesty/integrity
10. Work ethic*
10. Analytical/problem-solving skills*   *Tie

These relationships can be identified by the direction the communication flows, as discussed in the following sections.

Upward Communication: Talking with Your Boss

"Please place your suggestions in the suggestion box," announces the boss. The suggestion box is the symbol for upward communication. **Upward communication** involves the flow of communication from subordinates up to superiors. The only person in an organization who does not communicate upward is the boss, president, or chief executive officer (CEO). Even those individuals usually answer to a governing board or to stockholders. Although today's organizational emphasis on quality encourages communication from lower levels to higher levels, effective upward communication is still far from the norm. Many employees fear that their candid comments will not be well received. Others may wonder, "Why bother?" If managers offer no incentive for sharing information up the line, it is unlikely that their subordinates will make the effort. If a supervisor stays holed up in an office away from his or her employees, opportunities for sharing ideas will be limited. Remember the proximity hypothesis described in Chapter 9? People are more likely to talk with those people who are physically close to them.

If there is little upward communication, the organization may be in a precarious situation. Those lower down in the organization are often the ones who make contact with the customer, make the product, or work most closely with the development and delivery of the product or service; they hear feedback about the product's virtues and problems. If supervisors remain unaware of these problems, productivity or quality may suffer. In addition, if employees have no opportunities to share problems and complaints with their boss, their frustration level may be dangerously high. Upward communication helps managers to deal quickly with problems and to hear suggestions for improving processes and procedures.

The Broadway show *How to Succeed in Business Without Really Trying* suggests that you can get ahead by manipulating your boss. Although we do not encourage you to try this approach, we do suggest that developing a positive relationship with your supervisor can help you succeed. One pair of researchers suggests that subordinates can "manage up" by being sensitive to the needs of supervisors.[49] If you know what your boss's most important goals are, along with his or her strengths, weaknesses, and preferred working style, you will be in a good position to establish a more meaningful relationship that will benefit both of you.

This process of managing might be mediated by how influential subordinates perceive their superiors. In 1952, an organizational researcher discovered that subordinates were more satisfied in their jobs when they felt their immediate supervisor had influence on decisions made at higher levels.[50] This is called the Pelz effect, after its discoverer, Donald Pelz. Subsequent research by organizational communication scholar Fred Japlin, found when subordinates perceived their supervisors as supportive, the Pelz effect was particularly strong in creating a sense of openness and satisfaction.[51]

If you are a manager yourself, encourage your subordinates to share both good news and bad. Be visible and cultivate their trust by developing a system that elicits feedback and comments. Use a suggestion box (paper or electronic), informal discussions, or more formal meetings and presentations. Making time for these exchanges will pay off in the long run.

upper communication.
Communication that flows from subordinates to superiors.

Downward Communication: Talking with Your Subordinates

When the dean of your college tells your department chair that a course must be canceled because of low enrollment, the department chair tells your instructor, and your instructor tells you, you have experienced downward communication. **Downward communication** is the flow of information from those higher up in an organization to those of lower rank. It can happen via memo, newsletter, poster, or video or, of course, face-to-face. Most downward communication consists of instruction about how to do a job, rationales for doing things, statements about organizational policies and procedures, feedback about job performance, and information that helps develop the mission or vision of the organization.[52]

What is the best way to communicate with employees—in writing or face-to-face? It depends on the situation. Often the best method is oral, with a written follow-up. Table 11.1 suggests both effective and ineffective ways to communicate various categories of information to employees. In all these situations, the best managers take care to develop and send ethical, other-oriented messages. Then they follow up to ensure that the receiver understood the message, and that it achieved its intended

downward communication. Communication that flows from superiors to subordinates.

Table 11.1

Most Effective versus Least Effective Methods for Communicating with Employees in Ten Different Situations

Situation	Most Effective	Least Effective
1. Communicating information requiring immediate employee action	Oral followed by written	Written only
2. Communicating information requiring future employee action	Written only	Oral only
3. Communicating information of a general nature	Written only	Oral only
4. Communicating a company directive or order	Oral followed by written	Oral only
5. Communicating information on an important company policy change	Oral followed by written	Oral only
6. Communicating with your immediate supervisor about work progress	Oral followed by written	Oral only
7. Promoting a safety campaign	Oral followed by written	Oral only
8. Commending an employee for noteworthy work	Oral followed by written	Written only
9. Reprimanding an employee for work deficiency	Oral only	Written only
10. Settling a dispute among employees about a work problem	Oral only	Written only

Source: D. A. Level, Jr., "Communication Effectiveness: Method and Situation," *Journal of Business Communication,* 10 (Fall 1972): 19–25.

effect. Managers need to be especially other-oriented when they are sharing sensitive information or broaching personal topics.

At the opposite end of the spectrum, the worst managers indulge in an egocentric abuse of the legitimate power that accompanies their rank within an organization. Sexual harassment, which often takes place through downward communication channels, appears to be a growing problem in the workplace.

Some cases that have caught the national attention include the alleged sexual harassment of Paula Jones by then Gov. Bill Clinton, Anita Hill's claim of harassment by current Supreme Court Justice Clarence Thomas, Lt. Gen. Claudia Kennedy's (the highest-ranking woman in the Army) harassment claim against a fellow general, and the case of twenty-six women who sued the investment firm of Smith Barney for sexual harassment. Thousands of other cases are being dealt with throughout the United States. The U.S. Equal Employment Opportunity Commission (EEOC) received 15,222 sexual harassment complaints in 1999, resulting in settlements of over $50 million. Over 12 percent of these were complaints filed by men.

There are two types of harassment. The first type is **quid pro quo,** which translates from Latin as "You do something for me and I'll do something for you." A supervisor who says or implies, "Have sex with me or your job is in jeopardy" or "If you want the promotion you should have sex with me," is obviously using his or her power as a boss to trade sex for something the employee wants.

The second type of harassment involves creating a **hostile environment,** in which an employee feels his or her rights are being violated because of working conditions or offensive behavior on the part of other workers. Telling lewd or obscene stories or jokes about members of the opposite sex, using degrading terms to describe women or men, or displaying risqué photographs of nude or seminude people can contribute to a hostile working environment. A supervisor who either creates, or fails to change work situations that are threatening to a subordinate, is a party to sexual harassment. Jokes are not innocent and pictures are not "all in fun" if they make an employee feel degraded. Supervisors must adopt an other-oriented approach with respect to this issue; it is the receiver, not the sender, of the message who determines whether the behavior is hostile. Court cases have been won by defendants who were able to prove that a supervisor tolerated a hostile work environment, even if the supervisor did not directly participate in the offensive behavior. Wise supervisors do not wait for a problem to occur. They take a proactive approach, offering all workers seminars on how to avoid engaging in sexually offensive behavior and explicitly discussing what workers should do if they become the victims of sexual harassment.

Horizontal Communication: Talking with Your Colleagues

You poke your head into your coworker's office and say, "Did you hear about the possible merger between Byteware and Datamass?" Or while you are tossing a crust at the Pizza Palace, one of your fellow workers asks how much pepperoni to put on a Super Duper Supreme. Both situations illustrate horizontal communication. **Horizontal communication** refers to communication among coworkers at the same level within an organization. In larger organizations you may talk with other workers in different departments or divisions who perform similar jobs at a similar level; that, too, is horizontal communication. Most often you communicate with your colleagues to coordinate job tasks, share plans and information, solve problems,

quid pro quo. Latin phrase that can be used to describe a type of sexual harassment. The phrase means "You do something for me and I'll do something for you."

hostile environment. Type of sexual harassment that threatens an employee's rights through offensive working conditions or behavior on the part of other workers.

horizontal communication. Communication among colleagues or coworkers at the same level within an organization.

building your skills

What Is Sexual Harassment?

Read each of the following situations, and write an A in the blank if you agree that the situation depicts some form of sexual harassment, or D if you disagree. Share your answers with your classmates and discuss those situations over which you disagree. For those situations that everyone marked with an A, discuss whether the harassment is quid pro quo or whether it relates to a hostile environment.

_____ 1. Marcia is wearing a low-cut blouse and a miniskirt; a male coworker whistles at her as she is walking down the hall. In the past, Marcia has told her colleague that she does not appreciate his behavior. The male coworker is guilty of sexual harassment.

_____ 2. Susan is the branch manager of an insurance firm. She asks one of her employees, Steve, to stay after work and discuss some work-related ideas with her. When Steve arrives, the lights are dimmed, the door is locked, Susan offers Steve a glass of wine, and she asks Steve to sit next to her on the couch. Susan is guilty of sexual harassment.

_____ 3. Jed, Lee, and Fernando usually meet for lunch in the company cafeteria. They like to tell each other sexually explicit jokes that often portray women as sex objects. Juanita overhears the jokes and complains to her supervisor. Jed, Lee, and Fernando are guilty of sexual harassment.

_____ 4. Manny is a college professor who has a *Playboy* calendar displayed in his office. He requires all his students to visit him in his office for a private tutorial session in each of his classes. Manny is guilty of sexual harassment.

_____ 5. Cathy, Manny's department chair, has received several complaints from female students about the calendar that Manny displays on his wall. She has not asked Manny to remove the calendar. Cathy is guilty of sexual harassment.

_____ 6. At the weekly staff meeting several of the male workers secretly rate their female coworkers on a scale from 1 to 10 in terms of their physical attractiveness and then compare notes after the meeting. The supervisor knows this occurs but does not say anything about it. The supervisor is guilty of creating a hostile work environment.

_____ 7. Barbara has left Ricardo several notes asking him for a date. Ricardo keeps refusing Barbara's requests. Now Barbara sends him e-mail messages about three times each week asking Ricardo for a date. Ricardo asks Barbara to stop sending him messages, but she persists. Barbara is guilty of sexual harassment.

---

make sure you understand job procedures, manage conflict, or get a bit of emotional support on the job.[53]

"I Heard It Through the Grapevine," a popular song from the 1960s, describes the way gossip travels among friends. Messages travel through the workplace the same way. Grapevine messages tend to circulate within groups and departments rather than across departmental lines. Organizational communication researchers Davis and O'Connor found that information travels quickly through the organizational grapevine, and that it is also accurate from 75 to 90 percent of the time.[54] But errors do creep into these messages; details get lost and embellishments are added, much as when children play "Whisper Around the World" or "Telephone."

Although grapevine errors can cause problems for an organization, most continue to encourage coworker communication because it enhances teamwork and

He Said, She Said: Gender Styles Differ at Work

So you think you're bilingual, do you? You say you speak English and Spanish—or French, or German or New Yawk or Suuuuthe'n.

Impressive, but not good enough—not in today's workplace anyway. To be truly successful in the '90s, you also must be fluent in Femalespeak and Malespeak.

Conversation is rife with ritual, according to Deborah Tannen, author of *You Just Don't Understand* and *Talking from 9 to 5*. And men and women's conversational rituals often clash, leading to misinterpretation and, in the worst cases, hindering women's progress up the male-dominated corporate ladder.

On page after page in her latest tome, Tannen reiterates her theme: Both conversational styles—men tend to be direct, blunt; women indirect and vague—are valid. Either style can work well with others who share that style. But neither works well in every situation.

Tannen repeatedly pleads for both sexes to understand each other's style and to develop flexibility within those styles.

Men and women have very definite expectations of how members of their own sex should behave, Tannen writes.

Studies show that "individuals of both sexes who departed from the norms for their own sex were viewed negatively by subordinates of the same sex," she says.

In one study, "a male manager whose style approximated those of the women was seen as 'fairly meek' and 'weak' by men who worked for him, though he was highly praised by women subordinates," Tannen writes.

Conversely, or perversely, women managers whose style was more like those of the men in that study were criticized by female subordinates who saw them as cold and haughty.

What's a person to do?

Adapt to your audience, Tannen and others say.

For Moira Jamieson, an Orlando business consultant, the adapting has taken the form of becoming more comfy with Femalespeak, since Malespeak is her natural style. "One of the comments I've received throughout my life is that I'm blunt, I'm direct, I'm domineering like a man," says Jamieson, 39. "For this reason, I've had great relationships with men."

But not so great with women.

"Most women find me too pushy, assertive, forceful," she says. "On several occasions, I've been called a bitch for just being blunt."

So Jamieson is modifying her style.

"It takes a great deal of conscious effort," she says. "I think about things for a couple days before I know I'll have to say them."

---

allows the work group to develop a certain degree of independence. Some organizations even try to formalize it by forming *quality circles,* or groups of employees who meet together on a regular basis. These groups usually talk about such issues as how to improve the quality of services or products, reduce mistakes, lower costs, improve safety, or develop better ways of working together. This active participation in the work process encourages workers to do a better job. Moreover, the training they receive to participate in these groups—in group problem solving, decision-making skills, listening, relating, speaking, and managing conflict—applies to other areas of their work as well.

Outward Communication: Talking with Your Customers

"Attention, K-Mart shoppers: Submarine sandwiches are now a blue-light special, on sale for one dollar each for the next fifteen minutes." This is one kind of communication with customers. But in addition to just pitching to their customers, today's organizations are also asking customers what they think about the quality of the goods and services the organization produces. Increasingly, successful organ-

'Til Speech Do We Part
According to Deborah Tannen, these are the conversational rituals of women and men:*

Women

- Speaking indirectly, couching criticism and commands in praise or vagueness to avoid causing offense or hurt feelings.

- Maintaining an appearance of equality.

- Playing down their authority to avoid appearing egotistical or "bossy."

- Saying "I'm sorry" not as an apology but as a way of restoring balance to a conversation.

- Feeling discomfort with boasting; downplaying their accomplishments.

- Asking questions to elicit more information.

Men

- Speaking directly, whether giving criticism or orders.

- Using banter, teasing, and playful put-downs.

- Striving to maintain a one-up position in any interaction.

- Perceiving "I'm sorry" as putting oneself down or accepting blame.

- Boasting or "blowing their own horn" to highlight their accomplishments.

- Seeking information elsewhere rather than asking questions, for fear of appearing to lack knowledge.

According to Tannen and other researchers, here are some ways to bridge the gap between these different rituals:

Tips for Women

- Be cautious in offering unsolicited advice. Often, when men are given advice, they take it as criticism.

- Don't soften your opinions with qualifiers such as "I think" or "Maybe we should" or "Wouldn't it be a good idea if." Using such qualifiers weakens your message.

- Be wary of going into long explanations. Get to the point quickly—if more explanation is needed, provide it.

Tips for Men

- Don't minimize the importance of women's feelings with statements such as "Why are you so upset about that?" Women express their feelings more quickly and easily and need to have those feelings taken seriously.

- Don't remain silent and assume a woman will know you're absorbing what she's saying. Ask questions to show that you're interested and listening.

Note: Remember that these generalizations do not represent *all* men or *all* women.

Source: Excerpted and adapted from Loraine O'Connell, *Austin American-Statesman,* January 24, 1995.

izations are those that are other-oriented; they focus on the needs of those they serve through **outward communication.** They are spending time and money to find out what the *customer* perceives as quality, rather than relying solely on the judgments of their corporate executives. And they are training their staffs to develop more empathy, better listening skills, and more awareness of nonverbal messages from customers.

Enhancing Leadership Skills

The preceding discussion of upward and downward communication is a reminder that workplaces are hierarchies of power and influence. Some workers—those with such titles as boss or manager—have assigned leadership roles, while others follow their directives. The most successful workplaces have both effective leaders and effective followers. In most organizations today all workers are expected to exhibit some degree of leadership skill. The essence of **leadership** is the ability to influence others.

Around 700 B.C., Homer warned his Athenian audience to be selective in their attempts to assume control: "You will certainly not be able to take the lead in all

outward communication. Communication that flows to those outside an organization (such as customers).

leadership. Behavior that influences, guides, controls, or inspires others to take action.

"That was a fine report, Barbara. But since the sexes speak different languages, I probably didn't understand a word of it."

things yourself, for to one man a god has given deeds of war, and to another the dance, to another the lyre and song, and in another widesounding Zeus puts a good mind." The first qualification for leadership, as he was trying to tell them, is skill and knowledge about the task at hand. In addition, however, you need the skills necessary to motivate, inspire, and instruct others in their work. Because not all of us are born with these skills, Stephen Covey wrote a book called *The Seven Habits of Highly Effective People* to help those of us who want to sharpen our leadership skills. To be successful as a leader, Covey suggests the following:[55]

1. *Be proactive:* Don't wait until a situation becomes a problem to solve before starting to solve it. Don't simply react to problems, but anticipate them. Don't blame others. Accept responsibility for making decisions yourself.

2. *Begin with the end in mind:* Effective people have a vision of where they are going and what they want to accomplish.

3. *Put first things first:* In Covey's words, "Make sure the main thing is the main thing." Manage your time so that you can manage your life.

4. *Think win/win:* Don't assume someone must lose and someone must win. Approach situations attempting to maximize the benefits for all.

5. *Seek first to understand, then to be understood.* Listen effectively. Listening skills are essential in being other-oriented.

6. *Synergize:* Synergy means that working together results in more creativity than working alone.

7. *Sharpen the saw:* Take time out to enhance your skills rather than continuing to work with "unsharpened" tools.

The most effective leaders combine a task orientation with a relationship orientation to perform the following functions:[56]

Task Functions:

1. *Initiate* new ideas or approaches to achieving the task.

2. *Provide information,* such as facts, examples, statistics.

3. *Seek information* by asking for facts and other data that can help get the work done.

4. *Seek opinions* and ask for clarification of opinions expressed by others.

5. *Offer opinions* about issues and ideas under consideration.

6. *Elaborate* and amplify the ideas of others.

7. *Evaluate* the advantages and disadvantages of issues, ideas, or proposed solutions.

8. *Energize* and motivate the group to take action and be productive.

Relationship Functions:

9. *Encourage* others and offer praise and acceptance of others' ideas.

10. *Harmonize* and mediate disagreements and conflict.

11. *Compromise* and seek ways of finding common ground among group members.

12. *Be a gatekeeper* by encouraging less talkative members to participate and limiting lengthy orations from big talkers.

Enhancing Followership Skill

If you find yourself playing the role of follower in a group, remind yourself that you can still make an enormous contribution. Consider the following:

1. Seek opportunities to provide input and suggestions to leaders. Look for ways to communicate your interest in the goals of the group.

2. Listen well. This skill appears on any list for leaders or followers. Listening effectively and being able to comprehend and evaluate information is an essential followership skill.

3. Provide appropriate feedback. If you are not sure you understand directions from your superior, ask for further clarification.

4. Support your suggestions with evidence rather than with off-the-cuff opinions. Be able to document your suggestions with data, rather than relying only on emotion-based hunches. Although you should not ignore intuitive thoughts, most supervisors will respond more positively to those ideas you can support with evidence.

5. Don't abandon your ethical principles. If you are being asked to do something that violates your sense of right and wrong, you may need to suggest tactfully that the orders you have been given by your boss are not consistent with your ethical principles. "I was only following orders," or "I was just doing what I was told," usually don't hold up in court as an excuse for violating the law.

Interpersonal Relationships on the Internet

computer-mediated communication (CMC). Communication between and among people through the medium of computers (includes e-mail, chat rooms, bulletin boards, and newsgroups).

H omes and workplaces have been dramatically altered by the introduction of the personal computer and computer-mediated communication. **Computer-mediated communication (CMC)** was initially seen as a tool for accessing information, but it has quickly become an integral tool for human interaction. People have moved from using independent computers for word processing to using networked computers that allow them to send and receive messages and documents. This ability has proven invaluable at the workplace, where interoffice memos have been replaced by e-mail and attached documents. CMC has provided easy access to any member of an organization. The access may even be *too* easy, because e-mail addresses are readily available and messages can be composed and sent so quickly.

As the technology has been introduced to the home, more and more families use the Internet to keep in contact. E-mail and instant messaging provide another communication tool for maintaining interpersonal relationships with friends and lovers. With the introduction of chat rooms and discussion groups, you now have the ability to meet strangers and develop new interpersonal relationships. Thus, CMC allows you to meet two interpersonal goals: to make contact with strangers and thus initiate and develop new relationships; and to maintain existing relationships. These two goals differ greatly in directing your Internet interactions.

Computer-mediated communication has made it easy for us to have access to family, friends, co-workers, and even complete strangers. The key to success is to apply the same skills that you would in a face-to-face relationship. (Hyancith Manning/SuperStock)

e-connection
Cyberspace and Relationships

The development and maintenance of relationships in cyberspace is the subject of many articles and Web sites. The following Web site contains a number of interesting articles and links about various facets of computer-mediated communication, including cyberspace romance, identity management in cyberspace, and addiction to the Internet.

http://www.rider.edu/users/suler/psycyber/psycyber.html

The use of CMC as a surrogate for face-to-face encounters creates some unique and intriguing challenges. One overriding rule that you should follow when communicating on the Internet is to follow all the rules you would normally follow in face-to-face interactions.[57] For example, in getting acquainted with someone, don't disclose too much too soon. Be a good "listener," and confirm the statements made by your Internet partners. Be other-oriented by considering how your Internet partners will react to what you have written: What is their context for interpreting your messages; what do they know about you; what do you know about them?

The kind of information you provide and acquire through CMC has a direct impact on impression formation and relational attraction. Even though you are missing many of the usual nonverbal cues from which you draw impressions of other people (for example, their physical looks), you still form impressions about those with whom you interact. Prominent Internet researcher Joseph Walther has found that the impressions people develop about other people on the Internet become more similar to the impressions formed in face-to-face interactions the more users interacted.[58] In Chapter 3 you read about the various biases that affect your perception of others. These biases must be guarded against in computer-mediated interactions as well. You need different skills for ascertaining the personal qualities of an Internet partner from those you need in face-to-face relationships.

You can manage the impressions others form of you on the Internet through the control of the information you provide about yourself. In face-to-face encounters, your behaviors impact other people's impressions of you, whereas in Internet encounters there are fewer behaviors to observe. What you type and how you type are the major factors by which impressions are drawn. Impressions are also affected by your language selection, expression of sensitivity, and responsiveness to other peoples' messages.

Types of Computer-Mediated Communication (CMC)

Bulletin boards allow people to post messages without regard for who will read them, although threads often develop on bulletin boards where people respond to other postings. These can evolve into a kind of dialogue between or among posters, reaching a point at which controversies can erupt in "flaming," with individuals calling each other names and insulting one another. Regular reading of the same bulletin board often lets you develop a sense of the more active posters.

CMC is used as a replacement for traditional "snail" mail. People can send and receive "letters" (e-mail) with relative ease. In this way e-mail is not really a form of interpersonal communication, although it can be used to develop and maintain relationships. The speed by which people can send and receive letters through e-mail makes it seem a lot more interactive than traditional postal service. One emerging Internet norm is that you are expected to respond as soon as possible to your e-mail; failure to do so sometimes evokes resentment from correspondents.

Chat rooms (also referred to as Internet relay chat or IRC), where people are actively involved in sending and receiving messages, are more similar to face-to-face (FtF) interactions than is e-mail. Discussion groups or public chat rooms often involve many people engaging in a kind of group discussion. However, one intriguing aspect of public chat rooms is that even though ten or twelve people might be chatting at one time, the participants often pair up and simply respond to their partner's comments, ignoring the rest. Although at first confusing, chatters usually develop a knack for being able to discern relevant comments. Typed statements often start with the name to whom the message is intended. Such "interpersonal" dyadic exchanges often draw in the other chat room members, because everything that is written is open to public viewing. In this way it's like sitting in a small group in which you are talking with just one other member, but the other group members can still hear your conversation. Chatters often move to a "private room" where only those who are invited can participate. This allows chatters the privacy to carry on uninterrupted and confidential conversations. See if you can tell who is talking to whom in the following transcript of a fictional chat room:

SuperSteve:	Regis Philpin is cool.
Timeout:	I was bummed when they killed off the crew.
Beastie:	The first Star Wars is still the best—the story and effects were great.
SillySilk:	Can't believe the guy didn't know the Beatles made The White Album.
BrashnBold:	The effects stink. They're nothing compared to what they do now.
Super Steve:	Regis handled him well though—didn't make him feel too dumb.
BettyCracker:	But it was innovative for its time.
TinLizzie:	But if they were all saved, it wouldn't have been very realistic.
Beastie:	Yeah, and besides, Harrison Ford was great as Han.
Trouter:	I get enough realism from the news—I want to escape it at the movies.
BrashnBold:	I agree.
SillySilk:	I agree.
BettyCracker:	Right on.

In case you couldn't tell which comments went with which, we wrote this interaction so that all the names starting with the same letter are involved in a discussion with one another (regretfully, it doesn't happen this way on the Web). Often a chatter will use a unique color or font so that you can easily pick out his or her comments, and this does help in following a given thread.

Instant messaging is similar to private chat rooms. Most Internet providers allow their members to create a friends and family list. When any of the "buddies" you've put on your list are logged on to the Internet, it lets you know. You can then send them a message and engage them in an "instant" exchange of messages. Instant messaging approximates a personal conversation or a small-group discussion if you are connected with several people at the same time. One disadvantage of instant messaging is that you might be involved in some other activity when someone contacts you. This creates a "listening" problem for you, because you might try to continue your other computer activity while still instant-messaging; this results in dividing your attention and often causes delays or disconfirming responses to your partners. Handling this situation is similar to handling the same dilemma in a face-to-face situation; you should either tell your partner you can't talk right now, or you should postpone your other activity.

Comparing Face-to-Face (FtF) Communication to CMC

There are communication advantages and disadvantages to both FtF and computer-mediated interactions. In FtF people obtain a lot of information by seeing how the other person behaves, how they react, and how they look. However, such visual information has a down side when we base biased attributions on what we see (reacting to a person's age, sex, race, or physical size) that may not be readily apparent in CMC. We might engage in fruitful and fulfilling chat with someone online that we might have avoided if we first had seen what he or she looked like. Besides differing in the use of nonverbals, CMC has interesting characteristics related to the importance of the written word, how much time delay there is between the interactants' messages, the occurrence of deception, and ease of simply disappearing.

Nonverbal Communication

CMC is more limited in its use of nonverbal cues than FtF communication, lacking for instance the use of touch and smell and limited in the use of visual and aural cues. Thus words and graphics become more important in CMC than in FtF because you must rely solely on them to carry nonverbal messages. In FtF communication you can hear people's voices, see their facial expressions, and watch their body movements. These provide the context by which you attribute meaning to the words they speak. In CMC such cues are limited or nonexistent, which means words are taken at their face value. There are some basic things users do to add emotion to their messages, including CAPITALIZING THE MESSAGE (which is considered "yelling"), making letters **bold,** or using emoticons: keyboard combinations used to represent some emotion—smiley faces : -), frowning faces with glasses 8-(, and so on). Despite these efforts, the ability to tease or make sarcastic remarks is limited because there is no tone of voice in the written message, which means the author must usually write out an accompanying interpretation. For example, "Boy, am I insulted by that or what?!!!! (just kidding)."

Technology already has been developed that lets users go beyond the limitations of using only written words. Several chat rooms now feature the use of audio links and take on the feeling of a large telephone party line. The introduction of spoken instead of written messages on the Internet adds nonverbal information for listeners. Just like the telephone, audio chat rooms provide information that gives you hints about the person's age, sex, and ethnicity (through accents). In addition, people

can use the full range of vocal cues discussed in Chapter 7: pitch, tone, rate, volume, and silence. There are also visual chat rooms and teleconferencing that let you actually see the person with whom you are interacting. The use of video feed on the Internet makes it more and more like face-to-face interactions. Despite the availability of visual images, a recent visit by this author to such a site found most users posting surrogate images rather than actual ones.

Written Communication

Besides the restrictions on nonverbal communication, the use of the written word has other impacts on our Internet interactions. One online scholar suggests that a person's typing ability and writing skills affect the quality of any relationship that is developed.[59] The ability to encode thoughts quickly and accurately into written words is not a skill everyone has. Not only do writing skills affect your ability to express yourself and manage the relationship, but they also affect how you are perceived by others. Look at the following two e-mail messages and think about the impressions you form of the two authors.

GigoloMan: "Hey, babe, whad's up? no what im thnking now we shuld do?"

GentleJim: "Hi. Boy, have I been swamped with work lately. How's your day been?"

What's your impression of the two e-mailers? What affected your impression? The first example is filled with grammar and spelling errors that might create a negative impression because the author is not particularly skilled at writing. The second author uses correct grammar and spelling, which is more likely to produce a positive impression. The user name or nickname (also called a "nick" among CMC users) that is listed for each author also affects our impression.[60] "GigoloMan" sends a clear but politically incorrect message to those who see his moniker. The selection of words has a strong impact on the impression others draw about us from the Internet. All the material discussed in Chapter 6 on verbal communication and language is particularly relevant to the Internet, which is heavily word based.

One thing that has developed in CMC is the use of abbreviations to represent frequently used phrases, such as "K" for okay, or "L8er" for later (more of these can be found in the e-connections box that appears in Chapter 6.

Synchronous versus Asynchronous Interaction

In defining interpersonal communication in Chapter 1, we referred to the notion of being mutual. We described *mutual* as a transactional concept, meaning that the participants are influencing each other at the same time. In the cyber world, this notion is called *synchronicity*. A **synchronous interaction** involves both participants actively engaging in the interaction at the same time. Face-to-face interactions are, by their very nature, synchronous. Only some Internet interactions are synchronous, such as group or private chat sessions. Most Internet interactions are **asynchronous,** meaning that the participants are not necessarily logged on at the same time but rather send and receive posted messages. Bulletin boards, discussion forums, and e-mail represent asynchronous interactions. They are interactions to the degree that the participants post responses to what they have read. On bulletin boards a certain thread can continue for days or weeks about a particular subject. Your e-mails to friends often reflect responses to the e-mails they sent you, and they will then respond to your e-mails.

Even synchronous Internet interactions entail some response delay. It takes longer to formulate a typewritten response than a spoken or nonverbal one. The

synchronous interaction.
Occurs when participants are actively engaging in an interaction at the same time.

asynchronous interaction.
Occurs when participants send and receive messages from each other with extended periods of delay between reception and response.

amount of delay (which is similar to silence in FtF interactions) can have an impact on the interpretation of the message's meaning. In chat sessions, participants expect to see a response very quickly to their posting. This is one reason chat sessions often involve very short and concise messages that can be rapidly written and sent. Most chat sessions involve a rapid succession of short messages that foster a sense of synchronicity and interaction. By the time a long message gets written and sent, it is often no longer germane to the discussion. The exception to this is when people are in private or small-group chat sessions, where they ask questions for which a longer, more developed response is expected.

E-mailing someone allows you time to compose your message and craft it more carefully than you might in a FtF interpersonal interaction. You can take time to consider your message and delete it before sending if you don't feel you have worded the message the way you want. Even in chat sessions, you might finish typing a line and then decide to delete it and write something else. In face-to-face interactions, people can think about what they want to say; but once having spoken, they can not take it back. As a sender of Internet messages, you have more control over what you say and the impression you create; as the receiver of Internet messages, realize that the other person has had the chance to consider carefully his or her message for its greatest impact on you. Such deliberation is one reason you must be cautious about accepting the validity of Internet messages—deception is relatively easy.

● Deception and Disappearance

The detection of deception in face-to-face encounters is aided by the presence of nonverbal cues. A 50-year-old white male (named Sam) could not claim to be a 20-year-old Chinese female (Samantha) without a major makeover. However, online such deception is almost as easy as simply typing the words. We say almost, because you can assess the content of the written message for clues to deceit. Sam writing as Samantha might talk about how much "she" enjoyed watching the Beatles live on the Ed Sullivan TV show (they appeared in 1964 and 1965) when she was growing up. This should alert you to the fact that Samantha would have to be older than 20, and probably not from China. College student respondents in one study reported the most common form of deception detection occurred when someone made an implausible statement or bragged.[61] The criteria for detecting deception apparently change as the Internet relationship becomes more intimate. As "friendships" develop over the Internet, to detect deception people come to depend on the personal knowledge and impressions of their partners acquired over the course of their correspondence.[62] Interestingly, this study also found that those who reported lying most were the ones most likely to suspect other users of lying.[63]

The ease with which someone can create a false persona means that you need to be cautious in forming relationships with Internet strangers. Besides developing relationships with people who falsely present themselves, another aspect about Internet relationships is that a person can simply disappear or assume another nick without your ever knowing. Unless the person is using a site-specific user name, such as "iastate.edu" or "swt.edu," which represent university locations, you may have no direct knowledge about where they reside, much less their names. The use of an AOL, MSN, or Hotmail address means you are virtually in the blind about the people with whom you interact. People can simply change their e-mail addresses, and you are totally cut off. Disappearing is more difficult or at least impractical in face-to-face relationships; disappearing from a classmate with whom you've had a relationship would necessitate dropping the course and maybe even out of school.

Knowing that you will be continuing to see a person puts different kinds of demands on relationship management and termination from the demands of the Internet.

Comparing FtF Communication to CMC

Nonverbal Communication	The limitation of nonverbal cues in CMC means you depend on variations in the text to convey nonverbal meaning.
Written Communication	The selection and use of words conveys important information about the sender.
Synchronous versus Asynchronous Communication	The different types of CMC vary in terms of the transactional activity from almost simultaneous to highly delayed.
Deception and Disappearance	The lack of FtF nonverbal cues reduces your ability to detect deception in CMC. Individuals can change their e-mail address and stop corresponding.

Using CMC to Initiate New Relationships

People are forming personal relationships over the Internet. In a study reported in 1996 about discussion groups, over 60 percent of the survey respondents reported forming personal relationships with someone they met on the Internet.[64] Further analyses of these relationships revealed an almost equal number of mixed-sex (55 percent) and same-sex relationships (45 percent), and only 8 percent were considered romantic. Over half of the respondents reported communication with their "friend" at least once a week. Interestingly, this study found women were more likely to form personal relationships in these newsgroups than men (72 percent of the female respondents, as compared to 55 percent of the males). There is an increasing likelihood that you will find yourself in a position of initiating and forming relationships with people you have met through the Internet. In general, the same principles and skills you read about in the last two chapters apply to the Internet. For example, similar strategies are used in the opening and closing of FtF and computer-mediated interactions.[65] However, there are some unique issues you should understand as you enter the world of CMC relationships.

Choose the Right Chat Room

One way we normally make friends is by engaging in activities where we meet people with similar interests. You probably have made friends with people who are members of your church, softball team, or math class. One form of attraction discussed in Chapter 9 dealt with being attracted to those who share similar interests. This same form of attraction exists on the Internet and can be used as the basis for starting relationships. Finding people with similar interests on the Internet is relatively easy, because chat rooms are often organized according to topics and interest groups. There are chat rooms or discussion groups for almost every sport, activity, and interest that you can imagine. And if there isn't one, you can actually create your own. There are also general social chat rooms that are very unstructured and have the same feeling as visiting a bar that has the reputation for being a "meat" market or a pickup place. At times the new information highway seems more like Bourbon Street than Sesame Street. Being a regular contributor to the more topically based chat rooms usually provides a safer environment for getting to know other chatters. As chatters share thoughts on the given topic, they often share more and more personal information as well, which allows for the development of online relationships.

Accept the Slower Pace of Relational Development

As mentioned earlier, the development of impressions is slower in CMC than FtF. This means that the process of forming interpersonal relationships is also likely to be slower. The major reason for this difference is that almost all information on the Internet must be put into text, whereas FtF interactions use a variety of nonverbal channels. Early researchers disputed the notion that true interpersonal relationships could be formed online, but subsequent research has found that the kind of effects that occur quickly in FtF interactions also occur on the Internet but just require more time.[66] CMC users can self-disclose honestly and openly with each other, to the point of forming truly intimate relationships. One advantage of the text-only medium is a reduction in our perceptual biases about a person's physical attractiveness.[67] At some point in Internet relationships, the users often provide a physical description of themselves (people seem to want to know the other person's sex, age, and location at the very beginning); eventually they exchange photographs and even arrange to meet in person.

Participation in chat rooms or bulletin boards often involves exploring the unknown, and that uncertainty creates anxiety and restraint. However, the anonymity with which you can interact gives you a freedom to be open. The tension caused by these two forces is apparent when you begin interacting with strangers over the Internet. These are like the dialectical tensions discussed in Chapter 9 that explain relational development. Despite being able to choose a nick that hides your identity, most of us are still cautious about what we write and the information we disclose about ourselves. The process of building trust with another user to the point of feeling comfortable disclosing intimate information about yourself may take longer on the Internet than in person. Internet relationships can even reach a point of interdependence where you establish regular chat times or daily e-mail exchanges that are part of relational maintenance. You turn to your Internet partner for the same support, confirmation, and advice that your FtF relationships provide.

Apply Strong Verbal Skills

The point has been made repeatedly about the nonverbal communication limitations of CMC. Sending someone a hug and a kiss over the Internet does not provide the same kind of satisfaction as it does in person. Among the conversational skills used in FtF interactions are verbal and nonverbal expressiveness (including being articulate), listening and nonverbal sensitivity, humor, effective question asking, and responsiveness. These skills have their parallels in CMC, but for the most part are dependent on the ability to express yourself in writing. The reliance on verbal strategies is demonstrated by a study that found that e-mail pen pals apparently compensated for the lack of nonverbal feedback by increasing the use of personal questions.[68] Thus, having good questions-asking skills would prove advantageous on the Internet.

The most skilled Internet communicators know CMC shorthand, incorporate emoticons and other devices to enhance their text, and adapt to their partners. As a listener/respondent, you can't use eye contact, head nodding, and "uh-huhs" to let the person know you are attentive and interested. You must write responses that show you are listening. This reflects another advantage of the Internet over FtF—you have a record of what was sent by your partner. So instead of not hearing what he or she said because your mind was wandering, you can simply review what was written if you spaced out during a chat session. It's a good idea to hang on to e-mail so you can look through previous correspondence if you are afraid you have forgotten some information your partner shared.

People who are highly dependent on their nonverbal expressiveness and perceptiveness are disadvantaged on the Internet. People who express their emotions through nonverbal behaviors might find themselves having to literally "spell it out" on the Internet. The Internet can actually improve your FtF nonverbal skills because you develop a heightened awareness of your use of nonverbal behaviors to communicate. Having to write out an accompanying facial expression, tone of voice, or gesture increases your appreciation for how you use nonverbal communication. You might experience some frustration at the inability to express some things nonverbally, but you can develop ways to compensate for this limitation over time.

The limited nonverbal cues on the Internet mean that the principles of language discussed in Chapter 6 are probably more applicable to CMC than to FtF. The word is extremely important in our chat sessions and e-mails. However, we also have time to consider our words carefully before transmitting them. Our words have power and can have a dramatic impact on the success of our Internet interactions. The impact of words is obvious during flame wars. Flaming hurts feelings and causes people to be turned off to a particular individual or Web site. The management of such conflicts requires application of the skills discussed in Chapter 8.

You may unintentionally hurt someone's feelings by what you write, and can apologize and repair the damage. However, e-mail has become an increasing

e-connections
Netiquette: Network Etiquette

Various prescriptive lists of how to appropriately behave on the Internet. The following is one such list that provides ten rules of "Netiquette:"

Rule 1. Remember the human.

Rule 2. Adhere to the same standards of behavior online that you follow in real life.

Rule 3. Know where you are in cyberspace.

Rule 4. Respect other people's time and bandwidth.

Rule 5. Make yourself look good online.

Rule 6. Share expert knowledge.

Rule 7. Help keep flame wars under control.

Rule 8. Respect other people's privacy.

Rule 9. Don't abuse your power.

Rule 10. Be forgiving of other people's mistakes.

Source: The above core rules of *Netiquette* by Virginia Shea appear courtesy of the author and Albion.com. For a further discussion and explanation of these and other rules for behavior on the Internet, you can find *Netiquette* at the following Web site: http://www.albion.com/netiquette/book/index.html

medium for sexual harassment, aggressive behavior, and harsh and unbridled criticism in the workplace.[69] One possible reason is that people feel less inhibited about what they write because of the physical separation they have from the person to whom they send the e-mail.[70] One of your authors got into a situation with a colleague, sending back and forth e-mails that became more and more belligerent. Realizing this was happening, your author went down the hallway to the other person's office and sat down to discuss the issue they were e-mailing about. Both the tenor and success of the interaction improved when the interaction was conducted face-to-face.

Using CMC to Maintain Existing Relationships

A recent study found that the major use of home e-mail was for relationship maintenance.[71] This included using e-mail as a way to keep in touch with family and friends. E-mail is simple, quick, cheap, convenient, efficient, and provides a sense of interaction. For ongoing relationships, e-mail provides a kind of freedom from time zone and schedule conflicts allowing users to send out messages at their convenience. Survey respondents reported that e-mail made it easier to share ideas, express opinions, and provide information with friends and family all over the world.[72] As of July 2000, the Internet provider America On Line handled 110 million e-mails daily. Multiply this by the number of providers and add the growth that is occurring, and we get a glimpse of how important this medium is to interpersonal relationship maintenance. We use e-mail, instant chat, chat rooms, and discussion groups as a way of interacting with our friends and family. The expansion of CMC has begun to produce a virtual community, **computer-supported social networks (CSSN's).**[73] The development of social networks is enhanced by the ability of users to create buddy lists. These lists result in personal networks of friends with whom you can exchange group-addressed e-mails or create group chat sessions.

For the most part, the rules and principles discussed in the last chapter on how to maintain relationships apply to the use of CMC. The Internet simply provides another tool by which you can implement the strategies that were discussed in that chapter. For example, you can send e-mails in which you engage in a discussion about the nature of your relationship, express your emotions, or attempt to gain compliance for some request. In some ways, such discussions might be easier online than face-to-face. You have time to consider your statements and not having to face someone in person as you talk about sensitive issues may help reduce feelings of threat. The following are some of the ways you can use the Internet to help you maintain and even escalate existing interpersonal relationships.

Communicate!

The very act of sending regular e-mails or engaging in chat sessions is probably the primary way the Internet helps maintain relationships. Maintaining an active line of communication with people is one of the best ways to preserve the relationship. Interest in the other person and commitment to the relationship is reflected in the very act of communicating. However, the amount of communication that is needed is defined by the people in the relationship. You might have one friend whom you e-mail daily and another whom you e-mail two or three times a year. Are these relationships different? Is one less intimate than the other? The answers are not really cut and dry. You might feel as close to both people, but the daily

computer-supported social network (CSSN). A virtual community created by the social networking among individuals through CMC.

interactions create a sense of interdependence that is probably not found in the other relationship. Daily interactions mean you are both informed about each other's activities and probably providing daily support and confirming each other's value as a person.

Increases or decreases in how much you communicate with someone provides one way to signal your level of interest and commitment to the relationship. A change in the amount of communication represents a turning point in the relationship's development (as discussed in Chapter 9). You establish expectations about how often you e-mail a particular person, and deviations from those expectations signal a potential change in the relationship. You might become concerned about the status of a relationship if you have had daily exchanges of e-mails with a friend and then notice that he or she only responds every couple of days. This might prompt you to engage in a direct strategy and inquire about the status of the person and the relationship.

The Internet might actually result in increased communication among friends and lovers who are separated by distance. Information technologist Patricia Wallace speculates that the ease with which people can send each other things like e-mail greeting cards results in increased communication.[74] People are creative in the way they use the Internet to make contact and interact. One of your author's sons still manages to play games over the Internet with a school friend who has moved away. Wallace tells a story in her book, *The Psychology of the Internet,* about a couple who use the Internet to keep in contact when the husband is away on business trips and who link up to play bridge online with other people.[75]

● Use Relational Maintenance Strategies

Keeping in contact with someone is one way to maintain the relationship and show your interest. You can also use a variety of the other strategies discussed in Chapter 10. In your e-mails you should appropriately disclose information about yourself. Remember that self-disclosure is related to relational development. Don't disclose too much if you are not interested in escalating the relationship; however, not disclosing anything might create stagnation and de-escalation. Some of these disclosures might include sharing your emotions. Having limited nonverbal cues means that your partner depends on you verbalizing your feelings. You can describe the feelings you have about events in your life and you can also express your feelings toward your partner. Talking about your feelings for your friend and engaging in other relational talk as well is another way to maintain your relationships over the Internet. Relationship talk and expressing feelings are fruitful when done within the norms appropriate to the relational stage. The Internet can seduce you into being too open about your feelings and thoughts about your relationships, as compared to face-to-face discussions. Just as you need to show restraint in face-to-face disclosures, you need to do the same in CMC.

Dependence on verbal messages means that you need to monitor your perceptions to ensure that you have accurately interpreted your partner's messages. Asking for clarification, expressing misunderstanding, or paraphrasing back what you think your partner means are good ways to enhance the accuracy of messages. Such strategies help maintain relationships because they reduce the impact of conflicts and stress associated with misunderstanding. Apply the principles of listening discussed in Chapter 5 to your behavior during on-line relational interactions. Empathic listening on the Internet involves writing to let your partners know that you are sensitive to and understand their feelings. You can write back messages that show you are involved and engaged in the discussion of their situation. The use of confirming responses that show you understand their feelings will help maintain a positive relationship.

Be Other-Oriented and Adapt

The way you write back to your partner depends on your relationship and what you know about your partner. Throughout this text we have emphasized trying to look at interactions from your partner's perspective—to socially decenter and to empathize. This principle is no less applicable to the maintenance of Internet relationships. As you acquire more and more knowledge about your partner through both your FtF and CMC interactions, apply that knowledge by adapting your communication. If anything, CMC provides you more time to take into consideration what you know about another person and create appropriate messages. As you compose your words on the computer, it is easy to forget that another human

recap   Using CMC to Initiate and Maintain Relationships

Initiating

● Choose the right chat room.	Interact in places where you are likely to find other people who share your interests.
● Accept the slower pace of relational development.	The process of forming trust and getting to know another person online will probably be slower than FtF relationships.
● Apply strong verbal skills.	CMC favors those who have the ability to express themselves well in a written and graphic mode.

Maintenance

● Communicate.	The very act of regularly sending messages to another person is one way to help maintain the relationship.
● Use relational maintenance strategies.	Appropriate self-disclosing, sharing feelings, and relationship talk are among the strategies that can be used.
● Be other-oriented and adapt.	Use the knowledge you can about other people through CMC to adapt your communication.

being will be reading and interpreting those messages—and not just any anonymous human, but one with whom you have formed a defined relationship, one with whom you share a bond and commitment. Accordingly, compose messages that reflect your understanding and appreciation of that other person.

Summary

Interpersonal interactions occur in a variety of contexts. Communication principles and skills can be applied to interpersonal relationships at home, at work, and on the Internet.

A family unit is made up of any number of people who live in relationship with one another over time in a common living space and are usually, but not always, united by marriage and kinship. One model for describing families considers family cohesion and adaptability and the role of communication in affecting family members' roles and relationships. The term *cohesion* refers to the emotional bonding and the feeling of closeness that families experience. The term *family adaptability* refers to the flexibility of family members in responding to changes in family roles, rules, and relationships.

Communication among family members includes interactions between husbands and wives, between parents and their children, and among siblings. Married couples can be categorized as traditional (being interdependent, sharing, and compassionate), independent (allowing for individual space but exhibiting sharing and compassion), separates (supporting marriage but putting the individual above the couple), or mixed (displaying different styles from each other). The way parents interact with their children strongly affects the development of their children's interpersonal communication skills. As children grow up, the relationships with their parents often change a great deal. The communication skills covered in this text are as applicable to parents dealing with children as they are to any relationship. Siblings often provide each other with partners for discussing such issues as dating or negative experiences without having to worry about disapproval or disappointment (which their parents might display in discussing such matters).

There is no one best way to be a family. However, several skills and strategies can enhance the quality of family life: Take time to talk with other family members about relationship issues; listen to others; support and encourage one another; use productive strategies for managing conflict and stress.

Relationships at work can involve both a task and social dimension. Forming friendships at work is one way people meet social needs and often helps produce a positive work atmosphere. The challenge of workplace interpersonal relationships is maximizing the satisfaction derived from such relationships while minimizing any negative impact on work performance. Relationships are often defined by the organization, especially in terms of power.

In most organizations communication flows up, down, horizontally, and out to customers. Through upward communication you can share ideas and strategies for improving the work process; you can also enhance your relationship with your boss. Downward communication involves making contact with those who work for you. Decide whether you will send messages in writing, in person, or through mediated channels. Horizontal communication concerns the communication you have with your colleagues on your level throughout the organization; most of the time, however, horizontal communication will occur with those who work in your immediate vicinity. Most organizations are encouraging better communication with customers and clients. Contacting those outside the organization who receive the organization's goods and services is an important way to ensure that what the organization offers is of high quality.

Leadership skills are important for success in most jobs. To enhance your leadership skills, cultivate people management skills such as listening, responding, organizing, and inspiring others. Leaders also need to know how to organize work, accomplish tasks, and relate well to others. An effective follower—a role most people play in organizations—makes relevant contributions, listens, follows directions, supports suggestions with evidence, and doesn't abandon ethical principles.

A new context for interpersonal relationships is cyberspace or the Internet. From an interpersonal perspective, you can initiate and develop new relationships totally through computer-mediated communication (CMC) or you can use the Internet as a tool for maintaining existing relationships. CMC includes bulletin boards, e-mail, chat rooms (IRC—Internet relay chat), and instant messaging. Compared to face-to-face (FtF) communication, CMC offers fewer nonverbal cues, more reliance on the written word, variation in terms of being synchronous (interacting at the same time) or asynchronous (interactive but not at the same time), and the ability of posters to be deceptive or even simply disappear.

In initiating new relationships over the Internet, you need to participate in the right kind of a chat room, generally one that reflects your interests. Follow the same rules in developing a new relationship over the Internet as you would in person, realizing that the process is generally slower through CMC. People with strong verbal skills have an advantage in using the Internet for initiating and developing interpersonal relationships. More information must be put into written form for Internet interactions than for FtF interactions. The very act of keeping up with communication through the Internet helps maintain existing relationships. The amount of CMC and changes in the amount provide some indication of a person's interest in and commitment to the relationship. CMC can be used as a tool for implementing the various relational maintenance strategies discussed in Chapter 10. Being other-centered in your cyberinteractions will help you adapt your messages and responses to maintain your interpersonal relationships most effectively.

For Discussion and Review

● Focus on Comprehension

1. What is a family?

2. Identify interpersonal communication skills that can enhance the quality of family life.

3. What are some suggestions for improving upward, downward, horizontal, and outward communication?

4. How does computer-mediated communication (CMC) compare to face-to-face (FtF) communication?

5. What rules are suggested for initiating a relationship on the Internet? For maintaining an existing relationship on the Internet?

🔴 Focus on Critical Thinking

6. Steve and Yvette both have full-time jobs and are raising two children. A lot of the household chores simply aren't getting done, and this bothers Steve. How should Steve initiate and manage a discussion about how these chores should be done?

7. Do you think the institution of the family is deteriorating, or is it just changing? Support your answer.

8. What would the relationship be like for each of the six mixed types of married couples? To what degree does it matter which style the husband and wife enact?

9. Jerry is president of Southwest Technical Computing. He has a sense that his managers are not tapping the wealth of ideas and suggestions that lower-level employees might have for improving productivity. What specific strategies could Jerry implement to improve upward communication?

10. Despite the availability of relatively cheap interactive video setups for Internet use, people don't seem to be turning to them as much as they are to text-only interactions. Why might this be the case? Which would you use if you had a choice of the two? Why?

🔴 Focus on Ethics

11. Twelve-year-old Nathan consistently does not get along with his other brothers and sisters. He also is not doing well in school. His parents want to take him to a counselor, but Nathan does not want to go. Should Nathan's parents insist that he attend counseling?

12. Is it ethical to withhold honest thoughts and feelings from other family members? Should family members always "tell it like it is"? Should parents encourage their children to "tell everything" they know and feel?

13. Clayton has e-mail at work, but not at home. His brother has e-mail at his home. Is it ethical for Clayton to use the computer at work on company time to send and receive e-mail messages from his brother three or four times a week?

14. In chat sessions on the Internet, is it really wrong to present false information about yourself just for fun when you know you will never meet the other people with whom you are interacting? Under what circumstances is describing yourself over the Internet as being of a different sex, age, race, or ethnicity ethical or unethical?

For Your Journal

1. Select two TV situation comedies or dramas that revolve around a family. One program could be one that is still broadcast in reruns, such as *Leave It to Beaver, All in the Family,* or *The Brady Bunch,* and the other show could be a more contemporary program. Describe the communication patterns in the TV programs that you observe. Draw on the principles and skills presented in this chapter as you describe the family communication patterns. You may even want to discuss which of your TV families seems to do the most effective job of communicating with one another.

2. Describe what someone would learn about your family if they were to view only the nonverbal elements of the way your family interacts. For example, imagine someone viewing a videotape of your family's daily activities, with the "sound turned off." Consider not only such factors as facial expression, eye contact, touch, and use of personal space, but also the way your home is arranged and the overall appearance of your family's dwelling.

3. Log on to a social chat room and then onto a topic-specific chat room. You don't have to post any messages; just be a "lurker" and watch what happens. What do people do to compensate for the lack of nonverbal cues? What do you notice about the messages themselves (for example, how long are they, what is the vocabulary like, how is the grammar, what jargon or slang is used)? How do the two sites compare in terms of language? Focus on a couple of the posters on each site. What is your impression of these posters on the basis of what you observe?

Learning with Others

1. After you have indicated whether you agree or disagree with the following statements, break into small groups and try to agree or disagree unanimously with each statement. Try to find reasons for differences of opinion. If your group cannot reach agreement or disagreement, you may change the wording in any statement to promote unanimity.

Agree–Disagree Statements about Families

_____ 1. Most family members know how to communicate effectively; they just don't take the time to practice what they know.

_____ 2. Family conflict is a symptom rather than a cause of deteriorating family relationships.

_____ 3. Family conflict is harmful to family harmony, and all conflict should be avoided at all costs.

_____ 4. Most family conflict occurs because we don't understand the other family member; we fail to communicate effectively.

_____ 5. Families function best if there is one central leader of the family.

_____ 6. Ineffective communication is the single most important cause of family conflict, divorce, and family tension.

_____ 7. Nonverbal communication (facial expression, eye contact, tone of voice, posture, and so on) is more important than verbal communication; what you do is more important than what you say.

_____ 8. It is sometimes necessary to ignore the feelings of others in order to reach a family decision.

_____ 9. The best way to love your marriage partner is to care more for your partner than you care for yourself.

_____ 10. Generally speaking, the quality of family life is deteriorating today.

_____ 11. There is one best approach or set of rules and principles that will ensure an effectively functioning family.

2. Divide into teams of two or three people. Each team will interview a business-person or supervisor in a nonprofit organization such as a hospital or school about the issues covered in this chapter. Ask such questions as

- What do you do to enhance upward communication among the people you supervise?

- What is your approach to leading others? What works and what doesn't work with your subordinates?

Afterward, discuss your results with other groups and see what general conclusions you can reach.

3. This is a leadership exercise. Read the following case study and complete the instructions. Then compare your group's task list and communication strategies with those of other groups.

🌑 Hurricane Preparedness Case

Although you have idly watched local meteorologists track Hurricane Bruce's destructive course through the Caribbean for several days, you have not given any serious thought to the possibility that the number 3-rated storm might directly affect your coastal city. However, at about seven o'clock this morning, the storm suddenly veered northward, putting it on course for a direct hit. Now the National Hurricane Center in Miami has posted a hurricane warning for your community. Forecasters are predicting landfall in approximately nine to twelve hours. Having taken no advance precautions, you are stunned by the amount of work you now must do to secure your three-bedroom suburban home, which is about a half mile from the beach, and to protect your family—your spouse and two children ages 5 and 12.

You have enough food in the house for two days. You also have one candle and a transistor radio with one weak battery. You have no other hurricane supplies, nor have you taken any hurricane precautions. Your group's task is to identify specific strategies for (1) ensuring the survival and safety of your family and property, and (2) assigning appropriate tasks to family members to carry out these strategies. First, brainstorm a list or sequence of events or lists of tasks that you need to accomplish. Then arrange them in priority order. Finally, decide the best way to assign and explain these tasks to various family members. Make notes about your decisions.

Internet Study Group

Find three or four other students in your class with whom you feel comfortable and confident. Arrange some times where you can all be logged on to the Internet at the same time to do instant messaging, send e-mails copied to all the other group members, or create a chat room for your group. Share information with one another about the last assignments you had for this class such as examinations or papers. Discuss among yourselves through the Internet what is expected for the assignments, share any information each of you has that might help the others prepare better, and ask questions to help clarify information. If you are preparing for an exam, each of you might pose practice questions to the others, or each take a turn explaining some concept.

Notes

Chapter 1

1. E. T. Klemmer and F. W. Snyder, "Measurement of Time Spent Communicating." *Journal of Communication,* 20 (June 1972): 142.

2. F. E. X. Dance and C. Larson, *Speech Communication: Concepts and Behavior* (New York: Holt, Rinehart and Winston, 1972).

3. Dance and Larson, *Speech Communication.*

4 J. T. Masterson, S. A. Beebe, N. H. Watson, *Invitation to Effective Speech Communication* (Glenview, IL: Scott, Foresman, 1989).

5. M. Buber, *I and Thou* (New York: Scribners, 1958); Also see M. Buber, *Between Man and Man* (New York: Macmillan, 1965). For a detailed discussion of perspectives on interpersonal communication and relationship development, see G. H. Stamp, "A Qualitatively Constructed Interpersonal Communication Model: A Grounded Theory Analysis," *Human Communication Research,* 25(4), (June 1999): 531–547; J. P. Dillard, D. H. Solomon, and M. T. Palmer, "Structuring the Concept of Relational Communication," *Communication Monographs,* 66 (March 1999): 49–65.

6. Buber, *I and Thou.*

7. D. Yankelovich, *The Magic of Dialogue: Transforming Conflict into Cooperation* (New York: Simon & Schuster, 1999); for an excellent discussion of dialogue, also see S. W. Littlejohn and K. Domenici, *Engaging Communication in Conflict: Systemic Practice* (Thousand Oaks, CA: Sage, 2001), pp. 25–51

8. Buber, *I and Thou.*

9. V. Satir, *Peoplemaking* (Palo Alto, CA: Science and Behavior Books, 1972).

10. K. E. Davis and M. Todd, "Assessing Friendship: Prototypes, Paradigm Cases, and Relationship Description," in *Understanding Personal Relationships,* edited by S. W. Duck and D. Perlman (London: Sage, 1985); B. Wellman, "From Social Support to Social Network," in *Social Support. Theory, Research and Applications,* edited by I. G. Sarason and B. R. Sarason (Dordrecht, Netherlands:

Nijhoff, 1985); R. Hopper, M. L. Knapp, and L. Scott, "Couples' Personal Idioms: Exploring Intimate Talk," *Journal of Communication,* 31 (1981): 23–33.

11. M. Argyle and M. Hendershot, *The Anatomy of Relationships* (London: Penguin Books, 1985), 14.

12. See J. L. Winsor, D. B. Curtis, and R. D. Stephens, "National Preferences in Business and Communication Education: A Survey Update," *Journal of the Association for Communication Administration,* 3 (September 1997), 174.

13. M. Argyle, *The Psychology of Happiness* (London: Routledge, 1987).

14. J. J. Lynch, *The Broken Heart: The Medical Consequences of Loneliness* (New York: Basic Books, 1977).

15. R. Korbin and G. Hendershot, "Do Family Ties Reduce Mortality: Evidence from the United States 1968," *Journal of Marriage and the Family,* 39 (1977): 737–45.

16. D. P. Phillips, "Deathday and Birthday: An Unexpected Connection," in *Statistics: A Guide to the Unknown,* edited by J. M. Tanur (San Francisco: Holden Day, 1972).

17. H. Lasswell, "The Structure and Function of Communication in Society" in *The Communication of Ideas,* edited by L. Bryson (New York: Institute for Religious and Social Studies, 1948), 37.

18. See V. E. Cronen, W. B. Pearce, and L. M. Harris, "The Coordinated Management of Meaning: A Theory of Communication," in *Human Communication Theory: Comparative Essays,* edited by F. E. X. Dance (New York: Harper & Row, 1982), 61–89.

19. For an excellent discussion of the effects of computer-mediated communication and interpersonal communication, see J. B. Walther, ""Interpersonal Effects in Computer-Mediated Interaction: A Relational Perspective," *Communication Research,* 19 (1992): 52–90; J. B. Walther, "Relational Aspects of Computer-Mediated Communication: Experimental and Longitudinal Observations," *Organization Science,* 6 (1995): 186–203; J. B. Walther, J. F. Anderson, and D. Park.

"Interpersonal Effects in Computer-Mediated Interaction: A Meta-Analysis of Social and Anti-Social Communication, *Communication Research,* 21 (1994): 460–487; N. Negroponte, *Being Digital* (New York: Knopf, 1995); J. B. Walther and L. Tidwell, "When Is Mediated Communication Not Interpersonal?" in K. Galvin and P. Cooper, *Making Connections* (Los Angeles, CA: Roxbury Press, 1996); P. Wallace, *The Psychology of the Internet* (Cambridge, England: Cambridge University Press, 1999).

20. J. B. Walther and J. K. Burgoon, "Relational Communication in Computer-Mediated Interaction," *Human Communication Research,* 19 (1992): 50–88.

21. L. K. Trevino, R. L. Draft, and R. H. Lengel, "Understanding Managers' Media Choices: A Symbolic Interactionist Perspective," in *Organizations and Communication Technology,* edited by J. Fulk and C. Steinfield (Newbury Park, CA: Sage, 1990), 71–74.

22. Walther and Tidwell.

23. I. Reed, "The World Is Here," in *Writin' Is Fighting* (New York: Atheneum, 1988).

24. See D. Barnlund, *Interpersonal Communication: Survey and Studies* (Boston: Houghton Mifflin, 1968).

25. O. Wiio, *Wiio's Laws—and Some Others* (Espoo, Finland: WelinGoos, 1978).

26. S. B. Shimanoff, *Communication Rules: Theory and Research* (Beverly Hills: Sage, 1980).

27. M. Argyle, M. Hendershot, and A. Furnham, "The Rules of Social Relationships," *British Journal of Social Psychology,* 24 (1985): 125–39.

28. T. Watzlawick, J. Bavelas, and D. Jackson, *The Pragmatics of Human Communication* (New York: Norton, 1967).

29. See J. C. McCroskey and M. [J.] Beatty, "The Communibiological Perspective: Implications for Communication in Instruction," *Communication Education,* 49(1) (January 2000). 1–6; M. J. Beatty and J. C. McCroskey, "Theory, Scientific Evidence, and the Communibiological Paradigm: Reflections on Misguided

Criticism," *Communication Education,* 49(1), (January 2000): 36–44. Also see J. C. McCroskey, J. A. Daly, M. M. Martin, and M. J. Beatty, (eds.), *Communication and Personality: Trait Perspectives* (Cresskil, NJ: Hampton Press, 1998).

30. See J. Ayres and T. S. Hopf, "The Long-Term Effect of Visualization in the Classroom: A Brief Research Report," *Communication Education,* 39 (1990): 75–78; and J. Ayres and T. S. Hopf, "Visualization: A Means of Reducing Speech Anxiety," *Communication Education,* 34 (1985): 318–23.

31. For a discussion of criticism of the communibiological approach, see C. M. Condit, "Culture and Biology in Human Communication: Toward a Multi-Causal Model," *Communication Education,* 49(1), (January 2000): 7–24.

32. M. Argyle, *The Psychology of Interpersonal Behavior* (London: Penguin, 1983).

33. M. Argyle is widely acknowledged as the first scholar to suggest a systematic approach to apply learning theory to the development of social skills, including interpersonal communication skills. See M. Argyle, *The Psychology of Interpersonal Behavior.*

Chapter 2

1. K. Horney, *Neurosis and Human Growth* (New York: Norton, 1950), 17.

2. J. T. Masterson, *Speech Communication in Traditional and Contemporary Marriages* (doctoral dissertation, University of Denver, 1977). Also see S. A. Beebe and J. T. Masterson, *Family Talk: Interpersonal Communication in the Family* (New York: Random House, 1986), 91–100.

3. For an excellent discussion of the role of gender and communication, see J. C. Pearson, L. H. Turner, and W. Todd-Mancillas, *Gender and Communication,* 3d ed. (Dubuque, IA: William C. Brown, 1995). Also see D. K. Ivy and P. Backlund, *Exploring Genderspeak* (New York: McGraw-Hill, 2000).

4. Pearson, Turner, and Mancillas, *Gender and Communication;* Ivy and Backlund, *Exploring Genderspeak.*

5. D. G. Ancona, "Groups in Organizations: Extending Laboratory Models," in *Annual Review of Personality and Social Psychology: Group and Intergroup Processes,* edited by C. Hendrick (Beverly Hills,CA: Sage, 1987), 207–31. Also see D. G. Ancona and D. E. Caldwell, "Beyond

Task and Maintenance: Defining External Functions in Groups," *Group and Organizational Studies,* 13 (1988): 468–94.

6. S. L. Bem, "The Measurement of Psychological Androgyny," *Journal of Consulting and Clinical Psychology,* 42 (1974): 155–62.

7. L. A. Lefton, *Psychology* (Boston: Allyn & Bacon, 2000).

8. J. C. McCroskey and M. J. Beatty, "The Communibiological Perspective: Implications for Communication Instruction," *Communication Education,* 49 (January 2000): 1–28.

9. C. M. Condit, "Culture and Biology in Human Communication: Toward a Multi-Causal Model," *Communication Education,* 49 (January 2000): 7–24.

10. P. Zimbardo, *Shyness: What It Is, What to Do About It* (Reading, MA: Addison-Wesley, 1977).

11. S. Booth-Butterfield, "Instructional Interventions for Situational Anxiety and Avoidance," *Communication Education,* 37 (1988): 214–23.

12. J. C. McCroskey and V. P. Richmond, *Fundamentals of Human Communication: An Interpersonal Perspective* (Prospect Heights, IL: Waveland Press, 1996).

13. S. Booth-Butterfield, "Instructional Interventions."

14. Zimbardo, *Shyness.*

15. Our discussion of the Myers-Briggs Type Indicator is based on an excellent summary of research by L. A. Lefton, *Psychology* (Boston: Allyn and Bacon, 2000), 426–427.

16. E. Berne, *Games People Play* (New York: Grove Press, 1964).

17. L. Armstrong, *It's Not About the Bike: My Journey Back to Life* (New York: Putnam's, 2000), 146.

18. K. Sugarman, "Tennis and Positive Self-Talk," *WorldWide Tennis Ladder* (August 2000): http://www.sportsladders.com/tennis/tips/artcl-selftalk.asp.

19. Joe Ayres and Theodore S. Hopf, "The Long-Term Effect of Visualization in the Classroom: A Brief Research Report," *Communication Education,* 39 (1990): 75–78.

20. F. E. X. Dance and C. Larson, *The Functions of Human Communication* (New York: Holt, Rinehart and Winston, 1976), 141.

21. Our discussion of decentering specific-other and generalized other perspective is from M. V. Redmond, "The

Functions of Empathy (Decentering) in Human Relations," *Human Relations,* 42 (1993): 593–606. Also see M. V. Redmond, "A Multidimensional Theory and Measure of Social Decentering," *Journal of Research in Personality* (1995).

22. H. Brody. *The Placebo Response: How You Can Release Your Body's Inner Pharmacy for Better Health* (New York: HarperCollins, 2000). Also see H. Brody, "Tapping the Power of the Placebo," *Newsweek,* August 14, 2000, 68.

23. A. A. Milne, "Pooh Does a Good Deed," *Pooh Sleepytime Stories* (New York: Golden Press, 1979), 44.

24. Summarized by D. E. Hamachek, *Encounters with the Self* (New York: Holt, Rinehart and Winston, 1982), 3–5, and edited by R. B. Adler and N. Towne, *Looking Out/Looking In* (Fort Worth, TX: Harcourt Brace Jovanovich, 1993). Also see C. R. Berger, "Self Conception and Social Information Processing," in *Personality and Interpersonal Communication,* edited by J. C. McCroskey and J. A. Daly (1986): 275–303.

25. A. A. Milne, "Owl Finds a Home," in *Pooh Sleepytime Stories* (New York: Golden Press, 1979), 28.

26. Hamachek, *Encounters;* Berger, "Self-Conception."

27. W. C. Schutz, FIRO: *A Three-Dimensional Theory of Interpersonal Behavior* (New York: Holt, Rinehart & Winston, 1958).

28. McCroskey and Beatty, "Communibiological Perspective."

29. See J. C. McCroskey and V. P. Richmond, *Fundamentals of Human Communication.*

30. I. Altman and D. A. Taylor, *Social Penetration: The Development of Interpersonal Relationships* (New York: Holt, Rinehart & Winston, 1973).

31. J. Luft, *Group Process: An Introduction to Group Dynamics* (Palo Alto, CA: Mayfield, 1970).

32. J. Powell, *why am I afraid to tell you who I am?* (Niles, IL: Argus Communications, 1969), 12.

33. Powell, *why am I afraid.*

34. M. Argyle, M. Henderson, and A. Furnham, "The Rules of Social Relationships," *British Journal of Social Psychology,* 24 (1985): 125–39.

35. S. A. Beebe and J. T. Masterson, *Communicating in Small Groups: Principles and Practices* (New York: HarperCollins, 2000).

Chapter 3

1. C. R. Berger, "Self-Conception and Social Information Processing," In *Personality and Interpersonal Communication,* edited by J. C. McCroskey and J. A. Daly (Newbury Park, CA: Sage, 1987), 275–304.

2. P. R. Hinton, *The Psychology of Interpersonal Perception* (New York: Routledge, 1993).

3. D. W. Miller, "Looking Askance at Eyewitness Testimony," *Chronicle of Higher Education,* February 25, 2000: A19–20.

4. P. Watzlawick, J. Bevelas and D. Jackson, *The Pragmatics of Human Communication* (New York: Norton, 1967).

5. A. L. Sillars, "Attribution and Communication: Are People Naive Scientists or Just Naive?" in *Social Cognition and Communication,* edited by M. E. Roloff and C. R. Berger (Beverly Hills: Sage, 1982), 73–106.

6. Watzlawick et al., *The Pragmatics of Human Communication.*

7. R. D. Laing, H. Phillipson, and A. R. Lee, *Interpersonal Perception* (New York: Springer, 1966).

8. C. R. Berger and J. J. Bradac, *Language and Social Knowledge* (Baltimore: Edward Arnold, 1982).

9. S. Asch, "Forming Impressions of Personality," *Journal of Abnormal and Social Psychology,* 41 (1946): 258–290.

10. D. M. Wegner and R. R. Vallacher, *Implicit Psychology: An Introduction to Social Cognition* (New York: Oxford University Press, 1977).

11. S. Bruner and R. Tagiuri, "The Perception of People," in *Handbook of Social Psychology,* edited by G. Lindzey (Cambridge, MA: Addison-Wesley, 1954).

12. G. A. Kelly, *The Psychology of Personal Constructs* (New York: Norton, 1995).

13. F. Heider, *The Psychology of Interpersonal Relations* (New York: Wiley, 1958). Also see E. E. Jones and K. E. Davis, "From Acts to Dispositions: The Attribution Process in Person Perception," in *Advances in Experimental Social Psychology,* vol. 2, edited by L. Berkowitz (New York: Academic Press, 1965).

14. G. A. Kelly, *The Psychology of Personal Constructs* (New York: Norton, 1955).

15. R. Nisbett and L. Ross, *Human Inference: Strategies and Shortcomings of Social Judgment* (Englewood Cliffs, NJ: Prentice Hall, 1980).

16. Nisbett and Ross, *Human Inference.*

17. E. E. Jones and R. Nisbett, "The Actor and the Observer: Divergent Perceptions of the Causes of Behavior," in *Attribution: Perceiving the Causes of Behavior,* edited by E. E. Jones et al. (Morristown, NJ: General Learning Press, 1972), 79–94; D. E. Kanouse and L. R. Hanson, Jr., "Negativity in Evaluations," in Jones et al., *Attribution,* 47–62.

18. Nisbett and Ross, *Human Inference.*

19. Hinton, *The Psychology of Interpersonal Perception.*

20. M. V. Redmond, "The Functions of Empathy (Decentering) in Human Relations," *Human Relations,* 42(4), (1993): 593–606

Chapter 4

1. Chen and Starosta, "Intercultural Sensitivity," 5.

2. Chen and Starosta, "Intercultural Sensitivity," 5.

3. M. E. Ryan, "Another Way to Teach Migrant Students," *Los Angeles Times,* March 31, 1991, B20, as cited by M. W. Lustig and J. Koester, *Intercultural Competence: Interpersonal Communication Across Cultures* (New York: Longman, 1999), 11.

4. Lustig and Koester, *Intercultural Competence,* 8.

5. G. Chen and W. J. Starosta, "A Review of the Concept of Intercultural Sensitivity," *Human Communication,* 1, (1997) 7.

6. Lustig and Koester, *Intercultural Competence,* 10.

7. *Newsweek,* July 12, 1999, 51.

8. U.S. Bureau of the Census, *Statistical Abstract of the United States: 1996,* 116th ed. (Washington, DC: 1996) as cited by Lustig and Koester, *Intercultural Competence,* 8.

9. U.S. Bureau of the Census, *Report 1999,* as reported in Randolf E. Schmid, *Austin-American Statesman,* September 17, 1999, A20.

10. U.S. Bureau of the Census, *Report 1999,* A20.

11. "One Nation, One Language?" *U.S. News & World Report,* September 25, 1995, 40, cited by Lustig and Koester, *Intercultural Competence,* 10.

12. J. Malone, "Racial Categories in 2000 Census Reflect Diversity," *Austin-American Statesman,* March 11, 2000, A10.

13. Adapted from *Information Please Almanac* (Boston: Houghton Mifflin, 1990) and *World Almanac and Book of Facts* (New York: World Almanac, 1991), as cited by Lustig and Koester, *Intercultural Competence,* 11.

14. Lustig and Koester, *Intercultural Competence,* 9.

15. Lustig and Koester, *Intercultural Competence,* 318.

16. G. Smith (Ed.), *Communication and Culture* (New York: Holt, Rinehart & Winston, 1966).

17. G. Hofstede, *Culture's Consequences: International Differences in Work-Related Values* (Beverly Hills, CA: Sage, 1980).

18. P. Cateora and J. Hess, *International Marketing* (Homewood, IL: Irwin, 1979), 89; as discussed by L. A. Samovar and R. E. Porter, *Communication Between Cultures* (Belmont, CA: Wadsworth, 2001), 52.

19. Hofstede, *Culture's Consequences.*

20. For an extensive summary and critique of Hofstede's research, see M. W. Lustig and J. Koester, *Intercultural Competence,* 111.

21. G. Hofstede, Culture's Consequences; also see G. Hofstede, "Cultural Dimensions in Management and Planning," *Asia Pacific Journal of Management* (January 1984): 81–98.

22. For an extensive review of communication gender differences see L. H. Turner, K. Dindia, and J. C. Pearson, "An Investigation of Female/Male Verbal Behaviors in Same-Sex and Mixed-Sex Conversations," *Communication Reports,* 8 (Summer 1995): 86–96.

23. An excellent analysis and application of gender communication research has been compiled by A. Cornyn-Selby, "Are You from Another Planet or What?" presented at the Joint Service Family Readiness Matters Conference, July 14, 1999, Phoenix, Arizona.

24. See D. K. Ivy and P. Backlund, *Exploring GenderSpeak: Personal Effectiveness in Gender Communication* (New York: McGraw-Hill, 2000).

25. Hofstede, "Cultural Dimensions in Management and Planning."

26. Hofstede, *Culture's Consequences.*

27. W. B. Gudykunst, *Bridging Differences: Effective Intergroup Communication* (Newbury Park, CA: Sage, 1998), 45.

28. Gudykunst, *Bridging Differences.*

29. E. T. Hall, *Beyond Culture* (Garden City, NY: Doubleday, 1976).

30. Samovar and Porter, *Communication Between Cultures*, 234.

31. M. V. Redmond and J. M. Bunyi, "The Relationship of Intercultural Communication Competence with Stress and the Handling of Stress as Reported by International Students," *International Journal of Intercultural Relations*, 17 (1993): 235–54; R. Brislen, *Cross-Cultural Encounters: Face-to-Face Interaction* (New York: Pergamon Press, 1981).

32. W. G. Sumner, *Folkways* (Boston: Ginn, 1906), as cited by James W. Neuliep, *Intercultural Communication: A Contextual Approach* (Boston: Houghton Mifflin, 2000), 160.

33. Lustig and Koester, *Intercultural Competence*.

34. J. W. Neuliep and J. C. McCroskey, "The Development of a U.S. and Generalized Ethnocentrism Scale," *Communication Research Reports*, 14 (1997): 385–398.

35. R. E. Axtell, *Do's and Taboos of Hosting International Visitors* (New York: John Wiley & Sons, 1989), 118.

36. Kluckhohn and Murry, 1953 as quoted by J. S. Caputo, H. C. Hazel, and C. McMahon, *Interpersonal Communication* (Boston: Allyn and Bacon, 1994), 304.

37. S. Kamekar, M. B. Kolsawalla, and T. Mazareth, "Occupational Prestige as a Function of Occupant's Gender," *Journal of Applied Social Psychology*, 19 (1988): 681–88.

38. "Call to Oust Law Teacher Gets Louder," *Austin American Statesman*, September 13, 1997, A-1, A-11.

39. Eleanor Roosevelt, as cited by Lustig and Koester, *Intercultural Competence*.

40. For an excellent discussion of world view and the implications for intercultural communication, see C. H. Dodd, *Dynamics of Intercultural Communication* (New York: McGraw-Hill, 1998).

41. Dodd, *Dynamics*, 75.

42. J. T. Wood, *Communication Mosaics: A New Introduction to the Field of Communication* (Belmont, CA: Wadsworth, 2001), 207; C. C. Innman, "Men's Friendships: Closeness in the Doing," in Julia T. Wood (Ed.), *Gendered Relationships* (Mountain View, CA: Mayfield), 95–110.

43. R. Berger and R. J. Calabrese, "Some Explorations in Initial Interactions and Beyond," *Human Communication Research*, 1 (1975): 99–125.

44. B. J. Broome, "Building Shared Meaning: Implications of a Relational Approach to Empathy for Teaching Intercultural Communication," *Communication Education*, 40 (1991): 235–249.

45. R. L. Casmir and N. C. Asuncion-Lande, "Intercultural Communication Revisited: Conceptualization, Paradigm Building, and Methodological Approaches," in *Communication Yearbook*, edited by J. A. Anderson, vol. 12 (Newbury Park, CA: Sage, 1989), 278–309.

46. Broome, "Building Shared Meaning."

47. W. B. Gudykunst and Y. Kim, *Communicating with Strangers* (New York: Random House 1984); Gudykunst, *Bridging Differences*.

48. L. B. Szalay and G. H. Fisher, "Communication Overseas," in *Toward Internationalism: Readings in Cross-Cultural Communication*, edited by E. C. Smith and L. E Luce (Rowley, MA: Newbury House,1979). Also see Paul E. King and Chris R. Sawyer, "Mindfulness, Mindlessness and Communication Instruction," *Communication Education*, 47 (October 1998): 326–336.

49. M. V. Redmond, "The Functions of Empathy (decentering) in Human Relations," *Human Relations*, 42 (1993): 593–606. Also see M. V. Redmond, "A Multidimensional Theory and Measure of Social Decentering," *Journal of Research in Personality*, 29 (1995): 35–58; for an excellent discussion of the role of emotions in establishing empathy, see D. Goleman, *Emotional Intelligence* (New York: Bantam, 1995).

50. See H. Giles, A. Mulack, J. J. Bradac, and P. Johnson, "Speech Accommodation Theory: The First Decade and Beyond," in *Communication Yearbook*, edited by M. L. McLaughli, vol. 10 (Newbury Park, CA: Sage, 1987), 13–48. For an excellent summary and application of accommodation theory, see R. West and L. H. Turner, *Introducing Communication Theory: Analysis and Application* (Mountain View, CA: Mayfield, 2000).

51. L. J. Carrell, "Diversity in the Communication Curriculum: Impact on Student Empathy" *Communication Education*, 46 (October 1997): 234–244.

Chapter 5

1. H. J. M. Nouwen, *Bread for the Journey* (San Francisco: HarperCollins 1997), Entry for March 11.

2. Nowen, *Bread for the Journey*, March 11.

3. L. Barker et al., "An Investigation of Proportional Time Spent in Various Communication Activities of College Students," *Journal of Applied Communication Research*, 8 (1981): 101–09.

4. K. W. Watson, L. L. Barker, and J. B. Weaver, *The Listener Style Inventory* (New Orleans: SPECTRA, 1995).

5. S. L. Sargent and J. B. Weaver, "Correlates Between Communication Apprehension and Listening Style Preferences," *Communication Research Reports*, 14 (1997): 74–78.

6. M. D. Kirtley and J. M. Honeycutt, "Listening Styles and Their Correspondence with Second Guessing," *Communication Research Reports*, 13 (1996): 174–182.

7. Sargent and Weaver, "Correlates between Communication Apprehension."

8. W. Winter, A. J. Ferreira, and N. Bowers, "Decision-Making in Married and Unrelated Couples," *Family Process*, 12 (1973): 83–94.

9. O. E. Rankis, "The Effects of Message Structure, Sexual Gender, and Verbal Organizing Ability upon Learning Message Information," doctoral dissertation, Ohio University, 1981; C. H. Weaver, *Human Listening. Process and Behavior* (New York: Bobbs-Merrill, 1972); R. D. Halley, "Distractibility of Males and Females in Competing Aural Message Situations. A Research Note," *Human Communication Research*, 2 (1975): 79–82. Our discussion of gender-based differences and listening is also based on a discussion by S. A. Beebe and J. T. Masterson, *Family Talk.: Interpersonal Communication in the Family* (New York: Random House, 1986); J. Lurito, "Listening and Gender," paper presented at the Radiological Society of North America, Chicago (2000) as cited by L. Tanner, "Listening Study Finds Difference in the Sexes," *Austin-American Statesman*, (November 29, 2000), p. A11.

10. J. Stauffer, R. Frost, and W. Rybolt, "The Attention Factor in Recalling Network News," *Journal of Communication*, 33(1), (1983): 29–37.

11. This discussion is based on A. Vangelisti, M. Knapp, and J. Daly, "Conversational Narcissism," *Communication Monographs*, 57 (1990): 251–274.

12. J. Thurber, "The Secret Life of Walter Mitty," in *Literature for Composition*, 3d ed., edited by S. Barnet et al. (Glenview, IL: Scott, Foresman, 1992), 43.

13. R. Montgomery, *Listening Made Easy* (New York: Amacon, 1981); O. Hargie, C. Sanders, and D. Dickson, *Social Skills in Interpersonal Communication* (London: Routledge, 1994); O. Hargie (Ed.), *The Handbook of Communication Skills* (London: Routledge, 1997): Also see S. W. Littlejohn and K. Domenic, *Engaging Communication in Conflict: Systemic Practice* (Thousand Oaks, CA: Sage, 2001), 105–108.

14. R. G. Owens, "Handling Strong Emotions," in O. Hargie (Ed.), *A Handbook of Communication Skills* (London: Croom Helm/New York University Press, 1986).

15. K. B. Staples, "Black Men and Public Space," in *Literature for Composition*, 3rd ed., edited by S. Barnet et al. (Glenview, IL: Scott, Foresman, 1992), 73.

16. R. G. Nichols, "Factors in Listening Comprehension," *Speech Monographs*, 15 (1948): 154–63; G. M. Goldhaber and C. H. Weaver, "Listener Comprehension of Compressed Speech When the Difficulty, Rate of Presentation, and Sex of the Listener Are Varied," *Speech Monographs*, 35 (1968): 20–25.

17. J. Harrigan, "Listeners' Body Movements and Speaking Turns," *Communication Research*, 12 (1985): 233–SO.

18. S. Strong et al., "Nonverbal Behavior and Perceived Counselor Characteristics," *Journal of Counseling Psychology*, 18 (1971): 554–61.

19. See R. G. Nichols and L. A. Stevens, "Listening to People," *Harvard Business Review*, 35 (September–October 1957): 85–92.

20. C. W. Ellison and I. J. Firestone, "Development of Interpersonal Trust as a Function of Self-Esteem, Target Status and Target Style," *Journal of Personality and Social Psychology*, 29 (1974): 655–63.

21. O. Hargie, C. Sanders, and D. Dickson, *Social Skills in Interpersonal Communication* (London: Routledge, 1994); O. Hargie (Ed.), *Handbook*.

22. J. B. Weaver and M. B. Kirtley, "Listening Styles and Empathy," *The Southern Communication Journal*, 60 (1995): 131–40.

23. D. Goleman, *Emotional Intelligence* (New York: Bantam, 1995).

24. Goleman, *Emotional Intelligence*.

25. Hargie, Sanders, and Dickson, *Social Skills*; R. Boulton, *People Skills* (New York: 1981).

26. Boulton, *People Skills*. We also acknowledge others who have presented

excellent applications of listening and responding skills in interpersonal and group contexts: D. A. Romig and L. J. Romig, *Structured Teamwork Guide* (Austin, TX: Performance Resources, 1990); S. Deep and L. Sussman, *Smart Moves* (Reading: MA. Addison-Wesley, 1990); P. R. Scholtes, *The Team Handbook* (Madison, WI: Joiner Associates, 1992); Hargie, Sanders, and Dickson, *Social Skills*; Littlejohn and Domenici, *Engaging Communication in Conflict*.

27. This discussion of logic fallacies is based on our discussion in S. A. Beebe and S. J. Beebe, *Public Speaking: An Audience-Centered Approach* (Boston: Allyn & Bacon, 2000), 389–392.

28. S. Gilbert, "Self-Disclosure, Intimacy, and Communication in Families," *Family Coordinator*, 25 (1976).

Chapter 6

1. C. K. Ogden and I. A. Richards, *The Meaning of Meaning* (London: Kegan, Paul Trench, Trubner, 1923).

2. See G. H. Mead, *Mind, Self and Society* (Chicago: University of Chicago Press, 1934); H. Blumer, *Symbolic Interactionism: Perspective and Method* (Englewood Cliffs, NJ: Prentice Hall, 1969).

3. E. T. Hall, *Beyond Culture* (Garden City, NY: Doubleday, 1976).

4. L. A. Samovar and R. E. Porter, *Communication Between Cultures* (Belmont, CA: Wadsworth, 2001), 234.

5. A. Tan, "The Language of Discretion," in *About Language*, 3d ed., edited by W. H. Roberts and G. Turgeon (Boston: Houghton Mifflin, 1992), 142.

6. *The American Heritage Dictionary of the English Language* (Boston: Houghton Mifflin, 1969), 1162.

7. A. Korzybski, *Science and Sanity* (Lancaster, PA: Science Press, 1941).

8. G. Gusdorff, *Speaking* (Evanston, IL: Northwestern University Press, 1965), 9.

9. A. Ellis, *A New Guide to Rational Living* (North Hollywood, CA: Wilshire Books, 1977).

10. C. Peterson, M. E. P. Seligman, and G. E. Vaillant, "Pessimistic Explanatory Style Is a Risk Factor for Physical Illness: A 35-Year Longitudinal Study," *Journal of Personality and Social Psychology*, 55 (1988): 23–27.

11. E. K. Heussenstaumn, "Bumper Stickers and Cops," *Transaction*, 35 (1971): 32–33.

12. B. L. Whorf, "Science and Linguistics," in *Language, Thought and Reality*, edited by J. B. Carroll (Cambridge, MA: MIT Press, 1956), 207.

13. W. Johnson, *People in Quandaries* (New York: Harper & Row,).

14. A fascinating article "The Melting of a Mighty Myth" in *Newsweek* (July 22, 1991) suggests that, contrary to popular opinion, Eskimos do not have twenty-three words for snow, although they apparently do have more words to describe snow that most people who live in warm climates.

15. R. L. Howe, *The Miracle of Dialogue* (New York: The Seabury Press, 1963), 23–24.

16. H. S. O'Donnell, "Sexism in Language," *Elementary English*, 50 (1973): 1067–72.

17. See D. K. Ivy and P. Backlund, *Exploring Genderspeak* (New York: McGraw-Hill, 2000).

18. *Newsweek*, November 20 1995, 81.

19. We acknowledge and appreciate D. K. Ivy's contribution to this section on biased language. For an expanded discussion on this topic, see D. K. Ivy and P. Backlund, *Genderspeak* (New York: McGraw-Hill, 2000).

20. J. S. Seiter, J. Larsen, and J. Skinner, "'Handicapped' or 'Handicapable?': The Effects of Language about Persons with Disabilities on Perceptions of Source Credibility and Persuasiveness," *Communication Reports*, 11(1), (1998): 21–31.

21. D. O. Braithwaite and C. A. Braithwaite, "Understanding Communication of Persons with Disabilities as Cultural Communication," in *Intercultural communication: A Reader*, 8th ed., edited by L. A. Samovar and R. E. Porter (Belmont, CA: Wadsworth, 1997): 154–164.

22. D. Yankelovich, *The Magic of Dialogue: Transforming Conflict into Cooperation* (New York: Simon & Schuster, 1999).

23. J. R. Gibb, "Defensive Communication," *Journal of Communication*, 11 (1961): 141–48. Also see R. Bolton, *People Skills* (New York: Simon & Schuster, 1979), 14–26; O. Hargie, C. Sanders, and D. Dickson, *Social Skills in Interpersonal Communication* (London: Routledge, 1994); O. Hargie (Ed.), *The Handbook of Communication Skills* (London: Routledge, 1997); S. W. Littlejohn and K. Domenici, *Engaging Communication in Conflict* (Thousand Oaks, CA: Sage, 2001).

24. C. Rogers, *On Becoming a Person: A Therapist's View of Psychotherapy* (Boston: Houghton Mifflin, 1961); C. Rogers, *A Way of Being* (Boston: Houghton Mifflin, 1980); C. Rogers, "Comments on the Issue of Equality in Psychotherapy," *Journal of Humanistic Psychology,* 27 (1987): 38–39.

25. E. Sieburg and C. Larson, "Dimensions of Interpersonal Response," paper delivered at the annual conference of the International Communication Association, Phoenix, Arizona, April 1971.

26. J. Gottman, "Spotlighting the Family Communication Research of John Gottman," presentation at the National Communication Association annual conference, Seattle, Washington (November 2000).

27. G. Smalley and J. Trent, *The Language of Love* (Fort Worth: Word Publishers, 1993).

Chapter 7

1. A. Mehrabian, *Nonverbal Communication* (Chicago: Aldine Atherton, 1972), 108.

2. D. Lapakko, "Three Cheers for Language: A Closer Examination of a Widely Cited Study of Nonverbal Communication," *Communication Education,* 46 (1997): 63–67.

3. M. Zuckerman, D. DePaulo, and R. Rosenthal, "Verbal and Nonverbal Communication of Deception," *Advances in Experimental Social Psychology,* 14 (1981): 1–59.

4. P. Ekman and W. V. Friesen, "The Repertoire of Nonverbal Behavior: Categories Origins, Usage and Coding," *Semiotica,* 1 (1969): 49–98.

5. E. Hess, *The Tell-Tale Eye* (New York: Van Nostrand Reinhold, 1975).

6. R. L. Birdwhistell, *Kinesics and Context* (Philadelphia: University of Pennsylvania Press, 1970).

7. N. Zunin and M. Zunin, *Contact: The First Four Minutes* (New York: Signet, 1976).

8. J. H. Bert and K. Piner, "Social Relationships and the Lack of Social Relations," in *Personal Relationships and Social Support,* edited by S. W. Duck with R. C. Silver (London: Sage, 1989).

9. J. K. Burgoon, L. A. Stern, and L. Dillman, *Interpersonal Adaptation: Dyadic Interaction Patterns* (Cambridge, England: Cambridge University Press, 1995).

10. P. Ekman, "Communication Through Nonverbal Behavior: A Source of Information About an Interpersonal Relationship," in *Affect Cognition and Personality,* edited by S. S. Tomkins and C. E. Izard (New York: Springer, 1965).

11. M. Argyle, *Bodily Communication* (New York: Methuen, 1988).

12. W. G. Woodal and J. K. Burgoon, "The Effects of Nonverbal Synchrony on Message Comprehension and Persuasiveness," *Journal of Nonverbal Behavior,* 5 (1981): 207–23.

13. Argyle, *Bodily Communication.*

14. P. Ekman and W. V Friesen, "Constants Across Cultures in the Face and Emotion," *Journal of Personality and Social Psychology,* 17 (1971): 124–29; Argyle, *Bodily Communication,* 157; I. Eibl-Eibesfeldt, "Similarities and Differences Between Cultures in Expressive Movements," in *Nonverbal Communication,* edited by R. A. Hinde (Cambridge, England: Royal Society & Cambridge University Press, 1972); P. Collett, "History and Study of Expressive Action," in *Historical Social Psychology,* edited by K. Gergen and M. Gergen (Hillsdale, NJ: Erlbaum 1984); E. T. Hall, *The Silent Language* (Garden City, NY: Doubleday, 1959); R. Shuter, "Gaze Behavior in Interracial and Intraracial Interaction," *International and Intercultural Communication Annual,* 5 (1979): 48–55; R. Shuter, "Proxemics and Tactility in Latin America," *Journal of Communication,* 26 (1976): 46–52; E. T. Hall, *The Hidden Dimension* (New York: Doubleday, 1966). For an excellent discussion of world view and the implications for intercultural communication, see C. H. Dodd, *Dynamics of Intercultural Communication* (Dubuque, IA: Brown & Benchmark, 1995); G. W. Beattie, *Talk: An Analysis of Speech and Non-Verbal Behavior in Conversation* (Milton Keynes: Open University Press, 1983); O. Hargie, C. Sanders, and D. Dickson, *Social Skills in Interpersonal Communication* (London: Routledge, 1994); O. Hargie (Ed.), *The Handbook of Communication Skills* (London: Routledge, 1997).

15. K. N. Blurton-Jones and G. M. Leach, "Behavior of Children and Their Mothers at Separation and Parting," in *Ethological Studies of Child Behavior,* edited by N. Blurton-Jones (Cambridge, England: Cambridge University Press 1972).

16. This example originally appeared in P. Collett, "History and Study of Expressive Action."

17. R. Birdwhistell, *Kinesics and Context.* Also see D. G. Leathers, *Successful*

Nonverbal Communications and Applications (Boston: Allyn & Bacon, 1998).

18. A. E. Scheflen, "Quasi-Courtship Behavior in Psychotherapy," *Psychiatry,* 28 (1965): 245–57.

19. M. Moore, Journal of Ethology and Sociology (Summer 1994); also see D. Knox and K. Wilson, "Dating Behaviors of University Students," *Family Relations,* 30 (1981): 255–58.

20. M. Reece and R. Whitman, "Expressive Movements, Warmth, and Verbal Reinforcement," *Journal of Abnormal and Social Psychology,* 64 (1962): 234–36.

21. A. Mehrabian, *Silent Messages* (Belmont, CA: Wadsworth, 1972), 108.

22. Ekman and Friesen, "The Repertoire of Nonverbal Behavior."

23. A. T. Dittman, "The Body Movement–Speech Rhythm Relationship as a Cue to Speech Encoding," in *Studies in Dyadic Communication,* edited by A. W. Siegman and B. Pope (New York: Pergamon, 1972).

24. A. A. Cohen and R. P. Harrison, "Intentionality in the Use of Hand Illustrators in Face-to-Face Communication Situations," *Journal of Personality and Social Psychology,* 28 (1973): 276-79.

25. C. Darwin, *Expression of Emotions in Man and Animals* (Chicago: University of Chicago Press, 1965). Originally published 1872.

26. A. Mehrabian and M. Williams, "Nonverbal Concomitants of Perceived and Intended Persuasiveness," *Journal of Personality and Social Psychology,* 13 (1969): 37–58.

27. M. Argyle, E. Alkema, and R. Gilmour, "The Communication of Friendly and Hostile Attitudes by Verbal and Nonverbal Signals," *European Journal of Social Psychology,* 1 (1972): 385–402.

28. A. Kendon, "Some Functions of Gaze-Direction in Social Interaction," *Acta Psychologica,* 26 (1967): 22–63.

29. S. W. Duck, *Understanding Relationships* (New York: Guilford Press, 1991), 54.

30. M. Knapp and J. A. Hall, *Nonverbal Communication in Human Interaction* (Fort Worth, Texas: Harcourt Brace, 1997), 313.

31. P. Ekman, W, V. Friesen, and S. S. Tomkins, "Facial Affect Scoring Technique: A First Validity Study," *Semiotica,* 3 (1971): 37–58, P. Ekman and W. V. Friesen, *Unmasking the Face* (Englewood Cliffs, NJ: Prentice Hall, 1975).

32. A. Mehrabian, "Significance of Gesture and Position in the Communication of Attitude and Status Relationships," *Psychological Bulletin*, 71 (1969): 363.

33. Ekman and Friesen, *Unmasking the Face*; Ekman, Friesen, and Tomkins, "Facial Affect Scoring Technique."

34. Ekman and Friesen, *Unmasking the Face*; Ekman, Friesen, and Tomkins, "Facial Affect Scoring Technique."

35. A. Buck, R. E. Miller, and C. F. William, "Sex, Personality, and Physiological Variables in the Communication of Affect via Facial Expression," *Journal of Personality and Social Psychology*, 30 (1974):587–589

36. Ekman and Friesen, *Unmasking the Face*.

37. Ekman and Friesen, *Unmasking the Face*.

38. G. J. McHugo, "Emotional Reactions to a Political Leader's Expressive Displays," *Journal of Personality and Social Psychology*, 49 (1985); 513–29.

39. R. Davitz, *The Communication of Emotional Meaning*.

40. R. Davitz, *The Communication of Emotional Meaning*.

41. K. K. Sereno and G. J. Hawkins, "The Effect of Variations in Speakers' Nonfluency upon Audience Ratings of Attitude Toward the Speech Topic and Speakers' Credibility," *Speech Monographs*, 34 (1967): 58–74; G. R. Miller and M. A. Hewgill, "The Effect of Variations in Nonfluency on Audience Ratings of Source Credibility," *Quarterly Journal of Speech*, 50 (1964): 36–44; Mehrabian and Williams, "Nonverbal Concomitants of Perceived and Intended Persuasiveness."

42. T. Bruneau, "Communicative Silences: Forms and Functions," *Journal of Communication*, 23 (1973): 17–46.

43. S. J. Baker, "The Theory of Silence," *Journal of General Psychology*, 53 (1955): 145–67.

44. E. T. Hall, *The Hidden Dimension* (Garden City, NY: Doubleday, 1966).

45. R. Sommer, "Studies in Personal Space," *Sociometry*, 22 (1959): 247–60.

46. Sommer, "Studies in Personal Space."

47. See B. Stenzor, "The Spatial Factor in Face-to-Face Discussion Groups," *Journal of Abnormal and Social Psychology*, 45 (1950): 552–55.

48. A. Montague, *Touching: The Human Significance of the Skin* (New York: Harper & Row, 1978).

49. Montague, *Touching*.

50. N. M. Henley, *Body Politics: Power, Sex, and Nonverbal Communication* (Englewood Cliffs, NJ: Prentice Hall, 1977).

51. J. Kelly, "Dress as Non-Verbal Communication," paper presented to the annual conference of the American Association for Public Opinion Research, May 1969.

52. J. Lefkowitz, R. Blake, and J. Mouton, "Status Factors in Pedestrian Violation of Traffic Signals," *Journal of Abnormal and Social Psychology*, 51 (1970): 4–6.

53. J. T. Molloy, *Dress for Success* (New York: Warner Books, 1975), J. T. Molloy, *The Woman's Dress for Success Book* (Chicago: Follett, 1977).

54. Mehrabian, *Nonverbal Communication*.

55. L. Hinkle, "Nonverbal Immediacy Communication Behaviors and Liking in Marital Relationships," *Communication Research Reports*, 16(1), (1999): 81–90.

56. J. K. Burgoon and B. A. Le Poire, "Nonverbal Cues and Interpersonal Judgments: Participant and Observer Perceptions of Intimacy, Dominance, Composure, and Formality," *Communication Monographs*, 66 (1999): 105–124.

57. Argyle, *Bodily Communication*.

58. For an excellent review of gender and nonverbal cues, see J. Pearson, L. Turner, and W. Todd-Mancillas, *Gender and Communication* (Dubuque, IA: William C. Brown, 1991); D. K. Ivy and P. Backlund, *Exploring GenderSpeak: Personal Effectiveness in Gender Communication* (New York: McGraw Hill, 1994). Also see D. G. Leathers, *Successful Nonverbal Communication: Principles and Applications* (Boston: Allyn & Bacon, 1997).

59. Mehrabian, *Nonverbal Communication*.

60. Argyle, *Bodily Communication*.

61. Burgoon, Stern, and Dillman, *Interpersonal Adaptation*.

62. B. A. Le Poire and S. M. Yoshimura, "The Effects of Expectancies and Actual Communication on Nonverbal Adaptation and Communication Outcomes: A Test of Interaction Adaptation Theory," *Communication Monographs*, 66 (1999): 1–30.

63. See Birdwhistell, *Kinesics in Context*.

64. E. Hatfield, J. T. Cacioppo, and R. L. Rapson, *Emotional Contagion* (New York: Cambridge University Press, 1994).

65. For an excellent summary of the deception and nonverbal communication, see Leathers, *Successful Nonverbal Communication*, 253–274. Also see P. Ekman, M. O' Sullivan, W. V. Friesen, and K. R. Scherer, "Invited Article: Face, Voice, and Body in Detecting Deceit," *Journal of Nonverbal Behavior,* 15 (1991): 125–135; P. Ekman and W. Friesen, "Detecting Deception from the Body and Face," *Journal of Personality and Social Psychology,* 29 (1974): 288–298, M. Millar and K. Millar, "Detection of Deception in Familiar and Unfamiliar Persons: The Effects of Information Restriction," *Journal of Nonverbal Behavior,* 19 (1995): 69–84; D. B. Buller, J. K. Burgoon, A. Buslig, and J. F. Roiger, "Interpersonal Deception: VIII. Further Analysis of the Nonverbal Correlates of Equivocation from the Bavelas et al. (1990) Research," *Journal of Language & Social Psychology,* 13 (1994): 396–417.

66. Adapted from Leathers, *Successful Nonverbal Communication*, with supporting research from Ekman and Friesen, "Detecting Deception from the Face and Body"; M. Zuckerman, B. M. DePaulo, and R. Rosenthal, "Verbal and Nonverbal Communication of Deception," in L. Berkowitz (Ed.), *Advances in Experimental Social Psychology*, vol. 14 (New York: Academic Press, 1981), 1–60.

Chapter 8

1. J. W. Keltner, *Mediation: Toward a Civilized System of Dispute Resolution* (Annandale VA: Speech Communication Association, 1987); also see J. Hocker and W. Wilmot, *Interpersonal Conflict* (New York: McGraw-Hill, 2000).

2. R. J. Doolittle, *Orientations of Communication and Conflict* (Chicago: Science Research Associates, 1976), 7–9.

3. E. H. Mudd, H. E. Mitchell, and J. W. Bullard, "Areas of Marital Conflict in Successfully Functioning and Unsuccessfully Functioning Families," *Journal of Health and Human Behavior*, 3 (1962): 88–93; N. R. Vines, "Adult Unfolding and Marital Conflict," *Journal of Marital and Family Therapy*, 5 (1979): 5–14

4. B. A. Fisher, "Decision Emergence: Phases in Group Decision Making," *Speech Monographs*, 37 (1970): 60.

5. G. R. Miller and M. Steinberg, *Between People: A New Analysis of Interpersonal Communication* (Chicago: Science Research Associates, 1975), 264.

6. C. M. Hoppe, "Interpersonal Aggression as a Function of Subject's Sex Role Identification, Opponent's Sex, and Degree of Provocation," *Journal of Personality*, 47 (1979): 317–329.

7. W. Wilmot and J. Hocker, *Interpersonal Conflict* (New York: McGraw-Hill, 2000); also see S. W. Littlejohn and K. Domenici, *Engaging Communication in Conflict: Systemic Practice* (Thousand Oaks, CA: Sage, 2001).

8. J. M. Olsen, *The Process of Social Organization* (New York: Holt, Rinehart, & Winston, 1978).

9. J. M. Olsen, *The Process of Social Organization.*

10. S. Ting-Toomey, "A Face Negotiation Theory," in *Theories in Intercultural Communication,* edited by Y. Kim and W. Gudykunst (Newbury Park, CA: Sage, 1988).

11. S. Ting-Toomey, "A Face Negotiation Theory."

12. Wilmot and Hocker, *Interpersonal Conflict,* 15–16.

13. A. C. Filley, *Interpersonal Conflict Resolution* (Glenview, IL: Scott Foresman, 1975); R. H. Turner, "Conflict and Harmony," *Family Interaction* (New York: Wiley, 1970); K. Galvin and B. J. Brommel, *Family Communication: Cohesion and Change* (New York: Addison Wesley Longman, 2000).

14. Wilmot and Hocker, *Interpersonal Conflict,* 10.

15. Adapted from D. W. Johnson. *Reaching Out: Interpersonal Effectiveness and Self-Actualization* (Boston: Allyn & Bacon, 2000), 314.

16. M. Deutsch, *The Resolution of Conflict* (New Haven, CT: Yale University Press, 1973).

17. V. Satir, *Peoplemaking* (Palo Alto: Science and Behavior Books, 1972).

18. R. Kilmann and K. Thomas, "Interpersonal Conflict-Handling Behavior as Reflections of Jungian Personality Dimensions," *Psychological Reports,* 37 (1975): 971–80.

19. L. L. Putnam and C. E. Wilson, "Communicative Strategies in Organizational Conflicts: Reliability and Validity of a Measurement Scale," in *Communication Yearbook,* vol. 6, edited by M. Burgoon (Beverly Hills, CA: Sage, International Communication Association, 1982).

20. J. T. Tedeschi, "Threats and Promises," in *The Structure of Conflict,* edited by R. Swingle (New York: Academic Press, 1970).

21. See D. A. Infante and C. J. Wigley, "Verbal Aggressiveness: An Interpersonal Model and Measure," *Communication Monographs,* 53 (1986): 61–69; D. A. Infante and W. I. Gorden, "Superior and Subordinate Communication Profiles: Implications for Independent-Mindedness and Upward Effectiveness," *Central States Speech Journal,* 38 (1987): 73–80; D. A. Infante, B. L. Riddle, C. L. Horvath, and S. A. Tumlin, "Verbal Aggressiveness: Messages and Reasons," *Communication Quarterly,* 40 (1992): 116–126; D. E. Ifert and L. Bearden, "The Influence of Argumentativeness and Verbal Aggression on Responses to Refused Requests," *Communication Reports,* 11(2), (1998): 145–154; also see M. J. Beatty, K. M. Valencic, J. E. Rudd, and J. A. Dobos, "A 'Dark Side' of Communication Avoidance: Indirect Interpersonal Aggressiveness," *Communication Research Reports,* 16(2), (1999): 103–109.

22. See J. C. McCroskey and M. Beatty, "The Communibiological Perspective: Implications for Communication in Instruction," *Communication Education,* 49(1), (January 2000): 1–6; M. J. Beatty and J. C. McCroskey, "Theory, Scientific Evidence, and the Communibiological Paradigm: Reflections on Misguided Criticism," *Communication Education,* 49(1), (January 2000): 36–44. Also see J. C. McCroskey, J. A. Daly, M. M. Martin, and M. J. Beatty (Eds.), *Communication and Personality: Trait Perspectives* (Cresskil, NJ: Hampton Press, 1998).

23. Infante and Wigley, "Verbal Aggressiveness."

24. Infante et al., "Verbal Aggressiveness: Messages and Reasons."

25. R. Fisher and W. Ury, *Getting to Yes: Negotiating Agreement Without Giving In* (Boston: Houghton Mifflin, 1988). Also see D. Yankelovich, *The Magic of Dialogue: Transforming Conflict into Cooperation* (New York: Simon & Schuster, 1999).

26. Our discussion of conflict management skills is based on several excellent discussions of conflict management prescriptions. We acknowledge Fisher and Ury, *Getting to Yes;* R. Boulton, *People Skills* (New York: Simon & Schuster, 1979); D. A. Romig and L. J. Romig, *Structured Teamwork © Guide* (Austin, TX: Performance Resources, 1990); O. Hargie, C. Saunders, and D. Dickson, *Social Skills in Interpersonal Communication* (London: Routledge, 1994); S. Deep and L. Sussman, *Smart Moves* (Reading, MA: Addison-Wesley, 1990); and W. Wilmont and J. Hocker, *Interpersonal Conflict;* M. D. Davis, E. L. Eshelman, and M. McKay, *The Relaxation and Stress Reduction Workbook* (Oakland, CA: New Harbinger Publications, 1982). W. A. Donohue and R. Kolt, *Managing Interpersonal Conflict* (Newbury Park: CA: Sage, 1992); O. Hargie (Ed.), *The Handbook of Communication Skills* (London: Routledge, 1997); S. Littlejohn and K. Domenici, *Engaging Communication in Conflict;* M. W. Isenhart and M. Spangle, *Collaborative Approaches to Resolving Conflict* (Thousand Oaks, CA: Sage, 2000).

27. Boulton, *People Skills,* 217.

28. For additional strategies on managing emotion, see J. Gottman, *Why Marriages Succeed and Fail: And How You Can Make Yours Last* (New York: Simon & Schuster, 1994); J. Gottman, *The Seven Principles for Making Marriage Work* (New York: Crown, 1999). Also see D. W. Johnson, *Reaching Out.*

29. A. Ellis, *A New Guide to Rational Living* (North Hollywood, CA: Wilshire Books, 1977).

30. Fisher and Ury, *Getting to Yes;* Boulton, *People Skills;* Romig and Romig, *Structured Teamwork ® Guide;* T. Gordon, *Leader Effectiveness Training (L.E.T): The No-Lose Way to Release the Productive Potential of People* (New York: Wyden Books, 1977).

31. S. Deep and L. Susman, *Smart Moves* (New York: Addison-Wesley, 1990).

32. Ellis, *A New Guide to Rational Living.*

33. S. R. Covey, *The Seven Habits of Highly Effective People* (New York: Simon & Schuster, 1989), 235.

34. C. Pavitt and B. Kemp, "Contextual and Relational Factors in Interpersonal Negotiation Strategy Choice," *Communication Quarterly,* 47(2), (1999): 133–150.

35. Fisher and Ury, *Getting to Yes.*

36. E. Goffman, *Interaction Rituals: Essays on Face-to-Face Interaction.* Garden City, NY: Doubleday (1967).

37. S. Ting-Toomey, "Face and Facework: An Introduction," in S. Ting-Toomey (ED.), *The Challenge of Facework* (Albany, NY: SUNY Press, 1994), 1–14; S. Ting-Toomey, "Managing Intercultural Conflicts Effectively," in L. A. Samovar and R. E. Porter (Eds.), *Intercultural Communication: A Reader* (Belmont, CA: Wadsworth, 1994), 360–372. Also see S. Ting-Toomey and L. Chung, "Cross-Cultural Interpersonal Communication: Theoretical Trends and Research Directions," in W. B. Gudykunst, S. Ting-Toomey, and T. Nishida (Eds.), *Communication in Personal Relationships Across Cultures* (Thousand Oaks, CA: Sage, 1996), 237–261; M. W. Isenhart and M. Spangle, *Collaborative Approaches to Resolving Conflict,* 19–20.

38. Our prescriptions for assertiveness are based on a discussion by R. Boulton, People Skills. Also see J. S. St. Lawrence, "Situational Context: Effects on Perceptions of Assertive and Unassertive Behavior," *Behavior Therapy*, 16 (1985): 51–62; D. Borisoff and D. A. Victor, *Conflict Management: A Communication Skills Approach* (Boston: Allyn & Bacon, 1999).

39 D. Cloven and M. E. Roloff, "The Chilling Effect of Aggressive Potential on the Expression of Complaints in Intimate Relationships," *Communication Monographs*, 60 (1993):199–219.

40. J. W. Pfeiffer and J. E. Jones (Eds.), *A Handbook of Structured Experiences for Human Relations Training*, vol. 2 (La Jolla, CA: University Associates, 1974), 62–76.

Chapter 9

1. L. von Bertalanffy, "Der Organismus als physikalisches System betrachtet," *Die Naturwissenschaften*," 28 (1940), 521–31.

2. F. E. Millar and L. E. Rogers, "A Relational Approach to Interpersonal Communication," in *Explorations in Interpersonal Communication*, edited by G. R. Miller (Newbury Park, CA: Sage, 1976), 87–103.

3. A. P. Bochner, "On the Efficacy of Openness in Close Relationships," in *Communication Yearbook*, vol. 5, edited by M. Burgoon (New Brunswick, NJ: Transaction Books, 1982), 109–24.

4. Millar and Rogers, "A Relational Approach to Interpersonal Communication."

5. K. Chow, "Social Support and Subjective Well-Being Among Hong Kong Chinese Young Adults," *Journal of Genetic Psychology*, 160 (September 1999): 319–31.

6. W. Stoebe, "Self-Esteem and Interpersonal Attraction," in *Theory and Practice in Interpersonal Attraction*, edited by S. Duck (London: Academic Press, 1977).

7. S. W. Duck, *Personal Relationships and Personal Constructs: A Study of Friendship Formation* (New York: Wiley, 1993).

8. M. Sunnafrank, "A Communication-Based Perspective on Attitude Similarity and Interpersonal Attraction in Early Acquaintance," *Communication Monographs*, 51 (1984): 372–80.

9. M. Sunnafrank, "Interpersonal Attraction and Attitude Similarity: A Communication Based Assessment," in *Communication Yearbook*, vol. 14, edited by J. A. Anderson (Newbury Park: CA: Sage, 1991), 451–83.

10. Sunnafrank, "Interpersonal Attraction and Attitude Similarity."

11. W. Schutz, *Interpersonal Underworld* (Palo Alto, CA: Science and Behavior Books, 1966).

12. M. Sunnafrank, "Predicted Outcome Value During Initial Interaction: A Reformulation of Uncertainty Reduction Theory," *Human Communication Research*, 13 (1986): 3–33.

13. Sunnafrank, "Predicted Outcome Value During Initial Interaction.

14. M. V. Redmond and D. A. Vrchota, "The Effects of Varying Lengths of Initial Interaction on Attraction and Uncertainty Reduction," paper presented at the annual meeting of the National Communication Association, New Orleans (1994).

15. C. R. Berger, "Social Power and Interpersonal Communication," in *Handbook of Interpersonal Communication*, edited by M. L. Knapp and G. R. Miller (Newbury Park, CA: Sage, 1985), 439–499.

16. F. E. Millar and L. E. Rogers, "Relational Dimensions of Interpersonal Dynamics," in *Interpersonal Processes: New Directions in Communication Research*, edited by M. E. Roloff and G. R. Miller (Newbury Park, CA: Sage, 1987), 117–139.

17. J. R. P. French and B. H. Raven, "The Bases of Social Power," in *Group Dynamics*, edited by J. D. Cartwright and A. Zander (Evanston, IL: Row, Peterson, 1962), 607–622.

18. L. A. Baxter and C. Bullis, "Turning Points in Developing Romantic Relationships," *Communication Research*, 12 (1986): 469–493.

19. Baxter and Bullis, "Turning Points."

20. C. R. Berger and J. J. Bradac, *Language and Social Knowledge: Uncertainty and Interpersonal Relations* (Baltimore: Edward Arnold, 1982).

21. W. Douglas, "Question Asking in Same and Opposite Sex Initial Interactions: The Effects of Anticipated Future Interactions," *Human Communication Research*, 14 (1987): 230–245.

22. S. W. Duck, "A Topography of Relationship Disengagement and Dissolution," in *Personal Relationships 4: Dissolving Relationships*, edited by S. W. Duck (New York: Academic Press, 1982), 1–29.

23. Duck, "A Topography of Relationship Disengagement and Dissolution."

24. D. DeStephen, "Integrating Relational Termination into a General Model of Communication Competence," paper presented at the annual meeting of the National Communication Association, Denver (1985).

25. S. Duck, "Interpersonal Communication in Developing Relationships," in *Explorations in Interpersonal Communication*, edited by G. R. Miller (Newbury Park, CA: Sage, 1976), 127–47.

26. I. Atlman and D. A. Taylor, *Social Penetration: The Development of Interpersonal Relationships* (New York: Holt, Rinehart and Winston, 1973).

27. Sunnafrank, "Predicted Outcome Value During Initial Interaction.

28. J. W. Thibaut and H. H. Kelley, *The Social Psychology of Groups* (New York: Wiley, 1959).

29. G. R. Miller and M. R. Parks, "Communicating in Dissolving Relationships," in *Personal Relationships 4: Dissolving Personal Relationships*, edited by S. W. Duck (London: Academic Press, 1982), 127–154.

30. L. A. Baxter, "Dialectical Contradictions in Relationship Development," in *Handbook of Personal Relationships*, edited by S. W. Duck (Chichester, England: Wiley, 1988), 257–73; L. A. Baxter and B. M. Montgomery, "Rethinking Communication in Personal Relationships from a Dialectical Perspective," in *Handbook of Personal Relationships*, 2nd ed., edited by S. W. Duck (Chichester, England: Wiley, 1997), 325–349.

31. D. R. Pawlowski, "Dialectical Tensions in Marital Partners' Accounts of Their Relationships," *Communication Quarterly*, 46 (1998): 396–416.

32. M. V. Redmond, "Content Adaptation in Everyday Interactions," paper presented at the annual meeting of the National Communication Association, Chicago (1997).

33. Pawlowski, "Dialectical Tensions."

34. L. A. Baxter, "Interpersonal Communication as Dialogue: A Response to the 'Social Approaches' Forum," *Communication Theory*, 2 (1992): 330–338.

35. Baxter, "Interpersonal Communication as Dialogue."

Chapter 10

1. C. R. Berger and R. J. Calabrese, "Some Explorations in Initial Interaction and Beyond: Toward a Developmental Theory of Interpersonal Communication," *Human Communication Research*, 1, (1975): 99–112; C. R. Berger and J. J. Bradac, *Language and Social Knowledge:*

Uncertainty in Interpersonal Relations (Baltimore: Edward Arnold, 1982).

2. Berger and Bradac, *Language and Social Knowledge.*

3. S. Sunnafrank, "Predicted Outcome Value During Initial Interactions," *Human Communication Research,* 13 (1986): 3–33; and "Interpersonal Attraction and Attitude Similarity," in *Communication Yearbook,* vol. 14, edited by J. A. Anderson (Newbury Park, CA: Sage, 1991), 451–83.

4. Berger and Bradac, *Language and Social Knowledge.*

5. Adapted from K. Kellerman et al., "The Conversation MOP: Scenes in the Stream of Discourse," *Discourse Processes,* 12 (1989): 27–61.

6. M. Argyle and M. Henderson, *The Anatomy of Relationships* (New York: Guilford Press, 1991).

7. For an excellent review of the nature of friendship, see M. Argyle, *The Psychology of Interpersonal Behavior* (London: Penguin, 1983).

8. A. M. Nicotera, "The Importance of Communication in Interpersonal Relationships," in *Interpersonal Communication in Friend and Mate Relationships,* edited by A. M. Nicotera and Associates (Albany: State University of New York Press, 1993), 3–12.

9. D. T. Kenrick and M. R. Trost, "Evolutionary Approaches to Relationships," in the *Handbook of Personal Relationships,* 2d ed., edited by S. Duck (Chichester, England: Wiley, 1997), 151–177.

10. M. Argyle, *The Social Psychology of Everyday Life* (London: Routledge, 1991).

11. Nicotera, "The Importance of Communication in Interpersonal Relationships."

12. Argyle, *The Social Psychology of Everyday Life.*

13. Argyle, *The Social Psychology of Everyday Life,* 49.

14. P. Marsh, *Eye to Eye: How People Interact* (Topfield, MA: Salem House, 1988).

15. W. J. Dickens and D. Perlman, "Friendship over the Life-Cycle," in *Personal Relationships,* vol. 2. *Developing Personal Relationships,* edited by S. W. Duck and R. Gilmour (London: Academic Press, 1981).

16. R. L. Selman, "Toward a Structural Analysis of Developing Interper-

sonal Relations Concepts: Research with Normal and Disturbed Preadolescent Boys," in *Minnesota Symposia on Child Psychology,* vol. 10, edited by A. D. Pick (Minneapolis: University of Minnesota Press, 1976).

17. Dickens and Perlman, "Friendship over the Life-Cycle."

18. Z. Rubin, *Children's Friendship* (Cambridge, MA: Harvard University Press, 1980), 74.

19. Henry Van Dyke from E. Doan, *The Speaker's Sourcebook* (Grand Rapids, MI: 1960), 107.

20. S. M. Rose, "How Friendships End: Patterns Among Young Adults," *Journal of Social and Personal Relationships,* 1 (1984): 267–277.

21. H. J. Markman, F. Floyd, and F. Dickson, "Towards a Model for the Prediction of Primary Prevention of Marital and Family Distress and Dissolution," in *Personal Relationships,* vol. 4. *Dissolving Personal Relationships,* edited by S. W. Duck and R. Gilmour (London: Academic Press, 1982).

22. P. H. Zietlow and A. L. Sillars, "Life-Stage Differences in Communication During Marital Conflicts," *Journal of Social and Personal Relationships,* 5 (1988): 223–245.

23. S. H. Mathews, *Friendships Through the Life Course: Oral Biographies in Old Age* (Beverly Hills, CA: Sage, 1986).

24. S. J. Holladay and K. S. Kerns, "Do Age Differences Matter in Close and Casual Relationships? A Comparison of Age Discrepant and Age Peer Friendships," *Communication Reports,* 12 (1999): 101–114.

25. M. J. Collier, "Communication Competence Problematics in Ethnic Relationships," *Communication Monographs,* 63, (1996): 314–335.

26. Collier, "Communication Competence."

27. J. Crohn, *Mixed Matches: How to Create Successful Interracial, Interethnic, and Interfaith Relationships* (New York: Fawcett Columbine, 1995).

28. R. Suro, "Mixed Doubles," *American Demographics* (November 1999). Retrieved online at www.demographics.com/publications/AD/ December 20, 2000.

29. J. D. Cunningham and J. K. Antill, "Love in Developing Romantic Relationships," in *Personal Relationships,* vol 2. *Developing Personal Relationships,*

edited by S. W. Duck and R. Gilmour (London: Academic Press, 1981).

30. Z. Rubin, *Liking and Loving: An Invitation to Social Psychology* (New York: Holt, Rinehart & Winston, 1973).

31. A. Aron and E. N. Aron "Love," in *Perspectives on Close Relationships,* edited by A. Weber and J. Harvey (Boston: Allyn and Bacon, 1994).

32. R. J. Sternberg, "A Triangular Theory of Love," *Psychological Review,* 93 (1986): 119–135.

33. C. Hendrick and S. S. Hendrick, "Research on Love: Does It Measure Up?" *Journal of Personality and Social Psychology,* 56 (1989): 784–794.

34. R. Lemieux and J. L. Hale, "Intimacy, Passion, and Commitment in Young Romantic Relationships: Successfully Measuring the Triangular Theory of Love," *Psychological Reports,* 85 (1999): 497–504

35. J. A. Lee, "A Typology of Styles of Loving," *Personality and Social Psychology,* Bulletin 3 (1977): 173–182.

36. Holy Bible. *New International Version* (London: Hodder and Stoughton, International Bible Society, 1973), 1153–1154.

37. S. S. Hendrick and C. Hendrick, *Liking, Loving and Relating (Pacific Grove, CA: Brooks Cole, 1992).*

38. Hendrick and C. Hendrick, *Liking, Loving and Relating.*

39. R. A. Bell and J. A. Daly, "The Affinity Seeking Function of Communication," *Communication Monographs,* 51 (1984): 91–115.

40. Bell and Daly, "The Affinity Seeking Function of Communication."

41. A. L. Vangelisti, "Communication Problems in Committed Relationships: An Attributional Analysis," in *Attributions, Accounts, and Close Relationships,* edited by J. H. Harvey, T. L. Orbuch, and A. L. Weber, (New York: Springer Verlag, 1992), 144–164.

42. G. Levinger, and D.J. Senn, "Disclosure of Feelings in Marriage," *Merrill-Palmer Quarterly* 12, (1967): 237–49. A. Bochner, "On the Efficacy of Openness in Close Relationships," in *Communication Yearbook 5,* edited by M. Burgoon (New Brunswick, JNJ: Transaction Books, 1982), 109–24.

43. R. A. Clark and J. G. Delia, "Individuals' Preferences for Friends' Approaches to Providing Support in Distressing Situations," *Communication Reports,* 10 (1997): 115–121.

44. S. A. Westmyer and S. A. Myers, "Communication Skills and Social Support Messages Across Friendship Levels," *Communication Research Reports*, 13 (1996): 191–197.

45. J. K. Alberts, "An Analysis of Couples' Conversational Complaints," *Communication Monographs*, 55, (1988): 184–197.

46. M. A. Fitzpatrick and D. M. Badzinski, "All in the Family: Interpersonal Communication in Kin Relationships," in *Handbook of Interpersonal Communication*, edited by M. L. Knapp and G. R. Miller (Beverly Hills, CA: Sage, 1985), 687–736.

47. G. R. Miller and F. Boster, "Persuasion in Personal Relationship," in *A Handbook of Personal Relationships*, edited by S. Duck (New York: Wiley, 1988): 275–288; M. G. Garko, "Perspectives and Conceptualizations of Compliance and Compliance Gaining," *Communication Quarterly*, 38, no. 2 (1990): 138–157.

48. Miller and Boster, "Persuasion in Personal Relationship"; Garko, "Perspectives and Conceptualizations."

49. G. R. Miller and M. R. Parks, "Communication in Dissolving Relationships," in *Personal Relationships*, vol. 4. *Dissolving Personal Relationships*, edited by S. W. Duck (London: Academic Press, 1982), 127–154.

50. S. W. Duck, "A Topography of Relationship Disengagement and Dissolution," in *Personal Relationships*, vol. 4. *Dissolving Personal Relationships*, edited by S. W. Duck (London: Academic Press, 1982), 1–29.

51. Miller and Parks, "Communication in Dissolving Relationships."

52. M. J. Cody, "A Typology of Disengagement Strategies and an Examination of the Role Intimacy, Reactions to Inequity and Relational Problems Play in Strategy Selection," *Communication Monographs*, 49(3), (1982): 148–170.

53. Argyle and Henderson, *The Anatomy of Relationships*.

54. S. W. Duck, *Understanding Relationships* (New York: Guilford Press, 1991).

55. Duck, "A Typography."

56. Duck, *Understanding Relationships*.

57. J. M. Gottman and S. Carrere, "Why Can't Men and Women Get Along? Developmental Roots and Marital Inequities," in *Communication and Relational Maintenance*, edited by D. J. Canary and L. Stafford (San Diego: Academic Press, 1991): 203–129.

58. G. O. Hagestad and M. A. Smyer, "Dissolving Long-Term Relationships: Patterns of Divorcing in Middle Age," in Duck, *Personal Relationships*, vol. 4. *Dissolving Personal Relationships*, edited by S. Duck (London: Academic Press, 1982), 155–188.

59. L. A. Baxter, "Accomplishing Relationship Disengagement," in *Understanding Personal Relationships: An Interdisciplinary Approach*, edited by S. Duck and D. Perlman (Beverly Hills, CA: Sage, 1984): 243–265.

60. D. DeStephen, "Integrating Relational Termination into a General Model of Communication Competence," paper presented at the annual meeting of the Speech Communication Association, Denver, 1985.

61. Baxter, "Accomplishing Relationship Disengagement."

62. DeStephen, "Integrating Relational Termination."

63. Cody, "A Typology of Disengagement Strategies."

Chapter 11

1. J. M. McLeod and S. H. Chaffee, "The Construction of Social Reality," in *The Social Influence Processes*, edited by J. Tedeschi (Chicago: Aldine-Atherton, 1972), 50–59. D. H. L. Olson, H. L. McCubbin, H. L. Barnes, A. S. Larsen, M. J. Muxem, and M. A. Wilson, *Families, What Makes Them Work* (Beverly Hills, CA: Sage, 1983). L. D. Ritchie and M. A. Fitzpatrick, "Family Communication Patterns: Measuring Intrapersonal Perceptions of Interpersonal Relationships," *Communication Research*, 17 (1990): 523–544.

2. G. P. Murdock, *Social Structure* (New York: Free Press, 1965). Originally published in 1949.

3. G. D. Nass and G. W. McDonald, *Marriage and the Family* (New York: Random House, 1982), 5.

4. *The Miami Herald*, July 9, 1982, 12A.

5. A. P. Bochner, "Conceptual Frontiers in the Study of Communication in Families: An Introduction to the Literature," *Human Communication Research*, 2(4), (Summer 1976): 382.

6. V. Satir, *Peoplemaking* (Palo Alto, CA: Science and Behavior Books, 1972).

7. D. E. Beck and M. A. Jones, *Progress on Family Problems, A Nationwide Study of Clients' and Counselors' Views on Family Agency Services* (New York: Family Service Association of America, 1973).

8. Satir, *Peoplemaking*.

9. H. J. Markman, "Prediction of Mental Distress: A 5-Year Follow-Up," *Journal of Consulting and Clinical Psychology*, 49, (1981): 760–762.

10. A. Napier and C. Whitaker, *The Family Crucible* (New York: Bantam, 1978).

11. Napier and Whitaker, *The Family Crucible*.

12. D. H. Olson et al., *Families*.

13. M. A. Fitzpatrick, *Between Husbands and Wives: Communication in Marriage* (Newbury Park, CA: Sage, 1988).

14. D. L. Kelly, "Relational Expectancy Fulfillment as an Explanatory Variable in Distinguishing Couple Types," *Human Communication Research*, 25 (1999): 420–442.

15. Kelly, "Relational expectancy fulfillment."

16. Fitzpatrick, *Between Husbands and Wives*.

17. M. M. Martin, and C. M. Andersen, "Aggressive Communication Traits: How Similar Are Young Adults and Their Parents in Argumentiveness, Assertiveness, and Verbal Aggressiveness?" *Western Journal of Communication*, 61 (1997): 299–314.

18. L. D. Ritchie and M. A. Fitzpatrick, "Family Communication Patterns: Measuring Intrapersonal Perceptions of Interpersonal Relationships," *Communication Research*, 17 (1990): 523–544.

19. M. Booth-Butterfield and R. Sidelinger, "The Influence of Family Communication on the College-Aged Child: Openness, Attitudes and Actions About Sex and Alcohol," *Communication Quarterly*, 46 (1998): 295–308.

20. L. K. Guerrero and W. A. Afifi, "Some Things Are Better Left Unsaid: Topic Avoidance in Family Relationships," *Communication Quarterly*, 43 (1995): 276–296.

21. Guerrero and Afifi,. "Some things are better left unsaid."

22. V. Satir, *The New Peoplemaking* (Mountain View, CA: Science and Behavior Books, 1988), 4.

23. Satir, *Peoplemaking*, 13–14.

24. J. C. Pearson, *Lasting Love: What Keeps Couples Together* (Dubuque, IA: William C. Brown, 1992).

Index